BILLBOARD'S

HOTTEST HOT 100 HITS

FRED BRONSON

BILLBOARD BOOKS
An imprint of Watson-Guptill Publications/New York

To Favor,
who was constantly by my side as I wrote this book—
usually curled up on the floor, content to let me work.
I miss him very much.

First published 1991 by Billboard Books, an imprint of Watson-Guptill Publications, a division of BPI Communications, Inc. 1515 Broadway, New York, NY 10036.

Library of Congress Cataloging-in-Publication Data

Bronson, Fred.
   Billboard's hottest hot 100 hits / Fred Bronson.
     p.   cm.
   Includes index.
   ISBN 0-8230-7570-2
   1. Popular music—Discography. I. Title.
ML156.4.P6B77 1991
016.78242164'026'6—dc20   91-26029
                      CIP
                      MN

Manufactured in the United States of America
First printing, 1991

1 2 3 4 5 6 7 8 9 / 96 95 94 93 92 91

ACKNOWLEDGMENTS

My first thanks go to Brian Carroll, chief research assistant. A former writer for both Dick Clark and Casey Kasem, Brian gave unselfishly of his time and expertise. Also of major help were Brady L. Benton of BMI and Alex Lopez.

Many people assisted with the gigantic task of ranking the top hits of the rock era. Len Brugnano and Mark Sherwin added up most of the numbers; Ted Cordes and Bill Derby hosted a memorable marathon to track calculations. Joining them were Matt DeTroia, Russell Doe, Anthony Donato, Mark Gadoury, John Glueckert, Ernie Koneck, Frank Mason, Mike Resnick and John Zook.

Thanks to everyone at *Billboard*, particularly Michael Ellis, as well as Adam White, Jim Richliano and Mark Marone. I also appreciate the support of Louie Dorado, Mark Hahn, Louis Iacueo, Mike King, Marcia Rovins, Jana Wallace and Alan and Pat Warner. Susan Sackett, a special friend for the last 21 years, lent much love and support while we were working on our individual projects and a teleplay for "Star Trek: The Next Generation."

Many thanks to the following people at the Dick Clark Company: Dick and Kari, Larry Klein, Mark Young, Guy Aoki, Pam Miller-Algar, Mitch Plessner, Steve Nelson and Jim Zoller.

Dan Allen of MUSICbase deserves a special round of applause for personally installing the MUSICbase program, which includes all of the *Billboard* pop charts from the rock era as well as information about each song. Thanks also to the MUSICbase staff: Andrew Economos, Andy Craig, Chuck Dees and Ron Schumacher.

I've been fortunate enough to work with editors who have patience, understanding and a love for music. I'd like to thank senior editor Tad Lathrop and associate editor Fred Weiler of Billboard Books for their enthusiastic support.

To my family, thank you for your love and your belief in me. My father, Irving Bronson, and my aunt, Beatrice Goldman, have done so much for me over the years that just saying thanks isn't enough. My mother, Mildred Bronson, encouraged my talents at an early age, and I'll always remember her with love.

Other people made significant contributions to this book, and I want to thank them, too: Ric Alonso, Spence Berland, Bill Buster, Frank Catalano, Frank Ceraolo, Dennis Clark, Sherman Cohen, Mark Goodman, Michael Hill, Jeff James, Alan Jones, Danny Lemos, Mark Milett, Paul O'Dell, Dan Olmsted, Ernie Over, Gene Roddenberry, Steve Sabin, Ben Silliman, Horst Stipp, Phil Swern, Dorothee Wilk and Guy Zapoleon.

CONTENTS

THE PRODUCERS

THE LABELS

INTRODUCTION

I became fascinated with record charts just after turning 14. Every Friday afternoon, I made sure I was home from school by 3 p.m. to write down the KRLA Top 30 Tune-Dex. Soon, I found out those surveys were available at my local record store, and a few months later, I discovered that a weekly trade paper called *Billboard* published a national singles chart, the Hot 100.

As much as I enjoyed following the charts, I was frustrated when some of my favorite singles barely made it into the top 30, and other songs that I thought were dreadful sailed into the top 10. So I found a way to make sure that the songs I liked would become hits—I started keeping my own chart. Every Friday, I sat down at my typewriter and produced my own survey, deciding which songs would bullet up and which songs would tumble down. I kept abreast of new releases, and the ones I thought would be hits were "picked to click." The highlight of the year, of course, came in December, when I could take all of the charts from the preceding 12 months and figure out my own year-end survey. The accepted method was to assign points in descending order to each song on the chart. For a top 40, the number one song of the week would receive 40 points, the number two song would receive 39, and so on down the chart. When the points were added up, all of the songs that had made the chart that year could be ranked in order. Not surprisingly, I discovered that other "chart freaks" also performed this annual ritual.

Sometime later, I wondered what it would be like to apply this same process to the *Billboard* charts—*all* of the charts, dating back to the beginning of the rock era. One could then produce a master list of the biggest hits of all time, ranked in order.

It took almost two years to complete the research for this book, beginning with the process of compiling the top 3000 songs of the rock era. The method I used was very similar to my teenage practice of computing the biggest hits of the year. First, I assembled all of the *Billboard* pop singles charts dating back to July 9, 1955, the date that "(We're Gonna) Rock Around The Clock" by Bill Haley & His Comets went to number one.

The Hot 100, the definitive pop singles chart of the music industry, was first published on August 4, 1958. Prior to that date, *Billboard* published several different charts each week. The chart data in this book is based on the Best Sellers in Stores chart from July, 1955, to July, 1958, and the Hot 100 from that time forward.

Songs eligible for inclusion in this book were any titles that reached their peak position on or after July 9, 1955 and on or before December 29, 1990.

Every week that a song was number one, it was assigned 100 points. Each week that it was number two, it received 99 points. A number three song received 98 points, and so on, down the chart. Fifty bonus points were awarded for every week that a song was number one. For purposes of the Top 3000 list, a song was only tracked while it was in the top 30. This gave all songs of the rock era an equal chance, since the Best Sellers chart fluctuated in size from 20 to 50 positions.

All of the points were added up and entered into a database. Other information was included in that database, such as the writer and producer of the song, the label that released it, the gender of the lead vocalist and much more. When all of the information was entered, there were over 6,000 songs in the database. By manipulating the information, I was able to produce the list of the top 3000 songs of the rock era, as well as any other list I wanted, such as the top 100 songs that debuted at number 100, or the top 100 songs on Motown.

It's important to realize that all of the charts in this book, including the Top 3000, are based on *chart performance*. They are not ranked in the order of how many copies each title has sold, how critically acclaimed they are, or how much I like them personally. It is a totally objective ranking, based on the highest position reached and length of stay on the Hot 100.

This produced some interesting results. One might expect a song like the Beatles' "Yesterday" to rank fairly high. In truth, this number one single had a very short chart life—it was on the Hot 100 for only 11 weeks. Compare that with Laura Branigan's "Gloria," which peaked at number two, but was on the Hot 100 for 36 weeks. That is why "Gloria" ranks number 99 on the Top 3000 and "Yesterday" is much further down the list, at number 1243.

Many songs earned the same number of points, so there were multiple ties. These ties were broken by first determining the song's highest position on the chart and how many weeks it remained there. Remaining ties were broken according to how many weeks a title was in the top 10, the top 40 and the entire Hot 100. After all of these tiebreaking conditions were applied, there were no remaining ties.

A few singles have had more than one chart life, such as "Unchained Melody" by the Righteous Brothers. A hit in 1965, the original version re-entered the Hot 100 after it appeared in the 1990 movie *Ghost*. The song continued to accumulate points, and its ranking in the Top 3000 includes its entire chart life from 1965 and 1990. Other songs that had two chart runs include "The Twist" by Chubby Checker, "Wipe Out" by the Surfaris, "Monster Mash" by Bobby "Boris" Pickett, "Stand By Me" by Ben E. King, "Do You Love Me" by the Contours, "Twist And Shout" by the Beatles and "Into The Night" by Benny Mardones. Their listings on the Top 3000 include the original label and year of release. When an artist recorded a new version of his or her own previous

hit, the points were not added together. Neil Sedaka, for example, recorded a new version of his 1962 hit "Breaking Up Is Hard To Do" in 1975. Because they are different recordings, they are listed separately, as is the 1990 recording of "Unchained Melody" that the Righteous Brothers made for Curb Records.

Methods of compiling the Hot 100 have varied over the years. The chart is currently a combination of sales and airplay points. Singles earn those points by selling at the retail level or by being ranked on a local radio station's playlist. To be listed on the Hot 100, there must be a commercial single available for sale.

Over the years, the average number of weeks that a song stays on the chart has fluctuated. In 1956, for example, it was not unusual for a song to move up and down the Best Sellers chart very slowly. But in 1965, the aforementioned "Yesterday" zipped up and down in no time at all. By 1981, songs were having longer chart lives again, with "Bette Davis Eyes" spending nine weeks at number one. As a result, songs that were popular in the mid-'60s may be ranked lower than hits from 1956 or 1981. That could have been alleviated by artificially weighting songs from different years, but doing so would not have produced an accurate listing of how every song from the rock era has performed on the *Billboard* chart. I decided to forego any weighting system in favor of creating a clearer picture of *Billboard*'s biggest hits.

This book covers the first 35 years of the rock era. It includes artists as diverse as Teresa Brewer and Bon Jovi, the Partridge Family and Mariah Carey, and Conway Twitty and Culture Club. There's probably no radio station in America today that would play all six of those artists, or all 3000 of *Billboard*'s Hottest Hot 100 Hits. Compiling the data for this book helped me focus on the big picture of rock and roll that includes all of the artists, writers, producers and others involved in this business of music. If you're a Janet Jackson fan, you may not be familiar with the music of Perry Como. Conversely, if you stopped listening to music after "The Shifting Whispering Sands" was a hit, you may not know Paula Abdul from Vanilla Ice. As you read this book, you may also get a sense of that big picture, and join me in thanking all of the people whose musical contributions have enriched our lives.

FRED BRONSON
June 1991

THE ARTISTS

The first section of this book looks at the top songs of some of the leading artists of the rock era. The Top 100 Songs of the Beatles includes singles by the group as well as the four individual members when they went out on their own (or formed other bands). The Top 50 Songs of Diana Ross & the Supremes includes singles by the original trio as well as recordings by the "new" Supremes featuring Jean Terrell; the list also features solo and duet performances by Diana Ross. Similarly, The Top 50 Songs of the Jacksons includes group recordings by the Jackson Five and the Jacksons, as well as titles by Michael, Janet and Jermaine.

The balance of the artists in this section are treated in similar fashion. Peter Cetera's solo recordings are included with Chicago's top hits; Aretha Franklin's duets with George Michael and Elton John are included in her top 30. All present and previous members of Genesis and their spin-offs are included in the top 30 songs by that group. The top 20 songs of Crosby, Stills, Nash & Young also include efforts by the groups they were in, such as the Byrds, Buffalo Springfield and the Hollies.

It seems fitting to have the artists be up front in the book, because they always *are* up front. Supporting them behind the scenes are the writers, the producers and the labels listed in subsequent sections.

No group or individual has dominated the *Billboard* Hot 100 the way the Beatles did between the years 1964-70. Although their chart span as a foursome is brief compared to an artist like Ray Charles (with a chart span of 33 years, from 1957 to 1990), the Beatles set records that may never be toppled by anyone.

The Beatles made their first appearance on the British chart on October 11, 1962, when "Love Me Do" debuted. It would take them one year, three months and one week to have their first American chart entry: "I Want To Hold Your Hand" entered the Hot 100 on January 18, 1964. During that interval, they did have singles released in America, but Capitol Records declined to release their early material. "Love Me Do," "Please Please Me" and "From Me To You" were issued on the Chicago-based Vee Jay label and "She Loves You" came out on a Philadelphia label, Swan. Their highest chart ranking during this time was number 116 on the *Billboard*'s Bubbling Under chart with "From Me To You."

In November, 1963, Beatles manager Brian Epstein flew to New York with a demo of "I Want To Hold Your Hand." Brown Meggs, director of Eastern operations for Capitol, decided this song deserved to be on the label, and set a release date of January 13. But when Carroll Baker, a DJ at WWDC in Washington, D.C., played a copy he had received from a British flight attendant, other radio stations picked up on the record, and the date was advanced to December 26.

Beatlemania did not take long to catch on in America. Jack Paar showed a film clip of the Fab Four on his Friday night NBC series on January 3. Two weeks later, "I Want To Hold Your Hand" debuted on the *Billboard* chart at number 45. The next week, it moved to number three, and "She Loves You" debuted at number 69. The following week, "I Want To Hold Your Hand" was number one; "She Loves You" had moved to 21; and "Please Please Me" debuted at number 68. On March 14, those three songs held the top three positions on the chart. On March 28 "Twist And Shout" had joined them in the top four, and a week later, "Can't Buy Me Love" moved from number 27 to the top of the Hot 100—giving the Beatles an unprecedented hammerlock on the top five. One week later, the Beatles occupied 14 positions out of 100, another all-time record.

The top 100 Beatles songs include 14 songs from 1964 alone. The pace had settled down somewhat by 1965, although they did have 10 chart entries that year. Every new Beatles single went to number one, until "Nowhere Man" in early 1966—it stalled at number three. Later that year, "Yellow Submarine" stopped at number two, held back by the Supremes' "You Can't Hurry Love." But then the Beatles had three more chart-toppers, interrupted again by "Lady Madonna," which went to number four in 1968.

In the summer of that year, they released their first single on the Apple label. "Hey Jude" became the first single in the history of the Hot 100 to enter the chart in the top 10. On September 14, 1968, it debuted at number 10. The next week, it moved to number three, and the following week, to number one. "Hey Jude" stayed at the top for nine weeks—the longest of any Beatles single.

There would be only five more Beatles singles released in America while the group was still together. "Get Back" was next, and it matched "Hey Jude" by also debuting at number 10. "The Ballad Of John And Yoko" debuted when "Get Back" was in its fourth week at the top. "Come Together" and "Something" were back-to-back on the Beatles' final number one single of the '60s, and "Let It Be" was their first of the '70s. It entered the Hot 100 at number six, the highest debut of all time. The final original Beatles' single was "The Long and Winding Road," their 20th number one.

The release of solo Beatles singles had started as early as 1969, when John Lennon's "Give Peace A Chance" was released on Apple by the "Plastic Ono Band." It was recorded live in John and Yoko's hotel room in Montreal, where six months later they would hold a bed-in for peace. George was the first Beatle to have a solo number one. "My Sweet Lord," ranked number 11 on the top 100 Beatle songs, was inspired by the Edwin Hawkins Singers' "Oh Happy Day," according to George—although a judge would one day rule that it was unconsciously copied from Ronnie Mack's "He's So Fine," a chart-topper for the Chiffons in 1963.

Ringo also charted as a solo act in 1970 with the countrified "Beaucoups Of Blues," not one of his biggest hits. The following year, he made the top 10 with "It Don't Come Easy"; "Back Off Boogaloo" did the same in 1972. In 1973-74, he had two successive number one singles: "Photograph" (written by Ringo and George) and a cover of Johnny Burnette's "You're Sixteen." The latter is Ringo's most successful *Billboard* single, ranked number 26 on the list of top 100 Beatle songs.

Paul's first solo Hot 100 entry was "Another Day" backed with "Oh Woman Oh Why," number five in 1971. That was followed by his first post-Beatles number one hit, "Uncle Albert/Admiral Halsey." His next single was the first to credit Wings, but "Give Ireland Back To The Irish" was not a major hit, stalling at number 21. Paul hit a creative peak with "Band On The Run," number one in 1974, and a commercial peak with "Silly Love Songs," number one for five weeks in 1976. His most successful solo effort remains a live single, "Coming Up," recorded in Glasgow. His two most successful post-Beatles singles are superstar duets recorded with Michael Jackson and Stevie Wonder. Although they are considered to be among Paul's lighter material, "Say, Say, Say" and "Ebony And Ivory" proved to be the most popular with his fans, topping all other group and solo efforts by the Beatles save for "Hey Jude."

Following "Give Peace A Chance" and "Cold Turkey," the first solo record to bear John Lennon's name was "Instant Karma (We All Shine On)," which was on the chart at the same time as "Let It Be." John's singles were not as commercial as the other Beatles, and songs like "Mother" and "Woman Is The Nigger Of The World" found it tough going at top 40 radio. "Imagine" was an exception, played for weeks as an album track before its release as a single. Its late release resulted in an exceptionally short chart run of only nine weeks.

Lennon was the last of the Beatles to have a number one of his own. "Whatever Gets You Thru The Night," with Elton John on backing vocals, spent a week at the top in 1974. His next number one would be a posthumous achievement. After a five-year hiatus to raise his son Sean, John returned to the studio to record the *Double Fantasy* album with Yoko (he was one of the first artists signed to the Geffen label in 1980). The first single, "(Just Like) Starting Over," was climbing the chart when Lennon was murdered on December 8, 1980. Three weeks later, it was number one.

Thirty-nine of the top 100 Beatle hits are by the Beatles. Of the remaining 61 songs on the list, 29 are by Paul. John and George account for 12 each and Ringo for eight. None of the former Beatles made the Hot 100 during 1990, although all three surviving members were actively recording—Paul and Ringo released live albums, and George was part of the Traveling Wilburys.

Elvis Presley has had more song titles chart on the *Billboard* Hot 100 than any other artist. By the time of his death in 1977, he had amassed 146 chart entries, with three more posthumous ones to follow. His total of number one hits (17) is second only to the Beatles (20), although he spent more weeks at the top of the chart—80 compared to the Beatles' 59. He was the first artist in the rock era to have two consecutive number one songs. Only the Beatles, with three chart-toppers in a row, have matched or bested him.

Sun Records employee Marion Keisker could hardly have guessed what a phenomenon Elvis was going to become when she observed his first recording session in July, 1953. Working as a truck driver for Crown Electric in Memphis, Elvis took his lunch hour to record two songs on acetate as a birthday present for his mother. Keisker liked his voice, and quickly turned on a tape recorder so she could play "My Happiness" and "That's When Your Heartaches Begin" for the owner of the Memphis Recording Service (and Sun Records), Sam Phillips.

He didn't agree with Marion and was unimpressed with Elvis— even when the teenager returned on January 4, 1954, to record two more songs, "Casual Love Affair" and "I'll Never Stand In Your Way." Presley and Phillips didn't connect again until a few months later, when the studio owner needed a vocalist to record a song called "Without You." Keisker suggested Presley, and Sam couldn't find anyone else. The session didn't go well until Elvis ran through his repertoire of R&B, country, gospel and Dean Martin favorites. That led to a recording session on July 5, 1954, where Elvis started a jam session on "That's All Right Mama." Suddenly, Phillips realized he had the kind of singer he'd been looking for—a white kid who sounded black.

After five singles released on Sun, Elvis' new manager, Col. Tom Parker, let it be known that Presley's contract was for sale. Decca was willing to pay $5,000, but was quickly outbid by Dot with an offer of $7,500. Mercury was willing to sign Elvis for $10,000, and Parker used that information to get a bid from Mitch Miller at Columbia for $15,000. The Colonel told Mitch that RCA was going to offer $20,000. Atlantic upped that to $25,000, but RCA got Elvis for an unprecedented $35,000 plus a $5,000 bonus to Elvis for song royalties.

Elvis went into a Nashville studio on January 10, 1956, to record his first RCA single. Producer Steve Sholes brought in Sun musicians like Scotty Moore on guitar, Bill Black on bass and D.J. Fontana on drums. Five songs were recorded in two days, including "Heartbreak Hotel." It was released on January 27, and by April 21, "Heartbreak Hotel" was number one.

Elvis' most successful single was his third RCA 45, "Don't Be Cruel" backed with "Hound Dog." Together, they spent 11 weeks at the top of the chart, longer than any other single in the rock era. It is number two on the list of *Billboard*'s Top 3000 hits from 1955-1990.

Otis Blackwell, the composer of "Don't Be Cruel," was sitting in his publisher's office looking for inspiration when Al Stanton, one of the company's owners, walked in shaking a bottle of Pepsi. Two days later, Blackwell had written "All Shook Up."

Eight of Elvis' top 10 singles are from the '50s, and 18 of his top 50 are from that decade. He remained strong on the charts through 1963, but from 1964-1968 he had only one top 10 single, "Crying In The Chapel." His career was revived by a one-hour NBC-TV special directed by Steve Binder. The show closed with "If I Can Dream," written by Earl Brown specifically for the final segment. Released as a single, "If I Can Dream" reached number 12—the highest-charting Elvis single in almost four years. By the end of the decade, Elvis had topped the Hot 100 for the final time with "Suspicious Minds." Of Elvis' top 50 singles, 24 are from the '60s.

Eight songs on his top 50 are from the '70s. His highest-charting single of the decade was "Burning Love," which reached number two in 1972. "Way Down" had already peaked at number 31 when news of Elvis' death shocked the world. On September 3, "Way Down" started moving back up the Hot 100—finally stopping at number 18 on September 24.

DIANA ROSS & THE SUPREMES

The Supremes dominated the Hot 100 during the '60s in a way that no American group had done before. They had 12 number one songs in just over five years, and established the Motown sound as "The Sound of Young America."

While they are one of the most successful trios of the rock era, the Supremes actually began as a quartet. Milton Jenkins, manager of a male group known as the Primes, needed a female counterpart for the Primes, for personal appearances. Florence Ballard wanted to be a nurse, but her desire to sing was even stronger, so she accepted Jenkins' offer to form a group. She recruited Mary Wilson, and the two of them chose Betty Travis to be the third member. Paul Williams of the Primes found a young girl from the Brewster Projects (a Detroit public-housing project) to complete the quartet. Diane Ross was rehearsing with the other Primes when Betty Travis was pulled out of the group by her mother; she was replaced by Barbara Martin.

Diane's former neighbor, Smokey Robinson, introduced the girls to Motown founder Berry Gordy, Jr., but they were still in high school and he told them they weren't ready to record. They auditioned for another Detroit label, Lu-Pine, and were signed. After a couple of singles, they returned to Motown—Gordy still wasn't ready to sign them, but he let them hang around. Soon they were singing backing vocals for Marvin Gaye.

When Gordy did offer them a Motown contract, he asked the Primettes to change their name. The Primes had also signed with Motown and were known as the Temptations. Florence picked the name "Supremes" because it was the only one suggested that didn't end in "ette." Diana and Mary hated it.

Barbara Martin exited from the group, leaving them a trio. Berry released their first single on the Tamla label, but "I Want a Guy" failed to make the chart, as did their second single, "Buttered Popcorn," featuring Ballard on lead. Through their next five singles, issued on the Motown label, they earned the title "no-hit Supremes." That changed with their eighth release, a tune written and produced by Brian Holland, Lamont Dozier and Eddie Holland. The Marvelettes had turned down "Where Did Our Love Go," but the Supremes didn't have that kind of clout.

In a dramatic reversal of fortune, the Supremes scored five consecutive number one singles. They continued to work with Holland, Dozier and Holland, garnering four more number one songs. In 1967, Florence Ballard was asked to leave the group and was replaced by Cindy Birdsong of Patti LaBelle and the Bluebelles. When Holland-Dozier-Holland left Motown, other producers vied to work with the group, now billed as Diana Ross & the Supremes. Nick Ashford and Valerie Simpson were given first crack with "Some Things You Never Get Used To."

The Supremes had two more number one singles: "Love Child" and "Someday We'll Be Together." In 1970, after a final performance at the Frontier Hotel in Las Vegas, Diana officially was off on a solo career, so Jean Terrell took over lead vocal duties. Surprisingly, the first Supremes' single bested Diana's first solo 45: "Up The Ladder To The Roof" peaked at number 10, while Diana's "Reach Out And Touch (Somebody's Hand)" stopped at number 20. The Supremes continued to have hits, going as high as number seven with "Stoned Love." But in the long run, it was Diana who proved her longevity with six more number one singles—including "Ain't No Mountain High Enough," the Nile Rodgers-Bernard Edwards produced "Upside Down" and a duet with Lionel Richie, "Endless Love." The latter single is the number one Diana Ross song, the number one Motown song and the number one duet of the rock era.

Jean Terrell remained with the Supremes through the single "Bad Weather" in 1973. Scherrie Payne stepped in as lead singer, but the third position was a constantly-revolving door. Only Mary Wilson remained constant, and finally the Supremes faded away.

In 1981, Diana ended her association with Motown and signed with RCA for North America and EMI for the rest of the world. Her first release away from Berry Gordy was a new version of Frankie Lymon & the Teenagers' "Why Do Fools Fall In Love." By the end of the decade, Diana was back on Motown, which Gordy had sold to MCA.

THE JACKSONS

1. **SAY, SAY, SAY**
   Paul McCartney and Michael Jackson *Columbia* 83

2. **BILLIE JEAN**
   Michael Jackson *Epic* 83

3. **ROCK WITH YOU**
   Michael Jackson *Epic* 80

4. **BEAT IT**
   Michael Jackson *Epic* 83

5. **I'LL BE THERE**
   The Jackson Five *Motown* 70

6. **I WANT YOU BACK**
   The Jackson Five *Motown* 70

7. **MISS YOU MUCH**
   Janet Jackson *A&M* 89

8. **ESCAPADE**
   Janet Jackson *A&M* 90

9. **ABC**
   The Jackson Five *Motown* 70

10. **DANCING MACHINE**
    The Jackson Five *Motown* 74

11. **WHEN I THINK OF YOU**
    Janet Jackson *A&M* 86

12. **THE GIRL IS MINE**
    Michael Jackson and Paul McCartney *Epic* 83

13. **MAN IN THE MIRROR**
    Michael Jackson *Epic* 88

14. **THE LOVE YOU SAVE**
    The Jackson Five *Motown* 70

15. **WHAT HAVE YOU DONE FOR ME LATELY**
    Janet Jackson *A&M* 86

All nine of Joe and Katharine Jackson's children have been represented on the *Billboard* Hot 100. Michael, Jermaine, Tito, Jackie, Marlon, Randy, Janet, LaToya and Rebbie, in that order, have had singles enter the chart.

First there was the Jackson Five, featuring the lead vocals of 11-year-old Michael supported by his four eldest brothers. The group began as a trio with Sigmund Esco (Jackie), Toriano Adaryll (Tito) and Jermaine LaJaune. Marlon David and Michael Joe joined later. Michael was only five when the brothers—named the Jackson Five by a neighbor in Gary, Indiana—made their professional debut in a local nightclub. They became well-known to some of Motown's biggest acts by supporting them in local shows, and eventually Gladys Knight and Bobby Taylor put a word in Berry Gordy's ear about the talented brothers.

After a couple of singles on the Gary-based Steeltown label, the group was signed to Motown and moved to Los Angeles for a year of rehearsals. They opened for Diana Ross & the Supremes at the Forum in Inglewood, California, and in the fall of 1969, Motown released their first single, "I Want You Back." It was the first of four consecutive number one songs, including "ABC," "The Love You Save" and "I'll Be There." The latter is the most successful Hot 100 single by the five brothers.

In May, 1975, four of the Jacksons departed Motown for a new home at Epic Records; Jermaine, married to Berry Gordy's daughter Hazel, stayed behind. Motown claimed the rights to the name "Jackson Five," so with youngest brother Randy now on board, the brothers called themselves the Jacksons.

Michael had already been recording as a solo artist for Motown; the title song from the movie *Ben* had been a number one hit for him. While filming *The Wiz*, he approached Quincy Jones about producing his first solo LP for Epic. *Off the Wall* featured two number one hits, "Don't Stop 'Til You Get Enough" and "Rock With You." The first single from Michael's next album, *Thriller*, was "The Girl Is Mine," a duet with Paul McCartney. Michael returned the favor by guest-starring on McCartney's "Say, Say, Say," the most successful *Billboard* song for any Jackson. *Thriller*, with seven top 10 singles, became the best-selling record of all time, and *Bad* was the first album to yield five number one hits.

Jermaine's first solo chart single was "That's How Love Goes" in the fall of 1972, just one year after the release of Michael's "Got To Be There." His next Hot 100 single was a remake of Shep & the Limelites' 1961 recording, "Daddy's Home." Jermaine's version peaked at number nine on the Hot 100 and is ranked number 32 on the Jacksons' top 50. Jermaine's most successful solo effort was "Let's Get Serious," a song written by Stevie Wonder and Lee Garrett for Wonder to record. Jermaine's father-in-law heard the song and decided that Jermaine should record it instead. Jermaine's final chart single on Motown was "Let Me Tickle Your Fancy," a collaboration with Devo released in 1982. With Berry's blessing, Jermaine left Motown and signed with Clive Davis at Arista in 1984. That same year, Jermaine rejoined his brothers for the Jacksons' *Victory* album and tour. The LP included "State Of Shock," with Michael duetting with Mick Jagger. It is number 25 on the Jacksons' top 50.

Janet Jackson was only seven when she appeared with her brothers on stage at the MGM Grand Hotel in Las Vegas. She signed with A&M Records in November, 1982. Her first two albums failed to produce any top 40 hits, but that became irrelevant when her third LP, *Control*, hit the street. Produced by Jimmy Jam and Terry Lewis, the album rapidly yielded five top five hits: "What Have You Done For Me Lately" (number four), "Nasty" (number three), "When I Think Of You" (number one), "Control" (number five) and "Let's Wait Awhile" (number two). Janet kept up the barrage of hits with the *Rhythm Nation 1814* album. "Miss You Much" is her biggest *Billboard* hit to date. The album contained two other number one songs: "Escapade" and "Black Cat."

LaToya Jackson had recorded for Polydor before moving to the Private I label, where she charted on the Hot 100 with "Heart Don't Lie" (number 56 in 1984). The eldest Jackson sibling, Rebbie (nee Maureen), went to number 24 in 1984 with "Centipede," a song written and produced by her brother Michael.

The Beach Boys surprised everyone—perhaps even themselves—when "Kokomo," a single culled from the soundtrack of the Tom Cruise film *Cocktail*, surged to the top of the Hot 100 in November, 1988—24 years and four months after their first number one song, "I Get Around." That is the longest span of number one singles in the history of the rock era.

Brothers Brian, Dennis and Carl Wilson grew up in Hawthorne, California. In 1961, they formed the Beach Boys with cousin Mike Love and friend Al Jardine, and recorded "Surfin'"—their own composition—on the Candix label. "Surfin'" was a hit in Los Angeles, struggling to number 75 on the *Billboard* chart. The next year, the group signed a contract with Capitol Records; before long, the Beach Boys were scoring top 10 records like "Surfin' U.S.A." (number three), "Surfer Girl" (number seven), "Be True to Your School" (number six) and "Fun, Fun, Fun" (number five).

The group's seventh Capitol single, "I Get Around," became their first number one hit, and remains their most successful single to date. "Good Vibrations," their second biggest hit, was the most expensive, most elaborate single ever produced when it was released in October, 1966. According to Brian, it cost over $16,000 to record this one track, an amount unheard of in those days. The song was recorded in 17 sessions over a period of six months, at four different studios. Brian explained that each studio had its own unique sound, and that using all four contributed to the final version of the track.

First they were the Missing Links, then the Big Thing—until the band changed the name to Chicago Transit Authority. Mayor Richard Daley was not amused, especially since the group's first album for Columbia interspersed dramatic sounds from the 1968 Democratic Convention. A lawsuit was threatened, and the group shortened their name to Chicago.

Chicago achieved top 10 status with their second single, "Make Me Smile." By 1976, they had amassed nine more top 10 singles. In October of that year, Chicago had their first number one with "If You Leave Me Now." There would be only one more top 10 single in the decade—"Baby, What A Big Surprise" in 1977.

The band was badly shaken by the accidental shooting death of lead guitarist Terry Kath on January 23, 1978. Their albums suffered, and there was a further setback in 1981 when Columbia unceremoniously dropped the group from their roster. Manager Irving Azoff then signed them to his Full Moon label through Warner Brothers.

They were redeemed with their very first single for their new company, "Hard To Say I'm Sorry," from the soundtrack of the film *Summer Lovers.* The song fared much better than the movie—the single advanced to the top of the *Billboard* chart, to give Chicago their second number one single and their biggest hit of all time. Moving over to Warner Brothers' Reprise label, the group scored their third number one song with Diane Warren's "Look Away."

Four of the songs in Chicago's top 30 are by former lead singer Peter Cetera, who left the group in 1985.

Aretha Franklin was born in Memphis and raised in Detroit, the daughter of the Rev. C.L. Franklin. He was the pastor of the New Bethel Baptist Church, and Aretha grew up listening to artists like Mahalia Jackson and Clara Ward sing in her father's church.

In 1956, Aretha made her first recordings of gospel songs for the Checker label. Four years later, with encouragement from Sam Cooke, she moved to New York to perform more secular material. John Hammond heard one of her demo tracks, "Today I Sing The Blues," and signed her to Columbia Records, where she found herself stifled into recording show tunes and other standards with lush arrangements. Eight of her Columbia singles charted on the Hot 100, but in September, 1966, she decided not to renew her Columbia contract. She signed instead with Atlantic Records after Jerry Wexler encouraged Ahmet Ertegun to outbid CBS.

In January, 1967, Wexler brought Franklin to the Fame studios in Muscle Shoals, Alabama, using the same rhythm section that had worked with Wilson Pickett. The idea was to record material for an album, but after one day, an argument between Aretha's husband and a horn player led to Aretha's departure. Only one song had been completed, "I Never Loved A Man (The Way I Love You)." Aretha completed the flip side in New York and the single was released. Aretha's Atlantic debut soared to number nine on the *Billboard* chart; her follow-up, a version of Otis Redding's "Respect," went to number one for two weeks.

She remained prolific, with four top 10 singles released in 1968 alone. Her 27th Atlantic chart single became her biggest hit on the *Billboard* Hot 100. "Until You Come Back To Me (That's What I'm Gonna Do)" had actually been written and recorded by Stevie Wonder in 1967, but not released until after Aretha's version was a hit.

It was also her last top 10 single for Atlantic. A series of routine recordings and lackluster performances led to a slump in the late '70s. It wasn't until 1980 when she gave a rousing performance as a waitress in *The Blues Brothers* movie that the public "rediscovered" her. Working with producer Narada Michael Walden in 1985, she recorded her second biggest *Billboard* hit, "Freeway Of Love." The follow-up, "Who's Zoomin' Who," gave her two consecutive top 10 hits for the first time since 1971.

In 1987 Aretha was back on top of the Hot 100 for the second time with "I Knew You Were Waiting (For Me)," a duet with George Michael.

THE TOP 30 SONGS OF
GENESIS/PHIL COLLINS

The genesis of Genesis began in 1966 at the Charterhouse School, with Peter Gabriel, Mike Rutherford, Tony Banks and Anthony Phillips. After numerous shifts in personnel, the group was signed to Charisma Records in March, 1970. Five months later, when they needed a new drummer, they advertised anonymously in *Melody Maker*. Of the 14 people who auditioned, they chose a 19-year-old former child actor named Phil Collins.

Gabriel, who had sung a majority of the lead vocals, departed in August, 1975. When the search for a new lead singer proved unsuccessful, Collins stepped into the position. Hackett left in June, 1977, reducing Genesis to a trio. Less than a year later, they had their first top 30 hit in America, "Follow You Follow Me" (number 23).

In 1981, inspired by his divorce, Collins poured his feelings into his first solo album, *Face Value*. "I Missed Again" and "In The Air Tonight" both peaked at number 19. His second album, *Hello I Must Be Going*, provided him with a number 10 single, a faithful remake of the Supremes' "You Can't Hurry Love." In 1984, producer Taylor Hackford convinced Collins to sing the title song for his film *Against All Odds*; it went to number one. Collins' own movie *Buster* gave him two chart-toppers: a remake of the Mindbenders' "Groovy Kind Of Love" and a song written with Lamont Dozier, "Two Hearts."

Rutherford also scored a number one single with his own band, Mike + the Mechanics—"The Living Years." Despite the success of Collins and Rutherford away from Genesis, the band remains intact.

Elton John was born Reginald Kenneth Dwight in Pinner, Middlesex, England. A child prodigy in music, he took piano lessons at age four, and later won a scholarship to study part-time at the Royal Academy of Music in London. He resented studying, but absorbed knowledge about classical music and also became a fan of R&B. In 1961, he helped found Bluesology, a small outfit playing soul music that backed American R&B stars like Major Lance, Patti LaBelle and Billy Stewart on their British tours.

When Long John Baldry became front man for the group, Elton became disillusioned with playing in cabarets and left the group. He met Bernie Taupin at the office of music publisher Dick James; their first collaboration was a song called "Scarecrow." Reginald Dwight was now officially Elton John, a name culled from *Elton* Dean of Bluesology and Long *John* Baldry. Signed to MCA's Uni label for America, Elton went top 10 with his second single, "Your Song"—two years later, he had the first of his six number one singles, "Crocodile Rock."

Elton remained with MCA through 1980, coming out of a two-year slump with his third biggest hit, "Little Jeannie." But on December 21 of that year, he jumped ship, becoming one of the first artists signed to Geffen. Seven of his top 30 *Billboard* hits are on Geffen. Unhappy with the label, Elton left Geffen and returned to MCA. His first single for his old label was a live recording of "Candle In The Wind," a song originally heard on *Goodbye Yellow Brick Road* in 1973. Featuring the Melbourne Symphony Orchestra, "Candle In The Wind" peaked at number six.

THE ROLLING STONES

On July 12, 1962, a group consisting of Mick Jagger, Keith Richards, Brian Jones and Derek Taylor appeared at the Marquee in London as the Rollin' Stones, named after a Muddy Waters song. Bill Wyman replaced Derek Taylor on bass in December, and Charlie Watts became the band's drummer in January, 1963.

Their early demo tapes rejected by record companies, the Rollin' Stones took a regular Sunday job at the Crawdaddy Club in Richmond, Surrey. Andrew Loog Oldham, a 19-year old former publicist for the Beatles, saw the group there at the end of April and signed on as their manager.

Adding a "g" to make them the Rolling Stones, Oldham secured a record deal with Dick Rowe of Decca in May. The Rolling Stones' first British single, a cover of Chuck Berry's "Come On," peaked at number 21 in the U.K. in September. Through Oldham's contact with his former clients, the Stones were given a John Lennon-Paul McCartney song to record. "I Wanna Be Your Man" went to number 12 in the U.K. in December.

The Stones made their U.S. chart debut in May, 1964, with a cover of Buddy Holly's "Not Fade Away"; their first American top 10 single was "Time Is On My Side." But the record that established their reputation and reinforced their image as the bad boys of rock and roll was "(I Can't Get No) Satisfaction." It spent four weeks at number one in 1965, and is the Stones' fourth most successful chart single.

Their biggest American hit is "Honky Tonk Women," released one day after the funeral of Brian Jones. "Start Me Up" spent three weeks at number two in 1981, and—at 24 weeks on the Hot 100—is the Stones' second biggest single.

FRANKIE VALLI & THE 4 SEASONS

Francis Castelluccio released his first single in 1953. "My Mother's Eyes" featured his distinctive falsetto voice and the name "Frankie Valley" on the label—the first of many names he would use before settling on Frankie Valli.

By 1961, Frankie was singing with a group called the Four Lovers. Their songwriter and producer, Bob Crewe, had them doing background vocals for people like Bobby Darin, Freddy Cannon and Danny & the Juniors. The first release to feature their new name, inspired by a New Jersey bowling alley, was "Bermuda" by the Four Seasons. It failed to chart.

The group recorded five songs, including "Sherry." Crewe took the masters to a record convention in Miami, and word got around fast. Several different labels bid for them, but the winner was Chicago-based Vee Jay Records.

After "Sherry" spent five weeks at number one, Vee Jay released another of the five masters, "Big Girls Don't Cry"; it also spent five weeks at number one. A Christmas release of "Santa Claus Is Coming To Town" followed, then the Four Seasons had a third number one single: "Walk Like A Man."

By the end of 1963, the Four Seasons left Vee Jay because of royalty disputes, signing with Philips and releasing "Dawn (Go Away)." After their final top 30 hit on Philips in 1968, the Seasons experienced several years of chart obscurity. The success of Valli's "My Eyes Adored You," though, led to a new Four Seasons line-up. The group was signed to Warner/Curb, and "Who Loves You" put them back in the top 10 for the first time since 1967. The follow-up—"December, 1963 (Oh, What a Night)," originally written about Prohibition in the year 1933—was the Four Seasons' first number one record since "Rag Doll" in 1964.

THE TOP 20 SONGS OF
CROSBY, STILLS, NASH & YOUNG

David Crosby, Stephen Stills and Graham Nash found themselves spending a summer afternoon together in a Laurel Canyon home. The year was 1968, some time after Crosby had experienced success with the Byrds, Stills had found fame with Buffalo Springfield and Nash had helped form the Hollies.

A jam session developed in the living room, and with all three of them enjoying the spontaneous musical combustion, they decided it would be great to record together. Unfortunately, they were all signed to different labels. Fortunately, 26-year-old David Geffen was willing to work his way through the legal morass and sign the trio to Atlantic Records.

Crosby, Stills and Nash was released in June, 1969. The initial single, a Nash song that the Hollies had attempted to record, was "Marrakesh Express." It peaked at number 28 and was followed by Stills' ode to Judy Collins, "Suite: Judy Blue Eyes," which reached number 21.

Looking for musicians to support them on tour, they accepted the suggestion of Atlantic Records chief Ahmet Ertegun, who thought Neil Young would complement the trio. He agreed to be lead guitarist as long as he could continue recording with his own backup band, Crazy Horse, for Reprise—a label that shared corporate affiliation with Atlantic under the Warner-Elektra-Atlantic banner.

In March of 1970, the first Crosby, Stills, Nash and Young single was released: "Woodstock," written by Joni Mitchell. It went to number 11 on the *Billboard* chart. The group's second album—and the first to feature Young—was *Deja Vu*, which included the hits "Teach Your Children" (number 16) and "Our House" (number 30). Between those two singles, the quartet released a non-LP song, "Ohio." Young wrote the song after watching a TV report about the killing of four students at Kent State University by the National Guard earlier that day. "Ohio" ascended the chart at the same time as "Teach Your Children" and peaked at number 14.

The four musicians worked in different combinations during the '70s, recording solo material as well. Crosby, Stills and Nash continued to come together whenever the feeling struck them. The album *CSN*, released in 1977, contained their first top 10 single, "Just A Song Before I Go" (number seven). Their next LP didn't come out until 1982, but their fans were ready. "Wasted On The Way" peaked at number nine and is their most successful *Billboard* chart hit as a group. Six years later, Young joined them for the first time since January, 1975. The result was the album *American Dream*, which yielded "Got It Made" (number 69).

MADONNA

"I always thought of myself as a star, though I never in my wildest dreams expected to become this big," Madonna bluntly told Stephen Holden in the *New York Times*. Between 1983 and 1990, Madonna had 20 top 20 singles on the *Billboard* chart—her total output of releases. Of those, 16 in a row made the top five. And when "Vogue" went to number one, it gave her eight chart-topping singles, more than any other female soloist to that date.

Madonna Louise Veronica Ciccone was named after her mother, who died when she was six. She grew up in Michigan with her five brothers and two sisters. She studied piano and ballet and acted in plays in Catholic school. After a year at the University of Michigan on a dance scholarship, Madonna Louise moved to New York City at the suggestion of a ballet teacher.

She won another scholarship to study at Alvin Ailey's dance studio, and a brief detour took her to Paris, where she sang backing vocals for Patrick Hernandez ("Born To Be Alive"). She returned to Manhattan and formed a band, the Breakfast Club, with her boyfriend Dan Gilroy.

In 1980, Madonna left that group to form her own unit, Emmenon, later shortened to Emmy. But her big break came in 1982 when Mark Kamins, a DJ at the Danceteria, heard a tape that Madonna had made with Stephen Bray. Kamins introduced Madonna to Michael Rosenblatt of Sire Records, who liked her tape enough to play it for label head Seymour Stein.

Signed to Sire, Madonna released a single, "Everybody," which became a hit in dance clubs. "Physical Attraction," another club hit, followed, and in October, 1983, "Holiday" became Madonna's first Hot 100 entry.

Madonna's most successful *Billboard* single, "Like A Virgin," was originally written for a man to sing. Her second biggest single, "Vogue," was featured on *I'm Breathless*, an album "inspired" by the film *Dick Tracy* (but which had nothing to do with the soundtrack). Originally, Madonna thought that "Vogue" would make a good "B" side, but her label insisted that it was hit material. The number three single on her top 20, "Crazy For You," came from another movie, *Vision Quest*. Madonna has two other soundtrack singles on her top 20: "Live To Tell" and "Who's That Girl."

Almost from the beginning of her recording career, Madonna has been a media star. The press has covered the way she dresses, the Madonna wanna-be's who imitate her fashion, her marriage to and divorce from Sean Penn, her up-and-down film career and banned video on MTV. "I like challenge and controversy," she said to Holden. "I like to tick people off."

THE OSMONDS

"The [Mormon] church encourages talent, beginning with such things as singing, sports and speeches when the children are small. That's how the four boys got started singing together," Olive Osmond is quoted in Irwin Stambler's *The Encyclopedia Of Pop Rock And Soul*.

In 1959 Alan and three of his brothers—Wayne, Merrill and Jay—sang in church and rehearsed barbershop quartet songs at home. On a visit to Disneyland, the boys gave an impromptu performance with the park's barbershop quartet, the dapper Dans, and landed a gig with the "Disneyland After Dark" show. The Osmonds made their first network television appearance on Andy Williams' NBC variety show on December 20, 1962; one year later, on his sixth birthday, younger brother Donny made the Osmonds a quintet.

The brothers remained with Williams until his final broadcast in May, 1967. They were signed to Williams' Barnaby label, and then moved to MCA's Uni label, but without any chart hits. That changed in 1971, when they signed with MGM Records and Mike Curb set out to duplicate the success of another five brothers—the Jackson Five.

Curb sent the Osmonds to Rick Hall, owner of the Fame studios in Muscle Shoals, Alabama. One of his staff writers, George Jones, had already penned "One Bad Apple." The Osmonds' recording of it went to number one and stayed there for five weeks.

While "One Bad Apple" was still in the top 10, Donny's solo recording of an old Roy Orbison song debuted on the Hot 100. "Sweet And Innocent" peaked at number seven. His next single, a remake of "Go Away Little Girl," went to number one. Donny continued to record new versions of old songs, including Paul Anka's "Puppy Love," Johnny Mathis' "The Twelfth Of Never" and Freddie Scott's "Hey Girl." His sister Marie followed the same pattern when she began releasing singles in 1973. Donny and Marie also did a series of duets together, again specializing in remakes.

The Osmonds' chart attack ended in 1978. Without Donny, the four elder brothers reunited and became a country act in 1982, recording for Elektra, Warner Brothers, and EMI America. Marie also became a country singer, racking up three number one hits and moving from Elektra to RCA to Capitol. Donny dropped out of recording until 1988, when he signed with Virgin Records in the U.K. Unmarked copies of his single "Soldier Of Love" started getting airplay in the States, and listeners were surprised to find out they were enjoying Donny Osmond.

1 **GO AWAY LITTLE GIRL**
Donny Osmond *MGM* 71

2 **ONE BAD APPLE**
The Osmonds *MGM* 71

3 **YO-YO**
The Osmonds *MGM* 71

4 **PAPER ROSES**
Marie Osmond *MGM* 73

5 **SWEET AND INNOCENT**
Donny Osmond *MGM* 71

6 **DOWN BY THE LAZY RIVER**
The Osmonds *MGM* 72

7 **SOLDIER OF LOVE**
Donny Osmond *Capitol* 89

8 **PUPPY LOVE**
Donny Osmond *MGM* 72

9 **DEEP PURPLE**
Donny and Marie Osmond *MGM* 76

10 **I'M LEAVING IT (ALL) UP TO YOU**
Donny and Marie Osmond *MGM* 74

11 **THE TWELFTH OF NEVER**
Donny Osmond *MGM* 73

12 **HEY GIRL/I KNEW YOU WHEN**
Donny Osmond *MGM* 72

13 **MORNING SIDE OF THE MOUNTAIN**
Donny & Marie Osmond *MGM* 75

14 **WHY/LONELY BOY**
Donny Osmond *MGM* 72

15 **SACRED EMOTION**
Donny Osmond *Capitol* 89

16 **TOO YOUNG**
Donny Osmond *MGM* 72

17 **DOUBLE LOVIN'**
The Osmonds *MGM* 71

18 **LOVE ME FOR A REASON**
The Osmonds *MGM* 74

19 **CRAZY HORSES**
The Osmonds *MGM* 72

20 **HOLD HER TIGHT**
The Osmonds *MGM* 72

THE TOP 20 SONGS OF
SIMON & GARFUNKEL

1. **BRIDGE OVER TROUBLED WATER**
   Simon and Garfunkel *Columbia* 70
2. **50 WAYS TO LEAVE YOUR LOVER**
   Paul Simon *Columbia* 76
3. **MRS. ROBINSON**
   Simon and Garfunkel *Columbia* 68
4. **LOVES ME LIKE A ROCK**
   Paul Simon *Columbia* 73
5. **SLIP SLIDIN' AWAY**
   Paul Simon *Columbia* 78
6. **LATE IN THE EVENING**
   Paul Simon *Warner Bros* 80
7. **THE SOUNDS OF SILENCE**
   Simon and Garfunkel *Columbia* 66
8. **KODACHROME**
   Paul Simon *Columbia* 73
9. **CECELIA**
   Simon and Garfunkel *Columbia* 70
10. **MOTHER AND CHILD REUNION**
    Paul Simon *Columbia* 72
11. **I AM A ROCK**
    Simon and Garfunkel *Columbia* 66
12. **THE BOXER**
    Simon and Garfunkel *Columbia* 69
13. **ALL I KNOW**
    Art Garfunkel *Columbia* 73
14. **MY LITTLE TOWN**
    Simon and Garfunkel *Columbia* 75
15. **HOMEWARD BOUND**
    Simon and Garfunkel *Columbia* 66
16. **I ONLY HAVE EYES FOR YOU**
    Art Garfunkel *Columbia* 75
17. **SCARBOROUGH FAIR/CANTICLE**
    Simon and Garfunkel *Columbia* 68
18. **ME AND JULIO DOWN BY THE SCHOOLYARD**
    Paul Simon *Columbia* 72
19. **A HAZY SHADE OF WINTER**
    Simon and Garfunkel *Columbia* 66
20. **(WHAT A) WONDERFUL WORLD**
    Art Garfunkel w/James Taylor and
    Paul Simon *Columbia* 78

Paul Simon and Art Garfunkel met each other in 1953 during a sixth-grade production of *Alice In Wonderland*—Simon was the White Rabbit, Garfunkel was the Cheshire Cat. Two years later, they wrote their first song together, "The Girl For Me."

In 1957, their first record was released—"Hey, Schoolgirl" by Tom and Jerry, on the Big Top label. It went as high as number 49 on the Hot 100 and earned them an appearance on *American Bandstand*. Further Tom and Jerry singles didn't make the chart, and Simon and Garfunkel went separate ways after high school. Paul attended Queens College as an English major, and Art studied mathematics and architecture at Columbia University. Both continued their recording careers under a variety of assumed names. Simon made two more appearances on the Hot 100—as the leader of Tico & the Triumphs, with "Motorcycle," and as Jerry Landis, with "The Lone Teen Ranger." Art had two singles released as Artie Garr.

They remained friends and worked together in 1964, performing in Greenwich Village coffeehouses. A demo tape impressed Tom Wilson at Columbia Records, who signed the duo to the label. Paul moved to England, but came back to record *Wednesday Morning, 3 AM*. When a Boston radio station played one of the tracks, "The Sounds Of Silence," Wilson was encouraged to remix the acoustic cut with electric guitar, bass and drums. Paul received a phone call one day telling him the single had gone to number one on the *Billboard* chart.

Simon & Garfunkel's most successful Hot 100 single was released in 1970. Paul wrote "Bridge Over Troubled Water" during the summer of '69; the song was inspired by his love of gospel quartets, particularly the Swan Silvertones.

While it was their biggest hit yet, it also marked the end of Simon and Garfunkel working together. Disagreements and tension during the recording of the album had built to a point where both felt it was best to pursue individual careers. The two came back together in 1975 for a reunion single, "My Little Town." Six years later, Simon and Garfunkel reunited again to give a free concert in Central Park, which led to a tour of Europe and then the United States. A single from the Central Park concert, a revival of "Wake Up Little Susie," made the top 30 in 1982.

Garfunkel hit number one twice in Britain, with "I Only Have Eyes For You" and "Bright Eyes." Simon has won critical raves for albums like *Graceland* and *Rhythm of the Saints*, but has found it difficult to match that level of success on the singles chart.

THE TOP 20 SONGS OF
SONNY & CHER

Sonny Bono first made his mark in the record business as a songwriter, penning songs like "Needles And Pins" for Jackie DeShannon and the Searchers, and "Koko Joe" for the Righteous Brothers. When he met Cherilyn Sakisian LaPierre at a Hollywood coffee, he was working for producer Phil Spector. "I was his West Coast promotion man, I sang background and I hired the musicians and background singers," Sonny explains. He hired Cher to sing backing vocals on Spector tracks like the Crystals' "Da Doo Ron Ron" and the Ronettes' "Be My Baby."

At Sonny's request, Spector even produced a track for Cher, "Ringo, I Love You" (released under the name Bonnie Jo Mason). Then Sonny borrowed enough money to produce his own session for Cher. She was too nervous to sing by herself and asked Sonny to duet with her on "Baby Don't Go." Vault Records released a song by the duo, "The Letter," under the names Caesar and Cleo, and Cher was signed as a solo artist to Imperial.

Ahmet Ertegun signed the duo to Atco; their first single as Sonny & Cher was "Just You." They were all over the Hot 100 in 1965, starting with "I Got You Babe." Cher's version of Bob Dylan's "All I Really Want To Do" bested the Byrds recording of the same song, and Sonny's recording of "Laugh At Me"—inspired by being thrown out of Martoni's restaurant in Hollywood—was a top 10 entry.

It was a heady three years, but the top 10 hits stopped coming in 1967. Between 1968-70, neither Sonny nor Cher appeared on the *Billboard* Hot 100. Their return was spearheaded by Snuff Garrett, who was asked by Johnny Musso of Kapp Records to produce the couple's first efforts for their new label. (Garrett had known Sonny & Cher for some time—he was at Liberty Records when Cher recorded for the Imperial subsidiary, and he was their neighbor in the affluent community of Bel Air.) Garrett gave Sonny & Cher their biggest hits outside of "I Got You Babe." "All I Ever Need Is You," a remake of a song Garrett heard on a Ray Charles album, and "A Cowboy's Work Is Never Done" returned the husband and wife to the top 10. Garrett produced six of Sonny & Cher's top 10 hits, but moved on after 1974.

Sonny went into the restaurant business in West Hollywood before taking up politics. On April 13, 1988, he was elected mayor of Palm Springs. The day before, Cher received the Oscar for Best Actress for her performance in *Moonstruck*. Her film career had been doing so well that she had put aside recording, until she was signed to Geffen Records. In March, 1988, Cher had her first top 10 hit since 1979 with "I Found Someone."

When Rod Stewart went to number one on the *Billboard* Hot 100, he had a tendency to stay there. His top three singles, chart-toppers all, spent a total of 17 weeks at number one. That's the same number of weeks that the Supremes spent at the summit with their first *eight* number one songs.

Roderick David Stewart was born January 10, 1945, in the Highgate section of London. Inspired by the success of Bob Dylan, he hitchhiked around Europe in his teens playing guitar, until he was kicked out of Spain for vagrancy. Back in England, he worked as a gravedigger and joined the Five Dimensions.

After stints with blues singer Long John Baldry in the Hoochie Coochie Men and Steampacket, Rod found himself in the Shotgun Express with Mick Fleetwood and Peter Green. One single later, Rod moved on again, to sing vocals for ex-Yardbird Jeff Beck. In 1968, Rod signed a solo contract with Phonogram that allowed him to continue with the Jeff Beck Group. But that unit broke up, and Rod joined the Small Faces, who dropped the adjective in favor of just plain Faces.

Rod's first two solo albums, released on Mercury in America, were well-received, but didn't produce any hit singles. His first chart entry came from *Every Picture Tells a Story*. The original "A" side was a remake of Tim Hardin's "Reason To Believe"; it wasn't until its fifth week on the Hot 100 that "Maggie May" was even listed, and then only as the "B" side. The following week, "Maggie May" had taken over the lead position. Nobody liked it, Rod said in his liner notes for his *Storyteller* collection, and "if it wasn't for a diligent DJ in Cleveland who flipped it over, I would've still been digging graves."

"Maggie May" was the turning point in Rod's career. He continued with Phonogram until 1975, when he signed with Warner Brothers. His label debut, *Atlantic Crossing*, went top 10 but that success didn't cross over to the singles chart, where his version of the Sutherland Brothers' "Sailing" stalled at number 58. In the U.K., though, "Sailing" went to number one and became Stewart's biggest British hit of all time.

The Faces officially split at the end of 1975. Rod's solo career continued to shine, with the 1976 single "Tonight's The Night (Gonna Be Alright)" becoming his most successful American single. His next number one in America was savaged by critics for pandering to disco. Rod wrote about "Do Ya Think I'm Sexy?" in his liner notes for *Storyteller:* "It was frightening, stirring up so much love and hate at the same time; most of the public loved it; all the critics hated it."

THE TOP 20 SONGS OF
DIONNE WARWICK

1. **THAT'S WHAT FRIENDS ARE FOR**
   Dionne and Friends *Arista* 86
2. **I'LL NEVER LOVE THIS WAY AGAIN**
   Dionne Warwick *Arista* 79
3. **THEN CAME YOU**
   Dionne Warwicke & Spinners *Atlantic* 74
4. **HEARTBREAKER**
   Dionne Warwick *Arista* 83
5. **(THEME FROM) VALLEY OF THE DOLLS**
   Dionne Warwick *Scepter* 68
6. **I SAY A LITTLE PRAYER**
   Dionne Warwick *Scepter* 67
7. **THIS GIRL'S IN LOVE WITH YOU**
   Dionne Warwick *Scepter* 69
8. **WALK ON BY**
   Dionne Warwick *Scepter* 64
9. **I'LL NEVER FALL IN LOVE AGAIN**
   Dionne Warwick *Scepter* 70
10. **DO YOU KNOW THE WAY TO SAN JOSE**
    Dionne Warwick *Scepter* 68
11. **ANYONE WHO HAD A HEART**
    Dionne Warwick *Scepter* 64
12. **MESSAGE TO MICHAEL**
    Dionne Warwick *Scepter* 66
13. **LOVE POWER**
    Dionne Warwick and Jeffrey Osborne *Arista* 87
14. **DEJA VU**
    Dionne Warwick *Arista* 80
15. **ALFIE**
    Dionne Warwick *Scepter* 67
16. **YOU'VE LOST THAT LOVIN' FEELIN'**
    Dionne Warwick *Scepter* 69
17. **PROMISES, PROMISES**
    Dionne Warwick *Scepter* 68
18. **DON'T MAKE ME OVER**
    Dionne Warwick *Scepter* 63
19. **NO NIGHT SO LONG**
    Dionne Warwick *Arista* 80
20. **REACH OUT FOR ME**
    Dionne Warwick *Scepter* 64

Marie Dionne Warwick was born in East Orange, New Jersey, to a musical family—her father did gospel promotion for Chess Records, and her mother managed a church choir group. Forming a trio called the Gospelaires with her sister Dee Dee and cousin Cissy Houston, she did backing vocals for artists like Bobby Darin and the Drifters. One Drifters session found the girls singing background on "Mexican Divorce," written by Burt Bacharach and Bob Hilliard. Dionne asked to record some demos, so Florence Greenberg at Scepter Records suggested that Bacharach produce some sessions with Dionne. That resulted in a demo of "Don't Make Me Over."

Dionne charted with 38 different titles on Scepter between December, 1962 and August, 1971. All but five were written by Bacharach and David. Her most successful Scepter single was one of those five, "(Theme From) Valley Of The Dolls," written by Dory and Andre Previn. Originally, that song was released as the "B" side of Warwick's second most successful Scepter single, Bacharach-David's "I Say A Little Prayer."

Following her stint with Scepter, Dionne moved to Warner Brothers Records—without the services of her two main songwriters. Bacharach and David had split their partnership, and despite working with writer/producers like Brian Holland and Lamont Dozier, Dionne had no chart success on Warner Brothers. Her only hit between 1971 and 1978 was "Then Came You," produced by Thom Bell for Atlantic. Recorded with the Spinners, it was Dionne's first number one single.

Dionne's most successful single came about after the rift with Bacharach was repaired. When Bacharach and his wife Carole Bayer Sager were preparing material for Dionne to record in 1985, Carole remembered a song they had written three years earlier for the film *Night Shift*. Rod Stewart had recorded "That's What Friends Are For" for the closing credits, but Burt and Carole weren't happy with his rendition and it wasn't considered for single release.

Dionne thought the song would make a good duet with Stevie Wonder. When the two of them recorded the tune, Neil Simon and Elizabeth Taylor visited the studio. Knowing of Taylor's work against AIDS, Sager suggested that the proceeds from the song could be donated to the American Foundation for AIDS Research. Warwick, Wonder and Taylor were all enthusiastic about the idea. Then a third vocalist was added to the track—Gladys Knight. Clive Davis then suggested that Elton John add his voice, and agreed to also donate Arista's profits.

THE CARPENTERS

1 **(THEY LONG TO BE) CLOSE TO YOU**
70

2 **TOP OF THE WORLD**
73

3 **WE'VE ONLY JUST BEGUN**
70

4 **SUPERSTAR**
71

5 **RAINY DAYS AND MONDAYS**
71

6 **FOR ALL WE KNOW**
71

7 **YESTERDAY ONCE MORE**
73

8 **SING**
73

9 **PLEASE MR. POSTMAN**
75

10 **HURTING EACH OTHEP**
72

Richard and Karen Carpenter, having already cut four songs for RCA that were never released, were signed to Herb Alpert's A&M label after he heard a demo and liked Karen's voice. Their first hit was a song that had been previously recorded by Dionne Warwick and Richard Chamberlain. Alpert himself had turned it down when Burt Bacharach offered it to him, but suggested that the duo consider it. "(They Long To Be) Close To You" launched the Carpenters' career with a number one single, and remains their most successful Hot 100 entry.

The Carpenters mined many different sources for their singles. "We've Only Just Begun" was originally heard in a bank commercial. "Superstar" was a Leon Russell-Bonnie Bramlett tune that had been recorded several different times. "For All We Know" came from the film *Lovers and Other Strangers*; "Sing" was from "Sesame Street"; "Please Mr. Postman" was an early Marvelettes hit; and "Hurting Each Other" was originally recorded by Ruby & the Romantics.

HALL & OATES

1 **MANEATER**
82

2 **I CAN'T GO FOR THAT (NO CAN DO)**
82

3 **KISS ON MY LIST**
81

4 **OUT OF TOUCH**
84

5 **PRIVATE EYES**
81

6 **SAY IT ISN'T SO**
83

7 **RICH GIRL**
77

8 **SARA SMILE**
76

9 **YOU'VE LOST THAT LOVIN' FEELING**
80

10 **ONE ON ONE**
83

The Sound of Philadelphia was a strong influence on Daryl Franklin Hohl, who grew up in Pottstown, 40 miles west of the City of Brotherly Love. Daryl sang with street-corner groups, and at 17, he played keyboards for local bands. A year later, he was recording with the Romeos, a group that included future producer Kenny Gamble.

Hall and Tim Moore made one album together as Gulliver before Hall split to form a duo with John Oates. They signed with Atlantic, and their *Abandoned Luncheonette* album was produced by Arif Mardin. After one more Atlantic LP, they switched to RCA. Their first of six number one singles was "Rich Girl" in 1977. Three years later, they began to produce their own albums, unleashing a flood of hit 45s.

Their most successful Hot 100 single, "Maneater," sounded so much like the Supremes' "You Can't Hurry Love" that songwriter Lamont Dozier thought it was a cover of that hit the first time he heard the opening notes.

WHITNEY HOUSTON

1 I'M YOUR BABY TONIGHT
90

2 I WANNA DANCE WITH SOMEBODY (WHO LOVES ME)
87

3 GREATEST LOVE OF ALL
86

4 SO EMOTIONAL
88

5 HOW WILL I KNOW
86

6 SAVING ALL MY LOVE FOR YOU
85

7 DIDN'T WE ALMOST HAVE IT ALL
87

8 WHERE DO BROKEN HEARTS GO
88

9 YOU GIVE GOOD LOVE
85

10 ONE MOMENT IN TIME
88

When "I'm Your Baby Tonight" moved into the top spot on the Hot 100, Whitney Houston had her eighth number one single, equaling Madonna at that date as the female soloist with the most number one hits in the history of the *Billboard* chart.

Her first chart-topper, "Saving All My Love For You," started out as a duet between Marilyn McCoo and Billy Davis, Jr. Michael Masser, who wrote the tune with Gerry Goffin, altered it by removing the second bridge, and predicted it would be Whitney's first number one hit. "Greatest Love Of All," written by Masser and Linda Creed, was originally recorded by George Benson for the film *The Greatest*.

Whitney's second biggest *Billboard* single—"I Wanna Dance With Somebody (Who Loves Me)—was written by George Merrill and Shannon Rubicam, who had earlier penned "How Will I Know." Shannon says the song wasn't about disco dancing: "It was, 'I wanna do that dance of life with somebody.'"

GEORGE MICHAEL

1 CARELESS WHISPER
Wham! f/George Michael *Columbia* 85

2 FAITH
George Michael *Columbia* 87

3 WAKE ME UP BEFORE YOU GO-GO
Wham! *Columbia* 84

4 EVERYTHING SHE WANTS
Wham! *Columbia* 85

5 ONE MORE TRY
George Michael *Columbia* 88

6 FATHER FIGURE
George Michael *Columbia* 88

7 I WANT YOUR SEX
George Michael *Columbia* 87

8 I KNEW YOU WERE WAITING (FOR ME)
Aretha Franklin and George Michael *Arista* 87

9 MONKEY
George Michael *Columbia* 88

10 I'M YOUR MAN
Wham! *Columbia* 86

Georgios Panayiotou was 12 years old when he met Andrew Ridgely at the school in Bushey, England, where they were both students. As teenagers, they formed a band called the Executives, then signed with a small British label, Vision, as a duo called Wham!

After a few singles that did well in the U.K. but not America, Wham! released their breakthrough hit, "Wake Me Up Before You Go-Go." It went to number one in the U.S. as well as the U.K. "Careless Whisper" was released as a solo single by George at home, but in America, the label credit read "Wham featuring George Michael." Written while he was riding on a bus at age 16, "Careless Whisper" is Michael's most successful Hot 100 single.

In the fall of 1985, the pair split, and Michael went to work on his first solo effort, *Faith*. Five of the singles from that album are in his top 10: "Faith," "One More Try," "Father Figure," "I Want Your Sex" and "Monkey." His second album, *Listen Without Prejudice Vol. 1*, was released without a photo of George on the cover.

THE WRITERS

Long before the rock era began, America exalted its songwriters. Composers like Irving Berlin, George and Ira Gershwin, Cole Porter, Richard Rodgers and Lorenz Hart were as popular and as well-known as any performers of their day.

In the early days of rock and roll, astute record collectors who read the fine print on their 45s noticed some of the same names occurring underneath the titles of their favorite songs. Jerry Leiber and Mike Stoller, Doc Pomus and Mort Shuman, and Felice and Boudleaux Bryant were three teams who built up impressive repertoires during the '50s.

Many of the top chart hits in the first part of the '60s were written in or near the Brill Building, a latter-day Tin Pin Alley. Songsmiths pounded away on pianos in small cubicles, always within earshot of other writers working on similar tunes. Aldon Music, located at 1650 Broadway (across the street from the Brill complex), was a hotbed of activity. Al Nevins and Don Kirshner's publishing company was home to Gerry Goffin and Carole King, Barry Mann and Cynthia Weil, Neil Sedaka and Howard Greenfield, and Neil Diamond. In 1963 alone, the names "Goffin and King" appeared in parentheses under the titles of hits by the Cookies, the Drifters, Freddie Scott, the Chiffons, Little Eva, Lesley Gore, Skeeter Davis, Steve Lawrence and Dion.

The songs that Aldon's staff of composers were writing proved to have longer lifespans than the 10 or 12 weeks they might have spent on the Hot 100. It's unlikely that a single day has passed since 1965 that some radio station in the world hasn't played one of the many versions of Barry Mann and Cynthia Weil's "You've Lost That Lovin' Feelin'." Goffin and King's "The Loco-Motion" was a number one song in the '60s and '70s, and a number three hit in the '80s.

It will be up to future historians to decide if Bacharach and the Beatles belong in the same category as Bach and Beethoven. But we already know that the Lennon-McCartney songbook is still active two decades after the Beatles stopped recording as a group—and that the Holland-Dozier-Holland catalog is just as attractive to recording artists in the '90s as it was when the Marvelettes, the Supremes, the Four Tops and Martha & the Vandellas first recorded those songs a quarter of a century ago.

This section includes the greatest hits from long-established songwriters, as well as from relative newcomers who have made their mark in the last few years. Diane Warren may only be represented by a top 10 list—but as prolific as she is, she should work her way up to a top 100 in some future edition.

"We wanted to be the Goffin and King of England," is how John Lennon and Paul McCartney once described their goal as songwriters. Lennon and McCartney began writing songs the same time Gerry Goffin and Carole King did, in the late 1950s. They were prolific, and while the songs were freshman efforts, they often wrote at the top of their lyric sheets: "Another Lennon-McCartney Original."

Their talents as composers were not always recognized. When they recorded 15 songs for an audition tape for Decca Records, manager Brian Epstein suggested they stay away from original songs. Twelve of the tracks were versions of songs that ranged from Bobby Vee's "Take Good Care Of My Baby" to Guy Lombardo's 1937 hit "September In The Rain." The three Lennon-McCartney songs recorded for that audition tape were never released by the Beatles: "Love Of The Loved" (later given to Cilla Black), "Hello Little Girl" (recorded by the Fourmost) and "Like Dreamers Do" (a hit for the Applejacks from Birmingham).

Decca Records signed Brian Poole and the Tremeloes instead of the Beatles. Music publisher Syd Coleman suggested that Epstein contact George Martin, head of EMI's relatively small Parlophone label. Martin produced the Beatles' first session at Abbey Road studios on September 11, 1962; two of the songs recorded that day were "Love Me Do" and "P.S. I Love You." "I was convinced that I had a hit group on my hands if only I could get hold of the right songs," Martin said. When he couldn't find anything better than "Love Me Do" and "P.S. I Love You," he reluctantly agreed to release them back-to-back on the first single.

Martin, however, wasn't too keen on John and Paul's songwriting. He thought Mitch Murray's "How Do You Do It?" would be a better follow-up than Lennon and McCartney's "Please Please Me."

The Beatles agreed to record "How Do You Do It?," but it was never officially released. They prevailed, and "Please Please Me" was issued instead; it peaked at number two. "How Do You Do It?" was subsequently recorded by another Mersey group, Gerry and the Pacemakers. It was their first single, and it went to number one.

While the Beatles recorded a mix of original songs and remakes like "Twist And Shout" and "Money," their own songs were soon in demand by other artists. Another of Brian Epstein's groups, Billy J. Kramer and the Dakotas, were given Lennon-McCartney songs for their first three releases: "Do You Want To Know A Secret" (also recorded by the Beatles), "Bad To Me" (recorded by the Beatles but never officially released by them) and "I'll Keep You Satisfied," all charted in 1963.

"Do You Want To Know A Secret" had a U.S. release by Kramer on Liberty, but failed to chart. No one in America recognized the writers' names yet, although both the Vee-Jay and Swan labels released Beatles singles in the U.S. in 1963.

The first artist to take a Lennon-McCartney song into the *Billboard* Hot 100 was Del Shannon. When "From Me To You" was popular in Britain, Shannon was coming off a hit single, "Little Town Flirt." Appearing at the Royal Albert Hall on a bill that featured the Beatles, Shannon told Lennon he was going to record "From Me To You" for America. John's first response was, "That'll be fine." But as he turned to go on stage, John had second thoughts and shouted to Del, "Don't do that!"

John had apparently realized the consequences of having one of their tunes covered by an American artist for America—they were having trouble enough being accepted in the States.

Despite Lennon's plea, Shannon recorded the song. It entered the American Hot 100 on June 29, 1963. It had a brief four-week run on the chart and only reached number 77—but that was better than the original version, which debuted on *Billboard*'s Bubbling Under chart on August 3 and peaked at number 116.

Back in England, the Beatles continued to give songs away. Some did not fare well—like Tommy Quickly's "Tip of My Tongue" and Mike Shannon's "One And One Is Two." But in 1964, Peter and Gordon had a number one hit in the U.K. and the U.S. with "A World Without Love," a song given to them by Peter's friend, Paul McCartney. It helped that Paul was dating Peter's sister, actress Jane Asher. Peter and Gordon's next two singles—"Nobody I Know" and "I Don't Want To See You Again"—were also listed as Lennon-McCartney songs, although they were penned only by Paul. (The two Beatles had an agreement that both their names would go on all of their songs, no matter who wrote them.) For those who might have griped that Peter and Gordon had an advantage dipping into the Lennon-McCartney songbook, Paul

McCartney wrote the song "Woman" and listed the composer as "Bernard Webb." It peaked at number 14 in 1966.

As early as 1964, other artists included Lennon-McCartney songs in their repertoires. Bobby Vee cut "She Loves You" and "From Me To You" on his album *Bobby Vee Sings the New Sound from England.* Later that year, the Supremes recorded "I Want To Hold Your Hand," "Can't Buy Me Love," "You Can't Do That" and "A Hard Day's Night" on *A Little Bit of Liverpool.*

Some Lennon-McCartney covers were songs that the Beatles did not release as singles. In Britain, Marianne Faithfull released a 45 of "Yesterday" when the Beatles did not. "Michelle" was covered by the Overlanders (number one in the U.K.) and David and Jonathan (songwriters Roger Cook and Roger Greenaway). The latter peaked at number 18 on the Hot 100.

Of the Top 100 Lennon-McCartney songs, 37 of them were recorded by the Beatles. Another 40 were recorded by either Paul or John after the Beatles broke up. Fourteen are remakes of Beatle songs, and another nine were either never recorded or never released by the Beatles.

The most successful Lennon-McCartney song is "Hey Jude," number one for nine weeks in 1968. It was their first single on Apple Records, and was backed with a sped-up version of "Revolution." The original, slower version of that song was eventually released on *The Beatles,* a.k.a. the White Album. "Hey Jude" was composed by Paul as he was driving John's son Julian home one day. Some of the lyrics were meant as temporary, dummy lyrics ("the movement you need is on your shoulder"), but John liked them so much he insisted they stay.

The next two most popular Lennon-McCartney songs are also by Paul; they are his duets with Michael Jackson and Stevie Wonder.

The most successful remake of a Lennon-McCartney song is actually a remake of eight songs—the medley by Stars on 45 that begins with the introduction of Shocking Blue's "Venus." Oddly enough, the four Beatles songs in the medley that made the Hot 100 ("Do You Want To Know A Secret," "We Can Work It Out," "I Should Have Known Better" and "Nowhere Man") were all more successful in the Stars on 45 version than they had been when originally released.

The second most successful remake of a Beatles song is Elton John's "Lucy In The Sky With Diamonds," followed by Anne Murray's "You Won't See Me" and Sergio Mendes and Brasil 66's "The Fool On The Hill." None of those three songs were released as singles by the Beatles.

Although it's been almost 30 years since the first Lennon-McCartney song made the U.K. chart, there is no ebb to the release of new versions of their compositions. In 1990, the Pretenders recorded "Not A Second Time"; World Party covered "Happiness Is A Warm Gun"; and Candy Flip had a top five song in the U.K. with "Strawberry Fields Forever."

CAROLE KING

Brooklyn-born Carol Klein was only four when she learned to play the piano, and she started writing songs even then. The inspiration for her vocation came from going to see Alan Freed's rock and roll shows when she was 13. She specifically remembers being inspired by Chuck Berry, Jerry Lee Lewis and the Everly Brothers. "I wanted to be around these people, and get to know them personally, and have them like and respect me," she explains. "I thought the best way to do that would be to write songs for them."

In high school, Carol formed a quartet called the Co-Sines and wrote songs for the group. In 1958, she met Gerry Goffin when they were both students at Queens College. Gerry had been writing songs on his own since he was eight years old. They dated and began to collaborate on songs. His ambition was to write for the Broadway stage; she wanted to write rock and roll. They made a pact—Gerry would help Carol (who took the stage name Carole King) write lyrics for her rock songs, and she would help him write music for the Broadway show he had conceived.

Carole calls her early recordings "some of the worst songs you'd ever want to hear," including her first single, "Baby Sittin'," released on ABC-Paramount in March, 1959. That same year, she released "Short Mort" on RCA and "Oh! Neil"—a response to Neil

Sedaka's "Oh! Carol"—on Alpine.

Those early singles were surpassed in 1960 when Gerry and Carole went to work for Don Kirshner and Al Nevins' Aldon Music at 1650 Broadway—the legendary Brill Building—in Manhattan. Married and the parents of a young daughter, Louise, Goffin and King earned $50 a week as staff writers, working alongside other Aldon songwriting teams like Barry Mann and Cynthia Weil and Neil Sedaka and Howard Greenfield.

In 1960, Gerry and Carole wrote a four-and-a-half minute country and western song. Kirshner had them shorten it, and offered it to Johnny Mathis. After Johnny passed on it, the song went to producer Luther Dixon, who owed Goffin and King a favor. He played it for the Shirelles, who thought that "Will You Love Me Tomorrow" was terrible. But as Dixon worked on the arrangement, with Carole playing kettle drums herself, the girls changed their minds. It became the first number one record for the Shirelles as well as for Goffin and King.

"Will You Love Me Tomorrow" gave Gerry and Carole their first taste of economic freedom. They were soon in demand as songwriters, turning out hits for the Drifters ("Some Kind of Wonderful"), Bobby Rydell ("I've Got Bonnie") and Gene Pitney ("Every Breath I Take").

In 1962, Kirshner decided to take his demo singers—the Cookies, Little Eva and Carole—and transform them into recording artists. The first release was Carole's demo of "It Might As Well Rain Until September," written for Bobby Vee.

The years 1962-1963 were especially productive for Goffin and King, and they specialized in turning out follow-up hits like "Her Royal Majesty" for James Darren, "One Fine Day" for the Chiffons and "I Can't Stay Mad at You" for Skeeter Davis.

Lou Adler, who headed Dimension's publishing firm, formed the Ode label in 1967. A year later, Carole and Gerry moved to Los Angeles—but separately. The marriage was over. With Danny Kortchmar and Charles Larkey (who would become Carole's second husband), Carole formed a trio called the City and signed with Adler's label; one album later, the City disbanded. Carole recorded her first solo album in 1970, *Writer: Carole King*. But it was her second album for Ode that brought her worldwide fame. *Tapestry* was meant to be a way for other artists to hear Carole's songs—"I don't want to be a star," she said just before the album was released. When the album sold more than 15 million copies, she had little choice.

The only new Goffin-King song on *Tapestry* was "Smackwater Jack." While Carole had collaborated with others in the past—she wrote the Everly Brothers' "Crying In The Rain" with Howard Greenfield—she was now working regularly with writers like Toni Stern and Dave Palmer. Songs written with Goffin ("Ferguson Road," "High Out Of Time" and "Speeding Time") have turned up on Carole's albums through the years; two Goffin-King creations appeared on 1989's *City Streets*.

THE TOP 10 SONGS WRITTEN BY
GERRY GOFFIN

Gerry Goffin and Carole King sometimes wrote songs with other partners during their early days. Goffin often worked with Jack Keller, with whom he wrote Bobby Vee's "Run to Him," Gerry's most successful tune without Carole. Nine months after "Run to Him" entered the Hot 100, Goffin had a top 10 hit with "Who Put the Bomp (In the Bomp, Bomp, Bomp)," a collaboration with the song's artist, Barry Mann.

Just as Goffin and King teamed up to create hits for the Monkees in 1966-67, Goffin collaborated with Partridge Family producer Wes Farell to write "I'll Meet You Halfway," number nine in 1971.

Goffin teamed with Barry Goldberg to write "I've Got To Use My Imagination," covered by Gladys Knight & the Pips in 1974. But Goffin's most regular partner during the '70s and '80s was Michael Masser. Together, they wrote Diana Ross' "Theme from 'Mahogany' (Do You Know Where You're Going To)" and Whitney Houston's "Saving All My Love for You."

BARRY MANN & CYNTHIA WEIL

Don Kirshner with Cynthia Weil and Barry Mann

As a 12-year-old kid growing up in Brooklyn, Barry Mann was inspired by a friend who played piano to take lessons from his teacher. A year later, he had written his first song, an ode to an "Evil Horde" that he can still recite today.

He gave up the idea of being an architect to concentrate on songwriting. The first Barry Mann song ever recorded was "A Little Less Talk And A Little More Action," written with Joe Shapiro, whose hits included "Round And Round" for Perry Como. The first hit was the 1959 Diamonds song, "She Say (Oom Dooby Doom)." Barry's friend Jack Keller went to work for Don Kirshner and Al Nevins' publishing company, and suggested that Barry also be signed.

Barry had been with Aldon for about a year when he and Howard Greenfield played a song for singer Teddy Randazzo. "I walked in and saw this cute girl," he recalls. "She asked Teddy who I was and found out I worked for Aldon." Soon Cynthia Weil came up to the Aldon office to play her songs. "We became romantically involved before we started writing together," Barry says.

They were married in 1961, the same year their first song was recorded. "Painting The Town With Teardrops" didn't make it. Their second composition became their first hit—"Bless You," written for the Drifters but recorded by a teenaged Tony Orlando.

At the same time, Barry was moving up the Hot 100 with his own recording of "Who Put The Bomp (In The Bomp, Bomp, Bomp)," written with Gerry Goffin. It would be his only recording to make the upper half of the chart, although he would release singles on Red Bird, Scepter, United Artists, Warner Brothers, Arista and Casablanca.

On his Casablanca album, Barry introduced the song "Don't Know Much." Bill Medley released it as a single in 1981, and it peaked at number 88. Two years later, Bette Midler recorded it as "All I Need To Know," and it fared a little better, climbing to number 77. It wasn't until Linda Ronstadt asked Aaron Neville to record it with her that the song became a smash, reaching number two in 1989.

Number two on their list is "You've Lost That Lovin' Feelin'," originally recorded by the Righteous Brothers. It was specifically written for Bill Medley and Bobby Hatfield at the request of their producer, Phil Spector. It was the first Mann-Weil song to top the *Billboard* singles chart. The song appears three times on the Mann-Weil top 50: Dionne Warwick's version from 1969 is number 36, and Daryl Hall and John Oates' recording from 1980 is number eight. One of Barry and Cynthia's favorite versions was recorded by Long John Baldry and Kathi MacDonald; it peaked at number 89 in 1979. The fifth version to chart on the Hot 100 was by Roberta Flack and Donny Hathaway, number 71 in 1971.

Mann & Weil's most successful chart single is "Never Gonna Let You Go." "I spent three weeks on that melody," explains Barry. "I was going to write something for Maurice White. He asked me to come up with something for Earth, Wind and Fire." James Ingram sang the demo and Dionne Warwick first recorded it in 1982. Robby Buchanan passed the song to Sergio Mendes who liked it enough to record it, with Joe Pizzulo and Leza Miller on vocals.

Ingram also sang "Just Once," Cynthia's favorite song of all their compositions. It's Barry's second favorite, runner-up to "You've Lost That Lovin' Feelin'." They didn't write the song for anyone in particular, according to Cynthia. Barry had been recording many of their demos, but they thought it might be better to find an outstanding male R&B singer instead. Linda Perry at ATV Music suggested James Ingram. When they heard Ingram sing, "we looked at each other and became weak," Cybthia recalls. Barry adds: "I stopped him and said, 'You are the greatest singer I've heard in 20 years."

Their least favorite version of one of their songs is the Animals' "We Gotta Get Out Of This Place." Written for the Righteous Brothers, the song was passed to British producer Mickie Most by Allen Klein. "When I heard the Animals' record, I went berserk because they left out half the lyric," says Cynthia. "They changed it radically. I called Kirshner and begged him to stop the song from coming out. He said, 'It's number two in England, what do you want me to do?'"

JEFF BARRY & ELLIE GREENWICH

1 SUGAR, SUGAR
The Archies *Calendar* 69

2 CHAPEL OF LOVE
The Dixie Cups *Red Bird* 64

3 DO WAH DIDDY DIDDY
Manfred Mann *Ascot* 64

4 DA DOO RON RON
Shaun Cassidy *Warner/Curb* 77

5 LEADER OF THE PACK
The Shangri-Las *Red Bird* 64

6 HANKY PANKY
Tommy James & the Shondells *Roulette* 66

7 I HONESTLY LOVE YOU
Olivia Newton-John *MCA* 74

8 BE MY BABY
The Ronettes *Philles* 63

9 TAKE ME HOME TONIGHT
Eddie Money *Columbia* 86

10 BABY, I LOVE YOU
Andy Kim *Steed* 69

11 REMEMBER (WALKIN' IN THE SAND)
The Shangri-Las *Red Bird* 64

12 DA DOO RON RON (WHEN HE WALKED ME HOME)
The Crystals *Philles* 63

13 TELL LAURA I LOVE HER
Ray Peterson *RCA* 60

14 MONTEGO BAY
Bobby Bloom *L&R* 70

15 THEN HE KISSED ME
The Crystals *Philles* 63

Brooklyn-born Ellie Greenwich grew up in Levittown, Long Island. She loved music and her parents encouraged her to study the accordion, until she finally persuaded them to buy a piano. Through a local record store owner, she made contact with RCA Victor Records, and the label issued a single under the name Ellie Gaye. She met Jeff Barry at a Thanksgiving dinner hosted by her aunt. He had already written a song called "Tell Laura I Love Her," and he told Ellie that Ray Peterson had recorded it and that it was going to be a big hit. He was right.

Ellie was attending Hofstra University. After classes, she would head into Manhattan to record demos of Jeff's songs and was paid $15 per session. Following graduation, Ellie accepted a position as a high school teacher. Three-and-a-half weeks into the job, she quit to pursue a career in music.

Ellie had an appointment in the Brill Building with songwriter John Gluck, Jr., and was playing the piano in his office when a man walked in and mistakenly took her for Carole King. Ellie corrected him and played him some of her songs. Jerry Leiber said he liked her material and introduced her to his partner, Mike Stoller; Ellie was signed to their Trio Music publishing company for $75 a week. With Tony Powers, she wrote "He's Got The Power," the follow-up to the Exciters' "Tell Him."

Phil Spector liked a Greenwich-Powers song, "(Today I Met) The Boy I'm Gonna Marry," and asked to meet the writers. Meanwhile, Jeff and Ellie were married, and made a decision to only write with each other, much to Tony Powers' disappointment.

Barry and Greenwich's early collaborations included a number of Phil Spector productions: "Da Doo Ron Ron (When He Walked Me Home)" for the Crystals, "Wait Til' My Bobby Gets Home" for Darlene Love and "Be My Baby" for the Ronettes (all hits in 1963). That same year, Jeff and Ellie's demo of "What a Guy," a song they had written for the Sensations ("Let Me In"), was released under the name "The Raindrops" on Jubilee Records. The follow-up, "The Kind of Boy You Can't Forget," was a top 20 hit.

The Raindrops also recorded "Do Wah Diddy Diddy," originally cut by the Exciters ("Tell Him"). "Jeff and I really believed in that song," Ellie explains. "We got a call from Leiber and Stoller at the studio saying, 'You ought to forget about it. It was just shipped by Manfred Mann.' We had finished recording it, but we never mixed it."

Another Raindrops track—written in 20 minutes so they could have a "B" side for one of their singles—was a number one hit for Tommy James & the Shondells. "Hanky Panky" was a local hit in the tri-state area of Michigan, Indiana and Illinois two years before Roulette released it nationally.

Many other Barry-Greenwich hits were more successful when recorded the second time around. "Chapel Of Love" was written for the Ronettes, but when it wasn't released as a single, Jeff and Ellie produced it for the Dixie Cups. It was the first hit on Leiber and Stoller's Red Bird label. "Da Doo Ron Ron" was a bigger hit for Shaun Cassidy when he remade the Crystals song in 1977. "River Deep-Mountain High," considered a classic when Spector produced it for Ike and Tina Turner in 1966, didn't crack the top 30 until the Supremes and the Four Tops released it in 1971. The Ronettes' "Baby, I Love You" was a bigger hit when Barry produced it on his Steed label for Andy Kim. Kim also recorded "Be My Baby," a song that was heard again in 1986 when Eddie Money incorporated it (with vocals by Ronnie Spector) into his song "Take Me Home Tonight."

Through Don Kirshner, Jeff produced some of the early Monkees hits, including "I'm A Believer." Barry also started producing Andy Kim in 1968. The following year, they teamed up to write the biggest hit of Barry's career—"Sugar, Sugar," for the fictional Archies.

Barry continued to write with other collaborators, including Bobby Bloom ("Montego Bay" and "Heavy Makes You Happy") and Peter Allen ("I Honestly Love You"). Ellie was approached by Alan Pepper, one of the owners of Manhattan's Bottom Line, to put together a show based on her songs. After a successful off-Broadway run, *Leader of the Pack* moved to the Great White Way in March, 1985. The cast included Darlene Love and Ellie herself.

THE TOP 30 SONGS WRITTEN BY
NEIL SEDAKA

1 LOVE WILL KEEP US TOGETHER
Captain & Tennille *A&M* 75

2 LONELY NIGHT (ANGEL FACE)
Captain & Tennille *A&M* 76

3 LAUGHTER IN THE RAIN
Neil Sedaka *Rocket* 75

4 BREAKING UP IS HARD TO DO
Neil Sedaka *RCA* 62

5 WHERE THE BOYS ARE
Connie Francis *MGM* 61

6 BAD BLOOD
Neil Sedaka *Rocket* 75

7 OH! CAROL
Neil Sedaka *RCA* 59

8 YOU NEVER DONE IT LIKE THAT
Captain & Tennille *A&M* 78

9 HAPPY BIRTHDAY, SWEET SIXTEEN
Neil Sedaka *RCA* 62

10 CALENDAR GIRL
Neil Sedaka *RCA* 61

11 BREAKING UP IS HARD TO DO
Neil Sedaka *Rocket* 76

12 FRANKIE
Connie Francis *MGM* 59

13 NEXT DOOR TO AN ANGEL
Neil Sedaka *RCA* 62

14 BREAKIN' IN A BRAND NEW BROKEN HEART
Connie Francis *MGM* 61

15 STAIRWAY TO HEAVEN
Neil Sedaka *RCA* 60

16 SHOULD'VE NEVER LET YOU GO
Neil Sedaka and Dara Sedaka *Elektra* 80

17 THE DIARY
Neil Sedaka *RCA* 59

18 STUPID CUPID
Connie Francis *MGM* 58

19 YOU MEAN EVERYTHING TO ME
Neil Sedaka *RCA* 60

20 WORKIN' ON A GROOVY THING
5th Dimension *Soul City* 69

21 LITTLE DEVIL
Neil Sedaka *RCA* 61

22 ALICE IN WONDERLAND
Neil Sedaka *RCA* 63

23 LOVE IN THE SHADOWS
Neil Sedaka *Rocket* 76

24 SOLITAIRE
Carpenters *A&M* 75

25 PUPPET MAN
Tom Jones *Parrot* 71

26 THE IMMIGRANT
Neil Sedaka *Rocket* 75

27 PUPPET MAN
5th Dimension *Bell* 70

28 THAT'S WHEN THE MUSIC TAKES ME
Neil Sedaka *Rocket* 75

29 BREAKING UP IS HARD TO DO
The Partridge Family *Bell* 72

30 LET'S GO STEADY AGAIN
Neil Sedaka *RCA* 63

While attending the Juilliard School, Neil Sedaka would often neglect his study of classical music in favor of writing songs with Howard Greenfield. The two would peddle their songs to Manhattan music publishers, and one trip to the city found them in the Brill Building at 1650 Broadway. They knocked on the door of Aldon Music, and the next day, Don Kirshner and Al Nevins signed them to an exclusive contract.

Kirshner arranged for the two young songwriters to meet his friend Connie Francis, who had just scored her first hit, "Who's Sorry Now." Neil played her "Stupid Cupid"; Connie loved it, and invited Neil to play piano on the session. It was the first Sedaka-Greenfield hit, peaking at no. 14 on the Hot 100.

As an artist, Neil scored 12 top 30 hits between 1958-1963. Connie Francis continued to record his songs, but with the onset of the Beatles, Sedaka's chart fortunes sunk. It wasn't until the 5th Dimension re-made "Workin' on a Groovy Thing" (originally recorded by Patti Drew) in 1969 that Sedaka and Greenfield had another hit song. In 1970, the duo parted ways, and Sedaka's agent suggested he try for a comeback by performing in England. He recorded two albums there.

Collaborating with lyricist Phil Cody, Neil had a British hit with "Laughter In The Rain," which sailed up the British chart to number 15. Elton John signed him to his new label, Rocket Records, and a compilation LP with the title *Sedaka's Back* was released in the U.S. Neil and Elton agreed that "Laughter In The Rain" should be the first single—and it re-established Sedaka as an artist.

JERRY LEIBER & MIKE STOLLER

A mutual friend who knew that Jerry Leiber wanted to write blues songs and Mike Stoller played the piano suggested that the two 16-year-olds meet. Stoller was reluctant, but Leiber was persuasive and showed up at his house with a notebook full of lyrics. A writing partnership was born.

A few months later, Lester Sill of Modern Records wandered into the Los Angeles record store where Stoller was working. The teenager was bold enough to sing some of his material for Sill. He was impressed, and introduced the young songwriters to people in the music business. Two years later, the Robins recorded Leiber & Stoller's first song—"That's What The Good Book Says."

During the following year, Leiber-Stoller songs were recorded by Johnny Otis, Little Esther and Little Willie Littlefield, whose "K.C. Loving" later became "Kansas City," a number one single for Wilbert Harrison. Otis asked the two writers to come up with some material for one of the singers in his revue, Willie Mae "Big Mama" Thornton. They wrote "Hound Dog" in 15 minutes.

Four years after Big Mama's record topped the R&B chart, Elvis Presley heard "Hound Dog" performed by Freddie Bell and the Bellboys in the lounge at the Frontier Hotel in Las Vegas. Elvis' recording of "Hound Dog" is Leiber & Stoller's most successful chart song. In second place is the title song from *Jailhouse Rock* and its flip, "Treat Me Nice." (Leiber & Stoller were sent scripts from Elvis' films with places marked where the producers wanted songs.) In all, seven of Leiber & Stoller's top 30 songs were recorded by Elvis, including the title track from the film *Loving You* and "Love Me"—a song originally recorded by the duo of Willy and Ruth on Leiber & Stoller's Spark label in 1954.

Five of Leiber & Stoller's greatest hits were recorded by the group that evolved from the Robins—the Coasters. The two-sided hit "Searchin'"/"Young Blood" established the group; it was their third single. "Searchin'"/"Young Blood" ranks fourth on the list of the songwriting team's most successful chart singles.

Leiber & Stoller wrote and produced for the Drifters, and when Ben E. King left the group, they continued to work with him. "Stand By Me" is one of their most recorded songs, charting on the Hot 100 by King, Earl Grant, Spyder Turner, David and Jimmy Ruffin, John Lennon, Mickey Gilley and Maurice White.

In 1969, Leiber & Stoller returned to the Hot 100 with Peggy Lee's "Is That All There Is." The most recent Leiber-Stoller song on their top 30 is "I Keep Forgettin' (Every Time You're Near)" by Michael McDonald.

THE TOP 30 SONGS WRITTEN BY
NEIL DIAMOND

1 I'M A BELIEVER
The Monkees *Colgems* 66

2 LOVE ON THE ROCKS
Neil Diamond *Capitol* 80

3 YOU DON'T BRING ME FLOWERS
Barbra Streisand and Neil
Diamond *Columbia* 78

4 SWEET CAROLINE (GOOD TIMES NEVER SEEMED SO GOOD)
Neil Diamond *Uni* 69

5 CRACKLIN' ROSIE
Neil Diamond *Uni* 70

6 SONG SUNG BLUE
Neil Diamond *Uni* 72

7 RED RED WINE
UB40 *A&M* 88

8 HELLO AGAIN
Neil Diamond *Capitol* 81

9 AMERICA
Neil Diamond *Capitol* 81

10 HOLLY HOLY
Neil Diamond *Uni* 69

11 YESTERDAY'S SONGS
Neil Diamond *Columbia* 82

12 HEARTLIGHT
Neil Diamond *Columbia* 82

13 A LITTLE BIT ME, A LITTLE BIT YOU
The Monkees *Colgems* 67

14 I AM . . . I SAID
Neil Diamond *Uni* 71

15 LONGFELLOW SERENADE
Neil Diamond *Columbia* 74

16 IF YOU KNOW WHAT I MEAN
Neil Diamond *Columbia* 76

17 CHERRY, CHERRY
Neil Diamond *Bang* 66

18 THANK THE LORD FOR THE NIGHT TIME
Neil Diamond *Bang* 67

19 SEPTEMBER MORN'
Neil Diamond *Columbia* 80

20 WALK ON WATER
Neil Diamond *Uni* 72

21 DESIREE
Neil Diamond *Columbia* 78

22 PLAY ME
Neil Diamond *Uni* 72

23 GIRL, YOU'LL BE A WOMAN SOON
Neil Diamond *Bang* 67

24 STONES
Neil Diamond *Uni* 71

25 SOLITARY MAN
Neil Diamond *Bang* 70

26 I GOT THE FEELIN' (OH NO NO)
Neil Diamond *Bang* 66

27 BROTHER LOVE'S TRAVELLING SALVATION SHOW
Neil Diamond *Uni* 69

28 SUNDAY AND ME
Jay & the Americans *UA* 65

29 YOU GOT TO ME
Neil Diamond *Bang* 67

30 FOREVER IN BLUE JEANS
Neil Diamond *Columbia* 79

Brooklyn-born Neil Diamond was inspired to write songs after meeting folksinger Pete Seeger at summer camp. "I took to writing songs to satisfy my need for expression, to gain acceptance and recognition," Diamond said in 1971. "I was pretty much an outsider most of the time. I was never accepted. That's why I took to songwriting."

Diamond's first successful song was "Sunday And Me," recorded by Jay & the Americans in 1965. "Neil Diamond came to me with that one," Jay Black told Steve Kolanjian. "He sang it for us with his guitar, then we recorded it. We did that before he did 'Solitary Man.' Somebody told me that they had heard him say in a radio interview that the biggest thrill of his life was coming home from the hospital after his daughter was born and hearing Jay & the Americans sing 'Sunday And Me.' "

Diamond's career went into high gear when he met Ellie Greenwich, who was hired to record one of his demos. She and husband Jeff Barry were impressed with Diamond, and helped him get a contract with Bang Records. They produced his first efforts for the label, including "Solitary Man," "Cherry, Cherry" and "I Got The Feelin' (Oh No No)."

Barry was also responsible for Diamond's most successful chart song. Producer Don Kirshner felt the Monkees hadn't reached their full sales potential with their debut single, "Last Train To Clarksville," even though it went to number one. He asked Barry to help find a follow-up song that would sell millions of copies, and Barry suggested Diamond's song "I'm A Believer." It was number one for seven weeks.

After a long string of hits with MCA's Uni label, Neil signed a $4-million deal with Columbia in 1973. His first two Columbia singles failed to crack the top 30—but both were from the soundtrack of *Jonathan Livingston Seagull*, and the LP sold well. Then came "Longfellow Serenade," which peaked at number five in November, 1974. Diamond would not return to the top 10 until Bob Gaudio brought him into the studio to record a duet with Barbra Streisand. Their version of "You Don't Bring Me Flowers" is Diamond's third most successful chart song.

In second place is "Love On The Rocks," one of three singles from the soundtrack of *The Jazz Singer*. "Hello Again" and "America" are the other two records from the film.

In a 1988 *Rolling Stone* interview, Diamond told David Wild that his favorite cover of one of his songs is Frank Sinatra's take on "Sweet Caroline." "And I loved UB40's 'Red, Red Wine,' which came out of the blue."

HOLLAND-DOZIER-HOLLAND

1 **BABY LOVE**
The Supremes *Motown* 64

2 **COME SEE ABOUT ME**
The Supremes *Motown* 64

3 **BAND OF GOLD**
Freda Payne *Invictus* 70

4 **YOU CAN'T HURRY LOVE**
Phil Collins *Atlantic* 83

5 **I CAN'T HELP MYSELF (SUGAR PIE, HONEY BUNCH)**
Four Tops *Motown* 65

6 **WHERE DID OUR LOVE GO**
The Supremes *Motown* 64

7 **PLEASE MR. POSTMAN**
The Marvelettes *Tamla* 61

8 **REACH OUT I'LL BE THERE**
Four Tops *Motown* 66

9 **TWO HEARTS**
Phil Collins *Atlantic* 89

10 **YOU CAN'T HURRY LOVE**
The Supremes *Motown* 66

11 **HEAVEN MUST HAVE SENT YOU**
Bonnie Pointer *Motown* 79

12 **STOP! IN THE NAME OF LOVE**
The Supremes *Motown* 65

13 **YOU KEEP ME HANGIN' ON**
Kim Wilde *MCA* 87

14 **YOU KEEP ME HANGIN' ON**
The Supremes *Motown* 66

15 **LOVE IS HERE AND NOW YOU'RE GONE**
The Supremes *Motown* 67

Brian Holland, Lamont Dozier and Eddie Holland were three of the main architects of the Motown sound. Best known for producing number one hits for the Supremes and the Four Tops, they also worked with most of the artists on the Motown roster, including Marvin Gaye, the Temptations, the Miracles, Mary Wells and the Marvelettes.

Brian Holland was a teenager when he first met Berry Gordy. He was a recording engineer before he started to write and produce. Eddie recorded for Mercury and United Artists, also doing demos for Jackie Wilson, and was initially signed to Motown as an artist. Lamont Dozier first met Gordy in 1957 after forming the Romeos. They had one local hit in Detroit, "Fine Fine Baby," released on Fox Records and picked up nationally by Atlantic's subsidiary, Atco.

After the Romeos broke up, Dozier signed with Anna Records, the label owned by Berry's sister Gwen. He recorded "Popeye The Sailor Man" as Lamont Anthony. King Features didn't appreciate the copyright infringement, so the song was re-released as "Benny The Skinny Man." When Anna folded, Dozier signed with Berry's new company and had a single released on the Melody label, "Dearest One."

"As a producer, I had a budget that allowed me to record songs with other artists," Dozier explains. "At the end of the budget, if there weren't any songs worth releasing, I would be out on my can. I was down to my last two hundred dollars and had to come up with something fast. I figured it would help my chances if I would team up with some of the heavyweights. Brian Holland was doing fine with 'Please Mr. Postman' by the Marvelettes. His writing partner, Robert Bateman, was disenchanted and wanted to leave." Bateman and Dozier were neighbors, and Bateman offered to introduce Dozier to Brian Holland. "Brian and I got together on some songs I had already written, like 'Locking Up My Heart.' Since the Marvelettes were his, I said this was the way to save myself. We cut 'Locking Up My Heart' on the Marvelettes and my career was saved."

Eddie Holland joined the team. "Brian and I started turning out these hits. Eddie didn't want to be a singer anymore. We needed a third writer . . . Eddie came in as a lyricist." In 1963, H-D-H scored with "Heat Wave" for Martha & the Vandellas, "Can I Get A Witness" for Marvin Gaye, "Mickey's Monkey" for the Miracles and "You Lost The Sweetest Boy" for Mary Wells.

That same year, H-D-H wrote and produced "When The Lovelight Starts Shining Through His Eyes" for a group that had climbed no higher than number 75 on the Hot 100. That single peaked at number 23 for the Supremes. When the Marvelettes turned down H-D-H's "Where Did Our Love Go," it was given to the Supremes—who weren't too fond of it, either.

After "Where Did Our Love Go" went to number one, Gordy told H-D-H to come up with an album for the trio. "We put our nose to the grindstone," says Dozier. "Brian came up with the melody for 'Baby Love' and I came up with 'Come See About Me.'" Both songs were recorded the same week, and are the two most successful H-D-H songs on the *Billboard* chart.

H-D-H also had their first taste of a cover version when Scepter/Wand released "Come See About Me" by Nella Dodds while "Baby Love" was still on the chart. "We hadn't thought anyone would have the nerve to cover any of the songs," laughs Dozier. "We had to rush out 'Come See About Me,' which cut 'Baby Love's life short."

Artists have been covering H-D-H songs ever since. Ten of their top 50 are remakes; the most successful is Phil Collins' "You Can't Hurry Love." Dozier lists as his favorites "You Keep Me Hangin' On" by Vanilla Fudge and "Take Me In Your Arms (Rock Me)" by the Doobie Brothers.

Holland, Dozier and Holland left Motown in 1968 and started two labels of their own, Invictus and Hot Wax. Legal problems prevented them from taking songwriting credits on Freda Payne's "Band Of Gold" and the Chairmen of the Board's "Give Me Just A Little More Time."

The trio eventually split up to pursue separate projects, reuniting years later as free-lance producers for Motown.

SMOKEY ROBINSON

William Robinson, nicknamed Smokey Joe by an uncle, used to carry around a notebook when he was 16 years old so he could write down songs about his friends, his teachers and the ghetto in his hometown of Detroit. He had been composing since he was six years old, including some numbers for a school play in which he played the part of Uncle Remus.

Smokey was scheduled to begin college in September, 1957, to study dentistry. But before the semester began, he and friends Ronnie White, Pete Moore, and Bobby and Claudette Rogers auditioned for Jackie Wilson's manager. Five of the songs they performed were written by Smokey. The manager was unimpressed with the group but suggested that Smokey and Claudette form a duo along the lines of Mickey and Sylvia ("Love Is Strange").

One of Jackie Wilson's songwriters was at the audition. Berry Gordy, Jr., asked Smokey if he had written any more songs. Robinson took out his notebook and showed him over 100 songs. Gordy only liked one—"My Mama Done Told Me," which eventually became the flip side of the Miracles' first record, "Get A Job."

Smokey's songwriting wasn't confined to the Miracles. After Mary Wells' self-penned debut single, "Bye Bye Baby," Smokey was assigned to write for her, producing hits like "The One Who Really Loves You," "You Beat Me To The Punch" and "My Guy."

The Temptations were also early beneficiaries of Smokey's

talent. Their first Hot 100 single, "The Way You Do The Things You Do" would become one of Smokey's most enduring copyrights, charting for Rita Coolidge, Daryl Hall and John Oates (with former Temptations David Ruffin and Eddie Kendrick) and UB40. Smokey also gave the Temptations their first number one single, although the song was intended for the Miracles. After the Temps heard it, they pleaded with Smokey to give them "My Girl."

Before Holland-Dozier-Holland started a streak of number one hits for the Supremes, Smokey wrote one of their first singles, "Your Heart Belongs To Me." He would have another chance to write a Supremes hit after Holland-Dozier-Holland left the company: "The Composer" was the Supremes' second-to-last single with Diana Ross as lead vocalist. And in 1966, after a long period without any top 10 hits, Smokey breathed new life into the Marvelettes with "Don't Mess With Bill" and "The Hunter Gets Captured By the Game."

Many non-Motown artists have turned to the Smokey Robinson songbook for hit singles. Linda Ronstadt scored with "Ooh Baby Baby" and "The Tracks Of My Tears"; the latter was also a hit for Johnny Rivers. The second most successful non-Motown cover of a Smokey song is "More Love" by Kim Carnes. Written in a baseball park, "More Love" became a hit for the Miracles soon after they changed their billing to "Smokey Robinson and the Miracles" in 1967.

That same year, Smokey and company released an album called *Make It Happen*. The final track on that LP was "The Tears Of A Clown." When John Marshall of Motown's London office was looking for a follow-up to a re-release of "The Tracks Of My Tears" in 1970, he discovered that the Miracles had another "tears" song. "The Tears Of A Clown" became the Miracles' first and only number one song in Great Britain. A month after it topped the U.K. chart, Berry Gordy suggested an American release for "The Tears Of A Clown." It became their first number one single in America.

In 1971, Smokey told his fellow Miracles that he was going out on his own. Billy Griffin took over lead vocals and surprisingly, the Miracles fared better on the Hot 100 than Smokey. While he failed to make the top 20 with his first 11 solo efforts, the Miracles went to number one with "Love Machine." But that was the last Miracles single to chart, and Smokey rallied in 1980 with a number four hit, "Cruisin'," originally written as "Easy Rider" for a girl group. It is Smokey's second biggest chart single.

His most successful song came a year later. After Kim Carnes' good fortune with "More Love," Smokey sent additional material to her producer, George Tobin. But Tobin said he was no longer working with Carnes, and indicated that he would like to produce the songs with Smokey himself. "Being With You" soared to number two—held out of the top spot, ironically enough, by Carnes' "Bette Davis Eyes."

THE TOP 30 SONGS WRITTEN BY
NORMAN WHITFIELD

1 I HEARD IT THROUGH THE GRAPEVINE
Marvin Gaye *Tamla* 68

2 I CAN'T GET NEXT TO YOU
The Temptations *Gordy* 69

3 WAR
Edwin Starr *Gordy* 70

4 JUST MY IMAGINATION (RUNNING AWAY WITH ME)
The Temptations *Gordy* 71

5 CAR WASH
Rose Royce *MCA* 77

6 I HEARD IT THROUGH THE GRAPEVINE
Gladys Knight & the Pips *Soul* 67

7 BALL OF CONFUSION
The Temptations *Gordy* 70

8 SMILING FACES SOMETIMES
The Undisputed Truth *Gordy* 71

9 TOO BUSY THINKING ABOUT MY BABY
Marvin Gaye *Tamla* 69

10 PAPA WAS A ROLLIN' STONE
The Temptations *Gordy* 72

11 I WISH IT WOULD RAIN
The Temptations *Gordy* 68

12 RUN AWAY CHILD, RUNNING WILD
The Temptations *Gordy* 69

13 CLOUD NINE
The Temptations *Gordy* 69

14 PSYCHEDELIC SHACK
The Temptations *Gordy* 70

15 MASTERPIECE
The Temptations *Gordy* 73

16 BEAUTY IS ONLY SKIN DEEP
The Temptations *Gordy* 66

17 YOU'RE MY EVERYTHING
The Temptations *Gordy* 67

18 I WANNA GET NEXT TO YOU
Rose Royce *MCA* 77

19 (I KNOW) I'M LOSING YOU
Rare Earth *Rare Earth* 70

20 THAT'S THE WAY LOVE IS
Marvin Gaye *Tamla* 69

21 AIN'T TOO PROUD TO BEG
The Temptations *Gordy* 66

22 FRIENDSHIP TRAIN
Gladys Knight & the Pips *Soul* 69

23 WAR
Bruce Springsteen & the E Street Band *Columbia* 86

24 PRIDE AND JOY
Marvin Gaye *Tamla* 63

25 I COULD NEVER LOVE ANOTHER (AFTER LOVING YOU)
The Temptations *Gordy* 68

26 (I KNOW) I'M LOSING YOU
The Temptations *Gordy* 66

27 (LONELINESS MADE ME REALIZE) IT'S YOU THAT I NEED
The Temptations *Gordy* 67

28 THE END OF OUR ROAD
Gladys Knight & the Pips *Soul* 68

29 SUPERSTAR
The Temptations *Gordy* 71

30 TOO MANY FISH IN THE SEA
The Marvelettes *Tamla* 65

Norman Whitfield, born in New York City, made his professional musical debut playing tambourine for Popcorn & the Mohawks. He was more interested in writing and producing, though, so after working with some independent labels, he signed with Motown as a writer/producer. His first assignment: Marvin Gaye. In 1963, Whitfield, Gaye and Mickey Stevenson wrote "Pride And Joy," Gaye's first top 10 single.

Whitfield's next assignment was to work with the Temptations. For their debut album he wrote "The Further You Look, The Less You See" with the group's primary writer/producer, Smokey Robinson. Eventually, Smokey bowed out of the picture, convinced—especially after "Ain't Too Proud To Beg"—that the group was in good hands with Norman.

Whitfield's main collaborator on many of the Temptations' hits in 1966-67 was Eddie Holland. He was succeeded, in turn, by Barrett Strong, who had charted with one hit single in 1960, "Money (That's What I Want)." "Norman was always the producer," Strong said in Sharon Davis' *Motown: The History*. "I'd come in with my ideas and he would translate them."

In 1968, Temptations' lead singer David Ruffin went solo and was replaced by Dennis Edwards of the Contours. At the same time, Whitfield took the Temptations in an entirely new direction with a socially conscious song, "Cloud Nine." He used all five of the Temptations' voices—an approach that worked especially well on their most successful chart single, "I Can't Get Next To You."

Whitfield's biggest chart song is "I Heard It Through The Grapevine," originally recorded by a group Whitfield usually did not work with—Smokey Robinson and the Miracles. The Isley Brothers recorded it next, then Marvin Gaye. But the first group to actually release the song was Gladys Knight & the Pips. It peaked at number two; a year later, Marvin's version was number one for seven weeks, Motown's biggest single to that date.

Similarly, the Temptations cut "Too Busy Thinking About My Baby" before Marvin Gaye did; "War" was recorded by the Temptations but released on 45 by Edwin Starr; "Papa Was A Rollin' Stone" was first recorded by the Undisputed Truth before it was passed to the Temptations.

The writer/producer left Motown to start his own label, Whitfield, which he originally intended to be distributed by Motown. When the two parties couldn't come to terms, Whitfield Records went to Warner Brothers instead. Five singles from the label made the Hot 100: two by the Undisputed Truth, and three by Rose Royce.

THE TOP 30 SONGS WRITTEN BY
LIONEL RICHIE

The Commodores were signed to Motown in 1972, although they didn't have their first chart single until 1974, when the instrumental "Machine Gun" entered the Hot 100. In the meantime, Lionel Richie hung out with key Motown writer/producers like Norman Whitfield and Hal Davis, anxious to learn how to write songs. He would hum his musical ideas into a tape recorder, and approach his fellow Commodores with these snippets.

In December, 1974, the Temptations' "Happy People" entered the Hot 100. The songwriting credits listed Jeffrey Bowen, Donald Baldwin and a relative unknown—Lionel Richie. Lionel soon became known for writing ballads, giving a softer edge to the Commodores' funky sound. Their fourth chart single, "Sweet Love," propelled the group and songwriter Richie into the top five. After hits like "Just To Be Close To You" and "Easy," Richie's reputation as a songwriter was firmly established with the group's first number one single, "Three Times A Lady."

In 1980, Lionel met with Kenny Rogers in Las Vegas, and played him a demo of "Lady" and "Goin' Back To Alabama." Both songs were recorded the same night; "Lady" topped the Hot 100 for six weeks, becoming Richie's second most successful chart song.

Richie's biggest chart single, "Endless Love," was originally a "Love Story"-type instrumental theme that producer Jon Peters and director Franco Zeffirelli asked Lionel to write for their *Endless Love* movie. The success of "Lady" and "Endless Love" (a duet with Diana Ross) hastened Lionel's departure from the Commodores for a solo career.

NICK ASHFORD & VALERIE SIMPSON

1. **AIN'T NO MOUNTAIN HIGH ENOUGH**
   Diana Ross *Motown* 70
2. **AIN'T NOTHING LIKE THE REAL THING**
   Marvin Gaye and Tammi Terrell *Tamla* 68
3. **YOUR PRECIOUS LOVE**
   Marvin Gaye and Tammi Terrell *Tamla* 67
4. **YOU'RE ALL I NEED TO GET BY**
   Marvin Gaye and Tammi Terrell *Tamla* 68
5. **SOLID**
   Ashford and Simpson *Capitol* 85
6. **AIN'T NO MOUNTAIN HIGH ENOUGH**
   Marvin Gaye and Tammi Terrell *Tamla* 67
7. **REMEMBER ME**
   Diana Ross *Motown* 71
8. **THE BOSS**
   Diana Ross *Motown* 79
9. **I'M EVERY WOMAN**
   Chaka Khan *Warner Bros* 78
10. **REACH OUT AND TOUCH (SOMEBODY'S HAND)**
    Diana Ross *Motown* 70

Nick Ashford moved from his home state of Michigan to New York City, with hopes of becoming a singer or a dancer. He was 21 years old when he first saw 17-year-old Valerie Simpson at the White Rock Baptist Church in Harlem. Destitute, he was there for a free meal; she was there to sing during the service. The two started writing songs together—first gospel, then R&B. They recorded three singles for Glover Records before joining Scepter Records.

Ashford & Simpson had their first top 40 hit when Ray Charles recorded "Let's Go Get Stoned." Then the songwriting duo signed with Motown, and were assigned to write duets for Marvin Gaye and Tammi Terrell. They later wrote and produced Diana Ross' first post-Supremes album.

They left Motown in 1973 and signed as recording artists with Warner Brothers. A long string of singles failed to break the top 30 until Ashford & Simpson moved to Capitol in the early '80s. At the beginning of 1985, they went to number 12 with "Solid."

THE TOP 30 SONGS WRITTEN BY
KENNY GAMBLE & LEON HUFF

1 **DON'T LEAVE ME THIS WAY**
Thelma Houston *Tamla* 77

2 **ME AND MRS. JONES**
Billy Paul *PIR* 72

3 **TSOP (THE SOUND OF PHILADELPHIA)**
MFSB f/The Three Degrees *PIR* 74

4 **LOVE TRAIN**
The O'Jays *PIR* 73

5 **I LOVE MUSIC (PART 1)**
The O'Jays *PIR* 76

6 **IF YOU DON'T KNOW ME BY NOW**
Simply Red *Elektra* 89

7 **ENJOY YOURSELF**
The Jacksons *Epic* 77

8 **I'M GONNA MAKE YOU LOVE ME**
Diana Ross & the Supremes and the
Temptations *Motown* 69

9 **YOU'LL NEVER FIND ANOTHER LOVE
LIKE MINE**
Lou Rawls *PIR* 76

10 **USE TA BE MY GIRL**
The O'Jays *PIR* 78

11 **WHEN WILL I SEE YOU AGAIN**
The Three Degrees *PIR* 74

12 **EXPRESSWAY TO YOUR HEART**
Soul Survivors *Crimson* 67

13 **COWBOYS TO GIRLS**
The Intruders *Gamble* 68

14 **ONLY THE STRONG SURVIVE**
Jerry Butler *Mercury* 69

15 **TOGETHER**
Tierra *Boardwalk* 81

16 **THE LOVE I LOST (PART 1)**
Harold Melvin & the Blue Notes *PIR* 73

17 **BACK STABBERS**
The O'Jays *PIR* 72

18 **IF YOU DON'T KNOW ME BY NOW**
Harold Melvin & the Blue Notes *PIR* 72

19 **BREAK UP TO MAKE UP**
The Stylistics *Avco* 73

20 **FOR THE LOVE OF MONEY**
The O'Jays *PIR* 74

21 **PUT YOUR HANDS TOGETHER**
The O'Jays *PIR* 78

22 **DROWNING IN THE SEA OF LOVE**
Joe Simon *Spring* 72

23 **DO IT ANY WAY YOU WANNA**
People's Choice *TSOP* 75

24 **ENGINE NUMBER 9**
Wilson Pickett *Atlantic* 70

25 **HEY, WESTERN UNION MAN**
Jerry Butler *Mercury* 68

26 **I CAN'T STOP DANCING**
Archie Bell & the Drells *Atlantic* 68

27 **NEVER GIVE YOU UP**
Jerry Butler *Mercury* 68

28 **MOODY WOMAN**
Jerry Butler *Mercury* 69

29 **A BRAND NEW ME**
Dusty Springfield *Atlantic* 69

30 **WHAT'S THE USE OF BREAKING UP**
Jerry Butler *Mercury* 69

Kenny Gamble and Leon Huff both had their first chart records in 1964. Huff co-wrote "Mixed-Up, Shook-Up, Girl" for Patty & the Emblems, which debuted on the Hot 100 in June. Gamble co-wrote Candy and the Kisses' "The 81," which debuted in November. The former peaked at number 37, the latter at number 51.

A year later, Gamble and Huff were writing together. Their first effort to be recorded was "Gee I'm Sorry Baby," released on the flip side of the Saphires' "Gotta Have Your Love." With financial backing from a clothing manufacturer, Gamble and Huff started their own label, Excel, and signed their first act, the Intruders. After one release, they were legally challenged on the label name and changed it to Gamble.

While the Intruders were making inroads on the Hot 100, Philadelphia's Crimson label asked Gamble and Huff to write and produce for a group of young white kids, the Soul Survivors. "Expressway To Your Heart" peaked at number four in 1967. Six months later, the Intruders went to number six with "Cowboys To Girls." That established Gamble and Huff's Philadelphia sound, and soon they were being asked to write and produce for artists at major labels—like Jerry Butler at Mercury, and Wilson Pickett, Archie Bell & the Drells and Dusty Springfield at Atlantic.

Their own Gamble label remained small, though, and the two writer/producers wanted to affiliate with a larger label. They made a deal with Leonard Chess to form Neptune Records, and their first signing was the O'Jays. Billy Paul signed with the label, too. But a few months later, Chess died and the label was sold, effectively closing down Neptune.

Luckily, Columbia Records was looking to gain a stronger toehold in the R&B market, so the head of the label, Clive Davis, arranged to distribute Gamble and Huff's Philadelphia International Records. By the end of 1972, PIR had three smash records. "Back Stabbers" (the first pop hit for the label) was a number three hit for the O'Jays; "Me And Mrs. Jones," Gamble and Huff's second biggest chart single, was number one for Billy Paul; and "If You Don't Know Me By Now" was number three for Harold Melvin & the Blue Notes, with lead vocals by Teddy Pendergrass. Seventeen years later, "If You Don't Know Me By Now" would be a number one hit for the British band Simply Red.

The Gamble-Huff catalog has been richly mined by other artists. The duo's most successful chart song is "Don't Leave Me This Way" by Thelma Houston. It was first recorded by Harold Melvin & the Blue Notes, but failed to make the Hot 100.

1 **RAINDROPS KEEP FALLIN' ON MY HEAD**
   B.J. Thomas *Scepter* 70
2 **THAT'S WHAT FRIENDS ARE FOR**
   Dionne and Friends *Arista* 86
3 **ARTHUR'S THEME (BEST THAT YOU CAN DO)**
   Christopher Cross *Warner Bros* 81
4 **(THEY LONG TO BE) CLOSE TO YOU**
   Carpenters *A&M* 70
5 **MAGIC MOMENTS**
   Perry Como *RCA* 58
6 **ON MY OWN**
   Patti LaBelle and Michael McDonald *MCA* 86
7 **THIS GUY'S IN LOVE WITH YOU**
   Herb Alpert *A&M* 68
8 **ONE LESS BELL TO ANSWER**
   5th Dimension *Bell* 70
9 **BABY IT'S YOU**
   Smith *Dunhill* 69
10 **ONLY LOVE CAN BREAK A HEART**
   Gene Pitney *Musicor* 62
11 **HEARTLIGHT**
   Neil Diamond *Columbia* 82
12 **I SAY A LITTLE PRAYER**
   Dionne Warwick *Scepter* 67
13 **THE LOOK OF LOVE**
   Sergio Mendes & Brasil '66 *A&M* 68
14 **WISHIN' AND HOPIN'**
   Dusty Springfield *Philips* 64
15 **THIS GIRL'S IN LOVE WITH YOU**
   Dionne Warwick *Scepter* 69

Bert and Irma Bacharach expected their first child to be a girl, and when he wasn't, Bert wanted to name his son after himself. His wife disagreed, so they compromised and named him Burt. "We never anticipated any future problems over the different spellings of the same name because, quite truthfully, we never expected that either Big Bert [who was a clothing buyer for a department store at the time] or Little Burt would become known outside the neighborhood," the senior Bacharach wrote in the *Saturday Evening Post*.

Burt wanted to play high school football, but was too short. He studied piano, and after graduation, he played on USO tours. His first published song, "The Night Plane To Heaven," vanished into obscurity. He accompanied artists like Vic Damone and the Ames Brothers, all the while writing songs on the side. One day in 1957, he met songwriter Hal David in the offices of Paramount Music. David had written "Four Winds And Seven Seas" for Sammy Kaye, "Bell Bottom Blues" for Teresa Brewer and "My Heart Is An Open Book," later recorded by Carl Dobkins, Jr.

In 1958, Burt Bacharach and Hal David became the first writers to have consecutive number one singles in Britain. "The Story Of My Life" by Michael Holliday and "Magic Moments" by Perry Como had a combined 10-week run at the top of the U.K. chart.

In America, Marty Robbins had the original version of "The Story of My Life," and "Magic Moments" was the flip of Como's two-sided hit, "Catch A Falling Star." Those two songs established Bacharach's musical credentials and David's sensitive lyrics.

In 1961, Bacharach had two more significant hits: Gene McDaniels' "Tower Of Strength" and the Drifters' "Please Stay," both written with Bob Hilliard. It was during the recording of "Mexican Divorce" by the Drifters that Bacharach met a background singer named Dionne Warwick. By the end of 1962, Warwick had signed to Scepter and released her first Bacharach-David single, "Don't Make Me Over."

Their partnership flourished in the '60s, as Dionne had hits with Bacharach-David songs like "Anyone Who Had A Heart," "Walk On By," "I Say A Little Prayer" and "Do You Know The Way To San Jose."

In 1964, Bacharach's wife-to-be, actress Angie Dickinson, suggested to director Charles Feldman that her boyfriend score Feldman's next film, *What's New Pussycat?* The title track by Tom Jones went to number three. That led to other Bacharach film scores, including *Alfie* (with the title song released by Cilla Black, Cher and Dionne Warwick) and *Casino Royale* (featuring the title track by Herb Alpert & the Tijuana Brass and "The Look Of Love" by Dusty Springfield).

By the end of the decade, Bacharach and David had scored the film that would win them two Oscars: *Butch Cassidy and the Sundance Kid*. The hit song from the film, B.J. Thomas' recording of "Raindrops Keep Fallin' On My Head," is the most successful Bacharach song on the *Billboard* Hot 100.

In second place is another song originally written for a movie. Rod Stewart sang "That's What Friends Are For" over the end credits of the 1982 release *Night Shift*. Bacharach and wife Carole Bayer Sager were not happy with Stewart's rendition. A year later, Bacharach had a reunion with Warwick after not speaking with her for 10 years. Dionne had sued Bacharach and David after they split in 1971, for not fulfilling a contractual obligation.

Scheduled to produce new material for Dionne in 1985, Sager remembered "That's What Friends Are For." Dionne thought it would make a good duet with Stevie Wonder, and when friends Elizabeth Taylor and Neil Simon attended the recording session, Carole suggested the proceeds from the song be donated to the American Foundation for AIDS Research. Gladys Knight and Elton John added their vocals to the recording later. Number one for four weeks, it is Bacharach's second-ranked chart song.

In third place is another movie song, "Arthur's Theme (Best That You Can Do)" from *Arthur*. "I basically wrote it in one or two nights with Carole and Christopher," Burt recalls. One line came from an old Peter Allen song that had never been recorded. "Carole just asked Peter the next day if it was okay if she used this line." The song won an Oscar for all four composers.

THE GIBBS

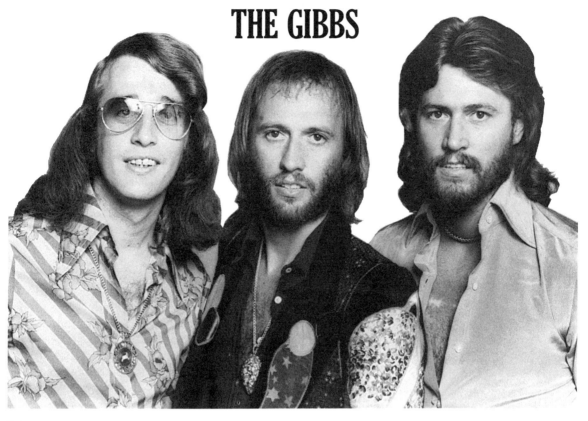

Barry Gibb is the only songwriter in the rock era to have four consecutive number one singles. "Stayin' Alive," "(Love Is) Thicker Than Water," "Night Fever" and "If I Can't Have You" had a 15-week lock on *Billboard*'s top spot from January 29-May 13, 1978.

Barry was nine and his twin brothers Robin and Maurice were seven when they first performed together professionally as the Rattlesnakes. They also called themselves Johnny Hays and the Bluecats, the Brothers Gibb and the B. G.'s before they decided on the Bee Gees. After emigrating to Brisbane. Australia, in 1958, the brothers signed with the Festival label and had a succession of hit singles. In February of that year, they sailed home to England and signed a five-year contract with manager Robert Stigwood. A month later, they were in the back stairway in the Polydor Records office building when they wrote "New York Mining Disaster 1941 (Have You Seen My Wife, Mr. Jones)." A song about the Aberfan mining disaster in Wales that killed over 200 children, it became their first chart hit in America, peaking at number 14 in July of 1967.

Just three weeks before "Stayin' Alive" went to number one, the songwriting brother team of Barry, Robin and Maurice Gibb were on top with the most successful song of their career, "How Deep

Is Your Love." "It's probably the nicest ballad we've ever written, apart from 'Words,' which will always be my favorite," says Barry.

"How Deep Is Your Love" was one of five songs written by the Gibbs for the film *Saturday Night Fever*. The movie was based on "Tribal Rites of the New Saturday Night," a *New York* magazine article by Nik Cohn. The Bee Gees were working on a studio album to follow *Children of the World* when producer Robert Stigwood called them at the Chateau D'Herouville in France. Barry recalls: "He said, 'Do you have any ideas either for the title of the film or a title song?'. . . . I scribbled down some titles within the next hour and called him back the same evening. 'Stayin' Alive' was one of them. 'More Than A Woman' was another. I said, 'What about something like 'Night Fever,' and he said it sounded pornographic. . . . That was the last conversation about the title, and the next thing I knew the film was called *Saturday Night Fever*."

After three number one singles from the soundtrack, radio stations played the Bee Gees' version of "More Than A Woman," but it was never released as a single. "Robert wanted us to go to number one for the fourth time or not at all," Barry explains. Another version from the soundtrack, by Tavares, was released instead.

The Gibbs have never kept all their songs for themselves. Their first number one single, "How Can You Mend A Broken Heart," was meant for Andy Williams, who passed on it. "How Deep Is Your Love" was written for Yvonne Elliman; instead she was given another song the Bee Gees had recorded but not yet released, "If I Can't Have You."

Other artists have approached the Gibbs for songs. Barbra Streisand asked Barry to produce an album for her. "Woman In Love," written by Barry and Robin, ranks sixth on the list of top 50 Gibb songs. When Kenny Rogers signed with RCA, he wanted Barry to produce his first album. Barry, Robin and Maurice penned "Islands In The Stream," recorded as a duet with Dolly Parton. It ranks seventh on the Gibb top 50.

The Gibbs had similar luck with Australian singer Samantha Sang ("Emotion") and Dionne Warwick ("Heartbreaker"). Despite the success of these songs for other artists, Barry says he has never regretted giving some of his better material to others. "I've never pulled back a song once I've written it for somebody else. I don't believe you should take a song back; if it's written for that person it should go to that person. So I never turn around and say, 'Whoops, this song turned out to be too strong.'"

Eight of the singles on the Gibb top 50 were recorded by the fourth Gibb brother, Andy. He was 18 when Stigwood signed him to RSO Records. He and Barry wrote four songs in two days, including Andy's first two singles: "I Just Want To Be Your Everything" (penned by Barry) and "(Love Is) Thicker Than Water" (by Barry and Andy). All four brothers teamed to write "Shadow Dancing," the third most successful Gibb song.

THE TOP 30 SONGS WRITTEN BY
BOB DYLAN

Robert Allen Zimmerman grew up in Hibbing, a mining town in Minnesota that was near the Canadian border. It was during a six-month tenure as a student at the University of Minnesota that be became Bob Dylan, performing at a coffeehouse on campus. At the end of 1960, he took off for New York City, where he visited the hospital bedside of his idol, Woody Guthrie (who was then dying of Huntington's disease).

Dylan went to the Manhattan office of music publisher Hill & Range seeking a $50-a-week staff writing job, but was turned down. Shortly after, he played harmonica on a recording session for folk singer Carolyn Hester. The producer of that session, Columbia Records executive John Hammond, was impressed enough to set up a recording session. *Bob Dylan* was released in March, 1962.

The Freewheelin' Bob Dylan was his second album. He sang the opening track, "Blowin' In The Wind," at the 1963 Newport Folk Festival, accompanied by Peter, Paul and Mary. The folk trio's versions of "Blowin' In The Wind" plus another track from *The Freewheelin' Bob Dylan*, "Don't Think Twice, It's All Right," were Dylan's first appearances in the top 10. "Blowin' In The Wind," the most successful Dylan song on the Hot 100, peaked at number two, and "Don't Think Twice" went to number nine.

In 1962, Dylan had his very own pop hit—"Like A Rolling Stone." He would only have two more top 10 singles of his own: "Rainy Day Women #12 & 35" and "Lay Lady Lay."

PRINCE

"**M**y songs are more about love than they are about sex," Prince once said. "I don't consider myself a great poet, or interpreter à la Moses. I just know I'm here to say what's on my mind, and I'm in a position where I can do that. It would be foolish for me to make up stories about going to Paris, knocking off the Queen and things of that nature."

Prince's first Hot 100 single, "Soft And Wet," peaked at number 92. A full year later, his second single went gold and climbed to number 11. "I Wanna Be Your Lover" established the young recording artist from Minneapolis, but he had already signed a three-album deal with Warner Brothers that allowed him to produce his own material.

The track that first put Prince Rogers Nelson in the top 10 was "Little Red Corvette." Then his previous single, "1999," was reissued and went to number 12. That was followed by another top 10 single, "Delirious." His real breakthrough, though, came with the release of his autobiographical film, *Purple Rain*. The soundtrack yielded five Hot 100 hits, including "When Doves Cry."

There was no official soundtrack to Prince's next film, *Under The Cherry Moon*, but the *Parade* album did feature songs from the movie. "Kiss" was the first single released from the album; it is Prince's fifth most successful song.

In the summer of 1989 came the long-awaited *Batman* film—and Prince's *Batman* album, with songs from and inspired by the movie. "Batdance" became Prince's fourth number one single.

THE TOP 10 SONGS WRITTEN BY
FELICE & BOUDLEAUX BRYANT

1 **BYE BYE LOVE**
Everly Brothers *Cadence* 57
2 **WAKE UP LITTLE SUSIE**
Everly Brothers *Cadence* 57
3 **ALL I HAVE TO DO IS DREAM**
Everly Brothers *Cadence* 58
4 **BIRD DOG**
Everly Brothers *Cadence* 58
5 **LOVE HURTS**
Nazareth *A&M* 76
6 **PROBLEMS**
Everly Brothers *Cadence* 58
7 **DEVOTED TO YOU**
Everly Brothers *Cadence* 58
8 **MEXICO**
Bob Moore *Monument* 61
9 **LET'S THINK ABOUT LIVING**
Bob Luman *Warner Bros* 60
10 **TAKE A MESSAGE TO MARY**
Everly Brothers *Cadence* 59

Boudleaux Bryant, born in Shellman, Georgia, played violin for the Atlanta Philharmonic Orchestra and radio station WSB. Felice grew up in Milwaukee, and was working at the Sherwood Hotel when she met Boudleaux—he was playing there with his jazz band. The two married in September, 1945, and began writings songs together just for fun—he wrote the music, she wrote the lyrics. They sent "Country Boy" to a publisher in Nashville, and in 1949 it was a number seven country hit for "Little" Jimmy Dickens. A year later, the Bryants decided to move to Nashville to be closer to the music scene.

In 1957, publisher Wesley Rose introduced them to an act he had signed with Archie Bleyer's New York-based label, Cadence. The Everly Brothers recorded the Bryants' "Bye Bye Love," and had their first chart entry, at number two. Phil and Don's follow-up was also written by the Bryants. Although Bleyer thought the song was too suggestive, "Wake Up Little Susie" went to number one, and ranks second on the list of the Bryants' greatest hits.

THE TOP 10 SONGS WRITTEN BY
MICHAEL MASSER

1 **TOUCH ME IN THE MORNING**
Diana Ross *Motown* 73
2 **GREATEST LOVE OF ALL**
Whitney Houston *Arista* 86
3 **SAVING ALL MY LOVE FOR YOU**
Whitney Houston *Arista* 85
4 **DIDN'T WE ALMOST HAVE IT ALL**
Whitney Houston *Arista* 87
5 **IT'S MY TURN**
Diana Ross *Motown* 81
6 **THEME FROM "MAHOGANY" (DO YOU KNOW WHERE YOU'RE GOING TO)**
Diana Ross *Motown* 76
7 **MISS YOU LIKE CRAZY**
Natalie Cole *EMI* 89
8 **IF EVER YOU'RE IN MY ARMS AGAIN**
Peabo Bryson *Elektra* 84
9 **TONIGHT, I CELEBRATE MY LOVE**
Peabo Bryson/Roberta Flack *Capitol* 83
10 **NOTHING'S GONNA CHANGE MY LOVE FOR YOU**
Glenn Medeiros *Amherst* 87

By the time Michael Masser was in his 20s, he knew he wanted to write songs for a living, but instead he married, and soon had two children. With a background in law, he became a stockbroker, all the while yearning to become a professional songwriter. As he drove to the Pan Am building each morning, he had a strong desire to take a left turn and head for Juilliard. Encouraged by Johnny Mercer, he made the transition to songwriting at age 31.

Michael took two songs to producer Bones Howe and was told to leave his tape. Bones liked what he heard, and suggested Michael work with lyricist Gerry Goffin. Their composition of "Turn Around To Me," recorded by the 5th Dimension, became Masser's first recorded work.

Then Masser met Motown executive Suzanne de Passe. "They were looking for a song for Diana Ross," he recalls. "Suzanne said, 'Why not start at the top?''Touch Me In The Morning' was my first time in the studio." It became his biggest chart hit of all time.

LAURA NYRO

1 **WEDDING BELL BLUES**
5th Dimension *Soul City* 69

2 **ELI'S COMING**
Three Dog Night *Dunhill* 69

3 **STONED SOUL PICNIC**
5th Dimension *Soul City* 68

4 **AND WHEN I DIE**
Blood, Sweat & Tears *Columbia* 69

5 **STONEY END**
Barbra Streisand *Columbia* 71

6 **SWEET BLINDNESS**
5th Dimension *Soul City* 68

7 **BLOWING AWAY**
5th Dimension *Soul City* 70

8 **SAVE THE COUNTRY**
5th Dimension *Bell* 70

9 **TIME AND LOVE**
Barbra Streisand *Columbia* 71

10 **FLIM FLAM MAN**
Barbra Streisand *Columbia* 71

After attending the High School of Music and Art in Manhattan, Laura Nyro moved to San Francisco and was booked for two months at the famous hungry i nightclub. Her first album, *More Than a New Discovery*, was released by Verve/Folkways in 1966. The next year, she appeared at the Monterey Pop Festival, but Jimi Hendrix and Janis Joplin fans didn't appreciate her quiet, thoughtful music.

In New York, Nyro hooked up with a young manager, David Geffen. He arranged for Laura to record *Eli and the 13th Confession*, her first album for Columbia. Geffen gave a demo of the album to producer Bones Howe, suggesting that "Stoned Soul Picnic" would be perfect for the 5th Dimension.

Howe continued to mine the Nyro catalog for the 5th Dimension. When he suggested they record "Wedding Bell Blues," Marilyn McCoo readily agreed. She was engaged to Billy Davis, Jr., of the group, and Laura's song began, "Bill, I love you so, I always will . . ."

DOC POMUS & MORT SHUMAN

1 **YOUNG BLOOD**
The Coasters *Atco* 57

2 **SAVE THE LAST DANCE FOR ME**
The Drifters *Atlantic* 60

3 **SURRENDER**
Elvis Presley *RCA* 61

4 **LITTLE CHILDREN**
Billy J. Kramer & the Dakotas *Imperial* 64

5 **CAN'T GET USED TO LOSING YOU**
Andy Williams *Columbia* 63

6 **A TEENAGER IN LOVE**
Dion & the Belmonts *Laurie* 59

7 **SUSPICION**
Terry Stafford *Crusader* 64

8 **TURN ME LOOSE**
Fabian *Chancellor* 59

9 **GO, JIMMY, GO**
Jimmy Clanton *Ace* 60

10 **THIS MAGIC MOMENT**
Jay & the Americans *UA* 69

Mort Shuman was a friend of the Pomus family, and liked going to New York nightclubs with Jerome "Doc" Pomus. Doc had already penned "Boogie Woogie Country Girl," a Joe Turner "B" side, and helped Leiber and Stoller with the Coasters' "Young Blood." When the two started writing together, Pomus did most of the work, and claimed 90 per cent of the song publishing. After their first year of collaborating, though, the songwriters changed the split to 50-50.

At the suggestion of Otis Blackwell, who wrote many Elvis Presley hits (including "Don't be Cruel"), Paul Case at Hill & Range Publishers signed Pomus and Shuman up in 1959. That same year, they scored with "A Teenager In Love," the first top 10 single for Dion & the Belmonts.

Leiber and Stoller were producing the Drifters, and looked for other songwriters to supply material. Pomus and Shuman contributed "Save The Last Dance For Me," which went to number one the week of October 17, 1960.

THE TOP 10 SONGS WRITTEN BY
BRUCE SPRINGSTEEN

1 **FIRE**
Pointer Sisters *Planet* 79

2 **DANCING IN THE DARK**
Bruce Springsteen *Columbia* 84

3 **HUNGRY HEART**
Bruce Springsteen *Columbia* 80

4 **BLINDED BY THE LIGHT**
Manfred Mann's Earth Band *Warner Bros* 77

5 **GLORY DAYS**
Bruce Springsteen *Columbia* 85

6 **COVER ME**
Bruce Springsteen *Columbia* 84

7 **THIS LITTLE GIRL**
Gary U.S. Bonds *EMI America* 81

8 **PINK CADILLAC**
Natalie Cole *EMI Manhattan* 88

9 **I'M ON FIRE**
Bruce Springsteen *Columbia* 85

10 **BORN IN THE U.S.A.**
Bruce Springsteen *Columbia* 85

Bruce Springsteen's first chart single, "Born To Run," was his only top 30 hit until "Hungry Heart" peaked at number five in 1980. Meanwhile, other artists were having better luck with his material. Manfred Mann's Earth Band covered "Spirit In The Night" (1975) and "Blinded By The Light" (1976); "Fire," originally recorded in 1977 by Robert Gordon, was the first top 10 single for the Pointer Sisters (1978).

"Fire" is the most successful Springsteen song on the Hot 100. In second place is "Dancing In The Dark." That song came about when Bruce's manager/producer, Jon Landau, insisted that *Born in the U.S.A.* needed a strong track for the first single. Springsteen said he didn't have a song like that, finally exploding, "Look, I've written 70 songs. You want another one, *you* write it," according to Dave Marsh in *Glory Days*. Alone in a hotel suite that night, Springsteen wrote "Dancing In The Dark." "It was just like my heart spoke straight through my mouth, without even having to pass through my brain. The chorus just poured out of me."

THE TOP 10 SONGS WRITTEN BY
BILLY STEINBERG & TOM KELLY

1 **LIKE A VIRGIN**
Madonna *Sire* 84

2 **ALONE**
Heart *Capitol* 87

3 **SO EMOTIONAL**
Whitney Houston *Arista* 88

4 **TRUE COLORS**
Cyndi Lauper *Portrait* 86

5 **ETERNAL FLAME**
Bangles *Columbia* 89

6 **HOW DO I MAKE YOU**
Linda Ronstadt *Asylum* 80

7 **IN YOUR ROOM**
Bangles *Columbia* 89

8 **I DROVE ALL NIGHT**
Cyndi Lauper *Epic* 89

9 **FIRE AND ICE**
Pat Benatar *Chrysalis* 81

10 **IN MY DREAMS**
REO Speedwagon *Epic* 87

Tom Kelly and Billy Steinberg both had songs on side one of Pat Benatar's *Precious Time* album. Tom had the hit single, "Fire And Ice" and Billy had the title tune. As a result, both of them were invited to producer Keith Olsen's housewarming party, where they met for the first time. Kelly discovered that Steinberg, once a member of the band Billy Thermal, had written one of his favorite songs—Linda Ronstadt's "How Do I Make You."

Their first collaboration was "Just One Kiss," recorded by Rick Springfield. Then they signed to Epic Records under the name i-Ten. One of the songs from their LP, "Alone," became their second biggest song—but not until it was recorded by Heart.

Steinberg and Kelly's most successful chart song, "Like A Virgin," was originally written for a man to sing. In fact, at the time, they didn't even know who Madonna was. Michael Ostin of Warner Brothers heard the song and played it for Madonna. "She went crazy," he says, "and knew instantly it was a song for her and that she could make a great record out of it."

THE TOP 10 SONGS WRITTEN BY
DIANE WARREN

1 **LOOK AWAY**
Chicago *Reprise* 88

2 **BLAME IT ON THE RAIN**
Milli Vanilli *Arista* 89

3 **NOTHING'S GONNA STOP US NOW**
Starship *Grunt* 87

4 **LOVE WILL LEAD YOU BACK**
Taylor Dayne *Arista* 90

5 **IF I COULD TURN BACK TIME**
Cher *Geffen* 89

6 **WHEN I SEE YOU SMILE**
Bad English *Epic* 89

7 **RHYTHM OF THE NIGHT**
DeBarge *Gordy* 85

8 **I GET WEAK**
Belinda Carlisle *MCA* 88

9 **I DON'T WANNA LIVE WITHOUT YOUR LOVE**
Chicago *Reprise* 88

10 **HOW CAN WE BE LOVERS**
Michael Bolton *Columbia* 90

Diane Warren's first top 10 hit was Laura Branigan's "Solitaire," but the California native wasn't that excited—she had simply written new lyrics for a French song. It was her next hit that brought her some attention: "Rhythm Of The Night."

By 1988, Diane's songs were all over the Hot 100. At one point, she had seven songs by seven different singers on the chart, and had the top two as well—"Blame It On The Rain" and "When I See You Smile."

"If I Could Turn Back Time" was picked out for Cher. "She didn't want to do it," Diane says. "Finally, just to get me out of there, she said, 'I'll do it.'"

Diane's most successful song on the Hot 100 is "Look Away." "A friend of mine who was divorced worked in my building," she recounts. "I was in her office and she was telling him she had met someone else she was going to marry. I thought, 'There's definitely a song here.'" Diane wrote the song from the man's point of view; it became Chicago's third number one single.

THE TOP 10 SONGS WRITTEN BY
JIMMY WEBB

1 **MACARTHUR PARK**
Donna Summer *Casablanca* 78

2 **WICHITA LINEMAN**
Glen Campbell *Capitol* 69

3 **WORST THAT COULD HAPPEN**
Brooklyn Bridge *Buddah* 69

4 **GALVESTON**
Glen Campbell *Capitol* 69

5 **MACARTHUR PARK**
Richard Harris *Dunhill* 68

6 **UP-UP AND AWAY**
5th Dimension *Soul City* 67

7 **ALL I KNOW**
Art Garfunkel *Columbia* 73

8 **HONEY COME BACK**
Glen Campbell *Capitol* 70

9 **BY THE TIME I GET TO PHOENIX**
Glen Campbell *Capitol* 67

10 **WHERE'S THE PLAYGROUND SUSIE**
Glen Campbell *Capitol* 69

Jimmy Webb played the piano and organ in his father's church, and was writing songs by the time he was 13. When his family moved to California, Webb enrolled in San Bernardino Valley College as a music major. Although he quit school during his second semester, Jimmy made an important contact—a DJ at local radio station KMEN heard his demo tapes, and suggested they collaborate on a documentary film about ballooning. The film was never produced, but Webb composed a song for it: "Up-Up And Away." Another Webb song was written after he broke up with a girl he was dating at college: "By The Time I Get To Phoenix."

Webb's most successful chart song, "MacArthur Park," was inspired by lunchtime walks with his girlfriend around the lake in Los Angeles' MacArthur Park. It has been recorded by actor Richard Harris, Waylon Jennings and the Four Tops. In 1978 Donna Summer recorded "MacArthur Park." Edited down from more than eight minutes to under four minutes for a single release, it became Webb's only number one song.

THE PRODUCERS

"I love producing," says Nile Rodgers, who has produced hit records for artists like Diana Ross, David Bowie, Madonna and his own group, Chic. "I really like making records, I think more than just about anything in the world. It's a great thing to start a project and then analyze the project in the middle and then finish it. It's the one thing that I really get emotional about. I love to make records."

Producers haven't always been acknowledged—or even paid—for their work. Phil Spector, architect of the famed "Wall of Sound," was one of the first producers to receive label credit. When Jerry Leiber and Mike Stoller asked Jerry Wexler at Atlantic Records for a printed credit, he exploded, according to Dorothy Wade and Justine Picardie in *Music Man*. "What the hell do you want your name on the label for?" he asked them. "Your name is on the label as writers. How many times do you want your names on the record? We tell everybody that you made the record, they all know." After Leiber and Stoller were given label credit, they also wanted a producer's royalty. Miriam Abramson, business manager for Atlantic, was outraged, according to *Music Man*. "At that time there weren't many producers—especially ones getting royalties," she explained. "As a principal in the company, I just didn't want to pay it."

Today, producers are not only acknowledged and paid, but sought-after. Jimmy Jam and Terry Lewis are as responsible for the success of *Control* as Janet Jackson. Clive Davis turned to L. A. Reid and Babyface to give Whitney Houston a rougher edge and re-establish her popularity at R&B radio. They came up with "I'm Your Baby Tonight," Houston's most successful chart single to date.

Producers also are known by their sound. Mike Stock, Matt Aitken and Pete Waterman are sometimes more identifiable than their artists. Kylie Minogue, Samantha Fox, Sonia and Sinitta could have recorded each other's vocals and the records would still be similar; take away their producers, and the songs would sound very different.

Not every producer becomes as well-known as Phil Spector or Quincy Jones, but Tom Dowd, Arif Mardin, Narada Michael Walden, Giorgio Moroder and the other producers listed in this section have created their own distinctive styles and reputations over the years. They are as respected and appreciated for their talent as much as any artist they have produced.

QUINCY JONES

1. **BILLIE JEAN**
   Michael Jackson *Epic* 83
2. **ROCK WITH YOU**
   Michael Jackson *Epic* 80
3. **BEAT IT**
   Michael Jackson *Epic* 83
4. **BABY, COME TO ME**
   Patti Austin w/James Ingram *Qwest* 83
5. **WE ARE THE WORLD**
   USA for Africa *Columbia* 85
6. **THE GIRL IS MINE**
   Michael Jackson and Paul McCartney *Epic* 83
7. **MAN IN THE MIRROR**
   Michael Jackson *Epic* 88
8. **IT'S MY PARTY**
   Lesley Gore *Mercury* 63
9. **STOMP!**
   Brothers Johnson *A&M* 80
10. **THE WAY YOU MAKE ME FEEL**
    Michael Jackson *Epic* 88
11. **GIVE ME THE NIGHT**
    George Benson *Warner Bros* 80
12. **WANNA BE STARTIN' SOMETHIN'**
    Michael Jackson *Epic* 83
13. **DON'T STOP 'TIL YOU GET ENOUGH**
    Michael Jackson *Epic* 79
14. **I'LL BE GOOD TO YOU**
    Brothers Johnson *A&M* 76
15. **DIRTY DIANA**
    Michael Jackson *Epic* 88

Quincy Delight Jones, Jr., was born in Chicago. He was 10 years old when his father got a job with the Bremerton Shipyards in Seattle. Quincy made his professional debut at age 14, playing trumpet at a YMCA dance—he was paid seven dollars.

"My arranging career really got started when I was around 14," Quincy told Nelson George in *Billboard*. "I met Count Basie and Lionel Hampton around the same time." He also met 16-year-old Ray Charles at that point, and the two formed a band, learning from each other.

A scholarship took him to the Berklee School of Music in Boston, after which Quincy moved to New York and worked with Dizzy Gillespie. At 19, he began a three-year stint playing in Lionel Hampton's band. By the end of the '50s, he was living in Paris as musical director for the Barclay label. Back in the States, he was hired by Mercury Records President Irving Green to be head of A&R for the Chicago-based label.

One day at a staff meeting, Quincy heard a voice he liked: the singer was 16-year-old Lesley Gore. "She was the first young artist that I heard sing in tune in a long time," Quincy told George. In February, 1963, Quincy showed up at Lesley's door with more than 250 demos so she could listen to them and select songs for her debut Mercury album. The first song they listened to was "It's My Party," written by John Gluck, Jr., Wally Gold and Herb Wiener. "It's My Party" was rush-released after Quincy ran into Phil Spector in front of Carnegie Hall and found out that Spector had just produced the same song with the Crystals. Four weeks after her record entered the Hot 100, Lesley was number one.

Quincy continued to work with Gore through 1965—ten of his top 50 songs are by the teenager from Tenafly, New Jersey. In 1965, Quincy also composed his first of more than 40 film scores, for *The Pawnbroker*. Four years later, he signed to A&M Records as an artist and released *Walking in Space*. His 1975 album *Mellow Madness* featured vocals by the Brothers Johnson; between 1976 and 1980, Quincy produced three top ten singles for the Los Angeles duo.

It was another film project that led Quincy to produce *Thriller*, the best selling album of all time. "I didn't want to do *The Wiz*," Quincy told Joe Smith in *Off the Record*. "Except for a couple of songs, I didn't like the music. But [director] Sidney Lumet, who I've done six movies with, said, 'You've got to do it,' and so I did it."

Jones had met Michael Jackson at Sammy Davis, Jr.'s house—when Michael was 12. But Quincy didn't get to know Michael until they worked on *The Wiz* together. "We talked and I started to see what a beautiful human being he was, how disciplined and talented," Quincy said in *Billboard*. "Really genius talent. Then I started to feel there was something inside of him that I had never heard before on his records. He kept asking me about [a] producer, so I said, 'You got a producer. I'll produce it.' So we went and did *Off the Wall* after that."

Michael had four top 10 singles from *Off the Wall*, including two number one hits. "And then came *Thriller*, which was mind-boggling," according to Quincy. *Thriller* yielded seven top 10 singles, including two more number one hits. The album sold more than 40 million copies, making it the best-selling record of all time.

Michael and Quincy did it again with *Bad*. This time, the first five singles from the album went to number one. In all, Michael has 18 songs on Quincy's top 50.

Michael co-wrote another Quincy Jones production: "We Are The World," recorded with an all-star supporting cast to raise money for the starving people of Africa and the United States. "The motivation behind involving me was, I believe, a song called 'State Of Independence' I'd done with Donna Summer three years before," Quincy told George. "Basically we have a third of 'We Are The World' on it: Stevie [Wonder], Michael, Lionel [Richie], Dionne Warwick, James Ingram . . . I would not have taken on that job if I hadn't done that three years before . . . when you can collectively get together and put all that energy together and make your voice felt in a whole sea of voices that have the same concern, they can really do something. It's not just the money. . . . If you sacrifice compassion, you're going to die as a human being."

THE TOP 50 SONGS PRODUCED BY
PHIL SPECTOR

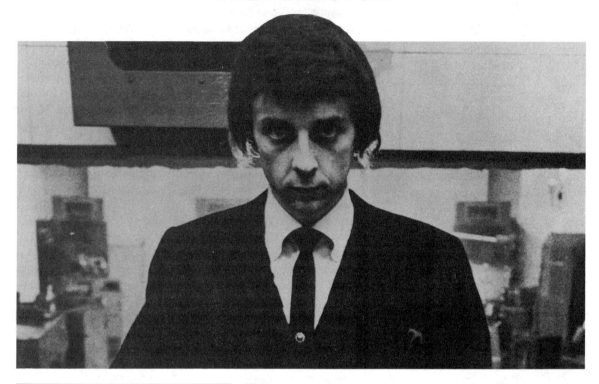

Phil Spector, creator of the "Wall of Sound," was born December 26, 1940, in the Bronx. His father died in 1949, and four years later, his family moved to Los Angeles. He was 16 when he performed Lonnie Donegan's "Rock Island Line" at a talent show at Fairfax High School.

In the spring of 1958, Phil raised enough money to secure two hours of recording time at Gold Star Studios. Contributing to the fund were Marshall Leib, Harvey Goldstein and Annette Kleinbard, and they joined Spector to record "Don't You Worry My Little Pet." That recording helped the group garner a deal with Era Records. At their next session, they recorded a song inspired by a photograph of the epitaph on the tombstone of Phil's father. "To Know Him Is To Love Him," recorded without Goldstein, became the Teddy Bears' first release on Era's Dore subsidiary.

Spector took the Teddy Bears to Imperial Records, but their next single failed to go higher than number 90 on the Hot 100, and after several more recordings, the trio went their separate ways. While recording *The Teddy Bears Sing!* album, Spector had met Lester Sill, a former promotion man who was a mentor to Jerry Leiber and Mike Stoller. After the demise of the Teddy Bears, Spector signed a contract with Sill to produce and record.

Sill arranged for Spector to apprentice with Leiber and Stoller in New York. He worked with the Coasters, the Drifters and Ben E. King; with Leiber, he wrote "Spanish Harlem" for King. Spector also produced records by Ray Peterson ("Corinna, Corinna") and Curtis Lee ("Pretty Little Angel Eyes").

Back in Hollywood, Spector agreed to produce one of Sill's acts. When Liberty and Capitol turned down the master, Sill formed a new label with Lee Hazlewood and released "Be My Boy" by the Paris Sisters on Gregmark. It faltered at number 58, but the follow-up, "I Love How You Love Me," peaked at number five.

Sill and Hazlewood split their business arrangement shortly after, and Phil suggested to Lester that they form a partnership. The result was Philles Records, named after both of them. Through Hill & Range Publishers, Spector found three groups he wanted to produce—the Ducanes, the Creations and the Crystals. The latter two were shuffled off to other companies, and Phil signed the five black teenage girls from Brooklyn known as the Crystals to his new label.

By the time "He's A Rebel" went to number one, Sill was out of the company, so Spector had the label all to himself. He created a new act called Bob B. Soxx & the Blue Jeans, featuring Darlene Love—who had actually sung the vocals on the Crystals' "He's A Rebel." Spector also released solo material by Darlene in 1963, the same year he released "Be My Baby" by the Ronettes. He was already in love with lead singer Veronica Bennett, and they married in 1967.

The Ronettes appeared at the Cow Palace in San Francisco during 1964; also on the bill were the Righteous Brothers. Spector was conducting the band for all the acts, and was so impressed with Bill Medley and Bobby Hatfield that he bought their contract from Moonglow Records and signed them to Philles. Spector asked Barry Mann and Cynthia Weil to write something for the duo, and "You've Lost That Lovin' Feelin'" was Philles' second number one single.

Spector's final signing to Philles was the husband-and-wife team of Ike and Tina Turner. But when "River Deep-Mountain High" failed to rise higher than number 88, Spector lost interest in his label and the recording industry.

He made a brief return in 1969 with a production deal for A&M Records. A Ronettes single flopped, but Spector was back on the Hot 100 with Sonny Charles and the Checkmates, Ltd. The A&M deal was short-lived, and Spector would have been out of the business again were it not for Allen Klein, who was managing the Beatles at the time. Through Klein, Spector was asked to work on the *Let It Be* tapes. First, Spector produced "Instant Karma" for John Lennon. That, in turn, led to producing George Harrison's triple solo album, *All Things Must Pass*. In 1971, Spector was named director of A&R for Apple Records. He only held the post for a year, but he produced Lennon's classic "Imagine," Harrison's "Bangla-Desh" and Ronnie Spector's "Try Some, Buy Some."

THE TOP 30 SONGS PRODUCED BY
PETER ASHER

1 **BLUE BAYOU**
Linda Ronstadt *Asylum* 77

2 **DON'T KNOW MUCH**
Linda Ronstadt f/Aaron Neville *Elektra* 89

3 **YOU'VE GOT A FRIEND**
James Taylor *Warner Bros* 70

4 **FIRE AND RAIN**
James Taylor *Warner Bros* 70

5 **WHEN WILL I BE LOVED**
Linda Ronstadt *Capitol* 75

6 **SOMEWHERE OUT THERE**
Linda Ronstadt and James Ingram *MCA* 87

7 **HANDY MAN**
James Taylor *Columbia* 77

8 **IT'S SO EASY**
Linda Ronstadt *Asylum* 77

9 **LONELY BOY**
Andrew Gold *Asylum* 77

10 **HURT SO BAD**
Linda Ronstadt *Asylum* 80

11 **OOH BABY BABY**
Linda Ronstadt *Asylum* 79

12 **HOW DO I MAKE YOU**
Linda Ronstadt *Asylum* 80

13 **YOU'RE NO GOOD**
Linda Ronstadt *Capitol* 75

14 **HEAT WAVE/LOVE IS A ROSE**
Linda Ronstadt *Asylum* 75

15 **AFTER ALL**
Cher and Peter Cetera *Geffen* 89

16 **THAT'LL BE THE DAY**
Linda Ronstadt *Asylum* 76

17 **HER TOWN TOO**
James Taylor and J.D. Souther *Columbia* 81

18 **BACK IN THE U.S.A.**
Linda Ronstadt *Asylum* 78

19 **DON'T LET ME BE LONELY TONIGHT**
James Taylor *Warner Bros* 73

20 **ALL MY LIFE**
Linda Ronstadt f/Aaron Neville *Elektra* 90

21 **YOUR SMILING FACE**
James Taylor *Columbia* 77

22 **THE TRACKS OF MY TEARS**
Linda Ronstadt *Asylum* 76

23 **HEART OF STONE**
Cher *Geffen* 90

24 **UP ON THE ROOF**
James Taylor *Columbia* 79

25 **I CAN'T LET GO**
Linda Ronstadt *Asylum* 80

26 **GET CLOSER**
Linda Ronstadt *Asylum* 82

27 **I KNEW YOU WHEN**
Linda Ronstadt *Asylum* 83

28 **SOMEONE TO LAY DOWN BESIDE ME**
Linda Ronstadt *Asylum* 77

29 **WHAT'S NEW**
Linda Ronstadt *Asylum* 83

30 **LONG AGO AND FAR AWAY**
James Taylor *Warner Bros* 71

Peter Asher admits, "I never liked performing very much. I liked singing, but I can still sing with friends on stage or on a record. But the responsibility and nervewracking obligation of entertaining an audience never particularly appealed to me."

In 1964, Peter Asher was part of the British invasion that swept through America. Partnered with Gordon Waller, he vaulted to the number one position his very first time out with a John Lennon-Paul McCartney song, "A World Without Love." Peter and Gordon had hits with a string of Lennon-McCartney tunes, including "Nobody I Know" and "I Don't Want To See You Again." The duo went their separate ways in 1967, and Peter produced a couple of records for former Manfred Mann lead singer Paul Jones. Paul McCartney was impressed with the results, and asked Asher to be head of A&R for Apple Records.

"James [Taylor] called me up one day," Peter recalls. "He'd been in a band with Danny Kortchmar called the Flying Machine in New York. Danny had been in a band called the Kingbees who had backed Peter and Gordon on a couple of American tours. Danny and I had become good friends. When the Flying Machine broke up, Kootch gave James my phone number in London." Peter listened to James' demo tape and promptly signed him up.

Taylor recorded one album for Apple. Asher left the label when Allen Klein started running the company, and eventually signed Taylor to Warner Brothers. The initial single from Taylor's first Warner album was "Fire And Rain"; nine months later, Taylor had his biggest success on the Hot 100 with a cover version of Carole King's "You've Got A Friend."

Twenty-seven of Asher's top 30 songs have been recorded either by Taylor or Linda Ronstadt. "I first met her on one of my early trips to New York," Peter says. He saw her perform at the Bitter End, and met her after the show through friends. Later, while changing managers, she asked Asher if he would like to be her new manager.

"The first thing we had to do was find a producer to finish the album she was working on then, *Don't Cry Now*. I ended up helping her finish some of that record and we liked working together, so we decided to do the next one together and that was *Heart Like a Wheel*." The initial single from that LP gave Linda her only number one single, "You're No Good."

It was a remake, like most of Ronstadt's hits—and most of Asher's. Of his top 30 productions, 18 of them are cover versions of older songs. His most successful chart single, Ronstadt's "Blue Bayou," was originally written and recorded by Roy Orbison.

TOM DOWD

Tom Dowd, a native of Manhattan, did some early engineering work for Atlantic Records, the label he would become associated with in the '50s. Tom was involved in recording many of the artists on the Atlantic roster, including LaVern Baker, the Coasters, the Drifters and Ray Charles. Although credited as an engineer, he would work directly with the artists, arrangers, and songwriters, often functioning more like a producer.

In the '60s, Dowd engineered recordings for Wilson Pickett and Otis Redding. He was the engineer on Redding's "Respect" as well as on the hit cover version by Aretha Franklin. Working with Jerry Wexler and Arif Mardin, he was credited as a producer on Aretha Franklin songs like "The Weight," "Share Your Love With Me" and "Eleanor Rigby."

With Mardin, he produced "Good Lovin'" for the Young Rascals, and then worked with Cream—back in the engineer's seat while Felix Pappalardi of Mountain produced the trio of Eric Clapton, Ginger Baker and Jack Bruce. As the decade closed, Dowd went to Memphis to produce another British artist—Dusty Springfield.

Through manager Phil Walden, Dowd produced the Allman Brothers second album, *Idlewild South*. While working with Duane Allman, Dowd was asked by Robert Stigwood at RSO Records if he would like to work with Clapton again. Dowd brought Clapton to an Allman Brothers concert, where he met Duane for the first time. "That's how the whole 'Layla' thing got to be—they just sat in the studio and traded instruments and licks for the next five days, and that made an album."

SNUFF GARRETT

Tommy Garrett quit school and went to California from Dallas, Texas, with a couple of DJ friends. He slept at night in Hollywood's Plummer Park. He looked for day work doing record promotion and met up with Al Bennett at Dot Records. Garrett had done some work for a record distributor in Dallas and had met Bennett; he was immediately hired as his assistant. But homesickness set in, and Garrett headed back to Texas.

While working as a DJ in Lubbock, Texas, Garrett—nicknamed "Snuff" after the well-known tobacco Garrett Snuff—met a local singer there, and they became best friends. The singer's name was Buddy Holly. Later, when Holly was successful and living in New York, he had plans to start a production company named Taupe, the color of his Cadillac. "He was going to hire three of us to come to New York and be with him," Snuff explains. "Bob Montgomery, a successful publisher and producer in Nashville; Waylon Jennings and myself. When Buddy died, a lot of our futures died with him. It was the only real link we had in those early days with the music business."

Hired by the Liberty label to do promotion, Snuff insisted on also being allowed to produce records. He had success with singles by Johnny Burnette ("Dreamin'," "You're Sixteen") and Bobby Vee ("Devil Or Angel," "Rubber Ball"), and was soon the head of A&R for Liberty. He produced singles for Gene McDaniels and actor Walter Brennan, but lost one he thought was going to be a hit. He had hired a young man named Phil Spector to work in Liberty's New York office. After cutting "He's A Rebel" for Vikki Carr, Garrett was shocked to learn that Spector had taken Gene Pitney's demo of the song and raced to Los Angeles to cut it with Darlene Love of the Blossoms on lead vocals. Spector released "He's A Rebel" as a Crystals single, and it went to number one.

In the mid-'60s, Garrett produced a string of hits for the son of his neighbor, Jerry Lewis. Gary Lewis & the Playboys started at the top by recording a song Bobby Vee had turned down, "This Diamond Ring."

Snuff was back on top of the Hot 100 in 1971 with Cher's "Gypsys, Tramps And Thieves" (which was originally titled "Gypsys and White Trash"). His most successful *Billboard* single is a song turned down by Liza Minnelli and Cher. "Sonny told me it was piece of junk and she would never record it," Snuff maintains. "Liza didn't like the song." So Snuff told songwriter Bobby Russell that his wife Vicki Lawrence should record "The Night The Lights Went Out In Georgia." Snuff recalls: "We did two or three sides in no more than two-and-a-half hours."

ARIF MARDIN

1 **AGAINST ALL ODDS (TAKE A LOOK AT ME NOW)**
Phil Collins *Atlantic* 84

2 **SEPARATE LIVES**
Phil Collins and Marilyn Martin *Atlantic* 85

3 **PEOPLE GOT TO BE FREE**
The Rascals *Atlantic* 68

4 **I FEEL FOR YOU**
Chaka Khan *Warner Bros* 84

5 **FROM A DISTANCE**
Bette Midler *Atlantic* 90

6 **UNTIL YOU COME BACK TO ME (THAT'S WHAT I'M GONNA DO)**
Aretha Franklin *Atlantic* 74

7 **YOU SHOULD HEAR HOW SHE TALKS ABOUT YOU**
Melissa Manchester *Arista* 82

8 **WIND BENEATH MY WINGS**
Bette Midler *Atlantic* 89

9 **WAITING FOR A STAR TO FALL**
Boy Meets Girl *RCA* 88

10 **PICK UP THE PIECES**
Average White Band *Atlantic* 75

11 **JIVE TALKIN'**
Bee Gees *RSO* 75

12 **GOOD LOVIN'**
The Young Rascals *Atlantic* 66

13 **SHE'S GONE**
Daryl Hall and John Oates *Atlantic* 76

14 **SPANISH HARLEM**
Aretha Franklin *Atlantic* 71

15 **NIGHTS ON BROADWAY**
Bee Gees *RSO* 75

16 **BRIDGE OVER TROUBLED WATER**
Aretha Franklin *Atlantic* 71

17 **RAINY NIGHT IN GEORGIA**
Brook Benton *Cotillion* 70

18 **YOU BELONG TO ME**
Carly Simon *Elektra* 78

19 **CUT THE CAKE**
Average White Band *Atlantic* 75

20 **FANNY (BE TENDER WITH MY LOVE)**
Bee Gees *RSO* 76

21 **DAY DREAMING**
Aretha Franklin *Atlantic* 72

22 **WHERE IS THE LOVE**
Roberta Flack and Donny Hathaway *Atlantic* 72

23 **SON-OF-A-PREACHER MAN**
Dusty Springfield *Atlantic* 69

24 **DON'T PLAY THAT SONG**
Aretha Franklin *Atlantic* 70

25 **GOOD TIME CHARLIE'S GOT THE BLUES**
Danny O'Keefe *Signpost* 72

26 **CALL ME**
Aretha Franklin *Atlantic* 70

27 **YOU KNOW I LOVE YOU ... DON'T YOU?**
Howard Jones *Elektra* 86

28 **ROCK STEADY**
Aretha Franklin *Atlantic* 71

29 **MOVE AWAY**
Culture Club *Epic/Virgin* 86

30 **SEND IN THE CLOWNS**
Judy Collins *Elektra* 77

A rif Mardin's credits as a producer include artists with many different visions, from Judy Collins to Culture Club, from Bette Midler to the Rascals. Mardin was born in Istanbul, Turkey, and was a jazz fan by the time he was 10. He came to the United States in 1958 as the recipient of a Quincy Jones music scholarship at Berklee College in Boston. Mardin met Nesuhi Ertegun of Atlantic Records, and was asked to join the label. "I started at the bottom and then I was given a production job with the Rascals in 1965. Tom Dowd and I were co-producing—it was the first time I was bitten by the pop bug." Mardin cites the Beatles, Motown and Stax as major influences.

Mardin worked with Dowd and Jerry Wexler on projects by Atlantic artists like Aretha Franklin and Dusty Springfield, and went solo on Brook Benton's "Rainy Night In Georgia." In the mid-'70s, he produced *Main Course*, the album that gave the Bee Gees a resurgence with "Jive Talkin'" and "Nights On Broadway." Mardin suggested they listen to current R&B records before recording the album. The producer recalls, "The rapport between the brothers and myself was fabulous. When we were in the studio together, one creative idea led to another." The Bee Gees wanted to continue to work with Mardin, but when Robert Stigwood moved his RSO label from Atlantic to Polydor, Mardin's services were no longer available.

Two of Mardin's top 10 singles are by Bette Midler. "'Wind Beneath My Wings' was chosen for the film *Beaches* before I joined the project," he explains. Director Garry Marshall used a rough mix during the filming. From the emotional reaction of the crew, Mardin knew the track was a hit.

Mardin came up with the idea of using Melle Mel's rap as an introduction to Chaka Khan's "I Feel For You." He recalls, "I thought Chaka's name was a great source for percussive singing. The hybrid really worked, combining the hip hop technology of the day."

Mardin's top two chart singles are both movie songs by Phil Collins. "Phil asked me to do some string arrangements on his first Atlantic solo album —we got along famously." Collins requested that Mardin produce "Against All Odds (Take A Look At Me Now)." The producer took a few days off from working with British trio Scritti Politti to record Phil's vocals in Los Angeles. The song "Separate Lives," from *White Nights*, was crying out for a duet, according to Doug Morris, president of Atlantic Records. "We overdubbed vocals by Marilyn Martin with great results," says Mardin.

RICHARD PERRY

Richard Perry grew up in Brooklyn. His doo-wop group Escorts signed with Coral Records, and had a local hit in Detroit with "Somewhere" from *West Side Story*.

After the Escorts, Perry wrote some songs with Kenny Vance of Jay & the Americans. Then he went to work in the West Coast A&R department of Kama Sutra Records, where he received his first production assignment: working with Captain Beefheart on the *Safe As Milk* album.

Next, Perry moved to Warner Brothers as a staff producer. He worked with Ella Fitzgerald, Fats Domino and Theodore Bikel, providing all three with a contemporary mix of songs that included a lot of Lennon-McCartney material. His first Hot 100 hit came not with any of those artists, but with the eccentric Herbert Khaury—better known as Tiny Tim.

Perry left Warner Brothers to become a free-lance producer, and was selected by Clive Davis at Columbia Records to produce Barbra Streisand. He gave Streisand her first top 10 hit since "People" in 1964 with Laura Nyro's "Stoney End."

Perry's next hit album was *Nilsson Schmilsson*. He had first met Harry Nilsson at a party Phil Spector threw for Tiny Tim in 1968. The first single from the album, a remake of Badfinger's "Without You," spent four weeks at number one. Perry had another chart-topper with Carly Simon's "You're So Vain"; more number one hits followed for Ringo Starr and Leo Sayer. The Pointer Sisters' version of Bruce Springsteen's "Fire" peaked at number two.

THE TOP 30 SONGS PRODUCED BY
NILE RODGERS & BERNARD EDWARDS

1 LE FREAK
Chic *Atlantic* 78

2 UPSIDE DOWN
Diana Ross *Motown* 80

3 LIKE A VIRGIN
Madonna *Sire* 84

4 LET'S DANCE
David Bowie *EMI America* 83

5 GOOD TIMES
Chic *Atlantic* 79

6 DANCE, DANCE, DANCE (YOWSAH, YOWSAH, YOWSAH)
Chic *Atlantic* 78

7 THE WILD BOYS
Duran Duran *Capitol* 84

8 A VIEW TO A KILL
Duran Duran *Capitol* 85

9 NOTORIOUS
Duran Duran *Capitol* 87

10 ADDICTED TO LOVE
Robert Palmer *Island* 86

11 I'M COMING OUT
Diana Ross *Motown* 80

12 DON'T YOU WANT ME
Jody Watley *MCA* 87

13 MY HEART CAN'T TELL YOU NO
Rod Stewart *Warner Bros* 89

14 WE ARE FAMILY
Sister Sledge *Cotillion* 79

15 MATERIAL GIRL
Madonna *Sire* 85

16 ROAM
The B-52's *Reprise* 90

17 I DIDN'T MEAN TO TURN YOU ON
Robert Palmer *Island* 86

18 I WANT YOUR LOVE
Chic *Atlantic* 79

19 ANGEL
Madonna *Sire* 85

20 WHEN SMOKEY SINGS
ABC *Mercury* 87

21 LAY YOUR HANDS ON ME
Thompson Twins *Arista* 85

22 HE'S THE GREATEST DANCER
Sister Sledge *Cotillion* 79

23 RUMORS
Timex Social Club *Jay* 86

24 KING FOR A DAY
Thompson Twins *Arista* 86

25 GET IT ON (BANG A GONG)
Power Station *Capitol* 85

26 CHINA GIRL
David Bowie *EMI America* 83

27 CRAZY ABOUT HER
Rod Stewart *Warner Bros* 89

28 DRESS YOU UP
Madonna *Sire* 85

29 THIS OLD HEART OF MINE
Rod Stewart w/Ronald Isley *Warner Bros* 90

30 FOREVER YOUNG
Rod Stewart *Warner Bros* 88

In 1973, Nile Rodgers and Bernard Edwards were backing up a Thom Bell group, New York City. When they broke up, Rodgers and Edwards decided to continue working together. They tried to get a record deal. Record companies liked their tapes but nobody wanted to sign them. "We had been writing songs all along, but they were all rock 'n' roll songs," says Nile. "Power chords and the whole bit. As soon as we did 'Dance, Dance, Dance,' our first disco song, we got a record deal."

"Le Freak," the third single by Chic, became Atlantic's most successful single of all time. While Chic was popular, Rodgers and Edwards toured and started to produce for other artists.

After "Good Times" hit number one in 1979, Chic never made the top 40 of the Hot 100 again. In 1980, Nile and Bernard were asked to produce an album for Diana Ross, *Diana*. "We had never worked with stars before," Rodgers admitted. "We didn't realize what producers did." The "Upside Down" single is Rodgers and Edwards' second biggest song on the *Billboard* chart.

By 1983, Chic had dissolved, and Rodgers was in a downswing. A chance meeting at an after-hours club with one of his long-time heroes, David Bowie, resulted in Nile producing Bowie's *Let's Dance* album; the title track became Bowie's most successful Hot 100 song, revitalizing his career. Nile went on to produce albums for Madonna as well as Duran Duran.

Bernard Edwards also worked with Duran Duran, Robert Palmer, ABC, Jody Watley and Rod Stewart.

THOM BELL

1 THE RUBBERBAND MAN
Spinners *Atlantic* 76

2 THEN CAME YOU
Dionne Warwick & the Spinners *Atlantic* 74

3 YOU MAKE ME FEEL BRAND NEW
The Stylistics *Avco* 74

4 BETCHA BY GOLLY, WOW
The Stylistics *Avco* 72

5 I DON'T HAVE THE HEART
James Ingram *Warner Bros* 90

6 YOU ARE EVERYTHING
The Stylistics *Avco* 72

7 MAMA CAN'T BUY YOU LOVE
Elton John *MCA* 79

8 COULD IT BE I'M FALLING IN LOVE
Spinners *Atlantic* 73

9 THEY JUST CAN'T STOP IT THE (GAMES PEOPLE PLAY)
Spinners *Atlantic* 75

10 LA-LA—MEANS I LOVE YOU
The Delfonics *Philly Groove* 68

Thom Bell teamed up with one of his sister Barbara's schoolmates, Kenny Gamble, to cut a song called "Someday," released on Jerry Ross' Heritage label. Later, with Kenny, he formed the Romeos, a group that became the house band at Cameo-Parkway Records in 1964. Two years later, Bell was the musical director for Chubby Checker's British tour.

After a brief stint with the Philly Groove label, where he produced the Delfonic's song "La La—Means I Love You," Tom worked with Gamble and his partner, Leon Huff. He arranged several Jerry Butler hits for them, and worked on a Dusty Springfield album recorded in Philadelphia. At the same time, Bell teamed up with Linda Creed to write songs.

Hugo Peretti and Luigi Creatore at Avco Records hired Bell to produce the Stylistics, who had immediate success with Bell-Creed songs like "You Are Everything," "Betcha By Golly, Wow" and "You Make Me Feel Brand New." Tom's later projects include the Spinners and Elton John.

MIKE CHAPMAN

1 MY SHARONA
The Knack *Capitol* 79

2 KISS YOU ALL OVER
Exile *Warner/Curb* 78

3 HOT CHILD IN THE CITY
Nick Gilder *Chrysalis* 78

4 THE TIDE IS HIGH
Blondie *Chrysalis* 81

5 STUMBLIN' IN
Suzi Quatro and Chris Norman *RSO* 79

6 RAPTURE
Blondie *Chrysalis* 81

7 HEART OF GLASS
Blondie *Chrysalis* 79

8 THE WARRIOR
Scandal f/Patty Smyth *Columbia* 84

9 LOVE TOUCH
Rod Stewart *Warner Bros* 86

10 CLOSE MY EYES (FOREVER)
Lita Ford w/Ozzy Osbourne *RCA* 89

Mike Chapman was working as a waiter in London in 1970 when he met Nicky Chinn. They decided to write songs together, and in less than a year they had their first top 20 hit in the U.K., "Funny Funny," the initial chart single by Sweet. They continued to turn out hits for the group.

Chapman's first real American triumph came in 1978, when he had two consecutive number one singles. After working with Exile for two years, he and Chinn wrote "Kiss You All Over" for the band. Mike also produced Nick Gilder's "Hot Child In The City" for Chrysalis, then worked with Blondie. Debbie Harry and Chris Stein were initially reluctant to have him produce, but Chapman won them over with a new arrangement for their song "Heart Of Glass."

Chapman's most successful chart song in America is the Knack's first single. "They approached me to produce them and the first song they played me was 'My Sharona,'" he recalled. "How could I not go into the studio with that song?"

JIMMY JAM & TERRY LEWIS

In January of 1981, Terry Lewis asked Jimmy Jam to join his band, Flyte Tyme. The other members included Alexander O'Neal, Jesse Johnson and Morris Day. When Prince offered Day a recording contract, he brought along the whole band, who shortened their name to the Time.

Jam and Lewis moonlighted as producers before leaving the Time to do full-time production work. Their early hits included "Tender Love" for the Force M.D.s and "Saturday Love" for Alexander O'Neal and Cherrelle. Then they produced Janet Jackson's third album, *Control*, which yielded six hit singles. Janet surpassed that feat with *Rhythm Nation 1814*, which contained three number one hits, including Jam and Lewis' most successful single, "Miss You Much."

The producers' success with Jackson resulted in a barrage of requests from artists who want to be produced by Jam and Lewis. They recently worked with the Human League, Herb Alpert, and George Michael.

THE TOP 10 SONGS PRODUCED BY
GIORGIO MORODER

1 **FLASHDANCE ... WHAT A FEELING**
Irene Cara *Casablanca* 83

2 **CALL ME**
Blondie *Chrysalis* 80

3 **HOT STUFF**
Donna Summer *Casablanca* 79

4 **BAD GIRLS**
Donna Summer *Casablanca* 79

5 **MACARTHUR PARK**
Donna Summer *Casablanca* 78

6 **LAST DANCE**
Donna Summer *Casablanca* 78

7 **HEAVEN KNOWS**
Donna Summer w/Brooklyn
Dreams *Casablanca* 79

8 **I FEEL LOVE**
Donna Summer *Casablanca* 77

9 **NO MORE TEARS (ENOUGH IS ENOUGH)**
Barbra Streisand and Donna
Summer *Columbia* 79

10 **DIM ALL THE LIGHTS**
Donna Summer *Casablanca* 79

Giorgio Moroder grew up in Italy, quitting school at 19 to become a professional musician. In 1972, his song "Nachts Schient Die Sonne"—translated into "Son Of My Father"— became a number one hit in the U.K. for Chicory Tip. In America, it was released on Dunhill by Giorgio himself, and charted at number 46.

After a three-year stay in Berlin, Moroder settled in Munich, where Donna Summer was also living. Summer recorded some early material with Moroder and his lyricist, Pete Bellotte. When they finally had a hit in France, Moroder sent a copy to Neil Bogart in the States and "Love To Love You Baby" introduced Donna in America. Giorgio's innovative use of synthesizers on Summer's "I Feel Love" started a wave of electronic pop hits. Eight of his top 10 chart singles are by Summer.

Giorgio won an Oscar with his first film score, for *Midnight Express*, and another one for composing the title song for *Flashdance*.

THE TOP 10 SONGS PRODUCED BY
MICHAEL OMARTIAN

1 **ARTHUR'S THEME (BEST THAT YOU CAN DO)**
Christopher Cross *Warner Bros* 81

2 **RIDE LIKE THE WIND**
Christopher Cross *Warner Bros* 80

3 **SHE WORKS HARD FOR THE MONEY**
Donna Summer *Mercury* 83

4 **UNDERCOVER ANGEL**
Alan O'Day *Pacific* 77

5 **HOW AM I SUPPOSED TO LIVE WITHOUT YOU**
Michael Bolton *Columbia* 90

6 **THE NEXT TIME I FALL**
Peter Cetera and Amy Grant *Full Moon* 86

7 **SAILING**
Christopher Cross *Warner Bros* 80

8 **GLORY OF LOVE**
Peter Cetera *Warner Bros* 86

9 **ROCK ME GENTLY**
Andy Kim *Capitol* 74

10 **INFATUATION**
Rod Stewart *Warner Bros* 84

Michael Omartian was encouraged by his parents to take piano lessons at four and drum lessons at six. He left Chicago in 1965 to move west and pursue a songwriting career, but found more success as a session keyboard player. He became an arranger before producing his first album, a project for Jay Gruska on ABC-Dunhill.

Omartian achieved success early in his producing career, coming up with "Rock Me Gently," a number one single for Andy Kim in 1974. He worked as a staff producer for ABC, then for Warner Brothers. Christopher Cross had submitted a tape to Warner Brothers, and asked Omartian to produce his album—mainly, according to Michael, "because I played a lot of keyboards on Steely Dan albums."

Michael's most successful production is "Arthur's Theme (Best That You Can Do)" by Cross (co-written with Peter Allen, Burt Bacharach and Carole Bayer Sager). He recalls: "There was no demo . . . we went in the studio and it took two days."

L.A. REID & BABYFACE

1 **I'M YOUR BABY TONIGHT**
Whitney Houston *Arista* 90

2 **ON OUR OWN**
Bobby Brown *MCA* 89

3 **EVERY LITTLE STEP**
Bobby Brown *MCA* 89

4 **CAN'T STOP**
After 7 *Virgin* 90

5 **THE LOVER IN ME**
Sheena Easton *MCA* 89

6 **GIRLFRIEND**
Pebbles *MCA* 88

7 **READY OR NOT**
After 7 *Virgin* 90

8 **DON'T BE CRUEL**
Bobby Brown *MCA* 88

9 **GIVING YOU THE BENEFIT**
Pebbles *MCA* 90

10 **SECRET RENDEZVOUS**
Karyn White *Warner Bros* 89

Antonio "L.A." Reid and Kenny "Babyface" Edmonds first met at the Zodiac nightclub in Indianapolis, where Reid was playing with his band, the Deele. Years later, while writing some songs for the Deele and working on their demos, L.A. invited Babyface to join the group. The Deele hit the Hot 100 in 1984, but their first real success came in May, 1988, with "Two Occasions." By this time, Reid and Babyface had written and produced a top 10 single, "Rock Steady" by the Whispers.

Reid and Babyface were soon in demand as songwriters and producers. In a three-year period, they produced hits for Bobby Brown, Karyn White, Pebbles (now Reid's wife) and After 7, a trio that included two of Babyface's brothers and L.A.'s cousin. In December, 1990, the two producers had their first number one single on the Hot 100 with Whitney Houston's "I'm Your Baby Tonight," a song designed to give a harder R&B edge to Houston. "I'm Your Baby Tonight" became L.A. Reid & Babyface's most successful chart single.

STOCK-AITKEN-WATERMAN

1 **NEVER GONNA GIVE YOU UP**
Rick Astley *RCA* 88

2 **VENUS**
Bananarama *London* 86

3 **TOGETHER FOREVER**
Rick Astley *RCA* 88

4 **THE LOCO-MOTION**
Kylie Minogue *Geffen* 88

5 **I HEARD A RUMOUR**
Bananarama *London* 87

6 **THIS TIME I KNOW IT'S FOR REAL**
Donna Summer *Atlantic* 89

7 **IT WOULD TAKE A STRONG STRONG MAN**
Rick Astley *RCA* 88

8 **YOU SPIN ME ROUND (LIKE A RECORD)**
Dead or Alive *Epic* 85

9 **BRAND NEW LOVER**
Dead or Alive *Epic* 87

10 **I SHOULD BE SO LUCKY**
Kylie Minogue *Geffen* 88

Mike Stock, Matt Aitken and Pete Waterman have had some measure of success in America, but in their native Britain, they have sold more than 10 million singles since 1984. Their 100th chart entry, "Use It Up And Wear It Out," was moving up the U.K. survey on April 14, 1990.

The trio's first collaboration was "The Upstroke," which Stock and Aitken recorded under the name Agents Aren't Airplanes. Their subsequent work with British singer Hazell Dean impressed Pete Burns from Dead or Alive. He asked the trio to be his producers; the result was their first U.K. number one and first U.S. chart hit, "You Spin Me Round (Like A Record)."

Stock-Aitken-Waterman's American successes include singles by Bananarama ("Venus," "I Heard A Rumour") and Rick Astley ("Never Gonna Give You Up"). They have also worked with Donna Summer, Cliff Richard and Samantha Fox. Their most consistent artists in the U.K. have been two actors from the Australian TV soap *Neighbours*—Kylie Minogue and Jason Donovan.

THE TOP 10 SONGS PRODUCED BY
NARADA MICHAEL WALDEN

1. **VISION OF LOVE**
   Mariah Carey *Columbia* 90
2. **I WANNA DANCE WITH SOMEBODY (WHO LOVES ME)**
   Whitney Houston *Arista* 87
3. **SO EMOTIONAL**
   Whitney Houson *Arista* 88
4. **NOTHING'S GONNA STOP US NOW**
   Starship *Grunt* 87
5. **HOW WILL I KNOW**
   Whitney Houston *Arista* 86
6. **WHERE DO BROKEN HEARTS GO**
   Whitney Houston *Arista* 88
7. **FREEWAY OF LOVE**
   Aretha Franklin *Arista* 85
8. **I KNEW YOU WERE WAITING (FOR ME)**
   Aretha Franklin and George Michael *Arista* 87
9. **SONGBIRD**
   Kenny G *Arista* 87
10. **WE DON'T HAVE TO TAKE OUR CLOTHES OFF**
    Jermaine Stewart *Arista* 86

Narada Michael Walden was 19 when he joined Deacon Williams and the Soul Revival Troupe. After hearing John McLaughlin's Mahavishnu Orchestra, he became interested in jazz fusion, and at 21, he replaced drummer Billy Cobham in that outfit. Walden also became interested in the teachings of McLaughlin's guru, Sri Chinmoy, who gave him the new first name of Narada ("supreme musician").

Walden worked with Jeff Beck and Weather Report, then recorded solo albums. His first experience as a producer was with jazz trumpeter Don Cherry; next he worked with pop artist Stacy Lattisaw. For Arista, he produced albums for Angela Bofill and Phyllis Hyman before taking on Aretha Franklin's *Who's Zoomin' Who?* album. He was planning to record "Freeway Of Love" for himself, but gave it to Aretha instead.

After working with Whitney Houston, Narada was called in by Tommy Mottola of Columbia Records to produce Mariah Carey—her "Vision Of Love" is Walden's most successful chart single.

THE LABELS

Record labels have their own distinct identities. Imagine "Baby Love" by the Supremes on Chrysalis or "That's Life" by Frank Sinatra on Island—it just wouldn't be the same.

Even though the concept of bonding a colorfully-designed piece of paper to the center portion of a disc died when vinyl records passed away, record companies will still be referred to as "labels" well into the future. But one should feel sorry for teenagers of the 21st century who will never know the joy of searching the singles wall at their local record store for the latest release featuring Motown's map of Detroit, Apple Records' Granny Smith apple, or the Elektra caterpillar that transformed into a butterfly on album labels.

Part of the fun of collecting 45s was enjoying the graphic designs of the artists employed by the various labels, noticing when colors were altered or whole new logos were introduced. The plastic-coated aluminum surface of a compact disc still allows for artists to use their imaginations, but it's not the same.

This section lists the most successful chart singles of 43 different labels. These companies vary in age, size and style. Columbia Records can trace its origins back to 1881; the company was pressing discs as early as 1901. Elektra Records marked its 40th anniversary in 1990 with the *Rubaiyat* collection of artists performing songs by former label artists. Arista celebrated its 15th birthday in 1990 with a concert to benefit the Gay Men's Health Crisis. Labels that are even younger are included, like the American arm of Virgin, established in 1987.

Labels that were owned or distributed by the same parent company are grouped together. Liberty—which bought Imperial, merged with United Artists, then was swallowed up by EMI—appears with all these labels in the same section as Capitol, the American label owned by Thorn-EMI of Great Britain. Decca and Uni were consolidated into MCA, so those three labels are grouped together.

Columbia and Epic, both owned by Sony, each have their own top 100 lists, as do most labels regardless of their affiliations. Exceptions were made for Motown, Stax and EMI. All Motown labels were included in that company's top 100. Similarly, Stax, Volt, Enterprise and KoKo singles are all included in the Stax list and EMI, EMI America, EMI Manhattan and Manhattan singles are grouped together under EMI.

Sadly, many of the label names featured in this section have gone to that great cut-out bin in the sky. The MGM logo has been dropped by its current owner, Polygram. ABC and Dot were purchased by MCA and laid to rest; Cameo-Parkway is dormant under the ownership of Allen Klein and his ABCKO Industries.

Of course, it's hard to keep a good label down. Warner Brothers reactivated its Reprise label in 1987, Atlantic has given new priority to Atco, and EMI revived Liberty for a short time.

Styx

The A&M record label can trace its origin to an obscure single called "Hooray For The Big Slow Train" by the Diddley Oohs. The "group" was made up of Herb Alpert and Jerry Moss, and while their ode to the Seattle World's Fair of 1962 might have been a bomb, their partnership would create one of the most successful independent labels of the rock era.

Louis and Tillie Alpert came home from a weekend trip and found their eight-year-old son Herb with a rented trumpet from school. Louis played the mandolin and Tillie had studied the violin, so they happily encouraged their boy to practice. By the time he was 15, Herb was playing local dates as part of the Colonial Trio. At the same time, he heard Ray Anthony's "Young Man With A Horn" on the radio, and became an avid record buyer.

Discharged from the army in 1956, Alpert met an insurance agent who wanted to be a lyricist. Herb agreed to collaborate with Lou Adler; their first sale was "Circle Rock," recorded by the Salmas Brothers on Keen. They were hired as staff writers for the label, where they worked with Sam Cooke and wrote "Wonderful World" with him. After Cooke signed with RCA, Alpert and Adler produced singles for Jan and Dean.

Jerry Moss grew up in the West Bronx, one of 11 children of Irving and Rose Moss. He worked as a page for ABC Television on the weekends while studying English at Brooklyn College. At a friend's wedding reception, a man named Marvin Cane suggested he would make a great promotion man, and in August of 1958 Moss went to work for Cane promoting "Sixteen Candles" by the Crests. After a year-and-a-half, he headed for Los Angeles.

Alpert's and Moss' paths kept crossing in Los Angeles music circles, and one day they agreed to form a partnership. They both put up $100 to form Carnival Records, and their first release was Herb's vocal rendition of his song "Tell It To The Birds," released under the name Dore Alpert. Herb wanted to record an instrumental song called "Twinkle Star," and a visit to a bullfight in Tijuana inspired them to add a mariachi beat and the sound of cheering spectators. Retitled "The Lonely Bull," the single was readied for release on Carnival, but someone else laid claim to the label name and the company had to be rechristened. The simplest thing to do was take their initials, A&M. Jerry decided the solo recording should be released under the name "The Tijuana Brass featuring Herb Alpert."

A&M moved offices from Herb's garage to the Sunset Strip. The Tijuana Brass recorded more albums, and promo man Gil Friesen joined the label. He suggested that Alpert create a real Tijuana Brass to play live dates, and as the TJB's popularity soared, the band had five albums in the top 20 of *Billboard's* album chart, including *Whipped Cream and Other Delights*.

The label also achieved early hits by the We Five ("You Were On My Mind"), Chris Montez, the Sandpipers and Sergio Mendes and Brasil '66. With a need for more office space, A&M moved to the former Charlie Chaplin movie studio at the corner of LaBrea and Sunset on November 6, 1966.

"At that moment," Moss told Timothy White, "I think our image was of a sort of semi-hip, jazz, Latin-sounding label using MOR stations to sell albums. At Monterey Pop in '67, the so-called underground emerged, and as successful as Herb was at that time, this new force was looked on as a different kind of medium. The movement was definitely towards rock 'n' roll."

Moss was depressed that A&M didn't have any artists at the Monterey Pop Festival. Shortly after, he traveled to England and signed Procol Harum and the Move for America. He made an agreement with Chris Blackwell of Island Records to license Jimmy Cliff, Cat Stevens, Spooky Tooth, Fairport Convention and Free for the U.S. Other British deals brought the Strawbs and Humble Pie to the label. American artists were added to the roster, including Phil Ochs, Lee Michaels and the Flying Burrito Brothers. When the Woodstock Music and Arts Festival took place in 1969, A&M had an artist on the bill: Joe Cocker.

As the new decade began, A&M was at the top of the Hot 100 with a new duo, the Carpenters. To many people, they were just another middle-of-the-road group. "The idea of a girl drummer who sang was shrugged off as too peculiar," Alpert told White, "but I heard something in Karen and Richard's music, a seductive delicacy. To go from early critical dismissal to selling 75 million records and holding an enormously loyal following was a very profound experience."

A&M fared well on the Hot 100 during the first half of the '70s with Billy Preston, the British duo Stealers Wheel (which included Gerry Rafferty), as well as Cat Stevens and Lee Michaels. In mid-decade, the label had its biggest hit to date with the Captain & Tennille's cover of Neil Sedaka's "Love Will Keep Us Together."

Humble Pie member Peter Frampton ventured out on his own as a solo artist and did well with his fourth LP, *Frampton*, in 1975. "After his 1975 album, we wanted Peter to do a live record," Moss said, "because his performances on the road in 1974-1975 were so electric, and we weren't selling as many records as we thought we should be from the studio work. I asked him for a concert record, and later, at Electric Lady Studios in New York, heard the tapes. I thought it was fantastic." "Show Me The Way," released previously as a studio cut, became a hit when a live version was released from *Frampton Comes Alive!*

A&M closed the '70s with hits from Styx, Rita Coolidge (who had been on Joe Cocker's *Mad Dogs and Englishmen* tour), Chuck Mangione and Supertramp. Alpert returned to the top of the Hot 100 with an instrumental, "Rise." "I know disco's not the rage anymore," Alpert said in *Rolling Stone* at the time, "but I also know that lots of people still dance. I wanted to plug into that—not to make another routine disco record, but to take some of those elements and come up with something I'd have fun playing."

A&M had more success in the '80s with British artists like Joe Jackson, the Human League and Simple Minds. Moss had returned to London in 1977, and met with Miles Copeland of the International Records Syndicate. "Miles had a group he was out to prove had something special," Moss said to White. "Derek Green, our managing director at A&M in England, obliged by signing them. I remember hearing the Police for the first time over the speakers in a New York club and I was gone—it totally nailed me. The record was called 'Roxanne.'"

The Police have six singles on A&M's top 100, including the label's most successful chart single, "Every Breath You Take." When the group split, lead singer Sting provided A&M with hits like "If You Love Somebody Set Them Free" and "We'll Be Together."

Canadian singer Bryan Adams gave the label a run of hit singles in the '80s. There were left-of-center singles from Suzanne Vega and Falco, and the British trio Breathe scored impressively with two ballads, "Hands To Heaven" and "How Can I Fall." But the ultimate success story of the last half of the decade was Janet Jackson, signed to A&M when she was just 16. Her first two albums, *Janet Jackson* and *Dream Street*, contained some juvenile pop songs, but the Jimmy Jam-Terry Lewis produced *Control* was her breakthrough, with five top five singles. *Rhythm Nation 1814* did even better, with four number ones, including "Miss You Much" (number nine on A&M's top 100).

Barry Manilow

When Alan Hirschfield, president of Columbia Pictures, wanted to strengthen the company's Bell Records subsidiary, he approached Clive Davis about heading up the label and offered him 20 percent of Bell's stock.

Davis, a lawyer educated at Harvard, had joined Columbia Records in 1960 as an attorney. Five years later, label president Goddard Lieberson asked the 33-year-old Davis to take the new position of administrative vice president. A year later, Clive was upped to vice president and general manager; in 1967, he was named president of Columbia Records. That was the year that the Monterey Pop Festival was taking place in California, and Davis thought it would be fun to go and mingle with people like Lou Adler, entertainment attorney Abe Somer, the Byrds and Simon and Garfunkel. Clive didn't expect to find any new talent there, but he saw Janis Joplin perform with Big Brother & the Holding Company and signed her away from the small Mainstream label.

Clive helped usher Columbia into the rock and roll era, signing Blood, Sweat and Tears, Santana, Chicago, Laura Nyro, Boz Scaggs, Johnny Winter and Loggins and Messina. When A&R executive John Hammond brought him Bruce Springsteen, Clive signed him, too.

In 1973, Davis was suddenly dismissed from the company, accused of misusing his expense account. He was indicted in 1975 on six counts of tax evasion in connection with those expenses, and in May, 1976, five of those counts were dismissed.

From mid-1973 to the spring of 1974, Davis took time out to write a biography, *Clive: Inside the Music Business.* He declined offers to work for Chris Blackwell of Island Records and Robert Stigwood, and accepted the Columbia Pictures offer in 1974.

Taking over Bell Records, Clive pared down the artist roster and concentrated on three acts: Barry Manilow, Melissa Manchester and the Bay City Rollers. Manilow had been signed to Bell by the company's former head, Larry Uttal.

In his book *Sweet Life,* Manilow said that Uttal's departure made him nervous about his future at the company, especially when Clive started dropping artists. "He would have gladly dropped me too, because he didn't like my first album. But two things stopped him: I was in the middle of making my second album and had already spent money on it; and everyone in the company believed in me."

Clive made a point to see Barry perform at a concert in Central Park and went backstage to meet him. He reassured Manilow that he was a part of the Bell family. Later, when Clive heard Barry's proposed second album, he told him he still needed some hit songs for it. He telephoned to suggest a song written by Scott English and Richard Kerr called "Brandy."

"It was a strange phone call and I didn't know exactly how to respond because I was supposed to be the songwriter," Manilow wrote. "Yet here was the president of my record company, whose support I needed, saying I should sing another songwriter's song."

To keep Clive as an ally, Manilow and producer Ron Dante agreed to record the song. They copied the tempo of the version recorded by English. When Davis showed up at the recording session, he hated the result. So Barry slowed it down, and Clive loved the song as a ballad. With a title change so as not to confuse the song with the Looking Glass tune "Brandy (You're A Fine Girl)," "Mandy" was released and went to number one. It was the last chart-topper to be issued on Bell. Clive changed the name of the label to Arista, after the honor society he belonged to when he attended public school in Manhattan.

In its first two years of operation, Arista also had hits from the other artists Davis had retained from the Bell roster, Melissa Manchester ("Midnight Blue") and the Bay City Rollers ("Saturday Night"). Davis expanded the label's horizons, with new wave artists like Patti Smith, Lou Reed and Graham Parker; R&B singers like Ray Parker, Jr.; and British groups like the Kinks and the Alan Parsons Project.

In 1979, Clive signed Dionne Warwick after her long dry spell on Warner Brothers. "I was flattered and touched that Dionne would sign with Arista for no guarantee beyond production costs, on the condition that I be involved," Davis said in *Rolling Stone.* Clive and Dionne debated who should produce her Arista debut, then Clive arranged for her to meet with Manilow. "Barry talked solidly for two hours," Warwick recalled to Stephen Holden in *Rolling Stone.* "He said, 'Honey, I've got to do this; nobody else can do it.' And at the end, I was totally convinced that this guy could do anything he wanted to."

The initial single—written by Will Jennings and "Mandy" co-writer Richard Kerr—was "I'll Never Love This Way Again," Dionne's first solo top 10 single in almost a decade. "I can see now that while I was at Warners, everything was wrong but me. Now, once again, everything is being done absolutely for *me*. There's no overshadowing, I'm sitting on top of everything, which is the way it should be," Dionne told Holden.

The same year Dionne had her first success with Arista, Hirschfield was fired from his post as CEO of Columbia Pictures. The studio's board of directors decided to sell off Arista. "[Hirschfield] believed in me and really was the main reason why Columbia Pictures financed the beginning of Arista," Davis said in Ted Fox' *In the Groove*. "I did feel a certain sense of alienation from the board of Columbia Pictures, and I motivated . . . the sale. . . . I came up with a purchaser of the stock of Arista, and recommended very highly to the board of Columbia Pictures that we both sell our interest in Arista to Bertelsmann [the German owners of Ariola Records]."

Arista moved into the '80s with a string of top 10 singles from the Australian duo Air Supply. Aretha Franklin signed with the label after a long run on Atlantic. And in 1983, Davis signed the artist that would assure the label of chart prominence through the rest of the decade and into the '90s. Her name was Whitney Houston.

Clive first saw her at the New York supper club Sweetwaters at the invitation of Gerry Griffith, then director of R&B music in Arista's A&R department. "From the moment he went down to Sweetwaters and heard her, he was relentless," Whitney's lawyer Paul Marshall said in Fredric Dannen's *Hit Men*. But there was competition for Whitney. CBS had expressed some interest, and Bruce Lundvall at Elektra wanted her. "Interestingly, [Clive] did not make the high bid," Marshall revealed. "Elektra kept upping their offer. And I finally recommended that she sign with Clive for less money." Whitney did sign with Arista, but included a key-man clause, stipulating that if Clive ever left the label, she would be free of her contract.

Joining her cousin Dionne Warwick on the Arista roster, Whitney didn't release an album until 1985. Her first single, "You Give Good Love," peaked at number three. Her next seven chart singles all went to number one, an unprecedented feat. All 11 of her chart singles between 1985 and 1990 are included in Arista's top 100.

That total is second only to Manilow, who has 12 songs in the top 100. Air Supply is in third place with eight, followed by Ray Parker, Jr., Taylor Dayne and Expose with seven each. Milli Vanilli—the group that caused Arista untold embarassment when it was revealed that Rob Pilatus and Fabrice Morvan did not record their own vocals—have five songs listed in the label's top 100.

The Partridge Family

Larry Uttal worked in his family's retail business. When the business was sold, he bought into a music publishing firm.

After that, he worked for small record companies, like Madison. Then he received a call from Al Massler, a record pressing-plant owner who had started his own record labels— Amy, Mala and Bell. Massler wanted Uttal to head up the labels. Uttal acquired half-ownership of the company and spent a lot of time in southern cities looking for material. One of the people he met down South was Chips Moman, who produced "Angel Of The Morning" by Merrilee Rush & the Turnabouts.

In 1969, Uttal sold the record company to Columbia Pictures. In 1970, producer Hank Medress brought Uttal a demo he had produced on a song called "Candida." Uttal recalls, "We both agreed the record was pretty bad." They decided to hold on to the track and find another artist to sing lead vocals. Two months later, Medress played a new version for Uttal but wouldn't tell him who was singing. At Uttal's insistence, Medress revealed that the singer was Tony Orlando. He was running CBS's April-Blackwood Music and didn't want to lose his job. "We had a hit record and nobody knew who the voice was," says Uttal. The billing continued to be "Dawn" through Bell's most successful chart single, "Tie A Yellow Ribbon Round The Ole Oak Tree."

By 1974, Uttal had signed Barry Manilow and Melissa Manchester to the label, and had released some early singles from a group that had signed to Bell in the U.K., the Bay City Rollers. Those three artists were the ones Clive Davis decided to concentrate on when he was named the new head of Bell. Most other artists were dropped, and Davis changed the name of the label to Arista. Uttal departed to create his own company, Private Stock.

Foreigner

Ahmet and Nesuhi Ertegun's father Munir was named Turkey's Ambassador to the United States in 1934. Ahmet, just 10 years old, had become fascinated with jazz music while his father was in his previous post as Ambassador to Britain. In Washington, Ahmet was befriended by Cleo Payne, a janitor at the Turkish embassy, who introduced the youngster to American R&B music. At 14, he accompanied the head of the Turkish Air Force on a trip to New York and managed to slip away long enough to visit nightclubs in Harlem.

When their father died in 1944, Ahmet and Nesuhi elected to stay in America while their mother and sister returned home to Turkey. With a $10,000 investment from his dentist, Dr. Vahdi Sabit, Ahmet partnered with Herb Abramson of National Records to start a new record company. When they launched their new venture in October, 1947, they called it Atlantic Records.

The label concentrated on jazz at first. In 1949, the first national hit on Atlantic was an R&B song, "Drinking Wine, Spo-Dee-O-Dee, Drinking Wine" by Stick McGhee. Atlantic expanded its R&B base by signing artists like Ruth Brown, Joe Turner and the Clovers. In 1952, Ahmet and Herb paid the Swingtime label $2,000 for Ray Charles, and a year later, Ahmet signed Clyde McPhatter, who became lead singer for the Drifters before recording on his own.

Abramson was drafted in 1953. His place at Atlantic was filled by a former *Billboard* reporter who was working for a music publisher, Jerry Wexler. With chief engineer Tom Dowd promoted to producer, Ertegun and Wexler turned out R&B hits like "Shake,

Rattle And Roll" for Joe Turner and "Tweedlee Dee" for LaVern Baker, but many of their songs were covered by white artists who outsold the originals.

When Abramson returned to the company in 1955, Wexler was an integral part of Atlantic and wasn't willing to give up his desk next to Ertegun. Abramson was given his own company to run, a subsidiary called Atco.

Nesuhi officially joined the company to supervise jazz recordings, and produced artists like John Coltrane, Ornette Coleman, Charles Mingus, Eddie Harris and the Modern Jazz Quartet.

In 1959, Atlantic and Atco were experiencing new heights of success, thanks mostly to Ray Charles and Bobby Darin. Then Charles left for ABC-Paramount, and later, Darin was wooed away by Capitol.

Atlantic survived. Jerry Leiber and Mike Stoller had joined the company as staff producers in 1956. After a series of hits with the Coasters on Atco, Leiber and Stoller turned their attention to the Drifters. They put strings on a song called "There Goes My Baby"; Wexler hated it, but the record went to number two. Just over a year later, the Drifters gave Atlantic a number one single with "Save The Last Dance For Me."

Atlantic prospered with a number of R&B artists like Wilson Pickett and Solomon Burke, and benefitted from its association with Stax Records in Memphis. In November, 1966, Wexler persuaded Ertegun to sign a woman who had been recording on Columbia for six years with little success. Wexler, Dowd and Arif Mardin brought Aretha Franklin to Rick Hall's Fame studios in Muscle Shoals, Alabama, for her first Atlantic session.

She recorded "I Never Loved A Man (The Way I Love You)" and it was a triumph. But when she tried to record a second track, "Do Right Woman—Do Right Man," it didn't work. An argument between Aretha's husband Ted White and Hall ensued, and Aretha left town without completing anything but the first song. Wexler brought some of the Muscle Shoals musicians to New York and finished the session. Aretha's second single, "Respect," brought her to the top of the *Billboard* Hot 100 in June of 1967.

In October of that year, Atlantic was sold to Warner Bros.-Seven Arts for $17.5 million. Wexler said it was half the amount the company was worth. When Ertegun tried to buy Atlantic back a year later for $40 million, he was turned down. But after another year, Ertegun forced a renegotiation by threatening a mass exit of Atlantic's top executives. He still wasn't thrilled with Elliot Hyman, head of Warner-Seven Arts, but then the company was sold to Kinney National Services, chaired by Steve Ross. "The only reason I'm here," Ertegun told Dorothy Wade and Justine Picardie in *Music Man*, "is because of Steve Ross, because I would have been long gone with the previous group. But Steve Ross has lived up to everything he ever said, and has given me total autonomy."

The company that had built its reputation with R&B artists built a pop base in the '60s. Buffalo Springfield were signed to Atco, and out of that group came Stephen Stills and Neil Young, who joined with David Crosby of the Byrds and Graham Nash of the Hollies to form Crosby, Stills, Nash and Young. At a party held in Wilson Pickett's honor in England, Ahmet first met Eric Clapton. Soon after, Clapton joined forces with Ginger Baker and Jack Bruce to form Cream; the trio was signed to Atco. Atlantic also had the British group Yes, and in 1968 Wexler took Dusty Springfield's suggestion and signed Led Zeppelin.

The label had a diverse artist roster in the '70s. When the Spinners left Motown, they were courted by Stax and Avco, but Aretha Franklin suggested they sign with Atlantic. Similarly, Atlantic jazz maestro Les McCann was so touched by seeing Roberta Flack perform at a benefit that he called Ertegun and staff producer Joel Dorn to arrange an audition for the high school teacher. She arrived with 600 songs under her arm, played 42 of them in three hours, and was awarded a contract. By the end of the '70s, Atlantic's hottest group was Chic. Their third chart single, "Le Freak," is Atlantic's most successful chart single.

After long negotiations with the Rolling Stones, Ertegun brought them to Atlantic on their own custom label, Rolling Stones Records. A deal with Stig Anderson's Polar Music of Sweden brought Abba to Atlantic for North America. The Anglo-American group Foreigner joined the company, as did pop diva Bette Midler.

In 1973, Atlantic president Jerry Greenberg closed the deal that brought Genesis to the label. With so many important British acts on the roster, Greenberg made several trips each year to the U.K. to look for new talent. "Genesis was the most intellectual band of its time and their songs weren't just rhymes or moon and June," Ertegun said in *Music Man*. After Peter Gabriel left the band, Ertegun worked closely with Genesis on the . . . *And Then There Were Three* album. He developed a mutual admiration society with Gabriel's replacement on lead vocals, Phil Collins.

Ertegun listened to a demo tape of some material Collins had recorded on his own. "I realized Phil could make a different sort of record than Genesis," Ahmet told Wade and Picardie. "I told him he should record those songs. There was something very magical about the original tape, so we used that. He produced it, and I helped a little bit at the end." Collins even took Ertegun's suggestion of adding extra drums to "In The Air Tonight" to give it a backbeat so it would be commercial enough for radio.

Seventeen of Atlantic's top 100 chart singles are by members of Genesis. Eleven of those belong to Collins, five to Genesis and one to Mike + the Mechanics, an extracurricular band formed by Mike Rutherford.

The diversity of Atlantic Records was well-demonstrated in 1987 at the marathon Madison Square Garden concert that celebrated the label's 40th anniversary. The all-day, all-night gala featured everyone from Ruth Brown and LaVern Baker to the Manhattan Transfer and the Rascals, from the label's youngest artist (Debbie Gibson) to Genesis, Foreigner and Led Zeppelin.

THE TOP 50 SONGS ON
ATCO

The Coasters

1 MACK THE KNIFE
Bobby Darin 59

2 SEARCHIN'/YOUNG BLOOD
The Coasters 57

3 OWNER OF A LONELY HEART
Yes 84

4 HOW CAN YOU MEND A BROKEN HEART
Bee Gees 71

5 STRANGER ON THE SHORE
Mr. Acker Bilk 62

6 DREAM LOVER
Bobby Darin 59

7 IF WISHES CAME TRUE
Sweet Sensation 90

8 CARS
Gary Numan 80

9 CHARLIE BROWN
The Coasters 59

10 TAKE A LETTER MARIA
R.B. Greaves 69

11 I GOT YOU BABE
Sonny and Cher 65

12 SIDESHOW
Blue Magic 74

13 YAKETY YAK
The Coasters 58

14 QUEEN OF THE HOP
Bobby Darin 58

15 APACHE
Jorgen Ingmann & His Guitar 61

The Atco label was created in 1955 as a subsidiary of Atlantic Records, as a company for Herb Abramson to run when he returned home after two years of military service.

Abramson, Ahmet Ertegun's original partner in the founding of Atlantic in 1947, was drafted in 1953. His place was taken by Jerry Wexler, a former *Billboard* staff reporter who loved jazz. Wexler loved the record business and he loved working with Ertegun. By the time Abramson was discharged, Wexler was occupying the desk next to Ahmet and there was no room—literally or figuratively—for Abramson. The tension was relieved when Ertegun created Atco for Herb to run. "Having gone away as the top executive—and being the president of the company even when I was away—when I came back I expected to carry on as usual," Abramson told Dorothy Wade and Justine Picardie in *Music Man.* "But I was surprised to see that there was not too much desire to work with me. They had a hot team going, and they wanted to keep it."

One of the first releases on Atco was "Smokey Joe's Cafe" by the Robins, originally issued on Spark, a label owned by writer-producers Jerry Leiber and Mike Stoller. When some of the Robins left the group, remaining members Carl Gardner and Bobby Nunn recruited Billy Guy and Leon Hughes to form the original line-up of the Coasters. Their second chart entry was a two-sided hit, "Searchin'" and "Young Blood." It ranks as the second most successful Atco single.

Atco's top-ranked chart single is "Mack The Knife" by Bobby Darin. Connie Francis' manager, George Scheck, helped Darin sign with Decca Records, but after four flop singles, he was dropped from the label. Darin had been writing songs with Don Kirshner, who told his friend Ahmet Ertegun about this hot new talent. Ertegun signed Darin to Atco.

"He started off really being a would-be R&B artist," Ertegun said in *Music Man*. "I thought he was a fantastic artist, and just needed to be recorded properly." Abramson disagreed, and wanted to drop Bobby from the label. Ertegun decided to produce Darin himself, and used Atlantic's new eight-track machine to record "Splish Splash." Doubting it would be a hit and assuming his contract would not be renewed, Darin went ahead and recorded "Early In The Morning" for Brunswick Records. When "Splish Splash" became a hit, Brunswick released their Darin recording under the name "the Rinky Dinks." Atco demanded that Brunswick recall their single; they complied and released the song by Buddy Holly instead.

At that point, the Erteguns bought out Abramson for $300,000, and he left the company. "Herb insisted on being bought out. He didn't have to go," Ahmet commented in *Music Man*.

Foreshadowing the company's future success with British artists, Atco had a number one hit in 1962 with Acker Bilk's "Stranger On The Shore." It was the first number one single by a British artist in America. The brother-and-sister act of Nino Tempo and April Stevens gave Atco another chart-topper in 1963 with "Deep Purple." Two years later, Sonny and Cher put the label back on top of the Hot 100 with "I Got You Babe."

Ertegun was impressed with the virtuoso guitar playing of Eric Clapton at a party for Wilson Pickett in England. When Clapton formed Cream with Jack Bruce and Ginger Baker, Ertegun suggested that Robert Stigwood manage them. Through Stigwood, Atco also signed the Bee Gees for North America.

During the latter half of the '70s, the Atco logo was practically dormant. Gary Numan brought the label back to the top 10 in 1980 with "Cars," and a re-formed Yes had a number one song on Atco with "Owner Of A Lonely Heart" in 1984. But the momentum wasn't sustained, and the label had a low profile until Derek Shulman was named president in 1988. The former lead singer of Gentle Giant had been senior vice president of A&R at Polygram before his Atco appointment. Shulman told Steve Gett in *Billboard* why he accepted the job: "Ahmet Ertegun, who built Atlantic and Atco Records, is probably one of my all-time heroes in this business. He is a music man, first and foremost."

Shulman returned the Atco label to the top in 1990 with a number one hit for Sweet Sensation, "If Wishes Came True."

CAPITOL

1 LISBON ANTIGUA
Nelson Riddle 56

2 SIXTEEN TONS
Tennessee Ernie Ford 55

3 MEMORIES ARE MADE OF THIS
Dean Martin 56

4 THE POOR PEOPLE OF PARIS
Les Baxter 56

5 A BLOSSOM FELL
Nat King Cole 55

6 LEARNIN' THE BLUES
Frank Sinatra 55

7 TRUE LOVE
Bing Crosby and Grace Kelly 56

8 ABRACADABRA
Steve Miller Band 82

9 MY SHARONA
The Knack 79

10 I WANT TO HOLD YOUR HAND
The Beatles 64

11 BOOGIE OOGIE OOGIE
A Taste of Honey 78

12 RHINESTONE COWBOY
Glen Campbell 76

13 WHAT'S LOVE GOT TO DO WITH IT
Tina Turner 84

14 SHAME ON THE MOON
Bob Seger & the Silver Bullet Band 83

15 TOM DOOLEY
The Kingston Trio 58

16 SEND FOR ME/MY PERSONAL POSSESSION
Nat King Cole 57

17 QUEEN OF HEARTS
Juice Newton 81

18 SILLY LOVE SONGS
Wings 76

19 YOU NEEDED ME
Anne Murray 78

20 LOVE ON THE ROCKS
Neil Diamond 80

21 BE-BOP-A-LULA
Gene Vincent 56

22 GONE
Ferlin Husky 57

23 RETURN TO ME
Dean Martin 58

24 LOVE AND MARRIAGE
Frank Sinatra 56

25 ALONE
Heart 87

26 ODE TO BILLIE JOE
Bobbie Gentry 67

27 THE JOKER
Steve Miller Band 74

28 THE SWEETEST THING (I'VE EVER KNOWN)
Juice Newton 82

29 I GET AROUND
The Beach Boys 64

30 YOUNG LOVE
Sonny James 57

Nat King Cole

Capitol Records, the first major label to be located in Los Angeles, was founded in 1942 by composer Johnny Mercer, record store owner Glenn Wallichs and movie producer B. G. "Buddy" DeSylva.

Capitol's initial batch of releases included the label's first hit, "Cow Cow Boogie" by Freddie Slack, with vocals by Ella Mae Morse. The label was innovative; Capitol was the first company to give free records to disc jockeys, record their masters on tape and, later, issue recordings in all three playing speeds.

Capitol expanded its roster in 1943, releasing material from Stan Kenton, Peggy Lee, Jo Stafford, Margaret Whiting and an artist would who account for one-quarter of the label's sales by 1950—Nat King Cole. A country and western division was set up in 1948. The roster included many best-selling C&W artists, such as Tex Ritter, Tennessee Ernie Ford, Faron Young, Hank Thompson, Merle Travis and Jean Sheppard, many of whom worked with staff producer Ken Nelson. In 1953, Capitol signed another important artist. After 10 years of recording on Columbia, Frank Sinatra moved over to the label and had a top 10 hit with his first Capitol single, "I'm Walking Behind You." Dean Martin, Les Paul and Mary Ford and Stan Freberg also had major hits on Capitol during the first half of the '50s.

Flush with success, the owners sold Capitol to EMI of Great Britain in 1955. On April 6, 1956, the famed Capitol Tower building had its grand opening in Hollywood. Billed as the world's first round office building, the Tower included recording studios, with echo chambers buried beneath the structure's parking lot.

Capitol took a tentative step into rock and roll in 1956 when Ken Nelson signed a 21-year-old rocker from Norfolk, Virginia. Gene Vincent wrote his early songs while recovering in a hospital from a motorcycle accident. One song was inspired by the comic strip Little Lulu—Vincent called it "Be-Bop-A-Lula." He acquired a manager, Bill "Sheriff Tex" Davis, who met Nelson at a DJ convention and told him about his new star. Capitol wanted their own white rock singer to compete with RCA's Elvis Presley, and signed Vincent to the label. His first recording session took place in Nashville on May 4, 1956. Nelson chose "Woman Love" as the first single, but DJs preferred "Be-Bop-A-Lula" on the "B" side.

Despite Vincent's immediate success, Capitol wasn't ready to make a full commitment to rock and roll. Most of the label's hits in the early years of the rock era belonged to artists like Sinatra, Cole, Martin and Ford as well as instrumentalists Les Baxter and Nelson Riddle, whose "Lisbon Antigua" ranks as Capitol's most successful chart single of the rock era.

The Kingston Trio signed with the label in January, 1958, after Bob Hope's agent saw them perform at the hungry i in San Francisco and told Voyle Gilmore of Capitol's A&R staff about them. Capitol also signed the Four Freshmen, the Four Preps and the Lettermen.

In the spring of 1962, Murry Wilson brought a demo tape of his sons' band, the Beach Boys, to Nick Venet at Capitol. The group had already released their debut single, "Surfin'," on Herb Newman's Candix label. Newman wasn't enthusiastic about the Beach Boys' other songs, including an early version of "Surfer Girl," and declined to release a follow-up. Venet played the tape for his boss, Gilmore, and within the hour Capitol agreed to sign the group.

Three months after the Beach Boys' first Capitol single entered the Hot 100, the first EMI single by the Beatles, released on the Parlophone label, started moving up the U.K. chart. But Capitol wasn't interested in releasing "Love Me Do," or any of the three singles that followed. "We don't think the Beatles will do anything in this market" is what one label executive told manager Brian Epstein. So the Beatles appeared on Vee Jay and Swan in the U.S., but they didn't chart. On October 19, 1963, the Beatles recorded "I Want To Hold Your Hand." Epstein took a demo copy with him when he flew to New York on November 5 so he could play it for Brown Meggs, director of eastern operations for Capitol. Meggs felt this record was right for America, and scheduled a release date of January 13, 1964. But when Carroll Baker, a DJ at WWDC in Washington, D.C., started playing an import copy, the demand caused Capitol to advance the release date to December 26 and increase the press run from 200,000 copies to one million. All of the earlier Beatles singles were re-released and charted. The official follow-up to "I Want To Hold Your Hand" was "Can't Buy Me Love," which had an advance order of 2,100,000 copies.

Capitol's most consistent artists of the '70s included Grand Funk, Steve Miller, Helen Reddy, Dr. Hook, Anne Murray, Bob Seger and Paul McCartney's second band, Wings. The label's biggest *Billboard* hit of the '70s is "My Sharona" by the Knack, a Los Angeles quartet who suffered for their comparisons to the Beatles.

Like the Knack, Grand Funk Railroad was never popular with the rock press, but they managed to sell millions of records anyway. The band's origins can be traced to the Flint, Michigan, band called Terry Knight & the Pack. After a series of singles on Cameo-Parkway's Lucky Eleven label, the Pack signed with Capitol in April, 1968. They returned to Lucky Eleven as the Fabulous Pack before breaking up. Mark Farner and Don Brewer then formed a new band, taking their name from Michigan's Grand Trunk Railroad. Knight became their manager and got them a deal with Capitol. Grand Funk's most successful chart single is their remake of Little Eva's "The Locomotion," produced by Todd Rundgren.

Capitol's biggest *Billboard* hit of the '80s is "Abracadabra," a track from Steve Miller's 12th album for the label. Miller formed his first band, the Marksmen Combo, back in 1955, when he was only 12. That ensemble featured future Steve Miller Band member Boz Scaggs. As the Ardells, they played Motown songs and other R&B covers, and while attending the University of Wisconsin, Miller and Scaggs fronted a group called the Fabulous Night Trains. After college, Miller teamed with Barry Goldberg in the Goldberg-Miller Blues Band, based in Chicago. Within four days of moving to San Francisco in 1966, Miller started a new outfit called the Steve Miller Blues Band. Their performance at the Monterey Pop Festival led to a contract with Capitol promising a $50,000 advance (astronomical at the time) and complete artistic freedom. Their first two albums were produced in Britain by Glyn Johns. Miller's eighth album yielded his first number one single, "The Joker"; the 1976 album *Fly Like an Eagle* contained his next number one hit, "Rock'n Me." Six years later, Miller had his third number one song, "Abracadabra."

Another important signing in the '80s was Tina Turner. After recording a searing version of the Temptations' "Ball Of Confusion" with Martyn Ware and Ian Craig Marsh of the British Electric Foundation (a spin-off of Heaven 17), Tina was signed to a worldwide deal by EMI. Her single "What's Love Got To Do With It" became the biggest hit of her career.

Capitol entered the '90s with hits from Heart, the Seattle-based band featuring sisters Ann and Nancy Wilson; and rapper M.C. Hammer, who topped the album chart for 21 weeks with *Please Hammer Don't Hurt 'Em.*

THE TOP 50 SONGS ON
EMI

The J. Geils Band

In America, the EMI label is a relatively recent newcomer to the charts. But in the United Kingdom, the name dates back to the 1931 merger of Columbia and the Gramophone Company, resulting in Electrical and Musical Industries, one of the world's major record companies. EMI's purchase of Capitol Records in 1955 gave it a strong presence in America, and at home, it operated three important labels: HMV, Parlophone and Columbia. In 1973, Gerry Oord from Holland set up an EMI label in Britain. One of the company's strongest artists, Cliff Richard, was shifted to the new division from Columbia, and in 1974 Queen had their debut single issued on EMI.

That same year, the EMI logo also appeared in America for the first time. The Swedish band Blue Swede gave the label a number one hit with a remake of "Hooked On A Feeling." In 1975, the Scottish quartet Pilot had an American hit with "Magic," produced by Alan Parsons. But the EMI label was shuttered soon after, not to appear in the U.S. again until 1978, when the EMI America label was created.

This time EMI had staying power. Set up as a separate division from EMI's other American label, Capitol, EMI America issued singles from both British and American artists. From the U.K. came Cliff Richard, Sheena Easton and Naked Eyes. From the

U.S. came Kim Carnes, the J. Geils Band, Robert John, the Stray Cats, Gary U.S. Bonds and Rocky Burnette.

In 1979, Robert John, who had recorded for Columbia, A&M, Atlantic and Ariola, gave the new label its first number one single on the Hot 100, "Sad Eyes." The following year, EMI had top 10 hits from Richard, Burnette and Carnes.

Cliff Richard had been a consistent hitmaker in the U.K. since 1958, when his debut single, "Move It," went to number two. Labels like ABC-Paramount, Epic and Uni had failed to break him in the States. It took Elton John and his Rocket label to finally land Cliff a top 10 hit in America with "Devil Woman" in 1976. But then he slipped back into obscurity until "We Don't Talk Anymore" went to number seven in January, 1980.

Rocky Burnette—the son of Johnny and nephew of Dorsey—made the British chart first with "Tired Of Toein' The Line." It was a minor hit in the U.K., but in America it went to number eight in July, 1980.

Kim Carnes was the first artist signed to EMI America by label president Jim Mazza. She went to number 10 with a remake of Smokey Robinson's "More Love" in August, 1980, but the song she will be remembered for is a remake of Jackie DeShannon and Donna Weiss' "Bette Davis Eyes," EMI's most successful chart single in America. Carnes credits Bill Cuomo, who played synthesizer on the track, for coming up with the arrangement that took the single to number one for nine weeks.

The label's British roots were helpful during the '80s, as David Bowie was signed to EMI worldwide after a long stint with RCA. In March of 1985, EMI in Britain signed the Pet Shop Boys. An earlier version of their "West End Girls" had been released on Epic; a newly-recorded version went to number one in Britain and America.

A new EMI label was set up under Bruce Lundvall. The name Manhattan had previously been used for a United Artists-distributed label run by Charles Koppelman. EMI's Manhattan label signed Glass Tiger, Robbie Nevil and, most importantly, Richard Marx (who has seven titles on EMI's top 50).

The EMI America and Manhattan labels were eventually merged, creating EMI Manhattan. But some artists, particularly the Pet Shop Boys, objected to having their records released on a label different from the one that had signed them. "Manhattan" was dropped, once again giving America an "EMI" label. One of the more unique releases on EMI Manhattan was "Don't Worry Be Happy," featuring the multi-tracked vocals of Bobby McFerrin, a San Francisco-based jazz singer. The song went to number one in 1988.

The company had a new success story in 1989 with the Swedish duo Roxette, who quickly racked up three number one songs: "The Look," "Listen To Your Heart" and, from the *Pretty Woman* soundtrack, "It Must Have Been Love."

THE TOP 50 SONGS ON
APPLE

The Beatles

The Beatles opened their own boutique on December 7, 1967, at 94 Baker Street in London. Paul McCartney described it as "a beautiful place where you could buy beautiful things." Inspired by a Magritte painting, Paul came up with the name of the new shop: Apple.

The exterior walls were painted in bright, psychedelic colors, shocking the neighbors. The goods flew out the door—sometimes in the hands of paying customers, but often fleeced by shoplifters. Business continued until July 30, 1968, when the Beatles decided to close up shop and give away all the remaining merchandise. By day's end, everything was gone.

Apple had other divisions, however. There was Apple Films, the production company that produced *Magical Mystery Tour*. There was the Apple Foundation for the Arts, designed to give grants to deserving artists. There was Apple Corps, which oversaw all of the Beatles' business interests. And there was Apple Records, headed by Ron Kass with Peter Asher in charge of A&R and Derek Taylor supervising publicity.

The record label and all of the other Apple businesses were housed in an elegant five-story Georgian building at 3 Savile Row. On August 11, 1968, the first four Apple singles were released. The new label sported a green Granny Smith on the "A" side and a halved apple on the "B" side. The Beatles' "Hey Jude," "Those Were The Days" by Mary Hopkin, "Sour Milk Sea" by Jackie Lomax and "Thingummybob" by the Black Dyke Mills brass band were hand-delivered in gift presentation boxes to Queen Elizabeth, Princess Margaret, the Queen Mother and Prime Minister Harold Wilson.

No word on what the Queen thought of "Thingummybob," but "Hey Jude" debuted at number 10 in America and held on to the number one spot for nine weeks, becoming Apple's most successful chart single. During "Hey Jude"'s sixth week at the top, "Those Were The Days" began a three-week stint at number two, giving the brand-new label the top two positions on the *Billboard* chart. In the U.K., "Those Were The Days" succeeded "Hey Jude" at number one.

Mary Hopkin had caught the attention of Twiggy after winning a talent contest on the TV series "Opportunity Knocks." The famed British model called Paul McCartney to tell him about the blonde singer from Wales. McCartney selected "Those Were The Days" for her to record.

The only other non-Beatle act to have more than one hit on Apple was a Welsh band, the Iveys. Their first single, "Maybe Tomorrow," flopped, and the group changed their name to Badfinger. Their next single was McCartney's "Come And Get It," from the film *The Magic Christian* starring Ringo Starr. It peaked at number seven, and was followed by two more top 10 singles.

Asher signed James Taylor to Apple, but the Boston-born singer didn't have a hit until he moved over to Warner Brothers. Billy Preston was also on the Apple roster, but aside from guest-starring on the Beatles' "Get Back," he didn't have chart success until he signed with A&M.

Apple had a short-lived subsidiary, Zapple, but it was shut down when Allen Klein took charge of the Beatles' business ventures. With Klein as the new head of Apple Corps, Kass and Asher were out, as were many other Apple executives and employees.

Apple Records continued to exist after the breakup of the Beatles, as all four members recorded their solo efforts for the label. But in 1975 their individual solo contracts with EMI came to an end, and so did Apple. "Junior's Farm" was McCartney's last single on the label. He remained with EMI, appearing on Capitol in the U.S. until he signed with Columbia in 1979; he returned to Capitol in 1985. "You" was George Harrison's last Apple single. His next release was on his own label, Dark Horse, distributed first through A&M, then through Warner Brothers. Ringo's swan song on Apple was "It's All Down To Goodnight Vienna." He subsequently recorded for Atlantic, Portrait, Boardwalk and Rykodisc. After his last Apple chart single, "Stand By Me," Lennon began a five-year hiatus from recording. He returned in 1980 with the *Double Fantasy* album on Geffen. After his death, unreleased material appeared on Polydor and Capitol.

Kenny Rogers

1 LADY
Kenny Rogers 80

2 WITCH DOCTOR
David Seville 58

3 TONIGHT YOU BELONG TO ME
Patience & Prudence 56

4 RUN TO HIM
Bobby Vee 61

5 WE'VE GOT TONIGHT
Kenny Rogers and Sheena Easton 83

6 SURF CITY
Jan and Dean 63

7 I DON'T NEED YOU
Kenny Rogers 81

8 A HUNDRED POUNDS OF CLAY
Gene McDaniels 61

9 TAKE GOOD CARE OF MY BABY
Bobby Vee 61

10 FOR YOUR EYES ONLY
Sheena Easton 81

11 THIS DIAMOND RING
Gary Lewis & the Playboys 65

12 DEVIL OR ANGEL
Bobby Vee 60

13 THE CHIPMUNK SONG
The Chipmunks w/David Seville 58

14 THE NIGHT HAS A THOUSAND EYES
Bobby Vee 63

15 COME BACK WHEN YOU GROW UP
Bobby Vee 67

Simon (Sy) Waronker and Jack Ames founded Liberty as a West Coast label in 1955. At first, the focus was on easy listening, jazz and pop. One of the label's earliest hits was "Cry Me A River" by Julie London, in December of 1955.

It didn't take long for Liberty to find its first rock and roll artist. Manager Jerry Capehart brought demos of his client Eddie Cochran to Waronker and Alvin (Al) Bennett, head of A&R and later an owner of the company. After meeting Cochran, they signed him to the label. Another Liberty artist, Lionel Newman, needed some performers for a film he was working on as musical director. He asked Waronker for suggestions, and the label head recommended Cochran. Eddie sang "Twenty Flight Rock" in *The Girl Can't Help It*, and Waronker planned to release it as his first single. At the same time, Waronker wanted to lease a song called "Sittin' In The Balcony," recorded by songwriter John D. Loudermilk as Johnny Dee on the Colonial label. When he couldn't buy the master, Waronker had Cochran cut a cover version and released it in March, 1957, as Eddie's debut single; it peaked at number 18. Just over a year later, Cochran had his biggest hit with "Summertime Blues," which went to number eight. Cochran never had another top 30 hit, and on April 17, 1960, he was killed in an automobile accident near Chippenham, England.

Liberty also had hits in the '50s with Patience and Prudence, two young sisters from Los Angeles; Billy Ward & His Dominoes, an R&B group that had recorded for Federal, King, Jubilee and Decca before moving to Liberty in 1957; Martin Denny, a composer/arranger who moved to Hawaii in the '50s; and Ross Bagdasarian, better known as David Seville.

Bagdasarian declined to join his family's grape-growing business in Fresno, California, and moved to New York to be an actor and work with his cousin, author William Saroyan. They collaborated on the song "Come On-A My House," later recorded by Rosemary Clooney. In 1956, Bagdasarian signed with Liberty and was persuaded to use a different name professionally. He had been stationed near Seville, Spain, while serving in the Air Force, so he created the alter-ego of David Seville. Ross had a number one single in 1958 that was inspired by a book in his library, *Duel With the Witch Doctor*. The novelty song "Witch Doctor" was followed eight months later by "The Chipmunk Song."

Snuff Garrett was asked by Al Bennett to join Liberty's promotion department; he agreed to do so if he could also produce records. His first two artists were Johnny Burnette and Bobby Vee, and both artists helped to establish Liberty's credentials in the early '60s. Garrett was named head of A&R for the label, and continued to produce hits for artists like Gene McDaniels and actor Walter Brennan. Garrett also brought Gary Lewis & the Playboys to Liberty in 1965. The label's other major act of the mid-'60s was Jan and Dean, signed to Liberty in 1961 after having hits on Dore and Challenge.

Through its history, Liberty expanded by buying other labels. In 1957, it absorbed the Pacific Jazz label, changing the name to World Pacific. Six years later, the Imperial label was purchased, and three years after that, Blue Note came into the fold. Liberty also bought the Seattle-based Dolton label, which it had been distributing. In 1967, Liberty was purchased by the conglomerate TransAmerica, which also owned the United Artists label. Eventually the Liberty logo was dropped, and all of the artists were moved over to United Artists.

In 1979, the British company EMI bought United Artists. EMI had launched the EMI America label in the U.S. in January, 1978, and in 1980, EMI reactivated the Liberty label. UA artists like Kenny Rogers and Dottie West were shifted to Liberty. Rogers' first single on Liberty was Lionel Richie's composition of "Lady," the label's most successful chart single. Liberty also released the soundtrack to *For Your Eyes Only*, as all previous James Bond soundtracks had been issued on United Artists. Sheena Easton, who recorded for EMI America, had her title song from the film released on Liberty as well.

The famed Statue of Liberty logo had a short second life, and the artists who remained with the label were transferred over to EMI America.

Fats Domino

F ive different labels have been named Imperial in the 20th century; the first one dates back to 1905. The Crystalate Gramophone Manufacturing Company Ltd. had an Imperial label in the U.K. from 1920-34. Domestic EMI labels in Brazil and Holland were also called Imperial, but the Imperial that had the greatest impact on rock and roll was the one created by Lew Chudd in Los Angeles back in 1947.

Chudd, a businessman who enjoyed electronics as a hobby, signed some jump blues bands to the label in its early days, but his real breakthrough came one evening in 1949 when he walked into the Bronze Peacock Club in Houston. He was heading home after traveling in Mexico to promote some Spanish records. Interested in signing some R&B artists, he stopped in at the club to check out Dave Bartholomew's band. They met later in New Orleans, where Chudd hired Bartholomew to produce records for Imperial.

Searching for talent, the two men found a 20-year-old boogie-woogie blues singer at the Hideaway Club in New Orleans. Antoine "Fats" Domino had been playing in local clubs since the age of 10. "Fats Domino was doing one of the things that the original, old guys used to sing," Bartholomew told Steve Kolanjian. "We used to call them jailhouse-type blues. At that time there wasn't anyone doing that type of thing. I was amazed at it. Being my first venture, I wanted it to be good. We changed the whole thing around and we called it 'The Fat Man.' That's the very first record we made." The single entered the *Billboard* R&B chart in February, 1950, and peaked at number six on the Best Sellers chart. Domino's next 10 singles all made the R&B top 10.

Domino crossed over to the top 20 of the pop chart in 1955 with "Ain't It A Shame," covered by Pat Boone as "Ain't That A Shame." A year later, he went to number four with "I'm In Love Again." Later in 1956, he recorded what would become his biggest hit, as well as Imperial's most successful chart single—"Blueberry Hill." Originally recorded by Glenn Miller, and sung in a film by Gene Autry, the song was recorded by Fats at Bunny Robine's studio during a trip to Los Angeles. Fats came up with the idea of recording the song but couldn't remember the bridge. His brother-in-law recalled the words. "Fats could hardly get through it," Bartholomew told Kolanjian. "So Bunny took a scissors to the tape and put it together. It's a common practice now but *that* was a long time ago."

Ricky Nelson sang a Domino tune, "I'm Walkin'," on the April 10, 1957 installment of "The Adventures of Ozzie and Harriet." Along with his older brother David, Ricky starred with his parents on their radio show and the weekly TV series.

His recording career began when 16-year-old Ricky was on a date with his girlfriend Arline. He was driving her home when an Elvis Presley song came on the radio. Arline said how much she loved Elvis, and a jealous Ricky boasted that he was going to have his own record released in a few weeks. Arline laughed, and although Ricky didn't have a recording contract with anyone, he became even more determined to make a record. Ricky asked his dad if he could use the TV series orchestra and picked the Fats Domino song because he knew the two chords. Ozzie helped him sign with Verve Records; after "I'm Walking" hit the charts, the flip side, "A Teenager's Romance," proved to be an even bigger hit, peaking at number two.

Ozzie suspected Verve wasn't paying Ricky all of the royalties he earned and shopped around for a new label. Chudd was anxious to sign young Nelson—at least he wouldn't be able to cover any more of Domino's material—and sent Ricky into the studio on August 18, 1957. That day, Ricky cut his first recordings for Imperial: "Be-Bop Baby" and "Have I Told You Lately That I Love You."

In 1963, Chudd sold his company to Liberty Records, and Ricky moved on to Decca Records. Imperial remained a strong pop label with Jackie DeShannon, Cher, Mel Carter, Johnny Rivers, the Classics IV and a handful of British groups, including Billy J. Kramer & the Dakotas and the Hollies. After TransAmerica purchased Liberty and merged it with United Artists, the Imperial logo was laid to rest. The last singles to appear on the label were released in 1970.

War

Like other major film studios, United Artists wanted to have its own record label primarily to release the company's motion picture soundtracks. Max Youngstein, a vice president of United Artists, started the record label in late 1957 with David Picker. UA did have soundtrack success with films like *The Apartment, The Great Escape, Irma La Douce, Mondo Cane, Tom Jones, A Man and a Woman* and the James Bond movies, beginning with *Dr. No* in 1963. But the label also built a roster of easy listening, rock and R&B artists and had its first number one single in 1961 with "Michael" by the Highwaymen.

UA's biggest hits from the early '60s were from Arthur Ferrante and Louis Teicher, pianists who first met when they were students at the Juilliard School of Music in Manhattan. After graduating, they did some concert work, then returned to the school to teach. In 1947, they gave up their faculty positions to perform full-time as a duo, appearing as regulars on ABC's "Piano Playhouse" and recording for Columbia, ABC-Paramount and MGM. In 1960, Ferrante and Teicher signed to United Artists and specialized in recording themes from films. Their two biggest hits are their twin-piano renditions of "Exodus" and "Theme From 'The Apartment.'" They also had a hit single with the theme from *Midnight Cowboy*.

In 1963, UA had pop and R&B success with the Exciters ("Tell Him") and Garnett Mimms & the Enchanters ("Cry Baby"). The Exciters were produced by Jerry Leiber and Mike Stoller, as were United Artists' most successful group of the '60s, Jay & the Americans. Leiber and Stoller signed the group to the label and were responsible for producing hits like "She Cried" and "Only In America." The latter was one of many songs by the group that made them sound like a white version of the Drifters—in fact, "Only In America" had been written for the Drifters, although they never recorded it. And one of Jay & the Americans' biggest hits was a remake of the Drifters' "This Magic Moment."

Bobby Goldsboro signed with UA after one minor hit on Laurie called "Molly." His biggest hit for the label was a song written by Bobby Russell, "Honey." Released in 1968, it is UA's second most successful Hot 100 single. That same year, TransAmerica purchased United Artists—including the film company, the publishing company and the record company. TransAmerica then bought the Liberty label and merged the two companies into Liberty-UA. Mike Stewart, who had been running UA on the East Coast, headed up the new label with Al Bennett, who had been in charge of Liberty on the West Coast. Eventually, Liberty was phased out, and its artists were moved over to the UA label.

In 1971, UA purchased the small Mediarts label, whose primary artist was a relatively unknown singer named Don McLean. His first album, *Tapestry*, was released on Mediarts in 1970, but only after 34 other labels had turned it down. McLean's second album included the title song "American Pie," which became the most successful chart single on United Artists.

During the '70s, UA flourished in different areas. Larry Butler ran the Nashville office and built up the country division with artists like Kenny Rogers and Crystal Gayle. The label also had an active office in the U.K., which provided the American company British artists like Maxine Nightingale and Gerry Rafferty. From Jet Records in the U.K. came the Electric Light Orchestra, and from Magnet Records came Chris Rea with "Fool (If You Think It's Over)."

Another major signing for UA in the '70s was Paul Anka, who hadn't had a top 10 single since 1961. His first UA single was "(You're) Having My Baby," which spent three weeks at number one and was the label's fourth chart-topping single. Anka followed that with two more top 10 singles, both duets with Odia Coates. Anka left UA in 1978 and went to one of his former labels, RCA.

In May, 1978, UA President Artie Mogull and his partner Jerry Rubinstein bought the company from TransAmerica for $30 million in a deal financed by EMI. Ten months later, Mogull and Rubinstein sold the company to EMI, and Jim Mazza was brought in to run UA. A year after that, the United Artists label disappeared after having chart hits with Kenny Rogers and the Dirt Band, who were shifted to the reactivated Liberty label.

Billy Joel

olumbia Records has been in business for more than a century, and the company's history parallels the history of the record business itself. The origins of the label can be traced back to 1881, when British inventors Chichester A. Bell and Charles Sumner Tainter received financial assistance from Bell's cousin, Alexander Graham Bell, to set up a laboratory in Washington, D.C. They were looking to improve upon Thomas A. Edison's 1878 patent for the phonograph machine.

Edison had recorded on tinfoil, but Bell and Tainter came up with the idea of recording on cardboard-coated wax. They received a patent on May 4, 1886 for such a disc, but chose to produce sounds on a cylinder. In early 1889, they demonstrated their Graphophone, a predecessor of the dictaphone recording device. Jesse Lippincott, a millionaire businessman from Pittsburgh, bought the rights to the machine as well as to Edison's patent and formed the North American Phonograph Company. Lippincott set up 33 franchises around the country, but only one survived: the Columbia Phonograph Company of Maryland, Delaware and the District of Columbia.

Doing business from Bridgeport, Connecticut, the company had a catalog of 200 cylinders of recorded music for sale by 1891. At the turn of the century, they were also manufacturing discs, which went on sale in 1901. A year later, Columbia and its chief rival, the Victor Talking Machine Company, agreed to standardize their product and release 7-inch and 10-inch single-sided discs. Double-sided discs were introduced in 1904.

Columbia flourished by releasing discs of military bands, love ballads, patriotic songs, comedy recordings and classical recordings leased from Europe. In 1912, cylinders fell by the wayside, and all music was released in disc form.

At the end of World War I, with the country facing a recession, Columbia was not in good financial shape. The British arm of Columbia was sold to its manager, Louis Sterling, in December, 1922. Two years later, Sterling paid $2.5 million for the American company, and in 1925, Columbia released the first electrically-recorded disc.

There were more financial woes during the depression of the '30s. Columbia merged with another British company, HMV, to form Electrical and Musical Industries, Ltd. Because of antitrust laws in the United States, EMI had to sell the American company. Columbia's new owners were Grigsby-Grunow, a refrigerator manufacturer. When that company went bankrupt in 1933, Columbia was purchased by the American Record Corporation, whose parent company was a button manufacturer. ARC had also purchased the Brunswick label, and in 1938 William S. Paley, the president of CBS, bought the controlling interest in ARC. CBS sold the Brunswick label to the American Decca company and would continue to run Columbia Records until January 5, 1988— the day the label was sold to the Sony Corporation of Japan.

The company prospered in the '40s, thanks in large part to a perceptive talent scout named John Hammond. He signed a number of big bands to the label as well as big band singers. In 1940, Columbia Records had the first-ever number one song in *Billboard*, "I'll Never Smile Again" by the Tommy Dorsey Orchestra, featuring the vocals of Frank Sinatra.

The man in charge of Columbia Records, Edward Wallerstein, had been at RCA Victor when that company tried to develop the long-playing record in 1931. Under Wallerstein's direction, CBS engineers, working with Dr. Peter Goldmark, came up with a 33⅓ RPM disc in 1948. The LP was born.

The new configuration helped usher in an age of Broadway musicals, overseen for CBS by Goddard Lieberson, who headed up the label in the 1950s.

One area Columbia did not rush into was rock and roll. While RCA Victor had the industry's hottest star in Elvis Presley, CBS avoided the trend (although they did bid for Presley). With Mitch Miller in charge of A&R, the company's stars of the '50s included Johnny Mathis, Doris Day, the Four Lads, Johnnie Ray and the man who recorded Columbia's most successful single of the rock era, Guy Mitchell.

Hammond moved the label in a new direction by signing Bob Dylan in 1962. Barbra Streisand also joined the company that year, and other rock or folk-rock acts were added to the roster, like Simon and Garfunkel, the Byrds and Paul Revere & the Raiders.

Clive Davis became head of the label in 1966. He attended the Monterey Pop Festival in 1967 and started to diversify the roster, signing acts like Big Brother & the Holding Company, Blood, Sweat & Tears, and Santana.

Davis resigned in 1975 and became the top executive at Arista. Lieberson returned briefly, but then the stewardship of the label was handed over to Walter Yetnikoff, who would remain at the top through the takeover by Sony.

Columbia's top 100 chart singles include recordings that span the rock era, from Mitch Miller to Mariah Carey. The label's top four singles are from 1955 and 1956; 16 of the top 100 are from the years 1955–59. There are only 13 titles from the '60s, including CBS's top 45 of the decade, Percy Faith's "Theme From 'A Summer Place.'" Also representing the '60s are Jimmy Dean, Marty Robbins, Johnny Horton, the Brothers Four, Steve Lawrence, Gary Puckett & the Union Gap, Simon and Garfunkel, the Byrds and O. C. Smith.

There are 22 songs from the '70s included on Columbia's top 100. The label's most successful single of the decade is "Best Of My Love" by the Emotions. Streisand has four singles from the '70s on the list: themes from the movies *A Star is Born* and *The Way We Were* and duets with Neil Diamond ("You Don't Bring Me Flowers") and Donna Summer ("Enough Is Enough"). The '80s are well represented, with 45 songs. Columbia signed Paul McCartney briefly for North America; he gave the label its top song of the decade with "Say, Say, Say," a duet with Michael Jackson. McCartney is also in the CBS top 100 with "Ebony and Ivory" and "Coming Up (Live At Glasgow)."

Columbia is off to a good start in the '90s, with four titles from 1990 in the top 100. Two are by Mariah Carey: "Love Takes Time" (number 17) and "Vision Of Love" (number 32). Michael Bolton and the New Kids on the Block are responsible for the other two 1990 singles.

The artist with the most singles on the top 100 is Billy Joel, with seven. Joel first recorded for CBS in 1970 as half of the rock duo Attila. An album was released on CBS's Epic subsidiary with little notoriety. Joel's first solo album, *Cold Spring Harbor*, was released through Paramount Records in November of that year. Under the name "Bill Martin," Joel played piano in a cocktail lounge in Los Angeles. In 1973, Clive Davis went to see him play and signed him to Columbia Records.

The *Piano Man* album only produced one top 30 single, the title track. Joel's first top 10 hit came in 1978 with "Just The Way You Are," number 41 on Columbia's top 100. His most successful chart single is "It's Still Rock And Roll To Me" from 1980 (number 24). Other Billy Joel songs included in Columbia's top 100 are "Uptown Girl" (number 46), "Tell Her About It" (number 55), "We Didn't Start The Fire" (number 56) and "My Life" (number 66).

1 BILLIE JEAN
Michael Jackson 83

2 ROCK WITH YOU
Michael Jackson 80

3 BEAT IT
Michael Jackson 83

4 PLAY THAT FUNKY MUSIC
Wild Cherry 76

5 KARMA CHAMELEON
Culture Club 84

6 EVERYDAY PEOPLE
Sly & the Family Stone 69

7 KEEP ON LOVING YOU
REO Speedwagon 81

8 TO SIR WITH LOVE
Lulu 67

9 BOOGIE NIGHTS
Heatwave 77

10 THE MOST BEAUTIFUL GIRL
Charlie Rich 73

11 FAMILY AFFAIR
Sly & the Family Stone 71

12 ROSES ARE RED (MY LOVE)
Bobby Vinton 62

13 I CAN SEE CLEARLY NOW
Johnny Nash 72

14 DO YOU REALLY WANT TO HURT ME
Culture Club 83

15 BRANDY (YOU'RE A FINE GIRL)
Looking Glass 72

16 BLUE VELVET
Bobby Vinton 63

17 CAN'T FIGHT THIS FEELING
REO Speedwagon 85

18 THERE! I'VE SAID IT AGAIN
Bobby Vinton 64

19 MORE THAN A FEELING
Boston 76

20 TAKE IT ON THE RUN
REO Speedwagon 81

21 FRANKENSTEIN
Edgar Winter Group 73

22 BABY, I LOVE YOUR WAY/FREEBIRD MEDLEY (FREE BABY)
Will to Power 88

23 COME AND GET YOUR LOVE
Redbone 75

24 MR. LONELY
Bobby Vinton 64

25 TIME (CLOCK OF THE HEART)
Culture Club 83

26 THE FLAME
Cheap Trick 88

27 THE GIRL IS MINE
Michael Jackson and Paul McCartney 83

28 DER KOMMISSAR
After the Fire 83

29 LADY MARMALADE
Labelle 75

Michael Jackson

Columbia Records announced the formation of a new subsidiary label in June, 1953. A story in *Billboard* promised that the Epic label would be "a full-fledged classical line." The story also cited the possibility of some of the pop artists on the Okeh label being transferred over to Epic.

The Okeh label dates back to September, 1918. It was founded by Otto Heinemann, who incorporated his initials as well as an American Indian word meaning "it is so" into the Okeh name. Heinemann remained president of the label after Columbia Records absorbed Okeh in 1926. Okeh was inactive from 1935 to 1940, when CBS renamed its Vocalion label Okeh.

More details on Epic were forthcoming in the September 19, 1953, issue of *Billboard*. An article headlined "Columbia's Epic to Bow With Classic, Pop Line" announced that the label's initial release would consist of classical LPs featuring the music of composers like Dvorak, Beethoven, Tchaikowsky, Schubert and Mozart. An EP of tunes from the British cast of *Call Me Madam* was also scheduled, as were EPs of older material from Al Jolson and Artie Shaw. The Epic pop roster was listed, including names like Helene Dixon, Dolores Hawkins, Sandy Stewart and June Anthony. Dixon and Stewart had already charted on Okeh. Another Okeh artist who joined the label was Roy Hamilton, who gave Epic a number 21 hit in February, 1954, with "You'll Never Walk Alone."

Some executives at Epic felt the label was considered second-class at Columbia Records. "Even here at CBS, we were treated as country cousins," former general manager Al Shulman said in *Billboard* on Epic's 25th anniversary. One problem was that Columbia had their own in-house distribution network, while Epic was handled by independent distributors. "It was tough," Shulman recalled. "We had to deal with indies, versus Columbia's power-house sales force."

Shulman helped turn Epic into the major label it became in the '60s. "Just before I left, I wrote a critique of the label, indicating what I thought should be done to make it a viable record making organization. We needed a larger A&R budget . . . and we had to be competitive to bid for talent. We needed a unified sales force. In short, Epic needed to be treated like a company."

In the '50s, Epic made the *Billboard* chart with hits from Somethin' Smith & the Redheads and Sal Mineo. But the label's first artist with staying power was Bobby Vinton, who has seven singles included in Epic's top 100. Bobby first recorded in 1960 when Pittsburgh DJ Dick Lawrence told him that End Records was interested in him. He recorded Bobby singing "I Love You The Way You Are," but then took it to CBS Records. Not wishing to offend an important disc jockey, the label signed Bobby to Epic. "They weren't really interested in my songs or me," Vinton admits, "they just signed me and Lawrence held on to the tape." Vinton's ambition was to be a big-band leader, and he recorded two albums of big-band music that were flops.

At a meeting with Epic executives, Bobby was told he was being dropped from the label. He protested, claiming his contract called for two more recordings. The executives excused themselves to discuss the situation. "They were figuring out how to get rid of me. I saw a pile of records that said, 'reject pile,' and they still weren't back. I noticed the record player was turning so I started to listen to some of the records they were throwing out and all of a sudden I heard, 'Roses are red, my love, violets are blue. . . .' When they came back, they said the band just wasn't making it. I said, 'I can sing a little, and there's a song you're throwing away that really sounds like something I would hear on the radio.'" They agreed to let Bobby record "Roses Are Red (My Love)." He cut it as an R&B song and hated it. He asked to record it again as a country song, and Epic agreed. The single became Epic's first number one hit.

Epic also did well in the '60s with artists from the U.K. Lulu, Donovan, Georgie Fame and the Hollies all had hits in America on the label. By the end of the decade, Epic's star attraction was Sly & the Family Stone, the San Francisco group that specialized in "psychedelic soul."

Sly & the Family Stone and the Hollies continued to have hits in the '70s as Epic's diverse roster grew to include LaBelle, Cheap

Trick, Charlie Rich, Boston, Engelbert Humperdinck and a former Motown group, the Jacksons.

Michael Jackson outlines his brothers' difficulties with Motown in his *Moonwalker* autobiography: "Our problems with Motown began around 1974, when we told them in no uncertain terms that we wanted to write and produce our own songs. Basically, we didn't like the way our music sounded at the time. We had a strong competitive urge and we felt we were in danger of being eclipsed by other groups who were creating a more contemporary sound." Motown wanted the group to continue using staff writers and producers, which led Michael to tell Berry Gordy that the Jackson Five were moving on.

Ron Alexenburg signed the group to Epic. Jermaine, who had become Berry's son-in-law, stayed behind and was replaced by the youngest Jackson brother, Randy. Motown laid claim to the name Jackson Five, so they called themselves the Jacksons. But Epic didn't give them *carte blanche* at first; Kenny Gamble and Leon Huff were named to write and produce their first album for their new label. The first track to be issued as a single was "Enjoy Yourself," which went to number six. But their next three singles failed to make the top 20. After their second album for the label, Michael and his father Joe met with Alexenburg and asked for the creative freedom they had wanted all along. They produced their third Epic album, *Destiny*, which included their most successful single for the label, "Shake Your Body (Down To The Ground)."

Meanwhile, Michael auditioned for the role of the Scarecrow in the film version of *The Wiz* and won the part. During production, he renewed his acquaintance with Quincy Jones, which led to Quincy producing Michael's first solo LP for Epic, *Off the Wall. Off the Wall* yielded two number one singles, "Don't Stop 'Til You Get Enough" and "Rock With You." The latter is Epic's second most successful chart single.

Off The Wall also sold over eight million copies, but that was miniscule compared to the sales figures of the follow-up album. With over 40 million copies sold, *Thriller* remains the best-selling record in history. The first single released was a duet with Paul McCartney, "The Girl Is Mine." It was followed by the most successful chart single in Epic's history, "Billie Jean," which remained on top of the Hot 100 for seven weeks.

Almost five years passed before Michael released his next solo album. "We worked on *Bad* for a long time. Years," Michael stated in *Moonwalker*. "There was a lot of tension because we felt we were competing with ourselves. It's very hard to create something when you feel like you're in competition with yourself because no matter how you look at it, people are always going to compare *Bad* to *Thriller*."

It didn't suffer in the comparison. Michael racked up five more number one singles from *Bad*, beginning with "I Just Can't Stop Loving You." In all, Michael has 14 singles included in Epic's top 100, plus three more with the Jacksons.

Olivia Newton-John

MCA Records was created in 1972 to consolidate all of the labels owned by MCA, Inc., into one company. Legendary names like Decca, Brunswick, Coral and Kapp disappeared, as did the company's youngest label, Uni. MCA Records inherited artists from its family of labels, and the very first single issued with the new logo was "Crocodile Rock" by Elton John, with the catalog number MCA 40000, followed by Ricky Nelson's "Palace Guard," MCA 40001.

The origin of MCA Records can be traced back to August 4, 1934, the day Decca Records was chartered as an American label. The founders were Jack Kapp, E.F. Stevens, Jr., and Milton R. Rackmil from America, and E.R. (Ted) Lewis from England. Lewis, a stockbroker, had formed Decca Records in the U.K. in 1929 by purchasing Barnett Samuel & Son Ltd., a company that manufactured portable gramophones under the name Decca.

Kapp had worked for Columbia Records from 1918-25, then was hired by Brunswick Records, where he became recording manager in 1930. Stevens and Rackmil also worked for Brunswick. On a trip to London, Kapp met with Lewis, who wanted to find an outlet for his product in America. When Columbia Records was up for sale in 1933, Lewis planned to buy it and have Kapp, Stevens and Rackmil run it. But the deal fell through, and Lewis suggested forming a brand-new company. He wanted to sell records for 35 cents, cheaper than the 75 cent product sold by other companies.

It was an excellent idea during the Depression, and helped bring the record industry out of the doldrums.

Now Kapp needed artists. He had worked closely with Bing Crosby at Brunswick, and Crosby had a clause in his contract that allowed him to leave if Kapp did. Bing joined the new company, and the first record issued, Decca 100, was his recording of "I Love You Truly" backed with "Just A-Wearyin' For You." Other Brunswick acts followed, including Guy Lombardo, the Mills Brothers, the Dorsey Brothers Orchestra and the Boswell Sisters. The roster expanded with the Andrews Sisters, Al Jolson, Judy Garland and Woody Herman. In 1939, Decca released the soundtrack to *The Wizard of Oz*.

During the '40s, Ella Fitzgerald, Louis Armstrong, Louis Jordan and the Ink Spots joined the company. The Coral label was created in November, 1948, to sign new artists and compete with independent labels, and the Brunswick name was purchased from Warner Brothers and reactivated as a label. But tragedy struck at the end of the decade—on March 25, 1949, Kapp died of a heart attack at age 47.

Rackmil succeeded him as president and oversaw the purchasing of 26 percent of the outstanding stock of the Universal Pictures Company, Inc., in the summer of 1951. Universal had been founded in 1912 by Carl Laemmle as an amalgamation of several corporations. On March 15, 1915, the gates to Universal City Studios were opened in the San Fernando Valley. By 1954, Decca owned 72.5 per cent of the stock. Rackmil became president of Universal, and the marriage of the two companies had immediate benefits: Decca released the soundtrack of Universal's *The Glenn Miller Story*.

Under Rackmil, Universal gradually stopped making "B" pictures and placed an emphasis on making fewer but better films. In 1962, Universal became a subsidiary of the Music Corporation of America, a talent booking agency founded by Jules Stein before World War II.

Jack Kapp's brother, Dave, continued managing A&R for the company after his brother's death, but he left to head A&R for RCA. In 1955, he formed his own label. Kapp Records had a number one single in its first year of operation with Roger Williams' "Autumn Leaves," the label's most successful chart single. The rest of Kapp's top 10: "Hello, Dolly!" by Louis Armstrong, "Fascination" by Jane Morgan, "Rainbow" by Russ Hamilton, "Gypsys, Tramps & Thieves" by Cher, "Half-Breed" by Cher, "Sailor (Your Home Is The Sea)" by Lolita, "Born Free" by Roger Williams, "Midnight In Moscow" by Kenny Ball & His Jazzmen and "Our Day Will Come" by Ruby & the Romantics. Kapp also had chart hits from the Searchers, Jack Jones, Jerry Keller and Joe Harnell. He sold his label to MCA in 1967; the only Kapp artist who continued to have hits on MCA was Cher.

In the '50s, the Coral and Brunswick labels were headed by Bob Thiele (who later married one of Coral's leading artists, Teresa

Brewer). When Decca Records allowed its contract with an unknown singer named Buddy Holly to lapse, Thiele signed him and his band, the Crickets. "That'll Be The Day," originally recorded but unreleased by Decca, was a number one single on Brunswick. Coral's most successful chart single is "Tammy" by Debbie Reynolds.

Olivia Newton-John and Elton John, two artists inherited from Uni, occupy the top six slots of MCA's top 100 chart singles. Olivia has a total of 12 singles on the label's top 100, and Elton has 17. Olivia left MCA, recording an album of lullabyes and children's songs for Geffen. Elton also left for Geffen, but it proved to be a hiatus—he returned to MCA in 1987.

MCA bought ABC Records in 1979, bringing the Dot and Dunhill catalogs to Universal City. Steely Dan and Jimmy Buffett, clients of Irving Azoff signed to ABC, were transferred to MCA. In 1983, Azoff himself moved to the label, by becoming its new president. It was a dramatic shot in the arm for the record company. By 1985, MCA's gross revenues had more than tripled over 1982's figures.

Azoff started by trimming the roster—from 46 acts down to five, according to Fredric Dannen in *Hit Men*. On July 8, 1989, MCA and the I.R.S. label, which it distributed, had the number one single ("Good Thing" by the Fine Young Cannibals) as well as the top three albums on *Billboard*'s LP chart.

Azoff built MCA back up by giving it a strong R&B base. Patti LaBelle joined the company and had a number one duet with Michael McDonald. Jody Watley, formerly of Shalamar, had solo success on MCA. Ready for the World, a sextet from Flint, Michigan, were signed to MCA by Jheryl Busby and went to number one with "Oh Sheila." And the members of New Edition proved to be a real bonanza. All teenagers when they signed with the label in 1983, the group itself only had two top 10 singles, "Cool It Now" and "If It Isn't Love." But lead singer Bobby Brown left the group in 1986 for a solo career and scored with a succession of top 10 singles; he has six titles in MCA's top 100. Ricky Bell, Michael Bivins and Ronald DeVoe of the group formed an extracurricular trio, Bell Biv Devoe, and have their first two singles ("Poison" and "Do Me!") in MCA's top 10. Two other group members, Johnny Gill and Ralph Tresvant, also developed successful solo careers.

Azoff, who became president of the MCA Music Entertainment Group, also brought Motown under MCA's distribution wing. In June of 1988, MCA and an outside investment group, Boston Ventures, purchased Motown for $61 million.

In August, 1988, Azoff brought in Al Teller, former president of CBS Records, to be president of the MCA label. Azoff left the company on September 5, 1989, to head up Giant Records, a new label financed by Warner Brothers.

In December, 1990, the Matsushita Electric Industrial Co. of Japan agreed to buy MCA Inc. for $6.13 billion, the largest purchase by a Japanese company in the United States.

THE TOP 50 SONGS ON
DECCA

Brenda Lee

Decca fielded a strong artist roster in the first half of the '50s, dominating the country chart with Red Foley, Webb Pierce and Kitty Wells, also remaining strong on the pop chart with Kitty Kallen, the Mills Brothers and the Four Aces. The label's presence on the R&B chart diminished after the death of founder Jack Kapp in 1949, but in the '40s, Decca had performed well with Louis Jordan, Buddy Johnson and Lionel Hampton.

Milt Gabler, the man in charge of finding new talent for Decca, had been brought into the company in 1941 by Kapp. Gabler had been running his own label, Commodore, with an artist roster that included Billie Holiday and Jelly Roll Morton. At Decca, he was in charge of producing records for Jordan as well as the Ink Spots, Louis Armstrong, Ella Fitzgerald, Burl Ives, the Weavers and Guy Lombardo, among others.

Gabler knew that rock and roll was the next big thing, so he gladly made an appointment with songwriter/music publisher Jim Myers to meet Bill Haley, who had been recording for the Essex label in Philadelphia. Myers and Max Freedman had written a song for Haley to record at Essex, but label owner Dave Miller disliked Myers and refused to let Haley record "(We're Gonna) Rock Around The Clock."

Gabler signed Haley instantly and took him into Decca's Pythian

Temple recording studio in New York City on April 12, 1954. Two songs were recorded that day, "Thirteen Women" and "Rock Around The Clock." Released as a single, the latter title entered the *Billboard* chart on May 29 and peaked at number 23. It sold well enough for Gabler to pick up Haley's option and record a follow-up. Haley selected "Shake, Rattle and Roll," an R&B hit by Joe Turner. It sold a million copies and went to number seven.

With the Comets, Haley had two more hits: "Dim, Dim The Lights" and "Mambo Rock." But Myers hadn't given up on "Rock Around The Clock." He sent copies to everyone he could think of in Hollywood. When the producers of *The Blackboard Jungle* used the song to open their film, there were riots in movie theaters. Decca re-serviced the single and it went to number one on July 9, 1955. Historians mark that date as the beginning of the rock era.

Decca continued to have chart hits in the latter half of the '50s with their pop artists. The Four Aces recorded the title song from the film *Love Is A Many Splendored Thing*. The Tommy Dorsey Orchestra, Victor Young, Elmer Bernstein and Sammy Davis, Jr. all had hits on the label.

In 1956 Decca signed an 11-year-old singer from Atlanta, Georgia. Brenda Lee was appearing on Peanut Faircloth's TV show in Augusta when Decca recording artist Red Foley and his manager, Dub Albritton, passed through town. Faircloth insisted they come and listen to Brenda sing. Foley and Albritton were impressed enough to have her open for Foley and appear on his ABC-TV series, "Ozark Jubilee."

Albritton brought Brenda to Decca. On July 30, 1956, she recorded two sides for her first single, "Jambalaya" and "BIgelow 6-200." By 1959 she still hadn't reached the upper portion of the Hot 100, so Albritton took her to Europe and then South America. Rave notices and international acclaim finally paid off at home: in April, 1960, Brenda had her first top 10 hit, "Sweet Nothin's." The follow-up was "I'm Sorry," but Decca was reluctant to let a 15-year-old sing about unrequited love. The ballad sat on a shelf for several months until it was released and became her first number one single. By the middle of 1963, Brenda had racked up 12 top 10 hits. Decca rewarded her in July of that year with a 20-year contract guaranteeing her $35,000 per year and a two-picture deal with Universal.

During the British invasion, Decca had one major U.K. group, the Who. Originally signed with Brunswick in the U.K., the Who remained with Decca in America despite litigation with Brunswick and a shift to Robert Stigwood's Reaction label.

The last single to be a hit on Decca was Dobie Gray's "Drift Away," which peaked at number five in May, 1973. Then Gray, along with Decca artists like Rick Nelson and the Who, were moved to MCA, which replaced all of the company's labels, including Coral, Brunswick and Uni. The Decca logo, an institution in America since 1934, disappeared into history.

Neil Diamond

1. **INCENSE AND PEPPERMINTS**
   Strawberry Alarm Clock 67
2. **SWEET CAROLINE (GOOD TIMES NEVER SEEMED SO GOOD)**
   Neil Diamond 69
3. **CRACKLIN' ROSIE**
   Neil Diamond 70
4. **BUILD ME UP BUTTERCUP**
   The Foundations 69
5. **SONG SONG BLUE**
   Neil Diamond 72
6. **GRAZING IN THE GRASS**
   Hugh Masekela 68
7. **HOLLY HOLY**
   Neil Diamond 69
8. **GYPSY WOMAN**
   Brian Hyland 70
9. **YOUR SONG**
   Elton John 71
10. **ROCKET MAN**
    Elton John 72
11. **BABY, NOW THAT I'VE FOUND YOU**
    The Foundations 68
12. **I AM ... I SAID**
    Neil Diamond 71
13. **ISRAELITES**
    Desmond Dekker & the Aces 69
14. **WALK ON WATER**
    Neil Diamond 72
15. **PLAY ME**
    Neil Diamond 72
16. **HONKY CAT**
    Elton John 72
17. **WALKIN' IN THE RAIN WITH THE ONE I LOVE**
    Love Unlimited 72
18. **STONES**
    Neil Diamond 71
19. **HE AIN'T HEAVY, HE'S MY BROTHER**
    Neil Diamond 70
20. **BROTHER LOVE'S TRAVELLING SALVATION SHOW**
    Neil Diamond 69

Uni Records was a subsidiary of MCA, the parent company of Universal. MCA was already operating its Decca and Brunswick subsidiaries when it started a newer, hipper label with psychedelic colors on the label. Russ Regan was national promotion director, and after the label's first seven months of operations, he was named general manager.

The first record Regan bought was the Strawberry Alarm Clock's "Incense And Peppermints," which turned out to be Uni's most successful chart hit. "I bought it for $2,500 in August—by November 18, it was a number one record," Regan recalls.

Regan traded the U.K. rights to "Incense And Peppermints" to Pye Records in Britain in exchange for the American rights to "Baby, Now That I've Found You" by the Foundations. Their third U.S. single, "Build Me Up Buttercup," is Uni's fourth biggest record.

Under Regan's administration, Uni signed three major artists: Neil Diamond, Elton John and Olivia Newton-John.

Diamond had been signed to Bang Records with a "main man" clause; when the head of the label, Bert Berns, passed away, Diamond was a free agent. "We went after him and got him," Regan reports. "We were very fortunate. He's one of the great talents. I was very honest with him; we had a great working relationship. I played devil's advocate and he trusted my ears. If I felt something wasn't up to snuff, I would tell him."

Regan was also responsible for signing Elton John to Uni. "I was at the Continental Hyatt House [on the Sunset Strip] in those days. A friend of mine named Lenny Hodes walked in; he was working for Dick James at the time."

James was a music publisher who started the Page One and DJM labels in the United Kingdom. Elton was signed to DJM. Hodes told Regan that five companies had already turned Elton down for the States, but he was a great talent, and Hodes wanted Regan to listen to *Empty Sky*. "I said if five companies have turned him down, he can't be much." Regan listened to the album that afternoon, and ended up signing Elton John to Uni.

Olivia Newton-John had her first two singles released on Uni; neither was a big hit. Her first top 10 single was "Let Me Be There," released on MCA.

Uni was reactivated briefly in 1988. The Scottish quartet Wet Wet Wet went to number 58 on the Hot 100 with "Wishing I Was Lucky." The label had two more chart singles—"Tell That Girl To Shut Up" by Transvision Vamp, and "Love Train" by Holly Johnson—before the logo was quietly retired for a second time.

MERCURY

The Platters

Mercury Records was established in Chicago in 1946. The independent company had hits in 1947 with Frankie Laine's "That's My Desire," which peaked at number four, and Vic Damone's "I Have But One Heart," which went to number seven. A year later, the label added another star to its roster—Patti Page.

Mitch Miller headed up pop A&R from 1948 to 1950 before moving to Columbia. Eventually Laine, Damone and Page would all follow him to CBS. Mercury's initial success in the rock era came from having white singers cover songs originally recorded by black artists. The Crew-Cuts had a number one record in 1954 by covering the Chords' "Sh-Boom," and the practice continued with Georgia Gibbs, who had pop hits with LaVern Baker's "Twee-dle Dee" and Etta James' "The Wallflower" (which became "Dance With Me Henry"). The Diamonds spent eight weeks at number two with a cover of the Gladiolas' "Little Darlin'," Mercury's most successful chart single of the rock era.

In the early part of 1955, the Penguins, a Los Angeles doo-wop group, had a top 10 single with "Earth Angel (Will You Be Mine)." Mercury wanted to sign them away from the DooTone label, and their manager Buck Ram agreed on one condition: Mercury also had to sign his other group, the Platters. John Sippel, a West Coast executive for Mercury, urged his superiors in Chicago to take both groups. The Penguins never had a chart single on Mercury and left in 1956 for Atlantic, but the Platters hit instantly and became the most popular vocal group of their day.

The Platters' first Mercury single was a re-working of an earlier release on Federal, "Only You (And You Alone)." It was issued on a purple Mercury label, indicating it was an R&B song. Ram insisted that the Platters were a pop group, so the single was reissued on the standard black Mercury label. "Only You" peaked at number five and was followed by "The Great Pretender," which went to number two on the Best Sellers chart. The Platters have 10 singles on Mercury's top 100; four of them are in the top 10.

In 1959, Brook Benton had his first hit on Mercury, "It's Just A Matter Of Time." Benton had recorded for Okeh, Epic and Vik before a fateful appointment at Meridian Music introduced him to Clyde Otis. Benton and Otis wrote "Looking Back," a number five song for Nat King Cole in 1958, and "A Lover's Question," a number seven hit for Clyde McPhatter at the beginning of 1957. The following year, Mercury A&R executive Art Talmadge went to New York and asked Otis to head up the creative department of Mercury's office there. "Up to that time, no black had enjoyed both administrative and creative responsibilities—only creative," Otis told Colin Escott. "I said I wanted both. Art wasn't prepared to offer that and went back to Chicago. Finally, the president of Mercury, Irving Green, offered me both." Atlantic Records wanted to sign Benton, but Otis grabbed him for Mercury. The association lasted through 1965.

Shelby Singleton headed up A&R in the South and brought artists like Johnny Preston and the Big Bopper to the label, giving Mercury hits like "Running Bear" and "Chantilly Lace." In 1959, Mercury created a subsidiary label, Smash, and Singleton was responsible for signing the artists that gave Smash its first two number one singles—Joe Dowell ("Wooden Heart") and Bruce Channel ("Hey! Baby").

In 1962, Mercury Records was sold to the Dutch multinational company Philips and became part of Polygram, which had been formed by a merger of Philips' Phonogram Records division and the German company, Polydor/Deutsche Grammophon. The Philips label was introduced in the U.S., followed later by the Fontana subsidiary. Green remained head of the company in Chicago, and one of his most important moves was bringing in Quincy Jones to head up the A&R department.

In the latter half of the '60s, Mercury had chart singles by the Blues Magoos, Manfred Mann and Keith. Jerry Butler began a run of hits in 1967, but the label's overall chart share was relatively insignificant. Gene Chandler and Daniel Boone had hits in the early '70s, and Rod Stewart gave the label its first number one single in eight years with "Maggie May" and "Reason To Believe." In the last half of the '70s, Mercury had a chart presence again with Bachman-Turner Overdrive, 10cc and the Ohio Players.

Mercury's most successful chart single of the '80s was a one-off from Donna Summer. She left Casablanca for Geffen in 1980, but still owed her former label one more album. Casablanca had been absorbed into Polygram, and after two albums on Geffen, Donna recorded *She Works Hard For the Money* for her old company. Issued on Mercury, the title track turned out to be one of her biggest hits.

Otherwise, Mercury's revitalization in the '80s was due to a combination of British and heavy-metal artists. Dexys Midnight Runners were signed to Phonogram in the U.K., and their "Come On Eileen" went to number one in Britain as well as America. The British duo Tears For Fears, who signed with Mercury in the U.K. in 1982, had two number one hits in the U.S. in 1985: "Everybody Wants To Rule The World" and "Shout." Martin Fry's ABC appeared on their own Neutron label at home in Britain; their American hits on Mercury included "The Look Of Love (Part One)," "Be Near Me" and "When Smokey Sings."

Mercury's most successful British heavy-metal band signed with Phonogram in the U.K. in 1979. Def Leppard formed in Sheffield in 1977 and had their first album released on the Vertigo subsidiary in November of '79. Their real breakthrough came with the 1983 album *Pyromania*, which gave them a number 12 single in the U.S., "Photograph." An automobile accident in which drummer Rick Allen lost his left arm resulted in a four-year delay between albums. When *Hysteria* was released in 1987, the group was poised for megastardom—"Pour Some Sugar On Me" went to number two on the Hot 100, followed by a number one hit, "Love Bites." The title track and "Armageddon It" were also hits, giving Def Leppard a total of five singles on Mercury's top 100.

Mercury's other heavy-metal band proved even more successful. Bon Jovi and lead singer Jon Bon Jovi have 10 singles on Mercury's top 100, matching the total set by the Platters. John Bongiovi formed his first band, Atlantic City Expressway, when he was in high school. His cousin Tony ran the Power Station recording studio in New York, home to Aerosmith, the Ramones and the Talking Heads. Jon (he dropped the "h") worked there for two years as a gofer, and was allowed to record in the studio during off hours. His song "Runaway" was included in radio station WAPP's *Homegrown* album and received some airplay around the country. He put together a band, and Derek Shulman signed them to Mercury. So that people would connect them with the "Runaway" track, they anglicized Jon's last name as the group name.

Bon Jovi's first two albums were mildly successful. But it wasn't until their third release, *Slippery When Wet*, that the band achieved multi-platinum status. The first single from *Slippery When Wet*, "You Give Love A Bad Name," went to number one in November, 1986. Three months later, the follow-up single, "Livin' On A Prayer," also went to number one. Bon Jovi's next album, *New Jersey*, produced a bumper crop of hit singles: "Bad Medicine" and "I'll Be There For You" both went to number one, and three other songs made the top 10.

THE TOP 30 SONGS ON
PHILIPS

N.V. Philips Gloeilampenfabrieken is the complete name of the Dutch manufacturer of audio equipment. Philips was also well-known as a classical record label, part of the company's Phonogram record division. In 1962, the Dutch company merged with Polydor/Deutsche Grammophon, a Germany company that dated back to 1898. The merger of Phonogram and Polydor resulted in a new corporate name, Polygram.

The Philips logo was seen in the U.K. on hits by the Springfields, the folk trio that included Dusty Springfield and her brother Tom. Polygram purchased the Chicago-based Mercury Records in 1962, and that year, the Philips label appeared in America as a subsidiary of Mercury. The Springfields had a top 20 hit in 1962 with "Silver Threads and Golden Needles." The following year, Philips had two number one hits in the U.S. First came "Hey Paula" by Paul and Paula, produced by Major Bill Smith. He had produced "Hey! Baby" by Bruce Channel, a number one hit on Mercury's Smash subsidiary 11 months earlier. Smith issued "Hey Paula" on his own LeCam label, and it sold so well in Atlanta that Shelby Singleton of Mercury Records picked it up for the new Philips label. In December of '63, Philips had its second number one in America with a song that was recorded under the auspices of the label's Brussels office. Sister Luc-Gabrielle and a friend had approached Philips about making a non-commercial recording of compositions they sang at their evening retreats at Fichermont Monastery. The result was so commercial that Philips released an album by *Soeur Sourire* throughout Europe. In America, the album was released under the name "The Singing Nun," but sales were sluggish until "Dominique" was released as a single.

While Philips also had a run of hits with Dusty Springfield, the label's primary source of record sales came from the Four Seasons. The New Jersey quartet signed with the label after a year of hits on Vee Jay. Unhappy with that label's accounting practices, the group looked for a better deal and found it with Philips. Seventeen of the label's top 30 songs are by the group or lead singer Frankie Valli.

Philips' most successful chart single is the instrumental "Love Is Blue," recorded in France by Paul Mauriat. It was just one of many cover versions included in his *Blooming Hits* album, alongside "Penny Lane," "This Is My Song" and "Somethin' Stupid." Written as "L'amour Est Bleu," it was Luxembourg's entry in the 1967 Eurovision song contest. Vicky Lenadros sang it in competition, and it only placed fourth. She recorded the song in 19 languages—but it took Mauriat's instrumental version to make "Love Is Blue" a worldwide hit.

Connie Francis

A label called Metro-Goldwyn-Mayer existed in 1928. The lion logo and *ars gratia artis* inscription were part of the label design, but the records were pressed by Columbia. The modern-day MGM Records was founded in 1946 by the motion picture company, primarily to issue film soundtracks of MGM musicals and other theatrical releases. In 1947, the label made its mark on the country charts with one of the most influential artists of all time, Hank Williams. His first massive hit was "Lovesick Blues," which topped the country Best Sellers chart for 16 weeks. MGM Records also made an impact on the R&B chart with Billy Eckstine (11 titles between 1948-52) and Ivory Joe Hunter (four titles in 1950). Tommy Edwards first made the pop chart in 1951, the same year Debbie Reynolds and Carleton Carpenter had a top three hit with "Aba Daba Honeymoon" from the soundtrack of the film *Two Weeks in Love*.

While the label had some success in the early years of the rock era with hits like Joni James' "You Are My Love" and Dick Hyman's "Moritat (A Theme From 'The Three Penny Opera')," the real breakthrough came in 1958 with a hat trick of number one singles from Tommy Edwards, Conway Twitty and Sheb Wooley, plus the chart debut of Connie Francis.

Tommy Edwards' first recording of "It's All In The Game"

peaked at number 18 in 1951. Seven years later, as Tommy was about to be dropped from the MGM artist roster, label executive Morty Craft asked him to re-record the song in stereo. The original arrangement was abandoned in favor of a rock and roll ballad; the single spent six weeks at number one, and became the most successful MGM chart single of the rock era.

"It's All In The Game" was knocked off the top of the chart by Conway Twitty's "It's Only Make Believe," the second most successful MGM chart single of the rock era.

Connie Francis was 16 years old when she was recording demos for music publishers. One of them put up $5,000 for her to have her own recording session. She was turned down by a number of labels, including Columbia, before Harry Myerson signed her to MGM. According to Connie, Myerson was interested because she had recorded a "dippy" song titled "Freddy," which happened to be the name of Myerson's son. "He thought it would be a cute birthday present," she explains. MGM released 10 singles on Connie without having any hits. The label lost interest in her and she was working on her final recording session when her father suggested she record a standard from 1923, "Who's Sorry Now." Francis has 20 singles on the MGM top 100, including the label's third most successful title of the rock era, "Everybody's Somebody's Fool."

While artists like Connie Francis saw their chart fortunes diminish during the British invasion, MGM performed strongly on the Hot 100 with two groups from the U.K.—Herman's Hermits and the Animals, both managed by Mickie Most. The Hermits, fronted by Peter Noone, were signed to EMI's Columbia label in the U.K. Their initial success in the States came with their first MGM single, a cover version of Earl-Jean's "I'm Into Something Good," written by Gerry Goffin and Carole King. The group formed in Manchester, England, as the Cyclones, and changed their name to the Heartbeats. Peter Noone joined the band in 1963 as lead vocalist. Bassist Karl Green pointed out Noone's resemblance to the cartoon character Sherman in the "Mr. Peabody" segments of TV's "The Bullwinkle Show," so the group was renamed Herman and the Hermits, later altered to Herman's Hermits.

Eric Burdon joined the Newcastle-based Alan Price Combo in 1962, forming the group that would change their name to the Animals a year later. Producer Most recorded a four-track E.P. with the group and got them a gig as the opening act for Chuck Berry on his U.K. tour. To provide some contrast to Berry's music, they included the bluesy "House Of The Rising Sun" in their act. After Most signed the Animals to EMI's Columbia label, they traveled to London via British Rail and recorded the song in two takes. It ran over four minutes, and Columbia was reluctant to release it as a single, but Most convinced the label it would be a hit.

In 1969, MGM Records was revitalized by a new president. Studio head Jim Aubrey asked Mike Curb to merge his Curb

Records with the MGM label and take charge of the new MGM Records. A week before he joined the company, Curb saw Burdon perform with the R&B band War. "When I got to MGM I found out there was no contract and they had new management, so I signed them," Curb recalls. A single was released. "The 'B' side was 'Spill The Wine,'" Curb confesses. "We flipped it after radio told us. I'm embarrassed to say I didn't know it was on there. I felt the other track was a hit."

Curb had already signed the Osmonds to Curb when the labels merged. "They hadn't hit yet. Right after we made the arrangement with MGM, our second single was 'One Bad Apple,' which was recorded in Muscle Shoals, Alabama. The idea was to use the Jackson Five sound. We changed the name Osmond Brothers to the Osmonds. Everyone thought they were a black group—before that, everyone thought they were a barbershop quartet."

Curb recorded Donny Osmond as a solo artist. His first hit was a remake of an obscure Roy Orbison song, "Sweet And Innocent." The follow-up was a remake of Steve Lawrence's "Go Away Little Girl," Curb's most successful chart single from his MGM tenure. He explains: "Most of the remakes were things I did. I've been a student of trivia . . . most of the things we brought back were songs that weren't closely identified with the artist." Curb followed that trend with the next Osmond to record solo: sister Marie. "Sonny James came up with the idea of recording 'Paper Roses,'" according to Curb. "I called Sonny and said I'd like to break Marie country and Sonny said she should do 'Paper Roses.'" The song, a number five hit for Anita Bryant in 1960, also went to number five for Marie. Counting all of the singles recorded by different members of the Osmond family, they are responsible for 20 of the top 100 MGM titles, the same number as Connie Francis.

The second biggest single of the Curb administration is "The Candy Man" by Sammy Davis, Jr. "We had a hit record with the Mike Curb Congregation's 'Burning Bridges' from the picture *Kelly's Heroes*," the former president remembers. "I recorded 'The Candy Man' to be a follow-up to that and released it on MGM and it wasn't breaking. So I asked Sammy to overdub his voice over the track of the Mike Curb Congregation and he gave me one of those looks that only Sammy can give you, but I convinced him to do it on the basis that we would try to make it like Frank Sinatra's 'High Hopes,' which had featured Sinatra with kids." Davis recorded the song in one take and was mixed in with the voices of the Mike Curb Congregation. It spent three weeks at number one.

During the years Curb headed MGM, he also signed Jim Stafford and Gloria Gaynor. But the label's identity disappeared after it was purchased by Polygram. The artists on the roster were moved over to the Polydor label and the lion logo was reserved for an occasional soundtrack before finally being put to rest. Curb, who would be elected Lieutenant Governor of California in 1978, took his label affiliation to Warner Brothers and had hits on Warner/Curb with Debby Boone, among others.

Lionel Richie

B erry Gordy had no interest in working in either of his father's businesses, printing or construction. He loved to listen to the radio and won first prize in a Detroit talent show by writing a song, "Berry's Boogie." He also had a passion for boxing, and after 15 amateur fights, he dropped out of high school to turn pro. During his amateur career, he met a Golden Gloves champ named Jackie Wilson.

After a two-year Army stint, Berry married and went to work in both of his father's businesses. In the summer of 1953, with a $700 loan from his father and his discharge pay from the Army, he opened the 3-D Record Mart, a store specializing in jazz. He was bankrupt in two years and went to work in a Ford assembly plant.

Two of his sisters, Anna and Gwen, were employed at the Flame Show Bar, where one night in 1957, Berry found out that talent manager Al Greene was looking for songs for an old acquaintance of Berry's—Jackie Wilson. With Gwen's friend Billy Davis (who used the name Tyran Carlo), Gordy wrote "Reet Petite," Wilson's first Hot 100 single. Over a two-year period, Wilson recorded several of Gordy and Davis' songs, including "To Be Loved," "Lonely Teardrops" and "That's Why (I Love You So)."

In 1958, Anna and Gwen Gordy, along with Billy Davis, formed their own record company, distributed by Chess. Among the artists signed to Anna were David Ruffin, Johnny Bristol, Lamont Dozier and Marvin Gaye (who worked as a session musician but never released anything on the label). Meanwhile, Smokey Robinson shared Berry Gordy's frustration in the agonizingly slow way they received their royalties from other companies, and urged him to start his own business like Anna and Gwen had. With an $800 loan from his family, Berry took Smokey's advice and formed not only his own record company, but a publishing firm (Jobete) and a talent agency to manage his artists. The Motown Record Corporation's first label was named Tammy after the Debbie Reynolds movie, but was changed for legal reasons to Tamla.

The company's first single was released in January, 1959. "Come To Me" by Marv Johnson was issued locally in Detroit as Tamla 101, but for national distribution, Gordy leased the track to United Artists. Another single, "Money" by Barret Strong, was also issued locally on Tamla but leased to Anna.

Then Berry decided to stop leasing his masters to other companies. Beginning with a Miracles single, "The Feeling Is So Fine," Tamla became a national label. That single was quickly withdrawn, however, in favor of "Way Over There," released in July, 1960. Three months later, Berry took a song Smokey had written for Barrett Strong and recorded it with the Miracles. "Shop Around" became the company's first major hit.

With the company settled in at the Hitsville offices, located at 2648 West Grand Boulevard in Detroit, the roster of artists, producers, writers and session players grew at a rapid rate. In September, 1961, a second label was added: "My Beloved" by the Satintones was the first release on Motown. The Temptations, who had recorded for the short-lived Miracle subsidiary in July, 1961, were the first artists released on the Gordy label when "Dream Come True" was issued in March, 1962. The Soul label was initiated in March, 1964, with Shorty Long's "Devil With The Blue Dress." Motown has had a number of other labels over the years, including V.I.P., Mowest, Prodigal, Chisa (for jazz), Melodyland and Hitsville (for country) and Rare Earth (for rock).

The company earned its first number one single on the Hot 100 in December, 1961, with "Please Mr. Postman" by the Marvelettes, five young girls from the suburb of Inkster, Michigan.

The drummer on "Please Mr. Postman" was 22-year-old Marvin Gaye. As a member of the Marquees, he was invited to join Harvey Fuqua in a revamped version of the Moonglows. When Fuqua went to work for Anna Records, he brought Gaye with him. Gordy first heard Gaye sing at a party in a Detroit nightclub. In May, 1961, Gaye's first single, "Let Your Conscience Be Your Guide," was released; Marvin later referred to it as one of Gordy's rare "lemons."

Mary Wells originally wanted to meet Berry Gordy because she had written a song she thought Jackie Wilson should record. Gordy said she should cut "Bye Bye Baby" herself and signed her. Mary was thrilled to be in the same company as the Miracles and the Marvelettes, but was disappointed to find out her records would not be issued on the famous Tamla label—instead, she was relegated to Berry's new label, Motown. Teamed up with writer/producer Smokey Robinson, she had a series of top 10 singles, topped by the first number one single on the Motown label itself, "My Guy."

The Temptations were created by a merger of two groups, the Primes and the Distants. They were to be called the Elgins until Motown employee Bill Mitchell came up with the name Temptations. Their initial success also came with a Smokey Robinson song, "The Way You Do The Things You Do" in 1964. A year later, they went to number one with Smokey's "My Girl."

The Primes' sister group, the Primettes, also had a name change. Diana Ross and Mary Wilson were shocked to find out Florence Ballard had picked "The Supremes" from a list of possibilities because they thought it sounded too masculine. The group's first two singles, "I Want A Guy" and "Buttered Popcorn," were issued on Tamla. They moved over to Motown with "Your Heart Belongs To Me," but they didn't become household names until they recorded "Where Did Our Love Go" in 1964 and began their run of five number one singles, all written and produced by Holland, Dozier and Holland.

Stevie Wonder came to the company through Ronnie White of the Miracles, who introduced him to Brian Holland. Berry Gordy was in the middle of a steak dinner when Holland called and told him he had to sign the 11-year-old genius. "Fingertips—Part 2" was Tamla's second number one single.

The Four Aims became the Four Tops and recorded for Chess and Columbia before signing to a relatively-unknown Motown subsidiary, Workshop. In 1964, they recorded Holland-Dozier-Holland's "Baby I Need Your Loving," the first of a series of hits released on the Motown label.

Motown secretary Martha Reeves had her first recording session when Mary Wells missed an appointment in the studio. "Come And Get These Memories" was the first Martha & the Vandellas hit in 1963. Oddly, none of Martha's songs registered in Motown's top 100. Her biggest hit, "Dancing In The Street," ranks number 103.

Motown's first number one single of the '70s was "I Want You Back" by the Jackson Five. By the end of the decade, the label's leading attraction was the group that had opened for the Jackson Five on their 1971 tour. The Commodores have seven titles listed in the top 100 Motown songs; Lionel Richie, who left the group for a solo career, has 10.

In June of 1988, after months of speculation and rumor, Berry Gordy sold one of the most successful black-owned companies in America. Motown was purchased by MCA and an outside investment group, Boston Ventures, for $61 million. Jheryl Busby, who had been the president of black music at MCA, was named the new president of Motown. The first artist to have a top 10 hit under the new administration was New Edition member Johnny Gill, who peaked at number three in 1990 with "Rub You The Right Way."

Elvis Presley

Emile Berliner built a gramophone machine in 1887 and invented the flat, laterally-recorded disc, as opposed to the cylinder phonograph of Thomas Edison. Eldridge R. Johnson designed the first spring-driven gramophone, and in 1901—with Berliner's blessing—incorporated the Victor Talking Machine Company of Camden, New Jersey.

Berliner sold the European rights to his invention to a group of English investors, who formed the Gramophone Company in 1898. While visiting London, Berliner saw a painting by Francis Barraud titled "His Master's Voice." It depicted Barraud's dog Nipper listening to a phonograph machine. The Gramophone Company had bought the painting and its copyright for £100, and Berliner asked permission to use the painting as a trademark in the U.S.

The Victor company had the first million-selling record, "Vesti La Giubba" from *Pagliacci* by Italian tenor Enrico Caruso, released in 1904. The company's Red Seal label specialized in classical music. Victor also recorded every U.S. President, from Theodore Roosevelt to Warren G. Harding. Billy Murray and Ada Jones, two of the most popular vocalists of the first quarter of the 20th century, recorded for Victor. The label also issued recordings of Broadway musicals, dance bands, marching bands and jazz.

Eldridge Johnson sold his company to a banking firm on December 7, 1926. On January 4, 1929, the bankers resold Victor to the Radio Corporation of America, the company founded by David Sarnoff. Record sales dropped dramatically after the Wall Street crash in October of that year, and the factory in Camden was converted to manufacture radios. "It looked like records were going out of style altogether—the 1930 catalog was a tiny little thing," explains Chic Crumpacker, a music historian who joined RCA in 1953. "The Depression made people return to records because they couldn't afford to go to movies or plays or shows. They could buy a 35 or 50 cent record. And by the mid- to late '30s, the catalog was back up to snuff." Helping RCA Victor survive the depression were artists like Benny Goodman, Glenn Miller, Tommy Dorsey and Fats Waller.

By the end of World War II, the popularity of big bands began to fade in favor of crooners like Frank Sinatra and Dinah Shore, who were signed to Columbia. By the time Crumpacker became the manager of country and western promotion for RCA, the label had a strong artists roster that included Eddy Arnold, Hank Snow and Chet Atkins.

RCA was doing well in the pop department, too, with Perry Como being the standard-bearer for that section of the label. Como signed with RCA on June 17, 1943. His first single was "Goodbye, Sue." He had eight number one singles between 1945 and 1954, and another, "Round And Round," in 1957. "Joe Carlton [head of the Pop A&R department] favored Como with the very best songs that came in," says Crumpacker.

RCA was an early entrant in the rhythm and blues field. Arthur "Big Boy" Crudup appeared on the R&B charts with singles issued on the Bluebird subsidiary in 1945. He later wrote "That's Alright Mama" and was cited by Elvis Presley as being a major influence. Another subsidiary label, Groove, specialized in R&B, and in 1951, RCA cut some sides on Little Richard. They were in a big-band R&B style, and were more blues-oriented than Little Richard's later Specialty singles.

In 1955, Crumpacker was directly involved in the signing of the artist who would insure RCA's fortunes for years to come. "I was the first New York home office person to see and meet Elvis. I brought some of the Sun records back to Steve Sholes, who was head of C&W Artists and Repertoires. He had heard through field reports about this guy. But he had been in the business for a long time and wasn't falling for anything that might be transient, a 'flash in the pan.' But a lot of people, including myself, said we didn't think this was the case. The guy was simply dynamite in front of an audience. And his records were very mesmerizing—the Sun records." Crumpacker suggested Sholes make an offer to buy Elvis' contract.

"Which he did—to his credit. He offered Sam Phillips $25,000 for Presley's contract. That was, I think, a record for RCA at the time in the country field. The bad news was that Mercury Records came in with a higher offer, and suddenly it looked like we'd lost the ball game. But Sholes persevered—he went back to Phillips and said, '$40,000, but that's it.' And the deal was made. When I met Elvis at the annual Disc Jockey convention in Nashville in November he said, 'Hey, it looks like I'm going to be with you guys.' In another few days, he was."

According to Crumpacker, there was resistance from the Pop side of the label to push Elvis' career. "Carlton detested rock music. When he left in '57 and Sholes took his place, he founded his own label, Carlton, which had nothing but the most old-line pop recordings. Anita Bryant was one of his artists. That was indicative of the way he felt about rock. So everybody felt Elvis would last 15 minutes."

The list of RCA's most successful chart singles is dominated by Elvis. He holds the top six positions, and seven out of the top 10. All of those are from the years 1956-57. He has 25 titles listed in the top 100. But Elvis wasn't RCA's only success story. The label's pop division continued to flourish in the opening years of the rock era with Kay Starr (signed from Capitol), the Ames Brothers, Harry Belafonte, the Browns, Eddie Fisher and a young songwriter from Brooklyn who joined the label in 1958—Neil Sedaka.

RCA sat out the British invasion of 1964. The label's artist roster was all-American—Henry Mancini, Skeeter Davis, Little Peggy March, Jim Reeves, Floyd Cramer, the Tokens—and the arrival of the Fab Four didn't change that. RCA's most successful post-Beatles single of the '60s is as American as one could get: "The Ballad Of The Green Berets" by S/Sgt. Barry Sadler.

RCA's most popular artist on the *Billboard* singles chart during the '70s was John Denver, who has five singles listed on the label's top 100. He originally recorded for Mercury during his three-year tenure with the Chad Mitchell Trio. His first album for RCA as a solo artist, *Rhymes and Reasons*, included his song "Leaving On A Jet Plane," which was covered by Peter, Paul and Mary. In 1974, Denver had the first of four number one singles, "Sunshine On My Shoulders."

Next to Elvis Presley, the act with the most titles on RCA's top 100 is Daryl Hall and John Oates. Originally signed to Atlantic, they failed to chart with their first album, *Whole Oats*. Their next two LPs were released in 1974. *Abandoned Luncheonette* peaked at number 33, but manager Tommy Mottola felt the album was full of hit songs and should have been more successful. *War Babies*, more experimental than the first album, ran out of steam at number 86. Atlantic wasn't too pleased with the album, giving Mottola a chance to shop the duo to another label. RCA signed up Hall and Oates and released a top five single in 1976, "Sara Smile." The following year, they hit number one with "Rich Girl."

The RCA record label was just one subsidiary of its parent company, which also included the NBC Television Network and a giant electronics manufacturing division. The entire company was purchased by General Electric in December, 1985. That marked the beginning of the end for RCA as a corporate entity. GE was not interested in running a record company. Thorn-EMI of Great Britain bid for the label, but the Bertelsmann Music Group of Germany already had an interest in RCA, and purchased the rest.

Rod Stewart

Warner Brothers' first attempt at running a record label took place in April, 1930, when the film studio purchased the American branch of Brunswick Records. Many of the stars under contract to the movie company recorded for Brunswick, including Gloria Swanson, Noah Beery, Harry Richman and Al Jolson. During this period, Brunswick also signed Bing Crosby, the Mills Brothers and the Boswell Sisters. But the Depression affected record sales, and the financial burden was too much to bear. In December, 1931, Warners sold Brunswick to the American Record Corporation, and eventually the label came under the jurisdiction of Decca and MCA.

In 1958, Jack Warner once again wanted the studio to have its own record company. He was tired of seeing some of Warner's best motion picture soundtracks sell well for other labels, like MGM and 20th Century Fox. He hired Jim Conkling away from Columbia Records, and with a $3-million investment, Warner Brothers Records opened offices above the studio's machine shop on March 19, 1958. The label began with a middle-of-the-road slant and a release of 12 albums, all in stereo.

But there were no hits. It took just over a year to have initial success on the Hot 100. The first Warner Brothers single to make the top 10 was "Kookie, Kookie (Lend Me Your Comb)" by Edd Byrnes (listed as Edward on the label) and Connie Stevens.

Byrnes played Kookie on the studio's popular television series, "77 Sunset Strip," and sang his hit in the first episode of the second season. Stevens starred as Cricket Blake in another Warner Brothers TV series, "Hawaiian Eye"; during that show's first season, Connie had a number three single of her own, "Sixteen Reasons," the label's second top 10 hit.

Despite the success of Byrnes' single, the label was $3 million in debt by December, 1959. Two months later, the staff had been trimmed and the label completely reorganized. On February 17, 1960, Warners made a major investment by signing the Everly Brothers away from Cadence Records. The 10-year contract was worth $1 million to Don and Phil, who were then under pressure from the label to come up with a hit single. They didn't like the first eight songs they wrote, and finally recorded "Cathy's Clown," Warner Brothers' first number one single.

Mike Maitland from Capitol Records was appointed the new president of Warner Brothers Records in 1961. He brought in a KFWB disc jockey and part-time promotion man to supervise the label's promotion department. Joe Smith turned down the job at first, but was eventually persuaded by Maitland to join the company.

The February 3, 1962 issue of *Billboard* announced that folk trio Peter, Paul & Mary had signed with Warner Brothers. In 1963, the threesome had two consecutive singles peak at number two on the Hot 100: "Puff The Magic Dragon" and "Blowin' In The Wind." In 1965, the label had another number one single with a track leased from Pye Records in Britain—Petula Clark's "Downtown." Warners bought the Valiant label, bringing the Association to the company and netting another number one song, "Windy." The next year, Warner Brothers acquired the Autumn label in San Francisco, and three new acts joined the roster: the Beau Brummels, the Mojo Men and the Tikis. The Tikis changed their name to Harpers Bizarre. Lenny Waronker, who went on to become president of Warner Brothers Records, produced their single "The 59th Street Bridge Song (Feelin' Groovy)"; group member Ted Templeman joined the company as a staff producer.

Jack Warner sold Warner Brothers to Seven Arts, a production and distribution company owned by Elliot Hyman, in 1967. The deal included the motion picture arm and the record label, and the company was renamed Warner Bros.-Seven Arts. Under this new banner, Warner Brothers purchased Atlantic Records. By 1969, the artist's roster included Van Morrison, Alice Cooper, the Grateful Dead and—from Apple Records—James Taylor. Seven Arts became debt-laden and was in turn acquired by Kinney National Services. Kinney was run by Steve Ross, who had built a family business in funeral parlors into a company that owned car-rental agencies, parking lots and the Ashley Famous Talent Agency. In 1971, the Kinney name was dropped from the parent company in favor of Warner Communications. Maitland left the company in 1970. Mo Ostin, who had headed the Reprise subsidiary, was named chairman of the Board, and Joe Smith became president of Warner Brothers Records. At the same time, the Warner-Elektra-Atlantic distribution system was set up, bringing the three companies together on the wholesale level.

In the first half of the '70s, Warner Brothers had consistent hitmakers in Seals and Crofts, America and the Doobie Brothers.

Dewey Bunnell, Gerry Beckley and Dan Peek were all sons of American servicemen stationed in the U.K. They formed a quintet called Daze and when the other two members left, they stayed together as an acoustic trio. Promoter Jeff Dexter introduced them to Ian Samwell, a staff producer at the London office of Warner Brothers. He outbid Atlantic and DJM to sign up America, whose biggest hit was "A Horse With No Name" in 1972.

The Doobie Brothers formed in San Jose, California, in March of 1970, as a group called Pud. They signed with Warner Brothers the following year, and their first album was produced by Waronker and Templeman. The Doobie Brothers' biggest hit was "What A Fool Believes," featuring Michael McDonald on lead vocals.

The two most successful Warner Brothers singles are both from the last half of the '70s. Debby Boone was signed by Mike Curb and appeared on the Warner/Curb label, as did Exile, Shaun Cassidy and the Four Seasons. "You Light Up My Life" was number one for 10 weeks, but was Debby's only single to make the upper portion of the Hot 100. Rod Stewart has proven to be a consistent hitmaker for the label, signed away from Mercury Records in December, 1974. Rod has had 11 top 10 singles on Warner Brothers, the most successful being "Tonight's The Night (Gonna Be Alright)."

Prince has the third most successful chart single on Warner Brothers with the first 45 from *Purple Rain*, "When Doves Cry." The label signed the musician from Minneapolis when he was just 18, agreeing that he could produce his own albums. He started his own custom label, Paisley Park, with a roster that included Sheila E. and the Family. With the 1985 release of "Raspberry Beret," Prince switched over to the Paisley Park label. The exception was his *Batman* soundtrack, released on Warner Brothers.

Before they became country stars, the members of Exile were playing pop music on Warner/Curb. They hailed from Richmond, Kentucky, and played together in a high school band called the Fascinations. They became the Exiles in 1965 and recorded a single for Columbia in 1969 before joining RCA's Wooden Nickel label. Upon hearing a demo tape by the band in 1975, British producer Mike Chapman signed them and shortened their name to Exile. Chapman produced a single called "Try It On," which was released on Rak in the U.K. and Atco in the States. Exile then shifted over to Warner/Curb with a single written by Chapman with his partner Nicky Chinn. "Kiss You All Over" was number one for four weeks, and is the fourth most successful Warner Brothers single.

REPRISE

The Kinks

1 LOOK AWAY
Chicago 88

2 SOMETHIN' STUPID
Nancy Sinatra and Frank Sinatra 67

3 EVERYBODY LOVES SOMEBODY
Dean Martin 64

4 HEART OF GOLD
Neil Young 72

5 LOVE SHACK
The B-52's 89

6 THE WRECK OF THE EDMUND FITZGERALD
Gordon Lightfoot 76

7 THESE BOOTS ARE MADE FOR WALKIN'
Nancy Sinatra 66

8 WELCOME BACK
John Sebastian 76

9 MIDNIGHT AT THE OASIS
Maria Muldaur 74

10 STRANGERS IN THE NIGHT
Frank Sinatra 66

11 SUNDOWN
Gordon Lightfoot 74

12 IF I HAD A HAMMER
Trini Lopez 63

13 I WANT TO BE YOUR MAN
Roger 88

14 SAY YOU LOVE ME
Fleetwood Mac 76

15 ROAM
The B-52's 90

Frank Sinatra quit his job as a sports writer for the *New Jersey Observer* after attending a Bing Crosby concert. Signed to Tommy Dorsey's orchestra, he had the top song ("I'll Never Smile Again") on the first singles chart ever published by *Billboard*.

By the end of the 1950s, though, Sinatra was unhappy at Capitol Records and wanted to leave. Not just for another company—he wanted to create his own record label, having also recorded for RCA Victor (with the Tommy Dorsey Orchestra) and Columbia. His contract with Capitol ran through 1962, but the label agreed to let him go if he would record four more albums for them. Sinatra asked a former controller at Verve Records, Mo Ostin, to run his new company as executive vice president. One day, while walking past the Capitol tower on Vine Street in Hollywood, Sinatra said to Ostin, "I helped build that. Now I'm going to build one of my own."

Offices were opened on Melrose Avenue, above a carpet warehouse. At first the roster consisted of Sinatra's friends—Sammy Davis, Jr., Dean Martin and Rosemary Clooney. But despite a top 20 single for Sammy ("What Kind Of Fool Am I") and a top three hit by Lou Monte ("Pepino The Italian Mouse"), the label did not get off to a good start. By the end of 1962, the company was $2 million in debt. In June, 1963, Sinatra's attorney, Mickey Rudin, approached Jack Warner about buying Reprise. Warner wanted

Sinatra to make films for the studio, and a deal was struck. Warner Brothers would buy two-thirds interest in Reprise for $10 million; Sinatra would retain one-third interest and make three movies.

Ostin relocated Reprise to the Burbank offices of Warner Brothers and the merged company became known as Warner-Reprise. The same deal that brought Petula Clark to Warner Brothers from Britain's Pye label gave Reprise access to the Kinks, who debuted in America in 1964 with "You Really Got Me." That same year, Dean Martin gave the label its biggest hit to date with a song previously recorded by Sinatra, "Everybody Loves Somebody." Sinatra continued to record for the label and achieved his own number one hit, "Strangers In The Night," in 1966. His daughter Nancy was also signed to Reprise.

"I wasn't really interested in a career," Nancy told Todd Everett. "I was a happily married young woman, who wanted to be a good wife and raise a family. But when I told my father that I thought I could make a hit record, he said, 'Try it.'" Nancy approached Disney's musical director, Tutti Camarata, and told him she wanted to cut the kind of material that Annette Funicello was recording. "Like I Do" was a hit in other countries but not at home. More singles were produced by Camarata, Don Costa and Jimmy Bowen. "By the end of my first contract, my records weren't selling as well. . . . I reminded Jimmy [Bowen], who was head of A&R at Reprise, that if my next single wasn't something very important, the label was going to drop me." Producer Lee Hazlewood asked Ostin and Bowen to give Nancy another chance and recorded three tracks, including "So Long, Babe." That was Nancy's first chart single in America.

Nancy wanted to follow up "So Long Babe" with a song she heard that had been written for a man to sing, but Hazlewood argued against it. Her father agreed that the song about the boots would be a hit. A year after "These Boots Are Made For Walkin'" was number one, Nancy recorded a duet with Frank. "We cut 'Somethin' Stupid' at the end of a session that dad was cutting with Antonio Carlos Jobim," Nancy told Everett. "We moved those musicians out, and mine in. We recorded the song in two takes." Ostin was in the studio and bet Sinatra two dollars that the song would not make the top 10. The check arrived already framed.

In 1976, the Reprise label was deactivated and most of the artists on the roster, like Fleetwood Mac and Gordon Lightfoot, were moved over to Warner Brothers. The name was kept alive by Neil Young, who continued to have his albums released on Reprise. The label was brought back to life in 1987, as new artists were signed and some Warner Brothers artists were reassigned to Reprise; among them were Roger (Troutman) and Chicago. The latter recorded the most successful Reprise chart single of all time, "Look Away," written by Diane Warren. Other former Warner Brothers acts like the B-52's and the Time were also added to the Reprise roster.

Madonna

At the age of 13, Seymour Stein paid a visit to Tommy Noonan, then head of the *Billboard* charts and research department, and asked permission to copy down in longhand the pop, R&B and country singles charts every week back to the year he was born. Two years later, the project was completed, and when he was 16, the boy with encyclopedic knowledge of the record industry was hired by Noonan to work in the chart department.

Stein left *Billboard* to work for Syd Nathan at King Records, then moved on to Red Bird, where his duties included chaperoning the Shangri-Las. After a stint as an independent promotion man, he formed Sire Productions with record producer Richard Gottehrer (of the Strangeloves) in 1966. Sire signed a distribution deal with Warner Brothers in 1976. In 1978, Stein sold half of his company to Warners; two years later, he sold the other half.

Sire's top 30 chart hits include songs by the Pretenders, Soft Cell, the Climax Blues Band, the Talking Heads, Tommy Page and a woman who uses just her first name—Madonna.

Stein first heard a demo tape from Madonna when he was recovering from endocarditis in the hospital. He listened to the song "Everybody" and told his assistant, Michael Rosenblatt, that he wanted to sign Madonna—right then and there. Stein asked for a new robe to be brought from home while Madonna was on her way to the hospital. "The minute she walked in the room, I knew," Stein said in *Rolling Stone*. "I just sensed that there was something there. I just wanted to rush right in and do a deal."

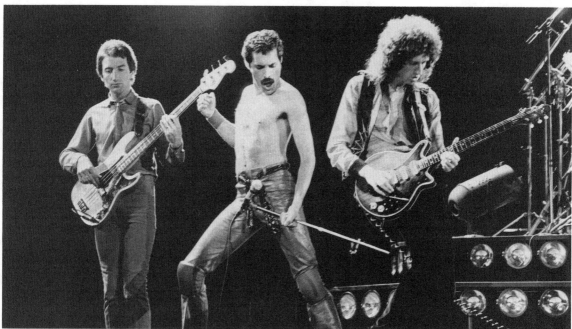

Queen

Jac Holzman was a student at St. John's College in Annapolis, Maryland, when he started Elektra Records in October, 1950, with $600 from his bar mitzvah money and $600 borrowed from a friend.

Jac was equally fascinated with audio engineering and music, and in December of 1950, he approached composer John Gruen and soprano Georgiana Bannister about recording their campus recital. The result was catalog number Elektra 101; although a few hundred copies were pressed, Holzman couldn't sell any of them.

The second Elektra release was an album of Appalachian mountain ballads, and for its first five years of existence the label released about thirty albums, none of which cost more than $45 to produce. Holzman paid the bills by doing hi-fi installations. The turning point came in 1955 when Holzman signed Josh White and Theodore Bikel. The label concentrated on folk music for the rest of the decade. "I expected the folk revival," Holzman told Lenny Kaye. "You could see it begin to happen in the festivals; it was easy music to make, friendly, collegiate."

The artist roster grew with the addition of Tom Paxton, Phil Ochs, Tom Rush and Judy Collins, whose recording of Joni Mitchell's "Both Sides Now" is the anchor recording on the list of top 50 Elektra songs.

It was a small step from folk to folk-rock, but Holzman was cautious and a subsidiary label, Bounty, was created to house acts like the Beefeaters—who would later sign to Columbia Records as the Byrds. Paul Butterfield, who participated in the *What's Shakin'* electric-guitar anthology album, was the first electric artist signed to the acoustic label. Elektra immersed itself in rock and roll after Holzman met Arthur Lee at the Bito Lito club in Los Angeles. His group, Love, was signed to the label, as were another Los Angeles club group—the Doors. Paul Rothchild, who joined the label in 1963, saw the Doors at the Whisky-a-Go-Go on the Sunset Strip and wanted to produce an album that would serve as an "aural commentary" on their live act. "Light My Fire" became Elektra's first number one single.

In July, 1970, Holzman sold his independent company to the Kinney National Services Corporation, then the parent company of Warner Brothers. The label continued to flourish with Bread, Carly Simon and Harry Chapin, but Holzman felt like he was repeating himself and took an extended sabbatical in Hawaii.

David Geffen, founder of Asylum Records, was brought in to run the company in 1973. He brought Asylum with him from Atlantic, another label under the Kinney banner, to form Elektra-Asylum. Two years later, he was named vice-chairman of Warner Brothers Pictures and Joe Smith took the helm. Under Smith's leadership, Elektra was well-represented on the Hot 100 with the Cars, Eddie Rabbitt and Queen.

The Cars were formed by Ric Ocasek and Ben Orr. They met in Columbus, Ohio, and had three earlier bands together before the Cars. Along with Greg Hawkes, Elliot Easton and drummer David Robinson, Ocasek and Orr made their first appearance as the Cars at Pease Air Force Base in New Hampshire on New Year's Eve, 1976. Two Boston radio stations popularized their demo tape of "Just What I Needed," which landed them a contract with Elektra.

Eddie Rabbitt, raised in East Orange, New Jersey, wrote his first published song while soaking in a bath in a Nashville hotel. "Working My Way Up To The Bottom" was recorded by Roy Drusky. Elvis Presley cut his "Kentucky Rain" in 1970, which led artists like Ronnie Milsap, Tom Jones and Dr. Hook covering Eddie's material. Elektra signed him in 1974.

The label's top two chart singles are both by Queen. Originally formed in 1971 in Middlesex, England, the band had their first American chart single with "Killer Queen" in 1975. "Crazy Little Thing Called Love" was a number two hit in Britain before it was released in the States. "We all felt it was a hit, except Elektra, who didn't want to release it," says lead singer Freddie Mercury. Radio stations started playing import copies. "That forced the single," according to Mercury. The follow-up was "Play The Game," but it peaked at number 42. Michael Jackson urged Freddie to release "Another One Bites The Dust" as the next single. It is Elektra's most successful chart hit to date.

The Eagles

After working as an usher at CBS and as a receptionist for a TV production company, 20-year-old David Geffen was hired to work in the mailroom of the William Morris agency in New York. He worked for William Morris until he was 23, then moved to the Ashley Famous agency. After hearing a tape of Laura Nyro he took her on as a client and made a deal with Clive Davis to sign her to Columbia. Then Geffen opened his own agency with Elliott Roberts, and in 1969 sold Nyro's publishing company to Columbia for $4.5 million worth of CBS stock, splitting the proceeds with her fifty-fifty. That same year, he engineered the deal that put Crosby, Stills and Nash on Atlantic.

Geffen's next two clients were Joni Mitchell and Jackson Browne. Mitchell was recording for Reprise and Browne needed a record deal. Geffen approached Ahmet Ertegun at Atlantic, but he wasn't interested. Geffen was inspired to start his own label. He convinced Atlantic to finance Asylum Records for three years in return for a share of the profits. In the second year of the deal he released Linda Ronstadt, Jackson Browne, the Eagles, and Joni Mitchell.

Two years into the Atlantic deal, Warner Communications chairman Steve Ross told Geffen to name a price for his label. Within 24 hours, Geffen sold Asylum for $5 million in Warner stock and $2 million cash. Elektra Records' Jac Holzman stepped down in 1973, and Warner was willing to merge Elektra and Asylum with Geffen overseeing both labels.

In 1975, Geffen was given another promotion: he was named vice-chairman of Warner Brothers Pictures.

Whitesnake

After a year as vice-chairman of Warner Brothers Pictures, David Geffen left the job. "I had to deal with bureaucracy and politics," he said in *Time*. "It just didn't work." Soon after leaving the post, he was diagnosed with cancer of the bladder. He spent the next four years collecting art and teaching at UCLA and Yale. Then he was told the original diagnosis had been incorrect. The tumor thought to be malignant had actually been benign, and there was no cancer. He took a trip to Barbados with Paul Simon and television producer Lorne Michaels and was advised to begin again in a field he already knew well: the record industry. Two days later, Warner Communications CEO Steve Ross agreed to finance a new record company headed by Geffen.

The label had no name when Geffen announced its creation in the May 15, 1980, issue of *Rolling Stone*. "I'm going to have a specialized, small record company," Geffen said in an article. "I think we'll be attractive both to established artists and new ones. . . . I think that I have a long history of being involved with the most creative, intelligent and productive artists, and I believe people will be attracted to what that's all about."

In mid-June, Geffen announced his first signing for his new label, which still didn't have a name. He paid $1.5 million for Donna Summer, who was suing her former company, Casablanca. Geffen said in an August 7, 1980 *Rolling Stone* news story, "Before I had announced the label, Donna called up and said, 'I hear you're starting a record company. Would you be interested in me?' And you know, of course, I thought it was a fake." The same article mentioned rumors of Geffen signing Jackson Browne, Elton John, Joni Mitchell and Neil Young. With the exception of Browne, he signed them all.

Elton was the second artist signed to the label, finally named after its founder. Then Yoko Ono called and Geffen had his third artist: John Lennon was ready to come out of retirement. "(Just Like) Starting Over" became a posthumous number one song and Geffen's most successful chart single.

Geffen stepped back from the day-to-day duties of running a record company. "I started to feel I was getting too old to go to clubs and hang out with teenagers and find music for their generation—I was no longer of their generation," Geffen said in *Forbes*. He relied on label president Ed Rosenblatt to helm the company and John Kalodner, Gary Gersh and Tom Zutaut to run the A&R department. Kalodner signed Aerosmith and thought Cher was ready to return to the charts; Zutaut brought in Guns n' Roses. Geffen wasn't completely removed from the process, however. He managed to sign Peter Gabriel and Ric Ocasek of the Cars.

The company also made major investments in Broadway musicals, including *Dreamgirls, Cats* and *Miss Saigon,* and did the same with motion pictures like *Risky Business, After Hours* and *Beetlejuice.*

In 1989, Time-Life and Warner merged into one company. *Forbes* reported that in addition to Steve Ross making $100 million in the deal, people like Steven Spielberg, Clint Eastwood and Barbra Streisand received generous stock options. "One of the things that really offended me was when I found out he had given these friends of his these stock options," Geffen said in *Forbes*. "Steve always told me that when the company got sold, he would buy my record company and I would be there for the ride. . . . But in the end no one thought that I should be included in the benefits from the success of the company." With his distribution agreement with Time Warner set to expire at the end of 1990, Geffen sold his record company in March of that same year. He spurned bids from Time Warner and Thorn EMI in favor of a deal with MCA that paid him $545 million in stock and gave him a 12 percent stake in MCA.

The deal became even sweeter eight months later when MCA was sold to Matsushita Electric Industrial Co. of Japan for $6.6 billion—Geffen netted $710 million from the deal. "It was smart to sell to MCA, but it was lucky that the Japanese bought it eight months later," Geffen said in *Vanity Fair*. "I had nothing whatever to do with it. The focus is only on me because I was the major beneficiary financially."

Ray Charles

1 AT THE HOP
Danny & the Juniors *ABC-Paramount* 58

2 DIANA
Paul Anka *ABC-Paramount* 57

3 I CAN'T STOP LOVING YOU
Ray Charles *ABC-Paramount* 62

4 LONELY BOY
Paul Anka *ABC-Paramount* 59

5 STAGGER LEE
Lloyd Price *ABC-Paramount* 59

6 YOU DON'T HAVE TO BE A STAR (TO BE IN MY SHOW)
Marilyn McCoo and Billy Davis, Jr. *ABC* 77

7 BAD, BAD LEROY BROWN
Jim Croce *ABC* 73

8 DIZZY
Tommy Roe *ABC* 69

9 BEFORE THE NEXT TEARDROP FALLS
Freddy Fender *ABC/Dot* 75

10 PUT YOUR HEAD ON MY SHOULDER
Paul Anka *ABC-Paramount* 59

11 PERSONALITY
Lloyd Price *ABC-Paramount* 59

12 TIME IN A BOTTLE
Jim Croce *ABC* 73

13 A ROSE AND A BABY RUTH
George Hamilton IV *ABC-Paramount* 56

14 (HEY WON'T YOU PLAY) ANOTHER SOMEBODY DONE SOMEBODY WRONG SONG
B.J. Thomas *ABC* 75

15 PRETTY BLUE EYES
Steve Lawrence *ABC-Paramount* 60

Back in the "old" days of broadcasting, all three of America's television networks were affiliated with record labels. Columbia Records was owned by the Columbia Broadcasting System; RCA was a subsidiary of the Radio Corporation of America, as was NBC; and ABC-Paramount Records shared the same parent company as ABC-TV, American Broadcasting-Paramount Theaters, Inc.

The impending creation of the ABC-Paramount label was first announced in the February 5, 1955, issue of *Billboard*. Datelined Hollywood, the story reported the parent company was planning a division expected to enter the record market.

By November, the label was a reality. Sam Clark was the president and Don Costa was director of A&R. *Billboard* reported that the label's initial single was a "dramatic rush affair." Eydie Gorme recorded a cover of Bubber Johnson's R&B song "Come Home" on October 20, and it was in the hands of disc jockeys on October 24. ABC wanted the pop hit on Johnson's song, but they needn't have hurried—it didn't chart, although Eydie did have a run of chart singles on the label. Husband Steve Lawrence had top 10 hits on ABC with "Pretty Blue Eyes" and "Footsteps."

ABC-Paramount's first number one hit was by a 15-year old boy from Ottawa in Ontario, Canada. Paul Anka had spent the summer in Los Angeles when he was 13 and dropped by the offices of Modern Records in Culver City. He recorded a single for them, but it didn't make it, and he returned home to Ottawa. The following summer, he won a Campbell's Soup contest; the prize was a train trip to Manhattan. He loved the city, and later borrowed $100 from his father to return with four new songs. The first person he went to see was Costa, who was so impressed with "Diana" that he told Paul to have his parents come to New York immediately so they could sign contracts. "Diana" is ABC's second most successful chart single. Anka, who has seven singles listed in ABC's top 50, left the label in 1962 for RCA.

Four months later, ABC-Paramount was back on top of the *Billboard* chart with the first chart entry from a Philadelphia quartet, Danny & the Juniors. Their song was originally written as "Do The Bop," but Dick Clark advised them that bop was passe, and suggested changing it to "At The Hop." Good advice: the song is ABC's most successful chart single.

In 1959, ABC-Paramount scored a coup by signing Ray Charles away from Atlantic Records. Ray told Ahmet Eretegun about ABC's generous offer, but Atlantic couldn't match it. Working with Sid Feller of ABC's A&R department, Charles first recorded for the label on December 29, 1959. There are five Ray Charles singles on the ABC top 50, including the label's third most successful chart song, "I Can't Stop Loving You."

Feller also worked with Lloyd Price, who had a number one hit with "Stagger Lee." Other artists who recorded for ABC-Paramount include the Impressions, George Hamilton IV, Tommy Roe and Brian Hyland.

The label's name was shortened to ABC in 1966. In its final decade, the label had a roster that included Jim Croce, B.J. Thomas, Bo Donaldson & the Heywoods and two acts managed by Irving Azoff—Steely Dan and Jimmy Buffett. The label also purchased the masters of Dot Records from Gulf + Western, and issued recordings by Freddy Fender and Donna Fargo on ABC/Dot.

The demise of ABC Records came suddenly on March 5, 1979, when all 300 employees were dismissed. A month before, MCA had bought the company for a reported price of $20 million. *Rolling Stone* reported that ABC staffers had been told up to the "very last minute" that the ABC label would remain autonomous from MCA. Instead, the roster was pared down, and those acts invited to remain were shifted to the MCA label. Regarding the future of his two ABC acts, Azoff was quoted, "We'll have to wait and see, but anything's better than ABC." John Hartmann, manager of Poco, said he had been dealing "with a lack of corporate commitment." He reported that ABC refused to give Poco a $17,000 advance to support a tour. Bob Siner, president of MCA Records at the time, advanced the amount by 10 A.M. on March 5, the day Poco became an MCA act.

Chubby Checker

Songwriters Kal Mann and Bernie Lowe formed the Cameo label in Philadelphia at the end of 1956. Their first signing was a 20-year old local singer who had starred in a 13-week TV series on a Pittsburgh station. Charlie Gracie sounded enough like Elvis to record Mann and Lowe's Presley-styled "Butterfly." Andy Williams released a cover version on Cadence, but Gracie had the bigger chart hit.

The company made the top 40 with comedian Timmie Rogers' "Back To School Again," but their next major hit was licensed from another label. The Rays had already recorded for Chess when they signed with Frank Slay's XYZ Records. Cameo licensed the doo-wop classic "Silhouettes," the Rays' only top 40 single.

In 1958, Cameo scored with singles by John Zacherle and Dave Appell's Applejacks. Zacherle, known as the "Cool Ghoul," hosted horror movies on WCAU-TV in Philadelphia. Appell was one of the label's most important signings, as he went on to write hits for the artists would who form the Cameo label's foundation in the early '60s.

Lowe and Mann expanded the company in 1959 by adding a second label, Parkway. Two important artists had their first chart entries that year—Robert Ridarelli and Ernest Evans. Ridarelli was in a band called Rocco & the Saints with Frankie Avalon. His first two singles—"Please Don't Be Mad" and "All I Want Is You"—failed to make the chart, but by the time "Kissin' Time" entered the Hot 100 in June, everyone knew the name Bobby Rydell. Ernest Evans was a chicken plucker working in a poultry market who was introduced to Kal Mann by his boss. Ernest's first single, "The Class," featured him impersonating Elvis Presley, Fats Domino and Ricky Nelson. His next two singles—"Whole Lotta Laughin'" and "Dancing Dinosaur"—disappeared without a trace, but his next release became the most successful single of the rock era. Renamed Chubby Checker by Dick Clark's wife Bobbie, he recorded a cover version of Hank Ballard's "The Twist" at Clark's suggestion. That led to a series of other twist songs, like "Let's Twist Again" and "Slow Twistin'," as well as a rash of other dance tunes like "Limbo Rock," "Pony Time," "The Fly," "Popeye The Hitchhiker" and "The Hucklebuck." Checker has 13 songs in Cameo-Parkway's top 50, tied with Bobby Rydell for the most hits by one artist on the label.

"Slow Twistin'" helped launch another successful career on Cameo. Dee Dee Sharp, signed to the company when she was 16, had been singing background vocals until she was brought to the front to duet with Checker on "Slow Twistin'." That song was recorded at 4:00 in the afternoon. After a dinner break, Dee Dee returned to the studio without Chubby and recorded a dance hit of her own, "Mashed Potato Time." The single spent two weeks at number two and the follow-up was icing on the cake: "Gravy (For My Mashed Potatoes)" peaked at number nine. Dee Dee's next two releases also made the top 10: "Raide!" and "Do The Bird."

Cameo-Parkway signed two groups in 1960. Dave Appell, placed in charge of A&R for the label, signed the Cashmeres. They were renamed the Dovells and hit with yet another dance song, "Bristol Stomp." It was number two for two weeks. Len Barry, lead singer of the Dovells, recommended a group called the Orlons to the label, and they had their first hit with their third release, "The Wah-Watusi." It spent two weeks at number two. The Orlons' next two singles, "Don't Hang Up" and "South Street," both made the top five.

The Tymes gave the company a number one single with "So Much In Love" in 1963. But with the onslaught of the Beatles and other British groups in 1964, the Cameo-Parkway star waned. Mann and Lowe sold the label that year to Texas financier William Bowen. The company was moved to New York, and a number of British masters were leased, although only one is listed in the label's top 50: "Cast Your Fate To The Wind" by Sounds Orchestral. Thom Bell and Kenny Gamble were writing and producing at the label, but their talents would blossom elsewhere. Neil Bogart signed artists like Bobby Sherman, Bob Seger, Evie Sands and the Ohio Express as well as a Michigan group that gave the company its final number one hit: "96 Tears" by ? (Question Mark) & the Mysterians. In the summer of '67, Cameo-Parkway was sold to Allen Klein and was absorbed into his ABKCO Industries.

CHRYSALIS

Huey Lewis & the News

C hris Wright was booking college dates for bands and running a blues club in Manchester when he found a band called the Jaybirds, a group that made demos for a music publisher and backed the British pop band Ivy League. "They knew I did bookings on the weekends, and they persuaded me to book them," Wright told Joe Smith in *Off the Record*. "Then they persuaded me to manage them when they got to Manchester." The band was renamed Ten Years After and signed with Decca's Deram label in the U.K.

In December, 1967, Jethro Tull signed on with the agency run by Wright and his partner Terry Ellis. Gary Wright of Spooky Tooth told Chris Blackwell at Island Records about Tull; Blackwell was intrigued. "I found out they were a new band managed by Terry Ellis, who at the time had a partnership with Chris Wright called the Ellis-Wright Agency," Blackwell told Ted Fox in *In the Groove*. "So I tracked him down. I made a deal with Terry Ellis. He wanted to start his own label. I told him that was great, I could really show him how to do it and guide him. He wanted to start it right away with Jethro Tull and I said, 'No, that doesn't make any sense, Island is really hot right now and our name is strong. It will help Jethro Tull to be on Island. What you do is this: when you have five chart entries—records in the top 40—on Jethro Tull or any other acts you bring through on the same deal, we'll start the Chrysalis label. All the acts will then go on Chrysalis.' Needless to say, Terry signed some other acts and worked them really hard and got five chart entries within a matter of a year. Then Chrysalis started and it was with us for about 10 years. Now they are one of our main competitors."

Jethro Tull's first five albums were released in America on Reprise. The first LP on Chrysalis in the States was *Living in the Past* in 1972. The title track is the earliest song on the Chrysalis top 50.

The most successful chart single for Chrysalis is "Call Me" by Blondie, from the film *American Gigolo*. Debbie Harry and Chris Stein first worked together in the Stilettos, a band that had been parodying girl group songs of the '60s. That group gave way to Angel and the Snakes before they renamed themselves after Chic Young's comic book heroine, Blondie. They became popular at the New York punk club CBGBs, and recorded an album with producer Richard Gottehrer that was released on Private Stock.

In August, 1977, Chrysalis bought Blondie's contract from Private Stock for $500,000. Two months later, the label released the *Plastic Letters* album. The single "Denis"—an updating of Randy & the Rainbows' "Denise"—was a European hit, but failed to crack the Hot 100. Blondie's first chart single in the U.S. was the Mike Chapman-produced "Heart Of Glass," which went to number one. "Call Me," produced by Giorgio Moroder, spent six weeks at number one, and was followed by two more chart-toppers: "The Tide Is High" and "Rapture."

The group with the highest number of singles (13) on the Chrysalis top 50 is Huey Lewis & the News. Huey joined the bar band Clover in Northern California in 1972. Manager Jake Riviera signed them to Phonogram's Vertigo label in the U.K. in 1976, where they released one album and backed Elvis Costello on *My Aim Is True*. They split in 1979, and Huey returned to Marin County. Along with some pals who jammed at a club called Uncle Charlie's in Corte Medera, Huey recorded a demo tape as "Huey Lewis and American Express." Manager Bob Brown hated their cover of the Supremes' "Stop! In The Name Of Love," but liked the band well enough to sign them. Only there was no band—just Huey and his friends, who agreed to become "the News." In 1980, they were signed to Chrysalis. With their breakthrough album, *Sports*, and its follow-up, *Fore!*, the News had chart success with songs like "I Want A New Drug," "The Power Of Love," "Stuck With You" and "Jacob's Ladder," the latter three reaching number one on the Hot 100.

Ten of Chrysalis' top 50 songs were recorded by Pat Benatar, an opera-trained singing waitress from Long Island, New York. She was appearing at Catch A Rising Star when club owner Rick Newman suggested he manage her career. Benatar developed a hard-rock vocal style and was signed to Chrysalis in 1978.

DOT

Pat Boone

After Randy Wood left the U.S. Air Force in 1945, he opened up an appliance shop in Gallatin, Tennessee. As a service to his customers, he stocked a few records in the store. Eventually, he was selling so many that he decided to open "Randy's Record Store," and by 1950 he had a huge mail-order following.

Wood bought a small local radio station and advertised his mail-order business. Soon he was spending his time after office hours producing sessions in the station's studio. He released recordings on his own label, Dot, and signed artists like Johnny Maddox, the Griffin Brothers, Margie Day and Mac Wiseman.

In 1952, Dot had its first top 10 single in *Billboard* with "Trying" by the Hilltoppers, a quartet from Western Kentucky College that included future Dot artist Billy Vaughn. In 1954, the Fontane Sisters switched from RCA to Dot and had a top 20 hit, "Happy Days And Lonely Nights." The Fontane Sisters' next chart single was a number one hit, "Hearts Of Stone." In 1955, Dot had top 10 hits with the star of "My Little Margie," Gale Storm, as well as Billy Vaughn and a clean-cut young man originally from Jacksonville, Florida: Pat Boone.

Pat was born Charles Eugene Boone on June 1, 1934, to a family that could trace its lineage back to frontiersman Daniel Boone. He advanced to the final round on Ted Mack's "Original Amateur Hour," but made the mistake of appearing professionally on "Arthur Godfrey's Talent Scouts." His $600 fee from that show disqualified him from winning Mack's amateur talent contest, so Boone lost out on a $6,000 college scholarship.

On his way home from appearing on those shows in New York, Pat stopped in Nashville to visit his parents. His friend Hugh Cherry, a disc jockey at WMAK, introduced him to Randy Wood. Dot's owner had seen Boone on both talent shows, and remarked that he should be making records.

"He called me up in Denton, Texas, in March, 1955, and said, 'I've got a song I want you to record,'" Boone told Jeff Tamarkin in *Goldmine.* "This was eight months after we'd agreed to record and I thought he'd forgotten all about me. He said he had a song he thought was a hit and wanted me to meet him in Chicago. I asked him what the song was and he said it was called 'Two Hearts' by Otis Williams and the Charms."

Boone assumed the R&B song was a ballad. "I get to Chicago and find it's a real rhythm 'n' blues jumper. . . . I tried my best to do it vocally, not having been very familiar with R&B. I tried my best to capture their flavor and feeling, and did."

Like other white pop singers, Boone continued to cover material by black R&B artists. His version of Fats Domino's "Ain't That A Shame" went to number two on the Best Sellers chart.

"Ninety per cent of radio stations in America wouldn't play R&B hits no matter how big they were," says Pat. "To get them on radio, other artists had to do them. I talked to Fats and Little Richard—there was a definite ceiling on how far they could go. When a white artist came along and sang their songs, they were introduced to audiences they couldn't reach themselves."

Wood moved Boone into a broader pop arena with ballads like "Love Letters In The Sand," "April Love" and "Friendly Persuasion." Wood suggested "Love Letters In The Sand" for Boone because so many people requested the song at his record store (Bing Crosby and Rudy Vallee had done earlier versions).

"It's always been a mystery to me why 'Love Letters' had universal appeal," Pat confesses. "There's nothing exciting about the arrangement or the way I sang it." Despite Boone's opinion, the single is Dot's most successful release.

The second most successful chart single on Dot is "The Green Door" by Jim Lowe, who was working in New York as a disc jockey when he wrote "Gambler's Guitar," a million-seller for Rusty Draper in 1953. Three years later, Lowe recorded Marvin Moore and Bob Davie's song.

Dot moved from Gallatin to Hollywood in 1956, and many of the label's biggest hits were leased from other labels: "Come Go With Me" by the Dell-Vikings, "The Fool" by Sanford Clark, "You Cheated" by the Shields, "Susie Darlin'" by Robin Luke, "Pipeline" by the Chantays and "Wipe Out" by the Surfaris.

Wood sold his company to Gulf + Western, owners of Paramount Pictures Corporation, in 1965. Later, the label was sold to ABC Records, which had hits with Donna Fargo and Freddy Fender under the ABC/Dot logo in the '70s. When ABC was sold to MCA, the Dot masters were included in the deal.

Andy Gibb

Robert Stigwood arrived in London from Adelaide, Australia, with less than six pounds in his pocket. He was a door-to-door vacuum cleaner salesman in Notting Hill Gate before finding work in the theater. Then he opened a model agency. One of his clients was an actor who could also sing. John Leyton's cover of "Tell Laura I Love Her" missed the charts, but "Johnny Remember Me" went to number one in the U.K. in 1961.

Stigwood expanded into other areas: he opened a television studio, published magazines and represented Motown in Britain. The companies prospered and then crashed. He was refinanced by people who believed in him, and through them, Stigwood met Brian Epstein, manager of the Beatles. Epstein's company, NEMS, bought the Robert Stigwood Organization with the provision that Stigwood could gain controlling interest. But when Epstein died, the deal fell apart and RSO went its separate way. Stigwood had financial backing from Polygram and had already signed the Bee Gees to a five-year contract.

Hugh Gibb, father of the Gibb brothers, had sent a copy of an Australian album by his sons to the NEMS office in London. Stigwood liked their sound, and within 24 hours of the Gibbs' arrival from Sydney, he arranged an audition for them at London's Savile Theatre.

In addition to the Bee Gees, Stigwood had Cream, perhaps the original "supergroup." Stigwood had represented the Graham Bond Organization, with Jack Bruce on bass and Ginger Baker on drums. Eric Clapton left John Mayall's Bluesbreakers to form Cream with Bruce and Baker, and they were signed to Stigwood's Reaction label in the U.K.

Stigwood also had a financial interest in Tim Rice and Andrew Lloyd Webber's *Jesus Christ Superstar*. He produced the movie version of the Who's *Tommy* and sold the TV series "Beacon Hill" to CBS. And his initials graced a new American label, RSO, distributed in the U.S. by Atlantic. Artists like the Bee Gees, whose records had been released on Atlantic's Atco subsidiary, were transferred to the RSO label, and in 1976, RSO shifted to Polygram.

RSO's golden period began in 1977, first with a number one single from Andy Gibb, and then with the first single from the soundtrack of *Saturday Night Fever*. "How Deep Is Your Love" is the most successful RSO chart single.

In 1978, RSO had a year that most record companies can only dream about. *Saturday Night Fever* produced four number one singles and became the best-selling album to that date. RSO had an unprecedented six consecutive number one singles on the *Billboard* chart, for 21 uninterrupted weeks at the top. There were three more number one songs that year. One was from Andy Gibb, and the other two were from the soundtrack of *Grease*. Parent company Polygram did $1.2 billion in record sales that year, a new high for any record company.

Al Coury, president of the label in America, ran the day-to-day operations for Stigwood. "We're a small, tightknit, young group of people, mostly street-oriented," he told *Rolling Stone* in 1978. "We all come from the practical end of the record business: we either sold, promoted or marketed. So when we do our thinking, we sit around here and put together some thoughts and ideas for a campaign; we think about it from a very practical level. We do things that instinctively feel good to us."

The top six singles on RSO are all from the Gibb family. In addition to "How Deep Is Your Love" at number one, the Bee Gees are also number four with "Stayin' Alive" and number five with "Night Fever." Younger brother Andy is number two with "I Just Want To Be Your Everything," number three with "Shadow Dancing" and number six with "(Love Is) Thicker Than Water."

Ranked number nine is "Disco Duck (Part 1)" by Rick Dees & His Cast of Idiots. Dees was handling the morning-drive shift at WMPS in Memphis when he recorded the song for Fretone, a local label owned by Stax Records co-founder Estelle Axton. When the song became popular in the South, Dees flew to Hollywood to land a deal with a major record label. Everyone passed on the song except for Al Coury, who played it for his kids. When they liked it, he leased "Disco Duck" for $3,500.

BUDDAH

Gladys Knight & the Pips

Neil Bogart (né Bogatz) was born and raised in Brooklyn. He was just 19 when he had his first and only chart record, "Bobby," recorded under the name Neil Scott. Neil joined the promotion department of MGM Records, then moved to Cameo-Parkway as vice president and sales manager. After Allen Klein took over that company, Bogart left for a new label, Buddah.

Buddah had been founded by Art Kass and his partner at Kama Sutra Records, Artie Ripp, as well as two other partners. Kass, who had worked at MGM with Bogart, convinced the others to hire the 24-year-old as the label's general manager.

All of Buddah's earliest hits were bubblegum music, exemplified by the inane lyrics of songs like "Yummy Yummy Yummy" and "Chewy Chewy" by the Ohio Express, and "1, 2, 3, Red Light" and "Indian Giver" by the 1910 Fruitgum Co. The Lemon Pipers didn't want to be a bubblegum group, but they were told to record "Green Tambourine" or be dropped from the label.

As the bubblegum fad faded, Buddah expanded its roster to include other musical styles. Buddah began the '70s with hits from Melanie and the group that Bogart brought from Cameo, the Five Stairsteps. But the label's most important signing happened in January, 1973, when Gladys Knight & the Pips moved over from Motown.

Bogart left Buddah in September, 1973, to move to California and start a new label, Casablanca. Kass remained, and in 1976, the label's parent company, Viewlex, went bankrupt. Kass bought the label back, but eventually found himself $10 million in debt, so Buddah was shut down for good.

THE TOP 30 SONGS ON
CADENCE

Andy Williams

Archie Bleyer was the on-camera bandleader for CBS' variety series "Arthur Godfrey and His Friends" from the program's debut on January 12, 1949, through his dismissal in 1954.

Bleyer had been leading his own dance band for 17 years when he started Cadence in 1952. A month later, the label had its first hit, "Anywhere I Wander"/"This Is Heaven" by Julius LaRosa. Cadence had several pre-rock era hits, including "The Ballad Of Davy Crockett" by Bill Hayes, "Mr. Sandman" by the Chordettes and Bleyer's own recording of "Hernando's Hideaway."

The Chordettes have four songs included in Cadence's top 30 chart hits; Bleyer produced them all.

In 1956, Bleyer signed Andy Williams, who covered Charlie Gracie's "Butterfly." After that one rock and roll outing, Williams turned to softer sounds for his subsequent releases.

Bleyer's most successful act was signed to Cadence in 1957. The Everly Brothers' "Bye Bye Love" peaked at number two, and is the most successful Cadence single on the *Billboard* chart.

The Everly Brothers left Cadence in February, 1960, and signed a million-dollar contract with Warner Brothers Records. Later that year, Johnny Tillotson, a singer from Jacksonville, Florida, had his first top 10 single on Cadence with "Poetry In Motion." Tillotson continued to have hits on Cadence until the label's demise in 1963. Bleyer sold the label's masters to Andy Williams, who released them on his Barnaby label.

1 FLASHDANCE ... WHAT A FEELING
Irene Cara 83

2 DO THAT TO ME ONE MORE TIME
Captain & Tennille 80

3 HOT STUFF
Donna Summer 79

4 Y.M.C.A.
Village People 79

5 BAD GIRLS
Donna Summer 79

6 MANIAC
Michael Sembello 83

7 MACARTHUR PARK
Donna Summer 78

8 FUNKYTOWN
Lipps, Inc. 80

9 LAST DANCE
Donna Summer 78

10 YES, I'M READY
Teri DeSario w/KC 80

11 HEAVEN KNOWS
Donna Summer w/Brooklyn Dreams 79

12 I FEEL LOVE
Donna Summer 77

13 BETH
Kiss 76

14 DIM ALL THE LIGHTS
Donna Summer 79

15 IN THE NAVY
Village People 79

16 ON THE RADIO
Donna Summer 80

17 I WAS MADE FOR LOVIN' YOU
Kiss 79

18 NEW YORK GROOVE
Ace Frehley 79

19 FLASH LIGHT
Parliament 78

20 LET ME LOVE YOU TONIGHT
Pure Prairie League 80

21 TAKE ME HOME
Cher 79

22 WHEN SHE WAS MY GIRL
Four Tops 81

23 ROCK AND ROLL ALL NITE
Kiss 76

24 HARD LUCK WOMAN
Kiss 77

25 CALLING DR. LOVE
Kiss 77

26 TEAR THE ROOF OFF THE SUCKER
Parliament 76

27 DON'T LET ME BE MISUNDERSTOOD
Santa Esmeralda 78

28 BABY MAKES HER BLUE JEANS TALK
Dr. Hook 82

29 THANK GOD IT'S FRIDAY
Love & Kisses 78

30 MACHO MAN
Village People 78

Donna Summer

In 1973, Mo Ostin of Warner Brothers agreed to finance a new label to be run by Neil Bogart of Buddah Records.

The Casablanca label's first important signing was a rock quartet from New York City—Kiss. But Bogart didn't believe that Warner Brothers supported the group, and in September of 1974 Bogart ended the label's affiliation with Warner Brothers.

The label's salvation came with a single from German producer Giorgio Moroder. Donna Summer's erotic "Love To Love You Baby" was released on Moroder's Oasis label through Casablanca. "Love To Love You Baby" helped establish a "new" genre of music—disco.

In 1977, Polygram gave the company a major cash infusion by buying half-interest in the label for $10 million.

Casablanca continued to pump out disco hits, particularly from Summer and a sextet formed by French producer Jacques Morali, the Village People.

Things began to fall apart in 1980. First, Summer sued for $10 million. Then Polygram bought the other 50 percent of Casablanca and, unhappy with diminishing profits, dismissed Bogart.

Casablanca continued under the stewardship of Bruce Bird for the first 10 months after Bogart's departure, and was eventually folded into the Polygram group as another subsidiary. The label's biggest hit came in 1983 with Irene Cara's title song from the movie *Flashdance*.

THE TOP 30 SONGS ON
CHESS

Chuck Berry

Brothers Leonard and Phil Chess, two Jewish immigrants from Poland, settled in Chicago in 1928. In 1947, the Chess brothers started a record company, Aristocrat, specializing in blues, jazz and pop. A blues pianist named Sunnyland Smith showed up for a recording date with a singer from Mississippi, Muddy Waters. He was given some recording time of his own; "I Can't Be Satisfied" was released as a single, and became a hit.

In 1950, the label name was changed to Chess, and material was released by Howlin' Wolf, Elmore James, Rosco Gordon and Willie Dixon.

In 1955, the Chess label signed Sonny Boy Williamson and Chuck Berry. Muddy Waters brought Berry to Phil Chess, who was impressed with Chuck's demo of "Ida Red." Leonard Chess suggested changing the name "Ida Red" to that of a cow in a children's story—Maybellene. "Maybellene" became Chess' first crossover hit, peaking at number five on the pop chart. That began a streak of hits for Berry, including such seminal songs as "Roll Over Beethoven," "School Day," "Rock & Roll Music," "Sweet Little Sixteen" and "Johnny B. Goode."

Leonard Chess died in 1969, and Chess was sold to tape manufacturer GRT. Phil left to manage the family-owned radio station, WVON, and Leonard's son Marshall headed up the Rolling Stones' record label. The Chess masters are now owned by MCA.

Johnnie Taylor

Jim Stewart, a Memphis bank teller who also played the fiddle, wanted to be a record producer. In 1958, he and his sister, Estelle Axton, bought some recording equipment and started Satellite Records in a storeroom 25 miles out of town.

"Someday" by the Veltones was Satellite's first release, but it was an inauspicious start for the label. Stewart moved back to the city in 1960, occupying a vacant theater on McLemore Street.

Stewart's house musicians, the Mar-Keys, gave Satellite its first—and last—national hit with the instrumental "Last Night." Another company claimed the Satellite name, so Jim and Estelle took the first two letters from their last names to form Stax.

The Mar-Keys recorded a couple of impromptu tracks that Stewart liked. He released them under the name Booker T. & the MG's (which stood for "Booker T. Jones and the Memphis Group"), and "Green Onions" peaked at number three. The MG's included Steve Cropper and Donald "Duck" Dunn.

Otis Redding was signed to Stax's new Volt subsidiary in 1962. He was on the brink of stardom when he died in a plane crash on December 10, 1967. Released posthumously, "(Sittin' On) The Dock Of The Bay" became Stax's most successful chart song.

Stax had multiple successes in the early '70s, but by 1974, financial problems did in the company, and the masters were sold to California-based Fantasy Records.

COLPIX

1 JOHNNY ANGEL
Shelley Fabares 62

2 BLUE MOON
The Marcels 61

3 GOODBYE CRUEL WORLD
James Darren 61

4 MY DAD
Paul Petersen 63

5 HER ROYAL MAJESTY
James Darren 62

6 HEY, GIRL
Freddie Scott 63

7 HEARTACHES
The Marcels 61

8 CONSCIENCE
James Darren 62

9 SHE CAN'T FIND HER KEYS
Paul Petersen 62

10 JOHNNY LOVES ME
Shelley Fabares 62

J onie Taps, an executive with Columbia Pictures, suggested to studio head Harry Cohn that the company start a record label so that they could issue their own soundtracks, instead of leasing them to other companies. Offices were opened in the Columbia Pictures building in New York, and Colpix Records was born.

Stu Phillips was hired as head of A&R for the label, and one of his first assignments was to produce a hit for the Skyliners. But when the Marcels unexpectedly showed up from Pittsburgh, Phillips snuck them into the studio late at night. With a few minutes of time left and one more song to record, Phillips produced Colpix's first number one single: a doo-wop version of Rodgers and Hart's "Blue Moon." He later produced hit singles for the teen-aged stars of "The Donna Reed Show," Shelley Fabares ("Johnny Angel") and Paul Petersen ("My Dad").

The name Colpix vanished and was replaced in 1966 by Columbia Pictures' new record label, Colgems.

ISLAND

1 UP WHERE WE BELONG
Joe Cocker and Jennifer Warnes 82

2 WITH OR WITHOUT YOU
U2 87

3 HIGHER LOVE
Steve Winwood 86

4 I STILL HAVEN'T FOUND WHAT I'M LOOKING FOR
U2 87

5 ADDICTED TO LOVE
Robert Palmer 86

6 WHILE YOU SEE A CHANCE
Steve Winwood 81

7 DESIRE
U2 88

8 I DIDN'T MEAN TO TURN YOU ON
Robert Palmer 86

9 THE FINER THINGS
Steve Winwood 87

10 ROMEO
Dino 90

C hris Blackwell started Island Records in Jamaica in 1959. Three years later, he had released two albums and 26 singles. In May of '62, he returned to England and started Island Records in the U.K.

Island's first international success was "My Boy Lollipop" by Millie Small, although Blackwell licensed it to Philips. After seeing the Spencer Davis Group—with 15-year-old Stevie Winwood—in a Birmingham club, he signed them on the spot; when the band broke up in 1967, Winwood and his new group, Traffic, remained with Island.

Blackwell added Cat Stevens, King Crimson, Jethro Tull and Emerson, Lake and Palmer to Island's roster in Britain, and continued to license them to other labels in America. In 1971, Blackwell signed Bob Marley, and two years later, he opened Island Records in the U.S.

Island continued to be strong in the '80s with chart hits by Robert Palmer and U2.

SUN

1. **WHOLE LOT OF SHAKIN' GOING ON**
   Jerry Lee Lewis 57
2. **BLUE SUEDE SHOES**
   Carl Perkins 56
3. **GREAT BALLS OF FIRE**
   Jerry Lee Lewis 58
4. **BREATHLESS**
   Jerry Lee Lewis 58
5. **GUESS THINGS HAPPEN THAT WAY**
   Johnny Cash 58
6. **BALLAD OF A TEENAGE QUEEN**
   Johnny Cash 58
7. **HIGH SCHOOL CONFIDENTIAL**
   Jerry Lee Lewis 58
8. **I WALK THE LINE**
   Johnny Cash 56
9. **THE WAYS OF A WOMAN IN LOVE**
   Johnny Cash 58
10. **WHAT'D I SAY**
    Jerry Lee Lewis 61

In 1950, former engineer and disk jockey Sam Phillips founded the Memphis Recording Service, the first permanent studio in the city. Many local black artists used the studio, including Bobby Bland, Howlin' Wolf and Jackie Brenston (who recorded what many consider to be the first rock and roll record—"Rocket 88"—in Phillips' studio). In 1952, Phillips started his own label, Sun Records, releasing singles by Rufus Thomas, Little Milton, Junior Parker and the Prisonaires. The first hit was Rufus Thomas' "Bear Cat," an answer song to Big Mama Thornton's recording of "Hound Dog."

Phillips' future was assured one summer day in July, 1953, when Elvis Presley stopped in on his lunch hour to record a couple of songs for his mother. Sun released five singles by Elvis between July, 1954 and November, 1955 before selling Presley's contract to RCA. Phillips used the income to invest in the Holiday Inn chain as well as other up-and-coming artists: Carl Perkins, Jerry Lee Lewis, Johnny Cash and Roy Orbison.

20TH CENTURY

1. **I LIKE DREAMIN'**
   Kenny Nolan 77
2. **LOVE'S THEME**
   Love Unlimited Orchestra 74
3. **DO YOU WANNA MAKE LOVE**
   Peter McCann 77
4. **BIGGEST PART OF ME**
   Ambrosia 80
5. **SOMETIMES WHEN WE TOUCH**
   Dan Hill 78
6. **NEVER, NEVER GONNA GIVE YA UP**
   Barry White 74
7. **THE MORNING AFTER**
   Maureen McGovern 73
8. **HEARTBEAT-IT'S A LOVEBEAT**
   DeFranco Family f/Tony DeFranco 73
9. **NEVER KNEW LOVE LIKE THIS BEFORE**
   Stephanie Mills 80
10. **KUNG FU FIGHTING**
    Carl Douglas 74

In the late '50s, 20th Century Fox followed the practice of other movie studios and started its own record label. Before it was shut down, two of its biggest hits were "Navy Blue" by Diane Renay and "The Little Drummer Boy" by the Harry Simeone Chorale. In 1972, Fox president Gordon Stulberg launched the 20th Century label, and hired Russ Regan away from MCA's Uni label to run the company. Regan had released a Love Unlimited album on Uni; he brought the female trio to 20th Century and signed their mentor, Barry White. He also licensed Carl Douglas' "Kung Fu Fighting" for U.S. release.

In 1974, Regan issued an album by the Eleventh Hour, the brainchild of Bob Crewe and Kenny Nolan. Nolan went on to record as a solo artist, giving the label its biggest hit with "I Like Dreamin'."

20th Century went out of business when Marvin Davis bought the film studio and decided he didn't want to be in the record business. He sold the company's assets to Polygram.

VEE JAY

1. **BIG GIRLS DON'T CRY**
   The Four Seasons 62
2. **SHERRY**
   The Four Seasons 62
3. **DUKE OF EARL**
   Gene Chandler 62
4. **WALK LIKE A MAN**
   The Four Seasons 63
5. **HE WILL BREAK YOUR HEART**
   Jerry Butler 60
6. **RAINDROPS**
   Dee Clark 61
7. **PLEASE PLEASE ME**
   The Beatles 64
8. **CANDY GIRL**
   The Four Seasons 63
9. **EVERY BEAT OF MY HEART**
   The Pips 61
10. **LET IT BE ME**
    Jerry Butler and Betty Everett 64

In 1953, Vivian Carter and her husband Jimmy Bracken formed the Vee Jay label to produce gospel recordings. They signed Maceo Smith, the Staple Singers and the Swan Silvertones, and converted their garage into a rehearsal studio. The label had its first hit in 1954 with the Spaniels' "Goodnite Sweetheart, Goodnite," a song covered for the pop chart by the McGuire Sisters. More success came with the Impressions and Dee Clark, whose earliest hits were on Vee Jay's Falcon subsidiary.

Vee Jay first went to number one on the Hot 100 with "Duke Of Earl" by Gene Chandler, in 1962.

Vee Jay's biggest success came from signing the Four Seasons in August, 1962. But in December, 1963, the Seasons left Vee Jay because of legal disputes over royalty payments, and moved to Philips. Vee Jay won the right to release Beatles singles in America when Capitol passed on some early songs, but the label never recovered from the loss of the Four Seasons and the Beatles, and finally had to shut its doors.

VIRGIN

1. **BACK TO LIFE**
   Soul II Soul (f/Caron Wheeler) 89
2. **ROLL WITH IT**
   Steve Winwood 88
3. **STRAIGHT UP**
   Paula Abdul 89
4. **OPPOSITES ATTRACT**
   Paul Abdul w/the Wild Pair 90
5. **FOREVER YOUR GIRL**
   Paula Abdul 89
6. **COLD HEARTED**
   Paula Abdul 89
7. **HEART AND SOUL**
   T'Pau 87
8. **(IT'S JUST) THE WAY THAT YOU LOVE ME**
   Paula Abdul 89
9. **THE WAY YOU DO THE THINGS YOU DO**
   UB40 90
10. **CAN'T STOP**
    After 7 90

Mike Oldfield was turned down by several British record companies when he proposed recording a 50-minute instrumental composition. He finally received financial backing from Richard Branson, owner of the Virgin record stores chain, who was planning to start his own label. That label was launched in May, 1973 with Oldfield's *Tubular Bells*. At first, Virgin would lease its artists to other American labels; as the Virgin empire grew to include an airline, so the roster grew to include Culture Club, Heaven 17, UB40 and Simple Minds.

Branson started talking to Jordan Harris of A&M Records about heading up the Virgin label in America as early as 1984. In '86, Harris approached a former A&M colleague, Jeff Ayeroff of Warner Brothers, about running the company with him, and the next year, they scored their first number one single on the Hot 100—Cutting Crew's "(I Just) Died In Your Arms."

Harris and Ayeroff outbid Island Records and signed Steve Winwood to a reported $13 million contract in February, 1987.

THE CHARTS

This section opens with The Top 100 Debut Songs, based on an artist's first appearance on the *Billboard* chart. The next two charts look at where a single debuted on the Hot 100. The first survey includes all songs that debuted at number 40 or higher. Today, a record company can manipulate a high debut by building up airplay over a period of weeks prior to a single's commercial release. "U Can't Touch This" by M.C. Hammer debuted at number 27 because of massive airplay that preceded the single's availability in stores. Two decades back, when "Let It Be" debuted at number six, it was the result of airplay and sales exploding at the same time. Following this chart is one that only includes songs that started at the bottom— literally. Proving that it's not impossible to overcome the odds, The Top 100 Songs That Debuted At Number 100 includes six singles that entered the chart at number 100 and eventually moved to number one.

One-hit wonders have been a topic for conversation among record enthusiasts for years; Wayne Jancik related many fascinating stories about them in *The Billboard Book of One-Hit Wonders*. Most recording artists don't plan to be one-hit wonders, but the curse strikes anyway. Being on the list of Top 100 One-Hit Wonders is a left-handed compliment; it says you were the best at having the shortest career.

It's a rare Hot 100 that doesn't include one or more remakes of previous hits. The next four charts focus on the most successful remakes of songs that were originally recorded after the rock era began in 1955, the biggest remakes of songs originally recorded before the rock era began, and the top remakes of Motown and Beatles songs.

Motion pictures were a source of hit songs long before the rock era began. One look at the Top 100 Songs From Motion Pictures proves that music and movies have been compatible in the age of rock and roll. The best example is the enormously successful *Saturday Night Fever*. That movie yielded four number one songs and resulted in the best-selling album of all time until *Thriller* came along. The theater has traditionally been another valuable source of hit songs, but the marriage of rock and the Broadway stage hasn't proved quite as successful.

The last chart in this section is based on songs where the lead singer's identity isn't revealed in the artist's name. The reason might be as simple as the fact that Teddy Pendergrass was the vocalist for the Blue Notes, not Harold Melvin. But there can also be some deception at work, as in the case of Darlene Love singing "He's A Rebel" instead of the Crystals, or Brad Howell and Johnny Davis not being identified as the real voices of Milli Vanilli.

THE TOP 100
DEBUT SONGS

Debby Boone

The list of top 100 debut songs includes the first *Billboard* chart entry by those artists who went on to have at least one more single make the chart. This eliminated all one-hit wonders, which by their definition must also be "debut" records. Artists who had made the charts before the rock era were disqualified—it would seem silly to include Bing Crosby or Frank Sinatra on the list, when they clearly made their debuts before 1955. Solo artists who had charted previously in groups were also not considered. Lionel Richie's first solo effort away from the Commodores should not be considered his debut on the Hot 100. And an artist who appeared on the chart under a different name was only counted the first time—so Simon and Garfunkel's debut was "Hey, Schoolgirl" recorded as Tom and Jerry in 1957, not "The Sounds of Silence" which went to number one in 1966. The only charts consulted were the Best Sellers in Stores (1955-58) and the Hot 100 (1958-90) lists. An artist who had previous hits on the R&B, Country or Adult Contemporary charts was still considered with their first single on the pop chart.

If there's one thing a new artist doesn't have, it's name value. There are exceptions; Andy Gibb wasn't a totally unknown entity when he released "I Just Want To Be Your Everything," because his three older brothers had been having hits for 10 years. Wilson Phillips were a new trio when "Hold On" was issued in 1990, but being related to a Beach Boy and a Mama and a Papa gave them instant identification. Tab Hunter was already a well-known actor when he covered "Young Love," and Ricky Nelson was appearing every week on his parents' television show when "A Teenager's Romance" came out on Verve. But names like Paul Anka, Mariah Carey and Christopher Cross meant nothing to radio when their first singles were released.

Still, some artists have managed to make breakthroughs. The second highest-ranking debut song is "You Light Up My Life" from Debby Boone. A cover version of the song performed by Kacey Cisyk in the movie *You Light Up My Life*, it spent 10 weeks at number one in 1977. Debby had previously recorded with her sisters on Motown as the Pat Boone Family, releasing a version of "Please Mr. Postman" almost simultaneously with the Carpenters. The Boones lost that cover battle, but Debby more than made up for it with her first chart entry. Unfortunately, she couldn't sustain her chart success. The follow-up to "You Light Up My Life" was "California," which peaked at number 50. She had only one more chart entry after that, the two-sided "God Knows"/"Baby, I'm Yours," which faltered at number 74.

Number three on the top 100 debut songs is one of the most auspicious beginnings in chart history. Elvis Presley had five singles released on the Sun label between July, 1954, and November, 1955. None made the pop chart, although "Baby Let's Play House"/"I'm Left, You're Right, She's Gone" went to number 10 on the country & western chart, and "Mystery Train" went to number one on that same chart. Elvis' first RCA release was a song written by Mae Boren Axton and Tommy Durden (Elvis also received co-writing credit). Axton handled public relations for Col. Tom Parker in Florida. When Parker became Elvis' manager, Mae told the singer: "You need a million seller, and I'm going to write it for you." When Durden showed her a page one newspaper story about a suicide victim who left a note reading "I walk a lonely street," Mae suggested they place a heartbreak hotel at the end of that street. In 22 minutes, they had written "Heartbreak Hotel."

The Beatles had different debut singles in the U. K. and the U. S. "Love Me Do" was their first chart single at home, where it peaked at number 17. Next was "Please Please Me," which went to number two. Then "From Me To You" became their first number one song. "She Loves You" and "I Want To Hold Your Hand" followed, both topping the U. K. chart. In America, the first four singles were duds until Capitol released "I Want To Hold Your Hand."

Other artists also have different debuts in Britain and America. Eurythmics first appeared on the U. K. chart in July, 1981, with "Never Gonna Cry Again," more than two years before "Sweet Dreams (Are Made Of This)" showed up on the Hot 100. Sinead O'Connor also had a two-year head start in the U. K. with "Mandinka" in January, 1988. "Nothing Compares 2 U" debuted on the *Billboard* chart in March, 1990. And Sheena Easton's first British hit was "Modern Girl," released in the States after "Morning Train (Nine To Five)."

Many artists besides Debby Boone and the Beatles had released singles before they had an entry on the Hot 100. Sam Cooke was the lead singer of the Soul Stirrers from 1950-56, and he recorded for Specialty as Dale Cook before moving to Keen and releasing "You Send Me." Rod Stewart recorded "Good Morning Little Schoolgirl" for the British Decca label in 1964 and Sam Cooke's "Shake" for an EMI label in 1966. Daryl Dragon and Toni Tennille recorded "The Way I Want To Touch You" for their own Butterscotch Castle label before signing with A&M and releasing "Love Will Keep Us Together." The Doors' "Break On Through" was a hit in their native Los Angeles, but they didn't debut on the Hot 100 until they released the follow-up, "Light My Fire." And the Jackson Five released a couple of singles on a local Gary, Indiana, label called Steeltown before moving to Motown and recording "I Want You Back."

Some of the artists included in the top 100 debut songs had relatively short chart careers after getting off to such a promising start. Bobby Lewis followed "Tossin' and Turnin'" with one top 10 hit ("One Track Mind"), and then only had two singles make the bottom portion of the chart. The Knack were promoted as the greatest new group since the Beatles, but "My Sharona" was followed by "Good Girls Don't" (number 11) and then three more minor hits. Phil Spector took the Teddy Bears to Imperial after "To Know Him Is To Love Him" was a number one hit on Dore. The good news was that both sides of their first Imperial single charted. The bad news was that they peaked at number 91 and 98, and never made the chart again. Phil did all right, though, and so did lead singer Annette Kleinbard, who changed her name to Carol Connors and wrote hits like "Hey Little Cobra" for the Rip Chords, "With You I'm Born Again" for Billy Preston and Syreeta and "Gonna Fly Now (Theme From 'Rocky')" with Bill Conti.

Artists conspicuously absent from the list include performers who debuted with a low-charting single and hit their peak later in their chart career. The Supremes aren't included because "Where Did Our Love Go" was their sixth single. "Your Heart Belongs To Me" was their first *Billboard* chart entry, and it went all the way to number 95. The Four Seasons were known as the Four Lovers when they appeared on the chart with "You're The Apple Of My Eye" in 1956, just over six years before "Sherry" went to number one. The Rolling Stones' first American single was a remake of Buddy Holly's "Not Fade Away"; it only went to number 48. "(I Can't Get No) Satisfaction" was their eighth chart entry. And as the National Academy of Recording Arts and Sciences pointed out when Whitney Houston failed to qualify for Best New Artist in 1985, she had already made the chart when she recorded "Hold Me," a duet with Teddy Pendergrass, in 1984.

Bob Seger & the Silver Bullet Band

Every week when *Billboard* publishes the Hot 100 singles, the song that is the highest new entry is designated the "Hot Shot Debut." Where a song enters on the chart is determined first, by the amount of airplay it receives, and second, by how many copies—if any—it has sold in its first week.

Radio stations that play contemporary hit music in the United States add new titles to their playlists each week—generally on Tuesday. In the first week of airplay, a single is usually not listed in the "top 30" songs that station is playing, but is considered an "extra." Within a week or two, depending on how popular the song is, it will debut on the station's survey and begin to move up the chart. *Billboard* keeps track of where that song is listed in the station's top 30 in order to determine airplay.

The more stations that add a record in its first week of release, the higher that song will debut on the Hot 100. "If every station in the country added your record, it would still be considered an 'add,' because very few stations are going to add it with a number (on their survey) out of the box," explains Michael Ellis, Director of Charts for *Billboard*. "So you might enter the chart in the high 30s if you got almost every station in the country, or the mid-30s if you got every single station to add it."

Ellis elaborates why a record would be prevented from debuting even higher than the mid-30s. "You're not going to get any sales points your first week. Maybe in the days of the Beatles, people would wait in the store for the record to come in, and they'd run out with it the minute the shipment arrived. Today, that happens to some degree with albums that will sell the second they hit the stores. People do wait for a new album by a certain superstar, and we've had some albums debut at number one. But for a single, almost inevitably, it's not going to get in all the stores the same day—and singles don't command the rabid fans the way albums do."

A single must be commercially available in order to appear on the Hot 100. "*Billboard*'s policy is that if a single is going on the stores that week, it can debut," Ellis confirms. "So in some cases, a new single may have no points at all from the stores."

There are exceptions to every rule, of course, and seven exceptional singles in the history of the Hot 100 have debuted in the top 20. The highest debut of all time is "Let It Be" by the Beatles, which entered the chart at number six on March 21, 1970. Tied for second place are two more Beatles singles. "Hey Jude," the most successful single to debut in the top 40, entered at number 10 on September 14, 1968. The follow-up, "Get Back," also entered at number 10, on May, 10, 1969. The next highest debut is "Mrs. Brown You've Got A Lovely Daughter" by Herman's Hermits. The single stormed onto the Hot 100 at number 12 on April 17, 1965. The only other singles to debut in the top 20 are "Something" by the Beatles, "Imagine" by John Lennon and "Thriller" by Michael Jackson. All entered at number 20, and the latter two had extensive airplay as album tracks before being released as singles.

Entering the chart in a high position does not automatically assure a single of going to number one. "Imagine" stopped at number three, probably for the same reason it had debuted at number 20. It had received so much airplay prior to its release that by the time it was a 45, the song was close to "burning out," so radio stations began to drop it from their playlists. It only spent nine weeks on the Hot 100, an unusually short term for a top three record.

Exactly 46 singles that debuted in the top 40 went on to become number one records; another 14 reached number two, and 11 peaked at number three. At the opposite end of the scale, some singles that debuted in the top 40 never even made the top 10. Most singles that have high debuts are new releases from proven artists. Radio stations in the U.S. would be inclined to add a new Madonna single in its first week of release, whereas a new single by an unknown artist—no matter how good the record is—would probably not get so much immediate airplay from as many radio stations. The songs that had high debuts and then failed to penetrate the top 10 were probably added to many radio stations right away because the artist had a track record, but then the songs fell short of the mark when it came to sales.

The song that fell the shortest is Paul Anka's "(All Of a Sudden)

66	STATE OF SHOCK [30]		
	The Jacksons *Epic* 84		
67	HELLO AGAIN [32]		
	Neil Diamond *Capitol* 81		
68	MISS ME BLIND [40]		
	Culture Club *Epic/Virgin* 84		
69	JACOB'S LADDER [40]		
	Huey Lewis & the News *Chrysalis* 87		
70	THE LONG RUN [33]		
	Eagles *Asylum* 80		
71	LONELY OL' NIGHT [40]		
	John Cougar Mellencamp *Riva* 85		
72	SATISFIED [39]		
	Richard Marx *EMI* 89		
73	I HEAR A SYMPHONY [39]		
	The Supremes *Motown* 65		
74	THE LONG AND WINDING ROAD/FOR YOU BLUE [35]		
	The Beatles *Apple* 70		
75	ALL THOSE YEARS AGO [33]		
	George Harrison *Dark Horse* 81		
76	PAPERBACK WRITER [28]		
	The Beatles *Capitol* 66		
77	BAD [40]		
	Michael Jackson *Epic* 87		
78	(SWEET SWEET BABY) SINCE YOU'VE BEEN GONE [31]		
	Aretha Franklin *Atlantic* 68		
79	CHERISH [37]		
	Madonna *Sire* 89		
80	I JUST CAN'T STOP LOVING YOU [37]		
	Michael Jackson and Siedah Garrett *Epic* 87		
81	REAL LOVE [40]		
	Doobie Brothers *Warner Bros* 80		
82	BLACK CAT [37]		
	Janet Jackson *A&M* 90		
83	IT'S RAINING AGAIN [31]		
	Supertramp *A&M* 82		
84	REVOLUTION [38]		
	The Beatles *Apple* 68		
85	LADY MADONNA [23]		
	The Beatles *Capitol* 68		
86	TRUE BLUE [40]		
	Madonna *Sire* 86		
87	IMAGINE [20]		
	John Lennon/Plastic Ono Band *Apple* 71		
88	THRILLER [20]		
	Michael Jackson *Epic* 84		
89	NOWHERE MAN [25]		
	The Beatles *Capitol* 66		
90	HE'LL HAVE TO STAY [37]		
	Jeanne Black *Capitol* 60		
91	I NEED YOUR LOVE TONIGHT [33]		
	Elvis Presley *RCA* 59		
92	NOBODY TOLD ME [36]		
	John Lennon *Polydor* 84		
93	BRILLIANT DISGUISE [40]		
	Bruce Springsteen *Columbia* 87		
94	HER TOWN TOO [38]		
	James Taylor and J.D Souther *Columbia* 81		
95	A LITTLE BIT ME, A LITTLE BIT YOU [32]		
	The Monkees *Colgems* 67		
96	(ALL OF A SUDDEN) MY HEART SINGS [39]		
	Paul Anka *ABC-Paramount* 59		
97	DRESS YOU UP [36]		
	Madonna *Sire* 36		
98	MY WISH CAME TRUE [39]		
	Elvis Presley *RCA* 59		
99	VALLERI [24]		
	The Monkees *Colgems* 68		
100	TONIGHT [37]		
	New Kids on the Block *Columbia*		

My Heart Sings," which debuted at number 39 on December 22, 1958; it only went as high as number 15. Aretha Franklin's "See Saw" entered at number 35, then stopped at number 14. (It just missed the top 100 songs that debuted in the top 40, ranking number 101). Two records that debuted in the top 40 both petered out at number 12, but both were flip sides of number one songs that were listed separately. Elvis Presley's "My Wish Came True" was the other side of "A Big Hunk O'Love" and the Beatles' "Revolution" was the "B" side of "Hey Jude." In 1983, "All Right" by Christopher Cross debuted at number 29 but only rose 17 places higher, stopping at number 12. "It's Raining Again" by Supertramp came on the chart at number 31, then peaked at number 11.

The Beatles have more records that debuted in the top 40 than any other artist. Thirteen of their singles started life at number 40 or above. Eight more of their solo efforts made the same start—four by John Lennon, three by Paul McCartney and one by George Harrison. Elvis and Madonna have each had five top 40 debuts, although all of Elvis' early hits are ineligible, as they predate the advent of the Hot 100, which began on August 4, 1958. Michael Jackson had four top 40 debuts on his own and two more with his brothers. Five artists had three high debuts: the Bee Gees, the Monkees, Kenny Rogers, Bruce Springsteen and Styx.

Few artists aside from the Beatles, Michael Jackson and Elvis Presley have managed to debut in the top 30. Aside from Herman's Hermits' extraordinary debut in 1965, only the Royal Guardsmen with "Snoopy Vs. The Red Baron" and the Monkees with "Valleri" managed to do it in the '60s.

The Bee Gees were the only ones to debut in the top 30 in the '70s. "Tragedy" debuted at number 29, following "How Deep Is Your Love," "Stayin' Alive," "Night Fever" and "Too Much Heaven." Like its predecessors, it went to number one.

In 1980, Bruce Springsteen debuted at number 30 with "Hungry Heart." It was Springsteen's first single to make the top 10 of the Hot 100, peaking at number five.

Darryl Hall and John Oates, Men at Work and Christopher Cross debuted in the top 30 during 1983. Hall and Oates did it with "Say It Isn't So," a single that spent four weeks at number two. Men at Work debuted at number 28 with "Overkill," the follow-up to two number one singles.

In 1984, Prince followed his number one hits "When Doves Cry" and "Let's Go Crazy" with the title track from his motion picture *Purple Rain*. That single debuted at number 28 and peaked at number two.

The following year, "We Are The World" made a spectacular debut at number 21 on the Hot 100 for the week ending March 23. The single had been released on Thursday, March 7, and by the weekend, all 800,000 copies that had been shipped were sold. The record moved to number one in its fourth week on the chart—the fastest-rising single since Elton John's "Island Girl" in November, 1975.

DEBUTED AT NO. 100

1 **THE NIGHT THE LIGHTS WENT OUT IN GEORGIA**
Vicki Lawrence *Bell* 73

2 **TEEN ANGEL**
Mark Dinning *MGM* 60

3 **JUNGLE BOOGIE**
Kool & the Gang *De-Lite* 74

4 **GO AWAY LITTLE GIRL**
Steve Lawrence *Columbia* 63

5 **KANSAS CITY**
Wilbert Harrison *Fury* 59

6 **NIGHTS IN WHITE SATIN**
The Moody Blues *Deram* 72

7 **MICHAEL**
The Highwaymen *UA* 61

8 **THE WAY YOU DO THE THINGS YOU DO**
UB40 *Virgin* 90

9 **DADDY DON'T YOU WALK SO FAST**
Wayne Newton *Chelsea* 72

10 **BALLROOM BLITZ**
Sweet *Capitol* 75

11 **WHEN A MAN LOVES A WOMAN**
Percy Sledge *Atlantic* 66

12 **SMOKIN' IN THE BOY'S ROOM**
Brownsville Station *Big Tree* 74

13 **THE BIRDS AND THE BEES**
Jewel Akens *Era* 65

14 **THE "IN" CROWD**
Ramsey Lewis Trio *Argo* 65

15 **PEOPLE**
Barbra Streisand *Columbia* 64

16 **DO YOU LOVE ME**
The Contours *Gordy* 62

17 **WASHINGTON SQUARE**
Village Stompers *Epic* 63

18 **IT'S IMPOSSIBLE**
Perry Como *RCA* 71

19 **SEALED WITH A KISS**
Brian Hyland *ABC-Paramount* 62

20 **WHICH WAY YOU GOIN' BILLY?**
The Poppy Family *London* 70

21 **TRAGEDY**
Thomas Wayne *Fernwood* 59

22 **RAINY NIGHT IN GEORGIA**
Brook Benton *Cotillion* 70

23 **CALENDAR GIRL**
Neil Sedaka *RCA* 61

24 **WHY ME**
Kris Kristofferson *Monument* 73

25 **THE COVER OF "ROLLING STONE"**
Dr. Hook & the Medicine Show *Columbia* 73

26 **HE AIN'T HEAVY, HE'S MY BROTHER**
The Hollies *Epic* 70

27 **BOTTLE OF WINE**
The Fireballs *Atco* 68

28 **COTTON FIELDS**
The Highwaymen *UA* 62

29 **CRY BABY**
Garnett Mims & the Enchanters *UA* 63

30 **TIME WON'T LET ME**
The Outsiders *Capitol* 66

Steve Lawrence

Record companies are not happy when their singles debut at number 100 on the Hot 100, explains Michael Ellis, Director of Charts for *Billboard*. "They're very upset by records making low debuts," he says. "I always tell them, it's not where you start, it's where you finish. But they're obsessed with the idea of a high debut being important."

To enter the Hot 100, a single must be heard on a minimum number of radio stations and have a minimum number of airplay points from those stations. Most singles debut in the 70s, 80s and 90s of the chart. Debuting in the 90s is not necessarily an indication of a weak record. Ellis points out that records often debut at number 95 or 96 and go to number one. It is more difficult, he concedes, to do that from number 100.

Still, six singles in the history of the Hot 100 have entered the chart in the anchor position and soared to number one. That includes the most successful single to ever debut at number 100, Vicki Lawrence's "The Night The Lights Went Out In Georgia." Released on Bell Records, the Snuff Garrett production entered the chart on February 10, 1973. The next week it moved to number 90 with a bullet. It moved at up at least 10 positions every week until it made the top 10, from 90-80-59-47-30-16-10. The following week it made the leap from 10 to number one, where it remained for two weeks.

The other number one singles to debut at number 100 include "Teen Angel" by Mark Dinning, "Go Away Little Girl" by Steve Lawrence, "Kansas City" by Wilbert Harrison, "Michael" by the Highwaymen and "When A Man Loves A Woman" by Percy Sledge.

All of them made major chart moves in their second week, with none making less than a 25-point move upward. Of the six, the record that made the biggest move in its second week was "Teen Angel," surging halfway up the chart from number 100 to number 50. All six singles spent exactly two weeks at number one.

At the other end of the scale—literally—there have been 104 singles that have debuted and peaked at number 100. The first record to do so was "Judy" by Frankie Vaughn, which made its debut on the very first Hot 100, on August 4, 1958. The next week it was off the chart, never to return. Two more singles ran out of gas at number 100 that year: "Going To Chicago Blues" by Count Basie and "Itchy Twitchy Feeling" by the Swallows.

Having previous hit singles was not an impediment to stopping at number 100. The Shirelles did it in 1963 with "Not For All The Money In The World," Andy Williams faltered in 1964 with "Charade" and the Ronettes failed with "I Can Hear Music" in 1966. The last single to peak at number 100 was "That's When I Think Of You" by the Australian quartet 1927 in August, 1989.

Superstardom didn't prevent many artists from debuting in the chart's lowest position. Neil Sedaka was already very successful when "Calendar Girl" came on the chart at number 100 on December 19, 1960; it eventually peaked at number four. The Buckinghams had already been to the top of the chart with "Kind Of A Drag" when "Don't You Care" debuted at the bottom on March 11, 1967. It went as high as number six. Stevie Wonder's "Uptight (Everything's Alright)," Cat Stevens' "Another Saturday Night" and the Ventures' "Hawaii Five-O" all made the top 10 after debuting at number 100. Elvis Presley, Paul McCartney and the Rolling Stones have also had singles start their chart life on the bottom rung. "If I Can Dream" was Elvis' comeback single from his NBC television special. It debuted on November 30, 1968, and zoomed to number 63 in its second week. "Hi, Hi, Hi" by Wings was Paul McCartney's fifth solo single. He had already racked up two top 10 singles by the time it debuted on December 16, 1972; success was assured in its second week, when it took a giant step to number 42. "It's All Over Now" was only the third American single for the Rolling Stones, and their highest chart ranking had been number 24 with "Tell Me (You're Coming Back)." "It's All Over Now" moved from 100 to 81 in its second week and managed to lose and regain its bullet for upward chart movement twice before peaking at number 26.

Several artists debuted at number 100 more than once. The Highwaymen's "Michael" debuted at the bottom but moved all the way to number one. Their second single, "Cotton Fields," also entered the chart at number 100, and went as high as number 13.

The Ramsey Lewis Trio's biggest chart hit, "The 'In' Crowd," came on at number 100 and peaked at number five. Four singles later, "Wade In The Water" also anchored the chart and eventually reached number 19. Dr. Hook & the Medicine Show's first two top 10 singles, both issued on Columbia, started out at the bottom. "Sylvia's Mother" went to number five and "The Cover Of 'Rolling Stone'" peaked at number six. Frankie Avalon had two top 30 singles begin life at 100: "I'll Wait For You" (number 15) and "Togetherness" (number 26).

The Poppy Family, the Canadian group that included the husband and wife team of Terry and Susan Jacks, experienced debuting at number 100 three times—with their first three chart singles. "Which Way You Goin' Billy?" did just fine, spending two weeks at number two in 1970. The follow-up, "That's Where I Went Wrong," peaked at number 29. "I Was Wondering" spent two weeks at number 100 in April, 1971.

Strangely, two versions of the same song both entered the Hot 100 in last place. Jerry Butler's recording of Burt Bacharach and Hal David's "Make It Easy On Yourself" anchored the survey on July 7, 1962. It rose as high as number 20. Three men from Los Angeles who recorded in England had a similar experience. The Walker Brothers' remake of the song entered the chart at number 100 on October 16, 1965. The trio bested Jerry Butler by peaking at number 16.

Singles continued to debut at the zenith of the *Billboard* chart on a regular basis from its inception in 1958 through 1977. The last record to enter at the bottom was "Discomania" by the Lovers on May 14, 1977. From that date until June 4, 1988, no singles debuted at number 100. The single that broke the spell was "Only A Memory" by the Smithereens, which peaked at number 92.

In 1990, UB40 may have finally laid to rest concern about starting in last place. (The group was used to being patient: "Red Red Wine," released in 1983, didn't go to number one until 1988). UB40's remake of the Smokey Robinson-penned "The Way You Do The Things You Do"—the Temptations' first hit—snuck onto the chart at number 100 on September 15, 1990. The song had been featured in the soundtrack of *Black Rain*, a film starring Michael Douglas, in October of 1989. When UB40's *Labour of Love II* album was released, Virgin issued "Here I Am (Come And Take Me)" as the first single. When it failed to chart, the label released "The Way You Do The Things You Do" in April, 1990. It was played on only 16 stations, according to Michael Plen, vice president of promotion at Virgin. The record "went away everywhere except for . . . Houston, Salt Lake City and Honolulu," Plen said in *Billboard*. "At this point, everybody in the industry thinks it's over." Plen convinced KIIS-FM in Los Angeles to add the record to its playlist; it spread nationally from there, peaking at number six in December. It ranks number eight on the top 100 songs that debuted at number 100.

ONE-HIT WONDERS

1 LITTLE STAR
The Elegants *Apt* 58

2 POP MUZIK
M *Sire* 79

3 DOMINIQUE
The Singing Nun *Philips* 63

4 WE ARE THE WORLD
USA for Africa *Columbia* 85

5 RAINBOW
Russ Hamilton *Kapp* 57

6 HE'S GOT THE WHOLE WORLD (IN HIS HANDS)
Laurie London *Capitol* 58

7 IN THE YEAR 2525 (EXORDIUM & TERMINUS)
Zager and Evans *RCA* 69

8 INTO THE NIGHT
Benny Mardones *Polydor* 80

9 DO YOU WANNA MAKE LOVE
Peter McCann *20th Century* 77

10 SUSIE DARLIN'
Robin Luke *Dot* 58

11 CINDY, OH CINDY
Vince Martin w/the Tarriers *Glory* 56

12 ALLEY-OOP
Hollywood Argyles *Lute* 60

13 MAKIN' IT
David Naughton *RSO* 79

14 CARS
Gary Numan *Atco* 80

15 FRIENDS AND LOVERS
Gloria Loring and Carl Anderson *Carrere* 86

16 PLAYGROUND IN MY MIND
Clint Holmes *Epic* 73

17 99 LUFTBALLONS
Nena *Epic* 84

18 SEA OF LOVE
Phil Phillips w/the Twilights *Mercury* 59

19 PUTTIN' ON THE RITZ
Taco *RCA* 83

20 MIAMI VICE THEME
Jan Hammer *MCA* 85

21 THE HAPPY WHISTLER
Don Robertson *Capitol* 56

22 TAINTED LOVE
Soft Cell *Sire* 82

23 WHEN I'M WITH YOU
Sheriff *Capitol* 89

24 GET A JOB
The Silhouettes *Ember* 58

25 THE ENTERTAINER
Marvin Hamlisch *MCA* 74

26 APACHE
Jorgen Ingmann & His Guitar *Atco* 61

27 SUNSHINE
Jonathan Edwards *Capricorn* 72

28 BOOK OF LOVE
The Monotones *Argo* 58

29 AXEL F
Harold Faltermeyer *MCA* 85

30 MULE SKINNER BLUES
The Fendermen *Soma* 60

The Elegants

A "one-hit wonder" is a recording by an artist who had one lone single solitary hit on the *Billboard* chart and nothing more. To determine the top 100 one-hit wonders of the rock era, a series of rules were established. First, the artist could only make one appearance on the Hot 100. This disqualified artists like Debby Boone, who spent 10 weeks at number one with "You Light Up My Life" and then never had anything chart higher than number 50 ("California").

Second, an artist could only have one appearance on the Hot 100 in any form. So if someone had hits with a group and also had a lone appearance as a solo artist, that solo performance would not count. That disqualified people like Frida, who had one hit on her own ("I Know There's Something Going On"), but 20 previous chart appearances with Abba.

Third, all chart appearances were considered, even if the artist used different names. While "Alley-Oop" by the Hollywood Argyles is generally considered to be a one-hit wonder, it was actually a solo effort by Gary Paxton, who had previously charted as the latter half of Skip and Flip ("It Was I," "Cherry Pie").

Fourth, an artist's entire career was considered, so someone who had registered on the *Billboard* chart before the rock era began, and then had only one hit after July 9, 1955, was not considered to be a one-hit wonder. This eliminated a singer like Jane Powell who had charted with Fred Astaire in 1951 before having a solitary rock era hit with a version of "True Love."

Finally, a cut-off date was established. The eligibility period was July 9, 1955-December 31, 1986. That eliminated Levert, M/A/R/R/S, Patrick Swayze and T'Pau, who all had one chart hit by the end of 1990.

Most artists who intend to have recording careers do not intentionally set out to be one-hit wonders. After experiencing success with an initial chart entry, it's reasonable to expect more. The reasons why some artists never experience a follow-up hit are diverse enough that there is no sure-fire way to prevent future one-hit wonders.

Seven records are the ultimate one-hit wonders of the rock era. They went to number one, then the artist never charted again.

The first of these is "Little Star" by the Elegants, the most successful one-hit wonder of all time. The founders of the group were from Staten Island, New York. Vito Picone, lead singer, and Carman Romano, baritone, were in a short-lived group called the Crescents. When they broke up in 1957, Vito and Carman recruited Artie Venosa to sing first tenor, Frankie Fardogno to sing second tenor and Jimmy Moschella to sing bass. They took their name from a billboard advertising Schenley's Whiskey as the "liquor of elegance." Vito and Artie adapted Mozart's "Twinkle, Twinkle, Little Star" into a rock and roll song, "Little Star." The Elegants were signed to Hull Records, which leased their first single to ABC-Paramount. "Little Star" was one of the first four singles released on ABC's Apt subsidiary. When the record hit, the group toured the continental United States and Hawaii, and didn't have time to go back in the studio. By the time they released "Goodnight" 18 months later, the Elegants had lost their momentum, and were never again to appear on the Hot 100.

The second biggest one-hit wonder of the rock era is by an artist with a short chart life—as well as the shortest name in the business. "Pop Muzik" was M's only chart appearance. "M" was actually British musician Robin Scott, who took his stage name from the large letter "M" that identified metro stations in Paris. The synthesized, electronic "Pop Muzik" was inspired by Donna Summer's "I Feel Love." Scott had three more pop hits in the U.K., including "Moonlight And Muzak," and released a 10th-anniversary edition of "Pop Muzik" in 1989 that also charted. In the U.S., he never returned to the Hot 100, either as M or as Robin Scott.

The third most popular one-hit wonder is "Dominique" by the Singing Nun. Sister Luc-Gabrielle composed songs for the sisters at Fichermont Monastery in Belgium to sing at their evening retreats. The convent asked Philips Records if they could press a few hundred copies of the songs to be given away as gifts, and the company agreed to a brief, non-commercial recording session. Philips was so impressed with the result that they released an album by *Soeur Sourire* (Sister Smile) in Europe. The American office of Philips changed the title to *The Singing Nun* for the U.S., but there was little reaction until "Dominique," a song eulogizing the founder of the Dominican order, was released as a single. Sister Luc-Gabrielle ended up singing on "The Ed Sullivan Show" and having Debbie Reynolds portray her in a film biography. After the movie was released, she left the convent and returned to private life as Jeanine Deckers. She recorded for Philips again, but songs like "Glory Be To God For The Golden Pill," an ode to birth control, didn't achieve commercial success.

The fourth most successful one-hit wonder is "We Are The World" by USA for Africa. The 45 artists who gathered at A&M Studios in Hollywood following the American Music Awards in 1985 only intended to record one song. They were there at the invitation of personal manager Ken Kragen, who had been approached by Harry Belafonte about raising money to feed the hungry people of Africa. Kragen suggested an American version of Band Aid, the Bob Geldof-inspired project that resulted in the recording of "Do They Know It's Christmas?" Kragen asked his client Lionel Richie to get involved, and approached Quincy Jones to produce. Lionel collaborated with Michael Jackson to write "We Are The World," and while ironically none of the performers who made up USA for Africa are one-hit wonders themselves, collectively they are classified as such.

The other three number one hits that are also one-hit wonders are "In The Year 2525 (Exordium & Terminus)" by Zager and Evans, "Miami Vice Theme" by Jan Hammer and "When I'm With You" by Sheriff.

Zager and Evans did release a follow-up single, but Denny Zager says he had already decided to quit the duo before "2525" fell off the chart. Hammer, a former keyboardist for the Mahavishnu Orchestra, composed his first film score for the 1983 movie *A Night in Heaven*. Producer Michael Mann asked him to score the pilot of "Miami Vice," which led to composing about 20 minutes of original music for every episode. When MCA released a soundtrack from the TV series, Hammer's title theme was released as a single. Sheriff's "When I'm With You" went to number one in their native Canada, but sputtered out at number 63 in America in 1983. The group split, with two of the members becoming Frozen Ghost and two others forming the group Alias. "When I'm With You" was revived by radio in 1988, and even though there was no more Sheriff, the song went to number one.

Some artists are only one-hit wonders in America. British singer Russ Hamilton had two pop hits in his home country, although neither one of them were "Rainbow." "Cars" was Gary Numan's only American hit, but he had 25 chart entries in England. The duo of Soft Cell hold the record for the single with the most weeks on the Hot 100. "Tainted Love," their only U.S. hit, remained on the chart for 43 weeks. In the U.K., they had nine different songs make the chart. Mungo Jerry, David Dundas, Argent, Mike Oldfield, the Korgis and Mac and Katie Kissoon are other U.K. artists who had more than one hit at home.

ROCK-ERA REMAKES

Chubby Checker

Some songs are so closely connected with the artists who recorded them, that to think of one automatically brings the other to mind. Chubby Checker and "The Twist" are inexorably linked, as are Debby Boone with "You Light Up My Life," and Kim Carnes with "Bette Davis Eyes." But like thousands of other songs, those three numbers were all originally recorded by someone else.

The practice of covering a song at the time of its release or remaking it years later is an old one. Music publishers earn royalties when the songs they own are recorded, and the more versions that are available, the more royalties they earn. Artists appreciate good material, which is why a song like "Cupid" can be a hit for Sam Cooke in 1961 and then chart again for Johnny Rivers in 1965, Johnny Nash in 1975, Dawn in 1976 and the Spinners, who used it in a medley in 1980. It went to number four on the Hot 100—the song's fifth and most successful chart run (so far).

In the '50s, it was common practice for white pop singers to cover songs written by black R&B artists. Radio stations that played rock and roll frequently would not give airplay to black artists, but would willingly play their songs if they were recorded by white singers. The highest-ranked example on the top 100 remakes of the rock era is Pat Boone's "Ain't That A Shame." The original recording by Fats Domino entered the R&B chart on May 14, 1955, and spent 11 weeks at number one. Dot Records owner Randy Wood had Pat Boone cover it, and his version entered the

Best Sellers chart on July 9, 1955—literally the beginning of the rock era. Boone's record went to number two, while Domino's entered the Best Sellers chart the following week and peaked at number 16.

Similarly, Teresa Brewer had a bigger pop hit with "Bo Weevil" than Fats Domino did. Cathy Carr had a pop hit with "Ivory Tower," first recorded by Otis Williams & His Charms, and Gale Storm had the pop hit with Smiley Lewis' "I Hear You Knocking." The Gladiolas, the group that became Maurice Williams & the Zodiacs ("Stay"), lost out when the Diamonds—a vocal quartet from Ontario, Canada—took their "Little Darlin' " to number two for eight weeks.

Not all of the songs remade in the '50s were new versions of R&B songs. Ric Cartey recorded a song he wrote with Carole Joyner, "Young Love," for RCA. When it failed to chart, Cartey played it for Sonny James, who liked it enough to record it on Capitol. At Dot, Wood thought James would have the country hit, and so he called actor Tab Hunter and asked him if he could carry a tune. Tab's version of "Young Love" went to number one on the Best Sellers chart, while James peaked at number two. Guy Mitchell had two number one hits by cutting pop versions of country recordings—first with Marty Robbins' "Singing The Blues" and then with Ray Price's "Heartaches By The Number."

The most successful cover version of the rock era is Chubby Checker's recording of "The Twist." Hank Ballard wrote the song after seeing teenagers in Tampa, Florida, dancing the Twist. He recorded it with his band, the Midnighters, and it was released on the flip side of their first pop hit, "Teardrops On Your Letter." When the dance became popular on "American Bandstand," Dick Clark suggested to Danny & the Juniors that they record a cover version of the song. When nothing materialized, Clark approached Philadelphia-based Cameo-Parkway Records and proposed that Checker record it. Chubby's version of "The Twist" was such a close copy that when Ballard first heard it, he thought he was listening to his own recording.

Motion picture soundtracks and Broadway scores have long been a source of recording material, and there have been many successful cover versions from the screen and stage. The most successful is Debby Boone's recording of the title song from *You Light Up My Life*, a film that starred Didi Conn as a young singer seeking fame. In the movie, Conn's vocals were provided by commercial jingle singer Kacey Cisyk. Mike Curb attended a screening of the film and thought the song would be perfect for Boone—so he borrowed the instrumental track from writer/producer Joe Brooks, dubbing Debby's vocal over it. Cisyk's version was also released, but the Arista single didn't even list her name: the label credit read "Original Cast."

Percy Faith had the number one single of 1960 by recording Max Steiner's theme music from *A Summer Place*. Arthur Ferrante and Louis Teicher, who met as children when they were both studying at the Juilliard School of Music in the '20s, had several chart hits by playing movie themes on their twin Steinway pianos. The most successful was their 1961 recording of Ernest Gold's theme from *Exodus*. Aubrey Woods sang Anthony Newley and Leslie Bricusse's "The Candy Man" in *Willie Wonka and the Chocolate Factory*, and although Newley was certain the song would not be a hit, Mike Curb, then president of MGM Records, came up with the idea of having Sammy Davis, Jr., record it.

The 5th Dimension had the biggest hit of their career when they recorded a medley of "Aquarius" and "Let The Sunshine In" from the Broadway musical *Hair*. The Cowsills also had their biggest hit by recording a version of the title song from that musical. Louis Armstrong made the title song of "Hello, Dolly!" his own, even though he wasn't in the stage musical. The Four Lads went to number three with "Standing On The Corner," originally heard in *The Most Happy Fella*.

Some original versions of songs remain obscure. Jackie De-Shannon recorded "Bette Davis Eyes," which she wrote with Donna Weiss, on a Columbia album from 1975, *New Arrangement*. "Gloria" was originally an Italian song, recorded by its composer, Umberto Tozzi, before Laura Branigan released it. The Arrows were an Anglo-American band recording for the Rak label in the U.K., and one of their "B" sides was a song written by group members Jake Hooker and Alan Merrill to counter the Rolling Stones' "It's Only Rock 'n Roll (But I Like It)." Joan Jett wanted to record "I Love Rock 'n Roll" when she was in the Runaways, but the other members declined. Her version with the Blackhearts was number one for seven weeks. "Whole Lot Of Shakin' Going On" was co-written by Roy Hall under the name Sunny David; his version was released on Decca in late 1955, but was preceded by a few months by an R&B version from Big Maybelle on the Okeh label. Jerry Lee Lewis made "Whole Lot Of Shakin' Going On" his own in 1957.

Steve Lawrence had the first hit with "Go Away Little Girl" and Donny Osmond remade it eight years later, but it originally appeared on an album by Bobby Vee. Vee had a chart single with "More Than I Can Say" 19 years before Leo Sayer took it to number two (the earliest version was by the Crickets.) All of the Supremes' singles from "I Want A Guy" to "No Matter What Sign You Are" were originals, so most people didn't realize that their final single with Diana Ross singing lead—"Someday We'll Be Together"—had actually been recorded nine years earlier by two of the song's composers, Jackie Beavers and Johnny Bristol, on the Tri-Phi label. David Martin, one of the writers of "Can't Smile Without You," recorded it in England before the Carpenters put it on one of their American albums; both versions preceded Barry Manilow's version. Bill Medley and Bette Midler each made the Hot 100 with earlier versions of Linda Ronstadt and Aaron Neville's hit "Don't Know Much," but the song first appeared on a 1980 Casablanca album by songwriter Barry Mann.

1 HOUND DOG
Elvis Presley [Big Mama Thornton, 1953]

2 ROCK AROUND THE CLOCK
Bill Haley & His Comets [Sonny Dae & the Knights, 1954]

3 AUTUMN LEAVES
Roger Williams [Joseph Kosma, 1947]

4 LOVE LETTERS IN THE SAND
Pat Boone [Ted Black & His Orchestra, 1931]

5 MACK THE KNIFE
Bobby Darin [OC/*The Threepenny Opera*, 1928]

6 LISBON ANTIGUA
Nelson Riddle [1937]

7 SO RARE
Jimmy Dorsey [Guy Lombardo, 1937]

8 JUST WALKING IN THE RAIN
Johnnie Ray [The Prisonaires, 1953]

9 THE YELLOW ROSE OF TEXAS
Mitch Miller [Traditional, Civil War]

10 SIXTEEN TONS
Tennessee Ernie Ford [Merle Travis, 1947]

11 LOVE ME TENDER
Elvis Presley [1861]

12 HONEYCOMB
Jimmie Rodgers [1954]

13 THE POOR PEOPLE OF PARIS
Les Baxter [Edith Piaf, 1954]

14 IT'S ALL IN THE GAME
Tommy Edwards [1912]

15 MOONGLOW AND THEME FROM "PICNIC"
Morris Stoloff [OC/*Blackbirds of 1934*, 1934]

16 THE BATTLE OF NEW ORLEANS
Johnny Horton [1815]

17 MY PRAYER
The Platters [1939]

18 BLUEBERRY HILL
Fats Domino [Glenn Miller/Gene Autry, 1940]

19 HOT DIGGITY (DOG ZIGGITY BOOM)
Perry Como [Chabrier, 19th century]

20 IT'S NOW OR NEVER
Elvis Presley [1901]

21 SAIL ALONG SILVERY MOON
Billy Vaughn [1937]

22 SMOKE GETS IN YOUR EYES
The Platters [OC/*Roberta*, 1933]

23 ARE YOU LONESOME TONIGHT?
Elvis Presley [1926]

24 UNCHAINED MELODY
The Righteous Brothers [Todd Duncan, 1955]

25 TOM DOOLEY
The Kingston Trio [Traditional, circa 1870]

26 A FIFTH OF BEETHOVEN
Walter Murphy & the Big Apple Band
[Ludwig van Beethoven, 1807]

27 HAVE I TOLD YOU LATELY THAT I LOVE YOU?
Ricky Nelson [Bing Crosby & the Andrews Sisters, 1950]

28 I ALMOST LOST MY MIND
Pat Boone [Ivory Joe Hunter, 1950]

29 FASCINATION
Jane Morgan [1904]

30 MY BLUE HEAVEN
Fats Domino [Paul Whiteman & His Orchestra, 1927]

31 STAGGER LEE
Lloyd Price [Archibald, 1950]

Bobby Darin

Many songs that have been popular in the rock era originated long before Bill Haley and His Comets ascended to number one with "(We're Gonna) Rock Around The Clock" on July 9, 1955. Even that rock classic had been recorded previously. Haley's recording first entered the *Billboard* chart on May 29, 1954, but it was preceded by an R&B recording of the song by Sonny Dae & the Knights.

The most successful remake of a pre-rock era song is "Hound Dog" by Elvis Presley. Jerry Leiber and Mike Stoller wrote it in 1952 when Johnny Otis asked them to come up with tunes for the singers in his band, Little Esther and Big Mama Thornton. Leiber and Stoller watched Thornton rehearse, then went home and wrote "Hound Dog" for her as a country blues song. They produced the song with Otis, and it entered the *Billboard* R&B Best Sellers chart on March 28, 1953. It spent six weeks at number one. Elvis heard the song while making his ill-fated debut in Las Vegas in April, 1956. The middle-aged audience that came to see the show didn't appreciate the future king, and the two-week engagement was cancelled at the end of the first week. One night during his run, Elvis walked into the lounge and saw Freddie Bell & the Bellboys perform a comedic version of "Hound Dog." Elvis liked how they did the song and performed it in June on Milton

Berle's TV show. He reluctantly recorded it in New York on July 2, at producer Steve Sholes' insistence. Along with "Don't Be Cruel," "Hound Dog" became Elvis' biggest hit of all time.

A number of rock era hits were first recorded in the early half of the '50s. Five inmates from Tennessee State Penitentiary, including songwriter Johnny Bragg, arrived at Sam Phillips' recording studio in Memphis on June 1, 1953, to rehearse some material they wanted to record. One of the songs they cut was an *a cappella* rendition of a song Bragg had written with Robert S. Riley, "Just Walking In The Rain." They returned to their prison cells, and six weeks later, Sun Records released the song on red vinyl with black stripes. Three years after that, Johnnie Ray recorded it, and it went to number three on the Best Sellers chart.

In 1954, "The Poor People Of Paris" was a hit for Edith Piaf in France under its original title, *La Goulante Du Pauvre Jean.* That should have translated as "The Ballad Of Poor John," but Capitol Records' Parisian representative substituted *gens* (meaning "people") for *Jean* when cabling the information to Hollywood.

Eight different artists have made the *Billboard* chart with "Unchained Melody," beginning with Les Baxter and Al Hibbler in 1955. The biggest hit version was by the Righteous Brothers, who enjoyed chart runs with the song in 1965 and 1990. The original version was sung by Todd Duncan in the film *Unchained.*

Ivory Joe Hunter took "I Almost Lost My Mind" to number one on the R&B Best Sellers chart in 1950, six years before Pat Boone made it a pop hit. Archibald, a New Orleans singer whose real name was Leon T. Gross, had an R&B top 10 hit with "Stack-A-Lee" in 1950, and Lloyd Price turned it into "Stagger Lee" for a number one hit on the Hot 100 in 1959. Tony Bennett peaked at number 16 with "Blue Velvet" in 1951, 12 years before Bobby Vinton made it a number one song. "Kansas City" was a Leiber-Stoller song first recorded as "K.C. Lovin'" by Little Willie Littlefield on Federal in 1952; Wilbert Harrison had a number one pop hit with the song in 1959. Elvis Presley recorded "Crying In The Chapel" in 1960, although it wasn't released until 1965. There were seven different versions of the song on the chart in 1953, including recordings by June Valli, Rex Allen and the Orioles. But the original was by 16-year-old Darrell Glenn from Waco, Texas; his father, Artie Glenn, wrote the song.

A lot of hits from the rock era originated in the '40s. "Autumn Leaves" was called "Les Feuilles Mortes" when Joseph Kosma wrote it in 1947, eight years before pianist Roger Williams had a number one hit with it. Merle Travis wrote and recorded "Sixteen Tons" in 1947 for an album titled *Folk Songs of the Hills.* Capitol wanted some mining songs on it, but Travis couldn't find any, so he wrote some. In 1955, Tennessee Ernie Ford took time out from his busy TV schedule to record Travis' song. Gene Autry sang "Blueberry Hill" in a 1940 movie; it was a number one song for Glenn Miller that same year, preceding Fats Domino's version by 17 years.

Twenty-three of the top 100 remakes of pre-rock era songs originated in the '30s. "Love Letters In The Sand" was recorded by Pat Boone because Dot Records founder Randy Wood had requests for the song over a 10-year period at the record store he owned in Gallatin, Tennessee. Bing Crosby and Rudy Vallee had recorded it, but it was first a hit for Ted Black & His Orchestra in the fall of 1931. Jimmy Dorsey had a hit with "So Rare" in 1957, 20 years after Guy Lombardo recorded it. Nelson Riddle's recording of "Lisbon Antigua" was an updating of a song written by three Portuguese writers in 1937 as "Lisboa Antigua," meaning "In Old Lisbon."

"Mack The Knife" was how Marc Blitzstein translated the song "Moritat" from *The Threepenny Opera* by Kurt Weill and Berthold Brecht. The show opened in Berlin in 1928. "Are You Lonesome Tonight?" was also from that decade; Roy Turk and Lou Handman wrote it in 1926. "My Blue Heaven," popularized by Fats Domino in 1956, was a hit for Paul Whiteman & His Orchestra in 1927.

"It's All In The Game" was first recorded by Tommy Edwards in 1951, the same year it was cut by Sammy Kaye, Carmen Cavallaro and Dinah Shore. Edwards recorded a new, pop version in stereo in 1958, and it went to number one. But the song's origins can be traced back to 1912, when Charles Gates Dawes—who would later be Vice President under Calvin Coolidge—wrote a tune called "Melody In A Major" (Carl Sigman added lyrics in 1951). Elvis Presley's recording of "It's Now Or Never" was a number one hit in 1960; the song is based on the Italian song "O Sole Mio," written in 1901.

Some rock and roll hits can be traced back to the 19th century. "The Yellow Rose Of Texas," number one for Mitch Miller in 1955, is an 1853 marching song written for traveling minstrel shows, and became popular during the Civil War. Elvis' "Love Me Tender" was based on "Aura Lee," a folk ballad from 1861. "The Battle Of New Orleans," a number one hit for Johnny Horton in 1959, descended from a folk song called "The Eighth Of January," the date Andrew Jackson's forces defeated the British at New Orleans in the final battle of the War of 1812. The song was written in 1815.

A number of rock era hits are based on pieces of classical music. Perry Como's "Hot Diggity (Dog Ziggity Boom)" was adapted from the first theme of Chabrier's "Espana Rhapsody," written in the 19th century. Walter Murphy gave Ludwig Van the disco treatment with the 1976 hit "A Fifth Of Beethoven." Della Reese' 1959 hit "Don't You Know" was based on Giacomo Puccini's "Musetta's Waltz," composed in 1896. Eric Carmen based his 1975 hit "All By Myself" on music from Rachmaninoff's "Second Concerto." Deodato's "Also Sprach Zarathustra" was a jazzy version of the dramatic theme heard in Stanley Kubrick's *2001: A Space Odyssey*; it was written by Richard Strauss in 1896. And Chopin's Prelude In C Minor provided the inspiration for Barry Manilow's third chart single, "Could It Be Magic."

MOTOWN REMAKES

The Temptations

1 **I HEARD IT THROUGH THE GRAPEVINE**
Marvin Gaye [Smokey Robinson & the Miracles]

2 **WAR**
Edwin Starr [The Temptations]

3 **AIN'T NO MOUNTAIN HIGH ENOUGH**
Diana Ross [Marvin Gaye and Tammi Terrell]

4 **UNTIL YOU COME BACK TO ME
(THAT'S WHAT I'M GONNA DO)**
Aretha Franklin [Stevie Wonder]

5 **I HEARD IT THROUGH THE GRAPEVINE**
Gladys Knight & the Pips
[Smokey Robinson & the Miracles]

6 **DEVIL WITH A BLUE DRESS ON & GOOD
GOLLY MISS MOLLY**
Mitch Ryder & the Detroit Wheels [Shorty Long]

7 **YOU CAN'T HURRY LOVE**
Phil Collins [The Supremes]

8 **GET READY**
Rare Earth [The Temptations]

9 **THE WAY YOU DO THE THINGS YOU DO**
UB40 [The Temptations]

10 **HEAVEN MUST HAVE SENT YOU**
Bonnie Pointer [The Elgins]

11 **TOO BUSY THINKING ABOUT MY BABY**
Marvin Gaye [The Temptations]

12 **MORE LOVE**
Kim Carnes [Smokey Robinson & the Miracles]

13 **YOU KEEP ME HANGIN' ON**
Kim Wilde [The Supremes]

14 **PAPA WAS A ROLLIN' STONE**
The Temptations [The Undisputed Truth]

15 **OOH BABY BABY**
Linda Ronstadt [The Miracles]

Berry Gordy established his own song publishing company in 1958. He named it Jobete, after his daughters Joy, Betty and Terry. The first song published by the new company was "I Need You," written by Gordy and recorded by Herman Griffin on the HOB label. Jobete would one day have one of the richest song catalogues in the world, in every sense of the word.

The earliest cover versions of Motown songs that were hits were released in 1964. The Kingsmen followed "Louie Louie" with a rendition of "Money," a song that went to number 23 in 1960 for Barrett Strong. The original version had been released on Anna, a label named for and run by Berry's sister, although "Money" also appeared later on Tamla. (The single by the Kingsmen fared even better than Strong's record, peaking at number 16.) Also in 1964, the Dave Clark Five released a remake of the Contours' 1962 hit "Do You Love Me," and the Beatles recorded three Motown songs—"Money," "Please Mr. Postman" and "You've Really Got A Hold On Me."

Later in the year, the Kingsmen's label, Wand, tried to cover a Holland-Dozier-Holland song. The Supremes were enjoying their second consecutive number one single with "Baby Love" when Wand released "Come See About Me" by Nella Dodds. Motown was planning to issue that track as the third single from the

Supremes' *Where Did Our Love Go* album, and had to rush it out to prevent the cover version from becoming a hit.

The next Motown song to be successfully covered was "Devil With A Blue Dress On," originally called "Devil With The Blue Dress" when Shorty Long released it as the first single on the Soul label. Mitch Ryder combined it with Little Richard's "Good Golly Miss Molly" in a medley that peaked at number four.

In 1967, Johnny Rivers remade the Four Tops' "Baby I Need Your Loving" and bested their version by peaking at number three (the Tops went to number 11). That same year, Bill Cosby put a new spin on Stevie Wonder's "Uptight" in a song called "Little Ole Man." Stevie had peaked at three and Cosby went to number four.

Motown did a great job of covering itself during the '60s and the first half of the '70s. In fact, four of the top five Motown remakes were recorded by Motown artists.

It wasn't unusual for Motown writer/producers to record one song with several different artists. The most successful Motown remake, "I Heard It Through The Grapevine," was originally recorded by Smokey Robinson & the Miracles, but not released until the 1968 album *Special Occasion*. The Isley Brothers recorded it next; their version was never released. Then Marvin Gaye cut it, but it was held back in favor of a version by Gladys Knight & the Pips. It was Gladys' first big hit for Motown, spending three weeks at number two at the end of 1967. In the fall of 1968, Gaye's version showed up on his *In the Groove* album, but it wasn't the first single released. When it was finally issued, it went to number one and stayed there for seven weeks.

Other Jobete songs covered by Motown artists include "War," an album track for the Temptations before it was a single for Edwin Starr; "Ain't No Mountain High Enough," a top 20 single for Marvin Gaye and Tammi Terrell three years before it was rearranged for Diana Ross; "Until You Come Back To Me (That's What I'm Gonna Do)," recorded by Stevie Wonder in 1967 but unreleased until after Aretha Franklin had a hit with it in 1974; "Get Ready," done in a rock version by Rare Earth four years after it was a hit for the Temptations; "Heaven Must Have Sent You," a bigger hit for Bonnie Pointer than for the Elgins; "Too Busy Thinking About My Baby," recorded by the Temptations on the *Gettin' Ready* album three years before it was a single for Marvin Gaye; and "Papa Was A Rollin' Stone," an album track for the Undisputed Truth before the Temptations took it to number one.

The passing of the years has not slowed down the number of Motown remakes. Many of the songs written by Motown's stable of writers have proved timeless, as Kim Wilde took "You Keep Me Hangin' On" to number one 21 years after the Supremes did; Rod Stewart had a top 10 hit with "This Old Heart Of Mine" 24 years after the Isley Brothers; Sweet Sensation updated "Love Child" 22 years after it was a hit for the Supremes; and UB40 had the most successful chart version of "The Way You Do The Things You Do" 26 years after it was recorded by the Temptations.

BEATLES REMAKES

1 MEDLEY: INTRO VENUS …
Stars on 45 *Radio* 81

2 LUCY IN THE SKY WITH DIAMONDS
Elton John *MCA* 75

3 YOU WON'T SEE ME
Anne Murray *Capitol* 74

4 THE FOOL ON THE HILL
Sergio Mendes & Brasil '66 *A&M* 68

5 I SAW HIM STANDING THERE
Tiffany *MCA* 88

6 GOT TO GET YOU INTO MY LIFE
Earth, Wind & Fire *Columbia* 78

7 HERE COMES THE SUN
Richie Havens *Stormy Forest* 71

8 WE CAN WORK IT OUT
Stevie Wonder *Tamla* 71

9 YOU'VE GOT TO HIDE YOUR LOVE AWAY
The Silkie *Fontana* 65

10 OH! DARLING
Robin Gibb *RSO* 78

The most successful remake of a Beatles song—or in this case, songs—on the Hot 100 is the medley recorded by producer Jaap Eggermont with studio musicians and singers collectively called Stars on 45. Recorded to prevent a similar bootleg medley from selling in Holland, it included pieces of "No Reply," "I'll Be Back," "Drive My Car," "Do You Want To Know A Secret," "We Can Work It Out," "I Should Have Known Better," "Nowhere Man" and "You're Going To Lose That Girl."

Of the nine other top 10 Beatle remakes, six were never released as singles by the Beatles. "Lucy In The Sky With Diamonds" (Elton John, with John Lennon guesting) came from the *Sgt. Pepper's Lonely Hearts Club Band* album; "You Won't See Me" (Anne Murray), from *Rubber Soul*; "The Fool On The Hill" (Sergio Mendes and Brasil '66), from *Magical Mystery Tour*; "Here Comes The Sun" (Richie Havens) and "Oh! Darling" (Robin Gibb), from *Abbey Road*; and "You've Got To Hide Your Love Away" (The Silkie), from *Help!*

Earth, Wind & Fire

MOTION PICTURES

1 HOW DEEP IS YOUR LOVE
Bee Gees [*Saturday Night Fever*]

2 TAMMY
Debbie Reynolds [*Tammy and the Bachelor*]

3 ENDLESS LOVE
Diana Ross and Lionel Richie [*Endless Love*]

4 JAILHOUSE ROCK/TREAT ME NICE
Elvis Presley [*Jailhouse Rock*]

5 (LET ME BE YOUR) TEDDY BEAR
Elvis Presley [*Loving You*]

6 EYE OF THE TIGER
Survivor [*Rocky III*]

7 FLASHDANCE ... WHAT A FEELING
Irene Cara [*Flashdance*]

8 LOVE ME TENDER
Elvis Presley [*Love Me Tender*]

9 CALL ME
Blondie [*American Gigolo*]

10 STAYIN' ALIVE
Bee Gees [*Saturday Night Fever*]

11 NIGHT FEVER
Bee Gees [*Saturday Night Fever*]

12 WHATEVER WILL BE, WILL BE
Doris Day [*The Man Who Knew Too Much*]

13 RAINDROPS KEEP FALLIN' ON MY HEAD
B.J. Thomas [*Butch Cassidy and the Sundance Kid*]

14 TRUE LOVE
Bing Crosby and Grace Kelly [*High Society*]

15 WHEN DOVES CRY
Prince [*Purple Rain*]

16 APRIL LOVE
Pat Boone [*April Love*]

17 IT'S NOT FOR ME TO SAY
Johnny Mathis [*Lizzie*]

18 HARD TO SAY I'M SORRY
Chicago [*Summer Lovers*]

19 LOVE THEME FROM "A STAR IS BORN"
Barbra Streisand [*A Star Is Born*]

20 MAGIC
Olivia Newton-John [*Xanadu*]

21 TO SIR WITH LOVE
Lulu [*To Sir With Love*]

22 MANIAC
Michael Sembello [*Flashdance*]

23 LOVE ON THE ROCKS
Neil Diamond [*The Jazz Singer*]

24 9 TO 5
Dolly Parton [*9 to 5*]

25 AGAINST ALL ODDS (TAKE A LOOK AT ME NOW)
Phil Collins [*Against All Odds*]

26 ARTHUR'S THEME (BEST THAT YOU CAN DO)
Christopher Cross [*Arthur*]

27 FOOTLOOSE
Kenny Loggins [*Footloose*]

28 THE WAY WE WERE
Barbra Streisand [*The Way We Were*]

29 IT MUST HAVE BEEN LOVE
Roxette [*Pretty Woman*]

30 GHOSTBUSTERS
Ray Parker Jr. [*Ghostbusters*]

"Tammy and the Bachelor"

It was obvious that rock and roll and the movies were meant for each other from the moment the curtain went up on *The Blackboard Jungle* in 1955 and Bill Haley's voice came thundering out of the giant theater speakers: "One, two, three o'clock, four o'clock rock . . . " There were riots in movie theaters; Clare Booth Luce denounced the film as degenerate, causing it to be pulled from a film festival in Venice. Haley's recording of "(We're Gonna) Rock Around The Clock," released in 1954 to a mediocre response, was re-released and shot to number one.

"Rock Around The Clock" wasn't written specifically for *The Blackboard Jungle*, so it's not included in the list of the top 100 songs from motion pictures. To qualify, a song had to be written or recorded specifically for a film. That eliminated cover versions of movie songs, like Debby Boone's "You Light Up My Life" and Meco's "Star Wars/Cantina Band." However, songs that weren't written for films were included if a version was recorded for a particular movie. "Wind Beneath My Wings," a top 10 country single for Gary Morris in 1983, qualifies because Bette Midler recorded it specifically for *Beaches*. The same holds true for Los Lobos' version of "La Bamba" from the Ritchie Valens film biography and Phil Collins' "Groovy Kind Of Love" from *Buster*.

The cinema welcomed rock and roll right from the beginning. Elvis Presley flew to Hollywood for a screen test with Hal Wallis at Paramount Pictures even before "Heartbreak Hotel" became his first number one hit. On April 1, 1956, Wallis signed Elvis to a three-picture deal. He was supposed to make his debut in *The*

Rainmaker with Burt Lancaster and Katherine Hepburn, but that was too serious a role by Col. Tom Parker's standards. He wanted Elvis to star in more lightweight fare, and he got his wish with 33 consecutive films.

Production on Elvis' first film started at 20th Century Fox on August 22, 1956. Originally titled *The Reno Brothers*, it was later renamed after one of the four songs included in the soundtrack, "Love Me Tender." Ken Darby, musical director of the film, wrote the tune based on a folk ballad from 1861, "Aura Lee," although the songwriting credits went to Darby's wife, Vera Watson, and Elvis.

Presley sang "Love Me Tender" when he made his first appearance on Ed Sullivan's show, on September 9—more than two months before the movie was released. His performance caused such a demand for the single that RCA was forced to issue it during the first week of October, and it went to number one 13 days before the opening of the movie.

Elvis' second film was *Loving You*, for Paramount. Kal Mann and Bernie Lowe wrote "(Let Me Be Your) Teddy Bear" for the movie, and it went to number one the day before the picture opened. The big production number in Elvis' third film gave him his most successful soundtrack single, "Jailhouse Rock." Jerry Leiber and Mike Stoller wrote the tune based on the script they received, which was marked where the songs were to be placed.

The most successful soundtrack single from the '50s is "Tammy," sung by Debbie Reynolds in the movie she starred in with Leslie Nielsen, *Tammy and the Bachelor*. Coral Records head Bob Thiele didn't expect the song to do very well, and released the unembellished version from the movie. Debbie's single went to number one; a version by the Ames Brothers, heard over the closing credits, went to number five.

There are only nine songs from the '60s included in the top 100 soundtrack singles. The highest-rated is the title song from *To Sir With Love*. Lulu was given a part in the film after director James Clavell saw her perform on the bill of a Beach Boys concert in London. The producers came up with several songs that could be used in the movie, but Lulu hated them all. She asked her friend Mark London to write something, and he came up with the music in five minutes. The next day, lyricist Don Black added the words. "I was over the moon, I just knew it was going to be a great song," says Lulu.

The Beatles were quickly recruited into the movies. Production on *A Hard Day's Night* began on March 2, 1964, at Paddington Station in London. John Lennon and Paul McCartney started working on the songs while in Paris two months earlier, and the Beatles recorded "A Hard Day's Night" on April 16. Almost a year later, they cut the title song for their second film, *Help!*

The best-selling soundtrack album of all time was released in the '70s: four of the songs from *Saturday Night Fever* went to number one, and all of them are included in the top 100 songs from motion pictures. Robert Stigwood, who produced the films *Tommy* and *Jesus Christ, Superstar*, bought the rights to Nik Cohn's article for *New York* magazine, "Tribal Rites of the New Saturday Night." The Bee Gees never saw the script for the film, but Stigwood verbally outlined the plot for them. Armed with that information and the fact that John Travolta was the lead, the Gibb brothers spent two-and-a-half weeks coming up with "Stayin' Alive" and "Night Fever." They had already written "If I Can't Have You" and the most successful chart single from a motion picture, "How Deep Is Your Love."

The second best-selling soundtrack album of the '70s was *Grease*. The Broadway musical had been a long-running success, and most of the songs were from the theatrical version, including "Summer Nights." But the three biggest songs from the film were original. Travolta and Newton-John duetted on "You're The One That I Want," Olivia soloed on "Hopelessly Devoted To You," and Frankie Valli was asked to sing Barry Gibb's title song.

One movie song from the '70s served triple duty. Barry De-Vorzon and Perry Botkin, Jr. composed the music for *Bless the Beasts and Children*. An instrumental track from the film, "Cotton's Dream," was appropriated as the theme music for CBS' daytime soap, "The Young And The Restless." After Romanian gymnast Nadia Comaneci used it as her theme music in the 1976 Olympics, it became a hit single under the title "Nadia's Theme (The Young And The Restless)."

The nature of soundtracks changed in the '80s. Record companies learned from the success of *Saturday Night Fever* and *Grease*, and became more interested in putting together collections of rock songs as soundtracks than issuing original instrumental background music. Sometimes the songs were integral to the plot, as in *Footloose*, and sometimes they were just used as incidental music, heard in filtered fragments as someone in the movie happened to be listening to the radio.

Music was employed well in films like *Dirty Dancing*, which produced two hit singles, and *Flashdance*, which yielded two number one singles. Prince triumphed with the critics in *Purple Rain* and had three hit singles in the top 100 from the soundtrack. Other films will be remembered for their music long after their place in cinematic history is reduced to a footnote. Eddie Rabbitt's "Drivin' My Life Away," for example, will still be played on the radio long after *Roadie* is forgotten, and Madonna's "Live To Tell" will survive *At Close Range*.

The *Rocky* series continued to produce hit singles in the '80s, following the tradition of Bill Conti's "Gonna Fly Now" from 1977. The group Survivor came up with "Eye Of The Tiger" for *Rocky III* and "Burning Heart" for *Rocky IV*. The James Bond series always included a title song over the opening credits. Carly Simon's "Nobody Does It Better" remains the most successful Bond song. Duran Duran had a number one hit with "A View To A Kill" in 1985, and Sheena Easton went to number three with "For Your Eyes Only" in 1981.

THE TOP 30 SONGS FROM
MUSICAL THEATER

1 MACK THE KNIFE
Bobby Darin [*The Three Penny Opera*]

2 AQUARIUS/LET THE SUNSHINE IN
5th Dimension [*Hair*]

3 HELLO, DOLLY!
Louis Armstrong [*Hello, Dolly!*]

4 SMOKE GETS IN YOUR EYES
The Platters [*Roberta*]

5 STANDING ON THE CORNER
The Four Lads [*The Most Happy Fella*]

6 HAIR
The Cowsills [*Hair*]

7 MORITAT (A THEME FROM "THE THREE PENNY OPERA")
Dick Hyman Trio [*The Three Penny Opera*]

8 ON THE STREET WHERE YOU LIVE
Vic Damone [*My Fair Lady*]

9 EASY TO BE HARD
Three Dog Night [*Hair*]

10 ONE NIGHT IN BANGKOK
Murray Head [*Chess*]

11 GOOD MORNING STARSHINE
Oliver [*Hair*]

12 PEOPLE
Barbra Streisand [*Funny Girl*]

13 SUMMER NIGHTS
John Travolta and Olivia Newton-John [*Grease*]

14 THE WAY WE WERE/TRY TO REMEMBER
Gladys Knight & the Pips [*The Fantasticks*]

15 I GOT RHYTHM
The Happenings [*Girl Crazy*]

16 I'VE TOLD EVERY LITTLE STAR
Linda Scott [*Music in the Air*]

17 I'LL NEVER FALL IN LOVE AGAIN
Dionne Warwick [*Promises, Promises*]

18 IF YOU LET ME MAKE LOVE TO YOU (THEN WHY CAN'T I TOUCH YOU)
Ronnie Dyson [*Salvation*]

19 I'VE GOTTA BE ME
Sammy Davis, Jr. [*Golden Rainbow*]

20 MY CUP RUNNETH OVER
Ed Ames [*I Do! I Do!*]

21 THEME FROM "THREE PENNY OPERA"
Richard Hayman and Jan August [*The Three Penny Opera*]

22 I DON'T KNOW HOW TO LOVE HIM
Helen Reddy [*Jesus Christ, Superstar*]

23 SUPERSTAR
Murray Head [*Jesus Christ, Superstar*]

24 WHAT KIND OF FOOL AM I
Sammy Davis, Jr. [*Stop the World—I Want to Get Off*]

25 I LOVES YOU, PORGY
Nina Simone [*Porgy and Bess*]

26 TONIGHT
Ferrante and Teicher [*West Side Story*]

27 SOME ENCHANTED EVENING
Jay & the Americans [*South Pacific*]

28 DAY BY DAY
Godspell [*Godspell*]

29 CORNER OF THE SKY
The Jackson Five [*Pippin*]

30 SEND IN THE CLOWNS
Judy Collins [*A Little Night Music*]

When *The Black Crook* opened in New York City on September 12, 1866, it ushered in a new era of American musical theater. At the start of the 20th century, that form was nurtured by Victor Herbert and George M. Cohan, who were followed by Jerome Kern, George and Ira Gershwin, Oscar Hammerstein II, Rodgers and Hart and Cole Porter. By the middle of the century, Broadway audiences were enjoying musicals like *Pal Joey* and *Oklahoma!*. But while Hollywood embraced rock and roll in 1955, Broadway theater resisted the new music. Twelve days after Elvis Presley made his first appearance on the *Billboard* singles chart, *My Fair Lady* opened on Broadway.

Pop artists had some success covering songs from Broadway shows in the '50s. *The Most Happy Fella* opened on Broadway on May 3, 1956, and the Four Lads recorded one of Frank Loesser's tunes from the show, "Standing On The Corner." Vic Damone had a top 10 single with "On The Street Where You Live" from *My Fair Lady*. In 1959, Bobby Darin recorded the most successful chart single to originate in a stage production. The song "Moritat" was from the 1928 German musical *The Threepenny Opera*, written by Kurt Weill and Bertholt Brecht. The show had a brief run in New York in 1933, and was revived off-Broadway on March 10, 1954 with a new translation by Marc Blitzstein—who turned "Moritat" into "Mack The Knife." With three songs in the top 30 stage songs list, *The Threepenny Opera* has proven to have more successful songs than any other show, with the exception of *Hair*.

One of the first new musicals of the new decade, *Bye, Bye Birdie*, took a good poke at rock and roll. But rock music and Broadway didn't successfully merge until *Hair* moved from off-Broadway to the Great White Way on April 29, 1968. Four songs from *Hair* are included in the top 30 songs from the stage: a medley of "Aquarius/Let The Sunshine In" by the 5th Dimension, "Hair" by the Cowsills, "Easy To Be Hard" by Three Dog Night and "Good Morning Starshine" by Oliver. No other Broadway show has had such an impact on the Hot 100.

In 1970, Andrew Lloyd Webber and Tim Rice oversaw production of an album version of *Jesus Christ, Superstar* a year before it opened at the Hellinger Theater in New York. Murray Head's "Superstar" was from the album, and Helen Reddy covered Yvonne Elliman's "I Don't Know How To Love Him." Fourteen years later, Rice repeated the formula with *Chess*, written with Benny Andersson and Bjorn Ulvaeus of Abba. Head had his second American hit with "One Night In Bangkok" before the show actually opened in London.

180

THE TOP 50
"WHO REALLY SANG THAT" SONGS

Milli Vanilli

The name on the label isn't always the name of the person singing the song. Sometimes it's accidental, sometimes it's for fun and sometimes it's deliberately misleading.

In the case of "The All American Boy," it was simply a mistake. The song was written by Bill Parsons and recorded by Bobby Bare. But when the single was issued on the Fraternity label in 1958, Parsons was listed as the artist. Bare was serving in the Army at the time, so Parsons made public appearances, lip synching to the record.

Many artists adapt stage names, and they are not included in the list. But those who have adapted strange nicknames are. British musician Robin Scott took the name "M" from the letter that identifies Metro stations in Paris. Jape Richardson used his initials, J.P., but most of the time he went by the name he used while working as a disc jockey during his high school days in Beaumont, Texas—he recorded for Mercury under that name, the Big Bopper. Sister Luc-Gabrielle, whose real name was Jeanine Deckers, was only identified as the Singing Nun on "Dominique." Kennedy Gordy, son of Motown founder Berry Gordy, recorded "Somebody's Watching Me" for his father's company under the name Rockwell. Gordon Sumner took the nickname Sting from a favorite black and yellow jersey, and Adam Ant was born Stuart Goddard.

Rappers rarely use their own names—would Marvin Young sell as many records as Young M.C., or would Stan Kirk Burrell be as popular as M.C. Hammer? And the name on the birth certificate isn't Vanilla Ice, Robert Van Winkle.

Some individuals have masqueraded as groups. Lipps, Inc. was the brainchild of a Minneapolis musician, Steven Greenberg. The New Vaudeville Band didn't exist when British composer Geoff Stephens recorded "Winchester Cathedral," but when the record became a hit, he put together an outfit that could tour. Gary Paxton was under contract to another label from his Skip & Flip days, so he recorded "Alley-Oop" and released it as by the "Hollywood Argyles." Gary De Carlo recorded "Na Na Hey Hey Kiss Him Goodbye," but released the single under the group name "Steam" so as not to detract from his "real" recordings. Stars on 45 was the credit on the medley of songs that included "Venus," "Sugar, Sugar" and eight Beatles songs, but the record was concocted by producer Jaap Eggermont using the voices of Bas Muys (as John Lennon), Okkie Huysdens (as Paul McCartney) and Hans Vermeulen (as George Harrison). Edison Lighthouse was one of many British studio groups fronted by vocalist Tony Burrows.

Some vocalists were simply not credited. Gladys Knight, Stevie Wonder and Elton John were listed as "and Friends" on Dionne Warwick's "That's What Friends Are For." Linda Greene assumed the role of Peaches when she sang duets with Herb. If it weren't for Bill Withers, Grover Washington, Jr. might have recorded "Just The One Of Us." Joe Pizzulo and Leza Miller supplied the vocals on Sergio Mendes' "Never Gonna Let You Go." Darlene Love recorded "He's A Rebel," and was surprised when Phil Spector released it as by the Crystals. Carolyn Willis and Odia Coates were the uncredited female singers on Seals and Crofts' "Get Closer" and Paul Anka's "(You're) Having My Baby," respectively. And Mickey Thomas was the guest vocalist on Elvin Bishop's "Fooled Around And Fell In Love."

Other singers didn't receive credit because their names weren't featured in the group name. J. Geils, Kool, Alan Parsons, Manfred Mann, and Mike of the Mechanics didn't sing lead on hits bearing their names. Other groups had names that sounded like real people, but weren't: Tommy Tutone, Tony! Toni! Tone! and Edward Bear.

That leaves the unusual case of Milli Vanilli. In November, 1990, producer Frank Farian called a press conference to tell the world that Rob Pilatus and Fabrice Morvan did not sing the vocals on the Milli Vanilli album. It was a defensive maneuver, as the dreadlocked duo had asked to really sing on the second Milli Vanilli album, and Farian had said no. Rob and Fab returned their Grammy for Best New Artist, and Brad Howell and Johnny Davis were identified as the real voices of Milli Vanilli.

THE CONFIGURATIONS

Age, gender, place of origin and family background are some of the factors that determine the charts in this section.

If any readers want proof that rock and roll has been dominated by men, they need only look at the number of singles eligible for the top 100 songs by male soloists and female soloists. The number by men is much, much greater, but male dominance might be a thing of the past. In 1990, women held the number one position on the Hot 100 for 31 weeks, as compared to 21 weeks for men.

Men and women aren't always competing with each other, as evidenced by the top 100 duets. Most of these are male-female duets, although gender was not a factor in this chart. A number of songs on the list of top 100 duets were performed by two superstars teaming up, such as Paul McCartney and Michael Jackson, Barbra Streisand and Donna Summer, and Diana Ross and Julio Iglesias.

There's nothing sexist about the term "girl groups." Although a phenomenon of the early '60s, modern-day acts like the Bangles, the Go-Go's and Wilson Phillips are commonly referred to as "girl groups." The top 100 chart for this section includes all groups made up exclusively of women, whether or not they were part of the "girl group" phenomenon.

The words won't get in the way of the next chart. Instrumentals are having a tough time making the chart in the '90s, but that wasn't so when the rock era began in 1955. In 1960, an instrumental was even the number one song of the year.

Tiffany and Debbie Gibson stand out for their youth in a time when many rock stars are over 40—some have even gone past the half-century mark. Back in the early '60s, being a teenaged rock star wasn't so unusual. Singles by artists who were teenagers or children are listed on this chart.

The following two charts are family-related. The first deals with groups that include blood relations, be they siblings, cousins or parents; the second concerns married couples.

The final chart in this section features the top 100 songs by artists from the United Kingdom. Countries in the U.K. include England, Scotland, Wales and Northern Ireland. By that definition, Irish artists like Sinead O'Connor and Gilbert O'Sullivan were not considered for this list.

MALE SOLO ARTISTS

1 THE TWIST
Chubby Checker *Parkway* 60

2 DON'T BE CRUEL/HOUND DOG
Elvis Presley *RCA* 56

3 SINGING THE BLUES
Guy Mitchell *Columbia* 56

4 LOVE LETTERS IN THE SAND
Pat Boone *Dot* 57

5 MACK THE KNIFE
Bobby Darin *Atco* 59

6 HEARTBREAK HOTEL
Elvis Presley *RCA* 56

7 ALL SHOOK UP
Elvis Presley *RCA* 57

8 I JUST WANT TO BE YOUR EVERYTHING
Andy Gibb *RSO* 77

9 JUST WALKING IN THE RAIN
Johnnie Ray *Columbia* 56

10 JAILHOUSE ROCK/TREAT ME NICE
Elvis Presley *RCA* 57

11 (LET ME BE YOUR) TEDDY BEAR
Elvis Presley *RCA* 57

12 SHADOW DANCING
Andy Gibb *RSO* 78

13 SIXTEEN TONS
Tennessee Ernie Ford *Capitol* 55

14 THE GREEN DOOR
Jim Lowe *Dot* 56

15 LOVE ME TENDER
Elvis Presley *RCA* 56

16 MEMORIES ARE MADE OF THIS
Dean Martin *Capitol* 56

17 HE
Al Hibbler *Decca* 55

18 HONEYCOMB
Jimmie Rodgers *Roulette* 57

19 CHANCES ARE/THE TWELFTH OF NEVER
Johnny Mathis *Columbia* 57

20 IT'S ALL IN THE GAME
Tommy Edwards *MGM* 58

21 MONSTER MASH
Bobby "Boris" Pickett & the Crypt
Kickers *Garpax* 63

22 TOSSIN' AND TURNIN'
Bobby Lewis *Beltone* 61

23 HURTS SO GOOD
John Cougar *Riva* 82

24 RAINDROPS KEEP FALLIN' ON MY HEAD
B.J. Thomas *Scepter* 70

25 A BLOSSOM FELL
Nat King Cole *Capitol* 55

26 LEARNIN' THE BLUES
Frank Sinatra *Capitol* 55

27 JESSIE'S GIRL
Rick Springfield *RCA* 81

28 THE BATTLE OF NEW ORLEANS
Johnny Horton *Columbia* 59

29 BILLIE JEAN
Michael Jackson *Epic* 83

30 LADY
Kenny Rogers *Liberty* 80

Elvis Presley

It shouldn't be any surprise that in the Eisenhower years of rock and roll, male singers dominated the *Billboard* chart. Forty-three of the top 100 songs by male solo artists are from the 1950s; in contrast, only 12 of the top 100 songs by female solo artists are from the same decade.

Elvis Presley dominates the men's top 100 with 10 songs listed, double the number of his closest competitor. Pat Boone has five titles in the top 100, and Rod Stewart, Michael Jackson and Andy Gibb have three each.

Elvis has four songs in the top 10, including the two-sided hit "Don't Be Cruel" and "Hound Dog," ranked number two. Eight of his 10 songs on the list are from the '50s; the ballads "It's Now Or Never" and "Are You Lonesome Tonight?" are his only two songs from the '60s in the top 100.

After Elvis, the most successful single by a male solo artist from the '50s is "Singing The Blues" by Guy Mitchell. Melvin Endsley wrote the song in 1954, but no one recorded it until Marty Robbins cut a version for Columbia Records in 1956. Robbins' single spent 13 weeks at number one on the country chart. Mitch Miller thought his company could have a pop hit with the same song, so he produced a cover version by Mitchell. His single topped the Best Sellers in Stores chart for nine weeks.

Pat Boone's "Love Letters In The Sand" is the next highest-ranked male solo performance from the '50s. Rudy Vallee and Bing Crosby had recorded it in decades gone by; a recording by Ted Black and His Orchestra reached the top 10 in 1931. Boone recorded it because Dot Records founder Randy Wood had been getting numerous requests for the song at the record shop he ran in Gallatin, Tennessee. After Boone cut the track, it remained on the shelf until the producers of the film *Bernadine* decided to take advantage of the fact that Boone was in the cast by including two of his songs in the film. Johnny Mercer wrote the title song, and "Love Letters In The Sand" was dusted off and added to the soundtrack.

Bobby Darin, Johnnie Ray, Tennessee Ernie Ford and Jim Lowe have one song each on the top 100. Darin's contribution is his version of "Mack The Knife," a song first heard in 1928 when Berthold Brecht and Kurt Weill wrote it for *The Threepenny Opera*. Inspired by Louis Armstrong's earlier recording of the song, Darin included it in his *That's All* album to demonstrate his diversity. It was released as a single against his wishes. Johnnie Ray first made the *Billboard* chart in 1951 when "Cry" was number one for 11 weeks. His most successful recording of the rock era, "Just Walking In The Rain," was originally recorded by the Prisonaires, a group of inmates from Tennessee State Penitentiary in Nashville. Tennessee Ernie Ford was so busy appearing on NBC five times a week with a daytime show that he fell behind in his recording schedule for Capitol Records. Pressed for time, he cut two songs he had performed on TV: "You Don't Have To Be A Baby To Cry" and a song written by Merle Travis in 1947, "Sixteen Tons." Jim Lowe was a disc jockey working for WNBC radio in New York when he recorded "The Green Door."

Chubby Checker's "The Twist" is the number one male vocal of the '60s and of the rock era. It is also the most successful chart single of the first 35 years of rock and roll. While Checker's chart fortunes don't match those of Elvis Presley, he did have success with a number of dance-oriented hits, including "Pony Time," "The Fly" and his other song listed in the top 100, "Limbo Rock" (number 81).

Bobby "Boris" Pickett's "Monster Mash" was a hit in two decades: it was a number one song in 1962, and returned to the top 10 in 1973. Ben E. King's "Stand By Me" was also a hit in two different decades—it peaked at number four in 1961, and was re-released in 1986 after Rob Reiner used it as the title song for his film *Stand By Me*. (It went to number nine on its second chart journey.) Marvin Gaye's "I Heard It Through The Grapevine" also spent seven weeks at number one, even though a version by Gladys Knight & the Pips had gone to number two a year earlier.

If they took a vote in 1964 to elect the artist most unlikely to knock the Beatles out of number one, Louis Armstrong might have been very near the top of the list—if anyone had thought of him at all. Nevertheless, Satchmo interrupted the Beatles after the Fab Four had spent 14 weeks at the top of the Hot 100 with three different singles. His recording of the title song from the Carol Channing musical *Hello, Dolly!* did the trick. Armstrong's success with the song led to him being cast in the film version of the play when Barbra Streisand took the title role in 1969.

The two highest-rated male vocal performances from the '70s are "I Just Want To Be Your Everything" (number eight) and "Shadow Dancing" (number 12) by Andy Gibb. He was the fourth son of Barbara and Hugh Gibb, and by the time he was 10, his three older brothers were already well known as the Bee Gees. "I Just Want To Be Your Everything" was written by Barry Gibb in a two-day session at Robert Stigwood's Bermuda estate; "Shadow Dancing" was written by Andy and his older siblings while they were filming *Sgt. Pepper's Lonely Hearts Club Band* in Los Angeles.

"Raindrops Keep Fallin' On My Head" by B.J. Thomas is the third most successful male solo performance from the '70s. It was the very first number one hit of the decade, available as a single as well as on the soundtrack of *Butch Cassidy and the Sundance Kid.* Written by Burt Bacharach and Hal David for the film, the song was submitted to singer Ray Stevens. Bacharach screened the film for him, but he turned down the opportunity to record the song. Thomas was recording for Scepter, the same label that was home to the most prominent interpreter of Bacharach's songs, Dionne Warwick. She told Burt about B.J., and Bacharach promised him a shot at the song.

Rod Stewart had three number one hits in the '70s, all included in the top 100 songs by male solo artists. The highest ranked is "Tonight's The Night (Gonna Be Alright)," which topped the Hot 100 for eight weeks. Paul Davis didn't get to number one with "I Go Crazy," but the single spent 40 weeks on the *Billboard* chart, a record at the time.

"Hurts So Good" by John Cougar (Mellencamp) is the most successful male solo recording from the '80s. Although it didn't go to number one, it did spend four weeks at number two and a total of 28 weeks on the Hot 100. The follow-up, "Jack and Diane," did go to number one and is also included in the top 100.

Australian Rick Springfield has the second most successful recording by a male performer in the '80s. "Jessie's Girl," the highest-ranked single by an Australian artist on the top 3000 songs of the rock era, was number one the day MTV debuted. That was appropriate, as Springfield's popularity was aided by his starring role on television's "General Hospital."

Michael Jackson's "Billie Jean" is the third highest-ranked male solo recording of the '80s. The second single to be released from *Thriller*, it remained on top of the Hot 100 for seven weeks. Jackson has two other singles included in the top 100 recordings by male solo artists: "Rock With You" and "Beat It," at number 38 and number 39, respectively.

Diana Ross

By the end of the 1950s, there were a number of male singers who had established themselves as consistent hitmakers. Elvis Presley led the pack, followed by artists like Pat Boone, Fats Domino and Ricky Nelson. While female singers like Gale Storm and Teresa Brewer had more than one top 10 hit, there weren't any women who were in the same class as Elvis, Ricky or Fats.

In the early '60s, Connie Francis and Brenda Lee challenged the men for chart superiority, but it wasn't until the '70s that female solo singers like Diana Ross, Donna Summer, Barbra Streisand and Olivia Newton-John could legitimately be called superstars. That trend continued in the '80s, and in the first year of the '90s, the women bested the men by a wide margin.

Twelve of the top 100 songs by female solo artists are from the '50s. Gogi Grant's "The Wayward Wind" is the highest-ranked of those 12 songs, placing number three on the top 100. The single was number one for six weeks and has the distinction of knocking off Elvis' first number one hit, "Heartbreak Hotel." Ironically, "The Wayward Wind" was written for a man to sing. Songwriter Herb Newman, owner of the Era label, had written "The Wayward Wind" with Stan Lebousky when they were students at UCLA. The lyrics were altered so a woman could sing the tune, and with 15 minutes of studio time left, Gogi recorded the song that would bring Elvis down.

The next biggest female solo recording from the '50s is Debbie

Reynolds' "Tammy," the first song by a solo female vocalist to go to number one since Gogi Grant's reign at the top 15 months earlier. Oddly, there was also a male interpretation of the song, a version by the Ames Brothers that was heard over the closing credits of the film. It would be almost three years before another female soloist would top the chart—Connie Francis ended the drought in June, 1960, with "Everybody's Somebody's Fool."

The other female singers from the '50s listed in the top 100 are Doris Day, Gisele MacKenzie, Kay Starr, Gale Storm, Patti Page, Jane Morgan, Cathy Carr, Teresa Brewer and Della Reese.

Brenda Lee has the top-rated female solo performance from the '60s with "I'm Sorry." She's listed twice in the top 100—"Sweet Nothin's" ranks number 83. The runner-up female solo single of the '60s is Lulu's "To Sir With Love," the title song from the motion picture she starred in with Sidney Poitier. Connie Francis places third for the '60s with "Everybody's Somebody's Fool." She's also listed with another of her three number one hits, "My Heart Has A Mind Of Its Own." After that comes Bobbie Gentry's "Ode To Billie Joe" and the Singing Nun's "Dominique." Other females from the '60s in the top 100 are Mary Wells, Connie Stevens, Petula Clark, Shelley Fabares and Dee Dee Sharp.

It wasn't until the '70s that solo female artists were truly competitive with the men. Heading the list is "You Light Up My Life" by Debby Boone, the most successful solo female recording of the rock era. The song was number one for 10 weeks, the longest run at the top since Elvis had an 11-week reign with "Don't Be Cruel" and "Hound Dog." Donna Summer has the runner-up female solo performance of the '70s with "Hot Stuff." She also appears on the top 100 with "Bad Girls," "MacArthur Park" and "She Works Hard For The Money."

Donna was the diva of disco, and the genre was also very good to Gloria Gaynor. Her recording of "I Will Survive" is the third most popular female solo performance of the '70s. After that comes Roberta Flack's interpretation of Ewan MacColl's "The First Time Ever I Saw Your Face." Flack is also on the top 100 with "Killing Me Softly With His Song," a tune inspired by a live performance by Don McLean.

Moving down the list, the next song from the '70s is "Love Theme From 'A Star Is Born' (Evergreen)" by Barbra Streisand. She is also on the list with another theme from one of her movies, "The Way We Were," as well as a song from the '80s, "Woman In Love."

Carole King, who wrote many hits in the '60s with her then husband, Gerry Goffin, came into her own as an artist in the '70s. The first single released from her *Tapestry* album was the two-sided hit "It's Too Late"/"I Feel The Earth Move," number 22 on the top 100 songs by female solo artists. Other women from the '70s on the list are Anne Murray, Alicia Bridges, Thelma Houston, Olivia Newton-John, Mary MacGregor, Dionne Warwick, Anita Ward, Carly Simon, Diana Ross, Crystal Gayle, Melanie, Vicki

Lawrence, Cher, Samantha Sang, Rita Coolidge, Maxine Nightingale, Dorothy Moore, Yvonne Elliman, Aretha Franklin, Janis Joplin, Amii Stewart and Linda Ronstadt.

Female singers continued to fare well in the '80s. There are 33 songs from that decade on the top 100, headed by Olivia Newton-John's "Physical." That is the only other single in the rock era besides "You Light Up My Life" to be number one for 10 weeks. Runner-up for the '80s is Kim Carnes' version of Jackie DeShannon and Donna Weiss' "Bette Davis Eyes." It held on to the top spot on the Hot 100 for nine weeks.

Irene Cara has the third most popular solo female recording of the '80s with "Flashdance . . . What A Feeling," from the film starring Jennifer Beals. Diana Ross, who scored in the '60s as lead singer for the Supremes and in the '70s as a solo artist, was also big in the '80s with "Upside Down," produced by the very chic team of Nile Rodgers and Bernard Edwards. Bonnie Tyler, a Welsh singer with a gravelly voice that prompted some to consider her a female Rod Stewart, did well with "Total Eclipse Of The Heart," a Jim Steinman epic that was number one in many countries around the world. Laura Branigan recorded a song that originated in Italy, "Gloria," and spent three weeks at number two. It was on the Hot 100 for 36 weeks. Tina Turner, who first hit the chart in August, 1960, made an impressive comeback in 1984 with "What's Love Got To Do With It." Juice Newton covered "Queen Of Hearts," the Hank DeVito song originally recorded by Dave Edmunds. Madonna first went to number one with "Like A Virgin," one of three songs by her on the top 100. Other female artists from the '80s on the list are Dolly Parton, Toni Basil, Sheena Easton, Chaka Khan, Donna Summer, Deniece Williams, Janet Jackson, Cyndi Lauper, Whitney Houston, Bette Midler, Paula Abdul, Debbie Gibson, Melissa Manchester, Belinda Carlisle and Tiffany.

The year 1990 was the best year yet for women in rock—eight songs on the top 100 are from that year. The success story of 1990 was Mariah Carey, who had the year's number one single with "Love Takes Time." Carey co-wrote the song, intending to save it for her second album. But a Columbia Records executive heard "Love Takes Time" and insisted that it be added to her debut disc. "Love Takes Time" ranks number 19 on the top 100 songs by female solo artists; Carey is also at number 44 with her first single, "Vision Of Love."

Sinead O'Connor, an Irish singer who covered an obscure song written by Prince, is the runner-up from 1990 with "Nothing Compares 2 U." Other female artists from 1990 included in the top 100 are Madonna, Alannah Myles, Whitney Houston, Bette Midler and Janet Jackson.

Houston appears on the top 100 more often than any other woman—five times in all. Diana Ross and Donna Summer each appear four times, and Olivia Newton-John, Barbra Streisand, Madonna and Bette Midler have three songs each on the list.

THE TOP 100
DUETS

Lionel Richie and Diana Ross

The dictionary defines "duet" as "a piece of music composed for two performers." That definition was expanded to compile the top 100 duets of the rock era, and some criteria were established. The list was limited to vocal duets. Individual artists who teamed up with groups were included, such as Dionne Warwick's collaboration with the Spinners and the Pet Shop Boys' team-up with Dusty Springfield on one of their hits. Two groups performing together were not included, thus eliminating the Supremes' collaborations with the Temptations and the Four Tops, as well as Earth, Wind & Fire's match-up with the Emotions.

Another qualification was that both artists had to be credited on the label. When Chubby Checker recorded "Slow Twistin'" with Dee Dee Sharp, he was the only performer listed. Similarly, Odia Coates was the anonymous female partnered with Paul Anka on "(You're) Having My Baby." Her name was included on subsequent releases, and they are included here. Andy Williams' recording of "I Like Your Kind Of Love" had an unusual label credit for Peggy Powers. The Cadence 45 lists her as "Andy's girlfriend played by Peggy Powers."

Excluded from the list are groups who happened to perform duets, and duos like the Righteous Brothers, the Everly Brothers and Daryl Hall and John Oates. Included are pairs of artists who by their very nature always recorded duets, such as Paul and Paula or Peaches and Herb.

A majority of the duets on the top 100 are one-time only collaborations between two well-established artists. The most successful duet of the rock era, "Endless Love," falls into this category. The song began as an instrumental theme for the film *Endless Love*, but director Franco Zeffirelli decided he wanted a title song with lyrics. Lionel Richie agreed to write some words for his theme, and then Zeffirelli suggested a duet would be appropriate—with someone like Diana Ross, for example. Diana had just left Motown for RCA, but arrangements were made for her to record the song for the soundtrack album, released on Mercury. The single was issued on Motown.

The second most successful duet of the rock era was another teaming of two superstars. Paul McCartney had already collaborated with Stevie Wonder a year earlier on "Ebony and Ivory" (number four), and had joined Michael Jackson for a track on his *Thriller* album, "The Girl Is Mine" (number 30). Jackson repaid the favor by working with McCartney on two tracks for the *Pipes of Peace* album. The only one released as a single was "Say, Say, Say," which spent six weeks at number one.

The third most popular duet of the rock era was from the film *High Society*. Bing Crosby and Grace Kelly sang "True Love" in the movie. The song marks the only appearance by the late Princess Grace on the *Billboard* chart. Crosby was frequently partnered with other singers; his chart duets include match-ups with Peggy Lee, Frank Sinatra, Louis Armstrong, Carol Richards, his son Gary and the Andrews Sisters.

The artist with the most songs included in the top 100 duets is Marvin Gaye, with seven. Early in his career, he was teamed with another Motown artist, Mary Wells, to record an album of duets. After one single was released, Wells left the label for 20th Century Fox Records. Gaye then recorded some tracks with an unknown female vocalist, Ona Page, but they were put on the shelf until they were unearthed for *The Marvin Gaye Collection* in 1990. Next, Motown paired Marvin with another female on the label's roster, Kim Weston. Two singles by this new duo were released before Kim departed for MGM Records. Marvin's next partner was born Thomasina Montgomery in Philadelphia. She recorded for Scepter/Wand, a James Brown label called Try Me and Checker before Berry Gordy signed Tammi Terrell to Motown.

Terrell had released two Motown singles of her own before her first duet with Marvin was issued: "Ain't No Mountain High Enough" peaked at number 19. But then the magic kicked in, and the team of Marvin Gaye and Tammi Terrell had four top 10 songs in a row: "Your Precious Love," "If I Could Build My Whole World Around You," "Ain't Nothing Like The Real Thing" and "You're All I Need To Get By." While she was achieving success on the charts, Tammi was suffering from a brain tumor, and her condition worsened. She died on March 16, 1970. Three years later, Motown teamed Marvin with another female singer—Diana Ross. Their vocals were recorded separately, and only one album was released. Two singles—"You're A Special Part Of Me" and "My Mistake (Was To Love You)"—made the top 20 of the Hot 100.

Cher has six singles on the list of the top 100 duets, five of which are recordings she made with her first husband, Sonny Bono. "Baby Don't Go," "I Got You Babe" and "The Beat Goes On" are from the '60s; "All I Ever Need Is You" and "A Cowboy's Work Is Never Done" are from the early '70s.

Peaches and Herb have four titles in the top 100. "Close Your Eyes," from 1967, was recorded by Herb Fame (ne Feemster) with the original Peaches, Francine Barker. The act broke up in 1970 when Herb joined the Washington, D.C. Police Department. By 1976, he was thinking about recording again, and producer Van McCoy found a new Peaches, singer Linda Greene. After one album on MCA, Peaches and Herb signed with Polydor and worked with producer Freddie Perren. "Shake Your Groove Thing," "Reunited" and "I Pledge My Love" were all from this period.

Diana Ross, Barbra Streisand and Olivia Newton-John all have four records each on the top 100. In addition to working with Lionel Richie and Marvin Gaye, Diana guest-starred on Julio Iglesias' "All Of You." Streisand is represented with two singles from *Guilty*, the album produced by Barry Gibb, as well as duets with Neil Diamond and Donna Summer. Olivia's two duets with John Travolta from *Grease* are on the top 100, as are pairings with Cliff Richard (from *Xanadu*) and Andy Gibb.

Kenny Rogers is on the list three times, with three different women. Dolly Parton, Kim Carnes and Sheena Easton were his singing partners, and all had top 10 singles. James Ingram also had three different collaborators: Patti Austin, Linda Ronstadt and Michael McDonald. Ronstadt is on the list an additional two times with Aaron Neville, and McDonald had a number one single when he teamed up with Patti LaBelle. Roberta Flack's three duets on the top 100 include two with the late Donny Hathaway and one with Peabo Bryson. Jennifer Warnes had two number one duets: her partners were Joe Cocker and Bill Medley.

There are two father-daughter duets on the list. Nancy and Frank Sinatra both had number one singles on their own in 1966; their recording of "Somethin' Stupid" went to number one in 1967. Dara Sedaka released a single of "My Guy" but it didn't make the chart; she did have a top 20 single, though, when she recorded "Should've Never Let You Go" with her father Neil.

Two sets of brothers and sisters are included in the top 100. Donny and Marie Osmond both established themselves as solo artists before recording a number of duets. Nino Tempo and April Stevens had also worked as solo artists before signing to Atco as a duo.

Surprisingly, there are only four married couples represented on the top 100. In addition to Sonny and Cher, there are Marilyn McCoo and Billy Davis, Jr., Carly Simon and James Taylor, and Jack Blanchard and Misty Morgan.

Wilson Phillips

In the vernacular of the '90s, "girl groups" would be a sexist term, but in the late '50s and early '60s, it was an accurate description of a genre of music that included groups like the Chantels, the Shirelles, the Ronettes, the Crystals and the Shangri-Las. The best songs by girl groups combined teen-age angst and innocence, with a wide appeal to the 15-year-old girls who were buying 45s.

Included in the list of the top 100 songs by girl groups are groups of three or more women who recorded together. Individual singers who personified the girl-group sound like Lesley Gore and Little Eva were not included, nor were any groups that included men, like the Orlons and the Exciters.

There were female singing groups long before there were girl groups. In the '30s, the Boswell Sisters from New Orleans had a number of successful records, including "The Object Of My Affection" and "Rock And Roll," the first hit song to ever use those words together in a title. After the Boswells came the Andrews Sisters, three siblings from Minneapolis. Patti, Maxene and LaVerne were the most successful female group before 1955.

There were three prominent female vocal groups at the beginning of the rock era. The Fontane Sisters had hits as early as 1951, and the Chordettes and the McGuire Sisters first hit the charts in

1954. On the R&B chart, Shirley Gunter & the Queens had a top 10 single in 1954 with "Oop Shoop." But the group that really initiated the girl-group sound was a quintet of teenagers from the Bronx, all students at Saint Anthony of Padua School. They took their name from their rival school, Saint Francis de Chantelle.

Arlene Smith was the leader of the Chantels, and her inspiration for forming her group was a man—or rather, a teen-age boy. "Alan Freed came on the radio and played Frankie Lymon & the Teenagers singing 'Why Do Fools Fall In Love,'" Smith told Charlotte Greig in *Will You Still Love Me Tomorrow?* "It was a lovely high voice and a nice song. Then Freed announces that Frankie is just 13! Well! I had to sit down. It was a big mystery, how to get into this radio stuff. I thought if he could do it. . . . It seemed so far removed, but I made a conscious decision to do the same."

When Frankie Lymon played a theater in the Bronx, Arlene took her group to meet Richard Barrett, Frankie's manager. Backstage, the Chantels sang an *a cappella* version of one of Arlene's songs, "The Plea." Barrett liked them enough to tell record company owner George Goldner that he wanted to sign them. Their first release was "He's Gone" on Goldner's End label; it peaked at number 71. Their next single, "Maybe," went to number 15.

The Chantels' success inspired four teen-aged girls from Passaic, New Jersey, to sing together. They even thought about calling themselves the Chanels, but that sounded too close. Eventually, they decided on "The Shirelles." A friend from school, Mary Jane Greenberg, wanted them to audition for her mother. Florence Greenberg signed the Shirelles to her Tiara label and released "I Met Him On A Sunday." The record became so popular that Decca bought the master, but subsequent releases were issued on Florence's Scepter label. In 1960, the Shirelles became the first girl group to have a number one song, when "Will You Love Me Tomorrow" moved to the top of the Hot 100.

The girl-group sound flourished on both coasts. In New York, writers like Barry Mann and Cynthia Weil, Carole King and Gerry Goffin, and Jeff Barry and Ellie Greenwich wrote hits for the Chiffons, the Cookies, the Crystals and the Ronettes. On the West Coast, Phil Spector was producing hits for the latter two groups at Gold Star Studios. The Crystals recorded "He's A Rebel," "Da Doo Ron Ron (When He Walked Me Home)" and "Then He Kissed Me." The Ronettes' first single was "Be My Baby," a number two hit in 1963. That same summer, the Angels went to number one with "My Boyfriend's Back."

In 1964, two labels figured in the surge of popularity for girl groups. George Goldner started the Red Bird label with Jerry Leiber and Mike Stoller. Their first release was "Chapel Of Love" by the Dixie Cups, three young girls from New Orleans. Red Bird also signed the Shangri-Las, two sets of sisters from Queens, New York. The Shangri-Las' first single, "Remember (Walking In The Sand)," seemed dramatic enough, but they went over the top with the sound effects-laden "Leader Of The Pack," an updating of the "He's A Rebel" theme.

The other label that fostered the girl group sound in 1964 was based in Detroit. Motown had experienced success with girl groups like the Marvelettes ("Please Mr. Postman") and Martha & the Vandellas ("Heat Wave"), but 1964 was the year the Supremes began their string of five consecutive number one singles. By the end of the '60s, the Supremes had established themselves as the most successful girl group of the rock era. They have 16 of the top 100 songs by girl groups, and "Love Child" is the third most successful girl group song of the rock era.

The first girl group to become successful in the '70s was the Honey Cone. Brian Holland, Lamont Dozier and Eddie Holland formed the Invictus and Hot Wax labels after leaving Motown. Darlene Love's sister, Edna Wright, asked her friend Eddie Holland to watch her sing backing vocals with Carolyn Willis and Shellie Clark on a Burt Bacharach TV special in 1969. Eddie suggested they form a group, and signed them to Hot Wax. "Want Ads" went to number one in 1971.

The female vocal groups of the '70s that followed the Honey Cone were influenced by the times. They were still working with male producers, but the lyrics were more assertive and the image was more aggressive. The most prominent female group of the '70s was the Pointer Sisters. They are second only to the Supremes, with eight titles listed in the top 100 songs by girl groups.

Most of the other female groups of the '70s were disco-oriented. The Emotions only had one big hit, "Best Of My Love," but it remains the most successful girl-group song of the rock era. Patti LaBelle and the Blue Belles had been making records since 1962's "I Sold My Heart To The Junkman," but they didn't become well-known until they changed their name to Labelle, adopted a space-age glitter image and recorded the disco smash "Lady Marmalade." Silver Convention began as three anonymous studio singers in Germany on "Fly, Robin, Fly"; they were replaced by three other women for their next hit, "Get Up And Boogie."

A new breed of girl groups became popular in the '80s. Their influences weren't the Chiffons or the Ronettes so much as the first female rock bands, like Fanny and the Runaways. The Go-Go's and the Bangles played their own instruments and wrote many of their own songs. There were still girl groups around who were produced by men, like Bananarama and Expose. The success of Expose gave rise to a whole slew of girl groups with little to distinguish themselves from each other: the Cover Girls, Seduction and Sweet Sensation were all cut from the same cloth.

In 1990, the girl-group tradition continued with the success of a trio of childhood friends. Chynna Phillips, daughter of John and Michelle, and Wendy and Carnie Wilson, daughters of Brian Wilson, have the second most popular girl-group song of the rock era with a song co-written by Chynna and Carnie with Glen Ballard, "Hold On."

THE TOP 100
INSTRUMENTALS

Roger Williams

In the opening years of the rock era, it was easy to have a hit with an instrumental recording. But as the decades have gone by, it has become increasingly difficult to succeed without lyrics. The evidence is the list of the top 100 instrumentals of the rock era. There are 31 titles on the list from the '50s, 40 from the '60s, 24 from the '70s, five from the '80s and none from 1990.

Exactly one-quarter of the songs on the list reached number one. The first instrumental to be number one in the rock era is also the most successful: "Autumn Leaves" remains the biggest chart instrumental of the years 1955-90. The tune was originally a French melody called "Les Feuilles Mortes," written by Joseph Kosma. French lyrics were added by Jacques Prevert, and English lyrics were later written by Johnny Mercer. There were many vocal versions of the song released in America—by artists like Bing Crosby and Jo Stafford—but no one had a hit with "Autumn Leaves" until Roger Williams played it on his piano.

The next instrumental to be number one is the second most successful of the rock era. Nelson Riddle heard about a Portugese melody called "Lisboa Antigua" ("In Old Lisbon") from the sister of Nat King Cole's manager. She was living near Mexico City and heard a local version by a band called Los Churambalis. Riddle was told by executives at Capitol Records to copy that version for his own recording.

Unlike "Autumn Leaves" and "Lisbon Antigua," the instrumental tune ranked number three on the top 100 was an original composition by the artist who recorded it. Bill Doggett, born in Philadelphia in 1916, formed his own band in 1938. He arranged material for the Ink Spots, Lionel Hampton, Louis Jordan and many others. He wrote "Honky Tonk" with Billy Butler, Shep Sheppard and Clifford Scott. Lyrics were later added by Henry Glover.

Other instrumentals that were successful in the '50s include "The Poor People Of Paris" by Les Baxter, "Moonglow And Theme From 'Picnic'" by Morris Stoloff, "Canadian Sunset" by Hugo Winterhalter with Eddie Heywood, "Sail Along Silvery Moon" and "Raunchy" by Billy Vaughn, and "Tequila" by the Champs.

"Tequila" was recorded when Dave Burgess, head of A&R for Challenge records, decided to cut a "B" side for one of his own songs recorded with session musician Danny Flores. With Gene Alden, Buddy Bruce and Cliff Hils, they cut a song Flores had written while visiting Tijuana. Released under the group name the Champs, "Tequila" soared to number one.

The most successful instrumental from the '60s is Percy Faith's version of "Theme From 'A Summer Place,'" composed for the film by Max Steiner. It is the only instrumental to be the number one record of the year, and its popularity remained strong enough for it to be included in the film *Batman* when the Joker invites Vicki Vale to lunch.

The second most popular instrumental of the '60s is conductor Paul Mauriat's "Love Is Blue." Mauriat was one of the writers of a previous number one hit, "I Will Follow Him" by Little Peggy March, but he didn't write "Love Is Blue." Andree Popp composed the music and Pierre Cour wrote the lyrics for the song, selected to be Luxembourg's entry in the 1967 Eurovision Song Contest. Vicky Leandros performed the song at that year's competition, held in Vienna. The song placed fourth, losing to the British entry, Sandie Shaw's "Puppet On A String." Vicki recorded the song in 19 different languages—but none of the versions, including the French "L'amour Est Bleu," was a hit. Mauriat included it on his *Blooming Hits* album; released as a single in America, "Love Is Blue" became the first instrumental to hit number one in more than five years.

The Surfaris' "Wipe Out" was a hit twice. The five teenagers from Glendora, California, first made the Hot 100 in 1963, when "Wipe Out" spent a week at number two. In 1966, the song peaked at number 16. The combined chart runs helped make the song the 11th most popular instrumental of the rock era.

The most successful instrumental of the '70s is Walter Murphy's "A Fifth of Beethoven." A Madison Avenue jingle writer, Murphy was fascinated with pop hits that had been adapted from classical music pieces, like "A Lover's Concerto" by the Toys and "Joy" by Apollo 100. He wanted to try the same thing, but with a disco beat. Murphy sent a demo tape of several classical tunes recorded with a contemporary rhythm to every record company in New York City. The response was underwhelming, but Larry Uttal at Private Stock Records liked what Murphy had done to *Symphony No. 5 in C Minor*, composed by Ludwig van Beethoven in 1807. Although Murphy played almost all of the instruments, his record label thought the song should be credited to a group, so the "Big Apple Band" was created in name only.

The second most successful instrumental of the '70s is from an artist who had scored with several instrumental hits in the '60s— as well as a number one vocal song. Herb Alpert's "Rise" was one of the last number one hits of the decade. Alpert had been absent from the Hot 100 for over five years when "Rise" debuted. He originally went into the studio to record a disco version of his very first hit, "The Lonely Bull." But 10 minutes into the session, he called a halt to the project, realizing how awful it sounded. Herb's cousin, writing under the name Randy Badazz, supplied his famous relative with a song he had written with Andy Armer. "Rise" was a dance song, but Alpert slowed down the beat so couples could dance and hug each other at last call. The song's popularity was bolstered by its use as a love theme on ABC-TV's "General Hospital."

Barry White's composition of "Love's Theme," recorded by his 40-piece Love Unlimited Orchestra, is the third biggest chart instrumental of the '70s. "Love's Theme" was the overture for an album by the female trio Love Unlimited, featuring White's wife, Glodean. The instrumental opening segued into the vocal track "Under The Influence Of Love," and the two tracks combined for eight minutes and 17 seconds of disco delight.

"Chariots Of Fire" is the most successful instrumental of the '80s. The opening track on the *Chariots of Fire* soundtrack, it was simply called "Titles" when first released. It wasn't re-titled until its eighth week on the Hot 100. Vangelis, born Evangelos Papathanassiou in Athens, Greece, was given his first major film-composing assignment by *Chariots* producer David Puttnam. Vangelis' work won an Oscar for Best Original Score.

The second biggest instrumental of the '80s is still the most recent instrumental to go to number one. Jan Hammer, born in Czechoslovakia, scored his first film, *A Night in Heaven*, in 1983. A year later, he met producer Michael Mann, who described a new project he was creating for NBC. Hammer scored the pilot of "Miami Vice" and ended up writing 20 minutes of original music for each episode. MCA released a soundtrack for the series, and Hammer's main title theme was issued as a single.

Harold Faltermeyer's "Axel F," from the soundtrack of *Beverly Hills Cop*, is the third most popular instrumental of the '80s. In fourth place is a rarity—an instrumental that was not a theme for a film or a TV series. Saxophonist Kenny G had his first top 10 hit in 1987 with "Songbird." The other instrumental from the '80s on the top 100 is "Hooked On Classics," a medley of classical pieces done disco-style by the Royal Philharmonic Orchestra.

TEENAGERS AND PRE-TEENS

1 I JUST WANT TO BE YOUR EVERYTHING
Andy Gibb *RSO* 77

2 AT THE HOP
Danny & the Juniors *ABC-Paramount* 77

3 DIANA
Paul Anka *ABC-Paramount* 57

4 I'LL BE THERE
The Jackson Five *Motown* 70

5 TO KNOW HIM IS TO LOVE HIM
The Teddy Bears *Dore* 58

6 (LOVE IS) THICKER THAN WATER
Andy Gibb *RSO* 78

7 I'M SORRY
Brenda Lee *Decca* 60

8 BE-BOP BABY/HAVE I TOLD YOU LATELY THAT I LOVE YOU
Ricky Nelson *Imperial* 57

9 THE TWIST
Chubby Checker *Parkway* 60

10 TO SIR WITH LOVE
Lulu *Epic* 67

11 VENUS
Frankie Avalon *Chancellor* 59

12 MR. BLUE
The Fleetwoods *Dolton* 59

13 LONELY BOY
Paul Anka *ABC-Paramount* 59

14 IVORY TOWER
Cathy Carr *Fraternity* 56

15 DONNA
Ritchie Valens *Del-Fi* 59

16 TONIGHT YOU BELONG TO ME
Patience and Prudence *Liberty* 56

17 WHY DO FOOLS FALL IN LOVE
The Teenagers f/Frankie Lymon *Gee* 56

18 WILL YOU LOVE ME TOMORROW
The Shirelles *Scepter* 61

19 GO AWAY LITTLE GIRL
Donny Osmond *MGM* 71

20 A TEENAGER'S ROMANCE/I'M WALKING
Ricky Nelson *Verve* 57

21 PONY TIME
Chubby Checker *Parkway* 61

22 LONESOME TOWN
Ricky Nelson *Imperial* 58

23 JUST A DREAM
Jimmy Clanton *Ace* 58

24 I WANT YOU BACK
The Jackson Five *Motown* 70

25 HE'S SO FINE
The Chiffons *Laurie* 63

26 THE LETTER
The Box Tops *Mala* 67

27 HE'S GOT THE WHOLE WORLD (IN HIS HANDS)
Laurie London *Capitol* 58

28 MY PREROGATIVE
Bobby Brown *MCA* 89

29 MY HEART IS AN OPEN BOOK
Carl Dobkins, Jr. *Decca* 59

30 COME SOFTLY TO ME
The Fleetwoods *Dolphin* 59

Paul Anka

Some people called Ricky Nelson a teen-age idol, and they were right. He was two days shy of his 17th birthday when his first single, "I'm Walking," made its debut on the *Billboard* chart. And by the time he turned 20, he had placed 20 different songs on the survey. Five of them are included in the top 100 songs by teenagers and pre-teens.

Being a teen-age idol had its high points as well as its low points. "The best thing was being able to get into the business I really wanted to be in at an early age," says Peggy March, who was just 15 when "I Will Follow Him" went to number one. To this day, she is still the youngest female singer to have a number one hit. "It was wonderful to have a career and have so many years experience before the age of 20, when most people were starting out. The only thing that was a drawback was not having a normal 'teenagehood.' I didn't go to football games or the senior prom and I didn't have dates, so I missed that."

To be considered for the top 100 songs by teenagers and pre-teens, an artist had to have not reached his or her 20th birthday by the day the record debuted on the *Billboard* chart. Groups were included only when a majority of the members were teenagers. This resulted in the Jackson Five being reconsidered after Jermaine left the group in 1975—his place was taken by the youngest Jackson brother, 13-year-old Randy.

While the average age of rock stars has increased over the years—Paul McCartney turned 40 in 1982, Mick Jagger passed that plateau in 1983 and Tina Turner hit the half-century mark in 1988—it was not at all unusual in the '50s to have teenagers performing their latest hits on "American Bandstand."

Danny & the Juniors got together while they were high school students, and lead singer Danny Rapp was only 16 when "At The Hop" went to number one. Paul Anka was 15 years old when he wrote "Diana." Phil Spector was 17 when "To Know Him Is To Love Him" by his group the Teddy Bears went to the top of the Hot 100. By comparison, Frankie Avalon was almost an adult when "Venus" went to number one—he was 19.

Several recording artists in the '50s were even younger. Patience and Prudence McIntyre were 11 and 14, respectively, when "Tonight You Belong To Me" entered the chart. Their father Mark heard them singing the song one day and brought them to his friend, Ross Bagdasarian, who had not yet assumed his identity of David Seville. Bagdasarian helped introduce the family to Liberty Records.

Frankie Lymon was a 13-year-old junior high student when he joined a group called the Premiers. Richard Barrett, a member of the Valentines, rehearsed at Lymon's school, and brought the young crooners to George Goldner. He recorded the group and issued Lymon's composition "Why Do Fools Fall In Love" on his Gee label. A saxophone player at the session suggested changing the group's name to the Teenagers, so the first single was credited to "The Teenagers featuring Frankie Lymon."

Other youngsters from the '50s included in the top 100 are Jimmy Clanton (17 when "Just A Dream" hit), Laurie London (14 years old when "He's Got The Whole World [In His Hands]" went to number two), Carl Dobkins, Jr. (18 when "My Heart Is An Open Book" peaked at number three), Robin Luke (16 years old when he wrote a song inspired by his younger sister, "Susie Darlin'"), the Bobettes (five girls ranging in age from 11 to 15 when they recorded "Mr. Lee"), the Crests (Johnny Maestro and his three friends were 18 and 19 when "Sixteen Candles" was a hit), Dodie Stevens ("Pink Shoe Laces" debuted one day before she turned 13), George Hamilton IV (19 when he recorded "A Rose And A Baby Ruth"), Little Anthony & the Imperials (all 18 and 19 when "Tears On My Pillow" was a hit), and Connie Francis (with six chart singles before she turned 20.)

Teen stars prospered in the '60s as well. Brenda Lee had turned professional when she was six; at 11, she recorded her first tracks for Decca Records. A promoter in Paris thought he was hiring an adult and threatened to cancel a scheduled performance. Brenda's manager secretly planted a story in the French newspapers that Brenda was a 32-year-old midget, then publicly denied it. The resulting controversy made Brenda so newsworthy, the promoter was forced to continue with the show. Brenda was 15 when "I'm Sorry" went to number one.

Chubby Checker's "The Twist" only ranks ninth on the list of the top 100 songs by artists under 20 because he was 18 when the record first debuted in 1960, but a ripe old 20 when it returned to the Hot 100 in November, 1961. Only the first chart run is counted for this list.

Lulu was an 18-year old Glaswegian when she starred in the movie *To Sir With Love* and sang the title song. Three of the Shirelles were 19 when "Will You Love Me Tomorrow" went to number one. The Chiffons were babies by comparison, just 15 and 16 years old. Alex Chilton of the Box Tops was 16 when he sang "The Letter." And Shelley Fabares was 18 when she recorded "Johnny Angel" against her wishes.

Other teen stars from the '60s include Dee Dee Sharp (16 when "Mashed Potato Time" was a hit), Kathy Young & the Innocents ("A Thousand Stars" debuted three days after her 15th birthday), Herman's Hermits (Peter Noone was 17 when "Mrs. Brown You've Got A Lovely Daughter" went to number one), the Dovells (lead singer Len Barry was 19 when "Bristol Stomp" debuted; he was the second oldest of the group), Stevie Wonder (only 12 when he recorded "Fingertips"), the Cowsills (all minors except for their mother, Barbara), Question Mark & the Mysterians (all minors except for lead singer Rudy Martinez), Bobby Vee (with 18 chart titles before he turned 20), Little Eva ("The Loco-Motion" debuted the day after her 17th birthday), Brian Hyland (16 when "Itsy Bitsy Teenie Weenie Yellow Polka Dot Bikini" was number one), the Marvelettes (all around 17 when "Please Mr. Postman" was released), and Dale and Grace (both 19 when they recorded "I'm Leaving It Up To You").

There were considerably fewer teen stars having hits in the '70s. Andy Gibb was 19 when he went to number one with "I Just Want To Be Your Everything," the most successful chart single by an artist under 20. The Jackson Five ranged in age from 11 to 18 when "I Want You Back" debuted. Donny Osmond was 13 when "Go Away Little Girl" was number one; the Osmonds were all under 20 except for Alan when "One Bad Apple" topped the chart. Shaun Cassidy was 17 when he had his first two hits, and the DeFranco Family ranged in age from 13 to 19 when they released "Heartbeat—It's A Lovebeat." The only other teen artists from the '70s listed on the top 100 are the Bay City Rollers, five Scottish lads—the three youngest members were 18 and 19.

The '80s was an even more difficult decade for young recording artists. Bobby Brown was 19 when "My Prerogative" went to number one, and was the 15-year-old senior member of New Edition when "Cool It Now" went top 10 in 1985. Debbie Gibson was 16 when she signed with Atlantic in 1987, and Tiffany was 15 when "I Think We're Alone Now" entered the chart. Berry Gordy's son Kennedy was 19 when he had a number two hit, "Somebody's Watching Me," as Rockwell. The only teen star from 1990 on the top 100 is Tommy Page, 19 when "I'll Be Your Everything" was number one.

THE TOP 100 SONGS BY
FAMILY MEMBERS

The Everly Brothers

"I've been blessed to work with families," says producer Freddie Perren, whose charges have included the Jackson Five, the Sylvers and Tavares. "There's usually a thread that holds them together—a low, middle and high singer. God seems to have made a person for each part that needs to be sung."

Barry Gibb agrees that there is some magic that takes place when families record together. "In the studio, yes, it's a very natural thing. I'm sure Freddie Perren wouldn't be able to explain it any more than I could. It's a thing that's just between brothers and it's very difficult to explain. There's no question about what we're going to do. We automatically know what our harmonies are and we automatically blend, and we think very much on the same level."

A majority of the top 100 songs by groups with family members include brothers—68 in all. The Bee Gees head the list with "How Deep Is Your Love" and "Stayin' Alive," number one and two, respectively. They have a total of nine records on the list, more than any other family act. At one point, however, the Bee Gees appeared to be finished as a group. After scoring several hits in the latter half of the '60s, Robin and Maurice weren't speaking, and Robin left the group. His father Hugh asked him to resolve the conflict, but Robin refused and recorded a solo album. In 1969, the Bee Gees were reduced to a duo. Barry and Maurice were planning to record solo projects when Robin reconciled. He said in

Time, "If we hadn't been related, we would probably have never gotten back together."

The Everly Brothers went through a similiar break-up, although theirs lasted much longer. As schoolkids, they performed on their family's half-hour radio show in Shenadoah, Iowa. When they were older, they went to Nashville to peddle songs and audition for record companies. After a brief stint at Columbia, the Everlys signed with Archie Bleyer's New York-based Cadence Records; their very first single, "Bye Bye Love," ranks number three on the family top 100. While performing at Knott's Berry Farm in California on July 13, 1973, Phil stormed off the stage and Don told a stunned audience that the Everly Brothers were through forever. That seemed true for 10 years, until their emotional reunion on September 22, 1983, at the Royal Albert Hall in London. They signed with Mercury Records and returned to the Hot 100 with a Paul McCartney composition, "On The Wings Of A Nightingale."

The Everlys have five songs on the family top 100, and so do the Jackson Five. Kool & the Gang (including brothers Robert and Ronald Bell) and Styx (with twin brothers John and Chuck Panozzo) have four each. Earth, Wind & Fire (with Maurice White and his brother Verdine) have three. Appearing twice on the list are Toto (Steve and Jeff Porcaro, later joined by a third brother, Mike), the Ames Brothers (Gene, Joe, Vic and Ed, who later recorded on his own), INXS (Tim, Andy and Jon Farriss), the Beach Boys (Brian, Carl and Dennis Wilson, plus their cousin Mike Love), New Kids on the Block (Jordan and Jon Knight), the Isley Brothers (O'Kelly, Ronald and Rudolph and later their younger brothers, Ernie and Marvin) and Creedence Clearwater Revival (John and Tom Fogerty).

Other brother acts in the top 100 include: Van Halen (Eddie and Alex Van Halen), Heatwave (Johnnie and Keith Wilder), Santo and Johnny (the Brooklyn-born Farina brothers), the Osmonds (Alan, Wayne, Merrill, Jay and Donny), Redbone (Pat and Lolly Vegas), the Tokens (Phil and Mitch Margo), Nelson (twins Gunnar and Matthew), the Crew-Cuts (John and Ray Perkins), Calloway (former Midnight Star members Reggie and Vincent Calloway), and Atlantic Starr (Wayne, David and Jon Lewis).

Twenty-four songs on the top 100 family songs include sisters. The Emotions are ranked number five with "Best Of My Love." Sheila, Wanda and Jeanette Hutchinson first sang in church with their father Joe as the Hutchinsons and later as the Heavenly Sunbeams. Their friends the Staple Singers introduced them to their record label, Stax/Volt. The sisters changed their name to the Emotions, as Jeanette left the group and was replaced by another sister, Pam. When Stax folded, the Emotions were signed by Earth, Wind & Fire's Maurice White, who co-wrote "Best Of My Love," released on Columbia.

The sister group that appears most often on the top 100 is the Pointer Sisters, with four titles. Ruth, Anita, Bonnie and June grew up in Oakland, the daughters of a minister. Bonnie and June first sang together as a duo until Anita joined them in 1969. Ruth left her office job in 1972 to complete the quartet, who recorded for Atlantic and Blue Thumb before signing with Richard Perry's Planet label in 1979. Bonnie had left the group in January, 1978, to record as a solo artist for Motown. The Pointers' first Planet effort, a version of Bruce Springsteen's "Fire," spent two weeks at number two.

The first three releases by Wilson Phillips are all included in the top 100. Sisters Wendy and Carnie Wilson, daughters of Beach Boy Brian Wilson, formed the trio with John and Michelle Phillips' daughter, Chynna. "Hold On," "Release Me" and "Impulsive" were the trio's first three singles.

The McGuire Sisters also have three songs in the top 100. Christine, Dorothy and Phyllis McGuire grew up in Middletown, Ohio. After winning a talent contest on Arthur Godfrey's Talent Scouts, they replaced the Chordettes when Godfrey fired them from his variety series. The Bangles and Heart each have two songs on the list. Vicki and Debbi Peterson grew up in Northridge, California, before they helped form the Bangles; Ann and Nancy Wilson were living in Seattle when they joined a band called the Army that eventually metamorphosed into Heart.

Other sister acts on the top 100 include Patience and Prudence (their last name was McIntyre and they were 11 and 14, respectively, when "Tonight You Belong To Me" was a hit), the Bobettes (a quintet that included Emma and Jannie Pought), the Angels (Barabara and Phyllis "Jiggs" Allbut), the Dixie Cups (Barbara Ann and Rosa Lee Hawkins) and the Fontane Sisters (Marge, Bea and Geri Rosse from New Milford, New Jersey).

Nine acts on the top 100 include brothers and sisters. The Carpenters have four songs on the list, as do Sly & the Family Stone (Sylvester Stewart's brother Freddie and sister Rosie were in the group). The Sylvers (nine brothers and sisters) and Cornelius Brothers and Sister Rose (Eddie and Carter and, of course, their sister Rose) have two songs each included in the top 100, as do Gladys Knight & the Pips. The group consists of Gladys, her brother Merald and cousins Edward Patten and Langston George.

Other brother-sister combinations on the top 100 are the Browns (Jim Ed, Maxine and Bonnie Brown), the Cowsills (brothers Bill, Bob, Paul, Barry and John; sister Sue; and their mother, Barbara) and the DeFranco Family (brothers Tony, Nino and Benny and sisters Merlina and Marisa).

The Staple Singers consisted of sisters Mavis, Cleo and Yvonne as well as their father, Roebuck ("Pops"). Brother Pervis left the group in 1971. Aside from the Staple Singers and the Cowsills, the only other parent-child relationship in the top 100 belongs to Nancy and Frank Sinatra.

In addition to the Beach Boys and Gladys Knight & the Pips, the other group with cousins singing together is the 5th Dimension: Billy Davis, Jr., and Lamonte McLemore are cousins.

HUSBANDS AND WIVES

1 **DO THAT TO ME ONE MORE TIME**
Captain & Tennille *Casablanca* 80

2 **COMING UP (LIVE AT GLASGOW)**
Paul McCartney & Wings *Columbia* 80

3 **HARDEN MY HEART**
Quarterflash *Geffen* 82

4 **SILLY LOVE SONGS**
Wings *Capitol* 76

5 **LOVE WILL KEEP US TOGETHER**
Captain & Tennille *A&M* 75

6 **YOU DON'T HAVE TO BE A STAR
(TO BE IN MY SHOW)**
Marilyn McCoo and Billy Davis, Jr. *ABC* 77

7 **MY LOVE**
Paul McCartney & Wings *Apple* 73

8 **ONE LESS BELL TO ANSWER**
5th Dimension *Bell* 70

9 **WEDDING BELL BLUES**
5th Dimension *Soul City* 69

10 **TAKE A CHANCE ON ME**
Abba *Atlantic* 78

11 **DANCING QUEEN**
Abba *Atlantic* 77

12 **WITH A LITTLE LUCK**
Wings *Capitol* 78

13 **THE WINNER TAKES IT ALL**
Abba *Atlantic* 81

14 **AFTERNOON DELIGHT**
Starland Vocal Band *Windsong* 76

15 **LONELY NIGHT (ANGEL FACE)**
Captain & Tennille *A&M* 76

16 **MUSKRAT LOVE**
Captain & Tennille *A&M* 76

17 **WAITING FOR A STAR TO FALL**
Boy Meets Girl *RCA* 88

18 **UNCLE ALBERT—ADMIRAL HALSEY**
Paul and Linda McCartney *Apple* 71

19 **ANYTHING FOR YOU**
Gloria Estefan & Miami Sound Machine *Epic* 88

20 **DON'T STOP**
Fleetwood Mac *Warner Bros* 77

21 **CONGA**
Miami Sound Machine *Epic* 86

22 **CALIFORNIA DREAMIN'**
The Mamas and the Papas *Dunhill* 66

23 **I GOT YOU BABE**
Sonny and Cher *Atco* 65

24 **DREAMS**
Fleetwood Mac *Warner Bros* 77

25 **I CAN'T WAIT**
Nu Shooz *Atlantic* 86

26 **MONDAY, MONDAY**
The Mamas and the Papas *Dunhill* 66

27 **GOODNIGHT TONIGHT**
Wings *Columbia* 79

28 **SHOP AROUND**
The Miracles *Tamla* 61

29 **LIVE AND LET DIE**
Wings *Apple* 73

30 **LISTEN TO WHAT THE MAN SAID**
Wings *Capitol* 75

Captain & Tenille

Paul and Linda McCartney are the couple with the most songs listed on the top 100 songs by husbands and wives. Linda Louise Eastman was born in Scarsdale, New York, on September 24, 1942. She turned down a chance to take piano lessons, but loved listening to rock music on the radio. After her mother was killed in a plane crash, she married, and had a daughter (Heather) before divorcing her husband. Linda became interested in photography while living in Tucson, and returned to New York to work for *Town and Country* magazine. While in London to shoot the group Traffic for an assignment in 1967, Jimi Hendrix's manager took her to a nightclub to see Georgie Fame perform. Paul was there to catch the show, and the two took notice of each other. He later paid her a visit in New York, and they went to California for a vacation. He asked her to come live with him in England, but marriage wasn't discussed. "One day I thought, okay, let's get married—we love each other, let's make it definite," Linda said in *Sounds*. Heather was a bridesmaid and Paul's brother Michael was best man when the two were wed at the Marylebone Register Office in London on March 12, 1969.

Marilyn McCoo and Billy Davis, Jr., have 11 songs on the top 100. McCoo was a founding member of the 5th Dimension, along with Lamonte McLemore. With two other friends, they formed the Hi-Fi's; when those friends split, McCoo and McLemore asked Florence LaRue to join them. McLemore then invited Ron

Townson to join, and for the fifth member, he recruited his cousin, Billy Davis, Jr. Davis had his own group, the Emeralds, in his native St. Louis. Johnny Rivers signed them to his Soul City label as the Versatiles, but suggested they change their name, so Townson and his wife Bobette came up with "The 5th Dimension." In 1969, their producer Bones Howe suggested they cover Laura Nyro's "Wedding Bell Blues" because Marilyn and Billy were engaged to be married. The couple remained part of the 5th Dimension until November, 1975, when they decided to break away for solo careers. Marilyn was working with producer Don Davis on a solo album when they changed course and decided to record an album of duets with Billy. "You Don't Have To Be A Star (To Be In My Show)" wasn't written as a duet, but producer Davis thought it would perfect for the couple and quickly came up with a new arrangement.

For some time, there were two married couples in the Swedish group Abba, represented on the top 100 songs by husbands and wives with 10 titles. Benny Andersson met Anni-Frid Lyngstad in 1969 when they performing at different nightclubs in Malmo, Sweden.

Bjorn Ulvaeus fell in love with Agnetha Faltskog's voice when he heard her sing "I Was So In Love" on the radio. She had signed with CBS Records in Sweden when she was only 17. They met when they both appeared on the same television show in Gothenburg in 1969. They were engaged the following year and on July 7, 1971, they were married in a church in southern Sweden.

Abba made their breakthrough in 1974 after winning the Eurovision Song Contest with "Waterloo." While they only had one number one hit in the States ("Dancing Queen"), they had nine chart-toppers in the U.K. and international record sales that made them Sweden's most successful export, even bigger than Volvo. On December 24, 1978, Bjorn and Agnetha separated, and a divorce was final the following year. Bjorn remarried in January, 1981, and a month later, Benny and Frida decided they, too, would divorce. While the group never announced a professional break-up, they did not record together after 1982.

Sonny and Cher have nine of their duets on the top 100 by husbands and wives. They met at a Hollywood coffee shop in 1963 while Sonny was working for Phil Spector. Sonny hired the background singers for Spector's sessions, and he gave Cher a job singing back-up vocals for the Crystals and the Ronettes. As Caesar and Cleo, they recorded "The Letter" for a Los Angeles-based label, Vault. In January of 1964, Sonny and Cher were married in Tijuana, Mexico. They were husband and wife for just over 10 years, as Cher filed for divorce on February 20, 1974. It was finalized on June 26 of that year; two days later, Cher married Gregg Allman. Nine days after that, she sought a divorce from Allman.

Three couples have eight songs each on the husbands and wives' top 100. The Captain & Tennille have the most successful chart single by a married couple, "Do That To Me One More Time." Toni Tennille met Daryl Dragon in the lobby of the Marines Memorial Theater in San Francisco. "It wasn't love at first sight," Toni recalls. "I don't believe in that. There was some kind of really strong vibration because I knew when I looked at him, in some way he would be important in my life." They met because Toni was looking for a keyboard player to come to Los Angeles and work in her musical *Mother Earth* at the Huntington Hartford Theater. When the show closed, Daryl asked Toni if she'd like to work with the Beach Boys. They toured together for a season and then returned to Southern California to work together as a duo. They got a gig at the Smoke House in Encino and recorded a couple of songs. They pressed 500 copies of "The Way I Want To Touch You" on their own Butterscotch Castle label and promoted the single themselves, stopping in Virginia City, Nevada, on Valentine's Day in 1974 to get married. A&M offered to sign them and let them produce themselves. A year later, they had a number one single with "Love Will Keep Us Together."

Gloria Estefan and the Miami Sound Machine also appear on the top 100 eight times. Emilio Estefan and some friends played local dates in Miami as the Miami Latin Boys. Gloria met him at a party one night where she was singing, and asked him for advice. Three months later, she reluctantly went to a wedding of a friend of her mother's. The Miami Latin Boys were playing at the wedding, and Emilio invited Gloria to sing with them. Later, he asked her to join the group, but she had plans to go to school, so she turned down the offer. Eventually, she decided to work with the band on weekends while studying for her degree in psychology at the Univeristy of Miami. A year later, Emilio and Gloria started dating, and in 1978, they were married.

The third married couple with eight songs on the top 100 are John and Michelle Phillips. John was in a folk trio called the Journeymen when he met Holly Michelle Gilliam at the hungri i night club in San Francisco. They were married shortly after, and when the Journeymen disbanded in 1964, Michelle and Denny Doherty formed the New Journeymen with John to fulfill contractual obligations. Cass Elliot, who had been in the Mugwumps with Denny, joined the other three in the Virgin Islands and then returned with them to California. An old friend, Barry McGuire, introduced them to Lou Adler at Dunhill Records, who hired them to sing backing vocals for McGuire's first album. Adler signed the four singers to Dunhill and they came up with a new name, the Magic Circle. That was discarded after John watched a TV documentary about the Hell's Angels. One of the members told an interviewer, "Some people call our women cheap—we call them mamas." The Mamas and the Papas broke up in July, 1968, and John and Michelle had a personal break-up at the same time. When the group was reformed in 1982, John's daughter MacKenzie took Michelle's place. Michelle's acting career blossomed, and she was signed to be a regular on CBS-TV's "Knots Landing."

U.K. ARTISTS

The Bee Gees

Pop music historians didn't pay much attention to the United Kingdom before 1964. America was the birthplace of rock and roll, and anyone who meant anything in the new idiom was from the good old U.S.A. There would be an occasional foray into the American charts by a British artist, but that was rare, and the momentum was usually not sustained.

Only four of the top 100 songs by U.K. artists are from the pre-Beatles era. The earliest entry is from Russ Hamilton, a Liverpudlian who was working as a singing waiter at the Ocean Hotel in Brighton when he was offered a record contract. His first of two British chart entries was "We Will Make Love." In America, the flip side, "Rainbow," went to number four and left him a one-hit wonder. The following year, another one-hit wonder migrated to the *Billboard* chart: Laurie London was 14 years old when his recording of an old gospel tune, "He's Got The Whole World (In His Hands)," went to number two.

In 1962, a clarinet player from Somerset, England, became the first British artist to top the Hot 100. Mr. Acker Bilk's instrumental "Stranger On The Shore" was originally titled "Jenny," named for one of his children. The song was renamed when the BBC asked Bilk if he would play the piece as the title tune for a children's TV series.

The first British group to top the American chart was the Tornadoes, five musicians assembled by producer Joe Meek.

The instrumental "Telstar" was number one on both sides of the Atlantic.

Other British artists crossed the pond before the Beatles, including Lonnie Donegan, Anthony Newley, Marty Wilde, Helen Shapiro, Frank Ifield and Matt Monro. But they were minor excursions, and even Britain's most popular male vocalist, Cliff Richard, could only get to number 30 in America with one of his biggest hits at home, "Living Doll."

Then came the Beatles. The impact was sudden and immediate. Within weeks of their arrival, they were followed by Peter and Gordon, Gerry & the Pacemakers, the Dave Clark Five, the Searchers, the Hollies, the Kinks, Cilla Black, Dusty Springfield, Herman's Hermits, the Zombies, and many, many others. Americans developed a wide fascination for anything British, and teen-aged Anglophiles could be heard using words like "fab," "gear" and "mod" and dropping names like "Carnaby Street" and "Piccadilly Circus."

The Beatles have seven songs on the top 100 U.K. songs, more than any other artist. The runners-up, with six apiece, are Paul McCartney and the Bee Gees. McCartney's popularity continued into the '70s as he recorded both on his own and with his second group, Wings. The brothers Gibb monopolized the charts in the last four years of the decade, especially with the Bee Gees' material from *Saturday Night Fever*. "How Deep Is Your Love" is the second most successful chart single by an artist from the U.K.

The Gibbs also have the second, third, fourth and fifth most successful U.K. singles from the '70s. The next two places from that decade are taken by Rod Stewart, born in London of Scottish roots. Other U.K. artists from the '70s included in the top 100 are: Nick Gilder (born in London, his family moved to Vancouver, British Columbia, when he was 10), Leo Sayer, Elton John, Eric Clapton, Olivia Newton-John (born in Cambridge, England; her family emigrated to Melbourne, Australia, when she was five), Heatwave, M (a.k.a. Robin Scott), George Harrison, Kiki Dee, Maxine Nightingale, the Rolling Stones, Chris Norman, Gerry Rafferty and the Anglo-American group Foreigner.

There were also many British musical influences that didn't translate to the U.S. charts in the '70s. The glitter rock movement almost passed America by completely, and artists like Gary Glitter, Alvin Stardust, Slade and the Rubettes didn't mean much in the States. Some U.K. songs were covered by American artists. Stories did their own take of Hot Chocolate's "Brother Louie" and Bo Donaldson & the Heywoods rushed out "Billy, Don't Be A Hero" before Paper Lace could score with it. Other U.K. artists like Mud, the Real Thing, Wizzard and Showaddywaddy all had number one hits at home but failed to make an impression in America.

The most successful U.K. chart single of the rock era is Olivia Newton-John's "Physical," number one for 10 weeks. Olivia nurtured her career while living in Australia. She played in coffeehouses on weekends and sang in a group with three other women, the Sol Four. Olivia won a Hayley Mills lookalike contest, and two years later, she won a talent contest that offered a trip to England as a prize. She was doing well in Australia and was reluctant to return home, but with encouragement from her mother, she traveled back to the U.K. with her friend Pat Carroll. They recorded together, and when Pat's visa ran out, Livvy became a regular on Cliff Richard's TV series and joined a Don Kirshner group, Toomorrow. She signed with Pye Records, and John Farrar of the Shadows produced a version of Bob Dylan's "If Not For You." Released on Uni in the States, "If Not For You" was Newton-John's first American chart entry, peaking at number 25. She had four number one singles to her credit by the time "Physical" was released. A well thought-out video campaign planted the idea that the song was about working out rather than *really* getting "physical," so a possible censorship campaign was averted. "Physical" became the biggest hit of her career and the tenth most popular chart single of the rock era.

The second most successful U.K. song of the '80s is "Another One Bites The Dust" by Queen, a group that started out with a glam-rock image. They broadened their musical horizons with subsequent releases, until they relied on a heavy urban influence for "Another One Bites The Dust."

In third place for the '80s is "Every Breath You Take" by the Police. The Anglo-American trio was formed by Stewart Copeland (born in Alexandria, Virginia) in 1977. Educated in Britain while his father worked for the CIA, Copeland played in a group called Curved Air and met Gordon Sumner (born in Wallsend) while he was playing bass with a jazz group called Last Exit. They teamed up with Andy Summers and several other musicians in an outfit called Strontium 90, and in June of 1977 Summers was invited to join the Police. In February, 1978, the group made their American debut—in a TV commercial for chewing gum, with their hair dyed blond. The following month, they were signed to A&M Records. Their first American chart entry was "Roxanne," which peaked at number 32 in April, 1979. The Police's first top 10 single was "De Do Do Do, De Da Da Da" in January, 1981, followed by another top 10 single, "Don't Stand So Close To Me." Their final album as a group, *Synchronicity*, was issued in the summer of 1983; the LP was preceded by "Every Breath You Take," which spent eight weeks at number one and 22 weeks on the Hot 100.

The '80s were a fertile decade for British artists, with a new wave of electronic, synthesized bands washing onto American shores. The Human League led this new British "invasion," and other artists from the '80s who made the U.K. top 100 list include Pink Floyd, Bonnie Tyler, Paul McCartney, Foreigner, John Lennon, Culture Club, Yes, Phil Collins, Wham! and George Michael, the Alan Parsons Project, Eurythmics, Joe Cocker, Elton John, the Rolling Stones, Sheena Easton, John Waite, Dire Straits, Soul II Soul, Steve Winwood, Tears For Fears, and Duran Duran.

THE YEARS

The final weekly *Billboard* issue of each year is devoted to a wrap-up of the previous 12 months. For chart enthusiasts, the most important section of that annual issue is the part that contains the top 100 singles and albums of the previous year. To be the number one song in any particular week is an achievement, but to be the number one song of the year—that's being a part of history.

The charts on the following pages are not meant to replace the year-end surveys *Billboard* has published over the years. Those charts are a matter of record. Rather, these lists are an opportunity to look at the biggest hits of each year from a different perspective.

One limitation of the annual charts published in *Billboard* is that they are not compiled on a calendar year basis—that is, they do not run from January to December. Because of publishing deadlines, the eligibility period has varied over the years but generally runs from November to November. In the past, this has penalized some records that were hits at the end of the year by leaving them caught in limbo between two particular years, not gaining enough points in either to register on any year-end chart. As a result, songs like "Big Girls Don't Cry" by the Four Seasons, "Come See About Me" by the Supremes and "I Think I Love You" by the Partridge Family never appeared on a *Billboard* year-end survey because they peaked in November or December.

The charts on the following pages list singles in the year that they peaked. "My Sweet Lord," which went to number one the week of December 26, 1970, is included in the top 100 songs of 1970. In the official *Billboard* charts, it was listed in 1971.

Records were given credit for their entire chart life, even if some weeks of that chart life took place in a different year. "Raindrops Keep Fallin' On My Head" by B.J. Thomas peaked on January 3, 1970; nine weeks of its chart life occurred in 1969. Those nine weeks were considered when calculating where the song should be listed in the year-end chart for 1970.

This sometimes affected the final choice for number one song of the year. On December 31, 1990, the most successful chart single of the year was "Hold On" by Wilson Phillips. But "Love Takes Time" by Mariah Carey and "Because I Love You (The Postman Song)" by Stevie B were still in the top 30 and were still accumulating points. By the time those songs dropped out of the top 30 in 1991, their point totals had surpassed "Hold On," making "Love Takes Time" and "Because I Love You (The Postman Song)" the number one and two singles of 1990, respectively.

The top 100 songs of each decade were compiled in the same manner. The list for the '50s includes songs that peaked on or after July 9, 1955. Traditionally, *Billboard* has not published the top singles by decades, so this information is being presented here for the first time in any form.

1. **DON'T BE CRUEL/HOUND DOG**
Elvis Presley *RCA*
2. **SINGING THE BLUES**
Guy Mitchell *Columbia*
3. **HEARTBREAK HOTEL**
Elvis Presley *RCA*
4. **LISBON ANTIGUA**
Nelson Riddle *Capitol*
5. **THE WAYWARD WIND**
Gogi Grant *Era*
6. **JUST WALKING IN THE RAIN**
Johnnie Ray *Columbia*
7. **THE GREEN DOOR**
Jim Lowe *Dot*
8. **HONKY TONK (PARTS 1 & 2)**
Bill Doggett *King*
9. **LOVE ME TENDER**
Elvis Presley *RCA*
10. **MEMORIES ARE MADE OF THIS**
Dean Martin *Capitol*
11. **THE POOR PEOPLE OF PARIS**
Les Baxter *Capitol*
12. **WHATEVER WILL BE, WILL BE**
Doris Day *Columbia*
13. **MOONGLOW AND THEME FROM "PICNIC"**
Morris Stoloff *Decca*
14. **TRUE LOVE**
Bing Crosby & Grace Kelly *Capitol*
15. **MY PRAYER**
The Platters *Mercury*
16. **CANADIAN SUNSET**
Hugo Winterhalter w/Eddie Heywood *RCA*
17. **IT'S ALMOST TOMORROW**
The Dream Weavers *Decca*
18. **I WANT YOU, I NEED YOU, I LOVE YOU**
Elvis Presley *RCA*
19. **THE GREAT PRETENDER**
The Platters *Mercury*
20. **HOT DIGGITY (DOG ZIGGITY BOOM)/
JUKE BOX BABY**
Perry Como *RCA*
21. **ROCK AND ROLL WALTZ**
Kay Starr *RCA*
22. **BAND OF GOLD**
Don Cherry *Columbia*
23. **ALLEGHENY MOON**
Patti Page *Mercury*
24. **I ALMOST LOST MY MIND**
Pat Boone *Dot*
25. **I'M IN LOVE AGAIN/MY BLUE HEAVEN**
Fats Domino *Imperial*
26. **STANDING ON THE CORNER**
The Four Lads *Columbia*
27. **MOONGLOW AND THEME FROM "PICNIC"**
George Cates *Coral*
28. **IVORY TOWER**
Cathy Carr *Fraternity*
29. **BLUE SUEDE SHOES**
Carl Perkins *Sun*
30. **IT ONLY HURTS FOR A LITTLE WHILE**
The Ames Brothers *RCA*
31. **TONIGHT YOU BELONG TO ME**
Patience and Prudence *Liberty*

Guy Mitchell

1956 was the year Capitol Records built a round office building in Hollywood that looked like a stack of records; Elvis Presley shook his hips on Milton Berle's television show; and Lerner and Loewe's *My Fair Lady* was the toast of Broadway.

Little Richard and Johnny Cash made their debuts on *Billboard*'s pop singles chart in 1956. Richard Penniman, born in Macon, Georgia, first went into a recording studio in October, 1951. Three years later he sent an audition tape to Specialty Records, but held back his wild rock songs in favor of blues material. He had a recording session in New Orleans for the label. "During a break . . . someone heard me playing 'Tutti Frutti' on the piano and asked me about the song. We ended up recording it and sold 200,000 copies in a week and a half," he told Robert Hilburn of the *Los Angeles Times*. "Long Tall Sally" was the number 58 song of 1956 and the follow-up, "Tutti Frutti," was number 96.

J.R. Cash, born in Kingsland, Arkansas, auditioned for Sam Phillips of Sun Records with some gospel songs, but Phillips didn't think there was much of a market for that kind of music. Then he heard a song Cash had written called "Hey Porter" and signed him and the Tennessee Two to the label. Phillips decided to call John R. Cash "Johnny." Soon after marrying his first wife, Vivian, Cash wrote "I Walk The Line" (the title was inspired by Carl Perkins) backstage at a club in Gladewater, Texas. It became his first pop hit and ranked number 93 for 1956.

Three rock and roll classics were among the top 100 songs of the year. "Blue Suede Shoes" by Carl Perkins ranked number 29. Perkins was originally signed by Sam Phillips to a Sun subsidiary label, Flip, as a country performer. After Elvis Presley left Sun for RCA, Perkins was moved over to the main label and told to write rock and roll songs. He took Phillips' advice and wrote "Blue Suede Shoes," a song promptly covered by Elvis.

"Why Do Fools Fall In Love" by the Teenagers featuring Frankie Lymon was the number 32 song of the year. Richard Barrett, lead singer of the Valentines, brought the young group to George Goldner, who owned a couple of record labels. There are differing accounts of how their first hit came to be. One version says that Lymon wrote a composition in school called "Why Do Fools Fall In Love"; another says that he wrote the song after being turned down by a girl. Yet another says that a neighbor had written a poem called "Why Do Birds Sing So Gay" and gave it to the group to adapt as a song. Whatever its origin, Goldner recorded it just after Thanksgiving, 1955, and released it on a new subsidiary, Gee.

"Be-Bop-A-Lula" by Gene Vincent was the number 34 song of 1956. Capitol Records wanted their own version of Elvis Presley, and label producer Ken Nelson thought Vincent would fill the bill. His first recording session for the label took place in Nashville on May 4, 1956. Among the three songs recorded that day were "Woman Love," the track Nelson chose for Vincent's first single. DJs liked the "B" side better and started giving airplay to a song inspired by a comic strip, Little Lulu. "Be-Bop-A-Lula" became a big hit (and the first record that Paul McCartney ever bought).

There were two instrumentals in the year's top 10. "Lisbon Antigua" by Nelson Riddle was number four and "Honky Tonk (Parts 1 & 2)" by Bill Doggett was number eight.

The number one single of 1956 was a two-sided hit, "Don't Be Cruel" and "Hound Dog" by Elvis Presley. The former was composed by Otis Blackwell, a Brooklyn-born songwriter who sold the rights to "Don't Be Cruel" and five other songs for $25 each on Christmas Eve of 1955. The latter was a Jerry Leiber-Mike Stoller song written for Willie Mae "Big Mama" Thornton, who topped the R&B chart with it in 1953. Elvis had two more songs in the top 10: "Heartbreak Hotel" at number three and "Love Me Tender" at number nine. "Heartbreak Hotel" was his first pop hit and his first recording for RCA Victor. Mae Axton, who handled public relations in Florida for Elvis' manager, Col. Tom Parker, was inspired to write the song when Tommy Durden showed her a story in the newspaper about someone who had committed suicide. He left a note that read, "I walk a lonely street." Mae suggested to Tommy they put a "heartbreak hotel" at the end of that lonely street, and in 22 minutes they wrote and recorded a demo of the song. "Love

Me Tender" was based on a folk ballad, "Aura Lee." Ken Darby, musical director of Elvis' first movie, wrote the song but gave the credit to his wife, Vera Watson.

"Singing The Blues" by Guy Mitchell was the second most popular chart single of 1956. Number one for nine weeks, it was originally recorded by Columbia artist Marty Robbins, who took it to number one on the country chart. Mitch Miller of Columbia's A&R department produced a pop version by Mitchell, and came up with two hits on the same song.

The highest-ranked female vocal of 1956 was "The Wayward Wind" by Gogi Grant. The only female vocal performance in the year-end top 10, it ranked number five for the year. After recording for RCA, she moved over to Herb Newman's Era label where her first single was "Suddenly There's A Valley." While recording the follow-up, "Who Are We," Gogi was shown a manuscript of a song Newman had written as a college student with Stan Lebousky. It was written for a man to sing, so Gogi changed the lyrics to suit a female singer and with 15 minutes of studio time left, recorded "The Wayward Wind." It knocked Elvis' first number one single off the top of the *Billboard* chart and remained there for six weeks.

The number six song of the year belonged to a man who turned down an offer to sign with CBS' Okeh label because he thought Capitol was going to sign him. When that Hollywood-based label turned him down, Johnnie Ray said OK to Okeh. His first chart single was a two-sided hit, "Cry" backed with "The Little White Cloud That Cried." The "A" side spent 11 weeks at number one at the beginning of 1952. Ray continued to have hits through the early '50s, but had a down period in 1955. A year later, Joe Johnson, who worked at Columbia Records in Nashville, heard Gene Autry's cover version of "Just Walking In The Rain." The song had originally been recorded in 1953 by the Prisonaires, a group of inmates at Tennessee State Penitentiary. Ray recorded the song at the tail end of a late-night recording session. Despite being tired and incensed at a rude remark made by Mitch Miller, Ray cut the song in two takes. It reached number three on the Best Sellers chart and was his biggest hit of the rock era.

Number seven for the year was "The Green Door" by Jim Lowe, a DJ at WNBC radio in New York. The song was released as the "B" side of "A Little Man In Chinatown" on Dot Records, but "The Green Door" proved to be more popular on the radio—that is, everywhere except New York City, where rival stations refused to play Lowe's hit.

Dean Martin had his only year-end top 10 single of the rock era with "Memories Are Made Of This," a song the Capitol A&R department didn't want him to record. But Dean insisted that the song, written by Terry Gilkyson, Richard Dehr and Frank Miller, had potential. The three songwriters formed a group called the Easyriders and backed Martin on the song, which spent five weeks at number one and ranked number 10 for the year.

Buddy Holly

1957 was the year Dick Clark convinced ABC to put his local "American Bandstand" show on the network; *Jailhouse Rock* premiered; and calypso music was popularized by Harry Belafonte and the "Banana Boat Song."

Four important artists of the rock era made their chart debuts in 1957. Ricky Nelson, already a familiar face to the 15 million people who watched "The Adventures of Ozzie and Harriet" on television every week, used his dad's studio orchestra to record a cover version of Fats Domino's "I'm Walkin.' " Ozzie filmed his son recording the song, and took the audio portion to various record companies; sixteen-year-old Ricky was signed to Verve. The company released the Domino tune backed with "A Teenager's Romance," and the two-sided hit was the number 29 song of 1957.

Paul Anka was even younger than Ricky when he recorded "Diana" for ABC-Paramount. The teenager from Ottawa, Canada, recorded his composition about his younger siblings' babysitter when he was just 15. The song spent one week on top of the *Billboard* Best Sellers chart, and ranked number 16 for the year.

The Everly Brothers made their first appearance on the chart with their debut Cadence recording, "Bye Bye Love." The record spent four weeks at number two and ranked number nine for the year. The follow-up, "Wake Up Little Susie," spent a week at number one and ranked number 14 for the year.

Jerry Lee Lewis of Ferriday, Louisiana, made his chart debut with "Whole Lot Of Shakin' Going On," the number 26 record of the year. Growing up with his cousins Mickey Gilley and Jimmy Swaggart, Lewis learned to play piano at age nine and made his first public appearance at an auto show in Natchez, Louisiana. With money earned from the sale of 33 dozen eggs, Lewis moved to Memphis in 1956. He auditioned for Jack Clement at Sun Records and was hired by label founder Sam Phillips. He played piano for artists like Carl Perkins and Billy Lee Riley and had his own single released—a verision of Ray Price's "Crazy Arms." While on tour with Sun artists Perkins and Johnny Cash, those two headliners suggested he "make a fuss" on stage. Lewis kicked back his piano stool and became a wild man, cementing his reputation as "The Killer." During his second session he recorded a version of "Whole Lot Of Shakin' Going On," previously cut by both co-writer Roy Hall and Big Maybelle. Jerry Lee's recording was considered "obscene" and was having trouble getting airplay—until he performed the song live on "The Steve Allen Show" on July 28, 1957. The national exposure and Lewis' crazed performance helped send the single up to number three on the *Billboard* chart.

For the second year in a row, Elvis Presley had a trio of singles in the year-end top 10: "All Shook Up" (number four), "Jailhouse Rock" backed with "Treat Me Nice" (number five) and "(Let Me Be Your) Teddy Bear" (number six).

For the last time in the rock era, all of the artists in the year-end top 10 were born in the U.S.A. Leading the list was a vocalist born in Jacksonville, Florida. Along with his brother Nick, Pat Boone sang at family gatherings and at church and school functions in Nashville. After appearing on Ted Mack's "The Original Amateur Hour" and "Arthur Godfrey's Talent Scouts" in New York, he was returning home to Denton, Texas, when he stopped to visit his parents in Nashville. His friend Hugh Cherry, a DJ at WMAK, introduced Pat to Dot Records founder Randy Wood, who had seen Boone on Mack and Godfrey's shows. Wood had a record shop in Gallatin, Tennessee, and often got requests for "Love Letters In The Sand," previously recorded by both Rudy Vallee and Bing Crosby. Wood had Boone record the song, but the track remained unreleased until the producers of the film *Bernadine* cast Pat in the lead and included the song in the movie. The single spent five weeks at number one, remaining on the Best Sellers chart for 23 weeks. It ranked number one for 1957, and was the number six single of the rock era.

"So Rare," the number two song of the year, was a successful end to a long career for bandleader Jimmy Dorsey. He was a teenager when he formed his first band, Dorsey's Novelty Six, with his younger brother Tommy. The Dorseys formed their own orchestra in 1934. A year later, they were performing at Glen Island Casino when they had a violent argument on stage that led to a long split. Jimmy and Tommy were rivals through the big-band era, and both were successful through the '40s. When Tommy died in 1956, Jimmy continued to lead the orchestra; at the suggestion of Harry Carlson of Fraternity Records, he recorded "So Rare," which had been a number one hit for Guy Lombardo in 1937. "So Rare" entered the chart in February of 1957 and was still in the top 10 when Dorsey died of cancer on June 12.

Debbie Reynolds was the only female vocalist in the year-end top 10 for 1957. She ranked number three with "Tammy," from the film *Tammy and the Bachelor* starring Debbie and Leslie Nielsen. The movie was released by Universal, which also owned Coral Records. Label head Bob Thiele was obligated to release the song, but he didn't think it would sell and decided to issue the track exactly as it was heard in the movie, rather than cut a new version. "Tammy" spent three weeks at number one and helped revive the film at the box office.

Jimmie Rodgers had the number seven single of 1957 with "Honeycomb." The singer from Camas, Washington, first heard the song at the Unique Club in Nashville, where he performed while serving at Stewart Air Force Base. Jimmie rearranged the song to match his own style. On a trip to New York, he appeared on "Arthur Godfrey's Talent Scouts" and auditioned for producers Hugo Peretti and Luigi Creatori at Roulette Records by singing "Honeycomb." Back home in Camas, Rodgers was renewing his wedding vows with his wife Colleen when a telegram arrived from Morris Levy, head of Roulette, asking him to return to New York and sign with the label. "Honeycomb" was his first single.

The number eight song of 1957 was "Come Go With Me" by the Dell-Vikings, an integrated doo-wop group formed at an Air Force Base in Pittsburgh. After winning an Air Force-sponsored talent contest in New York, they asked DJ Barry Kaye of WJAS in Pittsburgh if they could record some of their material in the studio he had built in the basement of his home. They recorded four songs, including the standard "The White Cliffs of Dover" and a tune written by their first tenor, Clarence Quick. That song was "Come Go With Me," and when Kaye played it on the air, Fee-Bee label owner Joe Averbach heard the song and signed the Dell-Vikings. He re-recorded the song, speeding up the tempo. After it became a local hit, it was picked up for national release by Dot Records. The follow-up, "Whispering Bells," was number 71 for the year.

The Coasters' second chart single, "Searchin'" backed with "Young Blood," was the number 10 record of 1957. The group's origin can be traced to the Robins, formed in 1949. They first worked with writer/producers Jerry Leiber and Mike Stoller in 1951, when they recorded "That's What The Good Book Says." The Robins recorded "Riot In Cell Block No. 9" for Leiber and Stoller's Spark label, but when the duo signed with New York-based Atlantic as independent producers, some members of the Robins didn't want to move to the East Coast. Bobby Nunn and Carl Gardner of the Robins recruited new members and followed Leiber and Stoller to New York as the Coasters.

1. **IT'S ALL IN THE GAME**
Tommy Edwards *MGM*
2. **AT THE HOP**
Danny & the Juniors *ABC-Paramount*
3. **TO KNOW HIM IS TO LOVE HIM**
The Teddy Bears *Dore*
4. **SAIL ALONG SILVERY MOON/RAUNCHY**
Billy Vaughn *Dot*
5. **TEQUILA**
The Champs *Challenge*
6. **TOM DOOLEY**
The Kingston Trio *Capitol*
7. **VOLARE (NEL BLU DIPINTO DI BLU)**
Domenico Modugno *Decca*
8. **DON'T/I BEG OF YOU**
Elvis Presley *RCA*
9. **ALL I HAVE TO DO IS DREAM**
Everly Brothers *Cadence*
10. **WITCH DOCTOR**
David Seville *Liberty*
11. **IT'S ONLY MAKE BELIEVE**
Conway Twitty *MGM*
12. **SUGARTIME**
McGuire Sisters *Coral*
13. **MY TRUE LOVE**
Jack Scott *Carlton*
14. **PATRICIA**
Perez Prado *RCA*
15. **LITTLE STAR**
The Elegants *Apt*
16. **CHANTILLY LACE**
The Big Bopper *Mercury*
17. **CATCH A FALLING STAR/MAGIC MOMENTS**
Perry Como *RCA*
18. **A WONDERFUL TIME UP THERE/ IT'S TOO SOON TO KNOW**
Pat Boone *Dot*
19. **TWILIGHT TIME**
The Platters *Mercury*
20. **RETURN TO ME**
Dean Martin *Capitol*
21. **LONESOME TOWN**
Ricky Nelson *Imperial*
22. **JUST A DREAM**
Jimmy Clanton *Ace*
23. **ROCKIN' ROBIN**
Bobby Day *Class*
24. **HE'S GOT THE WHOLE WORLD (IN HIS HANDS)**
Laurie London *Capitol*
25. **THE PURPLE PEOPLE EATER**
Sheb Wooley *MGM*
26. **BIRD DOG**
Everly Brothers *Cadence*
27. **POOR LITTLE FOOL**
Ricky Nelson *Imperial*
28. **SUSIE DARLIN'**
Robin Luke *Dot*
29. **GREAT BALLS OF FIRE**
Jerry Lee Lewis *Sun*
30. **TOPSY II**
Cozy Cole *Love*

Jerry Lee Lewis

1958 was the year Elvis Presley was inducted into the United States Army; RCA became the first major label to issue a wide selection of albums in stereo; and Jerry Lee Lewis admitted he had married his 14-year-old cousin.

It was a very good year for novelty songs—six of them were included in the top 100 songs of the year. The highest-ranked was "Witch Doctor" by David Seville at number 10. Written and produced by Seville under his real name, Ross Bagdasarian, "Witch Doctor" was inspired by a book in his library, *Duel with the Witch Doctor*. The music for the song was recorded two months before the vocals. That's how long it took Bagdasarian to figure out a way to record the voices at different speeds. The voice of the witch doctor was recorded at half-speed and played back at normal speed. That same device was used in Bagdasarian's other novelty number one song of 1958, "The Chipmunk Song" (number 44 for the year). After recording "Witch Doctor," Bagdasarian was driving through Yosemite Park in California. He encountered a stubborn chipmunk who refused to budge from the middle of the road.

That incident gave birth to the Chipmunks, named after Liberty Records executives Alvin (Al) Bennett, Simon (Sy) Waronker and Theodore (Ted) Keep. Bagdasarian's youngest son, Adam, was the role model for Alvin. As September rolled around each year, Adam would start asking if it was Christmas yet. Ross figured other children were probably pulling the same annoying stunt. The song went through several transformations before it was recorded as "The Chipmunk Song," including something called "In A Village Park."

Sheb Wooley hit number one in 1958 with another novelty song, "The Purple People Eater." It ranked number 25 for the year. Wooley got the idea for his novelty hit from a friend of his who repeated a joke his kids had heard in school. Soon after writing the song, Wooley had a meeting with the head of MGM Records. After hearing all of Wooley's ballads, the executive asked what else he had. Wooley said he had one more tune that was "the bottom of the barrel." Within three weeks of its release, it was the number one song in the country.

"Beep Beep" by the Playmates was the number 39 song of the year. Donny Conn, Morey Carr and Carl Cicchetti (a.k.a. Chic Hetti) met when they were students at the University of Connecticut. They were signed to Roulette Records as a calypso group and released a song called "Barefoot Girl," but then the calypso craze died and they had to come up with new material. They released a single called "Jo-Ann" that peaked at number 19 in February, 1958. Donny and Carl wrote "Beep Beep," a song about a comedic drag race between a Cadillac and a Nash Rambler. They performed it at a disc jockey convention in Kansas City. Their label didn't want to issue it as a 45 because it changed tempo, named commercial products and wasn't danceable. When it was included on an album, DJs played it anyway and forced its release as a single.

"Short Shorts" by the Royal Teens was the number 66 song of 1958. The five members of the New Jersey-based group recorded four songs during a session at Bell Sound Studios in Manhattan. With just a little studio time left, the Teens fooled around by playing one of their old instrumentals. Their manager, Leo Rogers, brought in two teenaged girls he saw in the lobby and asked them to sing something in front of the microphone—a silly phrase he made up, "Who wears short shorts?" The four ballads the group recorded were never heard again, but "Short Shorts" became a regional hit on the small Power label. The master was picked up by ABC-Paramount and went to number four on the Best Sellers chart. During a Baltimore television appearance, the Royal Teens met another group, the Four Lovers. One of the Teens, Bob Gaudio, struck up a friendship with Frankie Valli of the Four Lovers. Gaudio left the Royal Teens and worked in a printing factory before joining the Four Lovers, who became the Four Seasons.

"Western Movies" by the Olympics was the sixth novelty song on the top 100 of the year, ranked at number 82. The group was formed by students from two Southern California high schools, Centennial and Jordan. Singer Jesse Belvin introduced them to writer/producers Fred Smith and Cliff Goldsmith, who came up with "Western Movies." The song resembled the novelty hits of the Coasters, and lead singer Walter Ward's voice sounded like the Coasters' lead singer, Carl Gardner. The song made reference to popular TV westerns like "Maverick," "Cheyenne" and "Sugar-foot." Released on Liberty's Demon subsidiary, it peaked at number eight on the Hot 100.

The number one song of 1958 was Tommy Edwards' "It's All In The Game," originally written as an instrumental in 1912 by Charles Gates Dawes, who would later be Vice President of the United States under Calvin Coolidge. Carl Sigman added lyrics in 1951, the year Edwards first recorded the song. It peaked at number 18 during its original chart run, and seven years later MGM was ready to drop Edwards from its roster. But the label wanted to release singles in stereo, and executive Morty Craft asked Tommy to re-cut the song. The new, stereo version had an updated rock and roll ballad arrangement, and MGM had its biggest hit of the rock era. The follow-up, "Love Is All We Need," ranked number 99 for the year.

The ABC label's most successful chart single of the rock era was the number two song of 1958, "At The Hop" by Danny & the Juniors. Danny Rapp, Joe Terranova, Frank Maffei and Dave White started singing in high school as the Juvenairs. When Artie Singer caught their act, he changed their name to Danny & the Juniors and co-wrote a song for them, "Do The Bop." Dick Clark heard a demo of the song and suggested that because the Bop was already passé, they might want to change the lyrics to "At The Hop." Singer released the song on his own label, Singular, and it was picked up by ABC-Paramount.

Phil Spector had his most successful chart single of all time with his first production, "To Know Him Is To Love Him" by the Teddy Bears, ranked number three for the year. Spector wrote the song especially for lead singer Annette Kleinbard.

Billy Vaughn, born in Glasgow, Kentucky, was a member of the Hilltoppers before he was named musical director of Dot Records. As an orchestra leader, he was heard on Dot releases by the Fontane Sisters, Gale Storm and Pat Boone, among others. Under his own name, Billy specialized in covering other artists' recordings. His biggest hit of the rock era was the number four single of 1958, "Sail Along Silvery Moon," backed with "Raunchy." The former was a remake of a Bing Crosby hit from 1937; the latter was a cover of a song by Bill Justis. Vaughn's version hit the chart just two weeks after Justis and competed with it—Justis peaked at number two, Vaughn at number five. A third version, by Ernie Freeman, went to number 11 on the Best Sellers chart.

Domenico Modugno of Italy had the first song recorded in a foreign language to be a year-end top 10 single. "Volare (*Nel Blu Dipinto Di Blu*)," the number seven song of the year, was inspired by the back side of a pack of cigarettes. The song describes a dream in which a man paints his hands blue and flies through the air, the "blue painted in blue."

1 MACK THE KNIFE
Bobby Darin *Atco*

2 THE BATTLE OF NEW ORLEANS
Johnny Horton *Columbia*

3 SMOKE GETS IN YOUR EYES
The Platters *Mercury*

4 HEARTACHES BY THE NUMBER
Guy Mitchell *Columbia*

5 VENUS
Frankie Avalon *Chancellor*

6 MR. BLUE
The Fleetwoods *Dolton*

7 LONELY BOY
Paul Anka *ABC-Paramount*

8 STAGGER LEE
Lloyd Price *ABC-Paramount*

9 A LOVER'S QUESTION
Clyde McPhatter *Atlantic*

10 DONNA
Ritchie Valens *Del-Fi*

11 THE THREE BELLS
The Browns *RCA*

12 LONELY TEARDROPS
Jackie Wilson *Brunswick*

13 MY HEART IS AN OPEN BOOK
Carl Dobkins, Jr. *Decca*

14 COME SOFTLY TO ME
The Fleetwoods *Dolphin*

15 GOTTA TRAVEL ON
Billy Grammer *Monument*

16 PUT YOUR HEAD ON MY SHOULDER
Paul Anka *ABC-Paramount*

17 SLEEP WALK
Santo and Johnny *Canadian-American*

18 PERSONALITY
Lloyd Price *ABC-Paramount*

19 KANSAS CITY
Wilbert Harrison *Fury*

20 DREAM LOVER
Bobby Darin *Atco*

21 SIXTEEN CANDLES
The Crests *Coed*

22 DON'T YOU KNOW
Della Reese *RCA*

23 PINK SHOE LACES
Dodie Stevens *Crystalette*

24 WHY
Frankie Avalon *Chancellor*

25 IN THE MOOD
Ernie Fields *Rendezvous*

26 THE HAPPY ORGAN
Dave "Baby" Cortez *Clock*

27 PRIMROSE LANE
Jerry Wallace w/the Jewels *Challenge*

28 MY HAPPINESS
Connie Francis *MGM*

29 THE BIG HURT
Miss Toni Fisher *Signet*

30 ('TIL) I KISSED YOU
Everly Brothers *Cadence*

31 THE HAWAIIAN WEDDING SONG
Andy Williams *Cadence*

Frankie Avalon

1959 was the year Buddy Holly, Ritchie Valens and the Big Bopper were killed in a plane crash after a concert at Clear Lake, Iowa; the first Grammys were handed out; and Berry Gordy borrowed $800 to start his own record company.

Elvis Presley was absent from the year-end top 10 for the first time since his chart debut. It wasn't surprising, considering that Elvis spent all of 1959 in the U.S. Army. His only recording session during his military service resulted in five songs, including "A Big Hunk O'Love," his highest-ranked song of the year at number 39. Also recorded during that session was "(Now And Then There's) A Fool Such As I," the number 50 song of the year.

Also absent from the top 10 were female lead singers, although the Platters and the Fleetwoods counted women among their members. The only other year in the rock era that saw a shutout of female lead singers from the top 10 was 1976.

The number one song of the year was "Mack The Knife" by Bobby Darin. There had been many renditions of the song, written in 1928 by Kurt Weill and Bertold Brecht for *The Threepenny Opera*. Darin styled his version after Louis Armstrong's recording, and included it in his *That's All* album. He had recorded it to demonstrate his versatility, but didn't plan on having it released as a single. Atco Records overruled him, giving Darin the seventh most successful single of the rock era.

Runner-up to Darin's single was "The Battle Of New Orleans" by Johnny Horton. Its origin can be traced back to 1815, the year Andrew Jackson and his troops defeated the British forces of Commander Pakenham at New Orleans. The victory was soon commemorated with an instrumental folk song, "The Eighth Of January." In 1955, Arkansas schoolteacher Jimmy Driftwood wrote lyrics for the tune and retitled it, "The Battle Of New Orleans." Horton had been recording country songs since 1951. He was signed to the Cormac, Mercury and Abbott labels before moving to Columbia, the label that gave him his first entry on the country singles chart in 1956. "The Battle Of New Orleans" was his first single to make the pop chart.

The Platters achieved their highest year-end ranking with "Smoke Gets In Your Eyes," the number three song of 1959. The tune was written by Jerome Kern and Otto Harbach for the 1933 stage musical, *Roberta*.

Guy Mitchell, who had the number two song of 1956 with "Singing The Blues," was back in the upper reaches of the year-end chart with "Heartaches By The Number," the number four song of 1959. Like "Singing The Blues," "Heartaches By The Number" was first recorded by another artist on Columbia Records for the country charts. In this case, it was Ray Price who went to number one on the country singles chart with the Harlan Howard song. Mitch Miller produced Mitchell's version, which spent two weeks on top of the Hot 100.

The number five song of 1959 was "Venus" by Frankie Avalon. The Philadelphia native first wanted to be a boxer, but changed ambitions after seeing Kirk Douglas in the film *Young Man with a Horn*. Frankie's dad bought him a used trumpet from a pawn shop for $15. Manager Bob Marcucci persuaded Avalon to become a vocalist and signed him to the Chancellor label. Songwriter Ed Marshall came to Frankie's house and played "Venus" on the piano for him. Avalon asked if anyone else was interested in recording the song. Marshall told him Al Martino liked it very much. Three days later, Frankie was in the studio recording the song. Avalon had four other titles in the top 100 of the year: "Why" (number 24), "Just Ask Your Heart" (number 77), "Bobby Sox To Stockings" (number 86) and "A Boy Without A Girl" (number 96).

The Fleetwoods, a trio from Olympia, Washington, were in the year-end top 10 with "Mr. Blue," their second number one song in 1959. Their first, "Come Softly To Me," was number 14 for the year. Gretchen Christopher and Barbara Ellis, born nine days apart in the same hospital, became friends when they were five years old. In their senior year at Olympia High, Gretchen suggested forming a female quartet. When they couldn't find two other women who were suitable to join the group, they performed as a duo called the Saturns. After working up an arrangement of "Stormy Weather," they needed someone who could play blues trumpet and a friend suggested Gary Troxel. "He couldn't play in our key, and we couldn't sing in his," Gretchen remembers. But when he walked her downtown after school, he began humming a phrase that happened to be based on the same chord progression as a song Gretchen was writing, "Come Softly." The song was completed and performed at a couple of high school events. Record promoter Bob Reisdorff liked the song enough to sign the group and release "Come Softly To Me" on his own label, Dolphin. A conflict with a publishing company led him to change the name to Dolton. "Mr. Blue" was written for the Fleetwoods by Dewayne Blackwell, who met the group in a hotel room so they could hear his songs. Gretchen thought it was a great song and couldn't understand why Blackwell didn't record it himself. Blackwell explained that no one knew who he was, but if a group like the Fleetwoods recorded "Mr. Blue," every radio station in the country would play it. He was right.

Paul Anka had his highest year-end ranking with "Lonely Boy," the number seven song of the year. He wrote the song and performed it in the movie *Girls Town*, in which he starred with Mamie Van Doren and Mel Torme. It was one of four songs Anka placed in the top 100 of 1959. The others were "Put Your Head On My Shoulder" (number 16), "It's Time To Cry" (number 59) and "(All Of A Sudden) My Heart Sings" (number 93).

New Orleans artist Lloyd Price had three songs in the top 100 of 1959, including "Stagger Lee" at number eight. Born to a musical family, Price formed a five-piece group in high school. They performed on WBOK radio, and Price wrote jingles for station breaks. One was so popular that Price recorded a full-length version and took it to Specialty Records. The song, "Lawdy Miss Clawdy," topped the R&B chart in 1952. After a military stint, Price formed his own record company, Kent, and leased his masters to ABC-Paramount. With his business partner, Harold Logan, he adapted a folk song called "Stack-O-Lee" that had been a hit for another New Orleans singer, Archibald, in 1950. Price's "Stagger Lee" spent four weeks at number one. His other year-end hits in 1959 included "Personality" (number 18) and "I'm Gonna Get Married" (number 42).

Clyde McPhatter, formerly of the Dominoes and the Drifters, first made the year-end chart on his own in 1956 with "Treasure Of Love," number 92 for that year. He had his most successful chart single in 1959 with "A Lover's Question," the number nine song of the year.

Ritchie Valens, who perished in the plane crash that also took the lives of Buddy Holly and the Big Bopper, had the number 10 song of the year, "Donna." The song was written for his girlfriend, Donna Ludwig. It was his second release on Del-Fi, following "Come On, Let's Go," which peaked at number 42 on the Hot 100. "Donna" entered the chart on November 24, 1958. When Valens died on February 3, 1959, "Donna" was number three. It held that position for four weeks and then moved to number two.

1960

1 THEME FROM "A SUMMER PLACE"
Percy Faith Columbia

2 IT'S NOW OR NEVER
Elvis Presley RCA

3 HE'LL HAVE TO GO
Jim Reeves RCA

4 I'M SORRY
Brenda Lee Decca

5 ARE YOU LONESOME TONIGHT?
Elvis Presley RCA

6 THE TWIST
Chubby Checker Parkway

7 RUNNING BEAR
Johnny Preston Mercury

8 EVERYBODY'S SOMEBODY'S FOOL
Connie Francis MGM

9 CATHY'S CLOWN
Everly Brothers Warner Bros

10 EL PASO
Marty Robbins Columbia

11 LAST DATE
Floyd Cramer RCA

12 NORTH TO ALASKA
Johnny Horton Columbia

13 SAVE THE LAST DANCE FOR ME
The Drifters Atlantic

14 STUCK ON YOU
Elvis Presley RCA

15 MY HEART HAS A MIND OF ITS OWN
Connie Francis MGM

16 TEEN ANGEL
Mark Dinning MGM

17 GREENFIELDS
Brothers Four Columbia

18 SIXTEEN REASONS
Connie Stevens Warner Bros

19 SWEET NOTHIN'S
Brenda Lee Decca

20 HANDY MAN
Jimmy Jones Cub

21 THEME FROM "THE APARTMENT"
Ferrante and Teicher UA

22 A THOUSAND STARS
Kathy Young w/the Innocents Indigo

23 WILD ONE
Bobby Rydell Cameo

24 ONLY THE LONELY (KNOW HOW I FEEL)
Roy Orbison Monument

25 ALLEY-OOP
Hollywood Argyles Lute

26 SINK THE BISMARCK
Johnny Horton Columbia

27 ITSY BITSY TEENIE WEENIE YELLOW
POLKA DOT BIKINI
Brian Hyland Leader

28 PRETTY BLUE EYES
Steve Lawrence ABC-Paramount

29 WALK-DON'T RUN
The Ventures Dolton

30 CHAIN GANG
Sam Cooke RCA

The Little Dippers

1960 was the year Elvis Presley was discharged from the Army; Eddie Cochran was killed and Gene Vincent injured in an automobile accident in Chippenham, Wiltshire, England; and *Bye Bye Birdie* was a smash on Broadway.

Percy Faith, whose "Song From 'Moulin Rouge'" had been the number one song of 1953, repeated that feat in 1960 with another interpretation of a motion picture tune, "Theme From 'A Summer Place.'" The music was composed by Max Steiner for the 1959 film, which starred Dorothy McGuire, Richard Egan, Sandra Dee, Troy Donahue and Arthur Kennedy. "Theme From 'A Summer Place'" is the only instrumental number one song of the year in the rock era.

Faith was born in Toronto, Canada. The rest of the artists in the top 10 songs of 1960 were Americans. That makes 1960 the last time in the rock era that every song in the year-end top 10 was by an artist from North America.

Elvis Presley had more than one song in the year-end top 10 for the first time since 1957. Both were ballads. "It's Now Or Never," the number two song of the year, was based on an Italian song, "*O Sole Mio*," written in 1901 and popularized by Mario Lanza. Tony Martin sang an English adaptation in 1949 called "There's No Tomorrow." Aaron Schroeder and Wally Gold wrote new lyrics for

Elvis. "Are You Lonesome Tonight?" was written in 1926 and first recorded by Al Jolson. Jaye P. Morgan cut it for MGM in 1959; her version peaked at number 65 on the Hot 100. Elvis' version was the number five song of the year, marking the third time that Elvis had two of the year's top five songs.

The number three song of 1960 was by a man who might have been a star baseball pitcher if he hadn't broken both of his ankles while playing for the St. Louis Cardinals in 1947. Jim Reeves became a DJ for KGRI in Henderson, Texas, a station he later bought. Fabor Robinson of Abbott Records heard him singing on the radio and signed him. His first chart single was "Mexico Joe," which topped *Billboard*'s country chart for nine weeks in 1953. Reeves moved over to RCA in 1955 and continued to have success on the country chart. He crossed over to the pop chart in 1957 with "Four Walls." One day in 1959, he heard a song on his car radio written by Joe and Audrey Allison and recorded by Billy Brown. Reeves liked "He'll Have To Go," but didn't want to record it in case Brown's version turned out to be a hit. He waited six months and then recorded the song in Nashville. RCA released it as the "B" side of "In A Mansion Stands My Love." After that song floundered for a month, country radio DJs flipped the record. "He'll Have To Go" spent 14 weeks on top of the country chart and became Reeves' only top 10 pop hit, spending three weeks at number two. Jeanne Black, a singer from Pomona, California, recorded an answer record called "He'll Have To Stay," which went to number four on the Hot 100 and ranked number 73 for the year.

Brenda Lee made her first appearance on a year-end chart in 1960, with three titles in the top 100. "I'm Sorry" was the number four song of the year. It was recorded at the end of a session, with five minutes of studio time left. Brenda loved the song, but executives at Decca weren't sure that a 15-year-old girl should be singing about unrequited love. The label delayed release for several months, and then issued "I'm Sorry" as the flip side of "That's All You Gotta Do." Both sides charted on the Hot 100, the intended "A" side peaking at number six and "I'm Sorry" spending three weeks at number two. Brenda's two other year-end singles were "Sweet Nothin's" (number 19) and "I Want To Be Wanted" (number 34). Only two songs performed by women had ranked higher than "I'm Sorry" on a year-end chart in the rock era: "Tammy" by Debbie Reynolds and "To Know Him Is To Love Him" by the Teddy Bears were the number three song of 1957 and 1958, respectively. Patti Page, Gale Storm and Connie Francis had all placed three songs in a year-end top 100, but Brenda was the first to have all three in the top 40 portion of the chart.

Chubby Checker made his first appearance on a year-end survey with his cover version of Hank Ballard's "The Twist," the number six song of the year. Ballard had two recordings of his own in the top 100 of 1960: "Finger Poppin' Time" (number 40) and "Let's Go, Let's Go, Let's Go" (number 75).

The number seven song of 1960 was "Running Bear" by Johnny

Preston, a protégé of J. P. Richardson—better known as the Big Bopper. When Shelby Singleton signed Richardson to the Mercury label, he also signed Preston. Richardson discovered the teen-aged Preston singing in a club in Beaumont, Texas. A recording session was arranged, but Preston was nervous and the results were poor. Still, Richardson believed in his discovery and wrote a song for him inspired by a commercial for Dove soap. Preston didn't think much of "Running Bear," but he recorded it because his mentor believed in it. Mercury was ready to release the song when Richardson was killed on February 3, 1959, in the plane crash that also took the life of Buddy Holly and Ritchie Valens. "Running Bear" was put on hold until the fall of 1959. It entered the Hot 100 on October 12 and five weeks later had only climbed to number 71—then fell off the chart. After a one-week absence it returned and began its climb to number one, where it remained for three weeks.

Connie Francis had her first top 10 song of the year in 1960 with "Everybody's Somebody's Fool," ranked number eight. Her first hit, "Who's Sorry Now," was the number 40 song of 1958. The following year she had four songs on the year-end chart: "My Happiness" (number 28), "Lipstick On Your Collar" (number 36), "Frankie" (number 69) and "Among My Souvenirs" (number 80). In 1960, Connie had a very good idea of the type of song she wanted to record. Returning from a trip to Europe, she was looking for a country song she could record in different languages. She called Howard Greenfield, who had penned "Stupid Cupid" and "Lipstick On Your Collar" for Connie with his partner, Neil Sedaka. Writing with Jack Keller, Howard had come up with what he described as a LaVern Baker-type blues ballad. Connie told him to change it—"Just take your ballad and play it uptempo like 'Heartaches By The Number,'" she said. The result was "Everybody's Somebody's Fool," Francis' most successful chart single.

The Everly Brothers had the number nine song of the year—for the third time. They did it with "Bye Bye Love" in 1957, "All I Have To Do Is Dream" in 1958 and "Cathy's Clown" in 1960. The latter was their first single for Warner Brothers after nine consecutive hits on Cadence. One of their last singles for that label, "Let It Be Me," was the number 62 song of 1960. The Warner Brothers follow-up to "Cathy's Clown" was "So Sad (To Watch Good Love Go Bad)," the number 72 song of the year.

Marty Robbins first made the year-end chart in 1957, when "A White Sport Coat (And A Pink Carnation)" was the number 28 song of the year. He made his debut on the *Billboard* country chart in December, 1952, with "I'll Go On Alone," which went to number one. Robbins finally made it to number one on the pop chart in 1960 with "El Paso." With a running time of four minutes and 40 seconds, Columbia considered it too long to be a single. It appeared on the album *Gunfighter Ballads and Trail Songs* and proved to be so popular on radio that CBS relented and issued it as a 45 despite its length.

1 **TOSSIN' AND TURNIN'**
Bobby Lewis *Beltone*

2 **EXODUS**
Ferrante and Teicher *UA*

3 **WONDERLAND BY NIGHT**
Bert Kaempfert *Decca*

4 **BIG BAD JOHN**
Jimmy Dean *Columbia*

5 **TRAVELIN' MAN**
Ricky Nelson *Imperial*

6 **WILL YOU LOVE ME TOMORROW**
The Shirelles *Scepter*

7 **PONY TIME**
Chubby Checker *Parkway*

8 **RUNAWAY**
Del Shannon *Big Top*

9 **CALCUTTA**
Lawrence Welk *Dot*

10 **RUNAROUND SUE**
Dion *Laurie*

11 **THE LION SLEEPS TONIGHT**
The Tokens *RCA*

12 **BRISTOL STOMP**
The Dovells *Parkway*

13 **DEDICATED TO THE ONE I LOVE**
The Shirelles *Scepter*

14 **RUNNING SCARED**
Roy Orbison *Monument*

15 **BLUE MOON**
The Marcels *Colpix*

16 **RUN TO HIM**
Bobby Vee *Liberty*

17 **MOTHER-IN-LAW**
Ernie K-Doe *Minit*

18 **MICHAEL**
The Highwaymen *UA*

19 **PLEASE MR. POSTMAN**
The Marvelettes *Tamla*

20 **QUARTER TO THREE**
Gary U.S. Bonds *Legrand*

21 **HIT THE ROAD JACK**
Ray Charles *ABC-Paramount*

22 **SURRENDER**
Elvis Presley *RCA*

23 **THE BOLL WEEVIL SONG**
Brook Benton *Mercury*

24 **DON'T WORRY**
Marty Robbins *Columbia*

25 **A HUNDRED POUNDS OF CLAY**
Gene McDaniels *Liberty*

26 **TAKE GOOD CARE OF MY BABY**
Bobby Vee *Liberty*

27 **CRYING**
Roy Orbison *Monument*

28 **WHERE THE BOYS ARE**
Connie Francis *MGM*

29 **GOODBYE CRUEL WORLD**
James Darren *Colpix*

30 **WALK ON BY**
Leroy Van Dyke *Mercury*

Smokey Robinson & the Miracles

1961 was the year Ricky Nelson grew up and dropped the "y" from his first name; John Hammond signed Bob Dylan to Columbia Records; and Berry Gordy inaugurated a new label, Motown, with "My Beloved" by the Satintones.

Gordy's record company had its first showing on the year-end chart with two singles on the Tamla label. The first was by five high school girls from Inkster, Michigan, who had entered a school talent contest knowing the winners would be auditioned by Motown. They placed fourth, but their teacher asked the principal if they could join the top three groups for the audition. Motown liked the girls and told them to come up with some original material. Georgia Dobbins asked her songwriting friend, William Garrett, if he had anything they could sing. He suggested a blues song, "Please Mr. Postman." Georgia took the title and overnight wrote a new set of lyrics. Then she told group member Gladys Horton to learn how to sing it, because she was dropping out of the group to take care of her sick mother. With Wanda Young joining the group to replace Georgia, the girls went back to Motown and sang "Please Mr. Postman" for producers Brian Holland and Robert Bateman. They loved the song and recorded it, with 22-year-old Marvin Gaye on drums. Gordy named the girls the Marvelettes, and they gave the company its first number one single. "Please Mr. Postman" ranked number 19 for the year.

The other Tamla single on the year-end list was "Shop Around" by the Miracles. Smokey Robinson wrote the song in a few minutes. He wanted to give it to Barrett Strong, who had scored a hit with "Money" in April of 1960. But when Smokey played "Shop Around" for Gordy, the head of Motown records said he wanted the Miracles to record the song.

The single was in its second week of release, but Smokey wasn't able to promote it. He was bedridden with the flu. His telephone rang at three in the morning. Berry wanted to know what was happening. Not much, a sleepy Robinson told him. Berry told Smokey to come down to the studio right away—the musicians were already on their way in. Berry said he loved "Shop Around" but hated how it had turned out. He wanted to cut a new, faster version. The piano player didn't show up for the session, so Gordy played keyboards himself. The original version was withdrawn and the recut version released in its place. The new "Shop Around" went to number two, and ranked number 33 for the year.

The number one song of 1961 was "Tossin' and Turnin'" by Bobby Lewis. It was Lewis' initial chart entry, making it the first time in the rock era that a chart debut was the number one single of the year. Befriended by Jackie Wilson, Lewis accepted the singer's advice and financial support to leave Detroit for New York. During a week's stint at the Apollo Theater, Lewis gave some encouragement to a group of white singers, the Fireflies ("You Were Mine"). Three weeks later, Lewis knocked on the doors of Belltone Records for an audition and was surprised to run into the lead singer of the Fireflies, Ritchie Adams. Signed to Belltone himself, Adams listened to Lewis play his own songs, then suggested he try something Adams had written. The song was called "Tossin' and Turnin'," and it spent seven weeks at number one. It is the only single Lewis ever placed on a year-end chart, making him one of four artists who had a number one song of the year and then were never listed again on a year-end survey. The others are Percy Faith, Lulu and Debby Boone.

1961 is the only year in the rock era that two of the top three singles of the year were instrumentals. Pianists Ferrante and Teicher had the number two song of the year with their version of Ernest Gold's composition "Exodus," the main theme from the Otto Preminger film that starred Paul Newman and Eva Marie Saint in Leon Uris' stirring story of postwar Jewish refugees making the difficult journey to the new state of Israel.

German orchestra leader Bert Kaempfert had the number three song of the year with "Wonderland By Night," originally written as the instrumental title theme for *Wunderland Bei Nacht*, a film that told of the dark side of Germany's "economic miracle." There was a vocal version by Anita Bryant and another instrumental recording by Louis Prima. While all three made the Hot 100, Kaempfert's version fared the best, spending three weeks at number one.

There was one more instrumental in the top 10 songs of 1961:

"Calcutta" by Lawrence Welk was number nine. That makes 1961 the only year in the rock era aside from 1956 to have three instrumentals in the top 10 songs of the year. Like "Wonderland By Night," "Calcutta" was originally a German song. It was written in 1958 by Heino Gaze as "Tivoli Melody." It went through several other title changes before Randy Wood, founder of Dot Records, brought the song to Welk.

Jimmy Dean had the number four hit of 1961 with "Big Bad John," a song he wrote during a flight to Nashville. He was on his way to a recording session and only had three songs ready. "At that time, you recorded four sides a session," he explains. "I had to do something. I had worked with a guy in summer stock named John Mentoe. He was six-foot-five and skinny as a rail, but he was the only guy in the troupe taller than me, and I used to call him Big John. It had a powerful ring to it. So I put him in a mine and killed him . . . it took me an hour-and-a-half to write."

Ricky Nelson had his highest-ranked year-end song with "Travelin' Man," the number five single of 1961. His previous year-end high was "Lonesome Town," the number 21 song of 1958. Jerry Fuller wrote "Travelin' Man" while waiting in the park for his wife. He had a world atlas with him to help pick out different cities around the world. Fuller took a demo of the song performed by Glen Campbell to Sam Cooke's manager, J.W. Alexander, who didn't think much of it and threw the tape away. Lou Chudd, head of Ricky's label, Imperial, had an office next to Alexander, and bass player Joe Osbourne had heard the demo through the wall. He asked Alexander if he could hear the song again, and Alexander pulled it out of the trash can and gave it to him. The flip side of "Travelin' Man" was "Hello Mary Lou," written by Gene Pitney. It was the number 31 song of the year.

The Shirelles had the number six hit of 1961 with the first Gerry Goffin-Carole King song to make a year-end chart. Lead singer Shirley Owens heard Carole's demo of "Will You Love Me Tomorrow" and thought it sounded like a country and western song. She disliked it while rehearsing it, but changed her mind during the recording session when producer Luther Dixon turned it into a pop song.

Chubby Checker had a top 10 song of the year for the second year in a row. "The Twist" was the number six song of 1960; he came in one notch lower in 1961 with "Pony Time." It was adapted from a 1928 composition called "Boogie Woogie" by Clarence "Pinetop" Smith.

Del Shannon had the biggest hit of his career with his chart debut, "Runaway." The number eight song of 1961, it was recorded after DJ Ollie McLaughlin from WGRV in Ann Arbor, Michigan, suggested that Del write some uptempo material. Playing at the Hi-Lo club, Del stopped the show one night when organist Max Crook hit a chord change going from A-minor to G. Del incorporated that chord change into a new song, "Runaway."

1 THE TWIST
Chubby Checker *Parkway*

2 I CAN'T STOP LOVING YOU
Ray Charles *ABC-Paramount*

3 BIG GIRLS DON'T CRY
The Four Seasons *Vee Jay*

4 LIMBO ROCK
Chubby Checker *Parkway*

5 PEPPERMINT TWIST
Joey Dee & the Starliters *Roulette*

6 ROSES ARE RED (MY LOVE)
Bobby Vinton *Epic*

7 STRANGER ON THE SHORE
Mr. Acker Bilk *Atco*

8 THE STRIPPER
David Rose *MGM*

9 JOHNNY ANGEL
Shelley Fabares *Colpix*

10 RETURN TO SENDER
Elvis Presley *RCA*

11 SHERRY
The Four Seasons *Vee Jay*

12 MASHED POTATO TIME
Dee Dee Sharp *Cameo*

13 SOLDIER BOY
The Shirelles *Scepter*

14 HE'S A REBEL
The Crystals *Philles*

15 TELSTAR
The Tornadoes *London*

16 DUKE OF EARL
Gene Chandler *Vee Jay*

17 HEY! BABY
Bruce Channel *Smash*

18 THE WANDERER
Dion *Laurie*

19 THE LOCO-MOTION
Little Eva *Dimension*

20 BREAKING UP IS HARD TO DO
Neil Sedaka *RCA*

21 GOOD LUCK CHARM
Elvis Presley *RCA*

22 BOBBY'S GIRL
Marcie Blane *Seville*

23 RAMBLIN' ROSE
Nat King Cole *Capitol*

24 SHEILA
Tommy Roe *ABC-Paramount*

25 CAN'T HELP FALLING IN LOVE
Elvis Presley *RCA*

26 ALL ALONE AM I
Brenda Lee *Decca*

27 THE WAH-WATUSI
The Orlons *Cameo*

28 PALISADES PARK
Freddy Cannon *Swan*

29 MIDNIGHT IN MOSCOW
Kenny Ball & His Jazzmen *Kapp*

30 IT KEEPS RIGHT ON-A HURTIN'
Johnny Tillotson *Cadence*

Sam Cooke

1962 was the year the Beatles failed their audition with Decca Records in the U.K.; disc jockey Alan Freed went on trial for payola; and the first Motortown Revue played the Howard Theater in Washington, D.C.

"The Twist" by Chubby Checker made pop history when it returned to the *Billboard* Hot 100, less than a year after its original run. Ranked as the number six song of 1960, it did even better the second time around and was the number one song of 1962. Its two chart runs enabled "The Twist" to become the number one song of the rock era.

In 1960, the Twist was a popular dance with teenagers. They had moved on to other things by the time their parents discovered it at the end of 1961. Society columnist "Cholly Knickerbocker" wrote about the popularity of the Twist at the Peppermint Lounge on West 45th Street in Manhattan, and soon Chubby was invited to perform the song on "The Ed Sullivan Show." Radio stations were playing "The Twist" as often as brand-new hits, prompting Cameo-Parkway to re-release the single and promote it all over again.

As the Twist craze spread through America, other artists recorded songs about the dance. There were seven Twist songs included in the top 100 of the year. Joey Dee & the Starliters recorded one album for Scepter Records and asked staff producer Luther Dixon for some help in finding live work. He got them a one-night gig at the Peppermint Lounge. It was the morning after their performance that Knickerbocker wrote about Merle Oberon and Prince Serge Oblinski twisting the night away at the club. Joey and his band ended up playing the Peppermint Lounge for 13 months. The group's popularity led to contracts first with Capitol and then with Atlantic, but when nothing was released Roulette Records stepped in and rushed out the "Peppermint Twist" single (the number five song of 1962) and a live album recorded at the Peppermint Lounge.

Chubby Checker followed his "Twist" revival with one of the only ballads written about the dance. It was recorded with a 16-year-old teenager from Overbrook High School who had been hired to sing backing vocals for Cameo-Parkway. Dee Dee Sharp didn't receive any credit on "Slow Twistin'," the number 36 song of 1962, but it did lead to a recording session of her own and the number 12 song of the year, "Mashed Potato Time."

Gary U.S. Bonds followed "School Is In" with a song called "Havin' So Much Fun," but it wasn't getting any airplay. When Bob Schwartz at Laurie Records suggested promoting the flip side, a song about the Twist called "Dear Lady," writer/producer Frank Guida added the word "Twist" to the title. "Dear Lady Twist" went to number nine on the Hot 100 and ranked number 46 for the year. Bonds' next single, "Twist, Twist Senora," also peaked at number nine, and ranked number 98 for the year.

Sam Cooke took "Twistin' The Night Away" to number nine on the Hot 100. It was the number 61 song of the year. The other Twist song on the year-end chart was "Twist And Shout" by the Isley Brothers, number 89 for the year. When the Beatles covered it, most disc jockeys thought it was a remake of the "original" by the Isley Brothers. But the first group to record the Bert Berns-Phil Medley song was the Top Notes, featuring Derek Martin, on Atlantic. Jerry Wexler told Charlie Gillette about working with Phil Spector on that session: "He and I produced the record and it was horrible. Bert was such a newcomer, he was sitting in the spectator's booth, watching Phil and I butcher his song . . . we had the wrong tempo, the wrong feel, but we didn't realize that Bert could've produced it himself, and he just sat and watched us ruin it." Bert did produce it himself a year later with the Isley Brothers for Wand Records.

It was a good year for dances. Aside from the seven Twist songs and the Mashed Potato hit on the year-end chart, other dances represented were the Limbo, the Watusi, the Cha-Cha and a dance made up especially for a song, the Loco-Motion.

Ray Charles had his biggest hit of all time with "I Can't Stop Loving You," the number two song of 1962. Originally recorded by composer Don Gibson, Charles included the song in his landmark *Modern Sounds in Country and Western Music* album. Executives at his label, ABC-Paramount, discouraged Charles from attempting such a project, thinking he would lose his fans. Ray decided to do it anyway. "I didn't want to be a country-western singer," he told Ben Fong-Torres. "I just wanted to take country-western songs. When I sing 'I Can't Stop Loving You,' I'm not singing it *country-western*. I'm singing it like *me*."

The Four Seasons made their chart debut in 1962, after a brush with the Hot 100 in 1956 as the Four Lovers. "Sherry," written by Bob Gaudio in 15 minutes, was their first number one single. It spent five weeks atop the Hot 100 and came in at number 11 for the year. The follow-up, "Big Girls Don't Cry," was recorded at the same session and was strongly considered for the debut single. Like its predecessor, it spent five weeks at number one. It was the number three song of the year, and the highest-ranked year-end single of the Four Seasons' career.

Bobby Vinton experienced success with his first chart single, "Roses Are Red (My Love)." When Epic Records threatened to drop him, Vinton found the song in a pile of rejected records and told the label's attorneys they owed him two more recordings. "Roses Are Red" became Epic's first number one single and ranked number six for 1962.

Mr. Acker Bilk, a clarinet player from Somerset, England, became the first British artist to have a top 10 song of the year. His instrumental "Stranger On The Shore," originally called "Jenny" after one of his children, ranked number seven for the year. The song title was changed when it became the theme song for a BBC children's television series, "Stranger on the Shore."

David Rose was also in the top 10 with an instrumental, "The Stripper." Born in London, Rose moved to the U.S. when he was seven and later became an American citizen. "The Stripper" began as eight bars of music for a television show called "Burlesque" that Rose scored in 1958. Dan Dailey and Joan Blondell starred in the program, and minutes before they went on the air live, the producer asked Rose for some background music for a scene where the two stars argued behind a closed dressing room door. Soon after the broadcast, Rose was recording a new album and had 10 minutes of studio time remaining. He had the musicians record the song and, as a joke, had copies made for everyone so they could show their families what a "beautiful" string album they had been recording. Friends suggested he release the track, but MGM Records said no. Four years later Rose was rushed into the studio at MGM's request to record a version of "Ebb Tide" to help promote the film *Sweet Bird of Youth* with Paul Newman and Geraldine Page. There was no time to record something for the "B" side, so someone at MGM went to the master files and pulled the obscure, unreleased song. Los Angeles DJ Robert Q. Lewis liked the "B" side so much, he played it on the air continuously for 45 minutes. That stunt led to "The Stripper" topping the *Billboard* chart and placing number seven for the year.

Elvis Presley had four songs included in the top 100 of the year for the first time since 1959. Highest-ranked of the four was "Return To Sender" at number 10, Presley's final top 10 song on a year-end chart.

1963

1 SUGAR SHACK
Jimmy Gilmer & the Fireballs *Dot*

2 DOMINIQUE
The Singing Nun *Philips*

3 HE'S SO FINE
The Chiffons *Laurie*

4 BLUE VELVET
Bobby Vinton *Epic*

5 HEY PAULA
Paul and Paula *Philips*

6 GO AWAY LITTLE GIRL
Steve Lawrence *Columbia*

7 LOUIE LOUIE
The Kingsmen *Wand*

8 MY BOYFRIEND'S BACK
The Angels *Smash*

9 FINGERTIPS—PT 2
Little Stevie Wonder *Tamla*

10 SUKIYAKI
Kyu Sakamoto *Capitol*

11 I WILL FOLLOW HIM
Little Peggy March *RCA*

12 I'M LEAVING IT UP TO YOU
Dale and Grace *Montel*

13 SURF CITY
Jan and Dean *Liberty*

14 IT'S MY PARTY
Lesley Gore *Mercury*

15 WALK LIKE A MAN
The Four Seasons *Vee Jay*

16 YOU'RE THE REASON I'M LIVING
Bobby Darin *Capitol*

17 WALK RIGHT IN
Rooftop Singers *Vanguard*

18 EASIER SAID THAN DONE
The Essex *Roulette*

19 RHYTHM OF THE RAIN
The Cascades *Valiant*

20 THE END OF THE WORLD
Skeeter Davis *RCA*

21 THE NIGHT HAS A THOUSAND EYES
Bobby Vee *Liberty*

22 PUFF THE MAGIC DRAGON
Peter, Paul and Mary *Warner Bros*

23 SURFIN' U.S.A.
The Beach Boys *Capitol*

24 IF I HAD A HAMMER
Trini Lopez *Reprise*

25 DEEP PURPLE
Nino Tempo and April Stevens *Atco*

26 SO MUCH IN LOVE
The Tymes *Parkway*

27 SINCE I FELL FOR YOU
Lenny Welch *Cadence*

28 OUR DAY WILL COME
Ruby & the Romantics *Kapp*

29 EVERYBODY
Tommy Roe *ABC-Paramount*

30 IF YOU WANNA BE HAPPY
Jimmy Soul *SPQR*

Bobby Vinton

1963 was the year Frankie Avalon and Annette Funicello made the first *Beach Party* movie; Patsy Cline was killed in a plane crash in Tennessee; and Phil Spector asked stores to remove his Christmas album after the assassination of President Kennedy.

The number one song of 1963 was "Sugar Shack" by Jimmy Gilmer & the Fireballs. The song was produced by the same man who had worked with Buddy Holly, Norman Petty. "Sugar Shack" was co-written by Keith McCormick of another group Petty produced, the String-a-Longs ("Wheels").

Japan and Belgium were represented on the year-end chart for the first time, both in the top 10. "Dominique," the number two song of the year, was the Belgian entry. Kyu Sakamoto was number 10 with "Sukiyaki," a song originally titled "*Ue O Muite Aruko*," which translates "I Look Up When I Walk." Thinking that DJs would have a difficult time with the real title, Pye Records released it under a Japanese name most Westerners would recognize: "Sukiyaki." As *Newsweek* would later point out, it was like releasing "Moon River" in Japan under the title "Beef Stew."

For the first time in the rock era, there were four songs featuring female lead vocalists in the top 10. The Singing Nun was the highest-ranked woman in the top 10. Judy Craig sang lead on the number three song of the year, "He's So Fine" by the Chiffons. Along with her friends in the group Barbara Lee, Patricia Bennett and Sylvia Peterson, Judy had recorded for labels like Big Deal, Wildcat and Reprise, without much success. That all changed when songwriter Ronnie Mack asked them to record some of his songs as demos. Busy with high school graduation, they forgot about the session with Mack. But the writer was busy shopping his tunes around, and he hit paydirt when he walked into the offices of the Tokens ("The Lion Sleeps Tonight"). Phil Margo, Mitch Margo, Hank Medress and Jay Siegal had signed a production deal with Capitol, although they were still signed to RCA themselves. They produced "He's So Fine" for the Chiffons.

Jill Jackson was the third female in the top 10, with the number five song of the year. Jill's aunt ran a boarding house at Howard Payne College in Brownwood, Texas. Ray Hildebrand, a student on a basketball scholarship, was living in the house. Jill asked him to sing with her on a radio benefit for the American Cancer Society. They performed a song Ray had written in the school gym. A local DJ liked it so much, he taped their performance and played "Hey Paula" on his own show. A friend of Ray's suggested they meet with record producer Major Bill Smith in Fort Worth. When an artist failed to show for a session, the Major had Ray and Jill use the studio time he had already paid for to record "Hey Paula." Released on the Major's LeCam label, it sold well in Atlanta and Shelby Singleton of Mercury Records picked it up for the label's Philips subsidiary. Singleton only changed one thing—he thought Ray and Jill wouldn't sell as many records as "Paul and Paula," so he changed their names on the label.

The fourth female vocalist in the top 10 was Peggy Santiglia, lead singer for the Angels on "My Boyfriend's Back," the number eight song of 1963. Sisters Barbara and Phyllis Allbut formed the group while they were high school students in New Jersey. Along with Linda Jansen, they were signed to Caprice Records and had a hit in 1962 with " 'Til." After a follow-up single, Linda left and was replaced by Peggy, who had been appearing in *Do Re Mi* on Broadway. The Angels met writer/producers Robert Feldman, Jerry Goldstein and Richard Gottehrer and did some demo work for them. The three men wrote "My Boyfriend's Back" for the Angels and Mercury Records bought the master from Caprice for their Smash subsidiary.

Motown had its first top 10 song on a year-end chart in 1963. The company's youngest artist, Little Stevie Wonder, was number nine for the year with "Fingertips—Pt. 2." Stevie's first three singles for Motown failed to chart, but he did so well on the Motortown Revues that Berry Gordy decided to record him live. The result was an album called *Little Stevie Wonder—The 12-Year-Old Genius*. Reaction to the seven-minute track "Fingertips" was so positive that Gordy decided to split it into two parts and release it as a single. DJs preferred side two and Wonder had his first chart single and first number one hit. "Fingertips—Pt. 2" was one of five Motown singles on the top 100 of 1963, a new high for the Detroit record company.

Bobby Vinton, who had the number six song of 1962 with "Roses Are Red (My Love)," had his highest charted year-end single in 1963 with "Blue Velvet," the number four song of the year. After recording Burt Bacharach and Hal David's "Blue On Blue" (the number 50 song of the year), Bobby decided to do a theme album of all "blue" songs. "I picked songs like 'Blue Moon' and 'Blue Hawaii' and everything that was blue in the title," he explains. "Al Gallico, a well-known music publisher, said I ought to do 'Blue Velvet.' He gave his secretary a dollar to run down to the music store and buy the sheet music." An hour later, Bobby was recording the song, but he didn't think it would be the single. His pick was "Am I Blue." When Epic wanted to release "Blue Velvet," he told them he didn't think it was a good idea. The label put it out anyway. Originally a number 16 song for Tony Bennett in 1951, "Blue Velvet" put Bobby back on top of the Hot 100.

The number six song of the year was not written for the artist who recorded it. After Bobby Vee recorded a number of songs written by Gerry Goffin and Carole King, including "Take Good Care Of My Baby," "How Many Tears" and "Walkin' With My Angel," the husband-and-wife writing team gave Bobby his choice of songs to record next. "It was amazing," Vee told Steve Kolanjian. "I did one session where I recorded 'Sharing You,' 'Go Away Little Girl' and 'It Might As Well Rain Until September.' They all went on to become top 20 songs and were all written for me, but were not all hits for me. I thought they were all great. I was pleased with all of them. What happened was, when we said, 'We're going to put out "Sharing You," because we think that would be the best single,' they said, 'Well we can't wait for you to decide whether or not you're going to put out "Go Away Little Girl," we'll do it with someone else.' And so Steve Lawrence put it out. Of course it was a number one record, much bigger than 'Sharing You.'"

The number seven song of 1963 was one of the most controversial of the rock era. Richard Berry, a New Orleans musician who moved to Los Angeles in the early '40s, wrote and recorded "Louie Louie" in 1956 on the Flip label. It never made the Hot 100, but it was a regional hit in the Pacific Northwest and became a staple of garage bands in the state of Washington. The Frantics, a Seattle group signed to Dolton Records, included it in their shows but never recorded it. Another Seattle group, the Wailers, did commit it to vinyl, but it still wasn't a hit. In 1963, two groups from Portland, Oregon, happened to record "Louie Louie" within 24 hours of each other. Paul Revere and the Raiders cut it for the Sande label and it was picked up by Columbia Records. The Kingsmen recorded it for the Jerden label and six months later a DJ in Boston played their version. It was licensed by Scepter Records for their Wand label. The muffled vocals led many to believe the lyrics were obscene, although this was denied by both the Kingsmen and Richard Berry. "Louie Louie" was a hit at last, spending six weeks at number two on the Hot 100.

1 I WANT TO HOLD YOUR HAND
The Beatles *Capitol*

2 HELLO, DOLLY!
Louis Armstrong *Kapp*

3 OH, PRETTY WOMAN
Roy Orbison *Monument*

4 SHE LOVES YOU
The Beatles *Swan*

5 I GET AROUND
The Beach Boys *Capitol*

6 MY GUY
Mary Wells *Motown*

7 THERE! I'VE SAID IT AGAIN
Bobby Vinton *Epic*

8 BABY LOVE
The Supremes *Motown*

9 COME SEE ABOUT ME
The Supremes *Motown*

10 A HARD DAY'S NIGHT
The Beatles *Capitol*

11 MR. LONELY
Bobby Vinton *Epic*

12 EVERYBODY LOVES SOMEBODY
Dean Martin *Reprise*

13 WHERE DID OUR LOVE GO
The Supremes *Motown*

14 I FEEL FINE
The Beatles *Capitol*

15 CAN'T BUY ME LOVE
The Beatles *Capitol*

16 CHAPEL OF LOVE
The Dixie Cups *Red Bird*

17 SHE'S NOT THERE
The Zombies *Parrot*

18 DO WAH DIDDY DIDDY
Manfred Mann *Ascot*

19 WE'LL SING IN THE SUNSHINE
Gale Garnett *RCA*

20 RAG DOLL
The Four Seasons *Philips*

21 A WORLD WITHOUT LOVE
Peter and Gordon *Capitol*

22 LAST KISS
J. Frank Wilson & the Cavaliers *Josie*

23 HOUSE OF THE RISING SUN
The Animals *MGM*

24 BREAD AND BUTTER
The Newbeats *Hickory*

25 LOVE ME WITH ALL YOUR HEART
Ray Charles Singers *Command*

26 LOVE ME DO
The Beatles *Tollie*

27 PEOPLE
Barbra Streisand *Columbia*

28 RINGO
Lorne Greene *RCA*

29 LEADER OF THE PACK
The Shangri-Las *Red Bird*

30 FORGET HIM
Bobby Rydell *Cameo*

Herman's Hermits

1964 was the year Jan and Dean hosted the TAMI show; Jim Reeves was killed in a plane crash, Johnny Burnette drowned and Sam Cooke was shot to death; and 73 million Americans sat down in front of their television sets to watch the Beatles perform live on "The Ed Sullivan Show."

The Beatles dominated everything musical in 1964, right from the beginning of the year when "I Want To Hold Your Hand" debuted on the Hot 100 for the week ending January 18. It ended up as the number one song of the year, the first British recording to be the highest-ranked song of the year in the rock era. The Beatles were also in the year-end top 10 with "She Loves You" at number four and "A Hard Day's Night" at number 10. That equaled the record of three top 10 songs of the year set by Elvis Presley in 1956 and matched in 1957. Other Beatles songs included in the year's top 100 were: "I Feel Fine" (number 14), "Can't Buy Me Love" (number 15), "Love Me Do" (number 26), "Please Please Me" (number 36), "Twist And Shout" (number 42), "Do You Want To Know A Secret" (number 63) and "She's A Woman" (number 86). That gave them a total of 10 songs in the top 100 of the year, a record no one else has ever matched.

Prior to 1964, a total of eight records by artists from the U.K. had made the year-end surveys during the rock era; in 1964 there were 27 U.K. titles included in the top 100 of the year. Joining the Beatles on the chart were the Zombies (number 17 with "She's Not There"), Manfred Mann (number 18 with "Do Wah Diddy Diddy"),

Peter and Gordon (number 21 with "A World Without Love"), the Animals (number 23 with "House Of The Rising Sun"), Billy J. Kramer & the Dakotas (number 31 with "Little Children" and number 99 with "Bad To Me"), the Dave Clark Five (number 40 with "Glad All Over," number 49 with "Bits And Pieces," number 66 with "Because" and number 84 with "Can't You See That She's Mine"), Dusty Springfield (number 41 with "Wishin' and Hopin' "), the Rolling Stones (number 56 with "Time Is On My Side"), Gerry & the Pacemakers (number 57 with "Don't Let The Sun Catch You Crying"), the Honeycombs (number 61 with "Have I The Right?"), Herman's Hermits (number 65 with "I'm Into Something Good"), the Kinks (number 69 with "You Really Got Me") and Chad and Jeremy (number 76 with "A Summer Song").

While many American artists fell by the wayside in 1964, others maintained their strength despite the onslaught of British artists. The unlikely runner-up song of the year was "Hello, Dolly!" by Louis Armstrong. The jazz trumpeter known as Satchmo hadn't seen the Jerry Herman musical starring Carol Channing when he recorded the title song for an album of show tunes. Released as a single, "Hello, Dolly!" became the third most successful song from a stage production in the rock era. The song was so popular, most people believed Armstrong was starring in the show. He wasn't, but he did win a role in the film version produced in 1969. Unfortunately, he didn't get to work with Channing—Barbra Streisand played Dolly in the movie.

Roy Orbison made his first year-end chart appearance in 1960, when "Only The Lonely (Know How I Feel)" was the number 24 song of the year. In 1961 he was number 14 with "Running Scared" and number 27 with "Crying." A year later, "Dream Baby (How Long Must I Dream)" was number 80. In 1963, "In Dreams" was number 45 for the year and "Mean Woman Blues" was number 72. Orbison had the biggest hit of his career with "Oh, Pretty Woman," the number three song of 1964. His wife Claudette was the indirect inspiration for the song. She was leaving the house to go shopping one day and Roy asked if she needed any money. Songwriter Bill Dees suggested, "A pretty woman never needs any money," and thought it would make a good song title. By the time Claudette returned, Roy and Bill had written "Oh, Pretty Woman." Another Roy Orbison song, "It's Over," was the number 78 song of 1964.

The Beach Boys made their first appearance on a year-end chart in 1962, when "Surfin' Safari" was the number 67 song of the year. They fared better in 1963, when "Surfin' U.S.A." was number 23 for the year, "Surfer Girl" was number 31 and "Be True To Your School" was number 93. In 1964 they set their all-time high mark when "I Get Around" placed number five for the year. Two more Beach Boys songs graced the top 100: "Fun, Fun, Fun" at number 73 and "Dance, Dance, Dance" at number 90.

After registering its first top 10 song of the year in 1963, Motown landed an impressive three hits in the top 10 of 1964.

Mary Wells led the way with the Smokey Robinson-penned "My Guy," the first number one song on the Motown label itself. Wells had come to Berry Gordy's company as a songwriter, but her run of hits didn't begin until she teamed up with Robinson as her writer/producer. Mary had the number 76 song of 1972 with "The One Who Really Loves You" and the number 80 song of 1963 with "Two Lovers." After her success with "My Guy," she never appeared on a year-end chart again. At the height of her career she left Motown and signed with 20th Century Fox. Subsequent deals with Atco, Jubilee and Epic proved equally unsuccessful.

The other two Motown songs in the top 10 of 1964 were by the Supremes. "Baby Love" was number eight and "Come See About Me" was number nine. The only other American artists to have two songs in a top 10 of the year prior to the Supremes were Elvis Presley and Chubby Checker. The Detroit trio had one more song in the top 100, "Where Did Our Love Go" at number 13.

Bobby Vinton had a top 10 song of the year for the third year in a row. The only artists who had accomplished this prior to Vinton were Elvis Presley and Chubby Checker. The song that completed the hat trick for Bobby was "There! I've Said It Again," number seven for the year. Like his hit from 1963, "Blue Velvet," this was a recording of a song that was written prior to the rock era. "Blue Velvet" dated back to 1951; "There! I've Said It Again" went back even further. Vaughn Monroe recorded it in 1945 and had a six-week run at number one with the song. Bobby recorded his version after a long-haired DJ in Cincinatti surprised him by screaming at him as he walked on stage that he should record the song. "I still remember that recording session," says Bobby. "It was about 10 after seven and I sang it one time, and it was a quarter after seven. The session was supposed to go to ten o'clock and I said, 'That's it. I could sing this all night, but it's not going to get any better. It's a hit just the way it is, goodnight, everybody.'"

Barbra Streisand made her *Billboard* singles debut in 1964 with "People," a song she performed in the stage musical *Funny Girl*. It was the number 27 song of the year and Barbra's biggest hit of the decade.

The number one television series of the 1964-65 season was "Bonanza," and during that time the patriarch of the Cartwright clan, actor Lorne Greene, experienced being number one on another chart—the *Billboard* Hot 100. He did it with "Ringo," not a song about the Beatle but a spoken word recording about a sheriff who saved the life of gunman Johnny Ringo. Lorne's career as a pop star began when a producer at RCA Records suggested that the Cartwrights record an album. A Christmas LP featuring Greene with Michael Landon, Dan Blocker and Pernell Roberts sold well enough that a second album, *Welcome to the Ponderosa*, was recorded. A DJ in Lubbock, Texas, played "Ringo" from that LP and RCA was inundated with requests to release it as a single. It ended up as the number 28 song of the year.

THE TOP 100 SONGS OF
1965

1 (I CAN'T GET NO) SATISFACTION
The Rolling Stones *London*

2 YOU'VE LOST THAT LOVIN' FEELIN'
Righteous Brothers *Philles*

3 DOWNTOWN
Petula Clark *Warner Bros*

4 WOOLY BULLY
Sam the Sham & the Pharaohs *MGM*

5 MRS. BROWN YOU'VE GOT A LOVELY DAUGHTER
Herman's Hermits *MGM*

6 HELP!
The Beatles *Capitol*

7 I CAN'T HELP MYSELF (SUGAR PIE, HONEY BUNCH)
Four Tops *Motown*

8 LET'S HANG ON
The Four Seasons *Philips*

9 TURN! TURN! TURN!
The Byrds *Columbia*

10 MY GIRL
The Temptations *Gordy*

11 I GOT YOU BABE
Sonny and Cher *Atco*

12 YESTERDAY
The Beatles *Capitol*

13 THIS DIAMOND RING
Gary Lewis & the Playboys *Liberty*

14 STOP! IN THE NAME OF LOVE
The Supremes *Motown*

15 GET OFF OF MY CLOUD
The Rolling Stones *London*

16 HELP ME, RHONDA
The Beach Boys *Capitol*

17 KING OF THE ROAD
Roger Miller *Smash*

18 YOU WERE ON MY MIND
We Five *A&M*

19 THE BIRDS AND THE BEES
Jewel Akens *Era*

20 THE "IN" CROWD
Ramsey Lewis Trio *Argo*

21 HANG ON SLOOPY
The McCoys *Bang*

22 A TASTE OF HONEY
Herb Alpert & the Tijuana Brass *A&M*

23 I HEAR A SYMPHONY
The Supremes *Motown*

24 I GOT YOU (I FEEL GOOD)
James Brown *King*

25 CRYING IN THE CHAPEL
Elvis Presley *RCA*

26 1-2-3
Len Barry *Decca*

27 LOVE POTION NUMBER NINE
The Searchers *Kapp*

28 CAN'T YOU HEAR MY HEARTBEAT
Herman's Hermits *MGM*

29 MR. TAMBOURINE MAN
The Byrds *Columbia*

30 SHOTGUN
Jr. Walker & the All Stars *Soul*

The Byrds

1965 was the year the Beatles made their second movie, *Help!*, toured America for the second time and were awarded the MBE by Queen Elizabeth.

The British Invasion continued at full speed. There were four U.K. songs in the year-end top 10, and 32 in the top 100. The Beatles only had four titles on the list, compared to 10 the previous year. Herman's Hermits surpassed them, with five songs in the top 100 of the year. The Manchester group held down the number five spot with "Mrs. Brown You've Got A Lovely Daughter," written in 1963 and originally performed by actor Tom Courtenay in a British television play. Herman's Hermits' version was a track on their *Introducing Herman's Hermits* album, but radio airplay in America forced MGM to release it as a single. That didn't happen in Britain, where the track was never issued on a 45 rpm disc. Other Hermits' singles on the year-end chart included "Can't You Hear My Heartbeat" (number 28), an updating of the Rays' "Silhouettes" (number 41), a music hall song from 1911 called "I'm Henry VIII, I Am" (number 42) and a remake of Sam Cooke's "Wonderful World" (number 60).

American artists continued to hold their own, especially those signed to Motown. The Supremes weren't in the top 10 like they were in 1964, but they had three number one songs included in the year's top 100: "Stop! In The Name Of Love" (number 14), "I Hear A Symphony" (number 23) and "Back In My Arms Again" (number 45). The Temptations were in the top 10 for the first time with "My Girl," featuring a lead vocal by David Ruffin. After recording for Chess and Anna Records, David joined the Motown roster to become a Temptation—but only after brother Jimmy had turned the job down. Marvin Gaye had three songs on the year-end chart for 1965: "How Sweet It Is (To Be Loved By You)" (number 65), "Ain't That Peculiar" (number 66) and "I'll Be Doggone" (number 76). Jr. Walker & the All Stars were number 30 with "Shotgun" and Martha & the Vandellas were number 90 with "Nowhere To Run." But the highest-rated Motown song of the year was "I Can't Help Myself (Sugar Pie, Honey Bunch)" by the Four Tops. The number seven song of the year, it was written by Brian Holland, Lamont Dozier and Eddie Holland. It was the first chart-topper for the Tops, who first sang together at a party in 1954. That led to the formation of a group called the Four Aims and a deal with Chess Records in 1956. But their name sounded too much like the Ames Brothers. Their musical conductor asked how they had chosen their name, and Duke Fakir of the group replied they had been "aiming for the top." Their conductor suggested the Four Tops. They had brief tenures with the Red Top and Columbia labels before signing with a lesser-known Motown subsidiary called Workshop. After recording a jazz album, *Breaking Through*, they were assigned to Holland-Dozier-Holland and really broke through with "Baby I Need Your Loving," the number 62 song of 1964. While recording "I Can't Help Myself," lead singer Levi Stubbs wasn't happy with his vocals and asked to do a third take. Brian Holland insisted it was perfect, but agreed to let Levi try again the next day. There never was another session. "I Can't Help Myself" was released the way Levi sang it on take number two.

The number one song of 1965 was of British origin for the second consecutive year. The Rolling Stones' first number one single, "(I Can't Get No) Satisfaction," was the highest-ranked record of the year. The song's origin can be traced to Clearwater, Florida. Keith Richards was having trouble sleeping in a hotel room that night and thought up a chord progression. When he played it back the next morning for Mick Jagger, Keith had some words to go with the riff that was admittedly inspired by Martha & the Vandellas' "Dancing In The Street." Keith considered the lyric "I can't get no satisfaction" to be a working title, not believing it was commercial enough.

The runner-up song of the year was "You've Lost That Lovin' Feelin'" by the Righteous Brothers. Producer Phil Spector asked the husband-and-wife songwriting team of Barry Mann and Cynthia Weil to fly from New York to California to write the duo's debut song for Philles Records. Barry and Cynthia checked into the legendary Chateau Marmont hotel on the Sunset Strip and rented a piano. Their favorite song at the time was the Four Tops' "Baby I Need Your Loving," and that inspired them to come up with "You've Lost That Lovin' Feelin'," although they considered that to be a dummy title. Spector liked the original words enough to keep them.

Petula Clark was the lone female vocalist in the top 10. The first British female vocalist to have a number one song in America during the rock era, she was well-known around the world but a "newcomer" to the U.S. when "Downtown" was released. Living in Paris with husband Claud Wolff, Petula had been recording mostly in French, including *"Chariot,"* the original version of "I Will Follow Him." Tony Hatch of Pye Records in Britain told her it was time to record in English again, and she said she would—but only if she could find the right material. Hatch had written some new music and played one of his melodies while Petula went to the kitchen to make tea. She heard the music and came running back to tell Tony that if he could write suitable lyrics to match his title of "Downtown," she would record it. It became the number three song of the year. The follow-up, "I Know A Place," was the number 54 song of the year.

Sam the Sham & the Pharaohs were number four for the year with their first chart single, "Wooly Bully." Domingo Samudio played organ for Andy & the Night Riders until two members of the band quit, including Andy. When two new members joined, Samudio became the leader and renamed the band. His friends called him Sam, and the movie *The Ten Commandments* inspired the "Pharaohs." Given the opportunity to record, Sam used his cat's name, "Wooly Bully," to come up with a million-selling single.

The Four Seasons had their second top 10 song of the year with "Let's Hang On," the number eight single of 1965. It was their first time back in the top 10 since "Big Girls Don't Cry" had been the third most successful chart single of 1962.

The Byrds made their chart debut in 1965 and landed two songs on the year-end top 100. A song adapted by Pete Seeger from the Book of Ecclesiastes, "Turn! Turn! Turn!" was number nine for the year and an electrified Bob Dylan song, "Mr. Tambourine Man," was number 29. The Byrds recorded one single for Elektra as the Beefeaters, then were signed to Columbia Records.

A&M Records had its second year-end entry in 1965 with "You Were On My Mind" by the We Five, a group formed at Mount St. Antonio College in California. Mike Stewart, brother of John Stewart, was a member of the quintet and the song was originally written and recorded by Ian and Sylvia. The We Five version was the number 18 song of the year and the first A&M single on a year-end chart since "The Lonely Bull" by the Tijuana Brass featuring Herb Alpert was the number 46 song of 1962. The TJB were also back on the chart with "A Taste Of Honey," the number 22 song.

The Dunhill label made its first appearance on a year-end chart in 1965, thanks to Barry McGuire's "Eve Of Destruction," number 32 for the year. A former member of the New Christy Minstrels, McGuire had sung lead on their 1963 singles "Green, Green" and "Saturday Night."

1966

1 **I'M A BELIEVER**
The Monkees *Colgems*

2 **WINCHESTER CATHEDRAL**
New Vaudeville Band *Fontana*

3 **THE BALLAD OF THE GREEN BERETS**
S/Sgt Barry Sadler *RCA*

4 **96 TEARS**
?(Question Mark) & the Mysterians *Cameo*

5 **GOOD VIBRATIONS**
The Beach Boys *Capitol*

6 **DEVIL WITH A BLUE DRESS ON &
GOOD GOLLY MISS MOLLY**
Mitch Ryder & the Detroit Wheels *New Voice*

7 **LAST TRAIN TO CLARKSVILLE**
The Monkees *Colgems*

8 **REACH OUT I'LL BE THERE**
Four Tops *Motown*

9 **(YOU'RE MY) SOUL AND INSPIRATION**
Righteous Brothers *Verve*

10 **YOU CAN'T HURRY LOVE**
The Supremes *Motown*

11 **WE CAN WORK IT OUT**
The Beatles *Capitol*

12 **WHAT BECOMES OF THE BROKENHEARTED**
Jimmy Ruffin *Soul*

13 **CHERISH**
The Association *Valiant*

14 **CALIFORNIA DREAMIN'**
The Mamas and the Papas *Dunhill*

15 **THESE BOOTS ARE MADE FOR WALKIN'**
Nancy Sinatra *Reprise*

16 **POOR SIDE OF TOWN**
Johnny Rivers *Imperial*

17 **GOOD LOVIN'**
The Young Rascals *Atlantic*

18 **STRANGERS IN THE NIGHT**
Frank Sinatra *Reprise*

19 **BORN FREE**
Roger Williams *Kapp*

20 **YOU KEEP ME HANGIN' ON**
The Supremes *Motown*

21 **SNOOPY VS. THE RED BARON**
Royal Guardsmen *Laurie*

22 **MONDAY, MONDAY**
The Mamas and the Papas *Dunhill*

23 **WHEN A MAN LOVES A WOMAN**
Percy Sledge *Atlantic*

24 **SUMMER IN THE CITY**
The Lovin' Spoonful *Kama Sutra*

25 **THE SOUNDS OF SILENCE**
Simon and Garfunkel *Columbia*

26 **KICKS**
Paul Revere & the Raiders *Columbia*

27 **SUNSHINE SUPERMAN**
Donovan *Epic*

28 **PAINT IT, BLACK**
The Rolling Stones *London*

29 **HANKY PANKY**
Tommy James & the Shondells *Roulette*

30 **LIL' RED RIDING HOOD**
Sam the Sham & the Pharaohs *MGM*

The Monkees

1966 was the year John Lennon said, "The Beatles are probably bigger than Jesus"; NBC premiered "The Monkees" and "Star Trek" in the same week; and Brian Wilson finally completed "Good Vibrations."

There were four singles on the year-end chart by the Sinatra family. Frank had last appeared on a year-end singles chart in 1957, when "All The Way" was the number 67 song of the year. One year earlier, "Love And Marriage" had ranked 35 and "Hey! Jealous Lover" had been number 41. In 1966, Frank was number 18 with "Strangers In The Night" and number 59 with "That's Life." Jimmy Bowen, Sinatra's producer and A&R staffer for Reprise, found "Strangers In The Night" when publisher Hal Fine brought him instrumental tracks written for the movie *A Man Could Get Killed* by German orchestra leader Bert Kaempfert ("Wonderland By Night"). Bowen promised Sinatra would record the song if English lyrics were written. Charlie Singleton and Eddie Snyder came up with the words, but by the time Sinatra received the lyrics, Bobby Darin and Jack Jones had cut the song. With three days' notice that Jones' single was about to be released, Bowen asked Ernie Freeman to come up with an arrangement for Sinatra. Three days later a full orchestra was in place and Sinatra arrived at 8 p.m. to record the song. He was finished by 9, and 24 hours later Sinatra's version of "Strangers In The Night" was being played across the land.

31	MY LOVE Petula Clark *Warner Bros*
32	PAPERBACK WRITER The Beatles *Capitol*
33	MELLOW YELLOW Donovan *Epic*
34	FIVE O'CLOCK WORLD The Vogues *Co & Ce*
35	SUNNY Bobby Hebb *Philips*
36	DAYDREAM The Lovin' Spoonful *Kama Sutra*
37	A GROOVY KIND OF LOVE The Mindbenders *Fontana*
38	SEE YOU IN SEPTEMBER The Happenings *B.T. Puppy*
39	YOU DON'T HAVE TO SAY YOU LOVE ME Dusty Springfield *Philips*
40	WILD THING The Troggs *Fontana*
41	LIGHTNIN' STRIKES Lou Christie *MGM*
42	19TH NERVOUS BREAKDOWN The Rolling Stones *London*
43	BORN A WOMAN Sandy Posey *MGM*
44	RED RUBBER BALL The Cyrkle *Columbia*
45	I AM A ROCK Simon and Garfunkel *Columbia*
46	SUGAR TOWN Nancy Sinatra *Reprise*
47	NO MATTER WHAT SHAPE (YOUR STOMACH'S IN) The T-Bones *Liberty*
48	DID YOU EVER HAVE TO MAKE UP YOUR MIND The Lovin' Spoonful *Kama Sutra*
49	SHE'S JUST MY STYLE Gary Lewis & the Playboys *Liberty*
50	SECRET AGENT MAN Johnny Rivers *Imperial*
51	NOWHERE MAN The Beatles *Capitol*
52	TIME WON'T LET ME The Outsiders *Capitol*
53	WALK AWAY RENEE The Left Banke *Smash*
54	I'M SO LONESOME I COULD CRY B.J. Thomas & the Triumphs *Scepter*
55	HOORAY FOR HAZEL Tommy Roe *ABC*
56	LADY GODIVA Peter and Gordon *Capitol*
57	JUST LIKE ME Paul Revere & the Raiders *Columbia*
58	BANG BANG (MY BABY SHOT ME DOWN) Cher *Imperial*
59	THAT'S LIFE Frank Sinatra *Reprise*
60	RAINY DAY WOMEN #12 & 35 Bob Dylan *Columbia*
61	SLOOP JOHN B The Beach Boys *Capitol*
62	THE PIED PIPER Crispian St. Peters *Jamie*
63	I'M YOUR PUPPET James and Bobby Purify *Bell*
64	UPTIGHT (EVERYTHING'S ALRIGHT) Stevie Wonder *Tamla*
65	COOL JERK The Capitols *Karen*

The other Sinatra on the year-end chart was Frank's daughter Nancy. She came in three places ahead of her father, with "These Boots Are Made For Walkin'," the number 15 song of the year. Nancy had been recording for Reprise since 1961, when her first single was "Cufflinks And A Tie Clip." By 1965, she knew her time at the label was growing short unless she could come up with a hit record. Producer Lee Hazlewood managed to get her into the lower rungs of the Hot 100 with "So Long Babe." With backing from her father, Nancy insisted on recording "These Boots Are Made For Walkin'," even though Hazlewood had written it for a man to sing. After it went to number one, Nancy continued her association with Lee. A subsequent single, "Sugar Town," was the number 46 song of 1966.

The Four Tops and the Supremes represented Motown in the top 10 again, with "Reach Out I'll Be There" (number eight) and "You Can't Hurry Love" (number 10), respectively. But the highest-ranked Motown song of 1966 was a cover version. Mitch Ryder & the Detroit Wheels combined Motown artist Shorty Long's "Devil With The Blue Dress" and Little Richard's "Good Golly Miss Molly" in a medley that was the number six song of the year. Jimmy Ruffin, who passed on a chance to join the Temptations in favor of his brother David, gave Motown another year-end entry with "What Becomes Of The Brokenhearted" at number 12.

The New Vaudeville Band was the highest-ranked British act on the year-end chart with "Winchester Cathedral" at number two. Composer Geoff Stephens was the man behind the New Vaudeville Band. Working as a staff songwriter at a publishing company in Denmark Street, he stared at his calendar one day and was inspired by a picture of Winchester Cathedral. A fan of vaudeville music, he recorded the song himself with studio musicians and imitated the vocal style of Rudy Vallee, singing through a megaphone. When the song was so popular that he had to tour, Stephens put together a New Vaudeville Band to play live performances.

The Monkees joined the elite club of artists with two songs in the top 10 of a year. The only other members to date were Elvis Presley, Chubby Checker, the Beatles and the Supremes. The TV foursome had the number one song of 1966, "I'm A Believer," as well as the number seven song, "Last Train To Clarksville." The former was written by Neil Diamond and the latter by Tommy Boyce and Bobby Hart. The TV series was created by producers Bert Schneider and Bob Rafelson, who sold NBC on the idea of crossing the zaniness of the Beatles in *A Hard Day's Night* with the Marx Brothers. The original idea was to build a series around the Lovin' Spoonful, but the producers opted to create their own band. They ran an advertisement in a Hollywood trade paper seeking "four insane boys" to play rock musicians in a new TV series. Michael Nesmith, Micky Dolenz, Peter Tork and Davy Jones were cast as the Monkees. Don Kirshner was asked to find songs for the Monkees to record on the new Colgems label, owned by the studio that produced the Monkees, Columbia Pictures. Hart got the idea for "Last Train To Clarksville" after he heard the Beatles' "Paperback Writer" and mistakenly thought the song was about a "last train." For a follow-up single, Kirshner turned to producer Jeff Barry and asked him to find a song that would sell more copies than "Last Train To Clarksville." Barry had been working with Diamond and thought his "I'm A Believer" would be big for the Monkees. It spent seven weeks at number one.

The number three song of 1966 was an unlikely hit, "The Ballad Of The Green Berets" by S/Sgt. Barry Sadler. The Green Berets were an elite army combat unit called the Special Forces when they were created by President John F. Kennedy in 1961. Sadler had spent four years in the Air Force when he enlisted in the Army's airborne school and trained as a combat medic. His service with the Green Berets in Vietnam was cut short when he was injured in a booby trap. While recuperating back in the U.S., a friend suggested he write a song about the Special Forces. Sadler submitted his work to music publisher Chet Gierlach, who showed it to his friend Robin Moore, author of the book *The Green Berets*. Moore thought the song had potential and offered to rewrite it with Sadler. Recorded on a small budget and released just to the military, it became so popular that Moore asked RCA Records if they would be interested in releasing the song commercially. The label financed a new recording session with an orchestra and the new version became RCA's fastest-selling single to date.

The number four song of 1966 was first written as a poem called "Too Many Teardrops" by Rudy Martinez. Born in Mexico and raised in Michigan's Saginaw Valley, he set the tune to music with his band, XYZ. As ? (Question Mark) & the Mysterians, they recorded "96 Tears" and "Midnight Hour" in the living room of their manager, Lilly Gonzalez. She formed a label, Pa-Go-Go, and released the two songs. The band thought "Midnight Hour" would be the hit, but Martinez avidly pushed for "96 Tears."

The Beach Boys equaled their previous year-end high mark with "Good Vibrations," the number five song of 1966. Two years earlier, "I Get Around" had been the number five song of the year.

The Righteous Brothers had a top 10 single of the year for the second year in a row. "You've Lost That Lovin' Feelin'" was the number two song of 1965, but a year later producer Phil Spector had lost interest in the duo, and sold their contract to MGM for a million dollars. Looking for new material, Bill Medley and Bobby Hatfield turned to the writers of "Lovin' Feelin,'" Barry Mann and Cynthia Weil. They had written part of a song as a follow-up to "Lovin' Feelin,'" but stopped because they felt they were copying themselves. When Medley asked them to complete the song, Mann and Weil finished "(You're My) Soul And Inspiration" as a favor to the Righteous Brothers. Medley produced it and Cynthia says, "He made this terrific record, but it will always be 'Lovin' Feelin' sideways to me."

THE TOP 100 SONGS OF
1967

Sam & Dave

1967 was the year the Beatles released *Sgt. Pepper's Lonely Hearts Club Band*; Cindy Birdsong took Florence Ballard's place in the Supremes; and the Monterey Pop Festival kicked off the Summer of Love.

The focal point for the Summer of Love was San Francisco, the city that spawned the Jefferson Airplane. With lead vocals by Grace Slick, the Airplane landed two hits in the year-end top 100, "Somebody To Love" at number 82 and "White Rabbit" at number 86. The city itself was canonized in Scott McKenzie's "San Francisco (Be Sure To Wear Flowers In Your Hair)," the number 42 song of the year.

There were four female singers in the top 10, matching the record set in 1963. Three of them were American. Bobbie Gentry, born in Chickasaw County, Mississippi, grew up in the Delta. She was born Roberta Lee Streeter, but changed her name when she was 14 after seeing the movie *Ruby Gentry* with Jennifer Jones. While seeking a publishing deal for her songs, she was signed to Capitol as both songwriter and artist, much to her surprise. Her original recording of "Ode To Billie Joe" ran longer than seven minutes. Capitol edited it down and released it as the "B" side of "Mississippi Delta," but disc jockeys preferred "Ode To Billie Joe," which spent four weeks at number one and became the number four song of the year.

Nancy Sinatra, born in Jersey City, New Jersey, had the number

15 song of 1966 with "These Boots Are Made For Walkin'." She did even better in 1967, coming in at number seven for the year in her duet with her father Frank, "Somethin' Stupid." The song was a remake of a duet between composer C. Carson Parks and his wife, Gaile Foote. They had recorded their own album for Kapp Records and included a couple of Parks' songs to assure them of song royalties. "Cab Driver" was covered by the Mills Brothers and "Somethin' Stupid" was heard by Sinatra associate Sarge Weiss, who suggested Frank record it with Nancy.

Gladys Knight, born in Atlanta, Georgia, had her first year-end hit since "Every Beat Of My Heart," the number 55 song of 1961. Her recording of "I Heard It Through The Grapevine" with the Pips was the first version of the song to be released, but not the first recorded. Smokey Robinson & the Miracles, the Isley Brothers and Marvin Gaye had all cut the Norman Whitfield-Barrett Strong song before Gladys & the Pips, but theirs was the first released. It peaked at number two and ranked number nine for the year.

The non-American female vocalist in the top 10 was Lulu, born in Glasgow, Scotland. She and Davy Jones of the Monkees were the only non-Americans in the top 10. She was born Marie McDonald McLaughlin Lawrie, but manager Marian Massey renamed her because she was a "lulu of a kid." Marian's sister Felice worked for a film agent, and when she read the script for *To Sir With Love* suggested to Marian that Lulu try out for a role. Director James Clavell agreed to attend a Beach Boys concert in London that featured Lulu as a supporting act, and liked her enough to cast her in the film. She was signed to perform the title song, but didn't care for any of the tunes the producers had found. She asked her friend Mark London to write some music, and the next day lyricist Don Black penned the words. Although the song never made the British chart, it was number one in the States for five weeks, good enough to make it the highest ranking song of the year.

The number two song of 1967 was by a Los Angeles quartet formed by two graduates of the UCLA film school. Jim Morrison and Ray Manzarek started the band and recruited John Densmore and Robbie Krieger in a meditation class. Morrison was inspired to name the band after Aldous Huxley's *The Doors of Perception* as well as a passage written by William Blake: "There are things that are known and things that are unknown, in between the doors." The group's first single, "Break On Through (To The Other Side)," did not chart. Elektra Records was reluctant to release "Light My Fire" as a single because of its six minute, 50 second length. The Doors wanted the complete song released, but agreed to have the label edit it down. Unhappy with the result, the group asked producer Paul Rothchild to make a new edit by deleting a chunk of the instrumental break to bring it down to a time that radio would play. Ironically, most stations preferred the album-length version anyway and played that.

Another Los Angeles-based group, the Association, was number three for the year with "Windy." Their previous number one hit, "Cherish," had been the number 13 song of 1966. Songwriter Ruthann Friedman had submitted a demo tape of 22 songs to producer Bones Howe. His favorite was "Windy," but it was written as a waltz. A new arrangement with four beats to the bar gave the group their second chart-topping single. "Windy" was recorded in a marathon session that began in the afternoon and ended at 6:30 the next morning. Lead vocalists Larry Ramos and Russ Giguere were so burned out by the end of the session, they needed support from everyone present to record the multi-layered vocal chorus finale. Friedman joined in and can be heard singing counter harmony in the fade.

The number five song of the year was produced by Dan Penn for $800 at the American Recording Studios in Memphis. Larry Uttal of Bell Records liked the song enough to advance Penn the $800 and released "The Letter" by the Box Tops on the Mala subsidiary. Wayne Carson Thompson, who wrote the song, played guitar on the session and recalls the group didn't have a name yet. Someone suggested they have a contest to find a name, and invite people to send in 50 cents and a box top. Thompson and Penn looked at each other and knew they had found a new moniker for the band. Thompson didn't like the arrangement or 16-year-old Alex Chilton's lead vocals at first, and was bewildered when Penn added in the sound effect of a jet. Only one minute and 58 seconds in duration, "The Letter" shot up the Hot 100 and spent four weeks at number one.

The Monkees had their third top 10 song of the year with "Daydream Believer." Their recording of "I'm A Believer" had been the number one song of 1966, and "Last Train To Clarksville" was the number seven song of that year. The Turtles, yet another L.A. group in the top 10, were number eight for the year with "Happy Together." That was a vast improvement over their ranking in 1965, when they were number 95 for the year with "It Ain't Me Babe." The Santa Barbara, California, based group called the Strawberry Alarm Clock, with a name inspired in part by the Beatles' "Strawberry Fields Forever," had their only year-end hit with their debut single, "Incense and Peppermints."

The Beatles missed the year-end top 10 for the second year in a row. Their highest-ranking song of 1967 was "Hello Goodbye," at number 17. "All You Need Is Love" was number 34 for the year and "Penny Lane" was number 50.

Epic Records had their only year-end chart-topper with Lulu's "To Sir With Love." It replaced Bobby Vinton's 1962 recording of "Roses Are Red (My Love)" as Epic's most successful chart single to date. "Light My Fire" was Elektra's first number one single and its most successful chart single to date. "Incense and Peppermints" was Uni's first year-end chart listing, and the most successful single ever released on the label.

1968

1 HEY JUDE
The Beatles *Apple*

2 I HEARD IT THROUGH THE GRAPEVINE
Marvin Gaye *Tamla*

3 LOVE IS BLUE
Paul Mauriat *Philips*

4 LOVE CHILD
Diana Ross & the Supremes *Motown*

5 HONEY
Bobby Goldsboro *UA*

6 (SITTIN' ON) THE DOCK OF THE BAY
Otis Redding *Volt*

7 PEOPLE GOT TO BE FREE
The Rascals *Atlantic*

8 THIS GUY'S IN LOVE WITH YOU
Herb Alpert *A&M*

9 JUDY IN DISGUISE (WITH GLASSES)
John Fred & His Playboy Band *Paula*

10 WOMAN, WOMAN
Gary Puckett & the Union Gap *Columbia*

11 MRS. ROBINSON
Simon & Garfunkel *Columbia*

12 WHO'S MAKING LOVE
Johnnie Taylor *Stax*

13 HELLO, I LOVE YOU
The Doors *Elektra*

14 TIGHTEN UP
Archie Bell & the Drells *Atlantic*

15 YOUNG GIRL
Gary Puckett & the Union Gap *Columbia*

16 HARPER VALLEY P.T.A.
Jeannie C. Riley *Plantation*

17 THOSE WERE THE DAYS
Mary Hopkin *Apple*

18 LITTLE GREEN APPLES
O.C. Smith *Columbia*

19 THE GOOD, THE BAD AND THE UGLY
Hugo Montenegro *RCA*

20 BEND ME, SHAPE ME
American Breed *Acta*

21 CRY LIKE A BABY
The Box Tops *Mala*

22 MAGIC CARPET RIDE
Steppenwolf *Dunhill*

23 GREEN TAMBOURINE
The Lemon Pipers *Buddah*

24 MIDNIGHT CONFESSIONS
The Grass Roots *Dunhill*

25 FOR ONCE IN MY LIFE
Stevie Wonder *Tamla*

26 A BEAUTIFUL MORNING
The Rascals *Atlantic*

27 SPOOKY
Classics IV *Imperial*

28 ABRAHAM, MARTIN AND JOHN
Dion *Laurie*

29 STONED SOUL PICNIC
5th Dimension *Soul City*

30 CHAIN OF FOOLS
Aretha Franklin *Atlantic*

The Doors

1968 was the year Elvis Presley revived his career with a one-hour special on NBC; the Beatles launched their Apple label; and Peter Tork quit the Monkees, leaving them a trio.

"Love Is Blue" by Paul Mauriat, the number three song of the year, was the highest-ranked instrumental hit since "Exodus," by Ferrante and Teicher, which was the number two song of 1961.

"I Heard It Through The Grapevine," the number nine song of 1967 when it was recorded by Gladys Knight & the Pips, became the only song of the rock era to be in the year-end top 10 two years in a row. Marvin Gaye recorded his version of the Norman Whitfield-Barrett Strong song before Gladys did. The first recording, by Smokey Robinson and the Miracles, remained unreleased as a single. Marvin didn't want to release his version after Gladys had such a big hit with the song, but finally agreed. "I never thought a great deal about the song after recording it," he said in Sharon Davis' *Motown: The History*. "In fact, I wasn't too optimistic about it at all. I had no idea it would sell nearly four million records."

The other Motown song in the top 10 was "Love Child" by Diana Ross & the Supremes, ranked number four for the year. The Supremes had only scored three year-end top 10 hits prior to

"Love Child." In 1964, "Baby Love" and "Come See About Me" ranked numbers eight and nine, respectively. In 1966, "You Can't Hurry Love" ranked number 10, making "Love Child" their highest-ranked single of the rock era.

Memphis soul was also represented on the year-end chart. The Stax/Volt label had its two biggest hits to date with Otis Redding's "(Sittin' On) The Dock Of The Bay" at number six for the year and Johnnie Taylor's "Who's Making Love" at number 12. "Dock Of The Bay" was the first posthumous number one hit of the rock era. Otis wrote it (with Steve Cropper) in the summer of 1967 while staying on a houseboat anchored off of Sausalito, California, after performing at the Monterey Pop Festival. He recorded the song in Memphis on December 6 and 7. On the 8th, he flew to Nashville for a concert. He continued on to Cleveland for a TV appearance and another concert. On Sunday, December 10, he was on his way to Madison, Wisconsin, when his private twin-engine Beechcraft plane crashed into Lake Monoma. The 26-year-old singer was killed along with his pilot, valet and four members of the Bar-Kays.

Although "(Sittin' On) The Dock Of The Bay" would become a number one hit, it had its detractors. Stax founder Jim Stewart wasn't impressed with the recording. "To me, 'Dock Of The Bay,' when I first heard it, was not nearly as strong as 'I've Been Loving You Too Long.' Of course, it was a different kind of record for Otis." Redding's manager, Phil Walden, concurred. "It was a drastic change. Listening to it in retrospect now, it isn't that much (of a change) but for those times, it sounded like it might have been a little too pop."

Cropper, who also produced the recording, told Edna Gundersen of *USA Today* that Jerry Wexler at Atlantic Records (Stax' distributor) wanted the track remixed before being released. "Wexler thought the vocal wasn't big enough and that the ocean waves and gulls were too loud. It was hard enough to deal with Otis dying, and it was killing me to change the song. I listened to it one more time, put it in a different box and sent it back. With all due respect, Atlantic never realized it was the same mix."

Bobby Goldsboro, who had the number 95 song of 1964 with "See The Funny Little Clown," had his only other year-end hit in 1968 with "Honey," ranked number five for the year. The song was written by Bobby Russell, whose other hits include "Little Green Apples" by O.C. Smith (the number 18 song of 1968), "The Joker Went Wild" by Brian Hyland and "The Night The Lights Went Out In Georgia" by Russell's then-wife, Vicki Lawrence. "Honey" was originally recorded by Bob Shane, one of the founding members of the Kingston Trio. After Goldsboro heard the original version, he and producer Bob Montgomery asked Russell if they could also record it. Russell agreed as long as they wouldn't release it as a single to compete with Shane's version. They agreed to wait four weeks. While Shane's version sold around 100,000 copies, Goldsboro sold over five million.

The Rascals had their first year-end top 10 single with "People

Got To Be Free." They were number 17 in 1966 with "Good Lovin'" and number 11 in 1967 with "Groovin'." Felix Cavaliere found it difficult to cope with the assassinations of Martin Luther King, Jr. and Sen. Robert F. Kennedy in the spring of '68 and expressed his feelings by writing "People Got To Be Free" with Eddie Brigati. Cavaliere says that Jerry Wexler at Atlantic was reluctant to release a political song, as he thought it could hurt the career of the Rascals. Felix believed the song was important and needed to be heard. It was number one for five weeks, the biggest hit of the Rascals' career. Another political song that was also inspired by political assassinations was "Abraham, Martin and John," written by Dick Holler. Dion's recording of the song, number 28 for the year, gave the Bronx singer his first year-end hit since 1963.

The A&M label had its first year-end top 10 single with a vocal recording by one of the label's founders. "This Guy's In Love With You" was written by Burt Bacharach and Hal David and was one of 50 songs submitted to Herb Alpert for use on a CBS-TV special. Alpert sang the song to his (first) wife, Sharon, on the beach at Malibu. When CBS received thousands of calls from viewers asking where they could buy the song, A&M released it as a single the following day. Ranked number eight for the year, the song beats A&M's previous best, "You Were On My Mind" by the We Five, the number 18 song of 1965.

John Fred and His Playboy Band were ranked number nine for the year with a song inspired in part by an album released the year before, *Sgt. Pepper's Lonely Hearts Club Band*. When John Fred Gourrier first played that LP, he thought the Beatles were singing about "Lucy in disguise with diamonds." After seeing hundreds of girls wearing sunglasses on the beach in Florida, he came up with lyrics for a song called "Beverly In Disguise (With Glasses)." With writing partner Andrew Bernard, John Fred received another dose of inspiration from a TV commercial for Playtex living bras and finally came up with "Judy In Disguise (With Glasses)."

The original source of John Fred's inspiration, the Beatles, had the number one song of 1968 with "Hey Jude." It was the first time in the rock era that any artist had the number one single of the year for a second time ("I Want To Hold Your Hand" was the top-ranked single of 1964). "Hey Jude" was the first single released on the Beatles' new Apple label.

Apple was also represented on the year-end chart with "Those Were The Days" by Mary Hopkin, a music and drama student from Pontardawe, Wales, and with the Beatles' "Revolution."

Gary Puckett & the Union Gap, a group that formed in San Diego, California, had a sensational year in 1968, placing their first four singles on the year-end chart. Their debut release, "Woman, Woman" ranked number four for the year. The follow-up, "Young Girl," was number 15. "Lady Willpower" was number 43 and "Over You" was number 59. Their only other year-end chart single was "This Girl Is A Woman Now," the number 93 song of 1969.

1 AQUARIUS/LET THE SUNSHINE IN
5th Dimension *Soul City*

2 SUGAR, SUGAR
The Archies *Calendar*

3 HONKY TONK WOMEN
The Rolling Stones *London*

4 COME TOGETHER/SOMETHING
The Beatles *Apple*

5 EVERYDAY PEOPLE
Sly & the Family Stone *Epic*

6 CRIMSON AND CLOVER
Tommy James & the Shondells *Roulette*

7 I CAN'T GET NEXT TO YOU
The Temptations *Gordy*

8 GET BACK
The Beatles w/Billy Preston *Apple*

9 SOMEDAY WE'LL BE TOGETHER
Diana Ross & the Supremes *Motown*

10 DIZZY
Tommy Roe *ABC*

11 NA NA HEY HEY KISS HIM GOODBYE
Steam *Fontana*

12 LEAVING ON A JET PLANE
Peter, Paul and Mary *Warner Bros*

13 IN THE YEAR 2525 (EXORDIUM & TERMINUS)
Zager and Evans *RCA*

14 WEDDING BELL BLUES
5th Dimension *Soul City*

15 LOVE THEME FROM "ROMEO AND JULIET"
Henry Mancini *RCA*

16 HAIR
The Cowsills *MGM*

17 WICHITA LINEMAN
Glen Campbell *Capitol*

18 SWEET CAROLINE (GOOD TIMES NEVER SEEMED SO GOOD)
Neil Diamond *Uni*

19 SUSPICIOUS MINDS
Elvis Presley *RCA*

20 CRYSTAL BLUE PERSUSASION
Tommy James & the Shondells *Roulette*

21 BUILD ME UP BUTTERCUP
The Foundations *Uni*

22 IT'S YOUR THING
Isley Brothers *T-Neck*

23 PROUD MARY
Creedence Clearwater Revival *Fantasy*

24 ONE
Three Dog Night *Dunhill*

25 DOWN ON THE CORNER/FORTUNATE SON
Creedence Clearwater Revival *Fantasy*

26 TAKE A LETTER MARIA
R.B. Greaves *Atco*

27 HOT FUN IN THE SUMMERTIME
Sly & the Family Stone *Epic*

28 GET TOGETHER
The Youngbloods *RCA*

29 TOO BUSY THINKING ABOUT MY BABY
Marvin Gaye *Tamla*

30 I'LL NEVER FALL IN LOVE AGAIN
Tom Jones *Parrot*

The Rolling Stones

1969 was the year half a million people attended a three-day festival at Woodstock; Jim Morrison was arrested for indecent exposure at a concert in Miami; and Paul McCartney and John Lennon marched to the altar with Linda Eastman and Yoko Ono—respectively.

One of the bands appearing at Woodstock was Creedence Clearwater Revival. John Fogerty, Stu Cook and Doug Clifford had first played together as the Blue Velvets, a trio formed at El Cerrito Junior High in Northern California in 1959. John's brother Tom later joined the group. Their first recording deal was with the San Francisco Orchestra label in 1961. They were signed to Fantasy Records as the Golliwogs, and a cover version of Van Morrison's "Brown Eyed Girl" sold modestly.

In December, 1967, the group became Creedence Clearwater Revival. They had the number 95 song of 1968 with their first chart single, "Suzie Q. (Part One)." They fared a little better in 1969—placing four hits on the year-end chart. "Proud Mary" ranked highest at number 23, followed by "Down On The Corner"/ "Fortunate Son" (number 25), "Green River" (number 35) and "Bad Moon Rising" (number 36). "Proud Mary," "Bad Moon Rising" and "Green River" had all peaked at number two on the Hot 100 and "Down On The Corner" peaked at number three. That was as close as they ever came to having a number one single.

The Beatles and the Rolling Stones both had songs in the top 10; it was the first time since 1965 that they both registered in the year-end top 10. Both groups were bested by a band that didn't even exist. The Archies, featuring lead vocals by Ron Dante, had the number two song of the year with "Sugar, Sugar." The "Archie" comic strip had been created in 1942 by John L. Goldwater, and in 1968 Filmation Studios produced a Saturday morning cartoon show based on the strip. Don Kirshner, hired to supervise the music for the series, asked Jeff Barry to write and produce records for the "Archies." Dante, who had been the lead voice of the Laundromats in 1964 for their parody of the Shangri-Las' "Leader Of The Pack" called "Leader Of The Laundromat," multi-tracked his voice and was joined by singer Toni Wine. While "Sugar, Sugar" was in the top five, Dante had another top five single with "Tracy" by the Cuff Links, the number 83 song of the year.

The number one single of 1969 was a medley of two songs from the Broadway production of *Hair*. The 5th Dimension discovered the song while appearing at the Americana Hotel in New York City. Billy Davis, Jr. went shopping one afternoon and inadvertently left his wallet in a cab. The next passenger, one of the producers of *Hair*, found it and called him to return it. Billy was grateful and invited him to see their show at the Americana. In return, the producer invited the group to see *Hair*. They were all so taken with Ronnie Dyson's performance of the opening number, "Aquarius," that they wanted to record it. Producer Bones Howe felt it was only half a song and needed something more. When he saw *Hair* in New York he loved the show's finale, "The Flesh Failures (Let The Sunshine In)." Howe suggested they take the opening and closing numbers and "put them together like two trains."

"Aquarius/Let The Sunshine In" was the second song originally written for the stage to be the number one song of the year. The first was Bobby Darin's 1959 recording of "Mack The Knife" from *The Threepenny Opera*. Three other songs from *Hair* were also listed in the year-end top 100. Three Dog Night had the number 37 song of the year with "Easy To Be Hard," Oliver was number 39 with "Good Morning Starshine" and the Cowsills were number 16 with the title song, "Hair." Bill Cowsill, oldest brother of the Rhode Island family, says it was pure serendipity that the group recorded "Hair." They were signed as guest stars for a Carl Reiner television special. "Carl had this bent idea that it would be really cool to take the squeaky clean Cowsills with no make-up, let the zits show, chains, leather, hair and do the title track from the Broadway play," Bill explains. The four brothers went to a studio in Hollywood to record a track they would lip-synch to in the show. "Then we listened (to it). I looked at Bob—Bob looked at me— two thumbs up!" The Cowsills went to MGM and said they wanted to release "Hair" as a single. "They said, 'You're out of your mind, we're not releasing that! You'll blow your image!'" Bill recalls. While on tour in the Midwest, the Cowsills' father, Bud, convinced an MGM promo rep to take an acetate of the song to radio station WLS in Chicago. The program director agreed to play the song if he couldn't guess who was singing. He lost and the song was added to the playlist, and MGM was forced to release the single.

Psychedelic soul made its mark on the top 100 songs of the year thanks to Sly & the Family Stone. Former San Francisco DJ Sylvester Stewart had the number 58 song of 1968 with "Dance To The Music." In 1969 he had his highest year-end ranking by placing "Everyday People" at number five.

Another facet of psychedelia was "Crimson And Clover," according to Tommy James, who wrote and produced the song that placed number six for the year. " 'Crimson' and 'clover' were two of my favorite words that I put together," James explains. "We had the title before we wrote the song." Tommy and the Shondells placed two songs in the top 20 of 1969, the first time they had made the year-end top 20. "Crystal Blue Persuasion" ranked number 20 for 1969, a song that Tommy says is his favorite. "The title came right out of the Bible. 'Crystal Blue' meant truth. I said, 'What a title, I only wish it meant something.' "

The Temptations had their best-ever year-end ranking with "I Can't Get Next To You" at number seven. That beat their previous high, when they placed number 10 for 1965 with "My Girl." Inspired by Sly & the Family Stone, the Temptations turned to psychedelic soul under the aegis of producer Norman Whitfield. Their first effort in that field, "Cloud Nine," was the number 62 song of 1969. The follow-up, "Run Away Child, Running Wild" was two notches higher at number 60.

Diana Ross released her final single as lead singer of the Supremes in 1969. "Someday We'll Be Together" was their 12th number one hit, and the first of their chart-topping singles to be a remake of an older song. The original version by songwriters Jackie Beavers and Johnny Bristol had been written and recorded in 1960. Ranked number nine for 1969, the Supremes' version was their fifth year-end top 10 single.

Tommy Roe's first number one single, "Sheila," was the number 24 song of 1962, and in 1963 he placed number 29 for the year with "Everybody." He surpassed his previous record with "Dizzy," the number 10 song of 1969.

Elvis Presley returned to the top 20 portion of the year-end chart for the first time since 1962, when he was number 10 with "Return To Sender." His career revitalized by an NBC-TV special in 1968, he scored his 17th and final number one single with "Suspicious Minds," the number 19 song of 1969. His fellow Sun recording artist, Johnny Cash, had his first year-end placing since "Guess Things Happen That Way" in 1958. "A Boy Named Sue" was the number 33 song of 1969.

Peter, Paul and Mary's "Leaving On A Jet Plane," number 12 for the year, marked their first appearance on a year-end chart since their two Bob Dylan hits in 1963. Ray Stevens' "Gitarzan," number 77, was his first year-end hit since "Ahab The Arab" in 1962.

1 **RAINDROPS KEEP FALLIN' ON MY HEAD**
B.J. Thomas *Scepter*

2 **I'LL BE THERE**
The Jackson Five *Motown*

3 **I THINK I LOVE YOU**
The Partridge Family *Bell*

4 **BRIDGE OVER TROUBLED WATER**
Simon and Garfunkel *Columbia*

5 **(THEY LONG TO BE) CLOSE TO YOU**
Carpenters *A&M*

6 **MY SWEET LORD/ISN'T IT A PITY**
George Harrison *Apple*

7 **WAR**
Edwin Starr *Gordy*

8 **AMERICAN WOMAN/NO SUGAR TONIGHT**
Guess Who *RCA*

9 **LET IT BE**
The Beatles *Apple*

10 **I WANT YOU BACK**
The Jackson Five *Motown*

11 **THE TEARS OF A CLOWN**
Smokey Robinson & the Miracles *Tamla*

12 **WE'VE ONLY JUST BEGUN**
Carpenters *A&M*

13 **ONE LESS BELL TO ANSWER**
5th Dimension *Bell*

14 **AIN'T NO MOUNTAIN HIGH ENOUGH**
Diana Ross *Motown*

15 **ABC**
The Jackson Five *Motown*

16 **MAMA TOLD ME (NOT TO COME)**
Three Dog Night *Dunhill*

17 **BAND OF GOLD**
Freda Payne *Invictus*

18 **MAKE IT WITH YOU**
Bread *Elektra*

19 **SPIRIT IN THE SKY**
Norman Greenbaum *Warner Bros*

20 **BALL OF CONFUSION (THAT'S WHAT THE WORLD IS TODAY)**
The Temptations *Gordy*

21 **EVERYTHING IS BEAUTIFUL**
Ray Stevens *Barnaby*

22 **VENUS**
Shocking Blue *Colossus*

23 **GET READY**
Rare Earth *Rare Earth*

24 **CRACKLIN' ROSIE**
Neil Diamond *Uni*

25 **THANK YOU (FALETTINME BE MICE ELF AGIN)/EVERYBODY IS A STAR**
Sly & the Family Stone *Epic*

26 **FIRE AND RAIN**
James Taylor *Warner Bros*

27 **CANDIDA**
Dawn *Bell*

28 **WHOLE LOTTA LOVE**
Led Zeppelin *Atlantic*

29 **ALL RIGHT NOW**
Free *A&M*

30 **LOVE ON A TWO-WAY STREET**
The Moments *Stang*

The Carpenters

1970 was the year the Beatles movie *Let It Be* premiered; Janis Joplin overdosed in Hollywood; and four students were killed at Kent State University, inspiring Neil Young to write "Ohio."

The Beatles had their final year-end top 10 entry as a group. The single of "Let It Be" ranked number nine for the year. The follow-up, "The Long And Winding Road," was number 45. For the first time, solo recordings by the Beatles were listed on the year-end chart. George Harrison's two-sided hit "My Sweet Lord" and "Isn't It A Pity" bested "Let It Be" by coming in at number six for the year. John Lennon was listed at number 37 with the Phil Spector produced "Instant Karma (We All Shine On)." Another Apple signing, Badfinger, had two songs on the year-end chart, including the Paul McCartney composition "Come And Get It" at number 68.

The Motown family of labels had its best year-end showing of the rock era, with 16 titles listed on the top 100 songs of the year. Leading the pack was "I'll Be There," the most successful Jackson Five chart single of all time. It ranked number two for the year and was joined in the top 10 by the group's first Motown single, "I Want You Back." That song was originally written as "I Wanna Be Free" and was intended for Gladys Knight & the Pips, then for Diana

Ross. Berry Gordy suggested a rewrite that resulted in "I Want You Back" and gave it to the newly-signed quintet from Gary, Indiana. The Jackson brothers were also represented on the top songs of 1970 with "ABC" (number 15) and "The Love You Save" (number 32).

Another Motown artist in the year-end top 10 was Edwin Starr, with a reworking of "War," a song originally recorded by the Temptations. The label received a flurry of requests to release the Temptations' track as a single, but plans were underway to release "Ball Of Confusion (That's What The World Is Today)," which became the number 20 single of the year. Producer Norman Whitfield asked Starr if he'd like to record the song; having been out of the studio for six months he was happy to end his hiatus by recording "War."

Smokey Robinson & the Miracles had their biggest chart hit to date with a song from their 1967 album *Make It Happen*. When the British arm of Motown issued "The Tears Of A Clown" as a follow-up to a re-release of "The Tracks Of My Tears," it went to number one in the U.K. A month later, Motown had scheduled a new Miracles single for the States when Gordy suggested an American release of "The Tears Of A Clown." It was number one for two weeks and was number 11 for the year.

In 1970, Motown split its most successful act of the '60s in two. After a final performance at the Frontier Hotel in Las Vegas on January 14, 1970, Diana Ross stepped out of the Supremes for a solo career. Her place was taken by Jean Terrell. Diana went into the recording studio with producer Bones Howe and recorded tracks like "Stoney End" (later recorded by Barbra Streisand) and "Love's Lines, Angles and Rhymes" (later recorded by the 5th Dimension), but that material was shelved and she was placed under the supervision of Nickolas Ashford and Valerie Simpson. A remake of their song "Ain't No Mountain High Enough" gave Diana her first solo number one hit and the number 14 song of 1970. Jean Terrell, Mary Wilson and Cindy Birdsong made their first public appearance together on "The Ed Sullivan Show" as Jean introduced the first Supremes' single without Diana Ross, "Up The Ladder To The Roof." It became the number 78 song of 1970. Their third single, "Stoned Love," ranked number 35 for the year.

Other Motown artists included in the top 100 songs of 1970 were Rare Earth with "Get Ready" at number 23 and "(I Know) I'm Losing You" at number 94, R. Dean Taylor with "Indiana Wants Me" at number 34 and the Four Tops with "Still Water (Love)" at number 86.

The top 10 of the year included two songs written by Burt Bacharach and Hal David. They had the number one single of the year, "Raindrops Keep Fallin' On My Head" from the film *Butch Cassidy and the Sundance Kid*. It was only the second time during the rock era that a song from a movie was the number one hit of the year (the first was "To Sir With Love" in 1967). It was the first time that the top single of the year was also an Oscar winner. Ray

Stevens, who turned down the chance to record "Raindrops" after Bacharach screened the film for him, was ranked number 21 for the year with "Everything Is Beautiful."

The other Bacharach song in the top 10 was "(They Long To Be) Close To You" by the Carpenters. Burt had heard the duo's first single, a remake of the Beatles' "Ticket To Ride," on the radio and liked what he heard. When he found out the Carpenters were signed to A&M like he was, he asked Richard and Karen to open for him at a charity benefit for the Reiss-Davis Clinic at the Century Plaza Hotel in Los Angeles. When Burt asked Richard to arrange a medley of Bacharach songs, Richard searched for some of the composer's more obscure songs. Alpert suggested a song that had already been recorded by Dionne Warwick and Richard Chamberlain. The song didn't fit into the medley, but Richard couldn't get the tune out of his head and decided to record it.

Bacharach and David were also represented in the year-end chart with "One Less Bell To Answer" by the 5th Dimension. After recording for Johnny Rivers' Soul City label, the 5th Dimension wanted to sign with a new company. David Geffen, then an agent with CMA, let Larry Uttal at Bell Records know that the group was available. "We bought them from Johnny Rivers and we paid a big advance," Uttal recalls. "Bones Howe produced . . . the first album. The group wanted a record called 'The Declaration Of Independence' out. It was a real stiff. They had another one they wanted to come out, 'Puppet Man,' and that was a stiff and they were very adamant about it. Bones was siding with the group. There was a song on the album that I felt . . . was going to be a hit record, and that was 'One Less Bell To Answer.' The group didn't want it out, Bones didn't want it out, so we cut about 20 to 30 dubs, gave them out to the radio stations in the New Orleans area, the stations played the record and within a couple of days they got top 10 requests. So we put the record out. It was against the wishes of the group but we felt it was a hit record."

Uttal had an even bigger hit in 1970 with "I Think I Love You" by the Partridge Family. It was the number three song of the year, and marked the fourth time in a five year period that a television series-based group had a top 10 hit of the year (the Monkees in 1966 and 1967, the Archies in 1969). Uttal had sold Bell Records to Columbia Pictures, whose Screen Gems TV unit produced "The Partridge Family." "David Cassidy could really sing," Uttal notes. "So we could maintain legitimacy, we put the Partridge Family in the background. David sang up front and did a terrific job."

Simon and Garfunkel had their first year-end top 10 hit in 1970 with "Bridge Over Troubled Water," their third number one song. "The Sounds Of Silence" was the number 25 song of 1966 and "Mrs. Robinson" was number 11 for 1968. "Bridge" had been written in the same house in Los Angeles where George Harrison had written "Blue Jay Way." The instrumental track was recorded in Los Angeles and Paul and Art laid down the vocal tracks in New York.

THE TOP 100 SONGS OF
1971

1 **MAGGIE MAY/REASON TO BELIEVE**
Rod Stewart *Mercury*

2 **IT'S TOO LATE/I FEEL THE EARTH MOVE**
Carole King *Ode*

3 **JOY TO THE WORLD**
Three Dog Night *Dunhill*

4 **KNOCK THREE TIMES**
Dawn *Bell*

5 **HOW CAN YOU MEND A BROKEN HEART**
Bee Gees *Atco*

6 **BRAND NEW KEY**
Melanie *Neighborhood*

7 **GO AWAY LITTLE GIRL**
Donny Osmond *MGM*

8 **FAMILY AFFAIR**
Sly & the Family Stone *Epic*

9 **INDIAN RESERVATION (THE LAMENT OF THE CHEROKEE RESERVATION INDIAN)**
The Raiders *Columbia*

10 **JUST MY IMAGINATION (RUNNING AWAY WITH ME)**
The Temptations *Gordy*

11 **GYPSYS, TRAMPS & THIEVES**
Cher *Kapp*

12 **ONE BAD APPLE**
The Osmonds *MGM*

13 **ME AND BOBBY MCGEE**
Janis Joplin *Columbia*

14 **TAKE ME HOME, COUNTRY ROADS**
John Denver *RCA*

15 **YOU'VE GOT A FRIEND**
James Taylor *Warner Bros*

16 **TREAT HER LIKE A LADY**
Cornelius Brothers & Sister Rose *UA*

17 **THEME FROM "SHAFT"**
Issac Hayes *Enterprise*

18 **UNCLE ALBERT-ADMIRAL HALSEY**
Paul and Linda McCartney *Apple*

19 **GROOVE ME**
King Floyd *Chimneyville*

20 **MR. BIG STUFF**
Jean Knight *Stax*

21 **SUPERSTAR**
Carpenters *A&M*

22 **WHAT'S GOING ON**
Marvin Gaye *Tamla*

23 **SHE'S A LADY**
Tom Jones *Parrot*

24 **HAVE YOU SEEN HER**
The Chi-Lites *Brunswick*

25 **THE NIGHT THEY DROVE OLD DIXIE DOWN**
Joan Baez *Vanguard*

26 **WANT ADS**
The Honey Cone *Hot Wax*

27 **AIN'T NO SUNSHINE**
Bill Withers *Sussex*

28 **SMILING FACES SOMETIMES**
The Undisputed Truth *Gordy*

29 **ROSE GARDEN**
Lynn Anderson *Columbia*

30 **BROWN SUGAR**
The Rolling Stones *Rolling Stones*

Three Dog Night

1971 was the year the Rolling Stones launched their own record label; Jim Morrison died in Paris; and Andrew Lloyd Webber and Tim Rice were represented on Broadway with *Jesus Christ, Superstar.*

The Osmond family made a strong showing on the year-end chart, with four titles. That was one better than their friendly rivals, the Jackson family. The highest-rated Osmond single was Donny's "Go Away Little Girl," a remake of the Steve Lawrence hit originally recorded by Bobby Vee. It ranked number seven. It was one of four Carole King songs in the top 20. The Osmonds' "One Bad Apple," recorded at Rick Hall's Fame studios in Muscle Shoals, Alabama, was number 12 for the year. The Osmonds also scored with "Yo-Yo" (number 35) and Donny was number 41 with a remake of a Roy Orbison tune, "Sweet And Innocent."

As for the Jacksons, their highest-ranked single at year-end was the first solo single from Michael, "Got To Be There" (number 31). The Jackson Five was just one notch lower at number 32 with "Never Can Say Goodbye." "Mama's Pearl" was number 69 for the year.

Carole King and James Taylor's appearances on the chart heralded the beginning of the singer/songwriter era, a time of more personal and introspective music. King, who made her debut on the Hot 100 in 1962 with "It Might As Well Rain Until September," had her first year-end chart single in 1971 with a two-sided hit. "It's Too Late" and "I Feel The Earth Move" ranked number two for the year. Both tracks were lifted from her record-breaking *Tapestry* album. Another song on that LP, "You've Got A Friend," was covered and released as a single by Carole's friend, James Taylor. His version was the number 15 hit of the year.

Aside from Carole, the only other female lead vocalist in the top 10 was Melanie, number six for the year with "Brand New Key." Her previous hit, "Lay Down (Candles In The Rain)," recorded with the Edwin Hawkins Singers on the Buddah label, was the number 43 song of 1970. Melanie left Buddah and formed her own record label with husband/producer Peter Schekeryk. Her first release on Neighborhood was "Brand New Key," a song written in 15 minutes.

The number one song of the year was also a two-sided hit, "Maggie May" and "Reason To Believe" by Rod Stewart. It is the only time in the rock era that the top two singles of the year were double-sided hits. Stewart was only the fourth U.K. artist to top a year-end chart, after the Beatles, the Rolling Stones and Lulu. Rod would be the only British artist to have a number one song of the year in the '70s. "Maggie May" almost wasn't included on the *Every Picture Tells a Story* album. It wasn't intended to be the single—the remake of Tim Hardin's "Reason To Believe" was the original "A" side until DJs flipped it in favor of "Maggie May."

The number three song of the year had been written by Hoyt Axton for a children's animated television special, "The Happy Song." When the show wasn't produced, Axton tried to place the songs from the show with different artists. He had toured as an opening act for Three Dog Night, and dropped by the studio where they were recording one day to play "Joy To The World" for them. Cory Wells didn't think it would be a hit, but the rest of the band disagreed and voted to record it. Hoyt was disappointed with their version and was convinced it wouldn't sell. It was number one for six weeks and became the biggest hit of Three Dog Night's career as well as the most successful chart single on the Dunhill label.

Although he had recorded as early as 1961, Tony Orlando hadn't registered on the year-end chart until 1970, when "Candida" by Dawn was the number 27 song of the year. Orlando's name wasn't listed in the credits because he wanted to keep his day job at April-Blackwood Music. But after "Knock Three Times" was a hit (and the number four record of 1971), Orlando quit the music publisher and started a new career with Telma Hopkins and Joyce Vincent Wilson in Dawn.

The Bee Gees first made the Hot 100 in 1967. In 1970, they were number 36 for the year with "I've Gotta Get A Message To You." They made the year-end top 10 for the first time in 1971 with "How Can You Mend A Broken Heart" at number five. Barry and Robin Gibb had written the song for Andy Williams, but when he passed on it they decided to record it themselves.

Another group making the year-end top 10 for the first time was the Raiders. Billed as Paul Revere & the Raiders, they placed three songs in the top 100 of 1966: "Kicks" (number 26), "Just Like Me" (number 57) and "Hungry" (number 91). The following year they had "Good Thing" at number 45. They set a new high mark for themselves in 1971 with "Indian Reservation (The Lament Of The Cherokee Reservation Indian)." The song had been written and recorded in 1963 by Durham, North Carolina native John D. Loudermilk, whose pop hits included "Sittin' In The Balcony" by Eddie Cochran, "A Rose And A Baby Ruth" and "Abilene" by George Hamilton IV, "Norman" and "James, Hold The Ladder Steady" by Sue Thompson and "Tobacco Road" by the Nashville Teens. Loudermilk's version of "Indian Reservation" didn't make the chart—his biggest hit on his own was "The Language Of Love." In 1968, British singer Don Fardon, lead vocalist for the Sorrows, released a version of "Indian Reservation" in the U.K. It peaked at number three and was released in America, hitting number 20 on the Hot 100. Jack Gold at Columbia Records suggested to Mark Lindsay that Paul Revere & the Raiders cover the song. It became the Raiders' biggest hit as well as Columbia's best-selling single in history, to that date.

The highest-ranked Motown single of 1971 was "Just My Imagination (Running Away With Me)" by the Temptations, at number 10. It followed a series of socially relevant songs like "Cloud Nine," "Run Away Child, Running Wild" and "Don't Let The Joneses Get You Down" written for the group by Norman Whitfield and Barrett Strong. After missing the top 30 with "*Ungena Za Ulimwengu* (Unite The World)," Whitfield and Strong returned to the Tempts' earlier sound. "We needed to do something a little different," Barrett recalls. "We had thought of 'Just My Imagination' a year or two before we recorded it, but the timing wasn't right. Norman asked me, 'What was that song we were messing around with a year ago?' I played it on the piano and he said, 'Meet me in the studio because I'm gonna record it today.'" Eddie Kendricks, who sang lead on the Temptations' first hit, "The Way You Do The Things You Do," performed lead vocals on "Just My Imagination."

Motown didn't turn completely away from "socially relevant" songs. Marvin Gaye had the most critically acclaimed album of his career in 1971, *What's Going On*. The title track was the number 22 song of the year and the follow-up, "Mercy Mercy Me (The Ecology)" was number 67.

The second posthumous number one single of the rock era was "Me And Bobby McGee" by Janis Joplin, the number 13 song of 1971. The song first appeared in *Billboard* in 1969 when Roger Miller's version of the Kris Kristofferson tune peaked at number 12 on the country singles chart.

Cher equaled the mark set with husband Sonny in 1965 when "I Got You Babe" was the number 11 song of the year. In 1971, her number one hit "Gypsys, Tramps & Thieves" placed number 11.

1 AMERICAN PIE
Don McLean *UA*

2 THE FIRST TIME EVER I SAW YOUR FACE
Roberta Flack *Atlantic*

3 ALONE AGAIN (NATURALLY)
Gilbert O'Sullivan *MAM*

4 WITHOUT YOU
Nilsson *RCA*

5 I GOTCHA
Joe Tex *Dial*

6 LET'S STAY TOGETHER
Al Green *Hi*

7 THE CANDY MAN
Sammy Davis, Jr. *MGM*

8 I CAN SEE CLEARLY NOW
Johnny Nash *Epic*

9 A HORSE WITH NO NAME
America *Warner Bros*

10 ME AND MRS. JONES
Billy Paul *PIR*

11 BRANDY (YOU'RE A FINE GIRL)
Looking Glass *Epic*

12 BABY DON'T GET HOOKED ON ME
Mac Davis *Columbia*

13 LEAN ON ME
Bill Withers *Sussex*

14 NIGHTS IN WHITE SATIN
The Moody Blues *Deram*

15 I AM WOMAN
Helen Reddy *Capitol*

16 I'LL TAKE YOU THERE
The Staple Singers *Stax*

17 CLAIR
Gilbert O'Sullivan *MAM*

18 HEART OF GOLD
Neil Young *Reprise*

19 OH GIRL
The Chi-Lites *Brunswick*

20 SCORPIO
Dennis Coffey & the Detroit Guitar Band *Sussex*

21 BETCHA BY GOLLY WOW
The Stylistics *Avco*

22 (IF LOVING YOU IS WRONG) I DON'T WANT TO BE RIGHT
Luther Ingram *KoKo*

23 THE LION SLEEPS TONIGHT
Robert John *Atlantic*

24 TOO LATE TO TURN BACK NOW
Cornelius Brothers & Sister Rose *UA*

25 DADDY DON'T YOU WALK SO FAST
Wayne Newton *Chelsea*

26 SONG SUNG BLUE
Neil Diamond *Uni*

27 YOU ARE EVERYTHING
The Stylistics *Avco*

28 MY DING-A-LING
Chuck Berry *Chess*

29 LONG COOL WOMAN (IN A BLACK DRESS)
The Hollies *Epic*

30 BURNING LOVE
Elvis Presley *RCA*

The Staple Singers

1972 was the year John Lennon asked for American citizenship to avoid deportation; Diana Ross was nominated for an Oscar for portraying Billie Holiday in *Lady Sings the Blues;* and *Hair* closed on Broadway after 1,729 performances.

Elvis Presley made his first appearance in the top 30 portion of the year-end chart since 1969, when "Suspicious Minds" was number 19. "Burning Love," the number 30 song of 1972, marked Elvis' final appearance on a *Billboard* year-end singles chart.

Rick Nelson returned to the top 100 songs of the year after a long absence. He had last appeared in 1964 when "For You" was the number 75 song of the year. He had the number 37 song of 1972, "Garden Party," said to have been inspired by a Richard Nader Rock 'n' Roll Revival concert at Madison Square Garden where fans booed him for performing his contemporary material instead of his older songs. "I hate to ruin a legend," guitarist Allen Kemp told Todd Everett, "but after we left the stage, thinking that we had been booed for Dylan songs and long hair, we found out that some guys in the audience had gotten drunk and started a fight, and that the audience was booing them."

Returning after an even longer absence was Chuck Berry, who had the highest-ranking year-end song of his career with "My Ding-A-Ling," a rude novelty hit recorded live at the 1972 Arts Festival in Lanchester, England. It was the number 28 song of the year. Berry had two hits on the year-end chart for 1957 ("School Day" at number 45 and "Rock & Roll Music" at number 69) and two hits on the year-end chart for 1958 ("Johnny B. Goode" at number 60 and "Sweet Little Sixteen" at number 62).

For the first time since 1962, there were no Motown singles in the top 10 songs of the year. The highest-ranked Motown single of 1972 was the title song from the motion picture *Ben* by Michael Jackson at number 34. There were only three Motown singles included in the top 100 (the others: "Papa Was A Rollin' Stone" by the Temptations at number 35 and "Rockin' Robin," also by Michael, at number 40). That is the lowest total of Motown singles on a year-end chart since the pre-Supremes days of 1962.

The number one single of the year was a debut song, the first time an artist's initial chart single was the top record of the year since the Beatles' "I Want To Hold Your Hand" in 1964. Don McLean's "American Pie" was the first new number one song of 1972, in January. Although the eight minute and 36-second track was divided into two parts for release as a single, most radio stations played the song in its entirety. McLean was shocked to have a hit record—he was certain "American Pie" was too long to be played on the radio. But his time trip through rock and roll history was too compelling for music directors to ignore.

The number two single of 1972 had first appeared on an album released in 1969. Roberta Flack's *First Take* debut LP for Atlantic included a version of Ewan MacColl's "The First Time Ever I Saw Your Face." The song, written by MacColl for his wife Peggy (sister of Pete Seeger), was performed by Flack on a regular basis when she played piano and sang at a Washington, D.C. restaurant. When Clint Eastwood filmed *Play Misty for Me*, about a disc jockey stalked by a fatally attracted fan, he needed a romantic piece of music to underscore a scene with Donna Mills. He remembered "The First Time Ever I Saw Your Face" and asked Flack for permission to include her song in the movie. The demand for the song to be released as a single was so great that Atlantic edited it down for radio play and issued it. It spent six weeks at number one.

Another single that spent six weeks at number one was "Alone Again (Naturally)" by Gilbert O'Sullivan. The singer, born in Waterford, Ireland, as Raymond Edward O'Sullivan, was given his stage name by manager Gordon Mills, the same man who transformed Tommy Scott into Tom Jones and Arnold George Dorsey into Engelbert Humperdinck. The song sounded autobiographical, but even though O'Sullivan wrote it, he denied that it had anything to do with his own life.

The number four song of the year was "Without You," Nilsson's second appearance on a year-end chart following "Everybody's Talkin'," the number 84 song of 1969. He first heard the song while inebriated, and after sobering up tried to find the song on one of his Beatles' albums. The search proved fruitless until he realized it was another group on Apple Records—Badfinger. Nilsson took the song to producer Richard Perry and said it should be a number one hit. Perry helped make it so.

Joe Tex, who took his name from his home state of Texas, first appeared on a *Billboard* year-end chart in 1965 with "Hold What You've Got," ranked at number 86. In 1967, the former minister was number 71 for the year with "Skinny Legs And All." He had the biggest hit of his career in 1972 with "I Gotcha," the number five song of the year. Another minister, Al Green, had his most successful single of all time with "Let's Stay Together," the number six song of 1972.

Sammy Davis, Jr.'s two previous appearances on a year-end singles chart were both songs that had originated in Broadway shows. "What Kind Of Fool Am I," the number 92 song of 1962, was from *Stop the World—I Want to Get Off*. "I've Gotta Be Me," the number 85 song of 1969, was from *Golden Rainbow*. Davis had the biggest single of his career when he recorded a song from a movie, "The Candy Man," first heard in *Willie Wonka and the Chocolate Factory*. Mike Curb, head of MGM Records, released a version of the song by his own group, the Mike Curb Congregation. When it wasn't a hit, he convinced Davis to overdub his voice, and the recycled track went to number one on the Hot 100.

Like Joe Tex, Johnny Nash was also born in Texas. He competed in a local talent show that offered a chance to perform at the Apollo Theater in Harlem, but lost out to Tex. In 1972, he shared a spot in the top 10 songs of the year with Tex. "I Can See Clearly Now" was written and produced by Nash and recorded in Jamaica. Nash had first travelled there in 1957 while filming a part in the Burt Lancaster movie *Take a Giant Step*. Nash returned to Kingston in 1968 to record "Hold Me Tight," the number 54 song of that year. After a couple of top 10 singles in the U.K., Nash moved to London and signed with CBS Records, and hired a relatively unknown reggae singer named Bob Marley to write for him. Marley wrote "Stir It Up" and "Guava Jelly" for Nash.

America, a trio of Americans who met in London while attending a school for children of military families, had the number nine song of 1972. Gerry Beckley, Dewey Bunnell and Dan Peek played as an opening act for well-known groups like Pink Floyd and were well known in London before they signed with the British office of Warner Brothers Records. "A Horse With No Name" was written by Dewey, inspired by his feelings of homesickness for the desert countryside he remembered when he lived at Vandenberg, an Air Force base near San Luis Obispo, California.

Billy Paul had recorded for Kenny Gamble and Leon Huff's two previous labels, Gamble and Neptune, before signing with their new label, Philadelphia International Records. He gave that label its first number one single with "Me And Mrs. Jones," the number 10 song of 1972. The PIR label had two other songs included in the top 100 of 1972: "Back Stabbers" by the O'Jays was number 54 and "If You Don't Know Me By Now" by Harold Melvin & the Blue Notes was number 59.

1 TIE A YELLOW RIBBON ROUND THE OLE OAK TREE
Dawn *Bell*

2 LET'S GET IT ON
Marvin Gaye *Tamla*

3 KEEP ON TRUCKIN' (PART 1)
Eddie Kendricks *Tamla*

4 CROCODILE ROCK
Elton John *MCA*

5 THE MOST BEAUTIFUL GIRL
Charlie Rich *Epic*

6 YOU'RE SO VAIN
Carly Simon *Elektra*

7 TOUCH ME IN THE MORNING
Diana Ross *Motown*

8 KILLING ME SOFTLY WITH HIS SONG
Roberta Flack *Atlantic*

9 MIDNIGHT TRAIN TO GEORGIA
Gladys Knight & the Pips *Buddah*

10 BAD, BAD LEROY BROWN
Jim Croce *ABC*

11 TOP OF THE WORLD
Carpenters *A&M*

12 THE NIGHT THE LIGHTS WENT OUT IN GEORGIA
Vicki Lawrence *Bell*

13 MY LOVE
Paul McCartney & Wings *Apple*

14 BROTHER LOUIE
Stories *Kama Sutra*

15 WILL IT GO ROUND IN CIRCLES
Billy Preston *A&M*

16 HALF-BREED
Cher *Kapp*

17 FRANKENSTEIN
Edgar Winter Group *Epic*

18 TIME IN A BOTTLE
Jim Croce *ABC*

19 LOVES ME LIKE A ROCK
Paul Simon *Columbia*

20 PILLOW TALK
Sylvia *Vibration*

21 DELTA DAWN
Helen Reddy *Capitol*

22 ANGIE
The Rolling Stones *Rolling Stones*

23 JUST YOU 'N' ME
Chicago *Columbia*

24 THAT LADY (PART 1)
Isley Brothers *T-Neck*

25 YOU ARE THE SUNSHINE OF MY LIFE
Stevie Wonder *Tamla*

26 DRIFT AWAY
Dobie Gray *Decca*

27 WE'RE AN AMERICAN BAND
Grand Funk *Capitol*

28 SUPERSTITION
Stevie Wonder *Tamla*

29 LOVE TRAIN
The O'Jays *PIR*

30 PLAYGROUND IN MY MIND
Clint Holmes *Epic*

Stevie Wonder

1973 was the year Dr. Hook actually made the cover of *Rolling Stone*; Jim Croce was killed in a plane crash and Bobby Darin died after an operation on his heart; and Elvis and Priscilla Presley were divorced.

Paul McCartney, Ringo Starr and George Harrison were all represented on the year-end chart with number one songs. McCartney ranked number 13 with "My Love" and was also listed at number 43 with a number two song, "Live And Let Die." Ringo was number 39 for the year with "Photograph" and George was number 67 with "Give Me Love (Give Me Peace On Earth)." John Lennon, whose only chart single during 1973 was "Mind Games," was absent from the year-end chart.

Motown rebounded from being shut out of the top 10 the previous year with three titles in the first 10 positions, matching the record set by the label in 1964 and 1970. The Tamla label held down the number two and three slots with "Let's Get It On" by Marvin Gaye and "Keep On Truckin' (Part 1)" by Eddie Kendricks. It is the only year in history when Motown took two of the top three positions. Diana Ross was number seven for the year with "Touch Me In The Morning," her highest solo ranking so far.

Diana was joined in the top 10 by three other female lead vocalists. Carly Simon was the highest-ranked female vocalist of the year with "You're So Vain" at number six. Was it about Warren Beatty or James Taylor or Kris Kristofferson or Carly's backing vocalist on the song, Mick Jagger? She's never said, but she did reveal that when the song was originally written, it was called "Bless You Ben," a name later given to her son. In an interview with her younger brother Peter, she claimed the song wasn't written about a specific individual: "I would say I had about three or four different people in mind when I wrote that song . . . I actually did think specifically about a couple of people when I wrote it, but the examples of what they did was a fantasy trip."

Roberta Flack was back in the year-end top 10 for the second consecutive year. "Killing Me Softly With His Song" was inspired by a performance of the man who had the number one record of 1972. Singer Lori Lieberman saw Don McLean sing at the Troubadour in Los Angeles and went to writers Norman Gimbel and Charles Fox to put her thoughts into a song. Lieberman recorded the 10-minute epic, which was edited for single release. Flack was on a TWA flight from Los Angeles to New York when she plugged in her headphones and turned the pages of the in-flight magazine. She was intrigued with the title "Killing Me Softly With His Song" and made a point to listen for it. "By the time I got to New York I knew I had to do that song and I knew I'd be able to add something to it," Flack said in *High Fidelity*. She spent three months in the studio perfecting it; she was rewarded with a single that spent five weeks at number one.

The other female vocalist in the top 10 was Gladys Knight, who first made the year-end chart in 1961 with the Pips on "Every Beat Of My Heart." In 1967 the group had the number nine song of the year with "I Heard It Through The Grapevine," and in 1973 they equaled that mark with "Midnight Train To Georgia." The song had been originally written as "Midnight Plane To Houston" and recorded by its composer, Jim Weatherly. When Cissy Houston recorded it in Atlanta, Weatherly was asked if he minded the song being changed to "Midnight Train To Georgia." "I said, 'No, I don't mind—just don't change the rest of the song,'" he remembers. When Weatherly's publisher sent the song to Gladys Knight & the Pips, they retained the new title and had their first number one hit on the Hot 100.

The number one song of the year was "Tie A Yellow Ribbon Round The Ole Oak Tree" by Dawn. Tony Orlando, Telma Hopkins and Joyce Vincent Wilson were ready to disband the trio after six singles in a row failed to make the top 20. Then producers Hank Medress and Dave Appell called them to a recording session in New York to hear a new song written by Irwin Levine and L. Russell Brown. Tony admitted to Dick Clark on "Rock, Roll and Remember" that he wasn't that impressed with the material. "I said this was the corniest song I've ever heard in my life, no way am I singing this song. I called up Jimmy Darren and said, 'Listen, have I got a great song for you.' I sent it to him and he turned it down. Then I sent it to Bobby Vinton. Three or four months went by and I couldn't stop singing the chorus." Dawn had been accused of being a bubblegum group, and Tony wanted to shake that image. Telma and Joyce had sung backing vocals on Issac Hayes' "Theme From 'Shaft'" and Marvin Gaye's "I Heard It Through The Grapevine," and he wanted to show off their talent. He knew the group would be in for more criticism if they recorded a song like "Tie A Yellow Ribbon." "But . . . my publishing instincts came through," he told Clark. "I knew it was a great song . . . I remember standing behind that microphone and saying to myself, 'I'm going to think Bobby Darin. I'm going to think his attitude on this tune, and throughout 'Yellow Ribbon,' there were moments when I was doing Bobby. I was feeling him, I was acting like him on mike." When Tony accepted his American Music Award for the song, he told the audience, "This one's for Bobby Darin."

Elton John had his highest ranked year-end song to date with "Crocodile Rock," the number four song of 1973. Previously, he had the number 58 song of 1971 with "Your Song" and the number 67 song of 1972 with "Rocket Man." Elton admitted that "Crocodile Rock" was an amalgamation of several different songs, including "Little Darlin'" and "Oh, Carol" with some Beach Boys and Eddie Cochran thrown in. Some people felt there was a lot of Pat Boone's "Speedy Gonzales" in there as well.

Charlie Rich scored his first year-end chart single in 1973 with "The Most Beautiful Girl," number five for the year. He first made the Hot 100 in 1960 with "Lonely Weekends," on the Phillips label (as in Sam Phillips).

Jim Croce, who had the number 86 song of 1972 with his first chart single, "You Don't Mess Around With Jim," had the number 10 song of 1973 with "Bad, Bad Leroy Brown." Croce was inspired to write the song by a soldier who went AWOL from Fort Dix, New Jersey, while Croce was there learning how to be a telephone lineman. Croce also had the number 18 song of 1973 with the third posthumous number one hit of the rock era, "Time In A Bottle." The song was heard during the telecast of "She Lives," a TV movie starring Desi Arnaz, Jr., and Season Hubley on ABC-TV September 12, 1973. The night the movie aired, Croce completed his third album, *I Got a Name*. Eight days later, after giving a concert at Northwestern Louisiana University, he boarded his privately chartered plane to take him to his next college engagement, 70 miles away. The plane had an aborted take-off and crashed into a tree, killing Croce and five other people. "I Got A Name" was released as a single and ranked number 86 for 1973. The week it made the top 10, "Time In A Bottle" was issued.

"Monster Mash" by Bobby "Boris" Pickett & the Crypt Kickers made its second appearance on a year-end chart. It was the number 35 song of the year during its original release in 1962. It had a brief chart run in 1970, peaking at number 91 on the Hot 100. Almost three years later it returned to the *Billboard* singles chart for a third time, peaking at number 10. That was good enough to rank it number 81 for the year.

1 **THE WAY WE WERE**
Barbra Streisand *Columbia*

2 **SEASONS IN THE SUN**
Terry Jacks *Bell*

3 **BENNIE AND THE JETS**
Elton John *MCA*

4 **THE JOKER**
Steve Miller Band *Capitol*

5 **LOVE'S THEME**
Love Unlimited Orchestra *20th Century*

6 **THE STREAK**
Ray Stevens *Barnaby*

7 **TSOP (THE SOUND OF PHILADELPHIA)**
MFSB f/the Three Degrees *PIR*

8 **THEN CAME YOU**
Dionne Warwick & Spinners *Atlantic*

9 **UNTIL YOU COME BACK TO ME (THAT'S WHAT I'M GONNA DO)**
Aretha Franklin *Atlantic*

10 **JUNGLE BOOGIE**
Kool & the Gang *De-Lite*

11 **SHOW AND TELL**
Al Wilson *Rocky Road*

12 **YOU HAVEN'T DONE NOTHIN'**
Stevie Wonder *Tamla*

13 **DANCING MACHINE**
The Jackson Five *Motown*

14 **COME AND GET YOUR LOVE**
Redbone *Epic*

15 **YOU MAKE ME FEEL BRAND NEW**
The Stylistics *Avco*

16 **THE LOCO-MOTION**
Grand Funk *Capitol*

17 **HOOKED ON A FEELING**
Blue Swede *EMI*

18 **SPIDERS AND SNAKES**
Jim Stafford *MGM*

19 **BAND ON THE RUN**
Paul McCartney and Wings *Apple*

20 **SUNSHINE ON MY SHOULDERS**
John Denver *RCA*

21 **NEVER, NEVER GONNA GIVE YA UP**
Barry White *20th Century*

22 **(YOU'RE) HAVING MY BABY**
Paul Anka *UA*

23 **DO IT ('TIL YOU'RE SATISFIED)**
B.T. Express *Roadshow*

24 **NOTHING FROM NOTHING**
Billy Preston *A&M*

25 **LET ME BE THERE**
Olivia Newton-John *MCA*

26 **YOU'RE SIXTEEN**
Ringo Starr *Apple*

27 **BEST THING THAT EVER HAPPENED TO ME**
Gladys Knight & the Pips *Buddah*

28 **ROCK ON**
David Essex *Columbia*

29 **MIDNIGHT AT THE OASIS**
Maria Muldaur *Reprise*

30 **ANGIE BABY**
Helen Reddy *Capitol*

Barbra Streisand

1974 was the year Cass Elliott died while staying in Harry Nilsson's flat in London; Led Zeppelin launched their Swan Song label; and David Niven was surprised by a streaker at the Academy Awards.

Paul Anka returned to the year-end chart for the first time since 1960, when "Puppy Love" was number 53 and "My Home Town" was number 93. He did it with a number one song, "(You're) Having My Baby," written to express his joy at his wife's pregnancy. The single ranked number 22 for the year, but the National Organization of Women didn't share the joy. They awarded Anka their annual "Keep Her In Her Place Award." "It's the personal statement of a man caught up in the affection and joy of childbirth," Anka responded. Still, Anka changed the lyric in his live performances to "Having Our Baby," a new point of view that quieted his critics. "Baby" was supposed to be a solo effort, but Bob Skaff of United Artists Records suggested that Odia Coates duet with Paul on the track. Odia was a member of the Edwin Hawkins Singers while Paul was producing their album *Oh Happy Day*. After an audition in Las Vegas, Anka agreed to produce Coates for Buddah Records. Eventually she joined him on the UA roster.

Also returning to the year-end chart after an absence were the Righteous Brothers. The last time they showed up in the year-end tally was in 1966, when "(You're My) Soul And Inspiration" was number nine and "Ebb Tide" was number 83. Bill Medley went solo in 1968 while Bobby Hatfield kept the Righteous Brothers going with Jimmy Walker, formerly of the Knickerbockers ("Lies"). In February of 1974, Bill and Bobby got back together and announced their reunion on "The Sonny And Cher Comedy Hour." They had the number 70 song of 1974 with "Rock And Roll Heaven," a tune originally recorded by Climax ("Precious And Few").

Ray Stevens had the biggest hit of his career with a song that paid tribute to a current novelty, "The Streak." It was the number six song of the year, besting his previous year-end high in 1970 when "Everything Is Beautiful" was number 21 for the year. Stevens had read an article about the streaking fad on college campuses while flying from Nashville to Los Angeles. "It was a little bitty article about a college student who took off his clothes and ran through a crowd," Stevens explains. "The article called it 'streaking' and I said it had to be a great idea for a song." Stevens made some notes about it when he got to his hotel room and intended to finish the song when he returned home. "I didn't know it was going to be such a big fad. One morning I woke up and it was all over the news. Everywhere you turned, people were talking about streakers. So I built a fire under myself and went into the studio and rushed the record out."

Dionne Warwick, with an "e" added to the end of her name for "good luck," was teamed up with the Spinners by producer Thom Bell on "Then Came You." The song took both Warwick and the Spinners into the year-end top 10 for the first time. Dionne had asked the Spinners, a former Motown group that signed with Warner-owned Atlantic, to open for her on a five-week summer tour. That led Bell to suggest Dionne duet with lead singer Phillipe Wynne on "Then Came You." The song was Dionne's only hit during her long tenure with Warner Brothers, the label she joined after leaving Scepter.

There were two instrumentals in the year-end top 10 for the first time since 1962, when Mr. Acker Bilk's "Stranger On The Shore" and David Rose's "The Stripper" graced the upper portion of the year-end chart. "Love's Theme" by the Love Unlimited Orchestra was number five for the year, the highest-ranking instrumental on a year-end chart since "Love Is Blue" by Paul Mauriat was the number three song of 1968. The orchestra was a 40-piece studio band led by Barry White. The musicians were used to back White's female singing trio, Love Unlimited. They were originally signed to Uni Records, and when label head Russ Regan moved over to 20th Century he brought the group and Barry White with him. "He's a great talent," Regan says of White. "He had been around quite a while as a writer/producer but had never really done much as an artist." "Love's Theme" was written as an instrumental overture for a vocal album by the trio, *Under the Influence of Love Unlimited*. "'Love's Theme' was easy to break," according to Regan. "We sent it out to the clubs and to radio. Within a week there was a buzz on it."

The other instrumental in the top 10 was "TSOP (The Sound Of Philadelphia)" by MFSB featuring the Three Degrees. It was number seven for the year, the highest year-end ranking for any Philadelphia International Records single. Like the Love Unlimited Orchestra, MFSB was a collection of almost 40 session musicians. They were the house band at Sigma Sound Studios, the recording facility owned by Kenny Gamble and Leon Huff. Don Cornelius asked MFSB to fashion a theme song for his television series, "Soul Train." Gamble came up with the title and later used "TSOP" as a name for a new subsidiary label.

The number one song of 1974 was the title song from the movie *The Way We Were*. Barbra Streisand starred in the film as the liberal Katie Morosky, who falls in love with writer Hubbell Gardiner (Robert Redford). Her rendition of the title tune, written by Marvin Hamlisch and Alan and Marilyn Bergman, made her only the second female soloist to have a number one song of the year during the rock era. The first was Lulu, who also did it with the title song from a film that she starred in (*To Sir With Love*). This was the second number one song of the year to win an Oscar; "Raindrops Keep Fallin' On My Head" took the statue in 1970.

The runner-up song of the year was "Seasons In The Sun" by Canadian singer Terry Jacks. It became the highest ranked year-end single by an artist born in Canada since Percy Faith was number one in 1960 with "Theme From 'A Summer Place.'" Jacks had made the year-end chart in 1970 as half of the Poppy Family (with his wife Susan Jacks), when "Which Way You Goin' Billy?" was the number 50 song of the year. Terry had suggested that the Beach Boys record Jacques Brel's "*Le Moribond*" ("The Dying Man"), which had been given English lyrics by Rod McKuen. Jacks was familiar with a Kingston Trio version released in 1964. The Beach Boys took Terry's advice and recorded it, but never released it. Mourning a friend who passed away unexpectedly, Jacks decided to record it for himself. His version sat on a shelf for a year. It was only after a newspaper delivery boy heard it and asked if he could bring his friends over to hear it that Jacks was convinced it should be released.

Elton John bested his previous record by one notch, when "Bennie And The Jets" came in at number three for 1974. His "Crocodile Rock" had been the number four song of 1973. "Bennie" brought Elton to the *Billboard* R&B singles chart for the first time, an achievement that thrilled him.

Steve Miller, best known for being an album artist, also loved to make singles. "It's like a game, like a crossword puzzle," he said in *Guitar Player*. A song he didn't think would be a hit, "The Joker," ranked number four for the year.

Aretha Franklin had her only year-end top 10 single of the rock era in 1974 with a cover of an unreleased Stevie Wonder song from 1967. "Until You Come Back To Me (That's What I'm Gonna Do)" ranked number nine for 1974.

1975

1 **RHINESTONE COWBOY**
Glen Campbell *Capitol*

2 **PHILADELPHIA FREEDOM**
The Elton John Band *MCA*

3 **LOVE WILL KEEP US TOGETHER**
Captain & Tennille *A&M*

4 **FEELINGS**
Morris Albert *RCA*

5 **I'M SORRY/CALYPSO**
John Denver *RCA*

6 **BEFORE THE NEXT TEARDROP FALLS**
Freddy Fender *ABC/Dot*

7 **THAT'S THE WAY (I LIKE IT)**
KC & the Sunshine Band *TK*

8 **SHINING STAR**
Earth, Wind & Fire *Columbia*

9 **ONE OF THESE NIGHTS**
Eagles *Asylum*

10 **LAUGHTER IN THE RAIN**
Neil Sedaka *Rocket*

11 **FLY, ROBIN, FLY**
Silver Convention *Midland International*

12 **(HEY WON'T YOU PLAY) ANOTHER SOMEBODY DONE SOMEBODY WRONG SONG**
B.J. Thomas *ABC*

13 **LADY MARMALADE**
Labelle *Epic*

14 **PICK UP THE PIECES**
Average White Band *Atlantic*

15 **JIVE TALKIN'**
Bee Gees *RSO*

16 **THANK GOD I'M A COUNTRY BOY**
John Denver *RCA*

17 **FAME**
David Bowie *RCA*

18 **BOOGIE ON REGGAE WOMAN**
Stevie Wonder *Tamla*

19 **LOVIN' YOU**
Minnie Riperton *Epic*

20 **BLACK WATER**
Doobie Brothers *Warner Bros*

21 **LOVE WON'T LET ME WAIT**
Major Harris *Atlantic*

22 **MY EYES ADORED YOU**
Frankie Valli *Private Stock*

23 **BALLROOM BLITZ**
Sweet *Capitol*

24 **SKY HIGH**
Jigsaw *Chelsea*

25 **AT SEVENTEEN**
Janis Ian *Columbia*

26 **BEST OF MY LOVE**
Eagles *Asylum*

27 **FIGHT THE POWER (PART 1)**
Isley Brothers *T-Neck*

28 **FALLIN' IN LOVE**
Hamilton, Joe Frank & Reynolds *Playboy*

29 **BAD BLOOD**
Neil Sedaka *Rocket*

30 **WHY CAN'T WE BE FRIENDS?**
War *UA*

KC & the Sunshine Band

1975 was the year the Who's *Tommy* became a movie; Ron Wood joined the Rolling Stones; and Bruce Springsteen was *Born to Run.*

Several artists made surprise returns to the year-end chart. Simon and Garfunkel, who split up after releasing the *Bridge Over Troubled Water* album in 1970, temporarily reunited in 1975 and released one single, "My Little Town." It was the number 86 song of the year.

Another unexpected comeback was made by the Four Seasons, absent from the year-end singles chart since 1965, when "Let's Hang On" was the number eight song of the year. Signed with Warner/Curb, Frankie Valli and a new set of Four Seasons were number 34 for the year with "Who Loves You." Valli, signed as a solo artist to Private Stock Records, was on the year-end chart with a song originally recorded during his tenure with Motown. "My Eyes Adored You," which began life as "Blue Eyes In Georgia," was the number 22 song of 1975.

Neil Sedaka was another '60s artist who proved he could be contemporary in the '70s. He was last seen on the year-end chart in 1962, when he placed three songs in the top 100: "Breaking Up Is Hard To Do" (number 20), "Happy Birthday, Sweet Sixteen" (number 43) and "Next Door To An Angel" (number 69). He was responsible for writing three songs on the top 100 of 1975, two of which he also performed. "Laughter In The Rain" was his big comeback record, number 10 for the year. "Bad Blood," another number one hit, was number 29 for the year. And his composition of "Love Will Keep Us Together," released as a single by the Captain & Tennille, was the number three song of the year.

Toni Tennille was the only female voice in the top 10. She and her husband Daryl were also in the top 100 with "The Way I Want To Touch You" (number 38). That song had been recorded on their own Butterscotch Castle label after two disc jockeys saw the couple perform at the Smoke House in Encino, California, and promised to play their songs if they ever recorded anything. After "The Way I Want To Touch You" garnered some local airplay, it was picked up for distribution by Joyce Records. That led to four offers from major labels, including A&M. "A&M was what we wanted, because they were the only ones who would let us produce ourselves, and because Herb Alpert and Jerry Moss had done the kind of thing I always wanted to do," Daryl said in *Billboard*. "But I was afraid because they have the Carpenters, (they didn't) need another female singer/male keyboardist team."

Despite Daryl's considerations, A&M signed the duo. Kip Cohen of the label's A&R department asked them to listen to a track on the *Sedaka's Back* album, and both Daryl and Toni knew that "Love Will Keep Us Together" was right for them. Two weeks later they had a new arrangement for the song. Released as a single, it spent four weeks at number one.

Elton John bested his previous record by one notch once again. In 1973 he had the number four song of the year, "Crocodile Rock." In 1974 he had the number three song of the year, "Bennie And The Jets." And in 1975 he had his highest-ranked year-end song of the rock era, "Philadelphia Freedom," at number two. Elton says he wrote the song for Billie Jean King, coach of the Philadelphia Freedoms tennis team. After presenting Elton with a custom-made team warm-up suit, the singer told the coach: "Billie, I'm going to write a song for you." She dismissed the idea, but two months later Elton was recording at Caribou Studios in Colorado and showed up at the play-offs in Denver with a tape of "Philadelphia Freedom."

The number one song of 1975 was "Rhinestone Cowboy," written by Larry Weiss and recorded by Glen Campbell. Weiss recorded for 20th Century Records and released an album called *Black and Blue Suite* in 1974. "Rhinestone Cowboy" was pulled from the LP as a single, but failed to make the Hot 100. Campbell heard the song on KNX-FM, a Los Angeles adult contemporary station. He asked his secretary to find a copy of the song, although he wasn't sure who the artist was. Meanwhile, he dropped by Al Coury's office at Capitol Records and the label executive asked him to listen to a song—"Rhinestone Cowboy." Weiss was about to drop out of the music business and open a furniture store when he found out Campbell was recording his song. Glen first performed the tune on a telethon, and KHJ Radio program director Paul Drew called Capitol for a copy. The record wasn't pressed yet, but Drew obtained an acetate copy from producer Dennis Lambert and started playing it throughout the RKO radio chain. "In a sense, (Drew) forced everyone, Capitol primarily, to go into an even more accelerated rush release because now the record was on radio," Lambert explains.

Morris Albert had the number four song of the year with "Feelings," a number one hit in his native Brazil as well as Venezuela, Chile and Mexico before being released in the States by RCA. This is the highest-ranking song by a Brazilian artist in the rock era. Los Indios Tabajaras, two brothers from Brazil, had the number 81 song of 1963 with an instrumental version of "Maria Elena." Astrud Gilberto teamed with Stan Getz on "The Girl From Ipanema," the number 70 song of 1964. Sergio Mendes, born in Niteroi, Brazil, had two songs on the year-end chart of 1968: "The Look Of Love" (number 55) and "The Fool On The Hill" (number 79). And Deodato, a keyboardist from Rio de Janeiro, had the number 64 song of 1973 with a version of Richard Strauss' "Also Sprach Zarathustra."

John Denver had his first and only year-end top 10 listing with the two-sided hit "I'm Sorry" and "Calypso." In 1971 he had the number 14 song of the year, "Take Me Home, Country Roads." In 1973 he was number 53 with "Rocky Mountain High," and in 1974 he had three songs included in the top 100 of the year: "Sunshine On My Shoulders" (number 20), "Annie's Song" (number 37) and "Back Home Again" (number 74). *Newsweek* called him "the most popular singer in America," and for a time in the '70s, he was. But after "Fly Away," a duet with Olivia Newton-John that was the follow-up to "I'm Sorry" and "Calypso," he never returned to the top 20 portion of the Hot 100.

Disco music, which was represented on the year-end chart in 1974 with hits by the Love Unlimited Orchestra and MFSB as well as the Hues Corporation and George McCrae, continued to make an impact in 1975. KC & the Sunshine Band had the number seven song of the year with "That's The Way (I Like It)" as well as the number 81 song of the year with "Get Down Tonight." Earth, Wind & Fire's danceable "Shining Star" was number eight for the year. Other big disco hits on the year-end chart for 1975 included "Fly, Robin, Fly" by Silver Convention (number 11), "Lady Marmalade" by Labelle (number 13), "Jive Talkin'" by the Bee Gees (number 15), "You're The First, The Last, My Everything" by Barry White (number 48), "The Hustle" by Van McCoy (number 51), "Express" by B. T. Express (number 52), "Walking In Rhythm" by the Blackbyrds (number 58), "Doctor's Orders" by Carol Douglas (number 82), "Never Can Say Goodbye" by Gloria Gaynor (number 83) and "It Only Takes A Minute" by Tavares (number 98).

The Eagles' first song to make a year-end top 100 was "Witchy Woman," the number 78 song of 1972. In 1975 they had their highest-ranked year-end song with "One Of These Nights," number nine for the year. Two other Eagles' songs made the year-end chart: "Best Of My Love" at number 26 and "Lyin' Eyes" at number 84.

THE TOP 100 SONGS OF
1976

Boston

1976 was the year Peter Frampton came alive; Stevie Wonder finally released *Songs in the Key of Life*; and Paul McCartney flew his Wings Over America.

Frampton, the former guitarist for the British band Humble Pie, had two singles on the year-end chart from his *Frampton Comes Alive!* album: "Show Me The Way" was the number 47 song of the year and "Baby, I Love Your Way" just made the chart at number 99. It was a good year for U.K. artists—they were responsible for 25 of the year's top 100 songs, the highest mark since the heady British Invasion days of 1965, when there were 32 U.K. songs on the year-end chart.

Britain took the number one song of the year in the U.S., thanks to Rod Stewart's "Tonight's The Night (Gonna Be Alright)," which topped the Hot 100 for eight weeks. The only British artist to have a number one song of the year in the '70s, Rod also took top honors in 1971 with the two-sided hit "Maggie May" and "Reason To Believe." In 1976 Stewart became the first artist since the Beatles to have the highest-charted single of the year twice.

The only other British act in the top 10 was Paul McCartney's Wings, number five with "Silly Love Songs." It was McCartney's best showing on a year-end chart as lead vocalist since "Hey Jude" was the number one song of 1968.

Other U.K. artists performing well in 1976 included:

Elton John and Kiki Dee. Elton was a frequent visitor to the year-end chart, but Kiki Dee made her first appearance when she was invited to duet with Elton on "Don't Go Breaking My Heart," the number 15 song of the year. Born Pauline Matthews in Bradford, England, she was the first British female singer signed to Motown in the U.S. In 1973 Elton signed her to his Rocket label, and in 1974 she went to number 12 on the Hot 100 with "I've Got The Music In Me."

Maxine Nightingale. Raised in Wembley, she started doing session work at 18 and eventually moved to Los Angeles. Songwriters/producers Pierre Tubbs and Vince Edwards asked her to record their song, "Right Back Where We Started From." It went to number eight in the U.K. in 1975, but went even higher in the U.S. where it spent two weeks at number two, good enough to make it the number 16 song of 1976.

Hot Chocolate. Errol Brown, a vocalist from Jamaica, and Tony Wilson, a bass player from Trinidad, got their first break when Mary Hopkin recorded their song "Think About The Children" for Apple. A secretary at Apple suggested they call themselves Hot Chocolate, and they recorded a reggae version of "Give Peace A Chance" for the Beatles' label. They moved to the Rak label and had a number one hit in the U. K. with their song "Brother Louie," covered in the U.S. by Stories. They had their own hit in America in 1975 with "Emma," the number 95 song of the year, and an even bigger hit in 1976 with "You Sexy Thing," number 30 for the year.

Bee Gees. After making a comeback in 1975 with "Jive Talkin'," the number 36 song of the year, the Gibb brothers wanted to work with producer Arif Mardin on their next project. But with the RSO label shifting distribution from Atlantic to Polydor, the Bee Gees lost the services of Mardin, an in-house producer for Atlantic. After an attempt to work with producer Richard Perry failed, the trio produced themselves with the assistance of Albhy Galuten and Karl Richardson, who had worked with Mardin at Criteria Studios during the recording of *Main Course*. The result was the *Children of the World* album. The first single issued, "You Should Be Dancing," topped the Hot 100 and was the number 33 song of the year. The follow-up single, "Love So Right," ranked number 54 for the year.

Other U.K. artists who made the year-end chart in 1976 included Nazareth, a hard-rocking Scottish band that covered Boudleaux Bryant's "Love Hurts," previously recorded by the Everly Brothers and Roy Orbison; Queen, a glam-rock band fronted by Freddie Mercury that had hits in 1976 with "Bohemian Rhapsody" and "You're My Best Friend"; the Bay City Rollers, Scottish teen idols who inspired Rollermania on both sides of the pond, especially in America with their number one song "Saturday Night"; David Bowie, who had scored a hit in 1975 with "Fame" and was back again in 1976 with "Golden Years"; Fleetwood Mac, the Anglo-American outfit that had their first year-end chart hits with "Say You Love Me" and "Rhiannon (Will You Ever Win)"; Electric Light Orchestra, the Birmingham band led by Jeff Lynne that melded rock and classical music, resulting in hits like "Evil Woman"; Cliff Richard, who had been charting in England since 1958, but who didn't register on the American year-end chart until "Devil Woman" in 1976; Sweet, the British version of a bubblegum band, with "Fox On The Run" and the Beatles, who returned to the year-end chart for the first time since "Let It Be" and "The Long And Winding Road" in 1970, thanks to Capitol's issue of "Got To Get You Into My Life" as a single.

The number two song of 1976 was "Play That Funky Music" by Wild Cherry, a group that took its name from a box of cough drops. Bob Parissi, leader of the band, was in the hospital and anxious to get out so he could work with the group. They didn't have a name yet, and while the group was visiting him Parissi spied a box of cough drops. He jokingly suggested they name themselves after the flavor of the drops and his visitors took him seriously. The first incarnation of Wild Cherry was signed to the Brown Bag label, owned by Grand Funk manager Terry Knight. When that group broke up, Parissi formed a new Wild Cherry, a rock band frustrated by the popularity of disco music. When they played clubs like the 2001 disco in Pittsburgh, patrons requested that they "play that funky music." Parissi wanted to play rock music and please the people who wanted to hear dance music. Drummer Ron Beitle told him he should do what the customers wanted—"play that funky music, white boy."

The Miracles hit an all-time career high with "Love Machine (Part 1)," the number three song of 1976. Ironically, it was one of their post-Smokey Robinson hits. Their leader had left for a solo career, his place taken by vocalist Billy Griffin.

"A Fifth Of Beethoven" by Walter Murphy, the number four song of 1976, became the highest ranking instrumental on a year-end chart since Paul Mauriat's "Love Is Blue" was the number three song of 1968. Murphy, a Madison Avenue jingle writer and former arranger for Doc Severinsen and "The Tonight Show" orchestra, noted how two previous rock hits, "A Lover's Concerto" by the Toys and "Joy" by Apollo 100, had incorporated classical music into pop hits. He wanted to do the same, and made a demo tape of several classical and neo-classical works. Larry Uttal, founder of the Private Stock label, liked Murphy's disco treatment of Beethoven's *Symphony No. 5 in C Minor* and released the track as a single.

"Mandy" was Barry Manilow's first year-end chart listing, number 46 for the year 1975. He didn't write it, and vowed it would be the only "outside" song he would ever record. Then Clive Davis sent him "I Write The Songs," composed by Bruce Johnston. Barry went to the Arista office to tell Clive in person of his decision not to record the song. Fortunately, Barry later changed his mind. It ranked number six for the year and was his most successful chart single of all time.

Abba

1977 was the year the Sex Pistols went through three labels in less than six months; Studio 54 opened in Manhattan; and Elvis Presley was found dead on the floor of his bathroom at Graceland.

The Gibb family nabbed the number two and three positions on the year-end chart. The Bee Gees had the runner-up song of the year with the first single from *Saturday Night Fever*, "How Deep Is Your Love." Their youngest brother Andy was number three for the year with his first American single, "I Just Want To Be Your Everything." It was the only time in the rock era that brothers occupied two out of the top three slots on a year-end chart.

Half of the top 10 songs of the year featured female lead vocalists—the highest total of any year in the rock era to date. Debby Boone led the pack with the number one single of the year, "You Light Up My Life." Debby was only the third female soloist of the rock era to have the highest-ranked song of the year, following Lulu in 1967 with "To Sir With Love" and Barbra Streisand in 1974 with "The Way We Were." Like Lulu and Barbra, Debby did it with a song from a film. Unlike her predecessors, Debby did not appear in the movie, nor did she perform the song in the film. Didi Conn had the female lead in *You Light Up My Life*, and she lip-synched to vocals by commercial jingle singer Kacey Cisyk. "You Light Up My Life" is the third number one song of the year in the rock era to also be an Oscar winner, following "Raindrops Keep Fallin' On My Head" by B.J. Thomas in 1970 and "The Way We Were." Debby's father Pat had the number one song of 1957, "Love Letters In The Sand," making the Boones the only parent and child to both have number one records of the year.

The Emotions had the number four single of 1977 with "Best Of My Love," the highest-ranked girl group song of the rock era. Sisters Sheila, Wanda and Jeanette first performed in a gospel group with their father, Joe. Through the Staple Sisters, they were signed to Stax/Volt and recorded secular material. Sister Pam replaced Jeanette, and when Stax folded they were left without a label. They signed a production deal with Maurice White of Earth, Wind & Fire. White co-wrote and produced "Best Of My Love," which spent five weeks atop the *Billboard* Hot 100.

Barbra Streisand was number five for the year with only the second song she had ever written: the love theme from the third filmed version of *A Star Is Born.* Streisand starred in the film with Kris Kristofferson. The movie garnered only one Oscar nomination: for Best Original Song. The award went to Streisand and her co-writer, Paul Williams. "Evergreen" is Streisand's second-best showing on a year-end chart, topped only by "The Way We Were," the number one song of 1974.

Thelma Houston's remake of Harold Melvin & the Blue Notes' "Don't Leave Me This Way" was the number eight song of 1977. The most successful Kenny Gamble-Leon Huff recording of the rock era, it was a triumph for Houston, who had one minor chart hit on Dunhill before signing with Motown's west coast subsidiary, Mowest, in 1971. Producer Hal Davis admired Teddy Pendergrass' vocal on the original "Don't Leave Me This Way" and decided to have Houston cover it on the Tamla label.

Two of Houston's producers at Motown were Clayton Ivey and Terry Woodford. Although they were based in Muscle Shoals, they were signed to be staff producers for Motown after label executive Suzanne DePasse heard some material they produced for Capitol. Ivey and Woodford also wrote and produced for the Temptations and the Supremes while at the label, and when they left they looked for a new project to work on. They signed black vocalist Gwen Owens and then added two more female singers, Cathy Carson and Juanita Curiel, to create an interracial trio called Hot.

After recording some uptempo dance songs, Ivey and Woodford looked for a ballad. Tom Brasfield, a writer signed to their publishing company, had a title and first line for a country song he called "The Angel In Your Arms This Morning Is Gonna Be The Devil In Someone Else's Arms Tonight." Ivey and Woodford completed the song, shortened the title and overdubbed Brasfield's demo track with guitar, bass and keyboard. When LeBlanc and Carr, a duo signed to Big Tree Records, performed at a showcase in Muscle Shoals, Woodford tracked down label West Coast head Mardi

Nehrbass and played "Angel In Your Arms" for her. Nehrbass declared that the song was a hit, and leased the track.

Leo Sayer had three songs included in the top 100 of 1977. "You Make Me Feel Like Dancing" was his biggest hit, ranked number six for the year. Managed by former pop singer Adam Faith, Sayer's name first became known in America as the writer of "The Show Must Go On," a tune covered by Three Dog Night. Linked up with producer Richard Perry, Sayer recorded the *Endless Flight* album and recorded other people's material for the first time. He wrote the album's first number one single, "You Make Me Feel Like Dancing," but the next chart-topper, "When I Need You" (number 36 for the year), was penned by Albert Hammond and Carole Bayer Sager. The follow-up, "How Much Love" (number 97 for the year), was written by Sayer with Barry Mann.

Another songwriter in the top 10 was Kenny Nolan, who had written hits like "Lady Marmalade," "My Eyes Adored You" and "Get Dancin'." "I Like Dreamin' " was written for someone else to record, but when it was turned down a frustrated Nolan decided to record it himself. It became the biggest hit ever released by the 20th Century label.

"Boogie Nights" by the Anglo-American disco outfit known as Heatwave was the number 10 single of 1977. Brothers Johnny and Keith Wilder of Dayton, Ohio, served in the Army in West Germany and after being discharged decided to remain in Europe. British keyboard player Rod Temperton was working in Germany when he responded to an ad placed by the Wilders in a music paper. After playing clubs in Britain and Air Force bases throughout Europe, they were signed to the GTO label in the U.K. Barry Blue, who had several U.K. hits as a performer in 1973 and 1974, produced their album *Too Hot to Handle* and Temperton wrote their key hits, including "Boogie Nights" and "Always And Forever." He left the group in 1978 but continued to write for Heatwave as well as for some artists produced by Quincy Jones, including George Benson ("Give Me The Night") and Michael Jackson ("Rock With You," "Off The Wall" and "Thriller").

Marilyn McCoo and Billy Davis, Jr. made their first appearance on a year-end chart in seven years. As two/fifths of the 5th Dimension, they had the number 13 song of 1970, "One Less Bell To Answer." They came in one notch higher in 1977, number 12 for the year with their duet, "You Don't Have To Be A Star (To Be In My Show)." The husband and wife team departed the 5th Dimension in 1975, attributing their stepping out on their own to having completed the est training. Don Davis, producer of Johnnie Taylor's number one hit "Disco Lady," was preparing to record a solo album for Marilyn when Billy decided their first project away from the 5th Dimension should be an album of duets. Davis had a demo by songwriters James Dean and John Glover that wasn't written for two vocalists, but Davis thought it would be perfect for Marilyn and Billy to record together. Released as their second single, "You Don't Have To Be A Star" spent one week atop the Hot 100.

1978

1 **LE FREAK**
Chic *Atlantic*

2 **SHADOW DANCING**
Andy Gibb *RSO*

3 **STAYIN' ALIVE**
Bee Gees *RSO*

4 **NIGHT FEVER**
Bee Gees *RSO*

5 **I GO CRAZY**
Paul Davis *Bang*

6 **KISS YOU ALL OVER**
Exile *Warner/Curb*

7 **(LOVE IS) THICKER THAN WATER**
Andy Gibb *RSO*

8 **BOOGIE OOGIE OOGIE**
A Taste of Honey *Capitol*

9 **HOT CHILD IN THE CITY**
Nick Gilder *Chrysalis*

10 **BABY COME BACK**
Player *RSO*

11 **THREE TIMES A LADY**
Commodores *Motown*

12 **YOU NEEDED ME**
Anne Murray *Capitol*

13 **I LOVE THE NIGHTLIFE (DISCO 'ROUND)**
Alicia Bridges *Polydor*

14 **LAY DOWN SALLY**
Eric Clapton *RSO*

15 **MACARTHUR PARK**
Donna Summer *Casablanca*

16 **YOU'RE THE ONE THAT I WANT**
John Travolta & Olivia Newton-John *RSO*

17 **JUST THE WAY YOU ARE**
Billy Joel *Columbia*

18 **YOU DON'T BRING ME FLOWERS**
Barbra Streisand & Neil Diamond *Columbia*

19 **GREASE**
Frankie Valli *RSO*

20 **EMOTION**
Samantha Sang *Private Stock*

21 **CAN'T SMILE WITHOUT YOU**
Barry Manilow *Arista*

22 **MISS YOU**
The Rolling Stones *Rolling Stones*

23 **IF I CAN'T HAVE YOU**
Yvonne Elliman *RSO*

24 **TAKE A CHANCE ON ME**
Abba *Atlantic*

25 **HOW MUCH I FEEL**
Ambrosia *Warner Bros*

26 **BAKER STREET**
Gerry Rafferty *UA*

27 **FEELS SO GOOD**
Chuck Mangione *A&M*

28 **WITH A LITTLE LUCK**
Wings *Capitol*

29 **DANCE, DANCE, DANCE
(YOWSAH, YOWSAH, YOWSAH)**
Chic *Atlantic*

30 **THE CLOSER I GET TO YOU**
Roberta Flack w/Donny Hathaway *Atlantic*

Frankie Valli

1978 was the year the Bee Gees and Peter Frampton starred in *Sgt. Pepper's Lonely Hearts Club Band*; Lucille Ball asked for her photograph to be removed from the cover of the Rolling Stones' *Some Girls* album; and Keith Moon of the Who died.

British artists held down half of the positions in the year-end top 10, their best showing to date. Andy Gibb and the Bee Gees accounted for two each, and Nick Gilder, born in London but raised in Vancouver, Canada, was responsible for the fifth. There were 30 U.K. songs in the top 100 of the year, the highest total since 1965.

The films *Saturday Night Fever* and *Grease*, both of which starred John Travolta, were responsible for seven of the songs in the year's top 100. The Bee Gees led the charge with "Stayin' Alive" (number three) and "Night Fever" (number four), the first time in the rock era that two songs from the same film were in the top five singles of the year. The other song from *Saturday Night Fever* on the chart was "If I Can't Have You," written by the Bee Gees and performed by Yvonne Elliman.

Travolta and his co-star Olivia Newton-John placed two duets from *Grease* on the year-end chart. "You're The One That I Want," the number 16 song of 1978, was written for the movie while "Summer Nights," number 59 for the year, had been written for the original Broadway production. Olivia's "Hopelessly Devoted To You," number 31 for the year, was another song written for the film.

Robert Stigwood's RSO label had five songs in the top 10 and 14 songs in the top 100 of the year. That's the second-highest total of the rock era (Columbia had 15 singles on the year-end charts for 1982 and 1983). In addition to the songs from *Saturday Night Fever* and *Grease,* RSO scored with singles from Player, Eric Clapton and Andy Gibb.

The group Player was originally signed to Haven, a label owned by producers Dennis Lambert and Brian Potter. When the label folded, Lambert and Potter signed the group to RSO. Their first album had already been recorded, but not released. Peter Beckett, a guitarist from Liverpool, and John Charles Crowley, a musician from Galveston Bay, Texas, had written "Baby Come Back" after breaking up with their respective girlfriends. The song ranked number 10 for the year and the follow-up, "This Time I'm In It For Love," was number 89.

Eric Clapton, a bricklayer's son born in Ripley, England, had the number 14 song of the year, "Lay Down Sally." He first made the year-end chart in 1968 as part of Cream, when "Sunshine Of Your Love" was the number 56 song of the year. He equaled that mark in 1974, when "I Shot The Sheriff" came in at number 56. As a member of Derek & the Dominos, he ranked number 84 in 1972 with "Layla."

As songwriters, the Gibbs had nine songs included in the year's top 100. Aside from singles by the Bee Gees, Andy Gibb and their soundtrack material, the Gibbs came up with a tune for Australian vocalist Samantha Sang. She first met Barry Gibb in 1969 when he wrote and produced "Don't Let It Happen Again" for her, but it wasn't a hit. They reunited in Paris in 1977 and Samantha asked for another song. Barry gave her a choice between "Emotion" and "Our Love (Don't Throw It All Away)." She chose the former and the latter was recorded by Andy. Stigwood declined to release Samantha's Bee Gees-sounding single on RSO, and Larry Uttal picked it up for Private Stock. It was the number 20 song of the year.

The number one song of 1978 was the last song to top the Hot 100 in the calendar year. "Le Freak" by Chic moved into the number one position for the week ending December 9 and remained there for five weeks. Bernard Edwards and Nile Rodgers thought disco music "was like a gift from heaven." "Discos gave us the perfect opportunity to realize our concept, because it wasn't about being black, white, male or female. Further, it would give us a chance to get into the mainstream. We wanted millions of dollars, Ferraris and planes—and this seemed like the way to get them," Rodgers said in *Melody Maker.* Edwards confessed that at first, he hated disco. "I got into it, though, and realized that if we did it our way, it'd be pretty good." Despite two rejections by Atlantic Records, they were finally signed to the label. Their first hit, "Dance, Dance, Dance (Yowsah, Yowsah, Yowsah)," was the number 29 song of 1978. "Le Freak" was their third single. It became the most successful chart single issued on Atlantic and firmly established Rodgers and Edwards' reputation. They went on to produce, as a team and individually, artists as diverse as Diana Ross, David Bowie, Debbie Harry, Duran Duran, Madonna, Carly Simon and Sister Sledge.

Paul Davis had the number five song of the year with "I Go Crazy," a song originally written as a demo for Lou Rawls. Davis, who first made the Hot 100 with an updating of the Jarmels' "A Little Bit Of Soap," had decided to concentrate on songwriting instead of his recording career. He submitted "I Go Crazy" to Rawls' producer, Kenny Gamble at Philadelphia International Records. Gamble loved the song and wanted to cut it on Lou, but that response made Davis' label, Bang Records, take notice of the song. Reasoning that if the song was good enough for Lou Rawls, it was certainly good enough for Davis to record, Bang issued Davis' version in the summer of 1977. It began a long climb into the top 10, peaking at number seven in its 30th week on the chart. "I Go Crazy" was on the Hot 100 for a total of 40 weeks, a record at the time.

Songwriters Mike Chapman and Nicky Chinn had their first American number one hit with Exile's "Kiss You All Over," the number six song of 1978. "It's a very unusual song and is very much about what music in the U.S. is all about in 1978," Chapman told Jim McCullaugh in *Billboard* at the time.

A group named after a song, A Taste of Honey, had the number eight record of 1978 with their first chart single, "Boogie Oogie Oogie." The band was fronted by two female guitarists, Janice Marie Johnson and Hazel Payne. Johnson wrote "Boogie Oogie Oogie" with group member Perry Kibble after a frustrating gig at an Air Force club. "We were knocking ourselves out, but getting no reaction from the crowd," according to Janice. "In fact, they seemed to have contempt for two women who thought they could front a band." Angered at the military chauvinism she felt, Janice went home and started writing the song.

Nick Gilder's family moved from London, England, to Vancouver in British Columbia, Canada, when he was 10. After college, he formed a group called Sweeney Todd with guitarist Jimmy McCulloch. They signed with London records, and released a song called "Roxy Roller" in 1976. Group infighting led Gilder and McCulloch to split the band and relocate to Los Angeles. They signed with Chrysalis Records and their former label responded by reissuing "Roxy Roller" with a new lead vocalist. Chrysalis had Gilder record a new version, and a third version was released by a new incarnation of Sweeney Todd. All three singles bombed. Gilder worked with producers George Martin and Stuart Alan Love before Chrysalis teamed him with Mike Chapman. "Hot Child In The City" was one of three tracks recorded in a three-day period. Chapman wanted the label to release "All Because Of Love," but Chrysalis preferred "Hot Child In The City." It peaked at number one and was the number nine song of 1978.

1 **HOT STUFF**
Donna Summer *Casablanca*

2 **Y.M.C.A.**
Village People *Casablanca*

3 **MY SHARONA**
The Knack *Capitol*

4 **DA YA THINK I'M SEXY?**
Rod Stewart *Warner Bros*

5 **I WILL SURVIVE**
Gloria Gaynor *Polydor*

6 **BAD GIRLS**
Donna Summer *Casablanca*

7 **ESCAPE (PINA COLADA SONG)**
Rupert Holmes *Infinity*

8 **REUNITED**
Peaches and Herb *Polydor*

9 **A LITTLE MORE LOVE**
Olivia Newton-John *MCA*

10 **I'LL NEVER LOVE THIS WAY AGAIN**
Dionne Warwick *Arista*

11 **RING MY BELL**
Anita Ward *Juana*

12 **SAD EYES**
Robert John *EMI America*

13 **BABE**
Styx *A&M*

14 **POP MUZIK**
M *Sire*

15 **STILL**
Commodores *Motown*

16 **FIRE**
Pointer Sisters *Planet*

17 **RISE**
Herb Alpert *A&M*

18 **TOO MUCH HEAVEN**
Bee Gees *RSO*

19 **TRAGEDY**
Bee Gees *RSO*

20 **GOOD TIMES**
Chic *Atlantic*

21 **WHAT A FOOL BELIEVES**
Doobie Brothers *Warner Bros*

22 **STUMBLIN' IN**
Suzi Quatro & Chris Norman *RSO*

23 **SHARING THE NIGHT TOGETHER**
Dr. Hook *Capitol*

24 **HEART OF GLASS**
Blondie *Chrysalis*

25 **SEND ONE YOUR LOVE**
Stevie Wonder *Tamla*

26 **MY LIFE**
Billy Joel *Columbia*

27 **KNOCK ON WOOD**
Amii Stewart *Ariola*

28 **HEARTACHE TONIGHT**
Eagles *Asylum*

29 **MAKIN' IT**
David Naughton *RSO*

30 **HEAVEN KNOWS**
Donna Summer w/Brooklyn Dreams *Casablanca*

Chic

1979 was the year a Chicago DJ caused a riot at a White Sox game by burning a pile of disco records; Bette Midler starred in *The Rose*; and everybody wanted to *Get the Knack*.

For the first and only time in the rock era, the top two songs of the year were on the same label. Neil Bogart's Casablanca Records took the honors. There were nine Casablanca singles included in the top 100 songs of the year. That was one better than RSO, which had eight songs on the year-end chart for 1979.

Donna Summer became the first female solo artist in the rock era to have two singles in a year-end top 10. She had the number one record of the year, "Hot Stuff," as well as number six, "Bad Girls." She first appeared on a year-end chart in 1976, when "Love To Love You Baby" was the number 32 song of the year. In 1977, she ranked number 41 with "I Feel Love" and in 1978 she was number 15 with "MacArthur Park" and number 35 with "Last Dance." Her most successful chart single, "Hot Stuff" was written on an old piano in the coffee room of a studio on LaBrea Avenue in Hollywood, according to co-writer Keith Forsey. "It was modeled after the tempo of Rod Stewart's 'Da Ya Think I'm Sexy,'" he admits. Critics called it a successful merger of rock with disco. Summer had three other singles included in the top 100 of the year: "Heaven Knows" with Brooklyn Dreams at number 30, "No More Tears (Enough Is Enough)" with Barbra Streisand at number 32 and "Dim All The Lights" at number 35.

Casablanca's runner-up song was "Y.M.C.A." by the Village People. Jacques Morali, the French producer of the Ritchie Family's hits ("Brazil" and "The Best Disco In Town"), was inspired by all of the "macho men" he saw at Les Mouches, a gay disco in Greenwich Village. Felipe Rose was there that night, wearing an Indian costume. Morali later told *Rolling Stone*: "I say to myself, 'You know, this is fantastic—to see the cowboy, the Indian, the construction worker with other men around.' And also, I think to myself that the gay people have no group, nobody to personalize the gay people, you know?" Morali put all the stereotypes together and formed the Village People with Victor Willis as lead singer. "San Francisco (You've Got Me)" missed the pop singles chart, but "Macho Man" peaked at number 25. "Y.M.C.A." was their biggest hit, spending three weeks at number two and half a year on the Hot 100.

Casablanca was also represented on the year-end chart by Kiss and Cher. The glam-rock band was number 74 with "I Was Made For Lovin' You," and guitarist Ace Frehley had a solo hit at number 76 with a cover of Hello's "New York Groove." Cher was at number 82 with "Take Me Home."

There were six singles in the top 10 featuring female lead singers, a new record. In addition to the two titles by Donna Summer, the top 10 included Gloria Gaynor, Peaches (of Peaches and Herb), Olivia Newton-John and Dionne Warwick.

Gaynor first recorded in 1965 for Johnny Nash's Jocinda label. She had a brief tenure in the Soul Satisfiers group, then released "Honey Bee" on Columbia before signing with MGM. In 1975 she made the year-end chart for the first time with an updating of the Jackson Five's "Never Can Say Goodbye," an early disco record. It was the number 83 song of the year. Gaynor had been off the chart for three years when "I Will Survive" debuted. It was originally the "B" side of a single featuring a song called "Substitute." But discos and DJs preferred the defiant declaration of independence Gaynor made in "I Will Survive," and that side spent three weeks at number one.

Linda Greene was Peaches and Herb Fame was Herb on the duet "Reunited," the number eight song of 1979. Greene was the third vocalist to assume the role of "Peaches." Francine Barker was the lead singer of the Sweet Things when she was asked by producer Van McCoy to record a duet with record store clerk Herb Feemster. The original Peaches and Herb were signed to Columbia's Date label and first made the Hot 100 during the last week of 1966 with "Let's Fall In Love." The follow-up, "Close Your Eyes," was the number 88 song of 1967. Francine took a leave of absence in 1968 and was replaced by Marlene Mack. One day in 1970, Herb took an exam for the Washington, D.C. Police Department, and when he was given a job on the force he quit Peaches and Herb. Six years later he felt it was time to bring the duo back. McCoy told Herb about Linda Greene, and she became the new Peaches on an MCA album. Then the duo switched to Polydor and teamed with producer Freddie Perren. An upbeat single, "Shake Your Groove Thing," brought them back to the Hot 100 and ranked number 44 for 1979. "Reunited," a sweet ballad, was released as the follow-up.

Olivia Newton-John had never had a single in the year-end top 10 until 1979, when "A Little More Love" was the number nine song of the year. Her previous year-end high was "You're The One That I Want," her first duet from *Grease* with John Travolta. It was the number 16 song of 1978. Although "A Little More Love" only reached number three, it had a 20-week run on the Hot 100, ranking it higher than some of Olivia's number one hits, including "I Honestly Love You" and "Have You Never Been Mellow."

Dionne Warwick made the year-end top 10 for the second time, although it was her first time as a solo artist. She had the number eight song of 1974 when she teamed up with the Spinners for "Then Came You." Her first single for Arista, the Barry Manilow-produced "I'll Never Love This Way Again," was ranked number 10 for 1979.

The Knack had the number three song of the year with their debut single, "My Sharona." Doug Fieger, who said his life was changed when he saw the Beatles on "The Ed Sullivan Show," was inspired to write the song with Berton Averre after falling deeply in love with a girl named Sharona. The Knack became a hot attraction playing live dates in Southern California—so hot that 13 different labels were bidding for them. Capitol won out and teamed the group with producer Mike Chapman.

Rod Stewart made his third appearance in a year-end top 10 with "Da Ya Think I'm Sexy?" It was the number four song of 1979. His previous top 10 entries were both number one songs of the year: "Maggie May" backed with "Reason To Believe" in 1971 and "Tonight's The Night (Gonna Be Alright)" in 1976.

Rupert Holmes had the number seven song of the year with the final number one song of the '70s, "Escape (Pina Colada Song)." Holmes, who describes his career as "the *Poseidon Adventure* of pop," was born in England to an American G.I. and a British mother. The family moved to Nyack, New York, and Holmes wrote his first song when he was six years old. He formed a rock band, the Nomads, while in high school. He went to work for a music publisher in Manhattan and scored his first success in 1971 when he wrote "Timothy," a strange song about cannibalism recorded by the Buoys. It peaked at number 17 on the Hot 100. Three years later, Holmes was signed as an artist to Epic. He didn't have any hits of his own, but Barry Manilow and Dionne Warwick were among those recording his songs. Along with Jeffrey Lesser, he produced Barbra Streisand's *Lazy Afternoon* album and contributed songs to the soundtrack of *A Star Is Born*. Returning to England, Holmes produced albums for Sparks, the Strawbs, Sailor and John Miles. Back in the States, he signed with Private Stock. His single "Let's Get Crazy Tonight" was moving up the Hot 100 when the label folded. Holmes then signed with Infinity, an MCA-distributed label headed by Ron Alexenburg. "Escape" was moving up the Hot 100 when Infinity folded. This time, momentum was in Holmes' favor. He switched over to MCA and "Escape" kept moving up the chart, not stopping until it reached number one.

1. **ANOTHER ONE BITES THE DUST**
   Queen *Elektra*
2. **CALL ME**
   Blondie *Chrysalis*
3. **DO THAT TO ME ONE MORE TIME**
   Captain & Tennille *Casablanca*
4. **LADY**
   Kenny Rogers *Liberty*
5. **UPSIDE DOWN**
   Diana Ross *Motown*
6. **ANOTHER BRICK IN THE WALL**
   Pink Floyd *Columbia*
7. **ROCK WITH YOU**
   Michael Jackson *Epic*
8. **WOMAN IN LOVE**
   Barbra Streisand *Columbia*
9. **CRAZY LITTLE THING CALLED LOVE**
   Queen *Elektra*
10. **(JUST LIKE) STARTING OVER**
    John Lennon *Geffen*
11. **MAGIC**
    Olivia Newton-John *MCA*
12. **COMING UP (LIVE AT GLASGOW)**
    Paul McCartney & Wings *Columbia*
13. **PLEASE DON'T GO**
    KC & the Sunshine Band *TK*
14. **IT'S STILL ROCK AND ROLL TO ME**
    Billy Joel *Columbia*
15. **FUNKYTOWN**
    Lipps, Inc. *Casablanca*
16. **LITTLE JEANNIE**
    Elton John *MCA*
17. **RIDE LIKE THE WIND**
    Christopher Cross *Warner Bros*
18. **CRUISIN'**
    Smokey Robinson *Tamla*
19. **MASTER BLASTER (JAMMIN')**
    Stevie Wonder *Tamla*
20. **LOST IN LOVE**
    Air Supply *Arista*
21. **ALL OUT OF LOVE**
    Air Supply *Arista*
22. **MORE THAN I CAN SAY**
    Leo Sayer *Warner Bros*
23. **THE ROSE**
    Bette Midler *Atlantic*
24. **WORKING MY WAY BACK TO YOU/ FORGIVE ME, GIRL**
    Spinners *Atlantic*
25. **COWARD OF THE COUNTY**
    Kenny Rogers *UA*
26. **SEXY EYES**
    Dr. Hook *Capitol*
27. **BIGGEST PART OF ME**
    Ambrosia *20th Century*
28. **CUPID/I'VE LOVED YOU FOR A LONG TIME**
    Spinners *Atlantic*
29. **EMOTIONAL RESCUE**
    The Rolling Stones *Rolling Stones*
30. **HUNGRY HEART**
    Bruce Springsteen *Columbia*

The Spinners

1980 was the year of the *Urban Cowboy*; Pink Floyd built *The Wall*; and John Lennon was murdered in front of his apartment building in New York City.

Prince Rogers Nelson made his debut on a year-end chart with "I Wanna Be Your Lover," listed at number 91. Born in 1958, he became interested in music at the age of five and was proficient in piano by the time he was eight. A James Brown concert in 1968 was a strong influence on him, and in junior high he formed a band, Grand Central, with his cousin Charles Smith and Andre Cymone. In high school the band became Champagne. In 1977 Prince was signed to Warner Brothers after the label agreed he could produce himself. His first chart single, "Soft And Wet," peaked at number 92 in November, 1978. A year later, "I Wanna Be Your Lover" entered the Hot 100 and peaked at number 11.

Another newcomer was Christopher Cross, with two songs listed in the top 100 of 1980: "Ride Like The Wind" (number 17) and "Sailing" (number 38). Born Christopher Geppert in San Antonio, Texas, he formed a local band called Flash and by 1972 they were the top group in town. A year later Cross quit the group to focus on his songwriting. As early as 1975, Cross was sending audition tapes to Warner Brothers Records in Burbank, but with no interest from the label. In October of 1978, Michael Ostin of Warner Brothers' A&R staff saw Cross perform in Austin and helped sign him to the company. Producer Michael Omartian was assigned to work with Cross, and his debut album featured stellar guests like Michael McDonald, Don Henley, Nicolette Larson and J.D. Souther.

Also making their year-end chart debut in 1980 were the Australian duo known as Air Supply. "Lost In Love" was number 20 for the year and "All Out Of Love" was number 21. Graham Russell was born in Sherwood, Nottingham, England. His father and new stepmother moved to Australia when he was 13, but Graham ran away from home and didn't join them in Melbourne until three years later. He won a part in the chorus of *Jesus Christ, Superstar* and met fellow cast member Russell Hitchcock. They had a top three hit in Australia with "Love And Other Bruises." They opened for Rod Stewart in tours of Australia and the U.S. before Arista picked up "Lost In Love" for release in America.

The number one song of 1980 was "Another One Bites The Dust" by Queen, who were also in the year-end top 10 with "Crazy Little Thing Called Love" (number nine). Queen was only the third British group to have a number one song of the year in America, the others being the Beatles and the Rolling Stones.

Debbie Harry sang lead vocals on the number two song of the year, "Call Me." The Blondie tune was heard in the soundtrack of *American Gigolo*, starring Richard Gere. Producer Giorgio Moroder originally wanted Stevie Nicks of Fleetwood Mac to perform the tune. When she passed on it, Moroder turned to Harry, who agreed to write the lyrics. She viewed a rough cut of the film on video. "I went home and wrote the song immediately," she recalls. Neither Moroder nor director Paul Schrader restricted her creative freedom. The instrumental track was already recorded, and Harry only took a couple of hours to lay down her vocals, including the harmonies.

The Captain & Tennille equaled the mark they set in 1975 with "Love Will Keep Us Together" when they once again had the number three song of the year. "Do That To Me One More Time" was their debut single for Casablanca after a long run on A&M. Daryl Dragon and Toni Tennille first saw the end of their association with A&M coming at the company Christmas party. Toni was talking with Karen Carpenter, who complained that the label was forgetting "what made most of its money" in favor of a new wave of British artists. "We felt they weren't interested in what we were doing," Tennille explains. Toni and Daryl had met Casablanca founder Neil Bogart about a year before they left A&M at a dinner party arranged by Norman Brokaw, their agent at William Morris. Bogart wanted to expand Casablanca beyond its image as a disco label and thought the Captain & Tennille would bring the company some attention in the adult contemporary market. After signing with Casablanca, Bogart and label vice president Bruce Bird visited the couple in their Pacific Palisades home. "I had finished 'Do That To Me One More Time' and thought it was just a little tune—kind of nice, but it wasn't any big deal," Toni notes. "We played all the other things we had in mind, including some songs that were more powerful." Neil told them that the "little tune" was a smash and should be their first single. It became their second number one hit, and although it only spent one week at the top, it was on the Hot 100 for 27 weeks, good enough to rank it in the top 50 songs of the rock era.

Kenny Rogers, who first made a year-end chart in 1968 with the First Edition's "Ruby, Don't Take Your Love To Town" (number 91 for that year), had his most successful chart single in 1980. "Lady" ranked number four for the year. The song was written for Rogers by Lionel Richie. "I was about to explode," Rogers explained in *Billboard*. "I needed new input and that's where Lionel came in. I went to who I thought was the very best in the field." Richie flew to Las Vegas to meet with Rogers and played demos of "Lady" and "Goin' Back To Alabama." Both songs were recorded in eight-and-a-half hours. Rogers had two other songs on the year-end chart, both predecessors to "Lady." "Coward Of The County" was number 25 and "Don't Fall In Love With A Dreamer," a duet with Kim Carnes, was number 32.

Ranked number five for 1980 was "Upside Down" by Diana Ross, her most successful solo chart single. It was also one of her most controversial, as word leaked out about her displeasure with how Bernard Edwards and Nile Rodgers had produced the track. She felt her vocals were not prominent enough and wanted them brought forward. After asking them to remix the album they had produced for her, Diana was still not satisfied and mixed it again with assistance from Motown producer Russ Terrana. Rodgers told of his dismay in *Billboard*. "I was shocked. I was furious and got on the phone right away and called Motown. I was asked to listen to the album and then talk to Diana. I calmed down and listened to the album about 10 times. Then I had to say, 'Hey! I know where they're coming from. I understand what they're doing.' But initially I was not prepared for that kind of shock. I'm not as happy as I would be if it was the way we mixed it, but I'm happy with the album because Diana is happy with it."

Pink Floyd had their first and only year-end top 10 single with "Another Brick In The Wall," the number six single of 1980. Despite a run of successful albums, including the sturdy *Dark Side of the Moon*, Pink Floyd had only had one chart single prior to "Another Brick In The Wall." That was "Money," a track from *Dark Side* that peaked at number 13 in 1973.

Michael Jackson gave a hint of his chart dominance to come by placing "Rock With You" in the number seven position. The second number one hit from his *Off the Wall* album, it was written by Rod Temperton, formerly of Heatwave ("Boogie Nights"). The first number one single from the LP, "Don't Stop 'Til You Get Enough," had ranked number 50 for 1979. Two other songs from the album were on the list for 1980: "She's Out Of My Life" was number 77 and "Off The Wall" was number 90.

Barbra Streisand had her third year-end top 10 single with "Woman In Love," written by Barry and Robin Gibb.

John Lennon's posthumous number one song, "(Just Like) Starting Over," was the number 10 single of 1980.

THE TOP 100 SONGS OF
1981

Juice Newton

1981 was the year Bill Haley died in Texas; Bob Marley succumbed to cancer in Miami; and Harry Chapin was killed in an automobile accident on the Long Island Expressway.

Some long-absent artists returned to the year-end chart in 1981. Gary U.S. Bonds was listed for the first time since "Dear Lady Twist" and "Twist, Twist Senora" in 1962. The seeds of Bonds' return were sown in 1978 while he was playing the Red Baron club in New Jersey. A local guy who seemed pretty popular was in the audience, and Gary thought he'd give him a break by calling him up on stage. He had no idea who Bruce Springsteen was, but they sang a duet on "Quarter To Three," a song Bruce used as an encore in his own act. They remained in touch and Bruce asked Gary if they could work on an album together. Two years later, after completing *The River*, Springsteen kept his word and with Miami Steve Van Zandt, produced *Dedication*. The first single, "This Little Girl," ranked number 63 for the year.

The Moody Blues just eked on to the 1981 year-end chart with "Gemini Dream," number 100 for the year. It was their first year-end appearance since "Nights In White Satin" in 1972.

For the first time in the rock era, the top two songs of the year were by female vocalists. Olivia Newton-John had the number one song of 1981 with "Physical" and Kim Carnes was number two with "Bette Davis Eyes." Olivia's song was written by Steve Kipner and Terry Shaddick. Kipner recalls how the creative muse struck while he was driving to his manager's office: "I was at the corner of Fairfax and Sunset and it was the first time I sang, 'let's get physical.'" Kipner went running up to his manager's office, thinking he had come up with a good song for Rod Stewart.

Kim's song was written by Jackie DeShannon and Donna Weiss. Jackie recorded it on her 1975 album for Columbia, *New Arrangement*. Carnes' producer, George Tobin, gave Kim the song but she thought it wasn't a hit. When Carnes teamed up with a new producer, Val Garay, Weiss sent her the song again. Kim Carnes told Dick Clark who should get the credit for the new arrangement of "Bette Davis Eyes." "It's Bill Cuomo, my synthesizer player, who really came up with the new . . . feel, changing the chords. The minute he came up with that, it fell into place."

Diana Ross and Lionel Richie teamed up for "Endless Love," the number three song of 1981. The record also ranks as the most successful Motown chart single, the most successful duet and the third most successful soundtrack song of the rock era.

Rick Springfield made his first appearance on a year-end chart with "Jessie's Girl," his debut for RCA after charting on Capitol, Columbia and Chelsea. Born in Sydney and raised in Melbourne, he joined a succession of bands, including Rock House, Wackedy Wak and Zoot. That last group charted in Australia with "Speak To The Sky," and Rick recorded a new, solo version for America. Signed to a contract by Universal Studios, he had guest starring roles in "The Six Million Dollar Man," "The Rockford Files" and "The Incredible Hulk" before joining the cast of "The Young And The Restless." He was a regular in "General Hospital" when RCA released "Jessie's Girl," and his soap popularity helped the record sail to number one on the Hot 100. It ranked number four for the year.

Kool & the Gang were number five for 1981 with "Celebration," a song used to welcome home the American hostages held in Iran for 444 days. It was also the theme song for the 1981 Superbowl, and the first number one single for the group that had been together for 17 years. After a low point in 1978, Robert "Kool" Bell recruited James "J.T." Taylor to become the group's lead singer. A chance meeting with producer Eumir Deodato ("Also Sprach Zarathustra") led to the band's resurgence on the Hot 100. Bell talked about the origin of "Celebration" in the *Los Angeles Herald Examiner*. "The Bible describes life as a celebration and the idea came from our celebration of our return to the music business."

"Waiting For A Girl Like You," the song that remained at number two longer than any other in the rock era, ranked number six for the year. Foreigner spent 10 weeks in the runner-up spot on the Hot 100, most of that time behind "Physical." The Anglo-American outfit was formed by British musician Mick Jones. He heard two albums by a band called Black Sheep and invited their lead singer, Lou Gramm, to join Foreigner. Rick Wills and Dennis

Elliott were the other members of the quartet when "Waiting For A Girl Like You" was released.

Virginia-born Judy Cohen became Juice Newton and formed a couple of bands before recording on her own. With Otha Young, she organized Dixie Peach in 1971. The following year they formed Silver Spur. They were signed to RCA in 1975 and made the country singles chart in 1976 with "Love Is A Word." After two albums they moved to Capitol. Newton went solo in 1978 and had her first single on the pop chart, "It's A Heartache." Bonnie Tyler had the hit version while Newton stalled at number 86. She covered several pop songs and made the country charts with "Lay Back In The Arms Of Someone," "Any Way That You Want Me" and "Sunshine" before returning to the Hot 100 with a remake of Merilee Rush & the Turnabouts' "Angel Of The Morning," the number 39 song of 1981. Her next chart single was a cover of "Queen Of Hearts," written by Hank DeVito and first recorded by Dave Edmunds on his *Repeat When Necessary* album. "Queen Of Hearts" spent two weeks at number two and remained on the Hot 100 for 27 weeks. It was number seven for the year.

Daryl Hall and John Oates had their first year-end top 10 single in 1981 with "Kiss On My List," number eight for the year. They first appeared on a year-end chart in 1976, when "Sara Smile" was number 19 for the year and "She's Gone" was number 57. The following year, "Rich Girl" was number 21, and in 1980 they were number 44 for the year with their remake of "You've Lost That Lovin' Feelin'." "Kiss On My List" was the third single from their breakthrough album, *Voices*. Co-writer Jana Allen, younger sister of Daryl's girlfriend Sara, had never written a song before. She had some lyrics and music and sat down at a borrowed Wurlitzer with Daryl to finish the song. Oates pointed out that most people misunderstood the words, thinking they were singing "Kiss On My Lips." Hall and Oates had two more songs on the year-end chart for 1981: "Private Eyes" was number 18 and "You Make My Dreams" was number 57.

REO Speedwagon, named for the 1911 fire truck designed by Ransom Eli Olds, had their first year-end top 10 hit with "Keep On Loving You," the number nine song of the year. It was their first single to make the top 50 portion of the Hot 100. The band was already rolling when Kevin Cronin, lead singer and writer of "Keep On Loving You," joined. After their first album, guitarist Gary Richrath anonymously called the Musicians Referral Service in Chicago looking for a new lead vocalist. Cronin had started the service to help bands searching for musicians. Cronin told Richrath to come to his apartment to meet a new lead singer, and when he arrived Cronin sang an Elton John song and handed him a demo tape. Within a week, Cronin was the new lead singer of REO Speedwagon.

Neil Diamond had the number 10 song of 1981 with "Love On The Rocks," the first single from his soundtrack to *The Jazz Singer*. It is Diamond's only year-end top 10 single.

Toni Basil

1982 was the year E.T. phoned home; Trivial Pursuit was introduced; and the American media had a field day with Boy George.

For the first time since 1970, the top four songs of the year were by American artists. Survivor led the pack with "Eye Of The Tiger," from the soundtrack of *Rocky III*. It was the fourth number one song of the year to come from a movie, following "To Sir With Love," "Raindrops Keep Fallin' On My Head" and "The Way We Were."

The theme song from the first *Rocky* film, Bill Conti's "Gonna Fly Now," had ranked number 26 in 1977. Sylvester Stallone wanted a more rock-oriented theme for his third movie about the heavyweight champ. First he considered Queen's "Another One Bites The Dust," then he decided to commission a new song. Tony Scotti, one of the founders of the Scotti Brothers label, had issued a single by Frank Stallone. When he heard that brother Sly was looking for new material, he played Survivor's *Premonition* album for him. "Sylvester liked the beat and the drive of our music so he let us have a shot at writing the theme," Jim Peterik said in the *Los Angeles Times*. Stallone gave Peterik and Frankie Sullivan a video copy of the movie but little guidance as to what kind of song to write, other than telling them he wanted a strong beat and contemporary theme. Within 90 minutes of seeing the rough cut, they focused on the phrase "eye of the tiger" and wrote the first draft of the song that would top the Hot 100 for six weeks.

Coming in second place for the year was "Centerfold" by the J. Geils Band. The group solidified when former DJ Peter Wolf and drummer Stephen Jo Bladd teamed up with a Boston-based trio led by guitarist Jerome Geils in 1967. Keyboardist Seth Justman joined a year later. They signed with Atlantic in 1969 and turned down a chance to appear at Woodstock. "Three days in the mud, who needs it? That's where we were at," Wolf told Jeff Tamarkin in *Goldmine.* In 1978 the band switched to the new EMI-America label. "Centerfold" was their 12th chart single, and although they had never made the top 10 before, it shot to number one and remained there for six weeks.

John Cougar had his first year-end chart single in 1981 when "Ain't Even Done With The Night" was the number 91 song of the year. In 1982 he became the first American male solo artist since Elvis Presley and Chubby Checker to have two songs in the year-end top 10. "Hurts So Good" ranked number three and "Jack And Diane" was number 10. Born John Mellencamp in Seymour, Indiana, he was—much to his surprise—renamed Johnny Cougar by his first manager, Tony DeFries. Dropped from MCA, Mellencamp signed to Riva, a label formed by his new manager, Billy Gaff. He had only moderate chart success until the 1982 release of his *American Fool* album. The first single, "Hurts So Good," spent four weeks at number two and 28 weeks on the Hot 100. "Jack And Diane" was released so quickly, it was in the top 10 at the same time as "Hurts So Good." "Jack And Diane" spent four weeks at number one and 22 weeks on the Hot 100.

Steve Miller matched the high mark he had set in 1974 when "The Joker" was the number four song of the year. "Abracadabra" ranked fourth for 1982. It is Miller's most successful chart single of all time, number 69 on the top 3000.

"Don't You Want Me" by the Human League was the highest-ranked British single of 1982, number five for the year. The first edition of Human League had formed in Sheffield, England, in 1977. Ian Craig Marsh and Martin Ware teamed with vocalist Phil Oakey and took the name Human League from a computer game. In October of 1980, Ware and Marsh split to form the British Electric Foundation and an offshoot, Heaven 17. Oakey and Adrian Wright put together a revised version of the Human League. The band is credited with paving the way in America for a new wave British invasion, allowing groups like Culture Club, Dexys Midnight Runners and Duran Duran to chart.

Stevie Wonder returned to the year-end top 10 for the first time since his debut chart single, "Fingertips—Pt. 2," was the number nine song of 1963. He did it by pairing with Paul McCartney on "Ebony And Ivory," a song that "is supposed to say that people of all types could live together," according to McCartney. "It's just an idea that I had heard someone say once, you know the keyboard thing, you can play using just the black notes, or you can play using just the white notes, but combining them gives you great notes. That, I suppose, is a great analogy." Paul got word to Stevie through former Motown staffer Irv Beigel that he wanted to record together. Stevie suggested a tape be forwarded to his assistant. "I listened to the song and liked it very much," Wonder told Dick Clark. The two superstars met on the island of Montserrat in the West Indies to record "Ebony And Ivory," although the subsequent video found them recording their roles in separate locations.

Laura Branigan had her first year-end chart single with "Gloria," the number seven song of 1982. Educated at the Academy of Dramatic Arts in New York, Branigan, a former back-up singer for Leonard Cohen, was performing at Reno Sweeney's in Manhattan when Atlantic Records founder Ahmet Ertegun caught her act. "I was doing Barry Manilow songs, Edith Piaf numbers, things like that, plus some of my own material," Branigan told Todd Everett. "The other record company people seemed to think that I didn't fit in anywhere. Ahmet, I think, appreciated the fact that I had a real voice and wasn't a gimmick. I remember him saying that I had so much emotion in my voice." Once signed to Atlantic, Branigan was introduced to producer Jack White. He brought her "Gloria." "It was originally an Italian song recorded by Umberto Tozzi and sold 30 million copies in Europe," Branigan told Simon Tebbutt. "I liked it but I thought it was too European. So the lyrics were rewritten." Branigan elaborated in *Billboard*: "We took basically the same arrangement and just gave it that American kick. The Italian version is structurally the same but much softer; mine has more guts and a lot more punch." The song debuted on the Hot 100 on July 10 and began a slow climb. It peaked at number two in its 23rd week on the chart, and spent a total of 36 weeks on the survey.

The number eight song of 1982 was "I Love Rock 'n Roll" by Joan Jett & the Blackhearts. It was the debut chart single for Jett, a member of the female rock band the Runaways from 1975-78. While touring England with the Runaways, Joan saw the Anglo-American band the Arrows perform "I Love Rock 'n Roll" on their British TV series. The song was written by Jake Hooker and Alan Merrill of the group as a protest to the Rolling Stones "It's Only Rock 'n Roll (But I Like It)." Jett asked Hooker if she could cover the song, and he responded that she would do a better job than he did. But she couldn't convince the Runaways to record the tune, and had to wait until she was on her own to cut it. An early version was released as the flip side of a Dutch single, an updating of Lesley Gore's "You Don't Own Me." Jett recorded it a second time with the Blackhearts for release on Neil Bogart's Boardwalk Records. It spent seven weeks at number one.

Daryl Hall and John Oates were in the year-end top 10 for the second consecutive year. "Maneater," a song reminiscent of the Supremes' "You Can't Hurry Love," was the number nine single of 1982.

THE TOP 100 SONGS OF
1983

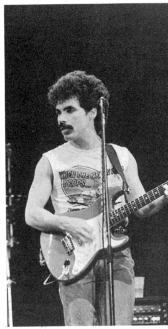

Hall & Oates

1983 was the year that compact discs were first sold in record stores; Jennifer Beals inspired women to tear their T-shirts; and Karen Carpenter died of cardiac arrest.

Michael Jackson had six titles on the year-end chart. Only the Beatles had more, when they placed 10 songs in the top 100 of 1964. Three of Michael's 1983 hits were in the year-end top 10. He is the only artist aside from Elvis Presley and the Beatles to have three songs in the top 10 of a year.

Michael's top-rated single of 1983 was "Say, Say, Say," his duet with Paul McCartney. Jackson contacted McCartney by telephone on Christmas Day, but the former Beatle didn't believe it was really Michael calling. When he finally convinced him, Michael told Paul he was coming to England and wanted to write some songs with Paul. The first record they released together was "The Girl Is Mine," the initial single from Michael's *Thriller* album. It was the number 36 song of 1983. Two more McCartney-Jackson collaborations appeared on Paul's *Pipes of Peace* album. "The Man" wasn't released as a single, but "Say, Say, Say" was. It was number one for six weeks and ranked number three for the year. Just one notch below it was "Billie Jean," the second single from *Thriller*. It was number one for seven weeks. Its follow-up, "Beat It," was number one for three weeks and ranked number seven for the year.

Michael's other year-end singles were "Wanna Be Startin' Somethin'" at number 60 and "Human Nature" at number 77.

The Police had the number 100 song of 1982, "Spirits In The Material World." In 1983, they appeared at the exact opposite end of the chart. Their single "Every Breath You Take" was the number one record of the year. That made them the fourth British group to have a number one song of the year, following the Beatles, the Rolling Stones and Queen. As Sting told Christopher Connelly in *Rolling Stone*, the song was not meant to be a sweet love song. "I consider it a fairly nasty song. It's about surveillance and ownership and jealousy."

The Anglo-American Police were part of the most successful year ever for U.K. artists. There were 33 songs in the year-end top 100 from the British Isles, breaking the record set in 1965. Aside from the Police and Paul McCartney, the other U.K. artist in the top 10 was Bonnie Tyler. She was born in Skewen, South Wales. After winning a local talent contest when she was 17, she quit her job as a candy store clerk to sing in Welsh nightclubs. A year-and-a-half later she developed nodules on her throat. They disappeared, but recurred twice until she had them surgically removed. That left her with a husky voice that reminded some of a female Rod Stewart. In 1978 she broke through in America with "It's A Heartache," which peaked at number three on the Hot 100 and was ranked number 36 for the year. But she tired of recording material written and produced by her managers and split from them. Under new management and signed with CBS Records, she expressed her wish to work with producer Jim Steinman (*Bat Out of Hell* for Meatloaf). He was busy with a film project and declined. Later, he surprised Bonnie when he called out of the blue and asked if she was still looking for a producer. She was invited to fly to New York and meet him in his apartment. There he played "Total Eclipse Of The Heart" for her on his grand piano. "When he plays he practically knocks it through the floor, he's incredible!" Bonnie gushed. After "Total Eclipse" went to number one on the U.K. singles chart, Columbia Records waited several months before releasing it in the States. They were rewarded with a song that topped the Hot 100 for four weeks and ranked number six for the year.

The most successful American single of 1983 was "Flashdance . . . What A Feeling" by Irene Cara. She had the number 53 song of 1980 with another motion picture theme song, "Fame." The Oscar-winning *Flashdance* theme was written by Cara and Keith Forsey while they were driving to a recording session. Cara hesitated from using Giorgio Moroder as a producer because she didn't want "flack" for using Donna Summer's producer. When critics compared Cara to the disco diva, she responded that such criticism was sexist. "There are so many records made by male artists today that sound alike. But nobody makes an issue of that," Cara said in *Songwriter Connection*. "Flashdance . . . What A Feeling," a song that never actually mentioned the word "flashdance" in the lyrics, was the number two record of 1983.

Lionel Richie was back in the year-end top 10 for the first time since "Endless Love" was the number three song of 1981. "All Night Long (All Night)" ranked in fifth place for the year. Lionel was worried about getting the right words for the Jamaican chant heard in the song and checked them out with his wife's Jamaican gynecologist.

"Down Under," the second most successful Australian single of the rock era, was the number eight song of the year. That bettered the mark set by Men at Work with their first single in 1982, "Who Can It Be Now," which ranked number 12. When Colin Hay and Ron Strykert first wrote "Down Under," producer Peter McIan felt it wasn't commercial. He took their simple flute and guitar arrangement and added more instruments to give it a reggae sound. Still, the Aussie lyrics left a memorable imprint. Americans even learned what vegemite sandwiches were. Men at Work had two other singles listed on the year-end top 100: "Overkill" was number 41 and "It's A Mistake" was number 71.

Dolly Parton was in the year-end top 10 for the first time, thanks to "Islands In The Stream," her duet with Kenny Rogers co-written and produced by Barry Gibb. Dolly's first year-end appearance was "Here You Come Again," the number 49 song of 1978. She just missed the top 10 in 1981 when the movie title theme "9 to 5" ranked number 11 for the year. Parton was the fourth female singer to chart in a duet with Kenny Rogers. He had already teamed with Kim Carnes ("Don't Fall In Love With A Dreamer"), Dottie West ("What Are We Doin' In Love") and Sheena Easton ("We've Got Tonight"). "Islands In The Stream" was Rogers' first single for RCA after a long run of hits on United Artists and Liberty.

Bob Seger, a native of Dearborn, Michigan, first appeared on a year-end chart in 1977 with "Night Moves," the number 70 song of that year. He made the year-end top 10 for the first time in 1983 with his remake of Rodney Crowell's "Shame On The Moon," the number 10 single of the year. He explained how he came to record the song: "Don Henley turned me on to Crowell, who he was listening to a lot, in 1980, but I didn't buy one of his records until '82. When I heard 'Shame On The Moon,' I just stopped and thought, 'Wow, this is a *great* song!' I played it for everyone in the band, and they said, 'Sure, let's do it.' We took it into the studio, and (producer) Jimmy Iovine didn't quite hear it at first, until he heard Glenn Frey and I do the back-up vocals, and then he decided it was a monster. It's more like a western song—a cowboy song—than it is a country and western song. And the track is *flawless*, the best and tightest track on the album. We cut it in like two hours, and everyone decided it was the miracle track. But then we had to decide whether to use it or not because *The Distance* was going to be a real rock album. . . . The next thing we know, the Capitol guys are saying, 'That's the single!'. . . . So thank you, Rodney. It's a great song and I'm beholden to the lad for writing it."

1 WHEN DOVES CRY
Prince *Warner Bros*

2 WHAT'S LOVE GOT TO DO WITH IT
Tina Turner *Capitol*

3 JUMP
Van Halen *Warner Bros*

4 KARMA CHAMELEON
Culture Club *Epic/Virgin*

5 LIKE A VIRGIN
Madonna *Sire*

6 HELLO
Lionel Richie *Motown*

7 OWNER OF A LONELY HEART
Yes *Atco*

8 AGAINST ALL ODDS
(TAKE A LOOK AT ME NOW)
Phil Collins *Atlantic*

9 FOOTLOOSE
Kenny Loggins *Columbia*

10 GHOSTBUSTERS
Ray Parker Jr. *Arista*

11 I JUST CALLED TO SAY I LOVE YOU
Stevie Wonder *Tamla*

12 OUT OF TOUCH
Daryl Hall & John Oates *RCA*

13 WAKE ME UP BEFORE YOU GO-GO
Wham! *Columbia*

14 I FEEL FOR YOU
Chaka Khan *Warner Bros*

15 MISSING YOU
John Waite *EMI America*

16 LET'S HEAR IT FOR THE BOY
Deniece Williams *Columbia*

17 TIME AFTER TIME
Cyndi Lauper *Portrait*

18 THE REFLEX
Duran Duran *Capitol*

19 DANCING IN THE DARK
Bruce Springsteen *Columbia*

20 CARIBBEAN QUEEN
(NO MORE LOVE ON THE RUN)
Billy Ocean *Jive*

21 TALKING IN YOUR SLEEP
The Romantics *Nemperor*

22 HARD HABIT TO BREAK
Chicago *Full Moon*

23 LET'S GO CRAZY
Prince & the Revolution *Warner Bros*

24 SELF CONTROL
Laura Branigan *Atlantic*

25 THE WILD BOYS
Duran Duran *Capitol*

26 HOLD ME NOW
Thompson Twins *Arista*

27 JUMP (FOR MY LOVE)
Pointer Sisters *Planet*

28 JOANNA
Kool & the Gang *De-Lite*

29 BREAK MY STRIDE
Matthew Wilder *Private I*

30 THE GLAMOROUS LIFE
Sheila E. *Warner Bros*

Cyndi Lauper

1984 was the year Ray Parker Jr. said he ain't afraid of no ghosts; Pink Floyd's *Dark Side of the Moon* passed the 500-week mark on the *Billboard* album chart; and Marvin Gaye was shot dead by his father on April 1.

Making her first appearance on a year-end chart, Madonna had three titles included in the top 100 songs of the year. "Like A Virgin," the number five song of the year, is her highest ranking on a year-end chart. "Borderline" was number 52 for the year and "Lucky Star" was number 62.

Another female singer who made her debut year-end appearance in 1984 was Cyndi Lauper, who was listed with her first four singles. Born in Queens, Cyndi grew up not understanding the creativity burning in her and thought she was crazy or stupid. After a difficult time in high school, she left home and hitchhiked through Canada with her dog Sparkle. She settled down at a Vermont college to study art, but didn't find her creative needs fulfilled. She returned home and sang with a couple of bands until her voice gave out. Doctors told her she would never sing again, but after working with a vocal coach for a year, her voice returned. With musician John Turi, she formed a group called Blue Angel in 1978. After their debut album for Polydor was released, the band broke up. Cyndi was singing in a Japanese piano bar and working in a clothing boutique when she met Dave Wolff, who became her boyfriend and manager. The song that introduced her to the world was "Girls Just Want To Have Fun," number 45 for the year. The follow-up, "Time After Time," was number 17. Her next single, "She Bop," ranked number 36. Her fourth single, "All Through The Night," was number 57.

The biggest comeback of the year was made by Tina Turner, who triumphed over personal adversity and achieved her greatest chart success. She had first appeared on the Hot 100 in the summer of 1960 coupled with her husband Ike on "A Fool In Love." According to Tina, the marriage started to decay after the first seven years. "I didn't plan to leave, but finally there was one last bit of real violence and I walked," she said in *USA Today*. With 36 cents, a gasoline credit card and the clothes she was wearing, she checked in to a Ramada Inn in Dallas where the manager gave her the best suite in the house. She called her friend Ann-Margret and asked her to buy an airline ticket so Tina could fly to Los Angeles. She stayed with Ann-Margret for six months while Ike searched for her. They were divorced in 1976. Tina's recording career was revived when the British band Heaven 17 asked her to participate in an album project. They produced her singing the Temptations' "Ball Of Confusion." She signed with Capitol Records and Heaven 17 produced her first single, a remake of Al Green's "Let's Stay Together." For her first Capitol album, manager Roger Davies assembled several producers. One of them was British songwriter Terry Britten. Tina heard the demo of a song he had written with Graham Lyle and hated it. Britten said he would arrange it to suit her, and "What's Love Got To Do With It" brought her to the top of the Hot 100 for the first time. It was the number two song of 1984. The follow-up, "Better Be Good To Me," ranked number 48.

"When Doves Cry" by Prince was the number one single of the year. It was the fifth song from a motion picture to top a year-end chart. It was the initial single from the soundtrack of *Purple Rain*, dubbed "the best rock film ever made" by critic Mikal Gilmore in the *Los Angeles Herald Examiner*. Sneaking in to a preview of the movie in San Diego, Gilmore wrote: "Prince fills the screen like the threat and promise that he is, inspiring the audiences in San Diego to the kind of uncalculated sexual hysteria I haven't heard since the Beatles tore across the opening frames of *A Hard Day's Night*."

The Southern California-based rock group Van Halen made their first year-end appearance in 1982, when they were listed at number 89 with "(Oh) Pretty Woman," a remake of the Roy Orbison song. In 1984 they had the biggest hit of their career. "Jump" was number one for five weeks and was ranked number three for the year. The music for "Jump" was written by Eddie Van Halen two years before David Lee Roth agreed to write lyrics and record the song. "Eddie wrote this thing on synthesizer," says producer Ted Templeman. "I really hadn't heard it for a long time, then he laid it down one night in the studio. . . . I heard it and it just killed me. It was perfect." Roth wrote the words in the backseat of a 1951 Mercury lowrider while cruising one afternoon through Los Angeles with one of the band's roadies. "Every hour and a half or so, I'd lean over the front seat and say, 'Lar, what do you think of this?' He's probably the most responsible for how it came out," Roth said in *Musician*.

Culture Club, the British band once known as In Praise of Lemmings and then the Sex Gang Children before Boy George renamed them, made their mark in America in 1983 with four singles on the year-end chart: "Do You Really Want To Hurt Me" (number 21), "Time (Clock Of The Heart)" (number 30), "Church Of The Poison Mind" (number 67) and "I'll Tumble 4 Ya" (number 78). Their fifth single, "Karma Chameleon," became their biggest hit, and was the number four song of 1984. The follow-up, "Miss Me Blind," ranked number 60 for the year.

"Hello," a song written for Lionel Richie's first solo album but not included, finally made it onto his second LP and became the number six song of 1984.

The British progressive rock group Yes had their first year-end chart hit 13 years after their debut single. The 1984 incarnation of the band started out as a group called Cinema, but by the time they added vocalist Jon Anderson there were so many former members of Yes in the band they realized they had accidentally reformed the group. "Owner Of A Lonely Heart" returned them to the Hot 100 after a long absence and was the number seven single of the year.

In addition to Prince's "When Doves Cry," there were three other soundtrack singles in the top 10. Phil Collins had his first number one hit with the title song from Taylor Hackford's *Against All Odds*. Hackford had to convince Collins to record a song for his film. He flew to Chicago to meet Phil after a Genesis concert. Hackford screened the movie for Collins in a hotel room and the drummer/vocalist agreed to write the title song, which was number eight for the year.

Kenny Loggins was ranked number nine with the title song from *Footloose*, written by Loggins and Dean Pitchford. Pitchford, who wrote the screenplay for the movie, wanted Loggins to perform the main title theme right from the beginning of the project. "It felt to me he was like the voice of the country," Pitchford explains. Three other songs from *Footloose* were included in the top 100 songs of the year: "Let's Hear It For The Boy" by Deniece Williams (number 16), "Almost Paradise" by Mike Reno and Ann Wilson (number 63) and "Dancing In The Sheets" by Shalamar (number 93).

Ray Parker Jr. had the number 10 song of 1984 with the title song from *Ghostbusters*. The most difficult problem in writing the song, Parker said in *USA Today*, was finding a word to rhyme with "ghostbusters." "I figured the best thing to do was to have somebody shout, 'Ghostbusters!' In order for that to work, I had to have something before or after it. That's when I came up with the line, 'Who you gonna call?'"

1 CARELESS WHISPER
Wham! f/George Michael *Columbia*

2 SAY YOU, SAY ME
Lionel Richie *Motown*

3 SEPARATE LIVES
Phil Collins and Marilyn Martin *Atlantic*

4 I WANT TO KNOW WHAT LOVE IS
Foreigner *Atlantic*

5 MONEY FOR NOTHING
Dire Straits *Warner Bros*

6 WE ARE THE WORLD
USA for Africa *Columbia*

7 BROKEN WINGS
Mr. Mister *RCA*

8 EVERYBODY WANTS TO RULE THE WORLD
Tears for Fears *Mercury*

9 THE POWER OF LOVE
Huey Lewis & the News *Chrysalis*

10 WE BUILT THIS CITY
Starship *Grunt*

11 ST. ELMO'S FIRE (MAN IN MOTION)
John Parr *Atlantic*

12 CAN'T FIGHT THIS FEELING
REO Speedwagon *Epic*

13 CRAZY FOR YOU
Madonna *Geffen*

14 EASY LOVER
Philip Bailey w/Phil Collins *Columbia*

15 EVERYTIME YOU GO AWAY
Paul Young *Columbia*

16 DON'T YOU (FORGET ABOUT ME)
Simple Minds *A&M*

17 TAKE ON ME
a-ha *Warner Bros*

18 PARTY ALL THE TIME
Eddie Murphy *Columbia*

19 EVERYTHING SHE WANTS
Wham! *Columbia*

20 SHOUT
Tears for Fears *Mercury*

21 ALIVE AND KICKING
Simple Minds *A&M*

22 I MISS YOU
Klymaxx *Constellation*

23 SEA OF LOVE
The Honeydrippers *Es Paranza*

24 COOL IT NOW
New Edition *MCA*

25 PART-TIME LOVER
Stevie Wonder *Tamla*

26 SAVING ALL MY LOVE FOR YOU
Whitney Houston *Arista*

27 SUSSUDIO
Phil Collins *Atlantic*

28 OH SHEILA
Ready for the World *MCA*

29 A VIEW TO A KILL
Duran Duran *Capitol*

30 ONE MORE NIGHT
Phil Collins *Atlantic*

Mr. Mister

1985 was the year Quincy Jones produced "We Are The World" to help feed millions of starving people in Africa and in America; Bob Geldof organized the Live Aid concert to help end the famine in Ethiopia; and Wham! became the first rock group to tour China.

With two singles included in the top 100 songs of the year, Whitney Houston made her first appearance on a year-end chart. Her debut single, "You Give Good Love," was number 55 for the year and the follow-up, "Saving All My Love For You," ranked number 26.

There were 33 titles on the top 100 by artists from the United Kingdom, matching the record set in 1983. That included the number one song of the year, "Careless Whisper" by Wham! featuring George Michael. It was the 10th U.K. single to be the number one record of the year in the rock era. Released in Britain as a solo single by George, it was written when he was 16. Employed as an usher at a cinema in his hometown of Bushey, he was bored with his job and spent his time writing lyrics. He thought up the melody to "Careless Whisper" while riding on a bus.

Phil Collins was responsible for five of the U.K. titles in the top 100 of 1984. Highest-ranked was his duet with Marilyn Martin on Stephen Bishop's song "Separate Lives." The song was composed after Taylor Hackford explained the plot of *White Nights* to Bishop in 1982. When the film project was turned down by several studios, Bishop grew tired of waiting and never recorded the song he had written. When the film was released in 1985, Collins and Martin sang the tune. Collins was also listed in the year's top 100 with "Easy Lover," a duet with Philip Bailey (number 14), "Sussudio" (number 27), "One More Night" (number 30) and "Don't Lose My Number" (number 39).

The Anglo-American group Foreigner had their first year-end entry since "Waiting For A Girl Like You" in 1981. "I Want To Know What Love Is" was the number four song of the year, their highest ranking on a year-end chart. Mick Jones said in *Billboard* that he was dubious about releasing the song as the first single from *Agent Provocateur* because it was a ballad. "I certainly want to retain the rock image," he explained. "We just put this out because the song was so strong, and because it was coming out at Christmas, and it had the right kind of mood."

Another U.K. band, Dire Straits, caused some controversy with "Money For Nothing," the number five song of the year. Mark Knopfler was inspired to write the song after shopping in an appliance store in the upper East Side of New York City. There was a wall of television sets tuned to MTV and a sales clerk that Knopfler described as a "blockhead." "I wanted to use a lot of the language that the real guy actually used when I heard him, because it was more real. It just went better with the song, it was more muscular," Knopfler told Bill Flanagan. But the reference to "little faggot" got Knopfler in trouble. "The same thing happened when Randy Newman recorded 'Short People,' a song that was clearly about the stupidity of prejudice," Knopfler said in the *New York Times*. "An editor of *Gay News* in England attacked the song. What surprises me is that an intelligent journalist can misunderstand it."

The other U.K. act in the top 10 was Tears for Fears. Curt Smith and Roland Orzabal met in Bath when they were 13 years old. Six years later they formed a band called Graduate, but they split after releasing one single, "Elvis Should Play Ska." They reformed as History of Headaches, but renamed themselves after a chapter title in Arthur Janov's *The Primal Scream*. "Everybody Wants To Rule The World" was recorded in three days and was the last song added to their *Songs from the Big Chair* album. It was the number eight song of 1985. The follow-up, "Shout," had taken four months to record. It was number 20 for the year.

The highest-ranked American single in the year's top 100 was "Say You, Say Me" by Lionel Richie. The number two song of 1985, it had something in common with the number three song: they were both from the film *White Nights*, although Lionel's song didn't appear on the Atlantic Records soundtrack album, at the request of Motown. Lionel was originally asked by Taylor Hackford to write the title theme for the movie, but Lionel's manager Ken Kragen called back to say that his client couldn't seem to write anything called "White Nights." Instead, he had something that he thought was one of his better songs and that it would work in the film. Hackford and Gary LeMel, then head of Columbia Pictures' music department, listened to "Say You, Say Me" and agreed. Richie and Collins shared a piece of chart history: 1985 was the first time that two songs from the same movie appeared in the top three songs of the year.

"We Are The World" by USA for Africa was the number six song of 1985. The idea to record the song originated with Harry Belafonte, who suggested the idea of a concert by black artists to raise money for Africa to Ken Kragen. Kragen thought a concert wouldn't raise the amount of money needed, and came up with the idea of an American version of Band Aid. That was the name used by the U.K. artists who recorded "Do They Know It's Christmas?," an effort organized by Bob Geldof prior to Live Aid. Kragen called Lionel Richie to tell him of Belafonte's idea and enrolled him in the project. Next he asked Quincy Jones to produce, and Quincy brought in Michael Jackson. Lionel and Michael wrote the song and Quincy sent out demo tapes to the artists invited to record the number, requesting they "check their egos at the door." The song was recorded at A&M Studios in Hollywood following the American Music Awards ceremony on January 28, 1985. Less than a year after the release of the "We Are The World" single and album, approximately $44 million had been raised.

"Broken Wings," the number seven single of 1985, was written in 20 minutes by Richard Page and Steve George of Mr. Mister with John Lang. "We weren't there to write," says Page. "The drum machine was going. I started with the bass line. Before I knew it, the song was done. It just sort of happened and luckily I had the tape machine on." RCA wanted to release an uptempo track as the first single from the *Welcome to the Real World* album, but the band felt "Broken Wings" was the best track.

Huey Lewis & the News had the third soundtrack single in the top 10. "The Power Of Love" from *Back to the Future* was the number nine song of the year. When Steven Spielberg, director Robert Zemeckis and producers Bob Gale and Neil Canton asked Lewis to write a song for the movie, he came up with a tune called "In The Nick Of Time." But as negotiations with managers and lawyers dragged on, Huey gave the song away to another movie— *Brewster's Millions*, starring Richard Pryor. "We thought we were going to get that song," laments music supervisor Bones Howe. "Everybody was really upset about it." Huey told them not to worry, he was writing another song for the film. He came up with "Back In Time." That was used in the film, but it was "The Power Of Love" that was released as a single. Michael J. Fox plays some riffs from it in a scene where Marty McFly is auditioning with his band to play at a high school dance. Huey played the part of the high school teacher who turned him down. A vocal version by Huey Lewis & the News was heard over a scene where Fox is riding his skateboard to school.

1 **THAT'S WHAT FRIENDS ARE FOR**
Dionne and Friends *Arista*

2 **WALK LIKE AN EGYPTIAN**
Bangles *Columbia*

3 **ON MY OWN**
Patti LaBelle and Michael McDonald *MCA*

4 **THE WAY IT IS**
Bruce Hornsby & the Range *RCA*

5 **YOU GIVE LOVE A BAD NAME**
Bon Jovi *Mercury*

6 **GREATEST LOVE OF ALL**
Whitney Houston *Arista*

7 **THERE'LL BE SAD SONGS
(TO MAKE YOU CRY)**
Billy Ocean *Jive*

8 **HOW WILL I KNOW**
Whitney Houston *Arista*

9 **KYRIE**
Mr. Mister *RCA*

10 **KISS**
Prince & the Revolution *Paisley Park*

11 **THE NEXT TIME I FALL**
Peter Cetera and Amy Grant *Full Moon*

12 **BURNING HEART**
Survivor *Scotti Bros*

13 **STUCK WITH YOU**
Huey Lewis & the News *Chrysalis*

14 **WHEN I THINK OF YOU**
Janet Jackson *A&M*

15 **ROCK ME AMADEUS**
Falco *A&M*

16 **WEST END GIRLS**
Pet Shop Boys *EMI America*

17 **SLEDGEHAMMER**
Peter Gabriel *Geffen*

18 **HUMAN**
Human League *A&M*

19 **SARA**
Starship *Grunt*

20 **HIGHER LOVE**
Steve Winwood *Island*

21 **GLORY OF LOVE**
Peter Cetera *Warner Bros*

22 **EVERYBODY HAVE FUN TONIGHT**
Wang Chung *Geffen*

23 **FRIENDS AND LOVERS**
Gloria Loring and Carl Anderson *Carrere*

24 **CONGA**
Miami Sound Machine *Epic*

25 **SECRET LOVERS**
Atlantic Starr *A&M*

26 **LIVE TO TELL**
Madonna *Sire*

27 **ADDICTED TO LOVE**
Robert Palmer *Island*

28 **I CAN'T WAIT**
Nu Shooz *Atlantic*

29 **WHAT HAVE YOU DONE FOR ME LATELY**
Janet Jackson *A&M*

30 **VENUS**
Bananarama *London*

Peter Gabriel

1986 was the year cassette singles first outsold their 7-inch vinyl counterparts; Aerosmith and Run-D.M.C. combined heavy metal with rap to "Walk This Way"; and the Rock and Roll Hall of Fame inducted its first honorees at a dinner in New York City.

Janet Jackson appeared on the year-end chart for the first time. Working with producers Jimmy Jam and Terry Lewis, she broke out of the teenybopper mold she had been in for her first two albums. She recorded *Control* after her marriage of six months to James DeBarge was annulled. Without the turmoil in her personal life, "The album wouldn't have been the same," she said in *Bam*. "I don't know what it would have been like." She made the album without any help from her father, brother Michael or any other members of her family. "I wanted the public to like my album because of *me*," she emphasized. Janet had three titles in the top 100 of the year: "When I Think Of You" (number 14), "What Have You Done For Me Lately" (number 29) and "Nasty" (number 41).

Past and present members of Genesis accounted for six of the year's top 100. Peter Gabriel, who left his post as lead vocalist in May, 1975, after a concert at St. Etienne, France, was number 17 for the year with "Sledgehammer." Genesis had two songs listed: "Invisible Touch" at number 52 and "Throwing It All Away" at number 55. Mike Rutherford's extracurricular band, Mike + the Mechanics, also had two titles on the chart: "All I Need Is A Miracle" at number 74 and "Silent Running (On Dangerous Ground)" at number 76. Phil Collins, the band's drummer and current lead vocalist, was number 83 with "Take Me Home."

Whitney Houston was in the year-end top 10 for the first time. Her remake of George Benson's "Greatest Love Of All" was number six and a song turned down by Janet Jackson, "How Will I Know" was number eight. That made her only the second female solo artist in the rock era to have two singles in the year-end top 10 (the first was Donna Summer in 1979).

The number one song of 1986 was by Whitney's cousin, Dionne Warwick. Accompanied by Gladys Knight, Stevie Wonder and Elton John, billed on the label as "and Friends," Dionne triumphed with a Burt Bacharach-Carole Bayer Sager song originally recorded by Rod Stewart in 1982 for the soundtrack of *Night Shift*. The song took on a new meaning when Sager suggested to her friend Elizabeth Taylor that proceeds from the song be donated to the American Foundation for AIDS Research. The song was Bacharach's second number one record of the year, after "Raindrops Keep Fallin' On My Head" by B.J. Thomas in 1970. Dionne, Gladys and Stevie waited longer than any other artist to have a number one single of the year. Gladys made her *Billboard* Hot 100 debut in 1961 with "Every Beat Of My Heart," Dionne's first chart appearance was in 1962 with "Don't Make Me Over" and Stevie debuted in 1963 with "Fingertips—Pt. 2."

The Bangles had the number two song of 1986 with "Walk Like An Egyptian," a song written by American expatriate Liam Sternberg. The title came to him while crossing the English Channel on a ferry. He recorded a demo of the song in Los Angeles with singer Marti Jones. Sternberg submitted it to Toni Basil ("Mickey"), who turned it down. David Kahne, producer for the Bangles, received a two-song demo tape from a publisher and was asked to consider the first, "Rock And Roll Vertigo," for the Bangles. But the order on the tape was reversed. "So I was listening to 'Walk Like An Egyptian' but thinking it was the other song," laughs Kahne. "I really liked the demo . . . Marti sang it with an offhand quality I thought was really great."

Patti LaBelle and Michael McDonald were both in the year-end top 10 for the first time. As lead singer for Labelle, Patti had the number 13 song of 1975, "Lady Marmalade." Michael joined the Doobie Brothers in 1976 and had the number 21 song of 1979 as lead singer on "What A Fool Believes." Their duet of "On My Own" was the number three song of 1986, giving Burt Bacharach and Carole Bayer Sager two of the year's top three songs. The only other songwriters to accomplish this in the rock era were Barry, Robin and Maurice Gibb, who wrote "Shadow Dancing" and "Staying Alive," the number two and three songs of 1978, respectively. Barry actually did it twice: in 1977 he was the writer of "How Deep Is Your Love" (number two) as well as "I Just Want To Be

Your Everything" (number three). Although Elvis Presley was listed as one of the songwriters on "Don't Be Cruel" and "Heartbreak Hotel" in 1956, it's commonly acknowledged that he didn't participate in composing either song.

Brothers Bruce and John Hornsby moved to Los Angeles in 1980 to try their luck at songwriting. As staff writers for 20th Century Fox's music publishing division they were asked to write formula disco songs. "We were terrible at it," Bruce admitted in *Rolling Stone*. Frustrated with trying to adapt to the latest trend, Bruce recorded a four-song demo tape that included "The Way It Is." He sent the tape to Windham Hill Records because he thought the tape sounded too organic to appeal to a major label. Windham Hill offered him a deal, but they weren't interested in his rock material. Paul Atkinson at RCA Records heard the tape and signed Hornsby to the label. Released as his second single, "The Way It Is" went to number one and was ranked number four for the year.

Derek Schulman of Polygram signed Bon Jovi to Mercury Records. The band had four chart singles beginning in 1984, all of which missed the top 30. Then they turned to Bruce Fairbairn (Loverboy, Honeymoon Suite) to produce them and Desmond Child to write songs with them. With Jon Bon Jovi and Richie Sambora of the group, Child wrote "You Give Love A Bad Name." It was their first number one song and the number five record of 1986.

Billy Ocean had his first top 10 song of the year in 1986. Two years earlier, he had the number 20 song of the year with "Caribbean Queen (No More Love On The Run)." In 1985 he had two songs in the top 100 of the year: "Loverboy" (number 46) and "Suddenly" (number 60). Born Leslie Sebastian Charles in Trinidad, he went through several stage names (including Joshua, Big Ben and Sam Spade) before naming himself Billy Ocean. He left his job installing windshield wipers at a Ford plant after his first chart single, "Love Really Hurts Without You." "There'll Be Sad Songs (To Make You Cry)" was one of the first tunes written for his *Love Zone* album. Co-writer Barry Eastmond relates, "I had the music in my head for a little while. It seemed perfect for Billy. The lyrics came out of a story my wife told me about a friend of hers. She had just broken up with the fellow she had been going out with for years. There was a particular song that always made her think of her boyfriend. She was at a party given by her new boyfriend and the song came on and reminded her of the old boyfriend. She broke down . . . we thought that was an interesting story so we wrote the song about it." The song that made her cry was Billy's 1985 hit, "Suddenly."

Mr. Mister had a year-end top 10 single for the second consecutive year. "Kyrie" was the number nine song of 1986.

Prince had his first year-end top 10 single since "When Doves Cry" was the number one record of 1984. "Kiss," the first single released from the *Parade* album, spent two weeks on top of the Hot 100 and ranked in tenth place for the year.

1987

1 FAITH
George Michael *Columbia*

2 ALONE
Heart *Capitol*

3 I WANNA DANCE WITH SOMEBODY (WHO LOVES ME)
Whitney Houston *Arista*

4 C'EST LA VIE
Robbie Nevil *Manhattan*

5 SHAKE YOU DOWN
Gregory Abbott *Columbia*

6 LA BAMBA
Los Lobos *Slash*

7 LIVIN' ON A PRAYER
Bon Jovi *Mercury*

8 HERE I GO AGAIN
Whitesnake *Geffen*

9 HEAVEN IS A PLACE ON EARTH
Belinda Carlisle *MCA*

10 (I'VE HAD) THE TIME OF MY LIFE
Bill Medley and Jennifer Warnes *RCA*

11 NOTHING'S GONNA STOP US NOW
Starship *Grunt*

12 I THINK WE'RE ALONE NOW
Tiffany *MCA*

13 WITH OR WITHOUT YOU
U2 *Island*

14 AT THIS MOMENT
Billy Vera & the Beaters *Rhino*

15 KEEP YOUR HANDS TO YOURSELF
Georgia Satellites *Elektra*

16 HEART AND SOUL
T'Pau *Virgin*

17 OPEN YOUR HEART
Madonna *Sire*

18 DIDN'T WE ALMOST HAVE IT ALL
Whitney Houston *Arista*

19 I STILL HAVEN'T FOUND WHAT I'M LOOKING FOR
U2 *Island*

20 LOOKING FOR A NEW LOVE
Jody Watley *MCA*

21 DON'T DREAM IT'S OVER
Crowded House *Capitol*

22 IS THIS LOVE
Whitesnake *Geffen*

23 SHAKE YOUR LOVE
Debbie Gibson *Atlantic*

24 SHAKEDOWN
Bob Seger *MCA*

25 NOTORIOUS
Duran Duran *Capitol*

26 I WANT YOUR SEX
George Michael *Columbia*

27 THE LADY IN RED
Chris DeBurgh *A&M*

28 ALWAYS
Atlantic Starr *Warner Bros*

29 HEAD TO TOE
Lisa Lisa & Cult Jam *Columbia*

30 MONY MONY
Billy Idol *Chrysalis*

Debbie Gibson

1987 was the year the Beatles' albums were first released on compact disc; Billy Joel was back in the U.S.S.R.; and U2 had their American breakthrough with *The Joshua Tree.*

The average age of artists in the year-end top 100 was reduced by the presence of two teenagers: Tiffany and Debbie Gibson.

Michael Jackson was back on the year-end chart with his first singles since *Thriller.* "Bad" was number 51 and "I Just Can't Stop Loving You," a duet with Siedah Garrett, was number 53.

For the second time, George Michael had the number one song of the year. The only artists to accomplish this prior to George were the Beatles (in 1964 and 1968) and Rod Stewart (in 1971 and 1976). "Careless Whisper" had been the top song of 1985 and "Faith," a song that George says described how hopeful and optimistic he felt at the time he wrote it, was the number one single of 1987.

In the runner-up position for the year was "Alone" by Heart. The group had first scored on a year-end chart with "Magic Man," the number 80 song of 1976. Nancy Wilson had joined the band just two years earlier, the same year their name was shortened from White Heart. Her sister Ann had joined in 1970. When Ann was offered a solo contract with Mushroom Records, she told them to take the whole band or nothing. After a short tenure with Mushroom, the group charged breach of contract and signed with Columbia's Portrait label. They reached a new pinnacle of chart success when they signed with Capitol. Billy Steinberg and Tom Kelly wrote "Alone" and had recorded an earlier version under the name i-Ten. Steinberg hated the original track and insisted on recording a new version before submitting it to producer Ron Nevison for Heart.

Whitney Houston had her highest-ranked year-end single when she recorded "I Wanna Dance With Somebody (Who Loves Me)." Written by the husband-and-wife team of George Merrill and Shannon Rubicam, the composers who provided Whitney with "How Will I Know," the song ranked number three for 1987. The follow-up, Michael Masser and Will Jennings' "Didn't We Almost Have It All," was number 18 for the year.

Chart newcomer Robbie Nevil, whose songs had been recorded by the Pointer Sisters, Sheena Easton, Al Jarreau and El DeBarge, gave EMI's Manhattan label its most successful chart single with "C'est La Vie," the number four song of 1987. The tune was written in a few hours while Nevil was messing around with his keyboard. He was concerned about releasing it as a single because as he told Holly Gleason, "It's so light. It doesn't represent the depth there is. It's a dance thing." Then he allowed, "I'd like to think that even if it's just a straight ahead dance song, people will hear an integrity that makes it more than another dance song."

Like Nevil, Gregory Abbott was new to the charts in 1987 when the Marvin Gaye-influenced "Shake You Down" became a hit. The number five song of the year, it was Abbott's first single for Columbia. Born in Harlem, he taught at the University of California at Berkeley before going to work as a researcher for a Wall Street brokerage. Some investment bankers financed a recording studio and record label for Abbott. He produced other artists for his label and spent three years writing songs for himself. He recorded 40 songs and chose the best three to submit to Columbia.

"La Bamba," a song that had been on the flip side of Ritchie Valens' "Donna" (the number 10 single of 1959), was updated by Los Lobos and used as the title song for the film biography of Valens' life starring Lou Diamond Phillips. The East Los Angeles group was signed to Slash Records on the recommendation of the label's leading group, the Blasters. Los Lobos had often performed "La Bamba," a traditional song dating back two centuries, before writer/director Luis Valdez suggested recording new music for the film rather than using Valens' original recordings. Phillips lip-synched to Los Lobos' pre-recorded tracks.

Bon Jovi were in the year-end top 10 for the second consecutive year. "Livin' On A Prayer," their second number one single, ranked number seven for 1987. The band had recorded more than 35 songs for their third album, and "Livin' On A Prayer" almost didn't make the cut. While writing the song with Richie Sambora and Desmond Child, Jon Bon Jovi told Sambora that they should submit the song for a movie soundtrack because it wasn't right for the band. Producer Bruce Fairbairn disagreed: "I really heard the lyric in that song as being something that spoke to a lot of people, so I liked it for that and I fought for the song. At some point it looked like it might not make the record. I convinced Jon and Richie that it was worth hanging in there, and sure enough, it started to develop. . . . By the time we finished it, everybody had the feeling that it was going to be a single. I thought it could be the biggest single on the record . . . as it turned out, it was."

The number eight song of 1987 had first charted five years earlier in Britain. David Coverdale of Whitesnake wrote "Here I Go Again" when he was in Portugal in 1981. It was recorded for the *Saints and Sinners* album that year, but that LP wasn't released in the U.S. Except for Coverdale, it was a new line-up of musicians in Whitesnake that re-recorded the song at the suggestion of John David Kolodner of Geffen Records. "I wanted to have a more positive backing track," Coverdale explains. "The only thing that stands up on the original version is the emotional security of the vocal performance. There's a very limp performance from some very exceptional musicians."

Belinda Carlisle first appeared on a year-end chart as a member of the Go-Go's. Their debut chart single, "Our Lips Are Sealed," was the number 94 song of 1981. The following year "We Got The Beat" ranked number 26. The Go-Go's announced their breakup on May 10, 1985. Belinda's first solo effort, "Mad About You," was the number 41 song of 1986. She set a new mark in 1987 with "Heaven Is A Place On Earth," number nine for the year. Producer Rick Nowels and his songwriting partner Ellen Shipley came up with the song and spent a month recording it with Belinda. Nowels liked the chorus but was uncomfortable with the verse, even after Belinda had finished cutting the track. Nowels asked Shipley to fly from New York to Los Angeles to rewrite the song. It took three days, and then Nowels had to break the news to Carlisle that she would have to record the song again. "I was very nervous about breaking this to her because I put her through a lot of changes to get her to sing the other vocal," the producer admits. But Belinda heard the rewrite and realized it was better. Joined by Michelle Phillips and songwriter Diane Warren on backing vocals, Carlisle re-recorded it and was rewarded with a number one single.

Bill Medley was in the year-end top 10 for the first time in 21 years. "(You're My) Soul And Inspiration" by the Righteous Brothers had been the number nine single of 1966. His singing partner back then had been Bobby Hatfield. Now he was teamed with another Orange County, California native, Jennifer Warnes, who had her first year-end chart single in 1977 when "Right Time Of The Night" was number 57 for the year. With Joe Cocker, she was ranked number 17 in 1982 with "Up Where We Belong." Medley and Warnes duetted on ("I've Had) The Time Of My Life" from the soundtrack of *Dirty Dancing*.

1988

Eric Carmen

1 **NEED YOU TONIGHT**
INXS *Atlantic*

2 **LOOK AWAY**
Chicago *Reprise*

3 **ROLL WITH IT**
Steve Winwood *Virgin*

4 **EVERY ROSE HAS ITS THORN**
Poison *Enigma*

5 **GOT MY MIND SET ON YOU**
George Harrison *Dark Horse*

6 **SO EMOTIONAL**
Whitney Houston *Arista*

7 **SEASONS CHANGE**
Expose *Arista*

8 **BABY, I LOVE YOUR WAY/FREEBIRD MEDLEY
(FREE BABY)**
Will to Power *Epic*

9 **COULD'VE BEEN**
Tiffany *MCA*

10 **NEVER GONNA GIVE YOU UP**
Rick Astley *RCA*

11 **SWEET CHILD O' MINE**
Guns n' Roses

12 **GET OUTTA MY DREAMS, GET INTO MY CAR**
Billy Ocean *Jive*

13 **THE FLAME**
Cheap Trick *Epic*

14 **GIVING YOU THE BEST THAT I GOT**
Anita Baker *Elektra*

15 **WAITING FOR A STAR TO FALL**
Boy Meets Girl *RCA*

16 **HANDS TO HEAVEN**
Breathe *A&M*

17 **HOW CAN I FALL?**
Breathe *A&M*

18 **ANYTHING FOR YOU**
Gloria Estefan & Miami Sound Machine *Epic*

19 **WISHING WELL**
Terence Trent D'Arby *Epic*

20 **HUNGRY EYES**
Eric Carmen *RCA*

21 **WILD, WILD WEST**
Escape Club *Atlantic*

22 **HOLD ON TO THE NIGHTS**
Richard Marx *EMI-Manhattan*

23 **MAN IN THE MIRROR**
Michael Jackson *Epic*

24 **LOVE BITES**
Def Leppard *Mercury*

25 **WHERE DO BROKEN HEARTS GO**
Whitney Houston *Arista*

26 **ONE MORE TRY**
George Michael *Columbia*

27 **GROOVY KIND OF LOVE**
Phil Collins *Atlantic*

28 **FATHER FIGURE**
George Michael *Columbia*

29 **BAD MEDICINE**
Bon Jovi *Mercury*

30 **DON'T WORRY BE HAPPY**
Bobby McFerrin *EMI-Manhattan*

1988 was the year Cher won an Oscar the day before Sonny was elected Mayor of Palm Springs; the Beatles were inducted into the Rock and Roll Hall of Fame; and Berry Gordy sold Motown to MCA.

It was a transition year for the label that had excelled with the Supremes, the Temptations, the Jackson Five, Lionel Richie and many other artists—for the first time since 1961, there were no Motown recordings included in the top 100 songs of the year.

In another first, the number one song of the year was by an Australian act. INXS was only the third Australian group in the rock era to have a number one song on the Hot 100. Air Supply was the first in 1981 and Men at Work reached the summit in 1982 and 1983. INXS lead singer Michael Hutchence was born in Hong Kong of Australian parents. The family moved back home to Sydney when he was 12. After his parents divorced, Hutchence lived with his mother for a year in North Hollywood, California. Then he returned to Sydney and found his childhood friend Andrew Farriss in a band with Garry Beers. Andrew's younger brother Jon and older brother Tim joined the group, as did Kirk Pengilly. With Hutchence handling the vocals, they lived in Perth for 10 months. A roadie suggested they call themselves "In Excess" and they did, but they spelled it "INXS." After experiencing chart success in Australia, they made the American chart with a single titled "The One Thing" in 1983. Their first major success in the U.S. came with "What You Need," the number 31 song of 1986. While recording their sixth album, they took a short break in Hong Kong where Andrew came up with a riff and Michael added some lyrics. They found a local studio and scheduled time to record "Need You Tonight."

The number two song of 1988 was a Diane Warren song, "Look Away" by Chicago. In 19 years of recording, it was their highest-ranked year-end song and their most successful chart single.

Steve Winwood first appeared on a year-end chart when he was 18 years old as lead singer for the Spencer Davis Group's "Gimme Some Lovin'," the number 83 song of 1967. His solo single "Higher Love" was the number 20 song of 1986. He set a new high mark in 1988 when the Stax-influenced "Roll With It" was in third place for the year. It was his first single for the Virgin label after a long association with Island Records. "I didn't say, 'I want to leave Island,'" Winwood told Pete Clark. "I just thought it was time to look at the options and see what other companies might do for me. I suppose changing record companies is a bit like changing insurance companies—there was no lover's tiff involved, it's just a business arrangement."

The number four single of the year was "Every Rose Has Its Thorn" by Poison. The group relocated from Harrisburg, Pennsylvania to Los Angeles in 1983, changed their name from "Paris" and became a sensation on the club circuit. Still, they couldn't get a record company deal until they were signed to the independent Enigma label.

George Harrison had the number five song of 1987, one notch higher than his ranking in 1970 when "My Sweet Lord" was the number six song of the year. He did it with a remake of an obscure song he had first heard in 1963 when he bought an album by James Ray. The LP contained a song the Beatles had been performing live, "If You Gotta Make A Fool Of Somebody." "The album itself was really terrible," George told Timothy White, "but the best three songs were written by this guy who discovered James Ray, a former mailman named Rudy Clark." One of the songs was "Got My Mind Set On You Part One/Part Two," although there was no break between the two parts. Harrison updated the song and changed the chords.

Whitney Houston was in the year-end top 10 for the third consecutive year. Her recording of Billy Steinberg and Tom Kelly's "So Emotional" was the number six song of 1988. It was the final track recorded for her second album. Clive Davis wanted one more uptempo number and asked the songwriters to submit material. Their demo sounded more like Prince than Whitney, but Clive loved it and passed it on to producer Narada Michael Walden. It took some time for Steinberg and Kelly to appreciate Whitney's recording. "If you fall in love with your version, and you're used to hearing it the way you conceived it, it's always hard to get used to," Kelly explains.

Whitney's labelmates Expose had the number seven song of the year, "Seasons Change." Jeanette Jurado, Gioia Bruno and Ann Curless were the second edition of Expose. The trio was put together by producer Lewis Martinee after he wrote a song called "Point Of No Return." He recorded the instrumental track and hired three session singers from Miami to record the vocals. But when it came time to record an album, an Arista Records source said the label felt the original singers didn't have enough "star potential" and were dismissed. Martinee sought replacements and found the three new singers. Jurado was his first discovery, and she recorded the ballad "Seasons Change" before Bruno and Curless came on board.

The number eight song of 1987 was a medley of Peter Frampton's "Baby, I Love Your Way" and Lynyrd Skynyrd's "Free Bird" put together by Miami disc jockey Bob Rosenberg. With vocalist Suzi Carr and saxophonist Dr. J, he formed a trio called Will to Power, a name inspired by the work of the 19th century German philosopher Friedrich Nietzsche. Rosenberg, a native of Philadelphia, is a second generation Hot 100 artist: his mother, Gloria Mann, charted in 1955 with cover versions of "Earth Angel" and "Teen Age Prayer." After attending college in Tampa, he worked as a mobile DJ and excelled in producing special mixes for radio. He recorded a rap song in 1984 called "Miami Vice," which was pulled when MCA, producers of the television series, threatened legal action. Then Rosenberg met Carr at a club in Ft. Lauderdale and asked her to sing on "Dreamin'," a single recorded in 1986 for his own Thrust label. The song became a local hit in Miami and was picked up nationally by Epic Records. While quickly recording his first album for the label, Rosenberg went into the studio on Christmas day and came up with the idea of combining "Baby, I Love Your Way" with "Free Bird."

Tiffany had her first year-end top 10 single in 1987 with "Could've Been," the number nine song of the year. Her second number one single, it was originally recorded by producer George Tobin as a demo by songwriter Lois Blaisch. Tobin loved the song and submitted it to Crystal Gayle, Dolly Parton, Natalie Cole and others, with no luck. Finally, he took Blaisch's vocal off the demo and had Tiffany record over the track.

British singer Rick Astley made his chart debut with "Never Gonna Give You Up," the number 10 song of the year. He was playing drums in a band called FBI and writing original material. The group played at a private club in Warrington, England, and producer Pete Waterman was invited to hear them. "He liked my vocals but wasn't all that interested in the band because we were still very young," Rick recalls. Astley was invited to work at Waterman's company, PWL, as a tape operator and tea boy. At night he recorded his own demos. He was signed to RCA under the aegis of producers Mike Stock, Matt Aitken and Waterman, the trio that wrote "Never Gonna Give You Up."

1989

Richard Marx

1989 was the year Prince and Danny Elfman both composed soundtracks for *Batman*; the New Kids on the Block were the latest teen idols; and former teen idol Donny Osmond made a surprising comeback.

Osmond had the number 60 song of the year with "Soldier Of Love," his first year-end chart appearance since "The Twelfth Of Never" was the number 93 song of 1973. Also making a comeback in 1989 was Donna Summer, ranked number 84 for the year with a Stock-Aitken-Waterman song, "This Time I Know It's For Real." It was Summer's first year-end chart appearance since 1983, when "She Works Hard For The Money" was number 17 for the year.

Phil Collins became only the third British male solo artist of the rock era to have a number one song of the year, following Rod Stewart and George Michael. "Another Day In Paradise" was the first single from his . . . *But Seriously* album. A song about homelessness, it inspired critics to question his sincerity. "The way they see it, I'm suddenly coming along and saying I've got a conscience," he complained to Gary Graff. "They don't believe me; they assume I'm doing it for the wrong reason. When I'm driving and I pass 60 or 100 homeless people on the street, I'm not immune to that. I have to write about them the same as Elvis Costello would want to write about them. But because of his track record, no one questions him. But I'm supposed to just go and record another 'Sussudio' or 'Groovy Kind Of Love.'"

After Janet Jackson's multi-platinum success with *Control*, A&M Records suggested a theme for her follow-up LP. It would be called *Scandal* and would be a concept album about her family. Janet wrote one song, "You Need Me," about a distant, neglectful father, but turned down the idea of an entire album about the Jackson family. "You Need Me" was released as the "B" side of "Miss You Much," the first single from *Rhythm Nation 1814*. Janet got the idea for the album when she read about the various communities (or "nations") formed in New York City by young people, mostly blacks, seeking a common identity. "I thought it would be great if we could create our own nation. . . . one that would have a positive message and that everyone would be free to join," she told Robert Hilburn in the *Los Angeles Times*. "Miss You Much" was number one for four weeks and is Janet's most successful chart single.

Beresford Romeo (better known as Jazzie B.) and Nellee Hooper had the number three single of 1989 as Soul II Soul. With Caron Wheeler guest starring as lead vocalist, their "Back To Life" peaked at number four on the Hot 100 and remained on the chart for 28 weeks. Jazzie was a tape operator in London and a DJ who brought his own sound system when he played records at unlicensed one-night warehouse parties. Hooper rented Jazzie B.'s system for a show in 1985 and ended up in a ferocious argument with him when Jazzie expected to play the gig as well as provide the audio equipment. They made up, became friends and started playing Sunday nights at the Africa Center in Covent Garden, where they met Wheeler. They recorded some material in 1987 and were signed to Virgin. After a couple of minor chart incursions, they scored heavily with the soft '70s soul sound of "Keep On Movin'," which ranked as the number 93 single of 1989.

Billy Joel had his first year-end top 10 single in 1989 with "We Didn't Start The Fire," the number four record of the year. His previous highest charted year-end single was "It's Still Rock And Roll To Me," number 14 for 1980. "We Didn't Start The Fire" compressed 40 years of history into a song that rhymed "Communist bloc" with "Rock Around The Clock" and "*Lawrence of Arabia*" with "Beatlemania." Billy Joel talked about the song with Edna Gundersen of *USA Today*: "I'm saying in the chorus that the world's always been a mess, the world's a mess now, it's going to be a mess when we're gone. But we *tried* to fight it. You can't drop out and fall into despair. It's easy to be a cynic."

The name Milli Vanilli will be accompanied into eternity by an asterisk, as pop historians explain about the two guys who really *weren't* Milli Vanilli. When Diane Warren's song "Blame It On The Rain" (number five for 1989) was on the Hot 100, everyone thought Rob Pilatus of Germany and Fabrice Morvan of France were the exciting dance duo known as Milli Vanilli. It was only when they insisted to producer Frank Farian that they *really* sing the vocals on their second album that Farian blew the whistle. He called a press conference to announce the rumors were true: Rob and Fab weren't the real thing. Charles Shaw, John Davis and Brad Howe provided the vocals on the album while the dreadlocked duo were the public faces of the group. Rob and Fab returned their Grammy at the request of the National Academy of Recording Arts and Sciences.

Former New Edition member Bobby Brown had five singles included in the top 100 of 1989. "My Prerogative," number six for the year, was his biggest hit, followed by "On Our Own" (number 27), "Every Little Step" (number 35), "Roni" (number 77) and "Rock Wit'cha" (number 92). Brown, only 14 when the Boston-based New Edition had their first chart single, left the group in 1985 to pursue more mature music. Brown wrote "My Prerogative" with Gene Griffin and says the lyrics are about breaking away from his former managers and New Edition and a response to false rumors about drug use.

First Paula Abdul was known as a cheerleader for the Los Angeles Lakers. Then she became a choreographer for Janet Jackson's videos and Tracey Ullman's television series. In 1989 she graduated to superstar status. Her third single for Virgin, "Straight Up," was the number seven record of the year.

Debbie Gibson achieved her highest ranking on a year-end chart in 1989 with "Lost In Your Eyes," the number eight single of the year. Interested in music from the age of two, Gibson became serious about it at age 12. A year later she wrote "Only In My Dreams," a song that would become her debut single for Atlantic Records three years later. By the time she cut her first album, she had written over 200 songs. "Lost In Your Eyes" was written a year-and-a-half before it was released; it was the lead-off single from her second album, *Electric Youth*, and spent three weeks at number one on the Hot 100.

Bette Midler made a dramatic return to the Hot 100 in 1989 with a song from the soundtrack of her film *Beaches*. "Wind Beneath My Wings," a number four song on the country chart by Gary Morris in 1983, was Bette's first number one hit after 17 years of recording. "I made that record against my better judgment, because two people—my hairdresser and my costumer—advised me to do it," she told Tom Green in *USA Today*. The number nine single of 1989, it revitalized Bette's recording career and won the Grammys for Record of the Year and Song of the Year.

Rap music made it into the year-end top 10 for the first time, thanks to Young M.C.'s "Bust A Move" at number 10. A 1988 graduate of USC with a degree in economics, Marvin Young intended to land a job on Wall Street. But an *a cappella* telephone audition with Michael Ross of Delicious Vinyl Records resulted in Young being signed to the label. Ross asked him to write the lyrics for Tone Loc's "Wild Thing," which went to number two on the Hot 100 (and was ranked at number 59 for 1989). Young helped write the follow-up, "Funky Cold Medina" (number 72 for the year), and then had success on his own with "Bust A Move."

1990

1 **LOVE TAKES TIME**
Mariah Carey *Columbia*

2 **BECAUSE I LOVE YOU (THE POSTMAN SONG)**
Stevie B *LMR*

3 **HOLD ON**
Wilson Phillips *SBK*

4 **IT MUST HAVE BEEN LOVE**
Roxette *EMI*

5 **NOTHING COMPARES 2 U**
Sinead O'Connor *Ensign*

6 **VISION OF LOVE**
Mariah Carey *Columbia*

7 **POISON**
Bell Biv Devoe *MCA*

8 **VOGUE**
Madonna *Sire*

9 **BLACK VELVET**
Alannah Myles *Atlantic*

10 **DO ME!**
Bell Biv Devoe *MCA*

11 **HOW AM I SUPPOSED TO LIVE WITHOUT YOU**
Michael Bolton *Columbia*

12 **I'M YOUR BABY TONIGHT**
Whitney Houston *Arista*

13 **CLOSE TO YOU**
Maxi Priest *Charisma*

14 **FROM A DISTANCE**
Bette Midler *Atlantic*

15 **PUMP UP THE JAM**
Technotronic f/Felly *SBK*

16 **ESCAPADE**
Janet Jackson *A&M*

17 **CRADLE OF LOVE**
Billy Idol *Chrysalis*

18 **HOLD ON**
En Vogue *Atlantic*

19 **OPPOSITES ATTRACT**
Paula Abdul w/the Wild Pair *Virgin*

20 **RUB YOU THE RIGHT WAY**
Johnny Gill *Motown*

21 **THE POWER**
Snap *Arista*

22 **ICE ICE BABY**
Vanilla Ice *SBK*

23 **SENDING ALL MY LOVE**
Linear *Atlantic*

24 **SHE AIN'T WORTH IT**
Glenn Medeiros f/Bobby Brown *MCA*

25 **BLAZE OF GLORY**
Jon Bon Jovi *Mercury*

26 **ALL AROUND THE WORLD**
Lisa Stansfield *Arista*

27 **STEP BY STEP**
New Kids on the Block *Columbia*

28 **SOMETHING TO BELIEVE IN**
Poison *Enigma*

29 **TWO TO MAKE IT RIGHT**
Seduction *Vendetta*

30 **I DON'T HAVE THE HEART**
James Ingram *Warner Bros*

New Kids on the Block

1990 was the year the world found out Milli Vanilli didn't sing, but the Simpsons and the Teenage Mutant Ninja Turtles did; MTV banned Madonna's "Justify My Love;" and obscenity charges were filed against 2 Live Crew and record-store owners who sold their album.

There were seven singles with lead vocals by women in the year-end top 10, a new record for the rock era. The previous high was in 1979, when there were six. Leading the way was Mariah Carey with two titles: "Love Takes Time," the number one single of the year, and "Vision Of Love," number six. Mariah became only the third female soloist in the rock era to have two year-end top 10 hits, after Donna Summer and Whitney Houston. Mariah was the first to accomplish this feat in her debut year.

Carey was raised by her mother, a jazz and classical vocalist who sang with the New York City Opera. At age 18, Mariah was singing backing vocals for Brenda K. Starr ("I Still Believe"). After winding up a four-month tour, Brenda talked Mariah into attending a CBS party with her. Mariah had one of her demo tapes and Brenda tried to hand it to a CBS label executive, who refused to take it. But CBS Records Group president Tommy Mottola observed the transaction and took the tape. On his way home from the party, Mottola listened to the cassette in his limo and liked what he heard so much that he returned to track down the vocalist. Mariah had already left, but he got her phone number and left a message for her.

Carey had been writing songs since high school with her friend Ben Margulies. They wrote Mariah's debut single for Columbia, "Vision Of Love." After it was recorded, Mottola and Columbia Records president Don Ienner asked Narada Michael Walden to polish the production. Walden's name was absent from the album credits but was later added, sharing producer credit with Rhett Lawrence on the track.

Hoping to defeat the sophomore jinx, Carey and Margulies wrote "Love Takes Time" and planned to save it for Mariah's second album. But after she played it for a Columbia Records executive during an airplane trip, label management insisted that "Love Takes Time" be added to her debut album. The decision was made so late that the song title didn't appear on the packaging for the CD and cassette during the initial press run.

Wilson Phillips bested their respective parents by placing number three for the year with "Hold On," their debut single. Carnie and Wendy Wilson's father, Brian Wilson, had the number five song of the year twice. He did it with the Beach Boys in 1964 ("I Get Around") and 1966 ("Good Vibrations"). Chynna Phillips' parents, John and Michelle, never made the year-end top 10 with the Mamas and the Papas; their highest-ranked year-end single was "California Dreamin,'" number 14 for 1966. The three offspring had been friends since they were small children and staged shows for their families and friends. But the concept of Wilson Phillips wasn't set into motion until Chynna and Owen Vanessa Elliot, daughter of the late Mama Cass, came up with the idea of recording an anti-drug song. Chynna invited Carnie and Wendy to participate, and although the project fizzled, the four women met with Richard Perry to discuss recording some demos. Elliot was dropped from the group, and Perry's management deal was cut off. The trio then signed with the new SBK label.

The Swedish duo of Marie Fredriksson and Per Gessle had the number four single of the year, "It Must Have Been Love," from the soundtrack of the Richard Gere/Julia Roberts film, *Pretty Woman*. The song had been a hit in Sweden before the film was produced; the lyrics were rewritten for the movie. Marie was a folk singer and Per was in a band called Gyllene Tider before they formed Roxette in 1986. Their first American chart single, "The Look," was the number 33 song of 1989. They were also number 36 for that year with "Listen To Your Heart." "It Must Have Been Love" was one of two songs from the *Pretty Woman* soundtrack on the year-end chart; the other was "King Of Wishful Thinking" by Go West at number 76.

Irish-born Sinead O'Connor made her Hot 100 debut with "Nothing Compares 2 U," the number five record of 1990. The song was written by Prince and originally recorded in 1985 on his Paisley Park label by the Family, a Minneapolis quintet. Although Sinead was managed by former Prince manager Steve Fargnoli when she recorded the tune, she learned about it from her former manager, Fatchna O'Ceallaigh.

Madonna scored her second year-end top 10 hit with "Vogue," a song she intended for release as a "B" side. But Sire Records thought better of the tune and released it as an "A" side. It spent three weeks at number one on the Hot 100. The only Madonna single to be more successful than "Vogue" was "Like A Virgin," number five for 1984.

The seventh female vocalist in the top 10 was Alannah Myles. The Canadian singer started performing in Toronto when she was 19; two years later she opened for the Christopher Ward Band. Ward, a VJ on the Canadian music television channel MuchMusic, collaborated with Myles on composing. Along with songwriter David Tyson, they worked on a three-song demo tape at Myles' ranch in Buckhorn, Canada. Based on that tape and a video clip, Myles was signed to Atlantic Records. Her first American chart single, "Black Velvet," was written by Ward and Tyson. The inspiration for the song came to Ward when he headed up a bus trip of Elvis Presley fans traveling from Toronto to Graceland.

The lone male soloist in the top 10 was Stevie B with the number two record of the year, "Because I Love You (The Postman Song)." Born Steven Bernard Hill in Miami, he opened a nightclub in Tallahassee while he was in college. He released "Sending Out For Love" on his own Midtown label in 1980 and had a duo called Friday Friday in 1985. After teaching himself the art of studio engineering, Stevie built his own studio. He concentrated on producing local artists, and in 1987, he decided to record himself once more. He had a local Miami hit that year with "Party Your Body," and was signed by Herb Moelis to his New York-based LMR Records. "Dreamin' Of Love" was Stevie B's first Hot 100 entry, peaking at number 80 in 1988. "Because I Love You," written in 1986 by Warren Allen Brooks (the other half of Friday Friday), became Stevie's first top 10 single in 1990, spending four weeks at number one.

The New Edition spin-off group of Bell Biv DeVoe had the number seven song of 1990 ("Poison") as well as the number 10 song ("Do Me!"). The only other groups to have two year-end top 10 hits are the Beatles, the Supremes, the Monkees, the Jackson Five, the Bee Gees and Queen. After working on New Edition's *Heart Break* album, producers Jimmy Jam and Terry Lewis suggested to Louis Silas, Jr., of MCA Records that Ricky Bell, Michael Bivins and Ronnie DeVoe record their own project. The other two members of New Edition—Ralph Tresvant and Johnny Gill—were off recording solo albums and Bell, Bivins and DeVoe were wondering what they were going to do in the meantime. They were in Silas' office when he wrote down "Bell Biv DeVoe" on a piece of paper and told them, "This is the new group that I want you guys to put together and work on." Both "Poison" and "Do Me!" proved to be bigger hits than any previous single by New Edition: the group's most successful chart single was "Cool It Now," the number 24 song of 1985.

THE TOP 100 SONGS OF
THE FIFTIES

The rock and roll era was officially ushered in on July 9, 1955, when "(We're Gonna) Rock Around The Clock" by Bill Haley & His Comets went to number one on the *Billboard* Best Sellers in Stores chart. The king of this music—music that was unlike any that had been heard before—was crowned in April, 1956, when Elvis Presley's "Heartbreak Hotel" became his first number one song. But there were detractors, too. Rev. John Carroll said, "Rock and roll inflames and excites youth, like jungle tom-toms readying warriors for battle. . . . The suggestive lyrics are, of course, a matter for law enforcement agencies."

The top 100 songs of the '50s include many titles that had nothing to do with rock and roll. While Elvis appears eight times, the list also includes Roger Williams, Jimmy Dorsey, Nelson Riddle, Johnny Mathis, Doris Day, Nat King Cole, Frank Sinatra and even the man who spoke out against rock, Mitch Miller.

And many of the songs were composed before the advent of rock and roll. Seven titles in the top 10 were recorded by other artists prior to 1955.

Elvis Presley

1 DON'T BE CRUEL/HOUND DOG
Elvis Presley *RCA* 56

2 (WE'RE GONNA) ROCK AROUND THE CLOCK
Bill Haley & His Comets *Decca* 55

3 AUTUMN LEAVES
Roger Williams *Kapp* 55

4 SINGING THE BLUES
Guy Mitchell *Columbia* 56

5 LOVE LETTERS IN THE SAND
Pat Boone *Dot* 57

6 MACK THE KNIFE
Bobby Darin *Atco* 59

7 MOMENTS TO REMEMBER
The Four Lads *Columbia* 55

8 HEARTBREAK HOTEL
Elvis Presley *RCA* 56

9 LISBON ANTIGUA
Nelson Riddle *Capitol* 56

10 SO RARE
Jimmy Dorsey *Fraternity* 57

11 THE WAYWARD WIND
Gogi Grant *Era* 56

12 TAMMY
Debbie Reynolds *Coral* 57

13 ALL SHOOK UP
Elvis Presley *RCA* 57

14 JUST WALKING IN THE RAIN
Johnnie Ray *Columbia* 56

15 THE YELLOW ROSE OF TEXAS
Mitch Miller *Columbia* 55

16 LOVE IS A MANY SPLENDORED THING
Four Aces *Decca* 55

17 JAILHOUSE ROCK/TREAT ME NICE
Elvis Presley *RCA* 57

18 (LET ME BE YOUR) TEDDY BEAR
Elvis Presley *RCA* 57

19 SIXTEEN TONS
Tennessee Ernie Ford *Capitol* 55

20 THE GREEN DOOR
Jim Lowe *Dot* 56

21 HONKY TONK (PARTS 1 & 2)
Bill Doggett *King* 56

22 LOVE ME TENDER
Elvis Presley *RCA* 56

23 MEMORIES ARE MADE OF THIS
Dean Martin *Capitol* 56

24 HE
Al Hibbler *Decca* 55

25 HONEYCOMB
Jimmie Rodgers *Roulette* 57

26 COME GO WITH ME
The Dell-Vikings *Dot* 57

27 BYE BYE LOVE
Everly Brothers *Cadence* 57

28 SEARCHIN'/YOUNG BLOOD
The Coasters *Atco* 57

29 THE POOR PEOPLE OF PARIS
Les Baxter *Capitol* 56

30 CHANCES ARE/THE TWELFTH OF NEVER
Johnny Mathis *Columbia* 57

THE TOP 100 SONGS OF
THE SIXTIES

Only five artists who were listed on the top 100 songs of the '50s were also included in the top 100 songs of the '60s: Elvis Presley, Ricky Nelson, the Everly Brothers, Johnny Horton and Frank Sinatra.

Still, the early part of the '60s didn't sound that different from the '50s. Hits like "Tossin' and Turnin'" and even "The Twist" could have been popular in either decade. One difference was the rising influence of women—Connie Francis and Brenda Lee were major artists, and the Shirelles were the first "girl group" to make an impact.

Then came January, 1964, and everything changed. The Beatles arrived from England, ushering in the British Invasion. Few American artists survived this period, though Bobby Vinton, the Four Seasons and the Beach Boys remained popular.

The '60s also saw the rise of Motown, beginning with the staggering hit streak of the Supremes in 1964. The label's success continued with Mary Wells, the Four Tops, the Temptations and Marvin Gaye.

The Beatles

1 THE TWIST
Chubby Checker *Parkway* 60

2 HEY JUDE
The Beatles *Apple* 68

3 THEME FROM "A SUMMER PLACE"
Percy Faith *Columbia* 60

4 TOSSIN' AND TURNIN'
Bobby Lewis *Beltone* 61

5 AQUARIUS/LET THE SUNSHINE IN
5th Dimension *Soul City* 69

6 SUGAR, SUGAR
The Archies *Calendar* 69

7 I WANT TO HOLD YOUR HAND
The Beatles *Capitol* 64

8 I HEARD IT THROUGH THE GRAPEVINE
Marvin Gaye *Tamla* 68

9 IT'S NOW OR NEVER
Elvis Presley *RCA* 60

10 HE'LL HAVE TO GO
Jim Reeves *RCA* 60

11 HELLO, DOLLY!
Louis Armstrong *Kapp* 64

12 I'M SORRY
Brenda Lee *Decca* 60

13 I'M A BELIEVER
The Monkees *Colgems* 66

14 I CAN'T STOP LOVING YOU
Ray Charles *ABC-Paramount* 62

15 LOVE IS BLUE
Paul Mauriat *Philips* 68

16 BIG GIRLS DON'T CRY
The Four Seasons *Vee Jay* 62

17 ARE YOU LONESOME TONIGHT?
Elvis Presley *RCA* 60

18 WIPE OUT
The Surfaris *Dot* 63

19 HONKY TONK WOMEN
The Rolling Stones *London* 69

20 COME TOGETHER/SOMETHING
The Beatles *Apple* 69

21 LOVE CHILD
Diana Ross & the Supremes *Motown* 68

22 EVERYDAY PEOPLE
Sly & the Family Stone *Epic* 69

23 SUGAR SHACK
Jimmy Gilmer & the Fireballs *Dot* 63

24 TO SIR WITH LOVE
Lulu *Epic* 67

25 LIMBO ROCK
Chubby Checker *Parkway* 62

26 HONEY
Bobby Goldsboro *UA* 68

27 PEPPERMINT TWIST
Joey Dee & the Starliters *Roulette* 62

28 EXODUS
Ferrante and Teicher *UA* 61

29 RUNNING BEAR
Johnny Preston *Mercury* 60

30 WONDERLAND BY NIGHT
Bert Kaempfert *Decca* 61

31 EVERYBODY'S SOMEBODY'S FOOL
Connie Francis *MGM* 60

32 (SITTIN' ON) THE DOCK OF THE BAY
Otis Redding *Volt* 68

33 CRIMSON AND CLOVER
Tommy James & the Shondells *Roulette* 69

34 CATHY'S CLOWN
Everly Brothers *Warner Bros* 60

35 BIG BAD JOHN
Jimmy Dean *Columbia* 61

36 I CAN'T GET NEXT TO YOU
The Temptations *Gordy* 69

37 TRAVELIN' MAN
Ricky Nelson *Imperial* 61

38 PEOPLE GOT TO BE FREE
The Rascals *Atlantic* 68

39 EL PASO
Marty Robbins *Columbia* 60

40 LAST DATE
Floyd Cramer *RCA* 60

41 GET BACK
The Beatles w/Billy Preston *Apple* 69

42 WILL YOU LOVE ME TOMORROW
The Shirelles *Scepter* 61

43 WINCHESTER CATHEDRAL
New Vaudeville Band *Fontana* 66

44 LIGHT MY FIRE
The Doors *Elektra* 67

45 NORTH TO ALASKA
Johnny Horton *Columbia* 60

46 ROSES ARE RED (MY LOVE)
Bobby Vinton *Epic* 62

47 OH, PRETTY WOMAN
Roy Orbison *Monument* 64

48 SAVE THE LAST DANCE FOR ME
The Drifters *Atlantic* 60

49 PONY TIME
Chubby Checker *Parkway* 61

50 STUCK ON YOU
Elvis Presley *RCA* 60

51 SHE LOVES YOU
The Beatles *Swan* 64

52 SOMEDAY WE'LL BE TOGETHER
Diana Ross & the Supremes *Motown* 69

53 WINDY
The Association *Warner Bros* 67

54 ODE TO BILLIE JOE
Bobbie Gentry *Capitol* 67

55 THIS GUY'S IN LOVE WITH YOU
Herb Alpert *A&M* 68

56 RUNAWAY
Del Shannon *Big Top* 61

57 DOMINIQUE
The Singing Nun *Philips* 63

58 DIZZY
Tommy Roe *ABC* 69

59 MY HEART HAS A MIND OF ITS OWN
Connie Francis *MGM* 60

60 HE'S SO FINE
The Chiffons *Laurie* 63

61 THE LETTER
The Box Tops *Mala* 67

62 CALCUTTA
Lawrence Welk *Dot* 61

63 TEEN ANGEL
Mark Dinning *MGM* 60

64 I GET AROUND
The Beach Boys *Capitol* 64

65 THE BALLAD OF THE GREEN BERETS
S/Sgt Barry Sadler *RCA* 66

66 MY GUY
Mary Wells *Motown* 64

67 NA NA HEY HEY KISS HIM GOODBYE
Steam *Fontana* 69

68 JUDY IN DISGUISE (WITH GLASSES)
John Fred & His Playboy Band *Paula* 68

69 GREENFIELDS
Brothers Four *Columbia* 60

70 STRANGER ON THE SHORE
Mr. Acker Bilk *Atco* 62

71 LEAVING ON A JET PLANE
Peter, Paul and Mary *Warner Bros* 69

72 IN THE YEAR 2525 (EXORDIUM & TERMINUS)
Zager and Evans *RCA* 69

73 BLUE VELVET
Bobby Vinton *Epic* 63

74 HEY PAULA
Paul and Paula *Philips* 63

75 DAYDREAM BELIEVER
The Monkees *Colgems* 67

76 (I CAN'T GET NO) SATISFACTION
The Rolling Stones *London* 65

77 WEDDING BELL BLUES
5th Dimension *Soul City* 69

78 YOU'VE LOST THAT LOVIN' FEELIN'
Righteous Brothers *Philles* 65

79 SIXTEEN REASONS
Connie Stevens *Warner Bros* 60

80 RUNAROUND SUE
Dion *Laurie* 61

81 THERE! I'VE SAID IT AGAIN
Bobby Vinton *Epic* 64

82 THE STRIPPER
David Rose *MGM* 62

83 SOMETHIN' STUPID
Nancy Sinatra and Frank Sinatra *Reprise* 67

84 BABY LOVE
The Supremes *Motown* 64

85 SWEET NOTHIN'S
Brenda Lee *Decca* 60

86 COME SEE ABOUT ME
The Supremes *Motown* 64

87 DOWNTOWN
Petula Clark *Warner Bros* 65

88 JOHNNY ANGEL
Shelley Fabares *Colpix* 62

89 RETURN TO SENDER
Elvis Presley *RCA* 62

90 GO AWAY LITTLE GIRL
Steve Lawrence *Columbia* 63

91 SHERRY
The Four Seasons *Vee Jay* 62

92 LOVE THEME FROM "ROMEO & JULIET"
Henry Mancini *RCA* 69

93 A HARD DAY'S NIGHT
The Beatles *Capitol* 64

94 MASHED POTATO TIME
Dee Dee Sharp *Cameo* 62

95 WOOLY BULLY
Sam the Sham & the Pharaohs *MGM* 65

96 HANDY MAN
Jimmy Jones *Cub* 60

97 LOUIE LOUIE
The Kingsmen *Wand* 63

98 HAPPY TOGETHER
The Turtles *White Whale* 67

99 THEME FROM "THE APARTMENT"
Ferrante and Teicher *UA* 60

100 A THOUSAND STARS
Kathy Young w/the Innocents *Indigo* 60

THE TOP 100 SONGS OF
THE SEVENTIES

To many baby-boomers who grew up in the '50s and '60s, the '70s paled by comparison. Contrasted to decades that gave birth to Elvis Presley and the Beatles, the '70s might suffer. But during the years 1970 and 1971, singer/songwriters like Carole King and James Taylor became successful with their personal, introspective music, and 1972 saw "American Pie" top the chart. The decade couldn't have been all that bad.

Only three artists who were listed on the top 100 songs of the '60s made it onto the list for the '70s: Marvin Gaye, the Four Seasons and Sly & the Family Stone. One could also include performers who left groups for solo careers: Diana Ross, Paul McCartney and George Harrison.

The latter part of the decade is hailed by some and condemned by others for the rise of disco music. The top songs of the decade include hits by Chic, Donna Summer, the Village People and Gloria Gaynor. Dominating the years 1977 through 1979 were the Bee Gees and their youngest brother Andy.

The Bee Gees

1 **YOU LIGHT UP MY LIFE**
Debby Boone *Warner/Curb* 77

2 **HOW DEEP IS YOUR LOVE**
Bee Gees *RSO* 77

3 **I JUST WANT TO BE YOUR EVERYTHING**
Andy Gibb *RSO* 77

4 **LE FREAK**
Chic *Atlantic* 78

5 **SHADOW DANCING**
Andy Gibb *RSO* 78

6 **STAYIN' ALIVE**
Bee Gees *RSO* 78

7 **NIGHT FEVER**
Bee Gees *RSO* 78

8 **RAINDROPS KEEP FALLIN' ON MY HEAD**
B.J. Thomas *Scepter* 70

9 **BEST OF MY LOVE**
The Emotions *Columbia* 77

10 **TONIGHT'S THE NIGHT (GONNA BE ALRIGHT)**
Rod Stewart *Warner Bros* 76

11 **HOT STUFF**
Donna Summer *Casablanca* 79

12 **I GO CRAZY**
Paul Davis *Bang* 78

13 **TIE A YELLOW RIBBON ROUND THE OLE OAK TREE**
Dawn *Bell* 73

14 **Y.M.C.A.**
Village People *Casablanca* 79

15 **MY SHARONA**
The Knack *Capitol* 79

16 **KISS YOU ALL OVER**
Exile *Warner/Curb* 78

17 **AMERICAN PIE**
Don McLean *UA* 72

18 **DA YA THINK I'M SEXY?**
Rod Stewart *Warner Bros* 79

19 **I WILL SURVIVE**
Gloria Gaynor *Polydor* 79

20 **I'LL BE THERE**
The Jackson Five *Motown* 70

21 **(LOVE IS) THICKER THAN WATER**
Andy Gibb *RSO* 78

22 **THE FIRST TIME EVER I SAW YOUR FACE**
Roberta Flack *Atlantic* 72

23 **BOOGIE OOGIE OOGIE**
A Taste of Honey *Capitol* 78

24 **I THINK I LOVE YOU**
The Partridge Family *Bell* 70

25 **ALONE AGAIN (NATURALLY)**
Gilbert O'Sullivan *MAM* 72

26 **RHINESTONE COWBOY**
Glen Campbell *Capitol* 75

27 **PLAY THAT FUNKY MUSIC**
Wild Cherry *Epic* 76

28 **LET'S GET IT ON**
Marvin Gaye *Tamla* 73

29 **HOT CHILD IN THE CITY**
Nick Gilder *Chrysalis* 78

30 **MAGGIE MAY/REASON TO BELIEVE**
Rod Stewart *Mercury* 71

THE TOP 100 SONGS OF
THE EIGHTIES

Half of the top 10 singles of the '80s feature women singing lead vocals, including the top two songs of the decade, "Physical" by Olivia Newton-John and "Bette Davis Eyes" by Kim Carnes. That's an improvement from the '50s and '60s, where only one female lead vocal was in the top 10, and the '70s, where there were three.

There are four singles taken directly from motion picture soundtracks in the top 10, equaling the number of movie songs in the top 10 of the '70s: "Endless Love," "Eye Of The Tiger," "Flashdance . . . What A Feeling" and "Call Me."

The decade's top 100 includes music of all genres, including disco or dance music like "Celebration" by Kool & the Gang; some classic British rock like "Owner Of A Lonely Heart" by Yes; Motown singles from Diana Ross, Stevie Wonder and Smokey Robinson; adult/contemporary hits like "Lady" by Kenny Rogers; country music from Eddie Rabbitt and Dolly Parton; and classic rock and roll from INXS and the J. Geils Band.

Michael Jackson

1 PHYSICAL
Olivia Newton-John *MCA* 81

2 BETTE DAVIS EYES
Kim Carnes *EMI America* 81

3 ANOTHER ONE BITES THE DUST
Queen *Elektra* 80

4 EVERY BREATH YOU TAKE
The Police *A&M* 83

5 ENDLESS LOVE
Diana Ross and Lionel Richie *Motown* 81

6 EYE OF THE TIGER
Survivor *Scotti Bros* 82

7 FLASHDANCE ... WHAT A FEELING
Irene Cara *Casablanca* 83

8 SAY, SAY, SAY
Paul McCartney and Michael Jackson *Columbia* 83

9 CALL ME
Blondie *Chrysalis* 80

10 CENTERFOLD
J. Geils Band *EMI America* 82

11 DO THAT TO ME ONE MORE TIME
Captain & Tennille *Casablanca* 80

12 HURTS SO GOOD
John Cougar *Riva* 82

13 JESSIE'S GIRL
Rick Springfield *RCA* 81

14 BILLIE JEAN
Michael Jackson *Epic* 83

15 LADY
Kenny Rogers *Liberty* 80

16 ABRACADABRA
Steve Miller Band *Capitol* 82

17 ALL NIGHT LONG (ALL NIGHT)
Lionel Richie *Motown* 83

18 DON'T YOU WANT ME
Human League *A&M* 82

19 UPSIDE DOWN
Diana Ross *Motown* 80

20 WHEN DOVES CRY
Prince *Warner Bros* 84

21 ANOTHER BRICK IN THE WALL
Pink Floyd *Columbia* 80

22 CELEBRATION
Kool & the Gang *De-Lite* 81

23 TOTAL ECLIPSE OF THE HEART
Bonnie Tyler *Columbia* 83

24 EBONY AND IVORY
Paul McCartney and Stevie Wonder *Columbia* 82

25 ROCK WITH YOU
Michael Jackson *Epic* 80

26 BEAT IT
Michael Jackson *Epic* 83

27 WOMAN IN LOVE
Barbra Streisand *Columbia* 80

28 DOWN UNDER
Men at Work *Columbia* 83

29 GLORIA
Laura Branigan *Atlantic* 82

30 WAITING FOR A GIRL LIKE YOU
Foreigner *Atlantic* 81

THE SUBJECTS

When Pam Miller-Algar writes each weekly edition of "Dick Clark's Rock, Roll and Remember," a nationally syndicated radio series, she has to come up with a number of songs that relate to each other, to be played in sets during the show. One segment might feature three songs about food, another could spotlight songs that have articles of clothing in the title. This section is dedicated to anyone in radio who has had to find three songs by artists born in Philadelphia on a Tuesday (when it was raining).

Strangely, this section was one of the more difficult ones to compile. Strict rules were set up to determine which songs belonged in a category. It wasn't so hard to decide if a song had a day of the week in the title; that was clear-cut. What constituted a song about a place was a trickier matter. Did "Chantilly Lace" qualify, even though the French town was being used as an adjective? Yes. Did fictional locations like Harper Valley count? Yes. What about "Margaritaville," which was a state of mind more than an actual location? In this case, no.

The list of top 100 songs about animals includes many songs that aren't actually about animals. "Cat's In The Cradle" refers to a children's game, not a feline, and "Hungry Like The Wolf" isn't about an actual wolf. Still, any song with an animal in its title—even a metaphoric animal—is on the list.

For those who are curious about subjects not included in this book, the top three songs that mention food or drink in the title are "Sugar, Sugar" by the Archies, "American Pie" by Don McLean and "Tequila" by the Champs.   The top three songs that have body parts in the title are "Bette Davis Eyes" by Kim Carnes, "Eye Of The Tiger" by Survivor and "Raindrops Keep Fallin' On My Head" by B.J. Thomas. The top three fashion-statement songs are "Blue Suede Shoes" by Carl Perkins, "A White Sport Coat (And A Pink Carnation)" by Marty Robbins and "The Ballad Of The Green Berets" by S/Sgt. Barry Sadler.   And the top three songs with land vehicles in the title are "Midnight Train To Georgia" by Gladys Knight & the Pips, "Morning Train (Nine To Five)" by Sheena Easton and "Chariots Of Fire" by Vangelis.

PLACES

Cal"California is the place that shows up the most often in the top 100 geographic songs. Considered for the list were any songs that mention a specific place in the title or were clearly about a specific geographic location. Continents, countries, states and cities qualified, and so did locales within a city, such as Baker Street or the West End in London, or Washington Square and Broadway in Manhattan. Locations were also included when used as adjectives, such as "Chantilly Lace" or "China Girl."

Six "California" songs are in the top 100, starting with "Hotel California" by the Eagles at number 18. The city with the most mentions is New Orleans, showing up in songs by Johnny Horton, Freddy Cannon, Gary U.S. Bonds and Fats Domino. Countries? The U.S.A. gets four mentions, and America gets two; other countries in the top 100 with one song each are Australia ("Down Under"), China, Mexico and Spain.

Mitch Miller

1 LISBON ANTIGUA
Nelson Riddle *Capitol* 56

2 THE YELLOW ROSE OF TEXAS
Mitch Miller *Columbia* 55

3 THE POOR PEOPLE OF PARIS
Les Baxter *Capitol* 56

4 THE BATTLE OF NEW ORLEANS
Johnny Horton *Columbia* 59

5 BLUEBERRY HILL
Fats Domino *Imperial* 57

6 DOWN UNDER
Men at Work *Columbia* 83

7 COMING UP (LIVE AT GLASGOW)
Paul McCartney *Columbia* 80

8 ALLEGHENY MOON
Patti Page *Mercury* 56

9 PHILADELPHIA FREEDOM
The Elton John Band *MCA* 75

10 MACARTHUR PARK
Donna Summer *Casablanca* 78

11 (SITTIN' ON) THE DOCK OF THE BAY
Otis Redding *Volt* 68

12 EL PASO
Marty Robbins *Columbia* 60

13 MIDNIGHT TRAIN TO GEORGIA
Gladys Knight & the Pips *Buddah* 73

14 CHANTILLY LACE
Big Bopper *Mercury* 58

15 WINCHESTER CATHEDRAL
The New Vaudeville Band *Fontana* 66

16 NORTH TO ALASKA
Johnny Horton *Columbia* 60

17 THE NIGHT THE LIGHTS WENT OUT IN GEORGIA
Vicki Lawrence *Bell* 73

18 HOTEL CALIFORNIA
Eagles *Asylum* 77

19 CALCUTTA
Lawrence Welk *Dot* 61

20 AFRICA
Toto *Columbia* 83

21 THE YELLOW ROSE OF TEXAS
Johnny Desmond *Coral* 55

22 TSOP (THE SOUND OF PHILADELPHIA)
MFSB f/The Three Degrees *PIR* 74

23 BAKER STREET
Gerry Rafferty *UA* 78

24 KANSAS CITY
Wilbert Harrison *Fury* 59

25 KEY LARGO
Bertie Higgins *Kat Family* 82

26 BRISTOL STOMP
The Dovells *Parkway* 61

27 WICHITA LINEMAN
Glen Campbell *Capitol* 69

28 TAKE ME HOME, COUNTRY ROADS
John Denver *RCA* 71

29 LAST TRAIN TO CLARKSVILLE
The Monkees *Colgems* 66

30 WEST END GIRLS
Pet Shop Boys *EMI America* 86

THE TOP 100 SONGS WITH
NAMES IN THE TITLE

Considering that love is the subject of most songs, it's not surprising that the name that appears the most often in the top 100 name songs is Venus, the goddess of love. Frankie Avalon's "Venus" is number 18. A different song called "Venus" by the Shocking Blue is number 70, and a piece of that song shows up in the Stars on 45 medley, listed at number 42.

The number one song is "Mack The Knife" by Bobby Darin from *The Threepenny Opera*. Many of the names in the top 100 are of characters from plays, films and literature, including Tammy, Dolly, Arthur, Rocky, Frankenstein, Romeo and Juliet, Mrs. Robinson, Alley-Oop and Shaft. Real people on the list are Bette Davis, Julian Lennon ("Hey Jude"), Beethoven, Mozart ("Rock Me Amadeus" by Falco), Nadia Comeneci, Duke Ellington ("Sir Duke"), Dominique and St. Elmo, girlfriends Sharona, Diana and Donna, and Theodore Roosevelt (as in "teddy bear").

Laura Branigan

1 **MACK THE KNIFE**
Bobby Darin *Atco* 59

2 **TAMMY**
Debbie Reynolds *Coral* 57

3 **BETTE DAVIS EYES**
Kim Carnes *EMI America* 81

4 **HEY JUDE**
The Beatles *Apple* 68

5 **(LET ME BE YOUR) TEDDY BEAR**
Elvis Presley *RCA* 57

6 **JESSIE'S GIRL**
Rick Springfield *RCA* 81

7 **BILLIE JEAN**
Michael Jackson *Epic* 83

8 **WAKE UP LITTLE SUSIE**
Everly Brothers *Cadence* 57

9 **MY SHARONA**
The Knack *Capitol* 79

10 **DIANA**
Paul Anka *ABC-Paramount* 57

11 **GLORIA**
Laura Branigan *Atlantic* 82

12 **JACK AND DIANE**
John Cougar *Riva* 82

13 **HELLO, DOLLY!**
Louis Armstrong *Kapp* 64

14 **MAGGIE MAY**
Rod Stewart *Mercury* 71

15 **TOM DOOLEY**
The Kingston Trio *Capitol* 58

16 **ROSANNA**
Toto *Columbia* 82

17 **A FIFTH OF BEETHOVEN**
Walter Murphy *Private Stock* 76

18 **VENUS**
Frankie Avalon *Chancellor* 59

19 **LAY DOWN SALLY**
Eric Clapton *RSO* 78

20 **ARTHUR'S THEME (BEST THAT YOU CAN DO)**
Christopher Cross *Warner Bros* 81

21 **PATRICIA**
Perez Prado *RCA* 58

22 **RUNNING BEAR**
Johnny Preston *Mercury* 60

23 **MACARTHUR PARK**
Donna Summer *Casablanca* 78

24 **STAGGER LEE**
Lloyd Price *ABC-Paramount* 59

25 **MICKEY**
Toni Basil *Chrysalis* 82

26 **CATHY'S CLOWN**
Everly Brothers *Warner Bros* 60

27 **BIG BAD JOHN**
Jimmy Dean *Columbia* 61

28 **DONNA**
Ritchie Valens *Del-Fi* 59

29 **BAD, BAD LEROY BROWN**
Jim Croce *ABC* 73

30 **LITTLE JEANNIE**
Elton John *MCA* 80

Dogs may be man's best friend, but more songs have been written about birds.

Perhaps it's because birds are considered to be more musical, although anyone who has heard the Singing Dogs warble "Jingle Bells" might disagree. To compute the top 100 songs about animals, all living creatures (except for humans, of course) were considered, even insects like the firefly and the ladybug. Metaphoric references were included, and so were mythical creatures like the unicorn and the dragon.

Birds of one type or another account for 24 of the top 100 songs. Doves and robins have three mentions each, while ducks have two. The highest ranking bird song is Prince's "When Doves Cry," from the soundtrack of *Purple Rain*.

Dogs placed a respectable second, with 11 songs included in the top 100; cats are right behind dogs with nine songs in the top 100.

Culture Club

31 THE CHIPMUNK SONG
The Chipmunks w/David Seville *Liberty* 58

32 MONKEY
George Michael *Columbia* 88

33 SNOOPY VS. THE RED BARON
The Royal Guardsmen *Laurie* 66

34 PUFF THE MAGIC DRAGON
Peter, Paul and Mary *Warner Bros* 63

35 BUFFALO STANCE
Neneh Cherry *Virgin* 89

36 THE BIRDS AND THE BEES
Jewel Akens *Era* 65

37 BEN
Michael Jackson *Motown* 72

38 MULE SKINNER BLUES
The Fendermen *Soma* 60

39 MOCKINGBIRD
Carly Simon and James Taylor *Elektra* 74

40 WILDFIRE
Michael Murphey *Epic* 75

41 SONGBIRD
Kenny G *Arista* 87

42 CAT'S IN THE CRADLE
Harry Chapin *Elektra* 74

43 ROCKIN' ROBIN
Michael Jackson *Motown* 72

44 THE HORSE
Cliff Nobles & Co. *Phil-L.A. of Soul* 68

45 PUPPY LOVE
Paul Anka *ABC-Paramount* 60

46 WINGS OF A DOVE
Ferlin Husky *Capitol* 61

47 BARRACUDA
Heart *Portrait* 77

48 FOX ON THE RUN
Sweet *Capitol* 76

49 THE FLY
Chubby Checker *Parkway* 61

50 HUMMINGBIRD
Les Paul and Mary Ford *Capitol* 55

51 THE LONELY BULL
The Tijuana Brass f/Herb Alpert *A&M* 62

52 ME AND YOU AND A DOG NAMED BOO
Lobo *Big Tree* 71

53 BLACK CAT
Janet Jackson *A&M* 90

54 ALLEY CAT
Bent Fabric & His Piano *Atco* 62

55 PUPPY LOVE
Donny Osmond *MGM* 72

56 TIGER
Fabian *Chancellor* 59

57 HEY LITTLE COBRA
The Rip Chords *Columbia* 64

58 SURFIN' BIRD
The Trashmen *Garrett* 64

59 WHAT'S NEW, PUSSYCAT?
Tom Jones *Parrot* 65

60 YELLOW BIRD
Arthur Lyman Group *Hi-Fi* 61

61 ALVIN'S HARMONICA
The Chipmunks & David Seville *Liberty* 59

62 SNOWBIRD
Anne Murray *Capitol* 70

63 THE UNICORN
The Irish Rovers *Decca* 68

64 HOUND DOG MAN
Fabian *Chancellor* 59

65 MOCKINGBIRD
Inez Foxx *Symbol* 63

66 WALKING THE DOG
Rufus Thomas *Stax* 63

67 TIE ME KANGAROO DOWN, SPORT
Rolf Harris *Epic* 63

68 BEATNIK FLY
Johnny & the Hurricanes *Warwick* 60

69 ELUSIVE BUTTERFLY
Bob Lind *World Pacific* 66

70 OLD RIVERS
Walter Brennan *Liberty* 62

71 THE MONKEY TIME
Major Lance *Okeh* 63

72 YEAR OF THE CAT
Al Stewart *Janus* 77

73 WALK THE DINOSAUR
Was (Not Was) *Chrysalis* 89

74 EDGE OF SEVENTEEN (JUST LIKE THE WHITE WINGED DOVE)
Stevie Nicks *Modern* 82

75 THE DUCK
Jackie Lee *Mirwood* 66

76 ONE MONKEY DON'T STOP NO SHOW (PART I)
The Honey Cone *Hot Wax* 72

77 FUNKY WORM
Ohio Players *Westbound* 73

78 WHITE RABBIT
Jefferson Airplane *RCA* 67

79 YOGI
The Ivy Three *Shell* 60

80 BEAST OF BURDEN
The Rolling Stones *Rolling Stones* 78

81 NASHVILLE CATS
The Lovin' Spoonful *Kama Sutra* 67

82 NIGHTINGALE
Carole King *Ode* 75

83 BUNGLE IN THE JUNGLE
Jethro Tull *Chrysalis* 75

84 TURTLE POWER
Partners In Kryme *SBK* 90

85 PUSSY CAT
The Ames Brothers *RCA* 58

86 RUN FOR THE ROSES
Dan Fogelberg *Full Moon* 82

87 BLACK DOG
Led Zeppelin *Atlantic* 72

88 LUCKY LADYBUG
Billy and Lillie *Swan* 59

89 HUMMINGBIRD
Seals and Crofts *Warner Bros* 73

90 PEPINO THE ITALIAN MOUSE
Lou Monte *Reprise* 63

91 FIREFLY
Tony Bennett *Columbia* 58

92 MICKEY'S MONKEY
The Miracles *Tamla* 63

93 LITTLE RED ROOSTER
Sam Cooke *RCA* 63

94 DO THE BIRD
Dee Dee Sharp *Cameo* 63

95 HONKY CAT
Elton John *Uni* 72

96 CRAZY HORSES
The Osmonds *MGM* 72

97 DEAD SKUNK
Loudon Wainwright III *Columbia* 73

98 ANIMAL
Def Leppard *Mercury* 87

99 WONDERING WHERE THE LIONS ARE
Bruce Cockburn *Millennium* 80

100 TENNESSEE BIRD WALK
Jack Blanchard and Misty Morgan *Wayside* 70

THE TOP 100 SONGS ABOUT
COLORS

The dictionary defines "blue" as the color of the clear sky and deep sea, or feeling melancholy or low. The latter definition has helped make "blue" the color of choice for most songwriters; 32 of the top 100 songs with colors in the title mention the color.

Songs with "blues" in the title were eliminated from the list, but metaphoric references were included, such as the themes from *The Man with the Golden Arm* and the song "Ivory Tower," which is listed twice.

Paul Mauriat's instrumental version of "Love Is Blue" leads the list of blue songs. In second place is a song about a man flying through the "blue painted in blue." That is the translation for "Volare (Nel Blu Dipinto Di Blu)" by Domenico Modugno.

Tied for second place are red and black, with 11 songs each on the top 100. Bobby Vinton's "Roses Are Red (My Love)" and Alannah Myles' "Black Velvet" are tops in their class.

Tony Orlando & Dawn

1 **THE YELLOW ROSE OF TEXAS**
Mitch Miller *Columbia* 55

2 **THE GREEN DOOR**
Jim Lowe *Dot* 56

3 **EBONY AND IVORY**
Paul McCartney and Stevie Wonder *Columbia* 82

4 **TIE A YELLOW RIBBON ROUND THE OLE OAK TREE**
Dawn *Bell* 73

5 **SAIL ALONG SILVERY MOON**
Billy Vaughn *Dot* 58

6 **LOVE IS BLUE**
Paul Mauriat *Philips* 68

7 **VOLARE (NEL BLU DIPINTO DI BLU)**
Domenico Modugno *Decca* 58

8 **MR. BLUE**
The Fleetwoods *Dolton* 59

9 **MY BLUE HEAVEN**
Fats Domino *Imperial* 56

10 **CRIMSON AND CLOVER**
Tommy James & the Shondells *Roulette* 69

11 **IVORY TOWER**
Cathy Carr *Fraternity* 56

12 **BLUE SUEDE SHOES**
Carl Perkins *Sun* 56

13 **DON'T IT MAKE MY BROWN EYES BLUE**
Crystal Gayle *UA* 77

14 **A WHITE SPORT COAT (AND A PINK CARNATION)**
Marty Robbins *Columbia* 57

15 **ROSES ARE RED (MY LOVE)**
Bobby Vinton *Epic* 62

16 **BLACK VELVET**
Alannah Myles *Atlantic* 90

17 **THE BALLAD OF THE GREEN BERETS**
S/Sgt. Barry Sadler *RCA* 66

18 **GREENFIELDS**
Brothers Four *Columbia* 60

19 **THE YELLOW ROSE OF TEXAS**
Johnny Desmond *Coral* 55

20 **THE PURPLE PEOPLE EATER**
Sheb Wooley *MGM* 58

21 **BLUE VELVET**
Bobby Vinton *Epic* 63

22 **MISTY BLUE**
Dorothy Moore *Malaco* 76

23 **BLUE BAYOU**
Linda Ronstadt *Asylum* 77

24 **PINK SHOE LACES**
Dodie Stevens *Crystalette* 59

25 **BLUE MOON**
The Marcels *Colpix* 61

26 **NIGHTS IN WHITE SATIN**
The Moody Blues *Deram* 72

27 **DEVIL WITH A BLUE DRESS ON & GOOD GOLLY MISS MOLLY**
Mitch Ryder & the Detroit Wheels *New Voice* 66

28 **ITSY BITSY TEENIE WEENIE YELLOW POLKA DOT BIKINI**
Brian Hyland *Leader* 60

29 **LITTLE RED CORVETTE**
Prince *Warner Bros* 83

30 **PRETTY BLUE EYES**
Steve Lawrence *ABC-Paramount* 60

1 SATURDAY NIGHT
Bay City Rollers *Arista* 76

2 RAINY DAYS AND MONDAYS
Carpenters *A&M* 71

3 MONDAY, MONDAY
The Mamas and the Papas *Dunhill* 66

4 MANIC MONDAY
Bangles *Columbia* 86

5 BLUE MONDAY
Fats Domino *Imperial* 57

6 RUBY TUESDAY
The Rolling Stones *London* 67

7 NEW MOON ON MONDAY
Duran Duran *Capitol* 84

8 PLEASANT VALLEY SUNDAY
The Monkees *Colgems* 67

9 SATURDAY IN THE PARK
Chicago *Columbia* 72

10 ANOTHER SATURDAY NIGHT
Cat Stevens *A&M* 74

11 SATURDAY NIGHT'S ALRIGHT FOR FIGHTING
Elton John *MCA* 73

12 ANOTHER SATURDAY NIGHT
Sam Cooke *RCA* 63

13 BEAUTIFUL SUNDAY
Daniel Boone *Mercury* 72

14 FRIDAY ON MY MIND
The Easybeats *UA* 67

15 NEVER ON SUNDAY
Don Costa *UA* 60

16 SATURDAY NITE
Earth, Wind & Fire *Columbia* 77

17 NEVER ON SUNDAY
The Chordettes *Cadence* 61

18 THAT SUNDAY, THAT SUMMER
Nat King Cole *Capitol* 63

19 LIVIN' IT UP (FRIDAY NIGHT)
Bell and James *A&M* 79

20 COME SATURDAY MORNING
The Sandpipers *A&M* 70

21 SATURDAY NIGHT AT THE MOVIES
The Drifters *Atlantic* 64

22 SUNDAY WILL NEVER BE THE SAME
Spanky & Our Gang *Mercury* 67

23 SUGAR ON SUNDAY
Clique *White Whale* 69

24 SUNDAY AND ME
Jay & the Americans *UA* 65

25 THANK GOD IT'S FRIDAY
Love & Kisses *Casablanca* 78

26 TUESDAY AFTERNOON (FOREVER AFTERNOON)
The Moody Blues *Deram* 68

27 SATURDAY MORNING CONFUSION
Bobby Russell *UA* 71

28 SATURDAY NIGHT SPECIAL
Lynyrd Skynyrd *MCA* 75

29 COME MONDAY
Jimmy Buffett *Dunhill* 74

30 SUNDAY MORNIN'
Spanky & Our Gang *Mercury* 68

The Mamas & the Papas

If Friday's Child is full of woe, it may be because she hasn't had very many songs written about her. There are only three "Friday" titles on the list of top 30 songs about days of the week, but that's better than Tuesday (2) and poor Wednesday and Thursday (with none).

The weekend is the most popular part of the week to write songs about. There are 10 "Saturday" songs, including the number one day-of-the-week hit, "Saturday Night" by the Bay City Rollers. Also in the top 10 are "Saturday In The Park" by Chicago and "Another Saturday Night" by Cat Stevens. Sam Cooke's original version of the latter is number 12.

Sunday is not far behind, with nine songs in the top 30. The top Sunday song is "Pleasant Valley Sunday" by the Monkees. Spanky & Our Gang especially loved the day, scoring with both "Sunday Will Never Be The Same" and "Sunday Mornin'."

Monday is a day of dread for many people, whether it's blue or manic. There are six "Monday" songs in the top 30, starting with the Carpenters' "Rainy Days And Mondays" at number two. Oddly, five of the six Monday songs are in the top 10, including the Mamas and the Papas' number one hit "Monday, Monday."

The "Friday" songs are led by the Easybeats' "Friday On My Mind." Tuesday is represented by the Rolling Stones with "Ruby Tuesday" and the Moody Blues with "Tuesday Afternoon."

There has only been one "Wednesday" song that made the *Billboard* chart during the entire rock era. The Royal Guardsmen's fourth single was titled "Wednesday," and it peaked at number 97.

THE TOP 3000 SONGS OF THE ROCK ERA

The Top 3000 Songs of the Rock Era are ranked in order of their chart performance on *Billboard*'s Hot 100—the weekly survey of the most popular singles in the U.S.A.—and the Hot 100's prior incarnation, the Best Sellers in Stores chart.

Singles eligible for inclusion in the Top 3000 reached their chart peaks between July 9, 1955, and December 29, 1990. Pop historians generally agree that the "rock era" began in July of 1955, when Bill Haley and His Comets' "(We're Gonna) Rock Around The Clock" went to number one.

Beginning with the chart of July 9, 1955, singles received 100 points for every week that they were in the number one position; 99 points for every week they were number two, 98 points for every week they were number three, and so on, down to number 30. Fifty bonus points were added to a song's total for every week that it was number one.

When all of the points were added up, there were multiple ties. Those were broken by considering each song's peak position and the number of weeks it spent in that peak position, in the top 10, in the top 40, and on the entire Hot 100. Remaining ties were broken by tracking the singles' entire chart life and assigning points for each week a song was listed between 31 and 100.

Billboard listed both sides of a single in the same chart position prior to the creation of the Hot 100 in August, 1958. After that date, "A" and "B" sides were ranked separately. That policy changed on November 29, 1969, and two-sided hits such as "Come Together" and "Something" by the Beatles were once again listed together. This practice was later discontinued, and today *Billboard* lists "A" and "B" sides separately.

Since both peak position and length of time on the Hot 100 figure into a single's point total, some rankings in the Top 3000 may be surprising at first. Many singles that reached number one had very short chart lives, and other singles that didn't even make the top five were on the chart for an extraordinarily long time. Extreme examples of this would be "I Hear A Symphony" by the Supremes, which topped the chart but only spent a total of 10 weeks on the entire Hot 100. On the other hand, "I Go Crazy" by Paul Davis peaked at number seven, but spent 40 weeks on the Hot 100. That is why "I Hear A Symphony" is ranked number 1821 on the Top 3000, and "I Go Crazy" is listed at number 87.

Strangely, many titles seem to be listed thematically. Who would have guessed that "King Of Pain" and "It Keeps Right On-A Hurtin'" would have the same point total, or that "My Dad" and "Color Him Father" would tie? "One Hell Of A Woman" and "Knockin' On Heaven's Door" are adjacent on the Top 3000, as are "Breathless" and "You Take My Breath Away" as well as "Somebody's Knockin'" and "At My Front Door." No human planned it that way—but the chart Muse must be having a good laugh.

THE ROCK ERA

1 **THE TWIST**
Chubby Checker *Parkway* 60

2 **DON'T BE CRUEL/HOUND DOG**
Elvis Presley *RCA* 56

3 **(WE'RE GONNA) ROCK AROUND THE CLOCK**
Bill Haley & His Comets *Decca* 55

4 **AUTUMN LEAVES**
Roger Williams *Kapp* 55

5 **SINGING THE BLUES**
Guy Mitchell *Columbia* 56

6 **LOVE LETTERS IN THE SAND**
Pat Boone *Dot* 57

7 **MACK THE KNIFE**
Bobby Darin *Atco* 59

8 **MOMENTS TO REMEMBER**
The Four Lads *Columbia* 55

9 **YOU LIGHT UP MY LIFE**
Debby Boone *Warner/Curb* 77

10 **PHYSICAL**
Olivia Newton-John *MCA* 81

11 **HEARTBREAK HOTEL**
Elvis Presley *RCA* 56

12 **LISBON ANTIGUA**
Nelson Riddle *Capitol* 56

13 **HOW DEEP IS YOUR LOVE**
Bee Gees *RSO* 77

14 **SO RARE**
Jimmy Dorsey *Fraternity* 57

15 **THE WAYWARD WIND**
Gogi Grant *Era* 56

16 **TAMMY**
Debbie Reynolds *Coral* 57

17 **ALL SHOOK UP**
Elvis Presley *RCA* 57

18 **BETTE DAVIS EYES**
Kim Carnes *EMI America* 81

19 **HEY JUDE**
The Beatles *Apple* 68

20 **I JUST WANT TO BE YOUR EVERYTHING**
Andy Gibb *RSO* 77

21 **JUST WALKING IN THE RAIN**
Johnnie Ray *Columbia* 56

22 **THE YELLOW ROSE OF TEXAS**
Mitch Miller *Columbia* 55

23 **LOVE IS A MANY SPLENDORED THING**
The Four Aces *Decca* 55

24 **ANOTHER ONE BITES THE DUST**
Queen *Elektra* 80

25 **EVERY BREATH YOU TAKE**
The Police *A&M* 83

26 **ENDLESS LOVE**
Diana Ross and Lionel Richie *Motown* 81

27 **JAILHOUSE ROCK/TREAT ME NICE**
Elvis Presley *RCA* 57

28 **(LET ME BE YOUR) TEDDY BEAR**
Elvis Presley *RCA* 57

29 **EYE OF THE TIGER**
Survivor *Scotti Bros* 82

30 **LE FREAK**
Chic *Atlantic* 78

31 **SHADOW DANCING**
Andy Gibb *RSO* 78

32 **FLASHDANCE ... WHAT A FEELING**
Irene Cara *Casablanca* 83

33 **SIXTEEN TONS**
Tennessee Ernie Ford *Capitol* 55

34 **THE GREEN DOOR**
Jim Lowe *Dot* 56

35 **HONKY TONK (PARTS 1 & 2)**
Bill Doggett *King* 56

36 **SAY, SAY, SAY**
Paul McCartney and Michael Jackson *Columbia* 83

37 **LOVE ME TENDER**
Elvis Presley *RCA* 56

38 **CALL ME**
Blondie *Chrysalis* 80

39 **CENTERFOLD**
J. Geils Band *EMI America* 82

40 **MEMORIES ARE MADE OF THIS**
Dean Martin *Capitol* 56

41 **THEME FROM "A SUMMER PLACE"**
Percy Faith *Columbia* 60

42 **STAYIN' ALIVE**
Bee Gees *RSO* 78

43 **HE**
Al Hibbler *Decca* 55

44 **HONEYCOMB**
Jimmie Rodgers *Roulette* 57

45 **COME GO WITH ME**
The Dell-Vikings *Dot* 57

46 **BYE BYE LOVE**
Everly Brothers *Cadence* 57

47 **NIGHT FEVER**
Bee Gees *RSO* 78

48 **SEARCHIN'/YOUNG BLOOD**
The Coasters *Atco* 57

49 **THE POOR PEOPLE OF PARIS**
Les Baxter *Capitol* 56

50 **DO THAT TO ME ONE MORE TIME**
Captain & Tennille *Casablanca* 80

51 **CHANCES ARE/THE TWELFTH OF NEVER**
Johnny Mathis *Columbia* 57

52 **IT'S ALL IN THE GAME**
Tommy Edwards *MGM* 58

53 **MONSTER MASH**
Bobby "Boris" Pickett & the Crypt-Kickers *Garpax* 62

54 **TOSSIN' AND TURNIN'**
Bobby Lewis *Beltone* 61

55 **WHATEVER WILL BE, WILL BE (QUE SERA, SERA)**
Doris Day *Columbia* 56

56 **MOONGLOW AND THEME FROM "PICNIC"**
Morris Stoloff *Decca* 56

57 **HURTS SO GOOD**
John Cougar *Riva* 82

58 **RAINDROPS KEEP FALLIN' ON MY HEAD**
B.J. Thomas *Scepter* 70

59 **A BLOSSOM FELL**
Nat King Cole *Capitol* 55

60 **LEARNIN' THE BLUES**
Frank Sinatra *Capitol* 55

Pat Boone

183 IT'S STILL ROCK AND ROLL TO ME
Billy Joel *Columbia* 80

184 QUEEN OF HEARTS
Juice Newton *Capitol* 81

185 BE-BOP BABY/HAVE I TOLD YOU LATELY THAT I LOVE YOU
Ricky Nelson *Imperial* 57

186 REUNITED
Peaches and Herb *Polydor* 79

187 HONKY TONK WOMEN
The Rolling Stones *London* 69

188 WITCH DOCTOR
David Seville *Liberty* 58

189 BECAUSE I LOVE YOU (THE POSTMAN SONG)
Stevie B *LMR* 90

190 LIKE A VIRGIN
Madonna *Sire* 84

191 THREE TIMES A LADY
Commodores *Motown* 78

192 SILLY LOVE SONGS
Wings *Capitol* 76

193 KISS ON MY LIST
Daryl Hall and John Oates *RCA* 81

194 HELLO
Lionel Richie *Motown* 84

195 IT'S ONLY MAKE BELIEVE
Conway Twitty *MGM* 58

196 HOLD ON
Wilson Phillips *SBK* 90

197 COME TOGETHER/SOMETHING
The Beatles *Apple* 69

198 LOVE CHILD
Diana Ross & the Supremes *Motown* 68

199 I ALMOST LOST MY MIND
Pat Boone *Dot* 56

200 EVERYDAY PEOPLE
Sly & the Family Stone *Epic* 69

201 SUGARTIME
McGuire Sisters *Coral* 58

202 OWNER OF A LONELY HEART
Yes *Atco* 84

203 KEEP ON LOVING YOU
REO Speedwagon *Epic* 81

204 KNOCK THREE TIMES
Dawn *Bell* 71

205 YOU MAKE ME FEEL LIKE DANCING
Leo Sayer *Warner Bros* 77

206 SEVENTEEN
Boyd Bennett & His Rockets *King* 55

207 PHILADELPHIA FREEDOM
The Elton John Band *MCA* 75

208 SUGAR SHACK
Jimmy Gilmer & the Fireballs *Dot* 63

209 YOU NEEDED ME
Anne Murray *Capitol* 78

210 TO SIR WITH LOVE
Lulu *Epic* 67

211 MANIAC
Michael Sembello *Casablanca* 83

212 LOVE ON THE ROCKS
Neil Diamond *Capitol* 81

213 FASCINATION
Jane Morgan *Kapp* 57

214 SILHOUETTES/DADDY COOL
The Rays *Cameo* 57

215 LOVE WILL KEEP US TOGETHER
Captain & Tennille *A&M* 75

216 I LIKE DREAMIN'
Kenny Nolan *20th Century* 77

217 I LOVE THE NIGHTLIFE (DISCO 'ROUND)
Alicia Bridges *Polydor* 78

218 DON'T LEAVE ME THIS WAY
Thelma Houston *Tamla* 77

219 LIMBO ROCK
Chubby Checker *Parkway* 62

220 9 TO 5
Dolly Parton *RCA* 81

221 MY TRUE LOVE
Jack Scott *Carlton* 58

222 AGAINST ALL ODDS (TAKE A LOOK AT ME NOW)
Phil Collins *Atlantic* 84

223 VENUS
Frankie Avalon *Chancellor* 59

224 WALK LIKE AN EGYPTIAN
Bangles *Columbia* 86

225 MR. BLUE
The Fleetwoods *Dolton* 59

226 KEEP ON TRUCKIN' (PART 1)
Eddie Kendricks *Tamla* 73

227 HONEY
Bobby Goldsboro *UA* 68

228 LAY DOWN SALLY
Eric Clapton *RSO* 78

229 ARTHUR'S THEME (BEST THAT YOU CAN DO)
Christopher Cross *Warner Bros* 81

230 ROUND AND ROUND
Perry Como *RCA* 57

231 I'M IN LOVE AGAIN/MY BLUE HEAVEN
Fats Domino *Imperial* 56

232 PATRICIA
Perez Prado *RCA* 58

233 ANGEL IN YOUR ARMS
Hot *Big Tree* 77

234 YOU AND I
Eddie Rabbitt w/Crystal Gayle *Elektra* 83

235 PEPPERMINT TWIST
Joey Dee & the Starliters *Roulette* 62

236 EXODUS
Ferrante and Teicher *UA* 61

237 FOOTLOOSE
Kenny Loggins *Columbia* 84

238 RUNNING BEAR
Johnny Preston *Mercury* 60

239 THE WAY WE WERE
Barbra Streisand *Columbia* 74

240 IT MUST HAVE BEEN LOVE
Roxette *EMI* 90

241 THEME FROM "GREATEST AMERICAN HERO" (BELIEVE IT OR NOT)
Joey Scarbury *Elektra* 81

242 WONDERLAND BY NIGHT
Bert Kaempfert *Decca* 61

243 I LOVE A RAINY NIGHT
Eddie Rabbitt *Elektra* 81

244 A LITTLE MORE LOVE
Olivia Newton-John *MCA* 79

245 GHOSTBUSTERS
Ray Parker Jr. *Arista* 84

246 MACARTHUR PARK
Donna Summer *Casablanca* 78

247 EVERYBODY'S SOMEBODY'S FOOL
Connie Francis *MGM* 60

248 (THEY LONG TO BE) CLOSE TO YOU
Carpenters *A&M* 70

249 LITTLE STAR
The Elegants *Apt* 58

250 STANDING ON THE CORNER
The Four Lads *Columbia* 56

251 I JUST CALLED TO SAY I LOVE YOU
Stevie Wonder *Motown* 84

252 BOOGIE NIGHTS
Heatwave *Epic* 77

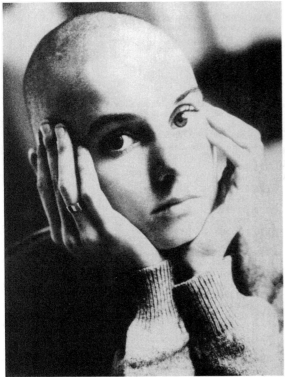

Sinead O'Connor

341

375 EVERY WOMAN IN THE WORLD
Air Supply *Arista* 81

376 AMERICAN WOMAN/NO SUGAR TONIGHT
The Guess Who *RCA* 70

377 CHARIOTS OF FIRE
Vangelis *Polydor* 82

378 JUST THE WAY YOU ARE
Billy Joel *Columbia* 78

379 MISSING YOU
John Waite *EMI America* 84

380 BENNIE AND THE JETS
Elton John *MCA* 74

381 SOMEDAY WE'LL BE TOGETHER
Diana Ross & the Supremes *Motown* 69

382 DARK MOON
Gale Storm *Dot* 57

383 ANOTHER DAY IN PARADISE
Phil Collins *Atlantic* 89

384 SHE WORKS HARD FOR THE MONEY
Donna Summer *Mercury* 83

385 JUST A DREAM
Jimmy Clanton *Ace* 58

386 ALONE
Heart *Capitol* 87

387 LET IT BE
The Beatles *Apple* 70

388 MASTER BLASTER (JAMMIN')
Stevie Wonder *Tamla* 80

389 MONEY FOR NOTHING
Dire Straits *Warner Bros* 85

390 LET'S STAY TOGETHER
Al Green *Hi* 72

391 MY LOVE
Paul McCartney & Wings *Apple* 73

392 WINDY
The Association *Warner Bros* 67

393 BLACK VELVET
Alannah Myles *Atlantic* 90

394 MOONLIGHT GAMBLER
Frankie Laine *Columbia* 57

395 ODE TO BILLIE JOE
Bobbie Gentry *Capitol* 67

396 YOU DON'T BRING ME FLOWERS
Barbra Streisand and Neil Diamond *Columbia* 78

397 DO ME!
Bell Biv Devoe *MCA* 90

398 THE SHIFTING WHISPERING SANDS (PARTS 1 & 2)
Billy Vaughn *Dot* 55

399 SOFT SUMMER BREEZE
Eddie Heywood *Mercury* 56

400 THIS GUY'S IN LOVE WITH YOU
Herb Alpert *A&M* 68

401 RISE
Herb Alpert *A&M* 79

402 HOTEL CALIFORNIA
Eagles *Asylum* 77

403 RUNAWAY
Del Shannon *Big Top* 61

404 DOMINIQUE
The Singing Nun *Philips* 63

405 I WANT YOU BACK
The Jackson Five *Motown* 70

406 DIZZY
Tommy Roe *ABC* 69

407 THE CANDY MAN
Sammy Davis, Jr. *MGM* 72

408 MY HEART HAS A MIND OF ITS OWN
Connie Francis *MGM* 60

409 THE TEARS OF A CLOWN
Smokey Robinson & the Miracles *Tamla* 70

410 UNDERCOVER ANGEL
Alan O'Day *Pacific* 77

411 HE'S SO FINE
The Chiffons *Laurie* 63

412 HOW AM I SUPPOSED TO LIVE WITHOUT YOU
Michael Bolton *Columbia* 90

413 GOT TO GIVE IT UP (PT. 1)
Marvin Gaye *Tamla* 77

414 THE LETTER
The Box Tops *Mala* 67

415 A TEAR FELL/BO WEEVIL
Teresa Brewer *Coral* 56

416 LET'S HEAR IT FOR THE BOY
Deniece Williams *Columbia* 84

417 CALCUTTA
Lawrence Welk *Dot* 61

418 MISS YOU MUCH
Janet Jackson *A&M* 88

419 I CAN SEE CLEARLY NOW
Johnny Nash *Epic* 72

420 THE JOKER
Steve Miller Band *Capitol* 74

421 LOST IN LOVE
Air Supply *Arista* 80

422 THE SWEETEST THING (I'VE EVER KNOWN)
Juice Newton *Capitol* 82

423 TOO MUCH HEAVEN
Bee Gees *RSO* 79

424 I'M YOUR BABY TONIGHT
Whitney Houston *Arista* 90

425 UPTOWN GIRL
Billy Joel *Columbia* 83

426 WE ARE THE WORLD
USA for Africa *Columbia* 85

427 TEEN ANGEL
Mark Dinning *MGM* 60

428 I GET AROUND
The Beach Boys *Capitol* 64

429 JUST THE TWO OF US
Grover Washington, Jr. *Elektra* 81

430 RAINBOW
Russ Hamilton *Kapp* 57

431 ALWAYS ON MY MIND
Willie Nelson *Columbia* 82

432 LET IT WHIP
Dazz Band *Motown* 82

433 FEELINGS
Morris Albert *RCA* 75

434 LOVE'S THEME
Love Unlimited Orchestra *20th Century* 74

435 JUST MY IMAGINATION (RUNNING AWAY WITH ME)
The Temptations *Gordy* 71

436 BACK TO LIFE
Soul II Soul (f/Caron Wheeler) *Virgin* 89

437 DISCO LADY
Johnnie Taylor *Columbia* 76

438 WE'VE ONLY JUST BEGUN
Carpenters *A&M* 70

439 YOUNG LOVE
Sonny James *Capitol* 57

440 NO, NOT MUCH
The Four Lads *Columbia* 56

441 THE BALLAD OF THE GREEN BERETS
S/Sgt. Barry Sadler *RCA* 66

442 CLOSE TO YOU
Maxi Priest *Charisma* 90

443 ALL OUT OF LOVE
Air Supply *Arista* 80

444 BROKEN WINGS
Mr. Mister *RCA* 85

Willie Nelson

497 IN THE YEAR 2525 (EXORDIUM & TERMINUS)
Zager and Evans *RCA* 69

498 BUTTERFLY
Charlie Gracie *Cameo* 57

499 INTO THE NIGHT
Benny Mardones *Polydor* 80

500 I'D REALLY LOVE TO SEE YOU TONIGHT
England Dan and John Ford Coley *Big Tree* 76

501 THE PURPLE PEOPLE EATER
Sheb Wooley *MGM* 58

502 WE BUILT THIS CITY
Starship *Grunt* 85

503 GOOD TIMES
Chic *Atlantic* 79

504 THE ROSE
Bette Midler *Atlantic* 80

505 THE STREAK
Ray Stevens *Barnaby* 74

506 ST. ELMO'S FIRE (MAN IN MOTION)
John Parr *Atlantic* 85

507 BLUE VELVET
Bobby Vinton *Epic* 63

508 PUMP UP THE JAM
Technotronic f/Felly *SBK* 90

509 BABY DON'T GET HOOKED ON ME
Mac Davis *Columbia* 72

510 HEY PAULA
Paul and Paula *Philips* 63

511 TSOP (THE SOUND OF PHILADELPHIA)
MFSB f/The Three Degrees *PIR* 74

512 NOBODY DOES IT BETTER
Carly Simon *Elektra* 77

513 MISTY BLUE
Dorothy Moore *Malaco* 76

514 DAYDREAM BELIEVER
The Monkees *Colgems* 67

515 NEVER GONNA LET YOU GO
Sergio Mendes *A&M* 83

516 EVERY ROSE HAS ITS THORN
Poison *Enigma* 88

517 TALKING IN YOUR SLEEP
The Romantics *Nemperor* 84

518 MISS YOU
The Rolling Stones *Rolling Stones* 78

519 CAN'T FIGHT THIS FEELING
REO Speedwagon *Epic* 85

520 ESCAPADE
Janet Jackson *A&M* 90

521 CAR WASH
Rose Royce *MCA* 77

522 MY PREROGATIVE
Bobby Brown *MCA* 89

523 CRADLE OF LOVE
Billy Idol *Chrysalis* 90

524 (I CAN'T GET NO) SATISFACTION
The Rolling Stones *London* 65

525 MEDLEY: INTRO VENUS . . .
Stars on 45 *Radio* 81

526 HOLD ON
En Vogue *Atlantic* 90

527 WHO'S CRYING NOW
Journey *Columbia* 81

528 FRIENDLY PERSUASION (THEE I LOVE)/CHAINS OF LOVE
Pat Boone *Dot* 56

529 WEDDING BELL BLUES
5th Dimension *Soul City* 69

530 CRAZY FOR YOU
Madonna *Geffen* 85

531 RICH GIRL
Daryl Hall and John Oates *RCA* 77

532 EASY LOVER
Philip Bailey w/Phil Collins *Columbia* 85

533 GREATEST LOVE OF ALL
Whitney Houston *Arista* 86

534 YOU'VE LOST THAT LOVIN' FEELIN'
Righteous Brothers *Philles* 65

535 IF I CAN'T HAVE YOU
Yvonne Elliman *RSO* 78

536 MY HEART IS AN OPEN BOOK
Carl Dobkins, Jr. *Decca* 59

537 COME SOFTLY TO ME
The Fleetwoods *Dolphin* 59

538 DAZZ
Brick *Bang* 77

539 TAKE A CHANCE ON ME
Abba *Atlantic* 78

540 WORKING MY WAY BACK TO YOU/FORGIVE ME, GIRL
Spinners *Atlantic* 80

541 C'EST LA VIE
Robbie Nevil *Manhattan* 87

542 SIXTEEN REASONS
Connie Stevens *Warner Bros* 60

543 SARA SMILE
Daryl Hall and John Oates *RCA* 76

544 RUNAROUND SUE
Dion *Laurie* 61

545 BIRD DOG
Everly Brothers *Cadence* 58

546 A WOMAN NEEDS LOVE (JUST LIKE YOU DO)
Ray Parker Jr. *Arista* 81

547 TINA MARIE
Perry Como *RCA* 55

548 HOW MUCH I FEEL
Ambrosia *Warner Bros* 78

549 STRAIGHT UP
Paula Abdul *Virgin* 89

550 THERE! I'VE SAID IT AGAIN
Bobby Vinton *Epic* 64

551 WHAT A FOOL BELIEVES
Doobie Brothers *Warner Bros* 79

552 THE STRIPPER
David Rose *MGM* 62

553 I WISH
Stevie Wonder *Tamla* 77

554 URGENT
Foreigner *Atlantic* 81

555 SOMETHIN' STUPID
Nancy Sinatra and Frank Sinatra *Reprise* 67

556 GOTTA TRAVEL ON
Billy Grammer *Monument* 59

557 BABY LOVE
The Supremes *Motown* 64

558 SOUTHERN NIGHTS
Glen Campbell *Capitol* 77

559 THEN CAME YOU
Dionne Warwick & Spinners *Atlantic* 74

560 SWEET NOTHIN'S
Brenda Lee *Decca* 60

561 LEAN ON ME
Bill Withers *Sussex* 72

562 SHAKE YOU DOWN
Gregory Abbott *Columbia* 87

563 BEFORE THE NEXT TEARDROP FALLS
Freddy Fender *ABC/Dot* 75

564 SWEET DREAMS
Air Supply *Arista* 82

565 LA BAMBA
Los Lobos *Slash* 87

566 COME SEE ABOUT ME
The Supremes *Motown* 64

Ricky Nelson

Blondie

The Four Tops

775 A ROSE AND A BABY RUTH
George Hamilton IV *ABC-Paramount* 56

776 STUCK WITH YOU
Huey Lewis & the News *Chrysalis* 86

777 FOREVER YOUR GIRL
Paula Abdul *Virgin* 89

778 ANGEL OF THE MORNING
Juice Newton *Capitol* 81

779 WHEN I THINK OF YOU
Janet Jackson *A&M* 86

780 867-5309/JENNY
Tommy Tutone *Columbia* 82

781 BLAZE OF GLORY
Jon Bon Jovi *Mercury* 90

782 CRYING
Don McLean *Millennium* 81

783 I'LL TAKE YOU THERE
The Staple Singers *Stax* 72

784 RUN TO HIM
Bobby Vee *Liberty* 61

785 ALL AROUND THE WORLD
Lisa Stansfield *Arista* 90

786 LEATHER AND LACE
Stevie Nicks w/Don Henley *Modern* 82

787 HELP!
The Beatles *Capitol* 65

788 I CAN'T HELP MYSELF (SUGAR PIE, HONEY BUNCH)
Four Tops *Motown* 65

789 HEARTACHE TONIGHT
Eagles *Asylum* 79

790 (YOU'VE GOT) THE MAGIC TOUCH
The Platters *Mercury* 56

791 SIR DUKE
Stevie Wonder *Tamla* 77

792 THAT'LL BE THE DAY
The Crickets *Brunswick* 57

793 ALLEY-OOP
The Hollywood Argyles *Lute* 60

794 KEEP IT COMIN' LOVE
KC & the Sunshine Band *TK* 77

795 CLAIR
Gilbert O'Sullivan *MAM* 72

796 GIVING YOU THE BEST THAT I GOT
Anita Baker *Elektra* 88

797 TEARS ON MY PILLOW
Little Anthony & the Imperials *End* 58

798 STEAL AWAY
Robbie Dupree *Elektra* 80

799 SEA OF LOVE
The Honeydrippers *Es Paranza* 85

800 SWAYIN' TO THE MUSIC (SLOW DANCIN')
Johnny Rivers *Big Tree* 77

801 ROCK ME AMADEUS
Falco *A&M* 86

802 HEART OF GOLD
Neil Young *Reprise* 72

803 YOU'VE GOT A FRIEND
James Taylor *Warner Bros* 71

804 TWIST AND SHOUT
The Beatles *Tollie* 64

805 REMINISCING
Little River Band *Harvest* 78

806 VENUS
Shocking Blue *Colossus* 70

807 FLY LIKE AN EAGLE
Steve Miller *Capitol* 77

808 STEP BY STEP
Eddie Rabbitt *Elektra* 81

809 STEP BY STEP
New Kids on the Block *Columbia* 90

810 LAST TRAIN TO CLARKSVILLE
The Monkees *Colgems* 66

811 OH GIRL
The Chi-Lites *Brunswick* 72

812 LOVES ME LIKE A ROCK
Paul Simon *Columbia* 73

813 LAST DANCE
Donna Summer *Casablanca* 78

814 PILLOW TALK
Sylvia *Vibration* 73

815 SWEET CAROLINE (GOOD TIMES NEVER SEEMED SO GOOD)
Neil Diamond *Uni* 69

816 LIVING INSIDE MYSELF
Gino Vannelli *Arista* 81

817 THE ONE THAT YOU LOVE
Air Supply *Arista* 81

818 TREAT HER LIKE A LADY
Cornelius Brothers & Sister Rose *UA* 71

819 IT'S A HEARTACHE
Bonnie Tyler *RCA* 78

820 STEPPIN' OUT
Joe Jackson *A&M* 82

821 THE WANDERER
Dion *Laurie* 62

822 JOANNA
Kool & the Gang *De-Lite* 84

823 SOMETHING TO BELIEVE IN
Poison *Enigma* 90

824 I'M WALKIN'
Fats Domino *Imperial* 57

825 YOU DON'T KNOW ME
Jerry Vale *Columbia* 56

826 YOU'RE IN MY HEART (THE FINAL ACCLAIM)
Rod Stewart *Warner Bros* 78

827 I JUST WANNA STOP
Gino Vannelli *A&M* 78

828 THE OTHER WOMAN
Ray Parker Jr. *Arista* 82

829 WHERE DID OUR LOVE GO
The Supremes *Motown* 64

830 THE FOOL
Sanford Clark *Dot* 56

831 GET READY
Rare Earth *Rare Earth* 70

832 COOL IT NOW
New Edition *MCA* 85

833 THE LOCO-MOTION
Little Eva *Dimension* 62

834 GIRL YOU KNOW IT'S TRUE
Milli Vanilli *Arista* 89

835 LOVE ME
Elvis Presley *RCA* 57

836 COLD HEARTED
Paula Abdul *Virgin* 89

837 DELTA DAWN
Helen Reddy *Capitol* 73

838 DON'T FALL IN LOVE WITH A DREAMER
Kenny Rogers w/Kim Carnes *UA* 80

839 SHINING STAR
The Manhattans *Columbia* 80

840 MELODIE D'AMOUR
The Ames Brothers *RCA* 57

841 YES, I'M READY
Teri DeSario w/KC *Casablanca* 80

842 WAITING FOR A STAR TO FALL
Boy Meets Girl *RCA* 88

843 SCORPIO
Dennis Coffey & the Detroit Guitar Band *Sussex* 72

844 MOTHER-IN-LAW
Ernie K-Doe *Minit* 61

Atlanta Rhythm Section

879 SO IN TO YOU
Atlanta Rhythm Section *Polydor* 77

880 (HEY WON'T YOU PLAY) ANOTHER SOMEBODY DONE
SOMEBODY WRONG SONG
B.J. Thomas *ABC* 75

881 THE HAPPY ORGAN
Dave "Baby" Cortez *Clock* 59

882 IF WISHES CAME TRUE
Sweet Sensation *Atco* 90

883 BAND ON THE RUN
Paul McCartney & Wings *Apple* 74

884 JUST YOU 'N' ME
Chicago *Columbia* 73

885 MAKIN' IT
David Naughton *RSO* 79

886 HEAVEN KNOWS
Donna Summer w/Brooklyn Dreams *Casablanca* 79

887 TOO HOT
Kool & the Gang *De-Lite* 80

888 HEAVEN ON THE 7TH FLOOR
Paul Nicholas *RSO* 77

889 THAT LADY (PART 1)
Isley Brothers *T-Neck* 73

890 (CAN'T LIVE WITHOUT YOUR) LOVE AND AFFECTION
Nelson *DGC* 90

891 YOU ARE THE SUNSHINE OF MY LIFE
Stevie Wonder *Tamla* 73

892 SLIP SLIDIN' AWAY
Paul Simon *Columbia* 78

893 SLEDGEHAMMER
Peter Gabriel *Geffen* 86

894 HEARTS
Marty Balin *EMI America* 81

895 LADY MARMALADE
Labelle *Epic* 75

896 LOVE YOU INSIDE OUT
Bee Gees *RSO* 79

897 DRIVIN' MY LIFE AWAY
Eddie Rabbitt *Elektra* 80

898 BLINDED BY THE LIGHT
Manfred Mann's Earth Band *Warner Bros* 77

899 SAILING
Christopher Cross *Warner Bros* 80

900 MORE, MORE, MORE (PT. 1)
Andrea True Connection *Buddah* 76

901 MORITAT (A THEME FROM "THE THREE PENNY OPERA")
The Dick Hyman Trio *MGM* 56

902 HUMAN
The Human League *A&M* 86

903 SUSSUDIO
Phil Collins *Atlantic* 85

904 SUSPICIOUS MINDS
Elvis Presley *RCA* 69

905 LITTLE RED CORVETTE
Prince *Warner Bros* 83

906 ANYTHING FOR YOU
Gloria Estefan & Miami Sound Machine *Epic* 88

907 SUNSHINE ON MY SHOULDERS
John Denver *RCA* 74

908 LOVE SHACK
The B-52's *Reprise* 89

909 ONLY THE LONELY
The Motels *Capitol* 82

910 THE BIBLE TELLS ME SO
Don Cornell *Coral* 55

911 WISHING WELL
Terence Trent D'Arby *Columbia* 88

912 GROOVE ME
King Floyd *Chimneyville* 71

913 I FEEL LOVE
Donna Summer *Casablanca* 77

914 PRIMROSE LANE
Jerry Wallace w/the Jewels *Challenge* 59

915 PRETTY BLUE EYES
Steve Lawrence *ABC-Paramount* 60

916 QUARTER TO THREE
Gary U.S. Bonds *Legrand* 61

917 SARA
Starship *Grunt* 86

918 EVERYTHING
Jody Watley *MCA* 90

919 HUNGRY EYES
Eric Carmen *RCA* 88

920 HELLO, I LOVE YOU
The Doors *Elektra* 68

921 WILD, WILD WEST
Escape Club *Atlantic* 88

922 DRIFT AWAY
Dobie Gray *Decca* 73

923 DUST IN THE WIND
Kansas *Kirshner* 78

924 WHY DO FOOLS FALL IN LOVE
Diana Ross *RCA* 81

925 PICK UP THE PIECES
Average White Band *Atlantic* 75

926 WE'RE AN AMERICAN BAND
Grand Funk *Capitol* 73

927 SUPERSTITION
Stevie Wonder *Tamla* 73

928 BONY MARONIE
Larry Williams *Specialty* 57

929 HIGHER LOVE
Steve Winwood *Island* 86

930 WALK—DON'T RUN
The Ventures *Dolton* 60

931 LADY (YOU BRING ME UP)
Commodores *Motown* 81

932 HIT ME WITH YOUR BEST SHOT
Pat Benatar *Chrysalis* 80

933 NO MORE TEARS (ENOUGH IS ENOUGH)
Barbra Streisand and Donna Summer *Columbia* 79

934 LOVE WILL LEAD YOU BACK
Taylor Dayne *Arista* 90

935 I'LL BE THERE FOR YOU
Bon Jovi *Mercury* 89

936 WHEN YOU'RE IN LOVE WITH A BEAUTIFUL WOMAN
Dr. Hook *Capitol* 79

937 TIGHTEN UP
Archie Bell & the Drells *Atlantic* 68

938 BREAKING UP IS HARD TO DO
Neil Sedaka *RCA* 62

939 SHE DRIVES ME CRAZY
Fine Young Cannibals *I.R.S.* 89

940 HIT THE ROAD JACK
Ray Charles *ABC-Paramount* 61

941 I'M LEAVING IT UP TO YOU
Dale and Grace *Montel* 63

942 TAKE IT TO THE LIMIT
Eagles *Asylum* 76

943 THE WAY YOU DO THE THINGS YOU DO
UB40 *Virgin* 90

944 THE STROLL
The Diamonds *Mercury* 58

945 GOOD LUCK CHARM
Elvis Presley *RCA* 62

946 CRYSTAL BLUE PERSUASION
Tommy James & the Shondells *Roulette* 69

947 LET'S HANG ON
The Four Seasons *Philips* 65

948 ANGELS IN THE SKY
The Crew-Cuts *Mercury* 56

949 LOTTA LOVE
Nicolette Larson *Warner Bros* 79

950 OH SHEILA
Ready for the World *MCA* 85

951 YOUNG GIRL
Gary Puckett & the Union Gap *Columbia* 68

952 MR. BIG STUFF
Jean Knight *Stax* 71

953 KEEP YOUR HANDS TO YOURSELF
Georgia Satellites *Elektra* 87

954 TELEPHONE LINE
Electric Light Orchestra *UA* 77

955 CARS
Gary Numan *Atco* 80

956 SURRENDER
Elvis Presley *RCA* 61

957 I'LL BE LOVING YOU (FOREVER)
New Kids on the Block *Columbia* 89

958 GET CLOSER
Seals and Crofts *Warner Bros* 76

959 ROCK-A-BYE YOUR BABY WITH A DIXIE MELODY
Jerry Lewis *Decca* 56

960 RELEASE ME
Wilson Phillips *SBK* 90

961 CINDY, OH CINDY
Eddie Fisher *RCA* 56

962 A VIEW TO A KILL
Duran Duran *Capitol* 85

963 BABY DON'T FORGET MY NUMBER
Milli Vanilli *Arista* 89

964 NEVER, NEVER GONNA GIVE YA UP
Barry White *20th Century* 74

965 JIVE TALKIN'
Bee Gees *RSO* 75

966 REACH OUT, I'LL BE THERE
Four Tops *Motown* 66

967 HOLD ON TO THE NIGHTS
Richard Marx *EMI Manhattan* 88

968 LOVE TRAIN
The O'Jays *PIR* 73

969 THE GLAMOROUS LIFE
Sheila E. *Warner Bros* 84

970 (YOU'RE MY) SOUL & INSPIRATION
Righteous Brothers *Verve* 66

971 MAN IN THE MIRROR
Michael Jackson *Epic* 88

972 SURF CITY
Jan and Dean *Liberty* 63

973 THE LIVING YEARS
Mike + the Mechanics *Atlantic* 89

974 BOBBY'S GIRL
Marcie Blane *Seville* 62

975 SOMEBODY'S WATCHING ME
Rockwell *Motown* 84

976 I DON'T NEED YOU
Kenny Rogers *Liberty* 81

977 FEELS LIKE THE FIRST TIME
Foreigner *Atlantic* 77

978 HEART AND SOUL
T'Pau *Virgin* 87

979 REMEMBER YOU'RE MINE
Pat Boone *Dot* 57

980 TWO HEARTS
Phil Collins *Atlantic* 89

981 LOVE BITES
Def Leppard *Mercury* 88

982 SUPERSTAR
Carpenters *A&M* 71

983 CAN'T TAKE MY EYES OFF YOU
Frankie Valli *Philips* 67

984 GLORY OF LOVE
Peter Cetera *Warner Bros* 86

985 OPEN YOUR HEART
Madonna *Sire* 87

986 LITTLE BIT O'SOUL
The Music Explosion *Laurie* 67

987 RUNNING WITH THE NIGHT
Lionel Richie *Motown* 84

988 BETH
Kiss *Casablanca* 76

989 YOU CAN'T HURRY LOVE
The Supremes *Motown* 66

990 DIDN'T WE ALMOST HAVE IT ALL
Whitney Houston *Arista* 87

991 IT'S MY PARTY
Lesley Gore *Mercury* 63

**992 THANK YOU (FALETTINME BE MICE ELF AGIN)/
EVERYBODY IS A STAR**
Sly & the Family Stone *Epic* 70

993 OLD CAPE COD
Patti Page *Mercury* 57

994 TURN! TURN! TURN!
The Byrds *Columbia* 65

995 I STILL HAVEN'T FOUND WHAT I'M LOOKING FOR
U2 *Island* 87

996 GIVING IT UP FOR YOUR LOVE
Delbert McClinton *Capitol* 81

997 PENNY LOVER
Lionel Richie *Motown* 84

998 ONE MORE NIGHT
Phil Collins *Atlantic* 85

999 CHAIN GANG
Sam Cooke *RCA* 60

1000 RAMBLIN' ROSE
Nat King Cole *Capitol* 62

1001 MY HAPPINESS
Connie Francis *MGM* 59

1002 COME SAIL AWAY
Styx *A&M* 78

1003 GIRL I'M GONNA MISS YOU
Milli Vanilli *Arista* 89

1004 HARPER VALLEY P.T.A.
Jeannie C. Riley *Plantation* 68

1005 DIM ALL THE LIGHTS
Donna Summer *Casablanca* 79

1006 ALL I WANNA DO IS MAKE LOVE TO YOU
Heart *Capitol* 90

1007 THAT'S ALL!
Genesis *Atlantic* 84

1008 IT'S MY TURN
Diana Ross *Motown* 81

1009 HEART ATTACK
Olivia Newton-John *MCA* 82

1010 THE BIG HURT
Miss Toni Fisher *Signet* 59

1011 THOSE WERE THE DAYS
Mary Hopkin *Apple* 68

1012 BUILD ME UP BUTTERCUP
The Foundations *Uni* 69

1013 (IF LOVING YOU IS WRONG) I DON'T WANT TO BE RIGHT
Luther Ingram *KoKo* 72

1014 ('TIL) I KISSED YOU
Everly Brothers *Cadence* 59

1015 THE HAWAIIAN WEDDING SONG
Andy Williams *Cadence* 59

1016 AFTER THE LOVE HAS GONE
Earth, Wind & Fire *ARC* 79

1017 WE CAN WORK IT OUT
The Beatles *Capitol* 66

1018 THE LION SLEEPS TONIGHT
Robert John *Atlantic* 72

Duran Duran

1053 FRIENDS AND LOVERS
Gloria Loring and Carl Anderson *Carrere* 86

1054 FIRE AND RAIN
James Taylor *Warner Bros* 70

1055 CANDIDA
Dawn *Bell* 70

1056 PLAYGROUND IN MY MIND
Clint Holmes *Epic* 73

1057 THAT GIRL
Stevie Wonder *Tamla* 82

1058 YOU ARE THE WOMAN
Firefall *Atlantic* 76

1059 CHAPEL OF LOVE
The Dixie Cups *Red Bird* 64

1060 FAME
David Bowie *RCA* 75

1061 GROOVY KIND OF LOVE
Phil Collins *Atlantic* 88

1062 FATHER FIGURE
George Michael *Columbia* 88

1063 OH SHERRIE
Steve Perry *Columbia* 84

1064 ELVIRA
Oak Ridge Boys *MCA* 81

1065 TOO LATE TO TURN BACK NOW
Cornelius Brothers & Sister Rose *UA* 72

1066 SHE BLINDED ME WITH SCIENCE
Thomas Dolby *Capitol* 83

1067 HEAVEN
Bryan Adams *A&M* 85

1068 99 LUFTBALLONS
Nena *Epic* 84

1069 LIKE A PRAYER
Madonna *Sire* 89

1070 DRIVE
The Cars *Elektra* 84

1071 TEEN BEAT
Sandy Nelson *Original Sound* 59

1072 DON'T WORRY
Marty Robbins *Columbia* 61

1073 HEAT OF THE MOMENT
Asia *Geffen* 82

1074 EVEN THE NIGHTS ARE BETTER
Air Supply *Arista* 82

1075 THIS IS IT
Kenny Loggins *Columbia* 80

1076 LOOKING FOR A NEW LOVE
Jody Watley *MCA* 87

1077 SHE'S NOT THERE
The Zombies *Parrot* 64

1078 DON'T DREAM IT'S OVER
Crowded House *Capitol* 87

1079 IT'S YOUR THING
Isley Brothers *T-Neck* 69

1080 I WANNA BE RICH
Calloway *Solar* 90

1081 THE MORNING AFTER
Maureen McGovern *20th Century* 73

1082 THE HEAT IS ON
Glenn Frey *MCA* 85

1083 LOWDOWN
Boz Scaggs *Columbia* 76

1084 UNSKINNY BOP
Poison *Enigma* 90

1085 DADDY DON'T YOU WALK SO FAST
Wayne Newton *Chelsea* 72

1086 WHAT IN THE WORLD'S COME OVER YOU
Jack Scott *Top Rank* 60

1087 SEA OF LOVE
Phil Phillips w/the Twilights *Mercury* 59

1088 IS THIS LOVE
Whitesnake *Geffen* 87

1089 BUTTERFLY
Andy Williams *Cadence* 57

1090 IT'S A SIN TO TELL A LIE
Somethin' Smith & the Redheads *Epic* 55

1091 BAD MEDICINE
Bon Jovi *Mercury* 88

1092 LONGER
Dan Fogelberg *Full Moon* 80

1093 DON'T STOP
Fleetwood Mac *Warner Bros* 77

1094 CONGA
Miami Sound Machine *Epic* 86

1095 DON'T WORRY BE HAPPY
Bobby McFerrin *EMI Manhattan* 88

1096 WANT ADS
The Honey Cone *Hot Wax* 71

1097 DEVIL INSIDE
INXS *Atlantic* 88

1098 BOOGIE ON REGGAE WOMAN
Stevie Wonder *Tamla* 75

1099 SECRET LOVERS
Atlantic Starr *A&M* 86

1100 A HUNDRED POUNDS OF CLAY
Gene McDaniels *Liberty* 61

1101 BEEP BEEP
The Playmates *Roulette* 58

1102 SHAKE YOUR LOVE
Debbie Gibson *Atlantic* 87

1103 SHAKEDOWN
Bob Seger *MCA* 87

1104 TAKE GOOD CARE OF MY BABY
Bobby Vee *Liberty* 61

1105 GOODBYE YELLOW BRICK ROAD
Elton John *MCA* 73

1106 PROUD MARY
Creedence Clearwater Revival *Fantasy* 69

1107 THE GOOD, THE BAD & THE UGLY
Hugo Montenegro *RCA* 68

1108 NOTORIOUS
Duran Duran *Capitol* 87

1109 HEAVEN MUST HAVE SENT YOU
Bonnie Pointer *Motown* 79

1110 TOO MUCH, TOO LITTLE, TOO LATE
Johnny Mathis and Deniece Williams *Columbia* 78

1111 HEAVEN
Warrant *Columbia* 89

1112 BEND ME, SHAPE ME
American Breed *Acta* 68

1113 CHERISH
The Association *Valiant* 66

1114 ON OUR OWN
Bobby Brown *MCA* 89

1115 THE WRECK OF THE EDMUND FITZGERALD
Gordon Lightfoot *Reprise* 76

1116 CRY LIKE A BABY
The Box Tops *Mala* 68

1117 CRYING
Roy Orbison *Monument* 61

1118 LITTLE WILLY
Sweet *Bell* 73

1119 WHOLE LOTTA LOVE
Led Zeppelin *Atlantic* 70

1120 DON'T WANNA FALL IN LOVE
Jane Child *Warner Bros* 90

1121 RASPBERRY BERET
Prince & the Revolution *Paisley Park* 85

1122 HERE COMES THE RAIN AGAIN
Eurythmics *RCA* 84

The Temptations

1175 BORN TO BE WITH YOU
The Chordettes *Cadence* 56

1176 THE END
Earl Grant *Decca* 58

1177 WELCOME BACK
John Sebastian *Reprise* 76

1178 STRAY CAT STRUT
Stray Cats *EMI America* 83

1179 IN THE NAVY
Village People *Casablanca* 79

1180 MAGIC CARPET RIDE
Steppenwolf *Dunhill* 68

1181 LAVENDER-BLUE
Sammy Turner *Big Top* 00

1182 ONE THING LEADS TO ANOTHER
The Fixx *MCA* 83

1183 ON AND ON
Stephen Bishop *ABC* 77

1184 THE LOVE YOU SAVE
The Jackson Five *Motown* 70

1185 POOR SIDE OF TOWN
Johnny Rivers *Imperial* 66

1186 SHORT PEOPLE
Randy Newman *Warner Bros* 78

1187 HOT FUN IN THE SUMMERTIME
Sly & the Family Stone *Epic* 69

1188 LIPSTICK ON YOUR COLLAR
Connie Francis *MGM* 59

1189 I LOVE MUSIC (PART 1)
The O'Jays *PIR* 76

1190 RED RIVER ROCK
Johnny & the Hurricanes *Warwick* 59

1191 DUNGAREE DOLL
Eddie Fisher *RCA* 56

1192 MIAMI VICE THEME
Jan Hammer *MCA* 85

1193 DREAMS
Fleetwood Mac *Warner Bros* 77

1194 YOU'RE SIXTEEN
Ringo Starr *Apple* 74

1195 DON'T RUSH ME
Taylor Dayne *Arista* 89

1196 HAZY SHADE OF WINTER
Bangles *Columbia* 88

1197 I'LL ALWAYS LOVE YOU
Taylor Dayne *Arista* 88

1198 PATCHES
Clarence Carter *Atlantic* 70

1199 STOMP!
Brothers Johnson *A&M* 80

1200 BLACK WATER
Doobie Brothers *Warner Bros* 75

1201 THE LADY IN RED
Chris DeBurgh *A&M* 87

1202 ON THE STREET WHERE YOU LIVE
Vic Damone *Columbia* 56

1203 ADDICTED TO LOVE
Robert Palmer *Island* 86

1204 DA DOO RON RON
Shaun Cassidy *Warner/Curb* 77

1205 GREEN TAMBOURINE
Lemon Pipers *Buddah* 68

1206 HERE YOU COME AGAIN
Dolly Parton *RCA* 78

1207 FREEWAY OF LOVE
Aretha Franklin *Arista* 85

1208 FOR YOUR EYES ONLY
Sheena Easton *Liberty* 81

1209 SHE BELIEVES IN ME
Kenny Rogers *UA* 79

1210 STAND BACK
Stevie Nicks *Modern* 83

1211 TEA FOR TWO CHA CHA
The Tommy Dorsey Orchestra *Decca* 58

1212 HULA LOVE
Buddy Knox *Roulette* 57

1213 ALWAYS
Atlantic Starr *Warner Bros* 87

1214 LOOKS LIKE WE MADE IT
Barry Manilow *Arista* 77

1215 I CAN'T WAIT
Nu Shooz *Atlantic* 86

1216 I KEEP FORGETTIN' (EVERY TIME YOU'RE NEAR)
Michael McDonald *Warner Bros* 82

1217 SPACE RACE
Billy Preston *A&M* 73

1218 THE HEART OF ROCK & ROLL
Huey Lewis & the News *Chrysalis* 84

1219 WE GOT LOVE
Bobby Rydell *Cameo* 59

1220 BROWN SUGAR
The Rolling Stones *Rolling Stones* 71

1221 (IT'S JUST) THE WAY THAT YOU LOVE ME
Paula Abdul *Virgin* 89

1222 THE THINGS WE DO FOR LOVE
10cc *Mercury* 77

1223 SHANNON
Henry Gross *Lifesong* 76

1224 LADIES NIGHT
Kool & the Gang *De-Lite* 80

1225 ENDLESS SUMMER NIGHTS
Richard Marx *EMI Manhattan* 88

1226 MY HEART BELONGS TO ME
Barbra Streisand *Columbia* 77

1227 LOVE WON'T LET ME WAIT
Major Harris *Atlantic* 75

1228 HEAD TO TOE
Lisa Lisa & Cult Jam *Columbia* 87

1229 IF I COULD TURN BACK TIME
Cher *Geffen* 89

1230 NAUGHTY GIRLS (NEED LOVE TOO)
Samantha Fox *Jive* 88

1231 MIDNIGHT CONFESSIONS
The Grass Roots *Dunhill* 68

1232 BOY FROM NEW YORK CITY
Manhattan Transfer *Atlantic* 81

1233 SONG SUNG BLUE
Neil Diamond *Uni* 72

1234 BORN TO BE MY BABY
Bon Jovi *Mercury* 89

1235 BACK ON THE CHAIN GANG
The Pretenders *Sire* 83

1236 LUCILLE
Kenny Rogers *UA* 77

1237 MY EYES ADORED YOU
Frankie Valli *Private Stock* 75

1238 DON'T GIVE UP ON US
David Soul *Private Stock* 77

1239 INDIANA WANTS ME
R. Dean Taylor *Rare Earth* 00

1240 BALLROOM BLITZ
Sweet *Capitol* 75

1241 LONESOME LOSER
Little River Band *Capitol* 79

1242 DO YOU WANT TO DANCE
Bobby Freeman *Josie* 58

1243 YESTERDAY
The Beatles *Capitol* 65

1244 I WANT TO BE WANTED
Brenda Lee *Decca* 60

1245 SKY HIGH
Jigsaw *Chelsea* 75

1246 WHAT HAVE YOU DONE FOR ME LATELY
Janet Jackson *A&M* 86

1247 VENUS
Bananarama *London* 86

1248 MONY MONY
Billy Idol *Chrysalis* 87

1249 BECAUSE THEY'RE YOUNG
Duane Eddy *Jamie* 60

1250 SHOW ME THE WAY
Peter Frampton *A&M* 76

1251 SHAKE YOUR BODY (DOWN TO THE GROUND)
The Jacksons *Epic* 79

1252 THIS DIAMOND RING
Gary Lewis & the Playboys *Liberty* 65

1253 THE LOOK
Roxette *EMI* 89

1254 BEST THING THAT EVER HAPPENED TO ME
Gladys Knight & the Pips *Buddah* 74

1255 ONLY IN MY DREAMS
Debbie Gibson *Atlantic* 87

1256 ONE ON ONE
Daryl Hall and John Oates *RCA* 83

1257 LET YOUR LOVE FLOW
Bellamy Brothers *Warner/Curb* 76

1258 AT SEVENTEEN
Janis Ian *Columbia* 75

1259 OH NO
Commodores *Motown* 81

1260 ALRIGHT
Janet Jackson *A&M* 90

1261 GET TOGETHER
The Youngbloods *RCA* 69

1262 AUTOMATIC
Pointer Sisters *Planet* 84

1263 ROCK ON
David Essex *Columbia* 74

1264 JUST BORN (TO BE YOUR BABY)/IVY ROSE
Perry Como *RCA* 57

1265 TOO BUSY THINKING ABOUT MY BABY
Marvin Gaye *Tamla* 69

1266 DON'T LOSE MY NUMBER
Phil Collins *Atlantic* 85

1267 WHAT YOU NEED
INXS *Atlantic* 86

1268 GOOD LOVIN'
The Young Rascals *Atlantic* 66

1269 YOUR MAMA DON'T DANCE
Loggins and Messina *Columbia* 73

1270 NEVER
Heart *Capitol* 85

1271 DEVIL OR ANGEL
Bobby Vee *Liberty* 60

1272 MIDNIGHT AT THE OASIS
Maria Muldaur *Reprise* 74

1273 KEEP THE FIRE BURNIN'
REO Speedwagon *Epic* 82

1274 BEST OF MY LOVE
Eagles *Asylum* 75

1275 ANGEL
Aerosmith *Geffen* 88

1276 STOP! IN THE NAME OF LOVE
The Supremes *Motown* 65

1277 IF YOU DON'T KNOW ME BY NOW
Simply Red *Elektra* 89

1278 THE WAY YOU MAKE ME FEEL
Michael Jackson *Epic* 88

1279 EVERY LITTLE STEP
Bobby Brown *MCA* 89

Janis Ian

1280 LAND OF CONFUSION
Genesis *Atlantic* 87

1281 LEAD ME ON
Maxine Nightingale *Windsong* 79

1282 SAILOR (YOUR HOME IS THE SEA)
Lolita *Kapp* 60

1283 ENJOY YOURSELF
The Jacksons *Epic* 77

1284 PLEASE HELP ME, I'M FALLING
Hank Locklin *RCA* 60

1285 RAG DOLL
The Four Seasons *Philips* 64

1286 TAKE MY BREATH AWAY
Berlin *Columbia* 86

1287 STRANGERS IN THE NIGHT
Frank Sinatra *Reprise* 66

1288 LISTEN TO YOUR HEART
Roxette *EMI* 89

1289 THESE DREAMS
Heart *Capitol* 86

1290 THINGS CAN ONLY GET BETTER
Howard Jones *Elektra* 85

1291 STONED LOVE
The Supremes *Motown* 70

1292 A WORLD WITHOUT LOVE
Peter and Gordon *Capitol* 64

1293 CONVOY
C.W. McCall *MGM* 76

1294 GIRLS JUST WANT TO HAVE FUN
Cyndi Lauper *Portrait* 84

1295 SHAKE YOUR GROOVE THING
Peaches and Herb *Polydor* 79

1296 FUNNY FACE
Donna Fargo *Dot* 73

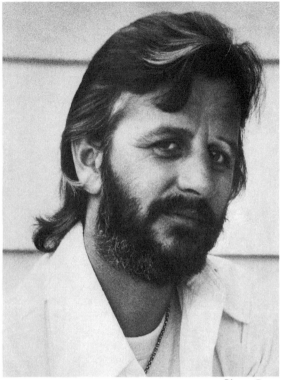

Ringo Starr

1349 TAINTED LOVE
Soft Cell *Sire* 82

1350 LIVING FOR THE CITY
Stevie Wonder *Tamla* 74

1351 KOKOMO
The Beach Boys *Elektra* 88

1352 YOU AIN'T SEEN NOTHING YET
Bachman-Turner Overdrive *Mercury* 74

1353 YAKETY YAK
The Coasters *Atco* 58

1354 BIG MAN
The Four Preps *Capitol* 58

1355 A SWEET OLD-FASHIONED GIRL
Teresa Brewer *Coral* 56

1356 NEVER CAN SAY GOODBYE
The Jackson Five *Motown* 71

1357 INFATUATION
Rod Stewart *Warner Bros* 84

1358 MORE LOVE
Kim Carnes *EMI America* 80

1359 A BIG HUNK O'LOVE
Elvis Presley *RCA* 59

1360 YOU KEEP ME HANGIN' ON
Kim Wilde *MCA* 87

1361 WHEN I'M WITH YOU
Sheriff *Capitol* 89

1362 ROCK ON
Michael Damian *Cypress* 89

1363 CAN'T STOP
After 7 *Virgin* 90

1364 THE RAIN, THE PARK & OTHER THINGS
The Cowsills *MGM* 67

1365 NEVER MY LOVE
The Association *Warner Bros* 67

1366 TOUCH ME (I WANT YOUR BODY)
Samantha Fox *Jive* 87

1367 BETTER BE GOOD TO ME
Tina Turner *Capitol* 84

1368 QUEEN OF THE HOP
Bobby Darin *Atco* 58

1369 HELLO GOODBYE
The Beatles *Capitol* 67

1370 YOU ARE EVERYTHING
The Stylistics *Avco* 72

1371 BAD BLOOD
Neil Sedaka *Rocket* 75

1372 LEAN ON ME
Club Nouveau *Warner Bros* 87

1373 DANCING ON THE CEILING
Lionel Richie *Motown* 86

1374 ELI'S COMING
Three Dog Night *Dunhill* 69

1375 THEME FROM "S.W.A.T."
Rhythm Heritage *ABC* 76

1376 I'M GONNA MAKE YOU LOVE ME
Diana Ross & the Supremes and the Temptations *Motown* 69

1377 WHY CAN'T WE BE FRIENDS?
War *UA* 75

1378 MAMA CAN'T BUY YOU LOVE
Elton John *MCA* 79

1379 SUNGLASSES AT NIGHT
Corey Hart *EMI America* 84

1380 THE HOUSE OF BLUE LIGHTS
Chuck Miller *Mercury* 55

1381 HARD HEADED WOMAN
Elvis Presley *RCA* 58

1382 RAINY DAYS AND MONDAYS
Carpenters *A&M* 71

1383 INSTANT KARMA (WE ALL SHINE ON)
John Ono Lennon *Apple* 70

1384 I'LL BE YOUR EVERYTHING
Tommy Page *Sire* 90

1385 A BOY NAMED SUE
Johnny Cash *Columbia* 69

1386 I CAN DREAM ABOUT YOU
Dan Hartman *MCA* 84

1387 (KEEP FEELING) FASCINATION
The Human League *A&M* 83

1388 YOU KEEP ME HANGIN' ON
The Supremes *Motown* 66

1389 GET A JOB
The Silhouettes *Ember* 58

1390 SPINNING WHEEL
Blood, Sweat & Tears *Columbia* 69

1391 YOU'LL NEVER FIND ANOTHER LOVE LIKE MINE
Lou Rawls *PIR* 76

1392 LOVE SO RIGHT
Bee Gees *RSO* 76

1393 I CRIED A TEAR
LaVern Baker *Atlantic* 59

1394 LAST KISS
J. Frank Wilson & the Cavaliers *Josie* 64

1395 TELL IT LIKE IT IS
Aaron Neville *Par-Lo* 67

1396 TIRED OF BEING ALONE
Al Green *Hi* 71

1397 HELP ME, RHONDA
The Beach Boys *Capitol* 65

1398 LOVE IS STRANGE
Mickey and Sylvia *Groove* 57

1399 TEEN-AGE CRUSH
Tommy Sands *Capitol* 57

1400 CAN'T HELP FALLING IN LOVE
Elvis Presley *RCA* 62

1401 CATCH ME (I'M FALLING)
Pretty Poison *Virgin* 87

1402 WHAT A DIFF'RENCE A DAY MAKES
Dinah Washington *Mercury* 59

1403 THE OTHER GUY
Little River Band *Capitol* 83

1404 I KNEW YOU WERE WAITING (FOR ME)
Aretha Franklin and George Michael *Arista* 87

1405 ANNIE'S SONG
John Denver *RCA* 74

1406 GREEN RIVER
Creedence Clearwater Revival *Fantasy* 69

1407 GOODBYE CRUEL WORLD
James Darren *Colpix* 62

1408 HOUSE OF THE RISING SUN
The Animals *MGM* 64

1409 (I JUST) DIED IN YOUR ARMS
Cutting Crew *Virgin* 87

1410 AMANDA
Boston *MCA* 86

1411 MY DING-A-LING
Chuck Berry *Chess* 72

1412 MONKEY
George Michael *Columbia* 88

1413 SISTER GOLDEN HAIR
America *Warner Bros* 75

1414 SNOOPY VS. THE RED BARON
The Royal Guardsmen *Laurie* 66

1415 LONG COOL WOMAN (IN A BLACK DRESS)
The Hollies *Epic* 72

1416 SISTER CHRISTIAN
Night Ranger *MCA/Camel* 84

1417 PAPA DON'T PREACH
Madonna *Sire* 86

1418 DESIRE
Andy Gibb *RSO* 80

The Animals

1453 HELLO MARY LOU
Ricky Nelson *Imperial* 61

1454 GOLDEN YEARS
David Bowie *RCA* 76

1455 SORRY (I RAN ALL THE WAY HOME)
The Impalas *Cub* 59

1456 GIVE ME THE NIGHT
George Benson *Warner Bros* 80

1457 START MOVIN' (IN MY DIRECTION)
Sal Mineo *Epic* 57

1458 BORDERLINE
Madonna *Sire* 84

1459 WHEN WILL I BE LOVED
Linda Ronstadt *Asylum* 75

1460 PURPLE RAIN
Prince & the Revolution *Warner Bros* 84

1461 SAIL ON
Commodores *Motown* 79

1462 BOOGIE DOWN
Eddie Kendricks *Tamla* 74

1463 DANIEL
Elton John *MCA* 73

1464 THE ENTERTAINER
Marvin Hamlisch *MCA* 74

1465 ALL ALONE AM I
Brenda Lee *Decca* 62

1466 BLACK MAGIC WOMAN
Santana *Columbia* 71

1467 LOVE SONG
Tesla *Geffen* 90

1468 RAUNCHY
Ernie Freeman *Imperial* 57

1469 ALL BY MYSELF
Eric Carmen *Arista* 76

1470 BREAD AND BUTTER
The Newbeats *Hickory* 84

1471 THE WAH-WATUSI
The Orlons *Cameo* 62

1472 SURFIN' U.S.A.
The Beach Boys *Capitol* 63

1473 EYES WITHOUT A FACE
Billy Idol *Chrysalis* 84

1474 GOODBYE BABY
Jack Scott *Carlton* 59

1475 APACHE
Jorgen Ingmann & His Guitar *Atco* 61

1476 SPILL THE WINE
Eric Burdon & War *MGM* 70

1477 EASY TO BE HARD
Three Dog Night *Dunhill* 69

1478 KING OF THE ROAD
Roger Miller *Smash* 65

1479 SWEET SOUL MUSIC
Arthur Conley *Atco* 67

1480 STONED SOUL PICNIC
5th Dimension *Soul City* 68

1481 RHYTHM OF THE NIGHT
DeBarge *Gordy* 85

1482 SIGNED, SEALED, DELIVERED (I'M YOURS)
Stevie Wonder *Tamla* 70

1483 BURNING BRIDGES
Jack Scott *Top Rank* 60

1484 ALL RIGHT
Christopher Cross *Warner Bros* 83

1485 SUNDOWN
Gordon Lightfoot *Reprise* 74

1486 SHATTERED DREAMS
Johnny Hates Jazz *Virgin* 88

1487 THE WANDERER
Donna Summer *Geffen* 80

1488 IT DON'T COME EASY
Ringo Starr *Apple* 71

1489 TOM'S DINER
DNA f/Suzanne Vega *A&M* 90

1490 LOLLIPOP
The Chordettes *Cadence* 58

1491 YOU MAKE MY DREAMS
Daryl Hall and John Oates *RCA* 81

1492 MARIANNE
Terry Gilkyson & the Easy Riders *Columbia* 57

1493 WHITE SILVER SANDS
Don Rondo *Jubilee* 57

1494 HEART TO HEART
Kenny Loggins *Columbia* 83

1495 CHAIN OF FOOLS
Aretha Franklin *Atlantic* 68

1496 LAST SONG
Edward Bear *Capitol* 73

1497 IT'S JUST A MATTER OF TIME
Brook Benton *Mercury* 59

1498 FAME
Irene Cara *RSO* 80

1499 THEME FROM MAHOGANY
(DO YOU KNOW WHERE YOU'RE GOING TO)
Diana Ross *Motown* 76

1500 AND WHEN I DIE
Blood, Sweat & Tears *Columbia* 69

1501 SHOP AROUND
The Miracles *Tamla* 61

1502 WE DON'T NEED ANOTHER HERO (THUNDERDOME)
Tina Turner *Capitol* 85

1503 FOOLED AROUND AND FELL IN LOVE
Elvin Bishop *Capricorn* 76

1504 SAY, HAS ANYBODY SEEN MY SWEET GYPSY ROSE
Dawn f/Tony Orlando *Bell* 73

1505 YOU WERE ON MY MIND
We Five *A&M* 65

1506 I THINK WE'RE ALONE NOW
Tommy James & the Shondells *Roulette* 67

1507 WE BELONG
Pat Benatar *Chrysalis* 85

1508 I NEVER CRY
Alice Cooper *Warner Bros* 77

1509 LIVE AND LET DIE
Wings *Apple* 73

1510 SPANISH HARLEM
Aretha Franklin *Atlantic* 71

1511 LOVERBOY
Billy Ocean *Jive* 85

1512 THERE GOES MY BABY
The Drifters *Atlantic* 59

1513 THE RAPPER
The Jaggerz *Kama Sutra* 70

1514 PALISADES PARK
Freddy Cannon *Swan* 62

1515 LOVE ME WITH ALL YOUR HEART
Ray Charles Singers *Command* 64

1516 QUIET VILLAGE
The Exotic Sounds of Martin Denny *Liberty* 59

1517 BURNING LOVE
Elvis Presley *RCA* 72

1518 WHO LOVES YOU
The Four Seasons *Warner/Curb* 75

1519 USE TA BE MY GIRL
The O'Jays *PIR* 78

1520 OH! CAROL
Neil Sedaka *RCA* 59

1521 MIDNIGHT IN MOSCOW
Kenny Ball & His Jazzmen *Kapp* 62

1522 RAMBLIN MAN
Allman Brothers Band *Capricorn* 73

1523 SUNSHINE
Jonathan Edwards *Capricorn* 72

1524 LONELY STREET
Andy Williams *Cadence* 59

1525 WHAT AM I LIVING FOR/HANG UP MY
ROCK AND ROLL SHOES
Chuck Willis *Atlantic* 58

1526 ALL I NEED
Jack Wagner *Qwest* 85

1527 IF I HAD A HAMMER
Trini Lopez *Reprise* 63

1528 LET 'EM IN
Wings *Capitol* 76

1529 DOUBLE VISION
Foreigner *Atlantic* 78

1530 MONY MONY
Tommy James & the Shondells *Roulette* 68

1531 TALK TO ME
Stevie Nicks *Modern* 86

1532 BABY, WHAT A BIG SURPRISE
Chicago *Columbia* 77

1533 ANGEL BABY
Rosie & the Originals *Highland* 61

1534 MAD ABOUT YOU
Belinda Carlisle *I.R.S.* 86

1535 PAPER ROSES
Anita Bryant *Carlton* 60

1536 DON'T CRY OUT LOUD
Melissa Manchester *Arista* 79

1537 WHIP IT
Devo *Warner Bros* 80

1538 DEEP PURPLE
Nino Tempo and April Stevens *Atco* 63

1539 I DON'T WANNA GO ON WITH YOU LIKE THAT
Elton John *MCA* 88

1540 NEVER SURRENDER
Corey Hart *EMI America* 85

1541 ONE NIGHT IN BANGKOK
Murray Head *RCA* 85

1542 EASY
Commodores *Motown* 77

1543 ON THE REBOUND
Floyd Cramer *RCA* 61

1544 AGAINST THE WIND
Bob Seger *Capitol* 80

1545 WHY BABY WHY
Pat Boone *Dot* 57

1546 CONTROL
Janet Jackson *A&M* 87

1547 DO YOU KNOW WHAT I MEAN
Lee Michaels *A&M* 71

1548 A LITTLE BIT MORE
Dr. Hook *Capitol* 76

1549 SO MUCH IN LOVE
The Tymes *Parkway* 63

1550 KING OF PAIN
The Police *A&M* 83

1551 MAKE ME LOSE CONTROL
Eric Carmen *Arista* 88

1552 IT KEEPS RIGHT ON A-HURTIN'
Johnny Tillotson *Cadence* 62

1553 WITH EVERY BEAT OF MY HEART
Taylor Dayne *Arista* 89

1554 WHEN
Kalin Twins *Decca* 58

1555 WANNA BE STARTIN' SOMETHIN'
Michael Jackson *Epic* 83

1556 DON'T FORGET ME (WHEN I'M GONE)
Glass Tiger *Manhattan* 86

1557 (NOW AND THEN THERE'S) A FOOL SUCH AS I
Elvis Presley *RCA* 59

1558 GOOD MORNING STARSHINE
Oliver *Jubilee* 69

1559 BUFFALO STANCE
Neneh Cherry *Virgin* 89

1560 COULDN'T GET IT RIGHT
Climax Blues Band *Sire* 77

1561 WITH YOU I'M BORN AGAIN
Billy Preston and Syreeta *Motown* 80

1562 SINCE I FELL FOR YOU
Lenny Welch *Cadence* 63

1563 I'M COMING OUT
Diana Ross *Motown* 80

1564 ALL THE WAY
Frank Sinatra *Capitol* 57

1565 DON'T STOP 'TIL YOU GET ENOUGH
Michael Jackson *Epic* 79

1566 OUTA-SPACE
Billy Preston *A&M* 72

1567 WHEN WILL I SEE YOU AGAIN
The Three Degrees *PIR* 74

1568 I'VE NEVER BEEN TO ME
Charlene *Motown* 82

1569 SHE'S LIKE THE WIND
Patrick Swayze f/Wendy Fraser *RCA* 88

1570 SMOKIN' IN THE BOY'S ROOM
Brownsville Station *Big Tree* 74

1571 WATERLOO
Stonewall Jackson *Columbia* 59

1572 SULTANS OF SWING
Dire Straits *Warner Bros* 79

1573 IT NEVER RAINS IN SOUTHERN CALIFORNIA
Albert Hammond *Mums* 72

1574 HOLD THE LINE
Toto *Columbia* 79

1575 I'VE GOT LOVE ON MY MIND
Natalie Cole *Capitol* 77

1576 THIS TIME
Troy Shondell *Liberty* 61

1577 WE'RE ALL ALONE
Rita Coolidge *A&M* 77

1578 I'VE GOT TO USE MY IMAGINATION
Gladys Knight & the Pips *Buddah* 74

1579 BOOK OF LOVE
The Monotones *Argo* 58

1580 HE DON'T LOVE YOU (LIKE I LOVE YOU)
Tony Orlando & Dawn *Elektra* 75

1581 LOVE ME DO
The Beatles *Tollie* 64

1582 DANGEROUS
Roxette *EMI* 90

1583 THE BIRDS AND THE BEES
Jewel Akens *Era* 65

1584 JUST WHEN I NEEDED YOU MOST
Randy Vanwarmer *Bearsville* 79

1585 KICKS
Paul Revere & the Raiders *Columbia* 66

1586 WHAT DOES IT TAKE (TO WIN YOUR LOVE)
Jr. Walker & the All Stars *Soul* 69

1587 PATCHES
Dickey Lee *Smash* 62

1588 WHEN THE GOING GETS TOUGH, THE TOUGH GET GOING
Billy Ocean *Jive* 86

1589 DOWNTOWN TRAIN
Rod Stewart *Warner Bros* 90

1590 WHEELS
The String-a-Longs *Warwick* 61

1591 IS THERE SOMETHING I SHOULD KNOW
Duran Duran *Capitol* 83

1592 LOVERGIRL
Teena Marie *Epic* 85

Wham!

1645 SUNSHINE SUPERMAN
Donovan *Epic* 66

1646 U GOT THE LOOK
Prince *Paisley Park* 87

1647 THE LOVER IN ME
Sheena Easton *MCA* 89

1648 I'M YOUR MAN
Wham! *Columbia* 86

1649 HANDY MAN
James Taylor *Columbia* 77

1650 SMOOTH OPERATOR
Sade *Portrait* 85

1651 MULE SKINNER BLUES
The Fendermen *Soma* 60

1652 I WANT A NEW DRUG
Huey Lewis & the News *Chrysalis* 84

1653 BLUE MONDAY
Fats Domino *Imperial* 57

1654 EVERYBODY
Tommy Roe *ABC-Paramount* 63

1655 NIGHT MOVES
Bob Seger *Capitol* 77

1656 GLORY DAYS
Bruce Springsteen *Columbia* 85

1657 SO MANY WAYS
Brook Benton *Mercury* 59

1658 WE DON'T TALK ANYMORE
Cliff Richard *EMI America* 80

1659 SOMETHING'S GOTTA GIVE
Sammy Davis, Jr. *Decca* 55

1660 RINGO
Lorne Greene *RCA* 64

1661 LEAVE ME ALONE (RUBY RED DRESS)
Helen Reddy *Capitol* 73

1662 HAVE YOU SEEN HER
M.C. Hammer *Capitol* 90

1663 THE WAY I WANT TO TOUCH YOU
Captain & Tennille *A&M* 75

1664 IF YOU LEAVE
Orchestral Manoeuvres in the Dark *A&M* 86

1665 HOOKED ON A FEELING
B.J. Thomas *Scepter* 69

1666 DON'T YOU WANT ME
Jody Watley *MCA* 87

1667 IF THIS IS IT
Huey Lewis & the News *Chrysalis* 84

1668 LET'S DO IT AGAIN
The Staple Singers *Curtom* 75

1669 26 MILES (SANTA CATALINA)
The Four Preps *Capitol* 58

1670 EXPRESSWAY TO YOUR HEART
Soul Survivors *Crimson* 67

1671 MISS ME BLIND
Culture Club *Epic/Virgin* 84

1672 LOVE WILL FIND A WAY
Pablo Cruise *A&M* 78

1673 SWEET THING
Rufus f/Chaka Khan *ABC* 76

1674 APPLES, PEACHES, PUMPKIN PIE
Jay & the Techniques *Smash* 67

1675 SOMEBODY'S BABY
Jackson Browne *Asylum* 82

1676 PAPA WAS A ROLLIN' STONE
The Temptations *Gordy* 72

1677 LEADER OF THE PACK
The Shangri-Las *Red Bird* 64

1678 THE LOCO-MOTION
Kylie Minogue *Geffen* 88

1679 SUDDENLY
Billy Ocean *Jive* 85

1680 WORD UP
Cameo *Atlanta Artists* 86

1681 WHOLE LOTTA LOVING
Fats Domino *Imperial* 59

1682 (OUR LOVE) DON'T THROW IT ALL AWAY
Andy Gibb *RSO* 78

1683 FORGET HIM
Bobby Rydell *Cameo* 64

1684 IT'S SO EASY
Linda Ronstadt *Asylum* 77

1685 ARE YOU SINCERE
Andy Williams *Cadence* 58

1686 INVISIBLE TOUCH
Genesis *Atlantic* 86

1687 BATDANCE
Prince *Warner Bros* 89

1688 COME BACK TO ME
Janet Jackson *A&M* 90

1689 I DON'T WANT YOUR LOVE
Duran Duran *Capitol* 88

1690 DAY AFTER DAY
Badfinger *Apple* 72

1691 MOCKINGBIRD
Carly Simon and James Taylor *Elektra* 74

1692 ETERNAL FLAME
Bangles *Columbia* 89

1693 WHAT'S ON YOUR MIND (PURE ENERGY)
Information Society *Tommy Boy* 88

1694 GOLD
John Stewart *RSO* 79

1695 GIRLFRIEND
Pebbles *MCA* 88

1696 COWBOYS TO GIRLS
The Intruders *Gamble* 68

1697 STUCK IN THE MIDDLE WITH YOU
Stealers Wheel *A&M* 73

1698 LONELY BOY
Andrew Gold *Asylum* 77

1699 I WANT YOU TO WANT ME
Cheap Trick *Epic* 79

1700 I LOVE HOW YOU LOVE ME
Bobby Vinton *Epic* 68

1701 JACOB'S LADDER
Huey Lewis & the News *Chrysalis* 87

1702 ONLY LOVE CAN BREAK A HEART
Gene Pitney *Musicor* 62

1703 SIGNS
Five Man Electrical Band *Lionel* 71

1704 SAD SONGS (SAY SO MUCH)
Elton John *Geffen* 84

1705 SMILE A LITTLE SMILE FOR ME
Flying Machine *Congress* 69

1706 TIMES OF YOUR LIFE
Paul Anka *UA* 76

1707 AMERICA
Neil Diamond *Capitol* 81

1708 LEADER OF THE BAND
Dan Fogelberg *Full Moon* 82

1709 HANGIN' TOUGH
New Kids on the Block *Columbia* 89

1710 I HEARD A RUMOUR
Bananarama *London* 87

1711 LITTLE LIES
Fleetwood Mac *Warner Bros* 87

1712 LUCKY STAR
Madonna *Sire* 84

1713 LONG TALL SALLY
Little Richard *Specialty* 56

1714 THE BALLAD OF BONNIE AND CLYDE
Georgie Fame *Epic* 68

1715 WHILE YOU SEE A CHANCE
Steve Winwood *Island* 81

1716 LAST NIGHT
Mar-Keys *Satellite* 61

1717 SOME KIND OF WONDERFUL
Grand Funk *Capitol* 75

1718 ENDLESS SLEEP
Jody Reynolds *Demon* 58

1719 BORN TOO LATE
Poni-Tails *ABC-Paramount* 58

1720 I'VE GOTTA GET A MESSAGE TO YOU
Bee Gees *Atco* 68

1721 ROCK & ROLL MUSIC
Chuck Berry *Chess* 57

1722 KIND OF A DRAG
The Buckinghams *U.S.A.* 67

1723 NO ONE IS TO BLAME
Howard Jones *Elektra* 86

1724 RUN TO YOU
Bryan Adams *A&M* 85

1725 TO BE A LOVER
Billy Idol *Chrysalis* 86

1726 THE LONG RUN
Eagles *Asylum* 80

1727 WILDFIRE
Michael Murphey *Epic* 75

1728 MY HEART CAN'T TELL YOU NO
Rod Stewart *Warner Bros* 89

1729 OBSESSION
Animotion *Mercury* 85

1730 ALMOST PARADISE
Mike Reno and Ann Wilson *Columbia* 84

1731 LITTLE CHILDREN
Billy J. Kramer & the Dakotas *Imperial* 64

1732 I'M NOT LISA
Jessi Colter *Capitol* 75

1733 GARDEN PARTY
Rick Nelson & the Stone Canyon Band *Decca* 72

1734 HAPPY, HAPPY BIRTHDAY BABY
The Tune Weavers *Checker* 57

1735 LOVE IS HERE AND NOW YOU'RE GONE
The Supremes *Motown* 67

1736 DARK LADY
Cher *MCA* 74

1737 18 AND LIFE
Skid Row *Atlantic* 89

1738 SONGBIRD
Kenny G *Arista* 87

1739 LONELY OL' NIGHT
John Cougar Mellencamp *Riva* 85

1740 A TASTE OF HONEY
Herb Alpert & the Tijuana Brass *A&M* 65

1741 I CAN'T TELL YOU WHY
Eagles *Asylum* 80

1742 JET AIRLINER
Steve Miller Band *Capitol* 77

1743 IF YOU WANNA BE HAPPY
Jimmy Soul *S.P.Q.R.* 63

1744 SOME LIKE IT HOT
The Power Station *Capitol* 85

1745 BLACK DENIM TROUSERS
The Cheers *Capitol* 55

1746 YOU'RE ONLY LONELY
J.D. Souther *Columbia* 79

1747 COVER ME
Bruce Springsteen *Columbia* 84

1748 PAINT IT, BLACK
The Rolling Stones *London* 66

1749 EVERY 1'S A WINNER
Hot Chocolate *Infinity* 79

1750 NIGHTS ON BROADWAY
Bee Gees *RSO* 75

1751 HURT SO BAD
Linda Ronstadt *Asylum* 80

1752 GRAZING IN THE GRASS
Hugh Masekela *Uni* 68

1753 SATISFIED
Richard Marx *EMI* 89

1754 READY OR NOT
After 7 *Virgin* 90

1755 IF IT ISN'T LOVE
New Edition *MCA* 88

1756 LOVE IS LIKE OXYGEN
Sweet *Capitol* 78

1757 GIVE ME JUST A LITTLE MORE TIME
Chairmen of the Board *Invictus* 70

1758 MORNING HAS BROKEN
Cat Stevens *A&M* 72

1759 ONLY SIXTEEN
Dr. Hook *Capitol* 76

1760 STONEY END
Barbra Streisand *Columbia* 71

1761 I LIKE IT
Dino *4th & B'dway* 89

1762 BOOGALOO DOWN BROADWAY
The Fantastic Johnny C *Phila-L.A. of Soul* 67

1763 LEGS
ZZ Top *Warner Bros* 84

1764 YOU DECORATED MY LIFE
Kenny Rogers *UA* 79

1765 STRUT
Sheena Easton *EMI America* 84

1766 AFFAIR OF THE HEART
Rick Springfield *RCA* 83

Jackson Browne

Linda Ronstadt

1767 I CAN'T STAND IT
Eric Clapton *RSO* 81

1768 RAINDROPS
Dee Clark *Vee Jay* 61

1769 YOU GOT IT (THE RIGHT STUFF)
New Kids on the Block *Columbia* 89

1770 THROWING IT ALL AWAY
Genesis *Atlantic* 86

1771 WHISPERING BELLS
The Dell-Vikings *Dot* 57

1772 CAT'S IN THE CRADLE
Harry Chapin *Elektra* 74

1773 I WANT TO BE YOUR MAN
Roger *Reprise* 88

1774 ANGELIA
Richard Marx *EMI* 89

1775 JUST BETWEEN YOU AND ME
Lou Gramm *Atlantic* 90

1776 ANGEL OF THE MORNING
Merrilee Rush & the Turnabouts *Bell* 68

1777 SURFER GIRL
The Beach Boys *Capitol* 63

1778 STILL THE ONE
Orleans *Asylum* 76

1779 YOUR LOVE
The Outfield *Columbia* 86

1780 HOLLY HOLY
Neil Diamond *Uni* 69

1781 WASTED DAYS AND WASTED NIGHTS
Freddy Fender *ABC/Dot* 75

1782 TOO SHY
Kajagoogoo *EMI America* 83

1783 SOMETHING ABOUT YOU
Level 42 *Polydor* 86

1784 DID IT IN A MINUTE
Daryl Hall and John Oates *RCA* 82

1785 COMIN' IN AND OUT OF YOUR LIFE
Barbra Streisand *Columbia* 82

1786 STAY
Maurice Williams & the Zodiacs *Herald* 60

1787 GEORGIA ON MY MIND
Ray Charles *ABC-Paramount* 60

1788 OOH BABY BABY
Linda Ronstadt *Asylum* 79

1789 PETER GUNN
Ray Anthony *Capitol* 59

1790 TELEFONE (LONG DISTANCE LOVE AFFAIR)
Sheena Easton *EMI America* 83

1791 JOHNNY B. GOODE
Chuck Berry *Chess* 58

1792 I GOT A FEELING
Ricky Nelson *Imperial* 58

1793 LOVE YOU SO
Ron Holden *Donna* 60

1794 HEY NINETEEN
Steely Dan *MCA* 81

1795 DIRTY DIANA
Michael Jackson *Epic* 88

1796 BREAKOUT
Swing Out Sister *Mercury* 87

1797 SECOND CHANCE
Thirty Eight Special *A&M* 89

1798 HEARTBREAKER
Dionne Warwick *Arista* 83

1799 FIRE
Ohio Players *Mercury* 75

1800 CLEAN UP WOMAN
Betty Wright *Alston* 72

1801 LET'S GO ALL THE WAY
Sly Fox *Capitol* 86

1802 MISS YOU LIKE CRAZY
Natalie Cole *EMI* 89

1803 CHURCH OF THE POISON MIND
Culture Club *Epic/Virgin* 83

1804 FIRE
The Crazy World of Arthur Brown *Atlantic* 68

1805 CAN I CHANGE MY MIND
Tyrone Davis *Dakar* 69

1806 WALK ON WATER
Eddie Money *Columbia* 88

1807 TAKE IT EASY ON ME
Little River Band *Capitol* 82

1808 HOOKED ON CLASSICS
Royal Philharmonic Orchestra *RCA* 82

1809 CANDLE IN THE WIND
Elton John *MCA* 88

1810 SAY YOU LOVE ME
Fleetwood Mac *Reprise* 76

1811 HANKY PANKY
Tommy James & the Shondells *Roulette* 66

1812 ROCKIN' ROBIN
Michael Jackson *Motown* 72

1813 TOUCH ME
The Doors *Elektra* 69

1814 LET THE LITTLE GIRL DANCE
Billy Bland *Old Town* 60

1815 LET'S TWIST AGAIN
Chubby Checker *Parkway* 61

1816 COOL NIGHT
Paul Davis *Arista* 82

1817 SOUL MAN
Sam and Dave *Stax* 67

1818 SWEET LITTLE SIXTEEN
Chuck Berry *Chess* 58

1819 TONIGHT SHE COMES
The Cars *Elektra* 86

1820 LET'S GET SERIOUS
Jermaine Jackson *Motown* 80

1821 I HEAR A SYMPHONY
The Supremes *Motown* 65

1822 DUELING BANJOS
Eric Weissberg and Steve Mandell *Warner Bros* 73

1823 GEORGY GIRL
The Seekers *Capitol* 67

1824 PUT YOUR HAND IN THE HAND
Ocean *Kama Sutra* 71

1825 WILDFLOWER
Skylark *Capitol* 73

1826 WHITE SILVER SANDS
Bill Black's Combo *Hi* 60

1827 (THEME FROM) VALLEY OF THE DOLLS
Dionne Warwick *Scepter* 68

1828 LIL' RED RIDING HOOD
Sam the Sham & the Pharaohs *MGM* 66

1829 JANIE'S GOT A GUN
Aerosmith *Geffen* 90

1830 THIS LITTLE GIRL
Gary U.S. Bonds *EMI America* 81

1831 MANDY
Barry Manilow *Bell* 75

1832 BORN TO BE WILD
Steppenwolf *Dunhill* 68

1833 WE ARE FAMILY
Sister Sledge *Cotillion* 79

1834 THE LONG AND WINDING ROAD/FOR YOU BLUE
The Beatles *Apple* 70

1835 ALL THOSE YEARS AGO
George Harrison *Dark Horse* 81

1836 ROCKY MOUNTAIN HIGH
John Denver *RCA* 73

1837 OVER THE MOUNTAIN; ACROSS THE SEA
Johnnie & Joe *Chess* 57

1838 SUDDENLY LAST SUMMER
The Motels *Capitol* 83

1839 HOW DO I MAKE YOU
Linda Ronstadt *Asylum* 80

1840 SWEETHEART
Franke & the Knockouts *Millennium* 81

1841 JENNY, JENNY
Little Richard *Specialty* 57

1842 YESTERDAY'S SONGS
Neil Diamond *Columbia* 82

1843 PRECIOUS AND FEW
Climax *Carousel* 72

1844 SLOW TWISTIN'
Chubby Checker *Parkway* 62

1845 HANG ON IN THERE BABY
Johnny Bristol *MGM* 74

1846 DE DO DO DO, DE DA DA DA
The Police *A&M* 81

1847 I CAN HELP
Billy Swan *Monument* 74

1848 MY LOVE
Petula Clark *Warner Bros* 66

1849 SOMEDAY
Glass Tiger *Manhattan* 87

1850 VALOTTE
Julian Lennon *Atlantic* 85

1851 BACKFIELD IN MOTION
Mel and Tim *Bamboo* 69

1852 YOU'VE MADE ME SO VERY HAPPY
Blood, Sweat & Tears *Columbia* 69

1853 LOVE (CAN MAKE YOU HAPPY)
Mercy *Sundi* 69

1854 SPLISH SPLASH
Bobby Darin *Atco* 58

1855 LET THERE BE DRUMS
Sandy Nelson *Imperial* 61

1856 DIAMOND GIRL
Seals and Crofts *Warner Bros* 73

1857 CAN'T GET USED TO LOSING YOU
Andy Williams *Columbia* 63

1858 THE HORSE
Cliff Nobles & Co. *Phil-L.A. of Soul* 68

1859 LADY WILLPOWER
Gary Puckett & the Union Gap *Columbia* 68

1860 PROBLEMS
Everly Brothers *Cadence* 58

1861 GIRLS NITE OUT
Tyler Collins *RCA* 90

1862 IF EVER YOU'RE IN MY ARMS AGAIN
Peabo Bryson *Elektra* 84

1863 TWILIGHT ZONE
Golden Earring *21 Records* 83

1864 YOU NEVER DONE IT LIKE THAT
Captain & Tennille *A&M* 78

1865 I HONESTLY LOVE YOU
Olivia Newton-John *MCA* 74

1866 JEAN
Oliver *Crewe* 69

1867 WASHINGTON SQUARE
Village Stompers *Epic* 63

1868 HOUSE OF THE RISING SUN
Frijid Pink *Parrot* 70

1869 STAND TALL
Burton Cummings *Portrait* 77

1870 MANHATTAN SPIRITUAL
Reg Owen *Palette* 59

1871 PAPERBACK WRITER
The Beatles *Capitol* 66

1872 DAWN (GO AWAY)
The Four Seasons *Philips* 64

1873 LADY
Little River Band *Harvest* 79

1874 YOU BELONG TO THE CITY
Glenn Frey *MCA* 85

1875 WAY DOWN YONDER IN NEW ORLEANS
Freddy Cannon *Swan* 60

1876 SHOP AROUND
Captain & Tennille *A&M* 76

1877 IT'S IMPOSSIBLE
Perry Como *RCA* 71

1878 MY BONNIE LASSIE
Ames Brothers *RCA* 55

1879 PUPPY LOVE
Paul Anka *ABC-Paramount* 60

1880 I LIKE IT LIKE THAT, PART 1
Chris Kenner *Instant* 61

1881 GET UP! (BEFORE THE NIGHT IS OVER)
Technotronic *SBK* 90

1882 DON'T BE CRUEL
Bobby Brown *MCA* 88

1883 DON'T STOP BELIEVIN'
Journey *Columbia* 81

1884 EVIL WOMAN
Electric Light Orchestra *UA* 76

1885 BE MY BABY
The Ronettes *Philles* 63

1886 I'M NOT IN LOVE
10cc *Mercury* 75

1887 CARRY ON WAYWARD SON
Kansas *Kirshner* 77

1888 YOU'RE THE FIRST, THE LAST, MY EVERYTHING
Barry White *20th Century* 75

Janet Jackson

1924 LIGHT MY FIRE
Jose Feliciano *RCA* 68

1925 THE DEVIL WENT DOWN TO GEORGIA
Charlie Daniels Band *Epic* 79

1926 SING
Carpenters *A&M* 73

1927 I'M GONNA LOVE YOU JUST A LITTLE MORE BABY
Barry White *20th Century* 73

1928 JAVA
Al Hirt *RCA* 64

1929 JULIE, DO YA LOVE ME
Bobby Sherman *Metromedia* 70

1930 MAYBELLENE
Chuck Berry *Chess* 55

1931 IF YOU WANT ME TO STAY
Sly & the Family Stone *Epic* 73

1932 RIDE CAPTAIN RIDE
Blues Image *Atco* 70

1933 (SWEET SWEET BABY) SINCE YOU'VE BEEN GONE
Aretha Franklin *Atlantic* 68

1934 ON THE RADIO
Donna Summer *Casablanca* 80

1935 BABY (YOU'VE GOT WHAT IT TAKES)
Dinah Washington and Brook Benton *Mercury* 60

1936 TYPICAL MALE
Tina Turner *Capitol* 86

1937 I WAS MADE FOR DANCIN'
Leif Garrett *Scotti Bros* 79

1938 BARRACUDA
Heart *Portrait* 77

1939 REAL LOVE
Jody Watley *MCA* 89

1940 PLEASE PLEASE ME
The Beatles *Vee Jay* 64

1941 WILD THING
Tone Loc *Delicious Vinyl* 89

1942 MIRACLES
Jefferson Starship *Grunt* 75

1943 POPSICLES AND ICICLES
The Murmaids *Chattahoochee* 64

1944 I KNOW (YOU DON'T LOVE ME NO MORE)
Barbara George *A.F.O.* 62

1945 UNDER THE BOARDWALK
The Drifters *Atlantic* 64

1946 PERFECT WAY
Scritti Politti *Warner Bros* 85

1947 DAYDREAM
The Lovin' Spoonful *Kama Sutra* 66

1948 SEALED WITH A KISS
Brian Hyland *ABC-Paramount* 62

1949 LONELY DAYS
Bee Gees *Atco* 71

1950 JUNIOR'S FARM
Wings *Apple* 75

1951 OUT OF THE BLUE
Debbie Gibson *Atlantic* 88

1952 REBEL-'ROUSER
Duane Eddy *Jamie* 58

1953 I CAN'T HOLD BACK
Survivor *Scotti Bros* 84

1954 WHICH WAY YOU GOIN' BILLY?
The Poppy Family *London* 70

1955 GREEN ONIONS
Booker T. & the MG's *Stax* 62

1956 NASTY
Janet Jackson *A&M* 86

1957 TRAGEDY
Thomas Wayne *Fernwood* 59

1958 A WHITER SHADE OF PALE
Procol Harum *Deram* 67

1959 DREAMIN'
Johnny Burnette *Liberty* 60

1960 BRASS IN POCKET (I'M SPECIAL)
The Pretenders *Sire* 80

1961 ALSO SPRACH ZARATHUSTRA
Deodato *CTI* 73

1962 SMOKE ON THE WATER
Deep Purple *Warner Bros* 73

1963 LA-LA - MEANS I LOVE YOU
The Delfonics *Philly Groove* 68

1964 IT'S TIME TO CRY
Paul Anka *ABC-Paramount* 59

1965 HEARTLIGHT
Neil Diamond *Columbia* 82

1966 SUMMER NIGHTS
John Travolta and Olivia Newton-John *RSO* 78

1967 RUBY TUESDAY
The Rolling Stones *London* 67

1968 CAN'T YOU HEAR MY HEARTBEAT
Herman's Hermits *MGM* 65

1969 A GROOVY KIND OF LOVE
The Mindbenders *Fontana* 66

1970 HEY THERE LONELY GIRL
Eddie Holman *ABC* 70

1971 R.O.C.K. IN THE U.S.A.
John Cougar Mellencamp *Riva* 86

1972 BRIDGE OVER TROUBLED WATER
Aretha Franklin *Atlantic* 71

1973 MR. TAMBOURINE MAN
The Byrds *Columbia* 65

1974 THE CISCO KID
War *UA* 73

1975 HEAT WAVE
Martha & the Vandellas *Gordy* 63

1976 SHORT SHORTS
Royal Teens *ABC-Paramount* 58

1977 DOESN'T SOMEBODY WANT TO BE WANTED
The Partridge Family *Bell* 71

1978 WHAT ARE WE DOIN' IN LOVE
Dottie West *Liberty* 81

1979 TIME OF THE SEASON
The Zombies *Date* 69

1980 SEE YOU IN SEPTEMBER
The Happenings *B.T. Puppy* 66

1981 GIRL WATCHER
The O'Kaysions *ABC* 68

1982 WOLVERTON MOUNTAIN
Claude King *Columbia* 62

1983 THINK I'M IN LOVE
Eddie Money *Columbia* 82

1984 THE HUSTLE
Van McCoy & the Soul City Symphony *Avco* 75

1985 I'M STILL IN LOVE WITH YOU
Al Green *Hi* 72

1986 WHERE OR WHEN
Dion & the Belmonts *Laurie* 60

1987 DON'T PULL YOUR LOVE
Hamilton, Joe Frank & Reynolds *Dunhill* 71

1988 RAINY NIGHT IN GEORGIA
Brook Benton *Cotillion* 70

1989 DECK OF CARDS
Wink Martindale *Dot* 59

1990 BABY, I'M FOR REAL
The Originals *Soul* 69

1991 GIVE ME LOVE (GIVE ME PEACE ON EARTH)
George Harrison *Apple* 73

1992 MR. CUSTER
Larry Verne *Era* 60

1993 DESIRE
U2 *Island* 88

Jerry Butler

1994 YOU CAN'T SIT DOWN
The Dovells *Parkway* 63

1995 NEVER BE ANYONE ELSE BUT YOU
Ricky Nelson *Imperial* 59

1996 GOIN' OUT OF MY HEAD
Little Anthony & the Imperials *DCP* 64

1997 SOLDIER OF LOVE
Donny Osmond *Capitol* 89

1998 I DIDN'T MEAN TO TURN YOU ON
Robert Palmer *Island* 86

1999 MOONLIGHT FEELS RIGHT
Starbuck *Private Stock* 76

2000 KOOKIE, KOOKIE (LEND ME YOUR COMB)
Edward Byrnes and Connie Stevens *Warner Bros* 59

2001 SHAKE IT
Ian Matthews *Mushroom* 79

2002 DIFFERENT DRUM
Stone Poneys f/Linda Ronstadt *Capitol* 68

2003 DON'T BREAK THE HEART THAT LOVES YOU
Connie Francis *MGM* 62

2004 FOOL #1
Brenda Lee *Decca* 61

2005 SOULFUL STRUT
Young-Holt Unlimited *Brunswick* 69

2006 CANDY GIRL
The Four Seasons *Vee Jay* 63

2007 MY CHERIE AMOUR
Stevie Wonder *Tamla* 69

2008 ONLY THE STRONG SURVIVE
Jerry Butler *Mercury* 69

2009 STORMY
Classics IV f/Dennis Yost *Imperial* 68

2010 CHERISH
Madonna *Sire* 89

2011 I GET WEAK
Belinda Carlisle *MCA* 88

2012 IN TOO DEEP
Genesis *Atlantic* 87

2013 EXPRESS
B.T. Express *Roadshow* 75

2014 TO ALL THE GIRLS I'VE LOVED BEFORE
Julio Iglesias and Willie Nelson *Columbia* 84

2015 TELL ME SOMETHING GOOD
Rufus *ABC* 74

2016 I DON'T WANNA LIVE WITHOUT YOUR LOVE
Chicago *Reprise* 88

2017 YOU DON'T HAVE TO SAY YOU LOVE ME
Dusty Springfield *Philips* 66

2018 SHOTGUN
Jr. Walker & the All Stars *Soul* 65

2019 ELECTION DAY
Arcadia *Capitol* 85

2020 POISON IVY
The Coasters *Atco* 59

2021 TICKET TO RIDE
The Beatles *Capitol* 65

2022 WHAT HAVE I DONE TO DESERVE THIS?
Pet Shop Boys w/Dusty Springfield *EMI Manhattan* 88

2023 YUMMY YUMMY YUMMY
Ohio Express *Buddah* 68

2024 DRAGGIN' THE LINE
Tommy James *Roulette* 71

2025 NICE TO BE WITH YOU
Gallery *Sussex* 72

2026 HOLD ME TIGHT
Johnny Nash *JAD* 68

2027 HAPPY BIRTHDAY, SWEET SIXTEEN
Neil Sedaka *RCA* 62

2028 FOR THE GOOD TIMES
Ray Price *Columbia* 71

2029 HAVE YOU NEVER BEEN MELLOW
Olivia Newton-John *MCA* 75

2030 EVE OF DESTRUCTION
Barry McGuire *Dunhill* 65

2031 CRADLE OF LOVE
Johnny Preston *Mercury* 60

2032 WHY CAN'T WE LIVE TOGETHER
Timmy Thomas *Glades* 73

2033 CECILIA
Simon and Garfunkel *Columbia* 70

2034 A MILLION TO ONE
Jimmy Charles *Promo* 60

2035 TALLAHASSEE LASSIE
Freddy Cannon *Swan* 59

2036 I JUST CAN'T STOP LOVING YOU
Michael Jackson and Siedah Garrett *Epic* 87

2037 TRACES
Classics IV f/Dennis Yost *Imperial* 69

2038 TURN BACK THE HANDS OF TIME
Tyrone Davis *Dakar* 70

2039 OH, BABE, WHAT WOULD YOU SAY?
Hurricane Smith *Capitol* 73

2040 I SAY A LITTLE PRAYER
Dionne Warwick *Scepter* 67

2041 THE LOOK OF LOVE
Sergio Mendes & Brasil '66 *A&M* 68

2042 SHE'S A FOOL
Lesley Gore *Mercury* 63

2043 DEVIL WOMAN
Cliff Richard *Rocket* 76

2044 RUBBER BALL
Bobby Vee *Liberty* 61

2045 GLAD ALL OVER
Dave Clark Five *Epic* 64

2046 DADDY'S HOME
Shep & the Limelites *Hull* 61

2047 WHO'S JOHNNY
El DeBarge *Gordy* 86

2048 MUSIC BOX DANCER
Frank Mills *Polydor* 79

2049 LA ISLA BONITA
Madonna *Sire* 87

2050 CALENDAR GIRL
Neil Sedaka *RCA* 61

2051 SUNSHINE OF YOUR LOVE
Cream *Atco* 68

2052 THESE EYES
The Guess Who *RCA* 69

2053 THE GROOVE LINE
Heatwave *Epic* 78

2054 WILD THING
The Troggs *Fontana/Atco* 66

2055 ALL YOU NEED IS LOVE
The Beatles *Capitol* 67

2056 LET'S WAIT AWHILE
Janet Jackson *A&M* 87

2057 FOX ON THE RUN
Sweet *Capitol* 76

2058 SORRY SEEMS TO BE THE HARDEST WORD
Elton John *MCA/Rocket* 76

2059 DANNY'S SONG
Anne Murray *Capitol* 73

2060 THE FLY
Chubby Checker *Parkway* 61

2061 TAKE IT AWAY
Paul McCartney *Columbia* 82

2062 GRAZING IN THE GRASS
Friends of Distinction *RCA* 69

2063 LUKA
Suzanne Vega *A&M* 87

2064 HOW CAN WE BE LOVERS
Michael Bolton *Columbia* 90

2065 SIGN YOUR NAME
Terence Trent D'Arby *Columbia* 88

2066 VOLARE
Bobby Rydell *Cameo* 60

2067 IT'S ALL RIGHT
The Impressions *ABC-Paramount* 63

2068 MOTHER AND CHILD REUNION
Paul Simon *Columbia* 72

2069 EVERYTHING I OWN
Bread *Elektra* 72

2070 LOOKIN' FOR LOVE
Johnny Lee *Full Moon* 80

2071 JAZZMAN
Carole King *Ode* 74

2072 PERFECT WORLD
Huey Lewis & the News *Chrysalis* 88

2073 PIPELINE
The Chantays *Dot* 63

2074 CARA, MIA
Jay & the Americans *UA* 65

2075 WHY ME
Kris Kristofferson *Monument* 73

2076 BURN THAT CANDLE/ROCK-A-BEATIN' BOOGIE
Bill Haley & His Comets *Decca* 55

2077 OVER AND OVER
Dave Clark Five *Epic* 65

2078 THE HAPPENING
The Supremes *Motown* 67

2079 MERCEDES BOY
Pebbles *MCA* 88

2080 YOU GOT IT ALL
The Jets *MCA* 87

2081 FREDDIE'S DEAD
Curtis Mayfield *Curtom* 72

2082 UP AROUND THE BEND/RUN THROUGH THE JUNGLE
Creedence Clearwater Revival *Fantasy* 70

2083 HOW SWEET IT IS (TO BE LOVED BY YOU)
James Taylor *Warner Bros* 75

2084 HEY DEANIE
Shaun Cassidy *Warner/Curb* 78

2085 WHO'S THAT GIRL
Madonna *Sire* 87

2086 HOW LONG
Ace *Anchor* 75

2087 1-2-3
Gloria Estefan & Miami Sound Machine *Epic* 88

2088 THE SHOW MUST GO ON
Three Dog Night *Dunhill* 74

2089 NEVER BEEN TO SPAIN
Three Dog Night *Dunhill* 72

2090 BRICK HOUSE
Commodores *Motown* 77

2091 FIRE LAKE
Bob Seger *Capitol* 80

2092 RUN AWAY CHILD, RUNNING WILD
The Temptations *Gordy* 69

2093 BEYOND THE SEA
Bobby Darin *Atco* 60

2094 DON'T MEAN NOTHING
Richard Marx *Manhattan* 87

2095 LET ME IN
The Sensations *Argo* 62

2096 LOVE SOMEBODY
Rick Springfield *RCA* 84

2097 REAL LOVE
Doobie Brothers *Warner Bros* 80

2098 MEMPHIS
Lonnie Mack *Fraternity* 63

2099 PLEASE LOVE ME FOREVER
Bobby Vinton *Epic* 67

2100 DO YOU REMEMBER?
Phil Collins *Atlantic* 90

2101 SING A SONG
Earth, Wind & Fire *Columbia* 76

2102 TOO LATE FOR GOODBYES
Julian Lennon *Atlantic* 85

2103 LIGHTNIN' STRIKES
Lou Christie *MGM* 66

2104 FREEDOM
Wham! *Columbia* 85

2105 GIVING YOU THE BENEFIT
Pebbles *MCA* 90

2106 STRAWBERRY LETTER 23
Brothers Johnson *A&M* 77

2107 IN MY HOUSE
Mary Jane Girls *Gordy* 85

2108 DOES ANYBODY REALLY KNOW WHAT TIME IT IS?
Chicago *Columbia* 71

2109 SUPERFLY
Curtis Mayfield *Curtom* 73

2110 FLOAT ON
The Floaters *ABC* 77

2111 TWO OF HEARTS
Stacey Q *Atlantic* 86

2112 IF
Bread *Elektra* 71

2113 SUMMER OF '69
Bryan Adams *A&M* 85

2114 (SHE'S) SEXY + 17
Stray Cats *EMI America* 83

2115 COME GO WITH ME
Expose *Arista* 87

2116 HELLO IT'S ME
Todd Rundgren *Bearsville* 73

2117 YOU MIGHT THINK
The Cars *Elektra* 84

2118 I'M ALRIGHT
Kenny Loggins *Columbia* 80

2119 ROCK THIS TOWN
Stray Cats *EMI America* 82

2120 RIGHT PLACE WRONG TIME
Dr. John *Atco* 73

2121 I LOVE YOU BECAUSE
Al Martino *Capitol* 63

2122 WILL YOU STILL LOVE ME?
Chicago *Full Moon* 87

2123 25 OR 6 TO 4
Chicago *Columbia* 70

2124 IF YOU LOVE ME (LET ME KNOW)
Olivia Newton-John *MCA* 74

2125 THE SWEETEST TABOO
Sade *Portrait* 86

2126 IT'S A MISTAKE
Men at Work *Columbia* 83

2127 THE JERK
The Larks *Money* 65

2128 DANCE WITH ME
Peter Brown *Drive* 78

2129 I SHOT THE SHERIFF
Eric Clapton *RSO* 74

2130 JACKIE BLUE
Ozark Mountain Daredevils *A&M* 75

2131 NEW SENSATION
INXS *Atlantic* 88

2132 CHEVY VAN
Sammy Johns *GRC* 75

2133 HIM
Rupert Holmes *MCA* 80

2134 WANTED DEAD OR ALIVE
Bon Jovi *Mercury* 87

2135 I WANT YOUR LOVE
Chic *Atlantic* 79

2136 WELCOME TO THE JUNGLE
Guns n' Roses *Geffen* 88

2137 LET IT BE ME
Everly Brothers *Cadence* 60

2138 TIGHTER, TIGHTER
Alive & Kicking *Roulette* 70

2139 SONG FOR A SUMMER NIGHT
Mitch Miller *Columbia* 56

2140 PRAYING FOR TIME
George Michael *Columbia* 90

2141 EVERYTHING YOUR HEART DESIRES
Daryl Hall and John Oates *Arista* 88

2142 DON'T BE CRUEL
Cheap Trick *Epic* 88

2143 DON'T DISTURB THIS GROOVE
The System *Atlantic* 87

2144 WE DON'T HAVE TO TAKE OUR CLOTHES OFF
Jermaine Stewart *Arista* 86

2145 WISHIN' AND HOPIN'
Dusty Springfield *Philips* 64

2146 WHEN I FALL IN LOVE
The Lettermen *Capitol* 62

2147 HUMMINGBIRD
Les Paul and Mary Ford *Capitol* 55

2148 SOMETHING HAPPENED ON THE WAY TO HEAVEN
Phil Collins *Atlantic* 90

2149 I'LL BE YOUR SHELTER
Taylor Dayne *Arista* 90

2150 THE LONELY BULL
The Tijuana Brass f/Herb Alpert *A&M* 62

2151 GOT TO GET YOU INTO MY LIFE
The Beatles *Capitol* 76

2152 DANCE TO THE MUSIC
Sly & the Family Stone *Epic* 68

2153 CHANGE OF HEART
Cyndi Lauper *Portrait* 87

2154 WHEN THE CHILDREN CRY
White Lion *Atlantic* 89

2155 TAKE ME HOME TONIGHT
Eddie Money *Columbia* 86

2156 WALKING IN RHYTHM
The Blackbyrds *Fantasy* 75

2157 TAKE GOOD CARE OF HER
Adam Wade *Coed* 61

2158 SLEEPING BAG
ZZ Top *Warner Bros* 85

2159 ONE GOOD WOMAN
Peter Cetera *Full Moon* 88

2160 ME AND YOU AND A DOG NAMED BOO
Lobo *Big Tree* 71

2161 PINK CADILLAC
Natalie Cole *EMI Manhattan* 88

2162 RHYTHM IS GONNA GET YOU
Gloria Estefan & Miami Sound Machine *Epic* 87

2163 ANGEL
Madonna *Sire* 85

2164 COME ON DOWN TO MY BOAT
Every Mothers' Son *MGM* 67

2165 SWEET FREEDOM
Michael McDonald *MCA* 86

2166 DELIRIOUS
Prince *Warner Bros* 83

2167 YOU'RE SIXTEEN
Johnny Burnette *Liberty* 60

2168 PLEASE MR. POSTMAN
Carpenters *A&M* 75

2169 SWEET LOVE
Commodores *Motown* 76

2170 CASANOVA
Levert *Atlantic* 87

2171 I'VE HAD IT
The Bell Notes *Time* 59

2172 SOLITAIRE
Laura Branigan *Atlantic* 83

2173 WALK THIS WAY
Run-D.M.C. *Profile* 86

2174 ALWAYS ON MY MIND
Pet Shop Boys *EMI Manhattan* 88

2175 BLACK CAT
Janet Jackson *A&M* 90

2176 WHEN SMOKEY SINGS
ABC *Mercury* 87

2177 IMAGE OF A GIRL
Safaris *Eldo* 60

2178 YOU MAY BE RIGHT
Billy Joel *Columbia* 80

2179 DEAR LADY TWIST
Gary U.S. Bonds *Legrand* 62

2180 POETRY MAN
Phoebe Snow *Shelter* 75

2181 COULD IT BE MAGIC
Barry Manilow *Arista* 75

2182 COME DANCING
The Kinks *Arista* 83

2183 ATLANTIS
Donovan *Epic* 69

2184 GET DOWN
Gilbert O'Sullivan *MAM* 73

2185 HARBOR LIGHTS
The Platters *Mercury* 60

Phoebe Snow

Van Halen

2272 FORTRESS AROUND YOUR HEART
Sting *A&M* 85

2273 BORN IN THE U.S.A.
Bruce Springsteen *Columbia* 85

2274 A LITTLE BITTY TEAR
Burl Ives *Decca* 62

2275 WATERLOO
Abba *Atlantic* 74

2276 ALL CRIED OUT
Lisa Lisa & Cult Jam w/Full Force *Columbia* 86

2277 BREAKING UP IS HARD TO DO
Neil Sedaka *Rocket* 76

2278 YOU AND ME
Alice Cooper *Warner Bros* 77

2279 THUNDER ISLAND
Jay Ferguson *Asylum* 78

2280 PLEASE MR. PLEASE
Olivia Newton-John *MCA* 75

2281 YOU BELONG TO ME
Carly Simon *Elektra* 78

2282 FOR WHAT IT'S WORTH (STOP, HEY WHAT'S THAT SOUND)
Buffalo Springfield *Atco* 67

2283 ENJOY THE SILENCE
Depeche Mode *Sire* 90

2284 ONLY YOU
Frank Pourcel's French Fiddles *Capitol* 59

2285 YOU CAN'T CHANGE THAT
Raydio *Arista* 79

2286 ALL SHE WANTS TO DO IS DANCE
Don Henley *Geffen* 85

2287 GOOD TIMIN'
Jimmy Jones *Cub* 60

2288 HELP ME MAKE IT THROUGH THE NIGHT
Sammi Smith *Mega* 71

2289 EASY COME, EASY GO
Bobby Sherman *Metromedia* 70

2290 REACH OUT OF THE DARKNESS
Friend and Lover *Verve Forecast* 68

2291 ON AND ON
Gladys Knight & the Pips *Buddah* 74

2292 VOICES CARRY
'Til Tuesday *Epic* 85

2293 HERE I AM (COME AND TAKE ME)
Al Green *Hi* 73

2294 THEY DON'T KNOW
Tracey Ullman *MCA* 84

2295 SHIPS
Barry Manilow *Arista* 79

2296 WE'LL BE TOGETHER
Sting *A&M* 87

2297 I'LL TUMBLE 4 YA
Culture Club *Epic/Virgin* 83

2298 HOLD ON TIGHT
Electric Light Orchestra *Jet* 81

2299 YOU'RE NO GOOD
Linda Ronstadt *Capitol* 75

2300 ALLEY CAT
Bent Fabric & His Piano *Atco* 62

2301 SOMETHING SO STRONG
Crowded House *Capitol* 87

2302 ONE MAN WOMAN/ONE WOMAN MAN
Paul Anka w/Odia Coates *UA* 75

2303 BABY, BABY DON'T CRY
Smokey Robinson & the Miracles *Tamla* 69

2304 BE NEAR ME
ABC *Mercury* 85

2305 IT'S RAINING AGAIN
Supertramp *A&M* 82

2306 I AIN'T GONNA STAND FOR IT
Stevie Wonder *Tamla* 81

2307 EIGHT DAYS A WEEK
The Beatles *Capitol* 65

2308 ALL THIS TIME
Tiffany *MCA* 89

2309 TOO MUCH TIME ON MY HANDS
Styx *A&M* 81

2310 SEVEN LITTLE GIRLS SITTING IN THE BACK SEAT
Paul Evans *Guaranteed* 59

2311 NEAR YOU
Roger Williams *Kapp* 58

2312 DON'T GET ME WRONG
The Pretenders *Sire* 86

2313 MARIANNE
The Hilltoppers *Dot* 57

2314 LITTLE WOMAN
Bobby Sherman *Metromedia* 69

2315 NITE AND DAY
Al B. Sure! *Warner Bros* 88

2316 STILL
Bill Anderson *Decca* 63

2317 KING OF WISHFUL THINKING
Go West *EMI* 90

2318 LIVING IN SIN
Bon Jovi *Mercury* 89

2319 FRANKIE
Connie Francis *MGM* 59

2320 WHEN IT'S LOVE
Van Halen *Warner Bros* 88

2321 HEART AND SOUL
Huey Lewis & the News *Chrysalis* 83

2322 EVERYBODY EVERYBODY
Black Box *RCA* 90

2323 RUBY BABY
Dion *Columbia* 63

2324 SUMMER BREEZE
Seals and Crofts *Warner Bros* 72

2325 CRUMBLIN' DOWN
John Cougar Mellencamp *Riva* 83

2326 EPIC
Faith No More *Slash* 90

2327 GET OFF
Foxy *Dash* 78

2328 IF I WERE YOUR WOMAN
Gladys Knight & the Pips *Soul* 71

2329 CUT THE CAKE
Average White Band *Atlantic* 75

2330 PARTY DOLL
Steve Lawrence *Coral* 57

2331 CRIMSON AND CLOVER
Joan Jett & the Blackhearts *Boardwalk* 82

2332 DON'T CRY
Asia *Geffen* 83

2333 SIMON SAYS
1910 Fruitgum Co. *Buddah* 68

2334 PRIVATE DANCER
Tina Turner *Capitol* 85

2335 IF YOU'RE READY (COME GO WITH ME)
The Staple Singers *Stax* 73

2336 BABY LOVE
Regina *Atlantic* 86

2337 SHE'S OUT OF MY LIFE
Michael Jackson *Epic* 80

2338 REVOLUTION
The Beatles *Apple* 68

2339 BETTER LOVE NEXT TIME
Dr. Hook *Capitol* 80

2340 SUDDENLY THERE'S A VALLEY
Gogi Grant *Era* 55

2341 MAGIC MAN
Heart *Mushroom* 76

2342 WHATCHA SEE IS WHATCHA GET
The Dramatics *Volt* 71

2343 VICTORY
Kool & the Gang *Mercury* 87

2344 DANCING IN THE MOONLIGHT
King Harvest *Perception* 73

2345 ROCK YOUR BABY
George McCrae *TK* 74

2346 A LOVER'S CONCERTO
The Toys *DynoVoice* 65

2347 REFLECTIONS
Diana Ross & the Supremes *Motown* 67

2348 I REMEMBER YOU
Skid Row *Atlantic* 90

2349 CLOSE MY EYES (FOREVER)
Lita Ford w/Ozzy Osbourne *RCA* 89

2350 FEEL LIKE MAKIN' LOVE
Bad Company *Swan Song* 75

2351 LOVE WILL TURN YOU AROUND
Kenny Rogers *Liberty* 82

2352 19TH NERVOUS BREAKDOWN
The Rolling Stones *London* 66

2353 FRESH
Kool & the Gang *De-Lite* 85

2354 I WON'T HOLD YOU BACK
Toto *Columbia* 83

2355 TWO OUT OF THREE AIN'T BAD
Meat Loaf *Epic* 78

2356 I'LL NEVER FIND ANOTHER YOU
The Seekers *Capitol* 65

2357 SPIES LIKE US
Paul McCartney *Capitol* 86

2358 SENTIMENTAL STREET
Night Ranger *MCA/Camel* 85

2359 C'MON AND GET MY LOVE
D-Mob i/Cathy Dennis *ffrr* 90

2360 REELING IN THE YEARS
Steely Dan *ABC* 73

2361 OH, BOY!
The Crickets *Brunswick* 58

2362 IN THE SUMMERTIME
Mungo Jerry *Janus* 70

2363 BIMBOMBEY
Jimmie Rodgers *Roulette* 58

2364 HURTING EACH OTHER
Carpenters *A&M* 72

2365 MEMPHIS
Johnny Rivers *Imperial* 64

2366 MY MARIA
B.W. Stevenson *RCA* 73

2367 DON'T DO ME LIKE THAT
Tom Petty & the Heartbreakers *Backstreet* 80

2368 JESSE
Carly Simon *Warner Bros* 80

2369 BORN A WOMAN
Sandy Posey *MGM* 66

2370 GARDEN OF EDEN
Joe Valino *Vik* 56

2371 MAKE YOU SWEAT
Keith Sweat *Vintertainment* 90

2372 BACK STABBERS
The O'Jays *PIR* 72

2373 BOTTLE OF WINE
The Fireballs *Atco* 68

2374 I GOT A NAME
Jim Croce *ABC* 73

2375 DISCO INFERNO
The Trammps *Atlantic* 78

2376 PROMISES, PROMISES
Naked Eyes *EMI America* 83

2377 YOU DON'T OWN ME
Lesley Gore *Mercury* 64

2378 LADY MADONNA
The Beatles *Capitol* 68

2379 GOT A HOLD ON ME
Christine McVie *Warner Bros* 84

2380 (DON'T FEAR) THE REAPER
Blue Oyster Cult *Columbia* 76

2381 THE ONE I LOVE
R.E.M. *I.R.S.* 87

2382 DANNY BOY
Conway Twitty *MGM* 59

2383 DEVOTED TO YOU
Everly Brothers *Cadence* 58

2384 LOVE IS ALL AROUND
The Troggs *Fontana* 68

2385 DON'T CLOSE YOUR EYES
Kix *Atlantic* 89

2386 MY ANGEL BABY
Toby Beau *RCA* 78

2387 LOVE ME
Yvonne Elliman *RSO* 76

2388 FOUR WALLS
Jim Reeves *RCA* 57

2389 BUSTED
Ray Charles *ABC-Paramount* 63

2390 SHE'S A BEAUTY
The Tubes *Capitol* 83

2391 I MADE IT THROUGH THE RAIN
Barry Manilow *Arista* 81

2392 THE PROMISE
When in Rome *Virgin* 88

2393 I WAS MADE FOR LOVIN' YOU
Kiss *Casablanca* 79

2394 WAKE UP EVERYBODY (PART 1)
Harold Melvin & the Blue Notes *PIR* 76

2395 SINCE I DON'T HAVE YOU
The Skyliners *Calico* 59

2396 DON'T LOOK BACK
Boston *Epic* 78

2397 TURN THE BEAT AROUND
Vicki Sue Robinson *RCA* 76

2398 HOW YOU GONNA SEE ME NOW
Alice Cooper *Warner Bros* 78

2399 ONLY WOMEN
Alice Cooper *Atlantic* 75

2400 CAUSING A COMMOTION
Madonna *Sire* 87

2401 RED RUBBER BALL
The Cyrkle *Columbia* 66

2402 TRUE BLUE
Madonna *Sire* 86

2403 EVERYBODY PLAYS THE FOOL
The Main Ingredient *RCA* 72

2404 PUPPY LOVE
Donny Osmond *MGM* 72

2405 FANNY (BE TENDER WITH MY LOVE)
Bee Gees *RSO* 76

2406 WAITING ON A FRIEND
The Rolling Stones *Rolling Stones* 82

2407 I'M STICKIN' WITH YOU
Jimmy Bowen w/the Rhythm Orchids *Roulette* 57

2408 DEDICATED TO THE ONE I LOVE
The Mamas and the Papas *Dunhill* 67

2409 WORST THAT COULD HAPPEN
Brooklyn Bridge *Buddah* 69

2410 I AM A ROCK
Simon and Garfunkel *Columbia* 66

2411 IMAGINE
John Lennon/Plastic Ono Band *Apple* 71

Steely Dan

377

2446 THE LITTLE OLD LADY (FROM PASADENA)
Jan and Dean *Liberty* 64

2447 RELEASE ME (AND LET ME LOVE AGAIN)
Engelbert Humperdinck *Parrot* 67

2448 THRILLER
Michael Jackson *Epic* 84

2449 ROCK 'N' ROLL FANTASY
Bad Company *Swan Song* 79

2450 I'M SORRY/HE'S MINE
The Platters *Mercury* 57

2451 DID YOU EVER HAVE TO MAKE UP YOUR MIND?
The Lovin' Spoonful *Kama Sutra* 66

2452 TRAVELIN' BAND/WHO'LL STOP THE RAIN
Creedence Clearwater Revival *Fantasy* 70

2453 SOUTH STREET
The Orlons *Cameo* 63

2454 HATS OFF TO LARRY
Del Shannon *Big Top* 61

2455 LAWYERS IN LOVE
Jackson Browne *Asylum* 83

2456 SOWING THE SEEDS OF LOVE
Tears for Fears *Fontana* 69

2457 BITS AND PIECES
Dave Clark Five *Epic* 64

2458 SURFIN' BIRD
The Trashmen *Garrett* 64

2459 SOMEONE SAVED MY LIFE TONIGHT
Elton John *MCA* 75

2460 AN AMERICAN DREAM
The Dirt Band *UA* 80

2461 CARRIE
Europe *Epic* 87

2462 WHAT'S NEW, PUSSYCAT?
Tom Jones *Parrot* 65

2463 SAN FRANCISCO (BE SURE TO WEAR FLOWERS IN YOUR HAIR)
Scott McKenzie *Ode* 67

2464 DEEP PURPLE
Donny and Marie Osmond *MGM* 76

2465 SHE'S JUST MY STYLE
Gary Lewis & the Playboys *Liberty* 66

2466 COME A LITTLE BIT CLOSER
Jay & the Americans *UA* 64

2467 DA DOO RON RON (WHEN HE WALKED ME HOME)
The Crystals *Philles* 63

2468 PROUD MARY
Ike and Tina Turner *Liberty* 71

2469 DON'T LET THE RAIN COME DOWN (CROOKED LITTLE MAN)
The Serendipity Singers *Philips* 64

2470 SERPENTINE FIRE
Earth, Wind & Fire *Columbia* 78

2471 SECRET AGENT MAN
Johnny Rivers *Imperial* 66

2472 EVERY BEAT OF MY HEART
The Pips *Vee Jay* 61

2473 MAY YOU ALWAYS
McGuire Sisters *Coral* 59

2474 HOW AM I SUPPOSED TO LIVE WITHOUT YOU
Laura Branigan *Atlantic* 83

2475 THE NIGHT CHICAGO DIED
Paper Lace *Mercury* 74

2476 CRY BABY
Garnet Mimms & the Enchanters *UA* 63

2477 MAKE A MOVE ON ME
Olivia Newton-John *MCA* 82

2478 G.T.O.
Ronny & the Daytonas *Mala* 64

2479 HEARD IT IN A LOVE SONG
Marshall Tucker Band *Capricorn* 77

2480 IF YOU DON'T KNOW ME BY NOW
Harold Melvin & the Blue Notes *PIR* 72

2481 NOWHERE MAN
The Beatles *Capitol* 66

2482 TRYIN' TO LIVE MY LIFE WITHOUT YOU
Bob Seger *Capitol* 81

2483 WHERE IS THE LOVE
Roberta Flack and Donny Hathaway *Atlantic* 72

2484 MANY TEARS AGO
Connie Francis *MGM* 60

2485 THE LOOK OF LOVE (PART ONE)
ABC *Mercury* 83

2486 BUT I DO
Clarence "Frogman" Henry *Argo* 61

2487 ANOTHER DAY/OH WOMAN OH WHY
Paul McCartney *Apple* 71

2488 GO, JIMMY, GO
Jimmy Clanton *Ace* 60

2489 SILHOUETTES
Herman's Hermits *MGM* 65

2490 HOT ROD HEARTS
Robbie Dupree *Elektra* 80

2491 I'M HENRY VIII, I AM
Herman's Hermits *MGM* 65

2492 IT MUST BE HIM
Vikki Carr *Liberty* 67

2493 I WISH IT WOULD RAIN DOWN
Phil Collins *Atlantic* 90

2494 IF YOU COULD READ MY MIND
Gordon Lightfoot *Reprise* 71

2495 TAKE TIME TO KNOW HER
Percy Sledge *Atlantic* 68

2496 TREAT HER RIGHT
Roy Head *Back Beat* 65

2497 MY BOY LOLLIPOP
Millie Small *Smash* 64

2498 TOWER OF STRENGTH
Gene McDaniels *Liberty* 61

2499 HURDY GURDY MAN
Donovan *Epic* 68

2500 BLAME IT ON THE BOSSA NOVA
Eydie Gorme *Columbia* 63

2501 BATTLE HYMN OF THE REPUBLIC
Mormon Tabernacle Choir *Columbia* 59

2502 MERCY MERCY ME (THE ECOLOGY)
Marvin Gaye *Tamla* 71

2503 MANDOLIN RAIN
Bruce Hornsby & the Range *RCA* 87

2504 YELLOW BIRD
Arthur Lyman Group *Hi-Fi* 61

2505 MY LOVE
Lionel Richie *Motown* 83

2506 LITTLE BITTY PRETTY ONE
Thurston Harris *Aladdin* 57

2507 MIDNIGHT BLUE
Melissa Manchester *Arista* 75

2508 GOING IN CIRCLES
Friends of Distinction *RCA* 69

2509 I GOT RHYTHM
The Happenings *B.T. Puppy* 67

2510 HELLO STRANGER
Barbara Lewis *Atlantic* 63

2511 PUT A LITTLE LOVE IN YOUR HEART
Jackie DeShannon *Imperial* 69

2512 CRYING IN THE RAIN
Everly Brothers *Warner Bros* 62

2513 AT MY FRONT DOOR (CRAZY LITTLE MAMA)
Pat Boone *Dot* 55

2514 SOMEBODY'S KNOCKIN'
Terri Gibbs *MCA* 81

2515 FERNANDO
Abba *Atlantic* 76

Cream

Bobby Brown

2620 JUST LIKE JESSE JAMES
Cher *Geffen* 89

2621 SHOWER ME WITH YOUR LOVE
Surface *Columbia* 89

2622 DREAMTIME
Daryl Hall *RCA* 86

2623 NOBODY TOLD ME
John Lennon *Polydor* 84

2624 HEAT OF THE NIGHT
Bryan Adams *A&M* 87

2625 THE SHOOP SHOOP SONG (IT'S IN HIS KISS)
Betty Everett *Vee Jay* 64

2626 TRANSFUSION
Nervous Norvus *Dot* 56

2627 CORINNA, CORINNA
Ray Peterson *Dunes* 61

2628 PLEASE COME TO BOSTON
Dave Loggins *Epic* 74

2629 WALKING TO NEW ORLEANS
Fats Domino *Imperial* 60

2630 ON BROADWAY
George Benson *Warner Bros* 78

2631 FORTY MILES OF BAD ROAD
Duane Eddy *Jamie* 59

2632 I'D WAIT A MILLION YEARS
The Grass Roots *Dunhill* 69

2633 JEANS ON
David Dundas *Chrysalis* 77

2634 SWEET TALKIN' WOMAN
Electric Light Orchestra *Jet* 78

2635 RONI
Bobby Brown *MCA* 89

2636 THERE'S A MOON OUT TONIGHT
The Capris *Old Town* 61

2637 RIKKI DON'T LOSE THAT NUMBER
Steely Dan *ABC* 74

2638 FOOLISH LITTLE GIRL
The Shirelles *Scepter* 63

2639 HAVE I THE RIGHT?
The Honeycombs *Interphon* 64

2640 YOU CAN DEPEND ON ME
Brenda Lee *Decca* 61

2641 LET ME BE THE ONE
Expose *Arista* 87

2642 ALL I EVER NEED IS YOU
Sonny and Cher *Kapp* 71

2643 BAD BOY
Miami Sound Machine *Epic* 86

2644 I'M SO LONESOME I COULD CRY
B.J. Thomas & the Triumphs *Scepter* 66

2645 MAYBE
The Chantels *End* 58

2646 PENNY LANE
The Beatles *Capitol* 67

2647 PETITE FLEUR (LITTLE FLOWER)
Chris Barber's Jazz Band *Laurie* 59

2648 THE BOXER
Simon and Garfunkel *Columbia* 69

2649 JUNGLE FEVER
Chakachas *Polydor* 72

2650 DARK MOON
Bonnie Guitar *Dot* 57

2651 BRILLIANT DISGUISE
Bruce Springsteen *Columbia* 87

2652 ANGEL EYES
Jeff Healey Band *Arista* 89

2653 I DON'T WANT TO LIVE WITHOUT YOU
Foreigner *Atlantic* 88

2654 I'VE FOUND SOMEONE OF MY OWN
Free Movement *Decca* 71

2655 TALL PAUL
Annette *Disneyland* 59

2656 BACK HOME AGAIN
John Denver *RCA* 74

2657 NO TIME
The Guess Who *RCA* 70

2658 MIDNIGHT BLUE
Lou Gramm *Atlantic* 87

2659 (YOUR LOVE KEEPS LIFTING ME) HIGHER AND HIGHER
Jackie Wilson *Brunswick* 67

2660 AMOS MOSES
Jerry Reed *RCA* 71

2661 I DON'T LIKE TO SLEEP ALONE
Paul Anka *UA* 75

2662 MR. BOJANGLES
Nitty Gritty Dirt Band *Liberty* 71

2663 LOVE IN AN ELEVATOR
Aerosmith *Geffen* 89

2664 STAND
R.E.M. *Warner Bros* 89

2665 TROGLODYTE (CAVE MAN)
Jimmy Castor Bunch *RCA* 72

2666 I WANT TO WALK YOU HOME
Fats Domino *Imperial* 59

2667 IF YOU REALLY LOVE ME
Stevie Wonder *Tamla* 71

2668 GITARZAN
Ray Stevens *Monument* 69

2669 WHY DON'T THEY UNDERSTAND
George Hamilton IV *ABC-Paramount* 58

2670 BLACK AND WHITE
Three Dog Night *Dunhill* 72

2671 ONE MOMENT IN TIME
Whitney Houston *Arista* 88

2672 CLAP FOR THE WOLFMAN
The Guess Who *RCA* 74

2673 YOU KEEP ME HANGIN' ON
Vanilla Fudge *Atco* 68

2674 STAY AWHILE
The Bells *Polydor* 71

2675 JOHNNY GET ANGRY
Joanie Sommers *Warner Bros* 62

2676 LET'S GET TOGETHER
Hayley Mills *Vista* 61

2677 FEVER
Peggy Lee *Capitol* 58

2678 LET THE MUSIC PLAY
Shannon *Mirage* 84

2679 SOCK IT TO ME-BABY!
Mitch Ryder & the Detroit Wheels *New Voice* 67

2680 DON'T YOU KNOW WHAT THE NIGHT CAN DO?
Steve Winwood *Virgin* 88

2681 WALKING ON SUNSHINE
Katrina & the Waves *Capitol* 85

2682 DON'T STAND SO CLOSE TO ME
The Police *A&M* 81

2683 MY DAD
Paul Petersen *Colpix* 63

2684 HOORAY FOR HAZEL
Tommy Roe *ABC* 66

2685 COLOR HIM FATHER
The Winstons *Metromedia* 69

2686 DON'T EXPECT ME TO BE YOUR FRIEND
Lobo *Big Tree* 73

2687 TIRED OF TOEIN' THE LINE
Rocky Burnette *EMI America* 80

2688 SNOWBIRD
Anne Murray *Capitol* 70

2689 COPACABANA (AT THE COPA)
Barry Manilow *Arista* 78

2690 A COWBOY'S WORK IS NEVER DONE
Sonny and Cher *Kapp* 72

2691 AFTER ALL
Cher and Peter Cetera *Geffen* 89

2692 I'LL NEVER FALL IN LOVE AGAIN
Dionne Warwick *Scepter* 70

2693 GOIN' OUT OF MY HEAD/CAN'T TAKE MY EYES OFF YOU
The Lettermen *Capitol* 68

2694 CAUGHT UP IN YOU
38 Special *A&M* 82

2695 HEARTBEAT
Don Johnson *Epic* 86

2696 OH MY MY
Ringo Starr *Apple* 74

2697 I GO TO EXTREMES
Billy Joel *Columbia* 90

2698 LADY GODIVA
Peter and Gordon *Capitol* 66

2699 DON'T YOU CARE
The Buckinghams *Columbia* 67

2700 NIKITA
Elton John *Geffen* 86

2701 HARD TO SAY
Dan Fogelberg *Full Moon* 81

2702 JUST TO SEE HER
Smokey Robinson *Motown* 87

2703 TAKE THE LONG WAY HOME
Supertramp *A&M* 79

2704 LET ME LOVE YOU TONIGHT
Pure Prairie League *Casablanca* 80

2705 LADY
Styx *Wooden Nickel* 75

2706 AL DI LA'
Emilio Pericoli *Warner Bros* 62

2707 THE UNICORN
The Irish Rovers *Decca* 68

2708 WHAT I AM
Edie Brickell & New Bohemians *Geffen* 89

2709 XANADU
Olivia Newton-John/Electric Light Orchestra *MCA* 80

2710 CHERRY BOMB
John Cougar Mellencamp *Mercury* 88

2711 KING FOR A DAY
Thompson Twins *Arista* 86

2712 GIMME LITTLE SIGN
Brenton Wood *Double Shot* 67

2713 KEEP A KNOCKIN'
Little Richard *Specialty* 57

2714 BABY, NOW THAT I'VE FOUND YOU
The Foundations *Uni* 68

2715 MAMA LOOK-A BOO-BOO
Harry Belafonte *RCA* 57

2716 LET'S DANCE
Chris Montez *Monogram* 62

2717 LONELY BLUE BOY
Conway Twitty *MGM* 60

2718 A DIFFERENT CORNER
George Michael *Columbia* 86

2719 WALK RIGHT BACK
Everly Brothers *Warner Bros* 61

2720 A ROCKIN' GOOD WAY
(TO MESS AROUND AND FALL IN LOVE)
Dinah Washington and Brook Benton *Mercury* 60

2721 I HATE MYSELF FOR LOVING YOU
Joan Jett & the Blackhearts *Blackheart* 88

2722 LOVE WILL CONQUER ALL
Lionel Richie *Motown* 86

2723 GINGER BREAD
Frankie Avalon *Chancellor* 58

2724 NIGHTS ARE FOREVER WITHOUT YOU
England Dan and John Ford Coley *Big Tree* 76

2725 STRANGE WAY
Firefall *Atlantic* 78

2726 ROMEO
Dino *Island* 90

2727 JUST TO BE CLOSE TO YOU
Commodores *Motown* 76

2728 JET
Paul McCartney & Wings *Apple* 74

2729 TAKE ME HOME
Cher *Casablanca* 79

2730 WALK AWAY FROM LOVE
David Ruffin *Motown* 76

2731 LOVE IS THE ANSWER
England Dan and John Ford Coley *Big Tree* 79

2732 MOTHER POPCORN (YOU GOT TO HAVE A MOTHER FOR ME) (PART 1)
James Brown *King* 69

2733 DON'T BE CRUEL
Bill Black's Combo *Hi* 60

2734 GET DOWN TONIGHT
KC & the Sunshine Band *TK* 75

2735 PARADISE CITY
Guns n' Roses *Geffen* 89

2736 BEACH BABY
First Class *UK* 74

2737 ALL OR NOTHING
Milli Vanilli *Arista* 90

2738 TIME IS TIGHT
Booker T. & the MG's *Stax* 69

2739 LIFE IN A NORTHERN TOWN
The Dream Academy *Warner Bros* 86

2740 THIS TIME I KNOW IT'S FOR REAL
Donna Summer *Atlantic* 89

2741 SHE WANTS TO DANCE WITH ME
Rick Astley *RCA* 89

2742 WRAPPED AROUND YOUR FINGER
The Police *A&M* 84

2743 THE WONDER OF YOU
Elvis Presley *RCA* 70

2744 JERK OUT
The Time *Reprise* 90

2745 HOUND DOG MAN
Fabian *Chancellor* 59

2746 WHAT KIND OF MAN WOULD I BE?
Chicago *Reprise* 90

2747 JUST LIKE PARADISE
David Lee Roth *Warner Bros* 88

2748 PROVE YOUR LOVE
Taylor Dayne *Arista* 88

2749 MASTERPIECE
The Temptations *Gordy* 73

2750 ALWAYS SOMETHING THERE TO REMIND ME
Naked Eyes *EMI America* 83

2751 BOBBY SOX TO STOCKINGS
Frankie Avalon *Chancellor* 59

2752 KEEP SEARCHIN' (WE'LL FOLLOW THE SUN)
Del Shannon *Amy* 65

2753 ARIZONA
Mark Lindsay *Columbia* 70

2754 I'M TELLING YOU NOW
Freddie & the Dreamers *Tower* 65

2755 PIANO IN THE DARK
Brenda Russell *A&M* 88

2756 THE TWELFTH OF NEVER
Donny Osmond *MGM* 73

2757 WHAT YOU DON'T KNOW
Expose *Arista* 89

2758 (I'VE BEEN) SEARCHIN' SO LONG
Chicago *Columbia* 74

2759 ALL I KNOW
Art Garfunkel *Columbia* 73

England Dan & John Ford Coley

2794 CIRCLE IN THE SAND
Belinda Carlisle *MCA* 88

2795 YOU WON'T SEE ME
Anne Murray *Capitol* 74

2796 HOLD ME, THRILL ME, KISS ME
Mel Carter *Imperial* 65

2797 POPCORN
Hot Butter *Musicor* 72

2798 TWISTIN' THE NIGHT AWAY
Sam Cooke *RCA* 62

2799 UP THE LADDER TO THE ROOF
The Supremes *Motown* 70

2800 FAITHFULLY
Journey *Columbia* 83

2801 CAN'T GET ENOUGH OF YOUR LOVE, BABE
Barry White *20th Century* 74

2802 I CAN'T STAY MAD AT YOU
Skeeter Davis *RCA* 63

2803 AIN'T NOTHING LIKE THE REAL THING
Marvin Gaye and Tammi Terrell *Tamla* 68

2804 WAIT
White Lion *Atlantic* 88

2805 I REMEMBER HOLDING YOU
Boys Club *MCA* 89

2806 DON'T SHED A TEAR
Paul Carrack *Chrysalis* 88

2807 YOU MAKE LOVING FUN
Fleetwood Mac *Warner Bros* 77

2808 STICK-UP
The Honey Cone *Hot Wax* 71

2809 HEAD OVER HEELS
The Go-Go's *I.R.S.* 84

2810 ENCHANTED
The Platters *Mercury* 59

2811 CHANSON D'AMOUR
Art and Dotty Todd *Era* 58

2812 WHATEVER GETS YOU THRU THE NIGHT
John Lennon w/the Plastic Ono Nuclear Band *Apple* 74

2813 HOLD YOUR HEAD UP
Argent *Epic* 72

2814 THE FOOL ON THE HILL
Sergio Mendes & Brasil '66 *A&M* 68

2815 FOOL (IF YOU THINK IT'S OVER)
Chris Rea *UA* 78

2816 LOLA
The Kinks *Reprise* 70

2817 FOR THE LOVE OF MONEY
The O'Jays *PIR* 74

2818 MAYBE I'M AMAZED
Wings *Apple* 77

2819 THE END OF THE INNOCENCE
Don Henley *Geffen* 89

2820 WESTERN MOVIES
The Olympics *Demon* 58

2821 YOU AND ME AGAINST THE WORLD
Helen Reddy *Capitol* 74

2822 TRACY
The Cuff Links *Decca* 69

2823 CRUEL SUMMER
Bananarama *London* 84

2824 MONEY HONEY
Bay City Rollers *Arista* 76

2825 IF I COULD REACH YOU
5th Dimension *Bell* 72

2826 TUBULAR BELLS
Mike Oldfield *Virgin* 74

2827 LET MY LOVE OPEN THE DOOR
Pete Townshend *Atco* 80

2828 TRYIN' TO GET THE FEELING AGAIN
Barry Manilow *Arista* 76

2829 ONE FINE DAY
Carole King *Capitol* 80

2830 NOTHING'S GONNA CHANGE MY LOVE FOR YOU
Glenn Medeiros *Amherst* 87

2831 I KNOW THERE'S SOMETHING GOING ON
Frida *Atlantic* 83

2832 (IF YOU LET ME MAKE LOVE TO YOU THEN)
WHY CAN'T I TOUCH YOU?
Ronnie Dyson *Columbia* 70

2833 NEVER CAN SAY GOODBYE
Gloria Gaynor *MGM* 75

2834 I JUST CAN'T HELP BELIEVING
B.J. Thomas *Scepter* 70

2835 THIS MASQUERADE
George Benson *Warner Bros* 76

2836 GO HOME
Stevie Wonder *Tamla* 86

2837 RHIANNON (WILL YOU EVER WIN)
Fleetwood Mac *Reprise* 76

2838 TEEN AGE PRAYER/MEMORIES ARE MADE OF THIS
Gale Storm *Dot* 56

2839 THE FLYING SAUCER (PARTS 1 & 2)
Buchanan and Goodman *Luniverse* 56

2840 FOREVER
Kiss *Mercury* 90

2841 YOU'RE ONLY HUMAN (SECOND WIND)
Billy Joel *Columbia* 85

2842 FAR FROM OVER
Frank Stallone *RSO* 83

2843 INVINCIBLE
Pat Benatar *Chrysalis* 85

2844 WHEN SHE WAS MY GIRL
Four Tops *Casablanca* 81

2845 SHA LA LA
Manfred Mann *Ascot* 65

2846 SHADOWS OF THE NIGHT
Pat Benatar *Chrysalis* 82

2847 DOWN BY THE STATION
The Four Preps *Capitol* 60

2848 ROCK WIT'CHA
Bobby Brown *MCA* 89

2849 NOBODY'S FOOL
Kenny Loggins *Columbia* 88

2850 SWEET LOVE
Anita Baker *Elektra* 86

2851 BE MY GUEST
Fats Domino *Imperial* 59

2852 YOUR WILDEST DREAMS
The Moody Blues *Threshold* 86

2853 THINK OF LAURA
Christopher Cross *Warner Bros* 84

2854 EVIL WAYS
Santana *Columbia* 70

2855 EVERYBODY'S TALKIN'
Nilsson *RCA* 69

2856 MONTEGO BAY
Bobby Bloom *L&R* 70

2857 KNOCKIN' BOOTS
Candyman *Epic* 90

2858 LOVIN' EVERY MINUTE OF IT
Loverboy *Columbia* 85

2859 (WHERE DO I BEGIN) LOVE STORY
Andy Williams *Columbia* 71

2860 BREATHLESS
Jerry Lee Lewis *Sun* 58

2861 YOU TAKE MY BREATH AWAY
Rex Smith *Columbia* 79

2862 SUSAN
The Buckinghams *Columbia* 68

2863 THAT'LL BE THE DAY
Linda Ronstadt *Asylum* 76

2864 I ONLY HAVE EYES FOR YOU
The Flamingos *End* 59

2865 YOU CAN'T TURN ME OFF
(IN THE MIDDLE OF TURNING ME ON)
High Inergy *Gordy* 77

2866 WALKING THE DOG
Rufus Thomas *Stax* 63

2867 SOMETHING'S BURNING
Kenny Rogers & the First Edition *Reprise* 70

2868 SWING THE MOOD
Jive Bunny & the Mastermixers *Music Factory* 90

2869 LOTTA LOVIN'/WEAR MY RING
Gene Vincent & His Blue Caps *Capitol* 57

2870 LYIN' EYES
Eagles *Asylum* 75

2871 ALONE AT LAST
Jackie Wilson *Brunswick* 60

2872 GET IT ON (BANG A GONG)
The Power Station *Capitol* 85

2873 MAKE ME SMILE
Chicago *Columbia* 70

2874 PORTRAIT OF MY LOVE
Steve Lawrence *UA* 61

2875 ONE TOKE OVER THE LINE
Brewer and Shipley *Kama Sutra* 71

2876 TIME HAS COME TODAY
Chambers Brothers *Columbia* 68

2877 MAGIC
The Cars *Elektra* 84

2878 GYPSY MAN
War *UA* 73

2879 SMOKE FROM A DISTANT FIRE
Sanford/Townsend Band *Warner Bros* 77

2880 IT'S A SIN
Pet Shop Boys *EMI America* 87

2881 BREAKIN' ... THERE'S NO STOPPING US
Ollie and Jerry *Polydor* 84

2882 OFF THE WALL
Michael Jackson *Epic* 80

2883 YES WE CAN CAN
Pointer Sisters *Blue Thumb* 73

2884 DARE ME
Pointer Sisters *RCA* 85

2885 BOOGIE WOOGIE BUGLE BOY
Bette Midler *Atlantic* 73

2886 OUR WINTER LOVE
Bill Pursell *Columbia* 63

2887 GO YOUR OWN WAY
Fleetwood Mac *Warner Bros* 77

2888 KEEP ON MOVIN'
Soul II Soul *Virgin* 89

2889 KEWPIE DOLL
Perry Como *RCA* 58

2890 EVERYBODY LOVES A LOVER
Doris Day *Columbia* 58

2891 I UNDERSTAND (JUST HOW YOU FEEL)
The G-Clefs *Terrace* 61

2892 DYNOMITE - PART I
Tony Camillo's Bazuka *A&M* 75

2893 CHINA GIRL
David Bowie *EMI America* 83

2894 PUT YOUR HANDS TOGETHER
The O'Jays *PIR* 74

2895 I SAY A LITTLE PRAYER
Aretha Franklin *Atlantic* 68

2896 SOMEBODY TO LOVE
Queen *Elektra* 77

2897 AIN'T NO STOPPIN' US NOW
McFadden and Whitehead *PIR* 79

2898 RUSH HOUR
Jane Wiedlin *EMI Manhattan* 88

2899 MY LITTLE TOWN
Simon and Garfunkel *Columbia* 75

2900 NEW MOON ON MONDAY
Duran Duran *Capitol* 84

2901 BROWN EYED GIRL
Van Morrison *Bang* 67

2902 THEME FROM "DR. KILDARE" (THREE STARS
WILL SHINE TONIGHT)
Richard Chamberlain *MGM* 62

2903 I WANNA BE YOUR LOVER
Prince *Warner Bros* 80

2904 STILL WATER (LOVE)
Four Tops *Motown* 70

2905 HER TOWN TOO
James Taylor and J.D. Souther *Columbia* 81

2906 THAT'S THE WAY OF THE WORLD
Earth, Wind & Fire *Columbia* 75

2907 EXPRESS YOURSELF
Charles Wright & the Watts 103rd Street Rhythm Band
Warner Bros 70

2908 NEVER ENDING SONG OF LOVE
Delaney and Bonnie *Atco* 71

2909 HELLO MUDDUH, HELLO FADDUH! (A LETTER FROM CAMP)
Allan Sherman *Warner Bros* 63

2910 SO FINE
The Fiestas *Old Town* 59

2911 BABY I NEED YOUR LOVING
Four Tops *Motown* 64

2912 SANDY
Larry Hall *Strand* 60

2913 ANTICIPATION
Carly Simon *Elektra* 72

2914 DO YOU WANT TO KNOW A SECRET
The Beatles *Vee Jay* 64

2915 IS IT LOVE
Mr. Mister *RCA* 86

2916 WHAT YOU WON'T DO FOR LOVE
Bobby Caldwell *Clouds* 79

2917 I'VE BEEN IN LOVE BEFORE
Cutting Crew *Virgin* 87

2918 BURNING DOWN THE HOUSE
Talking Heads *Sire* 83

2919 DENISE
Randy & the Rainbows *Rust* 63

2920 TWO OCCASIONS
The Deele *Solar* 88

2921 I COULD NEVER TAKE THE PLACE OF YOUR MAN
Prince *Paisley Park* 88

2922 I'VE GOTTA BE ME
Sammy Davis, Jr. *Reprise* 69

2923 DROWNING IN THE SEA OF LOVE
Joe Simon *Spring* 72

2924 I ONLY WANT TO BE WITH YOU
Bay City Rollers *Arista* 76

2925 IVORY TOWER
Otis Williams & His Charms *DeLuxe* 56

2926 LOOKIN' FOR A LOVE
Bobby Womack *UA* 74

2927 IT WOULD TAKE A STRONG STRONG MAN
Rick Astley *RCA* 88

2928 GEE WHIZ (LOOK AT HIS EYES)
Carla Thomas *Atlantic* 61

2929 YOU GOT THE LOVE
Rufus f/Chaka Khan *ABC* 74

2930 JUST LIKE ME
Paul Revere & the Raiders *Columbia* 66

2931 BLUE EYES
Elton John *Geffen* 82

2932 MIRACLE
Jon Bon Jovi *Mercury* 90

2933 TRUE LOVE
Jane Powell *Verve* 56

2934 WALK THIS WAY
Aerosmith *Columbia* 77

2935 WHAT ABOUT LOVE?
Heart *Capitol* 85

2936 YOU ARE MY LADY
Freddie Jackson *Capitol* 85

2937 WHAT'S YOUR NAME
Lynyrd Skynyrd *MCA* 78

2938 FOR THE LOVE OF HIM
Bobbi Martin *UA* 70

2939 I'LL HAVE TO SAY I LOVE YOU IN A SONG
Jim Croce *ABC* 74

2940 INDIAN LAKE
The Cowsills *MGM* 68

2941 COUNTRY BOY (YOU GOT YOUR FEET IN L.A.)
Glen Campbell *Capitol* 76

2942 LIGHTS OUT
Peter Wolf *EMI America* 84

2943 MISTY
Johnny Mathis *Columbia* 59

2944 ROUND AND ROUND
Ratt *Atlantic* 84

2945 RESPECT YOURSELF
The Staple Singers *Stax* 71

2946 ISN'T IT TIME
The Babys *Chrysalis* 77

2947 THE LONGEST WALK
Jaye P. Morgan *RCA* 55

2948 A LITTLE BIT ME, A LITTLE BIT YOU
The Monkees *Colgems* 67

2949 I THANK YOU
Sam and Dave *Stax* 68

2950 I FOUND SOMEONE
Cher *Geffen* 88

2951 SPANISH HARLEM
Ben E. King *Atco* 61

2952 ROMEO'S TUNE
Steve Forbert *Nemperor* 80

2953 THINKING OF YOU
Sa-Fire *Cutting* 89

2954 HOW 'BOUT US
Champaign *Columbia* 81

2955 (YOU'RE THE) DEVIL IN DISGUISE
Elvis Presley *RCA* 63

2956 GOOD GIRLS DON'T
The Knack *Capitol* 79

2957 ONE HELL OF A WOMAN
Mac Davis *Columbia* 74

2958 KNOCKIN' ON HEAVEN'S DOOR
Bob Dylan *Columbia* 73

2959 WHY ME?
Irene Cara *Geffen* 83

2960 YOUR LOVE IS DRIVING ME CRAZY
Sammy Hagar *Geffen* 83

2961 JAMAICA FAREWELL
Harry Belafonte *RCA* 57

2962 BABY I LOVE YOU
Aretha Franklin *Atlantic* 67

2963 WITCHY WOMAN
Eagles *Asylum* 72

2964 WIPEOUT
Fat Boys & the Beach Boys *Tin Pan Apple* 87

2965 DON'T YOU JUST KNOW IT
Huey "Piano" Smith & the Clowns *Ace* 58

2966 THE LONGEST TIME
Billy Joel *Columbia* 84

2967 BANG BANG (MY BABY SHOT ME DOWN)
Cher *Imperial* 66

2968 THE NAME GAME
Shirley Ellis *Congress* 65

2969 RUNNING ON EMPTY
Jackson Browne *Asylum* 78

2970 BLUER THAN BLUE
Michael Johnson *EMI America* 78

2971 HOLLYWOOD NIGHTS
Bob Seger & the Silver Bullet Band *Capitol* 78

2972 HURT SO BAD
The Lettermen *Capitol* 69

2973 DO I DO
Stevie Wonder *Tamla* 82

2974 BRING THE BOYS HOME
Freda Payne *Invictus* 71

2975 UM, UM, UM, UM, UM, UM
Major Lance *Okeh* 64

2976 DEDE DINAH
Frankie Avalon *Chancellor* 58

2977 EMPTY GARDEN (HEY HEY JOHNNY)
Elton John *Geffen* 82

2978 I'M INTO SOMETHING GOOD
Herman's Hermits *MGM* 64

2979 USE ME
Bill Withers *Sussex* 72

2980 THAT'S LIFE
Frank Sinatra *Reprise* 66

2981 YES, I'M READY
Barbara Mason *Arctic* 65

2982 PLEASE DON'T GO GIRL
New Kids on the Block *Columbia* 88

2983 GUESS THINGS HAPPEN THAT WAY
Johnny Cash *Sun* 58

2984 CRAZY ABOUT HER
Rod Stewart *Warner Bros* 89

2985 THINK TWICE
Brook Benton *Mercury* 61

2986 HEAD GAMES
Foreigner *Atlantic* 79

2987 I KNOW A PLACE
Petula Clark *Warner Bros* 65

2988 RESCUE ME
Fontella Bass *Checker* 65

2989 JUST A FRIEND
Biz Markie *Cold Chillin'* 90

2990 BABY, I LOVE YOUR WAY
Peter Frampton *A&M* 76

2991 GONNA GET ALONG WITHOUT YA NOW
Patience and Prudence *Liberty* 56

2992 COOL LOVE
Pablo Cruise *A&M* 81

2993 SALLY, GO 'ROUND THE ROSES
The Jaynetts *Tuff* 63

2994 AN OLD FASHIONED LOVE SONG
Three Dog Night *Dunhill* 71

2995 OH VERY YOUNG
Cat Stevens *A&M* 74

2996 WE'VE GOT TONITE
Bob Seger & the Silver Bullet Band *Capitol* 79

2997 BABY I NEED YOUR LOVIN'
Johnny Rivers *Imperial* 67

2998 MEAN WOMAN BLUES
Roy Orbison *Monument* 63

2999 LIVING IN THE PAST
Jethro Tull *Chrysalis* 73

3000 THE LANGUAGE OF LOVE
Dan Fogelberg *Full Moon* 84

INDEX TO THE TOP 3000 HITS

Can't Take My Eyes Off You
 The Lettermen*, 2693
 Frankie Valli, 983
 *Goin' Out Of My Head/Can't Take My Eyes Off You
Can't We Try
 Dan Hill w/Vonda Sheppard, 2610
Can't You Hear My Heartbeat
 Herman's Hermits, 1968
Car Wash
 Rose Royce, 521
Cara, Mia
 Jay & the Americans, 2074
Careless Whisper
 Wham! f/George Michael, 254
Caribbean Queen
 (No More Love On The Run)
 Billy Ocean, 466
Carrie
 Europe, 2461
Carry On Wayward Son
 Kansas, 1887
Cars
 Gary Numan, 955
Casanova
 Levert, 2170
Catch A Falling Star
 Perry Como, 330
Catch Me (I'm Falling)
 Pretty Poison, 1401
Cathy's Clown
 Everly Brothers, 284
Cat's In The Cradle
 Harry Chapin, 1772
Caught Up In You
 38 Special, 2694
Causing A Commotion
 Madonna, 2400
Cecilia
 Simon and Garfunkel, 2033
Celebration
 Kool & the Gang, 79
Centerfold
 J. Geils Band, 39
C'est La Vie
 Robbie Nevil, 541
Chain Gang
 Sam Cooke, 999
Chain Of Fools
 Aretha Franklin, 1495
Chains Of Love
 Pat Boone, 528
Chances Are
 Johnny Mathis, 51
Change Of Heart
 Cyndi Lauper, 2153
Chanson D'Amour
 Art and Dotty Todd, 2811
Chantilly Lace
 Big Bopper, 315
Chapel Of Love
 The Dixie Cups, 1059
Chariots Of Fire
 Vangelis, 377
Charlie Brown
 The Coasters, 1043
Cherish
 The Association, 1113
 David Cassidy, 2208
Cherish
 Kool & the Gang, 1036
Cherish
 Madonna, 2010
Cherry Bomb
 John Cougar Mellencamp, 2710
Chevy Van
 Sammy Johns, 2132
Chick-A-Boom (Don't Ya Jes' Love It)
 Daddy Dewdrop, 2223
China Girl
 David Bowie, 2893
Chipmunk Song, The
 The Chipmunks w/David Seville, 1344

Chuck E.'s In Love
 Rickie Lee Jones, 1902
Church Of The Poison Mind
 Culture Club, 1803
Cindy, Oh Cindy
 Eddie Fisher, 961
 Vince Martin w/the Tarriers, 657
Cinnamon
 Derek, 2783
Circle In The Sand
 Belinda Carlisle, 2794
Cisco Kid, The
 War, 1974
Clair
 Gilbert O'Sullivan, 795
Clap For The Wolfman
 The Guess Who, 2672
Classical Gas
 Mason Williams, 1598
Clean Up Woman
 Betty Wright, 1800
Close My Eyes (Forever)
 Lita Ford w/Ozzy Osbourne, 2349
Close To You
 Maxi Priest, 442
Closer I Get To You, The
 Roberta Flack and Donny Hathaway, 673
Cloud Nine
 The Temptations, 2196
C'mon And Get My Love
 D-Mob i/Cathy Dennis, 2359
Cold As Ice
 Foreigner, 625
Cold Hearted
 Paula Abdul, 836
Color Him Father
 The Winstons, 2685
Come A Little Bit Closer
 Jay & the Americans, 2466
Come And Get It
 Badfinger, 2587
Come And Get Your Love
 Redbone, 640
Come Back To Me
 Janet Jackson, 1688
Come Back When You Grow Up
 Bobby Vee, 1429
Come Dancing
 The Kinks, 2182
Come Go With Me
 The Dell-Vikings, 45
Come Go With Me
 Expose, 2115
Come In Stranger
 Johnny Cash, 2983
Come On Down To My Boat
 Every Mothers' Son, 2164
Come On Eileen
 Dexys Midnight Runners, 585
Come Sail Away
 Styx, 1002
Come See About Me
 The Supremes, 566
Come Softly To Me
 The Fleetwoods, 537
Come Together
 The Beatles, 197
Comin' In And Out Of Your Life
 Barbra Streisand, 1785
Coming Up (Live At Glasgow)
 Paul McCartney & Wings, 157
Conga
 Miami Sound Machine, 1094
Control
 Janet Jackson, 1546
Convoy
 C.W. McCall, 1293
Cool Change
 Little River Band, 2186
Cool It Now
 New Edition, 832
Cool Love
 Pablo Cruise, 2992

Cool Night
 Paul Davis, 1816
Copacabana (At The Copa)
 Barry Manilow, 2689
Corinna, Corinna
 Ray Peterson, 2627
Cotton Fields
 The Highwaymen, 2441
Could It Be I'm Falling In Love
 Spinners, 1601
Could It Be Magic
 Barry Manilow, 2181
Couldn't Get It Right
 Climax Blues Band, 1560
Could've Been
 Tiffany, 663
Count On Me
 Jefferson Starship, 2192
Country Boy
 (You Got Your Feet In L.A.)
 Glen Campbell, 2941
Cover Me
 Bruce Springsteen, 1747
Cover Of "Rolling Stone," The
 Dr. Hook, 2248
Coward Of The County
 Kenny Rogers, 577
Cowboys To Girls
 The Intruders, 1696
Cowboy's Work Is Never Done, A
 Sonny and Cher, 2690
Cracklin' Rosie
 Neil Diamond, 856
Cradle Of Love
 Billy Idol, 523
Cradle Of Love
 Johnny Preston, 2031
Crazy
 Hollywood Flames, 2570
Crazy About Her
 Rod Stewart, 2984
Crazy For You
 Madonna, 530
Crazy Little Thing Called Love
 Queen, 111
Crimson And Clover
 Tommy James & the Shondells, 276
 Joan Jett & the Blackhearts, 2331
Crocodile Rock
 Elton John, 260
Cross My Broken Heart
 The Jets, 2787
Cruel Summer
 Bananarama, 2823
Cruisin'
 Smokey Robinson, 369
Crumblin' Down
 John Cougar Mellencamp, 2325
Crush On You
 The Jets, 1612
Cry Baby
 Garnett Mimms & the Enchanters, 2476
Cry Like A Baby
 The Box Tops, 1116
Crying
 Don McLean, 782
 Roy Orbison, 1117
Crying In The Chapel
 Elvis Presley, 1896
Crying In The Rain
 Everly Brothers, 2512
Crystal Blue Persuasion
 Tommy James & the Shondells, 946
Cum On Feel The Noize
 Quiet Riot, 1123
Cupid/I've Loved You For A Long Time
 Spinners, 736
Cut The Cake
 Average White Band, 2329
Da Doo Ron Ron
 Shaun Cassidy, 1204
 The Crystals, 2467
Da Ya Think I'm Sexy?
 Rod Stewart, 114

Daddy Cool
 The Rays, 214
Daddy Don't You Walk So Fast
 Wayne Newton, 1085
Daddy's Home
 Jermaine Jackson, 1898
 Shep & the Limelites, 2046
Dance, Dance, Dance
 (Yowsah, Yowsah, Yowsah)
 Chic, 643
Dance To The Music
 Sly & the Family Stone, 2152
Dance With Me
 Peter Brown, 2128
Dance With Me
 Orleans, 2262
Dancing In The Dark
 Bruce Springsteen, 461
Dancing In The Moonlight
 King Harvest, 2344
Dancing In The Street
 Martha & the Vandellas, 1894
Dancing Machine
 The Jackson Five, 637
Dancing On The Ceiling
 Lionel Richie, 1373
Dancing Queen
 Abba, 598
Danger Zone
 Kenny Loggins, 1603
Dangerous
 Roxette, 1582
Daniel
 Elton John, 1463
Danny Boy
 Conway Twitty, 2382
Dare Me
 Pointer Sisters, 2884
Dark Lady
 Cher, 1736
Dark Moon
 Bonnie Guitar, 2650
 Gale Storm, 382
Dawn (Go Away)
 The Four Seasons, 1872
Day After Day
 Badfinger, 1690
Day Dreaming
 Aretha Franklin, 2439
Daydream
 The Lovin' Spoonful, 1947
Daydream Believer
 The Monkees, 514
 Anne Murray, 1922
Dazz
 Brick, 538
De Do Do Do, De Da Da Da
 The Police, 1846
Dead Man's Curve
 Jan and Dean, 2602
Dear Lady Twist
 Gary U.S. Bonds, 2179
December, 1963 (Oh, What A Night)
 The Four Seasons, 283
Deck Of Cards
 Wink Martindale, 1989
Dede Dinah
 Frankie Avalon, 2976
Dedicated To The One I Love
 The Mamas and the Papas, 2408
 The Shirelles, 709
Deep Purple
 Donny and Marie Osmond, 2464
 Nino Tempo and April Stevens, 1538
Delirious
 Prince, 2166
Delta Dawn
 Helen Reddy, 837
Denise
 Randy & the Rainbows, 2919
Der Kommissar
 After The Fire, 873
Desire
 Andy Gibb, 1418

Desire
U2, **1993**
Devil Inside
INXS, **1097**
Devil Or Angel
Bobby Vee, **1271**
Devil Went Down To Georgia, The
Charlie Daniels Band, **1925**
Devil With A Blue Dress On & Good
Golly Miss Molly
Mitch Ryder & the Detroit Wheels,
755
Devil Woman
Cliff Richard, **2043**
Devoted To You
Everly Brothers, **2383**
Diamond Girl
Seals and Crofts, **1856**
Diamonds
Herb Alpert, **2615**
Diana
Paul Anka, **96**
Did It In A Minute
Daryl Hall and John Oates, **1784**
Did You Ever Have To Make Up Your
Mind?
The Lovin' Spoonful, **2451**
Didn't I (Blow Your Mind This Time)
The Delfonics, **2432**
Didn't We Almost Have It All
Whitney Houston, **990**
Different Corner, A
George Michael, **2718**
Different Drum
The Stone Poneys f/Linda Ronstadt,
2002
Dim All The Lights
Donna Summer, **1005**
Dirty Diana
Michael Jackson, **1795**
Dirty Laundry
Don Henley, **872**
Disco Duck (Part 1)
Rick Dees & His Cast of Idiots, **262**
Disco Inferno
The Trammps, **2375**
Disco Lady
Johnnie Taylor, **437**
Disco Nights (Rock-Freak)
GQ, **2442**
Dizzy
Tommy Roe, **406**
Do I Do
Stevie Wonder, **2973**
Do It Again
Steely Dan, **2584**
Do It ('Til You're Satisfied)
B.T. Express, **1131**
Do Me!
Bell Biv Devoe, **397**
Do That To Me One More Time
Captain & Tennille, **50**
Do Wah Diddy Diddy
Manfred Mann, **1163**
Do What You Do
Jermaine Jackson, **2429**
Do You Believe In Love
Huey Lewis & the News, **2218**
Do You Know What I Mean
Lee Michaels, **1547**
Do You Love Me
The Contours, **176**
Do You Really Want To Hurt Me
Culture Club, **475**
Do You Remember?
Phil Collins, **2100**
Do You Wanna Make Love
Peter McCann, **624**
Do You Want To Dance
Bobby Freeman, **1242**
Do You Want To Know A Secret
The Beatles, **2914**
Doctor's Orders
Carol Douglas, **2792**

Does Anybody Really Know What Time
It Is?
Chicago, **2108**
Doesn't Somebody Want To Be Wanted
The Partridge Family, **1977**
Doing It All For My Baby
Huey Lewis & the News, **2761**
Dominique
The Singing Nun, **404**
Donna
Ritchie Valens, **302**
Don't
Elvis Presley, **169**
Don't Be Cruel
Bill Black's Combo, **2733**
Cheap Trick, **2142**
Elvis Presley, **2**
Don't Be Cruel
Bobby Brown, **1882**
Don't Break The Heart That Loves You
Connie Francis, **2003**
Don't Bring Me Down
Electric Light Orchestra, **1891**
Don't Close Your Eyes
Kix, **2385**
Don't Cry
Asia, **2332**
Don't Cry Daddy
Elvis Presley, **2217**
Don't Cry Out Loud
Melissa Manchester, **1536**
Don't Disturb This Groove
The System, **2143**
Don't Do Me Like That
Tom Petty & the Heartbreakers, **2367**
Don't Dream It's Over
Crowded House, **1078**
Don't Expect Me To Be Your Friend
Lobo, **2686**
Don't Fall In Love With A Dreamer
Kenny Rogers w/Kim Carnes, **838**
(Don't Fear) The Reaper
Blue Oyster Cult, **2380**
Don't Forbid Me
Pat Boone, **156**
Don't Forget Me (When I'm Gone)
Glass Tiger, **1556**
Don't Get Me Wrong
The Pretenders, **2312**
Don't Give Up On Us
David Soul, **1238**
Don't Go Breaking My Heart
Elton John and Kiki Dee, **458**
Don't Hang Up
The Orlons, **2427**
Don't It Make My Brown Eyes Blue
Crystal Gayle, **310**
Don't Know Much
Linda Ronstast f/Aaron Neville, **699**
Don't Leave Me This Way
Thelma Houston, **218**
Don't Let It End
Styx, **1329**
Don't Let The Rain Come Down
(Crooked Little Man)
The Serendipity Singers, **2469**
Don't Let The Sun Catch You Crying
Gerry & the Pacemakers, **2560**
Don't Look Back
Boston, **2396**
Don't Lose My Number
Phil Collins, **1266**
Don't Mean Nothing
Richard Marx, **2094**
Don't Pull Your Love
Hamilton, Joe Frank & Reynolds,
1987
Don't Rush Me
Taylor Dayne, **1195**
Don't Shed A Tear
Paul Carrack, **2806**
Don't Stand So Close To Me
The Police, **2682**
Don't Stop
Fleetwood Mac, **1093**

Don't Stop Believin'
Journey, **1883**
Don't Stop 'Til You Get Enough
Michael Jackson, **1565**
Don't Talk To Strangers
Rick Springfield, **286**
Don't Wanna Fall In Love
Jane Child, **1120**
Don't Wanna Lose You
Gloria Estefan, **1169**
Don't Worry
Marty Robbins, **1072**
Don't Worry Be Happy
Bobby McFerrin, **1095**
Don't You Care
The Buckinghams, **2699**
Don't You (Forget About Me)
Simple Minds, **579**
Don't You Just Know It
Huey "Piano" Smith & the Clowns,
2965
Don't You Know
Della Reese, **684**
Don't You Know What The Night Can
Do?
Steve Winwood, **2680**
Don't You Want Me
The Human League, **72**
Don't You Want Me
Jody Watley, **1666**
Double Vision
Foreigner, **1529**
Down By The Lazy River
The Osmonds, **1903**
Down By The Station
The Four Preps, **2847**
Down On The Corner
Creedence Clearwater Revival, **1145**
Down Under
Men at Work, **98**
Downtown
Petula Clark, **578**
Downtown Train
Rod Stewart, **1589**
Draggin' The Line
Tommy James, **2024**
Dream Lover
Bobby Darin, **667**
Dream On
Aerosmith, **2233**
Dream Weaver
Gary Wright, **1023**
Dreamin'
Johnny Burnette, **1959**
Dreaming
Cliff Richard, **2236**
Dreams
Fleetwood Mac, **1193**
Dreamtime
Daryl Hall, **2622**
Drift Away
Dobie Gray, **922**
Drive
The Cars, **1070**
Drivin' My Life Away
Eddie Rabbitt, **897**
Drowning In The Sea Of Love
Joe Simon, **2923**
Dueling Banjos
Eric Weissberg and Steve Mandell,
1822
Duke Of Earl
Gene Chandler, **694**
Dum Dum
Brenda Lee, **2412**
Dungaree Doll
Eddie Fisher, **119ʹ**
Dust In The Wind
Kansas, **923**
Dynomite—Part I
Tony Camillo's Bazuka, **2892**
Easier Said Than Done
The Essex, **1341**
Easy
Commodores, **1542**

Easy Come, Easy Go
Bobby Sherman, **2289**
Easy Lover
Philip Bailey w/Phil Collins, **532**
Easy To Be Hard
Three Dog Night, **1477**
Ebony And Ivory
Paul McCartney and Stevie Wonder,
84
Eight Days A Week
The Beatles, **2307**
867-5309/Jenny
Tommy Tutone, **780**
18 And Life
Skid Row, **1737**
El Paso
Marty Robbins, **301**
Election Day
Arcadia, **2019**
Electric Avenue
Eddy Grant, **629**
Electric Blue
Icehouse, **2264**
Eli's Coming
Three Dog Night, **1374**
Elvira
Oak Ridge Boys, **1064**
Emotion
Samantha Sang, **459**
Emotional Resuce
The Rolling Stones, **762**
Empty Garden (Hey Hey Johnny)
Elton John, **2977**
Enchanted
The Plaiters, **2810**
End, The
Earl Grant, **1176**
End Of The Innocence, The
Don Henley, **2819**
End Of The World, The
Skeeter Davis, **1420**
Endless Love
Diana Ross and Lionel Richie, **26**
Endless Sleep
Jody Reynolds, **1718**
Endless Summer Nights
Richard Marx, **1225**
Enjoy The Silence
Depeche Mode, **2283**
Enjoy Yourself
The Jacksons, **1283**
Entertainer, The
Marvin Hamlisch, **1464**
Epic
Faith No More, **2326**
Eres Tu (Touch The Wind)
Mocedades, **2780**
Escapade
Janet Jackson, **520**
Escape (Pina Colada Song)
Rupert Holmes, **177**
Eternal Flame
Bangles, **1692**
Eve Of Destruction
Barry McGuire, **2030**
Even The Nights Are Better
Air Supply, **1074**
Everlasting Love, An
Andy Gibb, **1173**
Every Beat Of My Heart
The Pips, **2472**
Every Breath You Take
The Police, **25**
Every Little Step
Bobby Brown, **1279**
Every Little Thing She Does Is Magic
The Police, **1299**
Every 1's A Winner
Hot Chocolate, **1749**
Every Rose Has Its Thorn
Poison, **516**
(Every Time I Turn Around)
Back In Love Again
L.T.D., **1430**

Going In Circles
Friends of Distinction, **2508**
Gold
John Stewart, **1694**
Golden Years
David Bowie, **1454**
Gone
Ferlin Husky, **354**
Gonna Fly Now (Theme From "Rocky")
Bill Conti, **589**
Gonna Get Along Without Ya Now
Patience and Prudence, **2991**
Good Girls Don't
The Knack, **2956**
Good Lovin'
The Young Rascals, **1268**
Good Luck Charm
Elvis Presley, **945**
Good Morning Starshine
Oliver, **1558**
Good Thing
Fine Young Cannibals, **1337**
Good Thing
Paul Revere & the Raiders, **2518**
Good Times
Chic, **503**
Good Timin'
Jimmy Jones, **2287**
Good Vibrations
The Beach Boys, **748**
Good, The Bad, And The Ugly, The
Hugo Montenegro, **1107**
Goodbye Baby
Jack Scott, **1474**
Goodbye Cruel World
James Darren, **1407**
Goodbye Girl
David Gates, **2591**
Goodbye Yellow Brick Road
Elton John, **1105**
Goodnight Tonight
Wings, **1431**
Goody Two Shoes
Adam Ant, **1157**
Got A Hold On Me
Christine McVie, **2379**
Got My Mind Set On You
George Harrison, **576**
Got To Be Real
Cheryl Lynn, **2769**
Got To Be There
Michael Jackson, **1334**
Got To Get You Into My Life
The Beatles, **2151**
Got To Give It Up (Pt. 1)
Marvin Gaye, **413**
Gotta Travel On
Billy Grammer, **556**
Grazing In The Grass
Friends of Distinction, **2062**
Hugh Masekela, **1752**
Grease
Frankie Valli, **445**
Great Balls Of Fire
Jerry Lee Lewis, **672**
Great Pretender, The
The Platters, **107**
Greatest Love Of All
Whitney Houston, **533**
Green Door, The
Jim Lowe, **34**
Green-Eyed Lady
Sugarloaf, **1435**
Green Onions
Booker T. & the MG's, **1955**
Green River
Creedence Clearwater Revival, **1406**
Green Tambourine
The Lemon Pipers, **1205**
Greenfields
Brothers Four, **464**
Groove Is In The Heart
Deee-Lite, **1146**
Groove Line, The
Heatwave, **2053**

Groove Me
King Floyd, **912**
Groovin'
The Young Rascals, **754**
Groovy Kind Of Love, A
Phil Collins, **1061**
The Mindbenders, **1969**
Guess Things Happen That Way
Johnny Cash, **2983**
Guilty
Barbra Streisand and Barry Gibb,
568
Gypsy Man
War, **2878**
Gypsy Woman
Brian Hyland, **1905**
Gypsys, Tramps and Thieves
Cher, **452**
Hair
The Cowsills, **726**
Half-Breed
Cher, **604**
Hands To Heaven
Breathe, **858**
Handy Man
Jimmy Jones, **644**
James Taylor, **1649**
Hang 'Em High
Booker T. & the MG',
Hang On In There Baby
Johnny Bristol, **1845**
Hang On Sloopy
The McCoys, **1630**
Hang Up My Rock And Roll Shoes
Chuck Willis, **1525**
Hangin' Tough
New Kids on the Block, **1709**
Hanky Panky
Tommy James & the Shondells, **1811**
Happening, The
The Supremes, **2078**
Happy Birthday, Sweet Sixteen
Neil Sedaka, **2027**
Happy, Happy Birthday Baby
The Tune Weavers, **1734**
Happy Organ, The
Dave "Baby" Cortez, **881**
Happy Together
The Turtles, **652**
Happy Whistler, The
Don Robertson, **1335**
Harbor Lights
The Platters, **2185**
Hard Day's Night, A
The Beatles, **631**
Hard Habit To Break
Chicago, **569**
Hard Headed Woman
Elvis Presley, **1381**
Hard To Get
Gisele MacKenzie, **116**
Hard To Say
Dan Fogelberg, **2701**
Hard To Say I'm Sorry
Chicago, **136**
Harden My Heart
Quarterflash, **178**
Harper Valley P.T.A.
Jeannie C. Riley, **1004**
Hats Off To Larry
Del Shannon, **2454**
Have I The Right?
The Honeycombs, **2639**
Have I Told You Lately That I Love You
Ricky Nelson, **185**
Have You Never Been Mellow?
Olivia Newton-John, **2029**
Have You Seen Her
The Chi-Lites, **1029**
M.C. Hammer, **1662**
Hawaiian Wedding Song, The
Andy Williams, **1015**
Hazy Shade Of Winter
Bangles, **1196**

He
Al Hibbler, **43**
McGuire Sisters, **1041**
He Ain't Heavy, He's My Brother
The Hollies, **2256**
He Don't Love You (Like I Love You)
*Jerry Butler**, **1314**
Tony Orlando & Dawn, **1580**
**He Will Break Your Heart*
He Will Break Your Heart
Jerry Butler, **1314**
*Tony Orlando & Dawn**, **1580**
**He Don't Love You (Like I Love You)*
Head Games
Foreigner, **2986**
Head Over Heels
Go-Go's 2809,
Head Over Heels
Tears for Fears, **1618**
Head To Toe
Lisa Lisa & Cult Jam, **1228**
Heard It In A Love Song
Marshall Tucker Band, **2479**
Heart And Soul
Huey Lewis & the News, **2321**
Heart And Soul
T'Pau, **978**
Heart Attack
Olivia Newton-John, **1009**
Heart Of Glass
Blondie, **619**
Heart Of Gold
Neil Young, **802**
Heart Of Rock And Roll, The
Huey Lewis & the News, **1218**
Heart To Heart
Kenny Loggins, **1494**
Heartache Tonight
The Eagles, **789**
Heartaches By The Number
Guy Mitchell, **171**
Heartbeat
Don Johnson, **2695**
Heartbeat—It's A Lovebeat
DeFranco Family f/Tony DeFranco,
1137
Heartbreak Hotel
Elvis Presley, **11**
Heartbreaker
Dionne Warwick, **1798**
Heartlight
Neil Diamond, **1965**
Hearts
Marty Balin, **894**
Heat Is On, The
Glenn Frey, **1082**
Heat Of The Moment
Asia, **1073**
Heat Of The Night
Bryan Adams, **2624**
Heat Wave
Martha & the Vandellas, **1975**
Linda Ronstadt, **2577**
Heaven
Bryan Adams, **1067**
Heaven
Warrant, **1111**
Heaven Help Me
Deon Estus, **2772**
Heaven Is A Place On Earth
Belinda Carlisle, **613**
Heaven Knows
Donna Summer w/Brooklyn Dreams,
886
Heaven Must Have Sent You
Bonnie Pointer, **1109**
Heaven On The 7th Floor
Paul Nicholas, **888**
He'll Have To Go
Jim Reeves, **122**
He'll Have To Stay
Jeanne Black, **2533**
Hello
Lionel Richie, **194**

Hello Again
Neil Diamond, **1629**
Hello, Dolly!
Louis Armstrong, **128**
Hello Goodbye
The Beatles, **1369**
Hello, I Love You
The Doors, **920**
Hello It's Me
Todd Rundgren, **2116**
Hello Mary Lou
Ricky Nelson, **1453**
Hello Mudduh, Hello Fadduh!
(A Letter From Camp)
Allan Sherman, **2909**
Hello Stranger
Barbara Lewis, **2510**
Help!
The Beatles, **787**
Help Me
Joni Mitchell, **2786**
Help Me Make It Through The Night
Sammi Smith, **2288**
Help Me, Rhonda
The Beach Boys, **1397**
Her Town Too
James Taylor & J.D. Souther, **2905**
Here And Now
Luther Vandross, **1050**
Here Comes The Rain Again
Eurythmics, **1122**
Here I Am (Come And Take Me)
Al Green, **2293**
Here I Am
(Just When I Thought I Was Over You)
Air Supply, **871**
Here I Go Again
Whitesnake, **605**
Here We Are
Gloria Estefan, **2773**
Here You Come Again
Dolly Parton, **1206**
He's A Rebel
The Crystals, **677**
He's Got The Whole World
(In His Hands)
Laurie London, **467**
He's Mine
The Platters, **2450**
He's So Fine
The Chiffons, **411**
He's So Shy
Pointer Sisters, **865**
He's The Greatest Dancer
Sister Sledge, **2230**
Hey! Baby
Bruce Channel, **702**
Hey Deanie
Shaun Cassidy, **2084**
Hey! Jealous Lover
Frank Sinatra, **626**
Hey Jude
The Beatles, **19**
Hey Little Cobra
The Rip Chords, **2426**
Hey Nineteen
Steely Dan, **1794**
Hey Paula
Paul and Paula, **510**
Hey There Lonely Girl
Eddie Holman, **1970**
(Hey Won't You Play)
Another Somebody Done Somebody
Wrong Song
B.J. Thomas, **880**
Higher Ground
Stevie Wonder, **1619**
Higher Love
Steve Winwood, **929**
Him
Rupert Holmes, **2133**
Hip To Be Square
Huey Lewis & the News, **1632**
Hit Me With Your Best Shot
Pat Benatar, **932**

Hit The Road Jack
Ray Charles, **940**
Hitchin' A Ride
Vanity Fare, **1300**
Hocus Pocus
Focus, **2779**
Hold Me
Fleetwood Mac, **649**
Hold Me Now
Thompson Twins, **742**
Hold Me, Thrill Me, Kiss Me
Mel Carter, **2796**
Hold Me Tight
Johnny Nash, **2026**
Hold On
En Vogue, **526**
Hold On
Wilson Phillips, **196**
Hold On To The Nights
Richard Marx, **967**
Hold The Line
Toto, **1574**
Hold Your Head Up
Argent, **2813**
Holding Back The Years
Simply Red, **1306**
Holly Holy
Neil Diamond, **1780**
Hollywood Nights
Bob Seger & the Silver Bullet Band,
2971
Honey
Bobby Goldsboro, **227**
Honeycomb
Jimmie Rodgers, **44**
Honky Tonk (Parts 1 & 2)
Bill Doggett, **35**
Honky Tonk Women
The Rolling Stones, **187**
Hooked On A Feeling
Blue Swede, **861**
B.J. Thomas, **1665**
Hooked On Classics
Royal Philharmonic Orchestra, **1808**
Hooray For Hazel
Tommy Roe, **2684**
Hopelessly Devoted To You
Olivia Newton-John, **692**
Horse, The
Cliff Nobles & Co., **1858**
Horse With No Name, A
America, **470**
Hot Blooded
Foreigner, **1032**
Hot Child In The City
Nick Gilder, **142**
Hot Fun In The Summertime
Sly & the Family Stone, **1187**
Hot Girls In Love
Loverboy, **2433**
Hot Line
The Sylvers, **874**
Hot Rod Hearts
Robbie Dupree, **2490**
Hot Stuff
Donna Summer, **85**
Hotel California
Eagles, **402**
Hotel Happiness
Brook Benton, **2527**
Hound Dog
Elvis Presley, **2**
Hound Dog Man
Fabian, **2745**
House Of Blue Lights, The
Chuck Miller, **1380**
House Of The Rising Sun, The
The Animals, **1408**
Frijid Pink, **1868**

How Am I Supposed To Live
Without You
Michael Bolton, **412**
Laura Branigan, **2474**
How 'Bout Us?
Champaign, **2954**
How Can I Fall?
Breathe, **866**
How Can We Be Lovers
Michael Bolton, **2064**
How Can You Mend A Broken Heart
Bee Gees, **277**
How Deep Is Your Love
Bee Gees, **13**
How Do I Make You
Linda Ronstadt, **1839**
How Do You Do?
Mouth and MacNeal, **2415**
How Long
Ace, **2086**
How Much I Feel
Ambrosia, **548**
How Sweet It Is (To Be Loved By You)
James Taylor, **2083**
How Will I Know
Whitney Houston, **681**
How You Gonna See Me Now
Alice Cooper, **2398**
Hula Love
Buddy Knox, **1212**
Human
The Human League, **902**
Human Nature
Michael Jackson, **2219**
Hummingbird
Les Paul and Mary Ford, **2147**
Humpty Dance, The
Digital Underground, **1135**
Hundred Pounds Of Clay, A
Gene McDaniels, **1100**
Hungry Eyes
Eric Carmen, **919**
Hungry Heart
Bruce Springsteen, **768**
Hungry Like The Wolf
Duran Duran, **479**
Hurdy Gurdy Man
Donovan, **2499**
Hurt So Bad
The Lettermen, **2972**
Linda Ronstadt, **1751**
Hurting Each Other
Carpenters, **2364**
Hurts So Good
John Cougar, **57**
Hustle, The
Van McCoy & the Soul City Symphony,
1984
I Ain't Gonna Stand For It
Stevie Wonder, **2306**
I Almost Lost My Mind
Pat Boone, **199**
I Am A Rock
Simon and Garfunkel, **2410**
I Am Woman
Helen Reddy, **772**
I Beg Of You
Elvis Presley, **169**
I Believe In You
Don Williams, **1921**
I Can Dream About You
Dan Hartman, **1386**
I Can Help
Billy Swan, **1847**
I Can See Clearly Now
Johnny Nash, **419**
I Can't Get Next To You
The Temptations, **290**
(I Can't Get No) Satisfaction
The Rolling Stones, **524**
I Can't Go For That (No Can Do)
Daryl Hall and John Oates, **163**
I Can't Help Myself
(Sugar Pie, Honey Bunch)
Four Tops, **788**

I Can't Hold Back
Survivor, **1953**
I Can't Stand It
Eric Clapton, **1767**
I Can't Stay Mad At You
Skeeter Davis, **2802**
I Can't Stop Loving You
Ray Charles, **148**
I Can't Tell You Why
Eagles, **1741**
I Can't Wait
Nu Shooz, **1215**
I Could Never Take The Place Of
Your Man
Prince, **2921**
I Cried A Tear
LaVern Baker, **1393**
I Didn't Mean To Turn You On
Robert Palmer, **1998**
I Don't Have The Heart
James Ingram, **875**
I Don't Like To Sleep Alone
Paul Anka, **2661**
I Don't Need You
Kenny Rogers, **976**
I Don't Wanna Go On With You
Like That
Elton John, **1539**
I Don't Wanna Live Without Your Love
Chicago, **2016**
I Don't Want Your Love
Duran Duran, **1689**
I Don't Want To Live Without You
Foreigner, **2653**
I Feel Fine
The Beatles, **1044**
I Feel For You
Chaka Khan, **368**
I Feel Love
Donna Summer, **913**
I Feel The Earth Move
Carole King, **151**
I Found Someone
Cher, **2950**
I Get Around
The Beach Boys, **428**
I Get Weak
Belinda Carlisle, **2011**
I Go Crazy
Paul Davis, **87**
I Go To Extremes
Billy Joel, **2697**
I Got a Feeling
Ricky Nelson, **1792**
I Got A Name
Jim Croce, **2374**
I Got Rhythm
The Happenings, **2509**
I Got Stung
Elvis Presley, **1635**
I Got The Feelin'
James Brown, **2552**
I Got You Babe
Sonny and Cher, **1162**
I Got You (I Feel Good)
James Brown, **1895**
I Gotcha
Joe Tex, **319**
I Guess That's Why They Call It
The Blues
Elton John, **1149**
I Hate Myself For Loving You
Joan Jett & the Blackhearts, **2721**
I Hear A Symphony
The Supremes, **1821**
I Hear You Knocking
Dave Edmunds, **
Gale Storm*, **155**
I Heard A Rumour
Bananarama, **1710**
I Heard It Through The Grapevine
Marvin Gaye, **113**
Gladys Knight & the Pips, **682**
I Honestly Love You
Olivia Newton-John, **1865**

I Just Called To Say I Love You
Stevie Wonder, **251**
I Just Can't Help Believing
B.J. Thomas, **2834**
I Just Can't Stop Loving You
Michael Jackson and Siedah Garrett,
2036
(I Just) Died In Your Arms
Cutting Crew, **1409**
I Just Fall In Love Again
Anne Murray, **2417**
I Just Wanna Stop
Gino Vannelli, **827**
I Just Want To Be Your Everything
Andy Gibb, **20**
I Just Want To Celebrate
Rare Earth, **2763**
I Keep Forgettin'
(Every Time You're Near)
Michael McDonald, **1216**
I Knew You Were Waiting (For Me)
Aretha Franklin and George Michael,
1404
I Know A Place
Petula Clark, **2987**
I Know There's Something Going On
Frida, **2831**
I Know (You Don't Love Me No More)
Barbara George, **1944**
I Like Dreamin'
Kenny Nolan, **216**
I Like It
Dino, **1761**
I Like It Like That, Part 1
Chris Kenner, **1880**
I Love A Rainy Night
Eddie Rabbitt, **243**
I Love How You Love Me
Paris Sisters, **2545**
Bobby Vinton, **1700**
I Love Music (Part 1)
The O'Jays, **1189**
I Love Rock 'n Roll
Joan Jett & the Blackhearts, **102**
I Love The Nightlife (Disco 'Round)
Alicia Bridges, **217**
I Love You
Climax Blues Band, **2435**
I Love You Because
Al Martino, **2121**
I Made It Through The Rain
Barry Manilow, **2391**
I Miss You
Klymaxx, **774**
I Need Your Love Tonight
Elvis Presley, **2561**
I Never Cry
Alice Cooper, **1508**
I Only Have Eyes For You
The Flamingos, **2864**
I Only Want To Be With You
Bay City Rollers, **2924**
I Ran (So Far Away)
A Flock of Seagulls, **2790**
I Remember Holding You
Boys Club, **2805**
I Remember You
Skid Row, **2348**
I Say A Little Prayer
Aretha Franklin, **2895**
Dionne Warwick, **2040**
I Second That Emotion
Smokey Robinson & the Miracles,
1448
I Shot The Sheriff
Eric Clapton, **2129**
I Still Believe
Brenda K. Starr, **2445**
I Still Can't Get Over Loving You
Ray Parker Jr.,
I Still Haven't Found What
I'm Looking For
U2, **995**
I Thank You
Sam and Dave, **2949**

It's Only Make Believe
Conway Twitty, **195**
It's Raining Again
Supertramp, **2305**
It's So Easy
Linda Ronstadt, **1684**
It's Still Rock And Roll To Me
Billy Joel, **183**
It's Time To Cry
Paul Anka, **1964**
It's Too Late
Carole King, **151**
It's Too Soon To Know
Pat Boone, **333**
It's You I Love
Fats Domino, **2225**
It's Your Thing
Isley Brothers, **1079**
Itsy Bitsy Teenie Weenie Yellow Polka
Dot Bikini
Brian Hyland, **860**
I've Been In Love Before
Cutting Crew, **2917**
(I've Been) Searchin' So Long
Chicago, **2758**
I've Done Everything For You
Rick Springfield, **2191**
I've Found Someone Of My Own
Free Movement, **2654**
I've Got Love On My Mind
Natalie Cole, **1575**
I've Got To Use My Imagination
Gladys Knight & the Pips, **1578**
I've Gotta Be Me
Sammy Davis, Jr., **2922**
I've Gotta Get A Message To You
Bee Gees, **1720**
I've Had It
The Bell Notes, **2171**
(I've Had) The Time Of My Life
Bill Medley and Jennifer Warnes, **646**
I've Never Been To Me
Charlene, **1568**
I've Told Every Little Star
Linda Scott, **2532**
Ivory Tower
Cathy Carr, **278**
Otis Williams & His Charms, **2925**
Ivy Rose
Perry Como, **1264**
Jack And Diane
John Cougar, **110**
Jack And Jill
Raydio, **1021**
Jackie Blue
Ozark Mountain Daredevils, **2130**
Jacob's Ladder
Huey Lewis & the News, **1701**
Jailhouse Rock
Elvis Presley, **27**
Jamaica Farewell
Harry Belafonte, **2961**
Jamie
Ray Parker Jr.,
Janie's Got A Gun
Aerosmith, **1829**
Java
Al Hirt, **1928**
Jazzman
Carole King, **2071**
Jean
Oliver, **1866**
Jeans On
David Dundas, **2633**
Jenny, Jenny
Little Richard, **1841**
Jeopardy
Greg Kihn Band, **740**
Jerk, The
The Larks, **2127**
Jerk Out
The Time, **2744**
Jesse
Carly Simon, **2368**

Jessie's Girl
Rick Springfield, **63**
Jet
Paul McCartney & Wings, **2728**
Jet Airliner
Steve Miller Band, **1742**
Jimmy Mack
Martha & the Vandellas, **2768**
Jive Talkin'
Bee Gees, **965**
Joanna
Kool & the Gang, **822**
Johnny Angel
Shelley Fabares, **588**
Johnny B. Goode
Chuck Berry, **1791**
Johnny Get Angry
Joanie Sommers, **2675**
Joker, The
Steve Miller Band, **420**
Jolly Green Giant, The
The Kingsmen, **2528**
Joy
Apollo 100, **2564**
Joy To The World
Three Dog Night, **152**
Judy In Disguise (With Glasses)
John Fred & His Playboy Band, **463**
Juke Box Baby
Perry Como, **109**
Julie, Do Ya Love Me
Bobby Sherman, **1929**
Jump
Van Halen, **149**
Jump (For My Love)
Pointer Sisters, **759**
Jumpin' Jack Flash
The Rolling Stones, **1900**
Jungle Boogie
Kool & the Gang, **582**
Jungle Fever
Chakachas, **2649**
Junior's Farm
Wings, **1950**
Just A Dream
Jimmy Clanton, **385**
Just A Friend
Biz Markie, **2989**
Just A Song Before I Go
Crosby, Stills and Nash, **2220**
Just Ask Your Heart
Frankie Avalon, **2544**
Just Between You And Me
Lou Gramm, **1775**
Just Born (To Be Your Baby)
Perry Como, **1264**
Just Don't Want To Be Lonely
The Main Ingredient, **1911**
Just Like Jesse James
Cher, **2620**
Just Like Me
Paul Revere & the Raiders, **2930**
Just Like Paradise
David Lee Roth, **2747**
(Just Like) Starting Over
John Lennon, **135**
Just My Imagination
(Running Away With Me)
The Temptations, **435**
Just The Two Of Us
Grover Washington, Jr., **429**
Just The Way You Are
Billy Joel, **378**
Just To Be Close To You
Commodores, **2727**
Just To See Her
Smokey Robinson, **2702**
Just Walking In The Rain
Johnnie Ray, **21**
Just When I Needed You Most
Randy Vanwarmer, **1584**
Just You 'n' Me
Chicago, **884**
Kansas City
Wilbert Harrison, **662**

Karma Chameleon
Culture Club, **181**
Keep A Knockin'
Little Richard, **2713**
(Keep Feeling) Fascination
The Human League, **1387**
Keep It Comin' Love
KC & the Sunshine Band, **794**
Keep On Dancing
The Gentrys, **2567**
Keep On Loving You
REO Speedwagon, **203**
Keep On Movin'
Soul II Soul, **2888**
Keep On Truckin' (Part 1)
Eddie Kendricks, **226**
Keep Searchin' (We'll Follow The Sun)
Del Shannon, **2752**
Keep The Fire Burnin'
REO Speedwagon, **1273**
Keep Your Hands To Yourself
Georgia Satellites, **953**
Kewpie Doll
Perry Como, **2889**
Key Largo
Bertie Higgins, **679**
Kicks
Paul Revere & the Raiders, **1585**
Kiddio
Brook Benton, **1348**
Killing Me Softly With His Song
Roberta Flack, **295**
Kind of A Drag
The Buckinghams, **1722**
King For A Day
Thompson Twins, **2711**
King Of Pain
The Police, **1550**
King Of The Road
Roger Miller, **1478**
King Of Wishful Thinking
Go West, **2317**
Kiss
Prince & the Revolution, **691**
Kiss And Say Goodbye
The Manhattans, **321**
Kiss On My List
Daryl Hall and John Oates, **193**
Kiss You All Over
Exile, **106**
Kisses Sweeter Than Wine
Jimmie Rodgers, **1151**
Knock On Wood
Amii Stewart, **664**
Knock Three Times
Dawn, **204**
Knockin' Boots
Candyman, **2857**
Knockin' On Heaven's Door
Bob Dylan, **2958**
Kodachrome
Paul Simon, **1916**
Kokomo
The Beach Boys, **1351**
Kookie, Kookie (Lend Me Your Comb)
Edward Byrnes and Connie Stevens,
2000
Kung Fu Fighting
Carl Douglas, **1315**
Kyrie
Mr. Mister, **690**
La Bamba
Los Lobos, **565**
La Isla Bonita
Madonna, **2049**
La-La—Means I Love You
The Delfonics, **1963**
Ladies Night
Kool & the Gang, **1224**
Lady
Little River Band, **1873**
Lady
Kenny Rogers, **67**
Lady
Styx, **2705**

Lady Godiva
Peter and Gordon, **2698**
Lady In Red, The
Chris DeBurgh, **1201**
Lady Madonna
The Beatles, **2378**
Lady Marmalade
Labelle, **895**
Lady Willpower
Gary Puckett & the Union Gap, **1859**
Lady (You Bring Me Up)
Commodores, **931**
Land Of Confusion
Genesis, **1280**
Language Of Love, The
Dan Fogelberg, **3000**
Last Dance
Donna Summer, **813**
Last Date
Floyd Cramer, **304**
Last Kiss
J. Frank Wilson & the Cavaliers,
1394
Last Night
Mar-Keys, **1716**
(Last Night) I Didn't Get To Sleep
At All
5th Dimension, **2260**
Last Song
Edward Bear, **1496**
Last Train To Clarksville
The Monkees, **810**
Late In The Evening
Paul Simon, **1174**
Laughter In The Rain
Neil Sedaka, **845**
Lavender-Blue
Sammy Turner, **1181**
Lawyers In Love
Jackson Browne, **2455**
Lay Down (Candles In The Rain)
*Melanie w/the Edwin Hawkins
Singers*, **1594**
Lay Down Sally
Eric Clapton, **228**
Lay Lady Lay
Bob Dylan, **2249**
Lay Your Hands On Me
Bon Jovi, **2270**
Lay Your Hands On Me
Thompson Twins, **2212**
Le Freak
Chic, **30**
Lead Me On
Maxine Nightingale, **1281**
Leader Of The Band
Dan Fogelberg, **1708**
Leader Of The Pack
The Shangri-Las, **1677**
Lean On Me
Club Nouveau, **1372**
Bill Withers, **561**
Learnin' The Blues
Frank Sinatra, **60**
Leather And Lace
Stevie Nicks w/Don Henley, **786**
Leave Me Alone (Ruby Red Dress)
Helen Reddy, **1661**
Leaving On A Jet Plane
Peter, Paul and Mary, **478**
Legs
ZZ Top, **1763**
Let 'Em In
Wings, **1528**
Let It Be
The Beatles, **387**
Let It Be Me
Jerry Butler and Betty Everett, **2574**
Everly Brothers, **2137**
Let It Whip
Dazz Band, **432**
Let Me Be The One
Expose, **2641**
Let Me Be There
Olivia Newton-John, **1168**

Papa Don't Preach
Madonna, **1417**
Papa Was A Rollin' Stone
The Temptations, **1676**
Paper Roses
Anita Bryant, **1535**
Marie Osmond, **1607**
Paperback Writer
The Beatles, **1871**
Paradise City
Guns n' Roses, **2735**
Part-Time Lover
Stevie Wonder, **852**
Party All The Time
Eddie Murphy, **705**
Party Doll
Buddy Knox, **352**
Steve Lawrence, **2330**
Passion
Rod Stewart, **732**
Patches
Clarence Carter, **1198**
Patches
Dickey Lee, **1587**
Patricia
Perez Prado, **232**
Peace Train
Cat Stevens, **2546**
Peggy Sue
Buddy Holly, **324**
Penny Lane
The Beatles, **2646**
Penny Lover
Lionel Richie, **997**
People
Barbra Streisand, **1640**
People Got To Be Free
The Rascals, **300**
Peppermint Twist—Part 1
Joey Dee & the Starliters, **235**
Perfect Way
Scritti Politti, **1946**
Perfect World
Huey Lewis & the News, **2072**
Personality
Lloyd Price, **647**
Peter Gunn
Ray Anthony, **1789**
Petite Fleur (Little Flower)
Chris Barber's Jazz Band, **2647**
Philadelphia Freedom
The Elton John Band, **207**
Photograph
Ringo Starr, **1307**
Physical
Olivia Newton-John, **10**
Piano In The Dark
Brenda Russell, **2755**
Pick Up The Pieces
Average White Band, **925**
Pillow Talk
Sylvia, **814**
Pink Cadillac
Natalie Cole, **2161**
Pink Houses
John Cougar Mellencamp, **2428**
Pink Shoe Laces
Dodie Stevens, **730**
Pipeline
The Chantays, **2073**
Play That Funky Music
Wild Cherry, **134**
Playground In My Mind
Clint Holmes, **1056**
Please Come To Boston
Dave Loggins, **2628**
Please Don't Go
KC & the Sunshine Band, **179**
Please Don't Go Girl
New Kids on the Block, **2982**
Please Help Me, I'm Falling
Hank Locklin, **1284**
Please Love Me Forever
Bobby Vinton, **2099**

Please Mr. Please
Olivia Newton-John, **2280**
Please Mr. Postman
Carpenters, **2168**
The Marvelettes, **867**
Please Please Me
The Beatles, **1940**
Poetry In Motion
Johnny Tillotson, **1434**
Poetry Man
Phoebe Snow, **2180**
Point Of No Return
Expose, **2269**
Poison
Bell Biv Devoe, **339**
Poison Ivy
The Coasters, **2020**
Pony Time
Chubby Checker, **356**
Poor Little Fool
Ricky Nelson, **575**
Poor People Of Paris, The
Les Baxter, **49**
Poor Side Of Town
Johnny Rivers, **1185**
Pop Life
Prince & the Revolution, **2775**
Pop Muzik
M, **288**
Popcorn
Hot Butter, **2797**
Popsicles and Icicles
The Murmaids, **1943**
Portrait Of My Love
Steve Lawrence, **2874**
Pour Some Sugar On Me
Def Leppard, **1153**
Power, The
Snap, **591**
Power Of Love, The
Huey Lewis & the News, **480**
Pray
M.C. Hammer, **2605**
Praying For Time
George Michael, **2140**
Precious And Few
Climax, **1843**
Pretty Blue Eyes
Steve Lawrence, **915**
Price Of Love
Bad English, **2254**
Primrose Lane
Jerry Wallace w/the Jewels, **914**
Private Dancer
Tina Turner, **2334**
Private Eyes
Daryl Hall and John Oates, **317**
Problems
Everly Brothers, **1860**
Promise, The
When in Rome, **2392**
Promises, Promises
Naked Eyes, **2376**
Proud Mary
Creedence Clearwater Revival, **1106**
Ike and Tina Turner, **2468**
Prove Your Love
Taylor Dayne, **2748**
Psychedelic Shack
The Temptations, **2611**
Puff The Magic Dragon
Peter, Paul and Mary, **1451**
Pump Up The Jam
Technotronic f/Felly, **508**
Puppy Love
Paul Anka, **1879**
Donny Osmond, **2404**
Purple People Eater, The
Sheb Wooley, **501**
Purple Rain
Prince & the Revolution, **1460**
Put A Little Love In Your Heart
Jackie DeShannon, **2511**
Put Your Hand In The Hand
Ocean, **1824**

Put Your Hands Together
The O'Jays, **2894**
Put Your Head On My Shoulder
Paul Anka, **580**
Puttin' On The Ritz
Taco, **1171**
Quarter To Three
Gary U.S. Bonds, **916**
Queen Of Hearts
Juice Newton, **184**
Queen Of The Hop
Bobby Darin, **1368**
Quiet Village
The Exotic Sounds Of Martin Denny,
1516
R.O.C.K. In The U.S.A.
John Cougar Mellencamp, **1971**
Rag Doll
The Four Seasons, **1285**
Rain, The Park, & Other Things, The
The Cowsills, **1364**
Rainbow
Russ Hamilton, **430**
Raindrops
Dee Clark, **1768**
Raindrops Keep Fallin' On My Head
B.J. Thomas, **58**
Rainy Days And Mondays
Carpenters, **1382**
Rainy Night In Georgia
Brook Benton, **1988**
Ramblin Man
Allman Brothers Band, **1522**
Ramblin' Rose
Nat King Cole, **1000**
Rapper, The
The Jaggerz, **1513**
Rapture
Blondie, **596**
Raspberry Beret
Prince & the Revolution, **1121**
Raunchy
Ernie Freeman, **1468**
Bill Justis, **706**
Billy Vaughn, **139**
Reach Out I'll Be There
Four Tops, **966**
Reach Out Of The Darkness
Friend and Lover, **2290**
Ready Or Not
After 7, **1754**
Real Love
Doobie Brothers, **2097**
Real Love
Jody Watley, **1939**
Reason To Believe
Rod Stewart, **143**
Rebel-'Rouser
Duane Eddy, **1952**
Red Red Wine
UB40, **1338**
Red River Rock
Johnny & the Hurricanes, **1190**
Red Rubber Ball
The Cyrkle, **2401**
Reeling In The Years
Steely Dan, **2360**
Reflections
Diana Ross & the Supremes, **2347**
Reflections Of My Life
Marmalade, **2261**
Reflex, The
Duran Duran, **451**
Release Me
Engelbert Humperdinck, **2447**
Release Me
Wilson Phillips, **960**
Remember (Walkin' In The Sand)
The Shangri-Las, **2443**
Remember You're Mine
Pat Boone, **979**
Reminiscing
Little River Band, **805**
Rescue Me
Fontella Bass, **2988**

Respect
Aretha Franklin, **1302**
Respect Yourself
The Staple Singers, **2945**
Return To Me
Dean Martin, **358**
Return To Sender
Elvis Presley, **603**
Reunited
Peaches and Herb, **186**
Revolution
The Beatles, **2338**
Rhiannon (Will You Ever Win)
Fleetwood Mac, **2837**
Rhinestone Cowboy
Glen Campbell, **131**
Rhythm Is Gonna Get You
*Gloria Estefan & Miami Sound
Machine*, **2162**
Rhythm Nation
Janet Jackson, **1889**
Rhythm Of The Night
DeBarge, **1481**
Rhythm Of The Rain
The Cascades, **1346**
Rich Girl
Daryl Hall and John Oates, **531**
Ride Captain Ride
Blues Image, **1932**
Ride Like The Wind
Christopher Cross, **341**
Right Back Where We Started From
Maxine Nightingale, **496**
Right Here Waiting
Richard Marx, **766**
Right Place Wrong Time
Dr. John, **2120**
Right Time Of The Night
Jennifer Warnes, **1328**
Rikki Don't Lose That Number
Steely Dan, **2637**
Ring My Bell
Anita Ward, **268**
Ringo
Lorne Greene, **1660**
Rise
Herb Alpert, **401**
Roam
The B-52's, **1920**
Rock-A-Beatin' Boogie
Bill Haley & His Comets, **2076**
Rock-A-Bye Your Baby With A
Dixie Melody
Jerry Lewis, **959**
Rock And Roll Heaven
Righteous Brothers, **2581**
Rock & Roll Music
The Beach Boys, **1620**
Chuck Berry, **1721**
Rock And Roll Waltz
Kay Starr, **120**
Rock Around The Clock
Bill Haley & His Comets, **3**
Rock Island Line
Lonnie Donegan & His Skiffle Group,
2579
Rock Me Amadeus
Falco, **801**
Rock Me Gently
Andy Kim, **1319**
Rock 'n' Roll Fantasy
Bad Company, **2449**
Rock On
Michael Damian, **1362**
David Essex, **1263**
Rock Steady
The Whispers, **2258**
Rock The Boat
Hues Corporation, **2211**
Rock The Casbah
The Clash, **1305**
Rock This Town
Stray Cats, **2119**

Rock Wit'cha
Bobby Brown, **2848**
Rock With You
Michael Jackson, **91**
Rock Your Baby
George McCrae, **2345**
Rock'n Me
Steve Miller, **680**
Rocket Man
Elton John, **2586**
Rocket 2 U
The Jets, **2187**
Rockin' Good Way
(To Mess Around And Fall In Love), A
Dinah Washington and Brook Benton,
2720
Rockin' Pneumonia—Boogie Woogie
Flu
Johnny Rivers, **1593**
Rockin' Robin
Bobby Day, **455**
Michael Jackson, **1812**
Rocky Mountain High
John Denver, **1836**
Roll With It
Steve Winwood, **468**
Romeo
Dino, **2726**
Romeo's Tune
Steve Forbert, **2952**
Roni
Bobby Brown, **2635**
Rosanna
Toto, **167**
Rose, The
Bette Midler, **504**
Rose And A Baby Ruth, A
George Hamilton IV, **775**
Rose Garden
Lynn Anderson, **1155**
Roses Are Red (My Love)
Bobby Vinton, **347**
Round And Round
Perry Como, **230**
Round And Round
Ratt, **2944**
Rub You The Right Way
Johnny Gill, **581**
Rubber Ball
Bobby Vee, **2044**
Rubberband Man, The
Spinners, **360**
Ruby Baby
Dion, **2323**
Ruby Tuesday
The Rolling Stones, **1967**
Rumors
Timex Social Club, **2251**
Run Away Child, Running Wild
The Temptations, **2092**
Run Through The Jungle
Creedence Clearwater Revival, **2082**
Run To Him
Bobby Vee, **784**
Run To You
Bryan Adams, **1724**
Runaround Sue
Dion, **544**
Runaway
Del Shannon, **403**
Running Bear
Johnny Preston, **238**
Running On Empty
Jackson Browne, **2969**
Running Scared
Roy Orbison, **722**
Running With The Night
Lionel Richie, **987**
Rush Hour
Jane Wiedlin, **2898**
Sad Eyes
Robert John, **269**
Sad Songs (Say So Much)
Elton John, **1704**

Safety Dance, The
Men Without Hats, **728**
Sail Along Silvery Moon
Billy Vaughn, **139**
Sail On
Commodores, **1461**
Sailing
Christopher Cross, **899**
Sailor (Your Home Is The Sea)
Lolita, **1282**
Sally, Go 'Round The Roses
The Jaynetts, **2993**
San Francisco
(Be Sure To Wear Flowers In
Your Hair)
Scott McKenzie, **2463**
Sandy
Larry Hall, **2912**
Sara
Fleetwood Mac, **2619**
Sara
Starship, **917**
Sara Smile
Daryl Hall and John Oates, **543**
Satisfied
Richard Marx, **1753**
Saturday Night
Bay City Rollers, **1298**
Save The Last Dance For Me
The Drifters, **355**
Saving All My Love For You
Whitney Houston, **868**
Say, Has Anybody Seen My Sweet
Gypsy Rose
Dawn f/Tony Orlando, **1504**
Say It Isn't So
Daryl Hall and John Oates, **329**
Say, Say, Say
Paul McCartney and Michael Jackson,
36
Say You Love Me
Fleetwood Mac, **1810**
Say You, Say Me
Lionel Richie, **263**
Say You Will
Foreigner, **2242**
School Day
Chuck Berry, **711**
School's Out
Alice Cooper, **2596**
Scorpio
*Dennis Coffey & the Detroit Guitar
Band*, **843**
Sea Of Love
The Honeydrippers, **799**
Phil Phillips w/the Twilights, **1087**
Sealed With A Kiss
Brian Hyland, **1948**
Search Is Over, The
Survivor, **1638**
Searchin'
The Coasters, **48**
Seasons Change
Expose, **628**
Seasons In The Sun
Terry Jacks, **373**
Second Chance
Thirty Eight Special, **1797**
Second Time Around, The
Shalamar, **2565**
Secret Agent Man
Johnny Rivers, **2471**
Secret Garden, The
*Quincy Jones f/El DeBarge, James
Ingram, Barry White and Al B. Sure!*,
Secret Lovers
Atlantic Starr, **1099**
Secret Rendezvous
Karyn White, **2215**
Secretly
Jimmie Rodgers, **1046**
See You In September
The Happenings, **1980**
See You Later, Alligator
Bill Haley & His Comets, **494**

Self Control
Laura Branigan, **610**
Send For Me
Nat King Cole, **165**
Send One Your Love
Stevie Wonder, **635**
Sending All My Love
Linear, **653**
Sentimental Lady
Bob Welch, **2557**
Sentimental Street
Night Ranger, **2358**
Separate Lives
Phil Collins and Marilyn Martin, **285**
Separate Ways (Worlds Apart)
Journey, **622**
September
Earth, Wind & Fire, **2558**
Serpentine Fire
Earth, Wind & Fire, **2470**
Seven Little Girls Sitting In The
Back Seat
Paul Evans, **2310**
Seventeen
Boyd Bennett & His Rockets, **206**
Fontane Sisters, **1139**
Sexual Healing
Marvin Gaye, **325**
Sexy Eyes
Dr. Hook, **602**
Sha La La
Manfred Mann, **2845**
Sha-La-La (Make Me Happy)
Al Green, **2271**
Shadow Dancing
Andy Gibb, **31**
Shadows Of The Night
Pat Benatar, **2846**
Shake It
Ian Matthews, **2001**
Shake It Up
The Cars, **293**
(Shake, Shake, Shake)
Shake Your Booty
KC & the Sunshine Band, **372**
Shake You Down
Gregory Abbott, **562**
Shake Your Body
(Down To The Ground)
The Jacksons, **1251**
Shake Your Groove Thing
Peaches and Herb, **1295**
Shake Your Love
Debbie Gibson, **1102**
Shakedown
Bob Seger, **1103**
Shambala
Three Dog Night, **1138**
Shame On The Moon
Bob Seger & the Silver Bullet Band,
141
Shannon
Henry Gross, **1223**
Sharing The Night Together
Dr. Hook, **600**
Shattered Dreams
Johnny Hates Jazz, **1486**
She Ain't Worth It
Glenn Medeiros f/Bobby Brown, **686**
She Believes In Me
Kenny Rogers, **1209**
She Blinded Me With Science
Thomas Dolby, **1066**
She Bop
Cyndi Lauper, **1047**
She Cried
Jay & the Americans, **2543**
She Drives Me Crazy
Fine Young Cannibals, **939**
She Loves You
The Beatles, **367**
She Wants To Dance With Me
Rick Astley, **2741**
She Works Hard For The Money
Donna Summer, **384**

Shelter Of Your Arms, The
Sammy Davis, Jr.,
She's A Beauty
The Tubes, **2390**
She's A Fool
Lesley Gore, **2042**
She's A Lady
Tom Jones, **1028**
She's Gone
Daryl Hall and John Oates, **1330**
She's Just My Style
Gary Lewis & the Playboys, **2465**
She's Like The Wind
Patrick Swayze f/Wendy Fraser, **1569**
She's Not There
The Zombies, **1077**
She's Out Of My Life
Michael Jackson, **2337**
(She's) Sexy + 17
Stray Cats, **2114**
Sheila
Tommy Roe, **1327**
Sherry
The Four Seasons, **623**
Shifting, Whispering Sands, The
Rusty Draper, **270**
Billy Vaughn, **398**
Shine A Little Love
Electric Light Orchestra, **2193**
Shining Star
Earth, Wind & Fire, **668**
Shining Star
The Manhattans, **839**
Ships
Barry Manilow, **2295**
Shoop Shoop Song
(It's In His Kiss), The
Betty Everett, **2625**
Shop Around
Captain & Tennille, **1876**
The Miracles, **1501**
Short Fat Fannie
Larry Williams, **641**
Short People
Randy Newman, **1186**
Short Shorts
Royal Teens, **1976**
Shotgun
Jr. Walker & the All Stars, **2018**
Should've Known Better
Richard Marx, **1333**
Shout
Tears for Fears, **756**
Show And Tell
Al Wilson, **590**
Show Me The Way
Peter Frampton, **1250**
Show Must Go On, The
Three Dog Night, **2088**
Shower Me With Your Love
Surface, **2621**
Sideshow
Blue Magic, **1325**
Sign 'O' The Times
Prince, **2438**
Sign Your Name
Terence Trent D'Arby, **2065**
Signed, Sealed, Delivered (I'm Yours)
Stevie Wonder, **1482**
Signs
Five Man Electrical Band, **1703**
Silent Running (On Dangerous Ground)
Mike + the Mechanics, **2255**
Silhouette
Kenny,
Silhouettes
Herman's Hermits, **2489**
The Rays, **214**
Silly Love Songs
Wings, **192**
Simon Says
1910 Fruitgum Co., **2333**
Simply Irresistible
Robert Palmer, **1165**

400

Since I Don't Have You
The Skyliners, **2395**
Since I Fell For You
Lenny Welch, **1562**
Since I Met You Baby
Ivory Joe Hunter, **1893**
Sincerely Yours
Sweet Sensation w/Romeo J.D.,
Sing
Carpenters, **1926**
Sing A Song
Earth, Wind & Fire, **2101**
Singing The Blues
Guy Mitchell, **5**
Sink The Bismarck
Johnny Horton, **855**
Sir Duke
Stevie Wonder, **791**
Sister Christian
Night Ranger, **1416**
Sister Golden Hair
America, **1413**
(Sittin' On) The Dock Of The Bay
Otis Redding, **257**
Sixteen Candles
The Crests, **683**
Sixteen Reasons
Connie Stevens, **542**
Sixteen Tons
Tennessee Ernie Ford, **33**
'65 Love Affair
Paul Davis, **1129**
Sky High
Jigsaw, **1245**
Sledgehammer
Peter Gabriel, **893**
Sleep Walk
Santo and Johnny, **594**
Sleeping Bag
ZZ Top, **2158**
Slip Away
Clarence Carter, **1892**
Slip Slidin' Away
Paul Simon, **892**
Slow Hand
Pointer Sisters, **326**
Slow Twistin'
Chubby Checker, **1844**
Small Town
John Cougar Mellencamp, **1642**
Smile A Little Smile For Me
Flying Machine, **1705**
Smiling Faces Sometimes
The Undisputed Truth, **1143**
Smoke From A Distant Fire
Sanford/Townsend Band, **2879**
Smoke Gets In Your Eyes
The Platters, **158**
Smoke On The Water
Deep Purple, **1962**
Smokin' In The Boy's Room
Brownsville Station, **1570**
Smooth Operator
Sade, **1650**
Snoopy Vs. The Red Baron
The Royal Guardsmen, **1414**
Snowbird
Anne Murray, **2688**
So Alive
Love and Rockets, **1633**
So Emotional
Whitney Houston, **612**
So Fine
The Fiestas, **2910**
So In To You
Atlanta Rhythm Section, **879**
So Many Ways
Brook Benton, **1657**
So Much In Love
The Tymes, **1549**
So Rare
Jimmy Dorsey, **14**
So Sad (To Watch Good Love Go Bad)
Everly Brothers, **2520**

Sock It To Me-Baby!
Mitch Ryder & the Detroit Wheels,
2679
Soft Summer Breeze
Eddie Heywood, **399**
Soldier Boy
The Shirelles, **675**
Soldier Of Love
Donny Osmond, **1997**
Solitaire
Laura Branigan, **2172**
Some Kind Of Wonderful
Grand Funk, **1717**
Some Like It Hot
The Power Station, **1744**
Somebody To Love
Queen, **2896**
Somebody's Baby
Jackson Browne, **1675**
Somebody's Knockin'
Terri Gibbs, **2514**
Somebody's Watching Me
Rockwell, **975**
Someday
Glass Tiger, **1849**
Someday We'll Be Together
Diana Ross & the Supremes, **381**
Someone Saved My Life Tonight
Elton John, **2459**
Somethin' Stupid
Nancy Sinatra and Frank Sinatra,
555
Something
The Beatles, **197**
Something About You
Level 42, **1783**
Something Happened On The Way
To Heaven
Phil Collins, **2148**
Something So Strong
Crowded House, **2301**
Something To Believe In
Poison, **823**
Something's Burning
Kenny Rogers & the First Edition,
2867
Something's Gotta Give
Sammy Davis, Jr., **1659**
McGuire Sisters, **1124**
Sometimes When We Touch
Dan Hill, **753**
Somewhere Out There
Linda Ronstadt and James Ingram,
1610
Song For A Summer Night
Mitch Miller, **2139**
Song Sung Blue
Neil Diamond, **1233**
Songbird
Kenny G, **1738**
Sorry (I Ran All The Way Home)
The Impalas, **1455**
Sorry Seems To Be The Hardest Word
Elton John, **2058**
Soul Limbo
Booker T. & the MG',
Soul Man
Sam and Dave, **1817**
Soulful Strut
Young-Holt Unlimited, **2005**
Sounds Of Silence, The
Simon and Garfunkel, **1446**
South Street
The Orlons, **2453**
Southern Nights
Glen Campbell, **558**
Sowing The Seeds Of Love
Tears for Fears, **2456**
Space Race
Billy Preston, **1217**
Spanish Harlem
Aretha Franklin, **1510**
Ben E. King, **2951**
Special Lady
Ray, Goodman & Brown, **1615**

Spiders And Snakes
Jim Stafford, **870**
Spies Like Us
Paul McCartney, **2357**
Spill The Wine
Eric Burdon & War, **1476**
Spinning Wheel
Blood, Sweat & Tears, **1390**
Spirit In The Sky
Norman Greenbaum, **729**
Splish Splash
Bobby Darin, **1854**
Spooky
Classics IV, **1441**
St. Elmo's Fire (Man In Motion)
John Parr, **506**
Stagger Lee
Lloyd Price, **266**
Stand
R.E.M., **2664**
Stand Back
Stevie Nicks, **1210**
Stand By Me
Ben E. King, **90**
Stand Tall
Burton Cummings, **1869**
Standing On The Corner
The Four Lads, **250**
Star Wars Theme/Cantina Band
Meco, **1026**
Stardust
Billy Ward & His Dominoes, **1445**
Start Me Up
The Rolling Stones, **323**
Start Movin' (In My Direction)
Sal Mineo, **1457**
State Of Shock
The Jacksons, **1611**
Stay
Maurice Williams & the Zodiacs,
1786
Stay Awhile
The Bells, **2674**
Stayin' Alive
Bee Gees, **42**
Steal Away
Robbie Dupree, **798**
Step By Step
New Kids on the Block, **809**
Step By Step
Eddie Rabbitt, **808**
Steppin' Out
Joe Jackson, **820**
Stick-Up
The Honey Cone, **2808**
Still
Bill Anderson, **2316**
Still
Commodores, **307**
Still The One
Orleans, **1778**
Still The Same
Bob Seger & the Silver Bullet Band,
1602
Still Water (Love)
Four Tops, **2904**
Stomp!
Brothers Johnson, **1199**
Stoned Love
The Supremes, **1291**
Stoned Soul Picnic
5th Dimension, **1480**
Stoney End
Barbra Streisand, **1760**
Stood Up
Ricky Nelson, **752**
Stop Draggin' My Heart Around
*Stevie Nicks w/Tom Petty & the
Heartbreakers*, **648**
Stop! In The Name Of Love
The Supremes, **1276**
Stormy
Classics IV f/Dennis Yost, **2009**
Straight Up
Paula Abdul, **549**

Strange Way
Firefall, **2725**
Stranger On The Shore
Mr. Acker Bilk, **477**
Strangers In The Night
Frank Sinatra, **1287**
Strawberry Letter 23
Brothers Johnson, **2106**
Stray Cat Strut
Stray Cats, **1178**
Streak, The
Ray Stevens, **505**
Stripper, The
David Rose, **552**
Stroll, The
The Diamonds, **944**
Strut
Sheena Easton, **1765**
Stuck In The Middle With You
Stealers Wheel, **1697**
Stuck On You
Elvis Presley, **366**
Stuck On You
Lionel Richie, **1030**
Stuck With You
Huey Lewis & the News, **776**
Stumblin' In
Suzi Quatro and Chris Norman, **586**
Suddenly
Billy Ocean, **1679**
Suddenly Last Summer
The Motels, **1838**
Suddenly There's A Valley
Gogi Grant, **2340**
Sugar Moon
Pat Boone, **2268**
Sugar Shack
Jimmy Gilmer & the Fireballs, **208**
Sugar, Sugar
The Archies, **101**
Sugar Town
Nancy Sinatra, **2414**
Sugartime
McGuire Sisters, **201**
Sukiyaki
Kyu Sakamoto, **713**
A Taste of Honey, **735**
Sultans Of Swing
Dire Straits, **1572**
Summer
War, **2257**
Summer Breeze
Seals and Crofts, **2324**
Summer In The City
The Lovin' Spoonful, **1439**
Summer Nights
John Travolta and Olivia Newton-John,
1966
Summer Of '69
Bryan Adams, **2113**
Summertime Blues
Eddie Cochran, **2767**
Sundown
Gordon Lightfoot, **1485**
Sunglasses At Night
Corey Hart, **1379**
Sunny
Bobby Hebb, **1923**
Sunshine
Jonathan Edwards, **1523**
Sunshine Of Your Love
Cream, **2051**
Sunshine On My Shoulders
John Denver, **907**
Sunshine Superman
Donovan, **1645**
Superfly
Curtis Mayfield, **2109**
Superstar
Carpenters, **982**
Superstition
Stevie Wonder, **927**
Surf City
Jan and Dean, **972**

Surfer Girl
The Beach Boys, **1777**
Surfin' Bird
The Trashmen, **2458**
Surfin' U.S.A.
The Beach Boys, **1472**
Surrender
Elvis Presley, **956**
Surrender To Me
Ann Wilson and Robin Zander, **2793**
Susan
The Buckinghams, **2862**
Susie Darlin'
Robin Luke, **642**
Suspicion
Terry Stafford, **1918**
Suspicious Minds
Elvis Presley, **904**
Sussudio
Phil Collins, **903**
Swayin' To The Music (Slow Dancin')
Johnny Rivers, **800**
Sweet And Innocent
Donny Osmond, **1643**
Sweet Caroline
(Good Times Never Seemed So Good)
Neil Diamond, **815**
Sweet Child O'Mine
Guns n' Roses, **676**
Sweet City Woman
Stampeders, **2766**
Sweet Dreams
Air Supply, **564**
Sweet Dreams (Are Made Of This)
Eurythmics, **261**
Sweet Freedom
Michael McDonald, **2165**
Sweet Home Alabama
Lynyrd Skynyrd, **2229**
Sweet Little Sixteen
Chuck Berry, **1818**
Sweet Love
Anita Baker, **2850**
Sweet Love
Commodores, **2169**
Sweet Nothin's
Brenda Lee, **560**
Sweet Old-Fashioned Girl, A
Teresa Brewer, **1355**
Sweet Soul Music
Arthur Conley, **1479**
(Sweet Sweet Baby) Since You've
Been Gone
Aretha Franklin, **1933**
Sweet Talkin' Woman
Electric Light Orchestra, **2634**
Sweet Thing
Rufus f/Chaka Khan, **1673**
Sweetest Taboo, The
Sade, **2125**
Sweetest Thing
(I've Ever Known), The
Juice Newton, **422**
Sweetheart
Franke & the Knockouts, **1840**
Swing The Mood
Jive Bunny & the Mastermixers, **2868**
Sylvia's Mother
Dr. Hook & the Medicine Show, **2583**
Tainted Love
Soft Cell, **1349**
Take A Chance On Me
Abba, **539**
Take A Letter Maria
R.B. Greaves, **1154**
Take Good Care Of Her
Adam Wade, **2157**
Take Good Care Of My Baby
Bobby Vee, **1104**
Take It Away
Paul McCartney, **2061**
Take It Easy On Me
Little River Band, **1807**
Take It On The Run
REO Speedwagon, **614**

Take It To The Limit
Eagles, **942**
Take Me Home
Cher, **2729**
Take Me Home
Phil Collins, **2568**
Take Me Home, Country Roads
John Denver, **761**
Take Me Home Tonight
Eddie Money, **2155**
Take Me To Heart
Quarterflash, **2613**
Take My Breath Away
Berlin, **1286**
Take My Heart
(You Can Have It If You Want It)
Kool & the Gang, **2571**
Take On Me
a-ha, **606**
Take The Long Way Home
Supertramp, **2703**
Take Time To Know Her
Percy Sledge, **2495**
Take Your Time (Do It Right)
S.O.S. Band, **1126**
Talk To Me
Stevie Nicks, **1531**
Talking In Your Sleep
The Romantics, **517**
Tall Paul
Annette, **2655**
Tallahassee Lassie
Freddy Cannon, **2035**
Tammy
Debbie Reynolds, **16**
Taste Of Honey, A
Herb Alpert & the Tijuana Brass,
1740
Tea For Two Cha Cha
Tommy Dorsey & the Orchestra, **1211**
Tear Fell, A
Teresa Brewer, **415**
Tears Of A Clown, The
Smokey Robinson & the Miracles, **409**
Tears On My Pillow
Little Anthony & the Imperials, **797**
Teen-Age Crush
Tommy Sands, **1399**
Teen Age Prayer
Gale Storm, **2838**
Teen Angel
Mark Dinning, **427**
Teen Beat
Sandy Nelson, **1071**
Teenager In Love, A
Dion & the Belmonts, **1907**
Teenager's Romance, A
Ricky Nelson, **345**
Telefone (Long Distance Love Affair)
Sheena Easton, **1790**
Telephone Line
Electric Light Orchestra, **954**
Tell Her About It
Billy Joel, **474**
Tell Him
The Exciters, **2534**
Tell Him No
Travis and Bob, **2777**
Tell It Like It Is
Heart, **2612**
Aaron Neville, **1395**
Tell It To My Heart
Taylor Dayne, **1322**
Tell Laura I Love Her
Ray Peterson, **2569**
Tell Me Something Good
Rufus, **2015**
Telstar
The Tornadoes, **687**
Temptation Eyes
The Grass Roots, **2539**
Tequila
The Champs, **160**
Thank God I'm A Country Boy
John Denver, **1035**

Thank You
(Falettinme Be Mice Elf Agin)
Sly & the Family Stone, **992**
That Girl
Stevie Wonder, **1057**
That Lady (Part 1)
Isley Brothers, **889**
That'll Be The Day
The Crickets, **792**
Linda Ronstadt, **2863**
That's All!
Genesis, **1007**
That's All There Is To That
Nat King Cole, **2548**
That's Life
Frank Sinatra, **2980**
That's Rock 'n' Roll
Shaun Cassidy, **764**
That's The Way (I Like It)
KC & the Sunshine Band, **630**
That's The Way Of The World
Earth, Wind & Fire, **2906**
That's What Friends Are For
Dionne & Friends, **145**
Theme From "A Summer Place"
Percy Faith, **41**
Theme From "Dr. Kildare"
(Three Stars Will Shine Tonight)
Richard Chamberlain, **2902**
Theme From "Greatest American
Hero" (Believe It Or Not)
Joey Scarbury, **241**
Theme From "Mahogany"
(Do You Know Where You're Going To)
Diana Ross, **1499**
Theme From "S.W.A.T."
Rhythm Heritage, **1375**
Theme From "Shaft"
Issac Hayes, **850**
Theme From "The Apartment"
Ferrante and Teicher, **661**
(Theme From) Valley Of The Dolls
Dionne Warwick, **1827**
Then Came You
Dionne Warwick & Spinners, **559**
Then You Can Tell Me Goodbye
The Casinos, **2618**
There Goes My Baby
The Drifters, **1512**
There! I've Said It Again
Bobby Vinton, **550**
There'll Be Sad Songs
(To Make You Cry)
Billy Ocean, **632**
There's A Kind Of Hush
Herman's Hermits, **2607**
There's A Moon Out Tonight
The Capris, **345**
(There's) No Gettin' Over Me
Ronnie Milsap, **743**
These Boots Are Made For Walkin'
Nancy Sinatra, **1164**
These Dreams
Heart, **1289**
These Eyes
The Guess Who, **2052**
They Don't Know
Tracey Ullman, **2294**
They Just Can't Stop It The
(Games People Play)
Spinners, **1634**
(They Long To Be) Close To You
Carpenters, **248**
Things Can Only Get Better
Howard Jones, **1290**
Things We Do For Love, The
10cc, **1222**
Think
Aretha Franklin, **2588**
Think I'm In Love
Eddie Money, **1983**
Think Of Laura
Christopher Cross, **2853**
Think Twice
Brook Benton, **2985**

Thinking Of You
Sa-Fire, **2953**
This Diamond Ring
Gary Lewis & the Playboys, **1252**
This Girl's In Love With You
Dionne Warwick, **2197**
This Guy's In Love With You
Herb Alpert, **400**
This Is It
Kenny Loggins, **1075**
This Is My Song
Petula Clark, **2526**
This Little Girl
Gary U.S. Bonds, **1830**
This Magic Moment
Jay & the Americans, **2553**
This Masquerade
George Benson, **2835**
This Time
Troy Shondell, **1576**
This Time I Know It's For Real
Donna Summer, **2740**
This Will Be
Natalie Cole, **2617**
Those Were The Days
Mary Hopkin, **1011**
Thousand Stars, A
Kathy Young w/the Innocents, **674**
Three Bells, The
The Browns, **361**
Three Times A Lady
Commodores, **191**
Thriller
Michael Jackson, **2448**
Throwing It All Away
Genesis, **1770**
Thunder Island
Jay Ferguson, **2279**
Ticket To Ride
The Beatles, **2021**
Tide Is High, The
Blondie, **253**
Tie A Yellow Ribbon Round The Ole
Oak Tree
Dawn, **88**
Tiger
Fabian, **2425**
Tighten Up
Archie Bell & the Drells, **937**
Tighter, Tighter
Alive and Kicking, **2138**
('Til) I Kissed You
Everly Brothers, **1014**
Time After Time
Cyndi Lauper, **447**
Time (Clock Of The Heart)
Culture Club, **725**
Time Has Come Today
Chambers Brothers, **2876**
Time In A Bottle
Jim Croce, **655**
Time Is On My Side
The Rolling Stones, **2550**
Time Is Tight
Booker T. & the MG's, **2738**
Time Of The Season
The Zombies, **1979**
Time Passages
Al Stewart, **1343**
Time Won't Let Me
The Outsiders, **2563**
Times Of Your Life
Paul Anka, **1706**
Tin Man
America, **2592**
Tina Marie
Perry Como, **547**
Tired Of Being Alone
Al Green, **1396**
Tired Of Toein' The Line
Rocky Burnette, **2687**
To All The Girls I've Loved Before
Julio Iglesias and Willie Nelson, **2014**
To Be A Lover
Billy Idol, **1725**

Yesterday Once More
Carpenters, **1913**
Yesterday's Songs
Neil Diamond, **1842**
Yo-Yo
The Osmonds, **1419**
You Ain't Seen Nothing Yet
Bachman-Turner Overdrive, **1352**
You And I
Eddie Rabbitt w/Crystal Gayle, **234**
You And Me
Alice Cooper, **2278**
You And Me Against The World
Helen Reddy, **2821**
You Are
Lionel Richie, **607**
You Are Everything
The Stylistics, **1370**
You Are My Lady
Freddie Jackson, **2936**
You Are The Sunshine Of My Life
Stevie Wonder, **891**
You Are The Woman
Firefall, **1058**
You Belong To Me
Carly Simon, **2281**
You Belong To The City
Glenn Frey, **1874**
You Can Depend On Me
Brenda Lee, **2640**
You Can Do Magic
America, **608**
You Can't Change That
Raydio, **2285**
You Can't Hurry Love
Phil Collins, **769**
The Supremes, **989**
You Can't Sit Down
The Dovells, **1994**
You Can't Turn Me Off
(In The Middle Of Turning Me On)
High Inergy, **2865**
You Decorated My Life
Kenny Rogers, **1764**
You Don't Bring Me Flowers
Barbra Streisand and Neil Diamond, **396**

You Don't Have To Be A Baby To Cry
The Caravelles, **2559**
You Don't Have To Be A Star
(To Be In My Show)
Marilyn McCoo and Billy Davis, Jr., **305**
You Don't Have To Say You Love Me
Dusty Springfield, **2017**
You Don't Know Me
Ray Charles, **2530**
Jerry Vale, **825**
You Don't Own Me
Lesley Gore, **2377**
You Give Good Love
Whitney Houston, **1625**
You Give Love A Bad Name
Bon Jovi, **490**
You Got It All
The Jets, **2080**
You Got It (The Right Stuff)
New Kids on the Block, **1769**
You Got The Love
Rufus f/Chaka Khan, **2929**
You Got What It Takes
Marv Johnson, **1444**
You Haven't Done Nothin'
Stevie Wonder, **597**
You Keep Me Hangin' On
The Supremes, **1388**
Vanilla Fudge, **2673**
Kim Wilde, **1360**
You Light Up My Life
Debby Boone, **10**
You Make Loving Fun
Fleetwood Mac, **2807**
You Make Me Feel Brand New
The Stylistics, **717**
You Make Me Feel Like Dancing
Leo Sayer, **205**
You Make My Dreams
Daryl Hall and John Oates, **1491**
You May Be Right
Billy Joel, **2178**
You Might Think
The Cars, **2117**

You Needed Me
Anne Murray, **209**
You Never Done It Like That
Captain & Tennille, **1864**
You Ought To Be With Me
Al Green, **1906**
You Send Me
Sam Cooke, **115**
You Sexy Thing
Hot Chocolate, **712**
You Should Be Dancing
Bee Gees, **857**
You Should Hear How She Talks
About You
Melissa Manchester, **592**
You Take My Breath Away
Rex Smith, **2861**
You Were On My Mind
We Five, **1505**
You Won't See Me
Anne Murray, **2795**
You'll Never Find Another Love
Like Mine
Lou Rawls, **1391**
You'll Never Never Know
The Platters, **2784**
Young Blood
The Coasters, **48**
Young Girl
Gary Puckett & the Union Gap, **951**
Young Love
Tab Hunter, **138**
Sonny James, **439**
Young Turks
Rod Stewart, **617**
Your Love
Marilyn McCoo and Billy Davis, Jr.,
Your Love
The Outfield, **1779**
Your Love Is Driving Me Crazy
Sammy Hagar, **2960**
(Your Love Keeps Lifting Me) Higher
And Higher
Rita Coolidge, **484**
Jackie Wilson, **2659**
Your Mama Don't Dance
Loggins and Messina, **1269**

Your Song
Elton John, **2239**
Your Wildest Dreams
The Moody Blues, **2852**
(You're) Having My Baby
Paul Anka, **1125**
You're In My Heart (The Final Acclaim)
Rod Stewart, **826**
(You're My) Soul And Inspiration
Righteous Brothers, **970**
You're No Good
Linda Ronstadt, **2299**
You're Only Human (Second Wind)
Billy Joel, **2841**
You're Only Lonely
J.D. Souther, **1746**
You're Sixteen
Johnny Burnette, **2167**
Ringo Starr, **1194**
You're So Vain
Carly Simon, **292**
(You're The) Devil In Disguise
Elvis Presley, **2955**
You're The First, The Last, My
Everything
Barry White, **1888**
You're The Inspiration
Chicago, **1136**
You're The One That I Want
John Travolta and Olivia Newton-John,
362
You're The Reason I'm Living
Bobby Darin, **1039**
You've Got A Friend
James Taylor, **803**
(You've Got) The Magic Touch
The Platters, **790**
You've Lost That Lovin' Feelin'
Daryl Hall and John Oates, **1140**
Righteous Brothers, **534**
You've Made Me So Very Happy
Blood, Sweat & Tears, **1852**
You've Really Got A Hold On Me
The Miracles, **2776**
Yummy Yummy Yummy
Ohio Express, **2023**

About the Author

Fred Bronson is the author of *The Billboard Book of Number One Hits*. He has also written numerous television and radio projects for Dick Clark, including the two-hour ABC-TV special "America Picks the Number One Songs." He co-wrote the "Menage a Troi" episode of "Star Trek: The Next Generation" with Susan Sackett, and wrote "The Counter-Clock Incident" segment of the animated "Star Trek" series.

He has also produced segments for "2 on the Town" on KCBS-TV in Los Angeles; written for *Emmy,* the magazine produced by the Academy of Television Arts and Sciences; adapted children's musicals for the Theater of Light in Hollywood; and written a Hollywood-based column for the British pop weekly *Record Mirror.* He spent 12 years in the press and publicity department at NBC-TV in Burbank, where he was the publicist for series like "Bonanza," "Sanford and Son," "The Bionic Woman," "The Hollywood Squares" and the Bob Hope specials.

Photo Credits

Courtesy of Frank Driggs: Pages 34, 49, 86, 143, 156, 162, 165, 202. Courtesy of Photofeatures International: 17, 18, 20, 21, 43, 60, 79 (David Wainwright), 95, 110, 171. Courtesy of the Michael Ochs Archive/Venice, CA: 33, 41 (BMI), 62. Courtesy of Sherry Rayn Barnett: 31, 68. Courtesy of Starfile: 71 (Vinnie Zuffante), 168. Courtesy of Ebet Roberts: 69, 74. Courtesy of Ellie Greenwich: 36.